GOOD HOUSEKEEPING

THE NEW
COOKERY
ENCYCLOPEDIA

GOOD HOUSEKEEPING

THE NEW COOKERY ENCYCLOPEDIA

EBURY PRESS · LONDON

First published by Ebury Press
an imprint of The Random Century Group
Random Century House 20 Vauxhall Bridge Road London SW1V 2SA

Reprinted 1990

British Library Cataloguing in Publication Data
Good Housekeeping The new cookery encyclopedia.
1.Cookery
1.Good Housekeeping Institute
641.5

ISBN 0-85223-806-1

Compiled by Helen Southall
Designed by Gwyn Lewis

Typeset in Palatino from disk by Saxon Printing Ltd, Derby
Printed and bound in Great Britain by Butler & Tanner Ltd, Frome and London

CONTENTS

Cookery Notes   7

Introduction   9

THE ENCYCLOPEDIA   11

Recipes illustrated on colour pages   439

COOKERY NOTES

When using the recipes in this book, follow either metric or imperial measures as they are not interchangeable

All spoon measures are level unless otherwise stated

Sets of measuring spoons are available in both metric and imperial sizes to give accurate measurement of small quantities

When measuring milk, the exact conversion of 568ml (1 pint) has been used

Size 4 and 3 eggs should be used except where otherwise stated

METRIC CONVERSION CHARTS

SOLID

Imperial	Exact conversion	Recommended g
1 oz	28.35 g	25 g
2 oz	56.7 g	50 g
4 oz	113.4 g	100 g
8 oz	226.8 g	225 g
12 oz	340.2 g	350 g
14 oz	397.0 g	400 g
16 oz (1 lb)	453.6 g	450 g

1 kilogram (kg) equals 2.2 lb

LIQUID

Imperial	Exact conversion	Recommended ml
¼ pint	142 ml	150 ml
½ pint	284 ml	300 ml
1 pint	568 ml	600 ml
1½ pints	851 ml	900 ml
1¾ pints	992 ml	1 litre

INTRODUCTION

Visit the kitchens of the Good Housekeeping Institute in London's West End on any weekday and you will soon realize why the information in the following pages can be trusted: apart from thorough research into all the entries, every technique and recipe has been tried and tested, as the words of Good Housekeeping Institute's famous Seal of Approval attest. Tried and tested not by kitchen technicians from whom a combination of ingredients is a mathematical problem to be solved. Far from it. Tried and tested by people with a genuine love of food; both cooking it and eating it. By people whose knowledge extends beyond cooking techniques to food hygiene, beyond calories to nutritional content, beyond national boundaries to encompass some of the best techniques from around the world. For this reason, whether you want to know the meaning of a culinary term, how to use an unusual ingredient, how to make the most of your microwave or create the perfect sauce, the Encyclopedia will provide the answer. It has over 3000 entries listed in alphabetical order and is comprehensively cross-referenced to cover essential information on all aspects of cookery.

The Good Housekeeping Institute, a complex of kitchens and equipment testing areas, is the place from which much of the information in this book emanates. The Institute, which is the largest department of Good Housekeeping magazine, has been disseminating advice and creating wonderful meals for the magazine's readers since 1924, and for readers of Good Housekeeping books since the late thirties. During the war years, the Institute was a vital part of the war effort, advising people how best to make imaginative use of wartime rations while preserving the nutritional balance. These were the days when everything the Institute preached actually came out of the real experience of serving the public. In 1927 the magazine had opened a restaurant in Oxford Street, opposite Selfridges, where tea and cakes were served. No better proof of the success of recipe pages than the public's active approbation. During the war, the magazine ran a wartime meals centre in Victoria, as well as beginning the publishing venture, which today produces all Good Housekeeping cookbooks.

All the information gleaned over the past 65 years is what makes Good Housekeeping's cookery books unique. The knowledge gathered by so many caring hands through the decades gives The New Cookery Encyclopedia an authority which few other cookbooks merit. Good Cooking!

Noëlle Walsh
Editor, Good Housekeeping Magazine

A

ABAISSE A French name given to a piece of pastry that is rolled out thinly and used as a base. The name also applies to a biscuit or piece of sponge cake to be topped with jam, icing or cream.

ABALONE (Ormer, Sea-ear) The abalone is a single-shelled (univalve) mollusc found mostly in warm waters off the Californian coast and the Channel Islands. It is also found in Australia and features in the cooking of both Japan and China as well as the Mediterranean. There are two main varieties: the European Ormer is smaller than the Californian Abalone. All varieties are well known for their ornamental shells which have a fine lining reminiscent of mother-of-pearl. Their nickname, sea-ear, comes from the shape of the shell.

The edible part of the abalone is its muscular 'foot' which it uses to move along and to attach itself to rocks on the sea-bed. The flavour of the white meat is similar to that of scallops.

To prepare: Being a muscle, the 'foot' tends to be a tough morsel which needs tenderizing before cooking. After cutting it away from the shell, remove the inedible parts and beat the remainder with a meat mallet or rolling pin.

To cook: Small tender abalone should be sliced, marinated and eaten raw, while larger abalone should be sliced and lightly fried before serving. Overcooking will make them tough.

ABERNETHY BISCUIT A plain, sweet biscuit, flavoured with caraway.

ABRICOTINE (Apricot Brandy) A liqueur made from brandy, sugar and apricots (or apricot kernels).

ACETIC ACID The essential constituent of vinegar, amounting to not less than 4 per cent. It is produced when wine is left exposed to the air and the alcohol in the wine reacts with bacteria, turning it to acetic acid. A dilute solution of acetic acid (4-5 per cent) is sometimes used as a cheap substitute for white wine vinegar for pickling purposes. Acetic acid is also used in very small quantities to make some sweets. (*see also* VINEGAR)

ACETO-DOLCE An Italian pickle, consisting of fruits preserved in a syrup of vinegar and honey. It is chiefly used as an appetizer.

ACHARD A pickle consisting of a mixture of chopped fruits and vegetables in a spicy sauce. Originating in India, it was brought to Europe by the English in the eighteenth century.

ACKEE (*see* AKEE)

ACID An acid substance will give off hydrogen ions when combined with water and the degree to which this occurs (the pH or 'hydrogen potential') determines the acidity of the substance. Acidity is measured on a scale of 0 (very acid) to 14 (very alkaline). Some common acid substances include lemon juice (pH2) and apple juice (pH3), while pure water is neutral (pH7).

Acids exist in many natural ingredients – citric acid in lemon juice, acetic acid in vinegar, tartaric acid in wine and unripe fruit, lactic acid in sour milk and malic acid in sour apples. Acids have many important uses in cookery. Foods which contain acid will stay in good condition longer as micro-organisms leading to deterioration cannot develop easily in a low pH environment. This is why vinegar is used to preserve foods in pickles, chutneys and relishes. An acid such as lemon juice can be used to halt the deterioration which leads to discoloration of peeled and cut bananas, avocados or Jerusalem artichokes (*see* ACIDULATE). Finally, the amount of acid in food determines how sour it will taste, so a squeeze of lemon juice can make all the difference to the flavour of a sweet or savoury dish.

ACIDULATE To make something acid by adding a little lemon juice, vinegar or other acid. Acidulated water is used when preparing some fruits and vegetables, such as apples, celeriac and Jerusalem artichokes, to prevent them turning brown when their cut surfaces are exposed to the air. The pieces of food should be dropped straight into acidulated water after peeling and/or cutting.

ACITRON A candied cactus made in Mexico and used as a stuffing for meats.

ADDITIVE Any substance added to processed food to perform a special function: this may be to prevent spoilage, or to enhance texture, flavour or appearance. The purposes legally acceptable are: preserving; colouring; flavouring (including sweetening); emulsifying and stabilizing (ensuring ingredients do not separate); improving. Other substances may also be used to control the acidity of a product (so-called 'buffers' and 'bases'), to prevent fats from going rancid (antioxidants) and to stop food drying out (humectants). Many additives are of natural origin, but some are synthetic, laboratory-produced and developed to perform a specific function. Natural additives include pectin (E440) and vitamin C (E300), both of which are naturally present in everyday foods.

An increasing demand for convenience foods has led to more and more food processing, which in turn has led to the use of more and more additives, many of which are added simply to conceal the effects of processing, such as loss of real colour. There are approximately 3,500 additives in use, a number which has given rise to a considerable amount of concern. Many people have begun to question whether so many additives are really necessary, and have expressed doubts as to the safety and long-term effects of consuming so many artificial substances. It is thought likely that a small proportion of people could be adversely affected by consuming too many additives, or could exhibit a reaction to one particular additive. Symptoms ranging from vomiting to asthma and, in the case of some children, hyperactivity, have all been linked to the consumption of particular additives. However, it is important to balance the risks with the benefits – without additives many of the fresh foods we take for granted would be unavailable

and the 'shelf-life' of many foods would be drastically reduced. In particular, we would have to learn to accept food that was far less presentable in appearance.

As a result of the controversy, however, new regulations introduced in 1986 have led to stricter controls being placed on the use of additives. All pre-packed food products sold in Britain must now list additives individually amongst other ingredients on the label or packet. Vague terms like 'permitted colouring and preservatives' are no longer acceptable. (Food sold loose, however, does not have to comply with this law, which does not help to inform the consumer about certain 'hidden' additives that are used in food production, such as colouring in hen feed and antibiotics in meat.) As well as this, the EC Scientific Committee is responsible for drawing up a list of additives permitted for use in foods sold within EC countries. These permitted additives are given an 'E' number by which they can be identified. Additives with a number but no 'E' prefix have been approved in the country in which they are used but not throughout the EC. To introduce a new additive in the UK, the Food Advisory Committee (FAC) have to be persuaded that it is both essential and safe. After testing, it may be approved for use. (*see also* ADULTERANT, ALAR, ANTIBIOTIC, COLOURINGS, FLAVOURINGS, PRESERVATIVES, SWEETENERS)

ADUKI BEAN (*see* ADZUKI BEAN)

ADULTERANT A substance which is added to another (usually food) in order to increase the bulk and reduce the cost, with intent to defraud. The adulterant is usually similar in consistency and colour to the food in question and the flavour is either similar or neutral. Common examples of adulterants that were formerly used include: starch in spices, curry powder and cocoa; water in milk, butter and beer; turmeric in mustard; chicory in coffee.

Since the first Food and Drugs Act of 1860, control of adulteration of foods has improved considerably and there are laws governing the preparation and labelling of food as well as the content. These laws are continually being revised. For most food products, the manufacturer must now print on the packaging a list of the ingredients it contains. The ingredients must be listed according to the proportions in which they are used, the greatest being at the top of the list. (*see also* ADDITIVE)

ADVOCAAT A Dutch liqueur, thick and creamy, made from fresh egg yolks and brandy.

ADZUKI BEAN (Aduki Bean) These small, round, reddish brown beans are grown in China and Japan and are available dried in Britain. They need overnight soaking before being boiled rapidly for 10 minutes, then simmered for about 30 minutes, depending on the age of the beans. They may be used whole in casseroles, soups and other savoury dishes. Ground to a powder, the unusual sweet flavour of the dried beans makes them also suitable for cakes, breads and pastry. (*see also* PULSES)

AGAR-AGAR (Japanese Gelatine, Kanten) A tasteless white powder derived from seaweed that has useful gelling properties and can be used as a vegetarian substitute for gelatine. It is also available in sheets or threads. Unlike gelatine, which dissolves at a much lower temperature, agar-agar will only dissolve in boiling water. Follow the manufacturer's instructions carefully when using in both sweet and savoury dishes.

AGARIC A family of fungi, containing many different types of both edible and poisonous mushrooms. (*see also* FUNGUS, MUSHROOM)

AIGUILLETTE A French name given to a thin strip of cooked poultry, meat or fish.

AILLADE A French word used to describe various sauces and accompaniments to salads, all strongly flavoured with garlic, for example *sauce aillade.*

AÏOLI A mayonnaise-like sauce made from olive oil, egg yolks and garlic. It may be served with cold fish, potatoes, hard-boiled eggs, snails or cold meats.

AJOWAN A spice seed that is closely related to caraway and looks similar to celery seed. It has a strong thyme-like flavour and is often used in Indian recipes.

AKEE (Ackee) A tropical fruit from the Caribbean that is available canned elsewhere. Inside this bright red pear-shaped fruit are three black seeds which are surrounded by soft, creamy flesh, the only edible part of the fruit. Akee is eaten as a vegetable and is used in a traditional West Indian dish, Salt Fish and Akee. The fruit must be absolutely ripe when eaten as it is poisonous when unripe or over-ripe.

ALAR A chemical used to spray apple trees to regulate apple growth. Research has shown that Alar permeates the skin and fruit of apples and could constitute a health hazard. Although the Government has declared the chemical safe, the manufacturers of Alar are no longer producing it for use on food crops grown in Britain.

ALASKA, BAKED (*see* BAKED ALASKA)

ALBUMEN POWDER A commercially produced dried form of egg albumen (*see* ALBUMIN) which can be used as a substitute for egg whites when making meringues or royal icing. Royal icing made with albumen powder has the advantage of being softer than that made with egg whites. Albumen powder has come into more common use since it became advisable to avoid eating raw egg which could be infected with salmonella bacteria. (*see also* EGGS)

ALBUMIN (Albumen) A soluble protein which is found in blood, milk and egg white. When gently heated to 70°C (150°F), or when mixed with alcohol, it coagulates into a flocculent mass. Egg white is commonly known as albumen.

ALCOHOL Alcohol is a liquid produced by the fermentation of sugary substances, followed by a distillation process. There are many types of alcohol, but only one, ethyl alcohol, is suitable for consumption. It is produced by the fermentation of fruits, cereals and root vegetables (potatoes in particular), and is a component of all alcoholic drinks – wines, spirits, liqueurs, beers.

The alcoholic content of a drink can be measured in a number of ways which vary from country to country. In Europe, the Gay-Lussac (degrees GL) scale is most commonly used and expresses what proportion of a liquid's volume is alcohol at a certain temperature.

Alcohol has antiseptic and preservative properties and some nutritive value in the form of sugars. The effects of consuming too much alcohol are well known, though many unpleasant 'hangover' symptoms are caused by the so-called 'congenerics', or by-products, of the fermentation process, rather than by the alcohol itself.

In cookery, alcohol is used in marinades, sauces and stuffings as well as in a number of recipes for casseroles, pâtés, cakes and desserts. It can also be used to stunning effect in dishes that are 'flambéed' (*see* FLAMBÉING).

AL DENTE An Italian expression used to describe the consistency of pasta when it is cooked to perfection. Its literal translation is 'to the tooth', meaning that cooked pasta should still feel slightly firm to the bite. (*see also* PASTA)

ALE An alcoholic drink brewed from malt and hops. The name is generally confined to the lighter-coloured malt liquors or beers, though before the introduction of hops it also applied to all malt beer. (*see also* BEER)

ALECOST (*see* COSTMARY)

ALEWIFE (*see* HERRING)

ALFALFA This leguminous European plant with clover-like leaves is primarily a fodder food, but its seed has become popular as one of a number of seeds that can be 'sprouted' at home for use in salads or as a garnish. It has a mild and pleasant flavour and is an excellent vegetable source of protein, vitamins and minerals although excessive amounts (more than 25 g/1 oz per day) have been linked to an inflammatory disease, systemic lupus erythematosis. (*see also* BEAN SPROUTS)

ALGAE (*see* SEA VEGETABLES)

ALGINATES (*see* SEA VEGETABLES)

ALISIER (*see* EAU-DE-VIE)

ALKALI An alkaline substance can be said, in simple terms, to be the opposite of an acid. It will turn litmus paper blue, while an acid turns it red. Like acids, the alkalinity of a substance is measured on the pH scale (*see* ACID) but it registers at the other end of the scale. An alkali can be defined by its ability to neutralize acids, to combine with them to form base salts, then to dissolve in water.

The alkali most commonly used in cooking is bicarbonate of soda. Its flavour is familiar in soda bread, scones and griddle scones. Combined in a recipe with an acid, such as sour milk, buttermilk, lemon juice or cream of tartar, it reacts, giving off gases that have a leavening effect. Bicarbonate of soda is one of the ingredients of baking powder.

ALKANET (*see* ALKANNA)

ALKANNA (Alkanet) A plant of the borage family which grows in Mediterranean countries and in south-east Europe. Although its leaves were once eaten as a vegetable, its major use today is in the production of a red food dye which is extracted from the roots of the plant. It is used to colour wine, drinks, oils, ices and sausage skins.

ALLEMANDE, À L' A French term applied to dishes garnished with such German specialities as *sauerkraut*, smoked sausage, pickled pork, potato dumplings or noodles tossed in butter, or to dishes served with the classic French *sauce allemande*. In French cuisine, the term also refers to a method of preparing game.

ALLIGATOR PEAR (*see* AVOCADO)

ALLIS (*see* SHAD)

ALLSPICE (Jamaican Pepper, Myrtle Pepper, Pimento) A spice from the West Indies sold as small dried berries or ready ground. The whole berries are an ingredient of pickling spice. The flavour of allspice is a mixture of cloves, cinnamon and nutmeg (hence its name) and it can be used whole in marinades, meat dishes, pickles, chutneys and with poached fish, or ground in pickles, relishes, soups, sauces, vegetable dishes, beef stews, baked ham, lamb dishes, boiled fish, oyster stew, cakes, milk puddings and fruit pies.

ALLUMETTES Potatoes cut in 'matchsticks' and fried; sometimes called 'straw potatoes'. The name is also given to narrow pastry fingers, sweet or savoury.

ALMOND This popular nut is the seed of a tree belonging to the peach family which grows in the hot dry climate of such countries as Sicily, Spain and California. There are two varieties of almond – bitter and sweet. Bitter almonds contain prussic acid and are poisonous if eaten in large quantities. They are used mainly for making essences and oils.

Sweet almonds are available in their shells and in many shelled forms – whole, split, flaked, chopped and ground. Whole and split almonds are used in baking, whole blanched almonds being a traditional decoration for Dundee cake. Split almonds are traditionally served with trout in *truite aux amandes*. Flaked almonds are often toasted and used as a garnish or decoration, while chopped almonds may be sprinkled over desserts and ice creams. Ground almonds are used to make almond paste (*see* ALMOND PASTE) and macaroons, amongst many other things.

When almonds are first shelled, they are coated

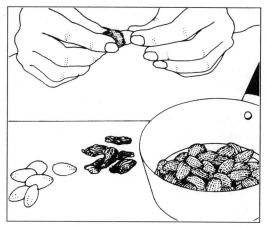

Gently squeezing almonds to remove them from their skins after blanching and cooling slightly.

in a thin but tough brown skin. This is easily removed by blanching.
To blanch: Cover the almonds with boiling water and leave for a few minutes, then rinse in cold water and remove the skins.

ALMOND ESSENCE This is made from bitter almonds by a process of fermentation and distillation. It is not widely available but is sometimes sold at herbalists. Synthetic almond flavouring is sold in most supermarkets. Either can be used in baking.

ALMOND OIL An oil obtained by pressing bitter almonds. It is very expensive and is therefore occasionally adulterated with oil from peach or apricot kernels (*see* ADULTERATE). The flavour of almond oil is very delicate and its uses are limited to sweet-making and oiling moulds for desserts.

ALMOND PASTE (Marzipan) This firm, sweet paste is used as a coating for cakes (often to provide a smooth surface for royal icing), or it can be moulded into decorative shapes. It is also popular as a stuffing for dried fruits (especially dates) and chocolates.

The almond paste of classic French cooking is

made by stirring ground almonds into hot sugar syrup, but a simpler version is more usually made by binding ground almonds and icing sugar with whole eggs, egg yolks or egg whites. Almond paste should always be made from freshly ground almonds as they quickly lose their flavour. The egg should be added very gradually and the paste kneaded well, to soften it and to bring out the natural oil. It may be coloured as required. Several brands of commercially manufactured almond paste are available.

Almond Paste
225 g (8 oz) icing sugar
225 g (8 oz) caster sugar
450 g (1 lb) ground almonds
2 eggs, lightly beaten
5 ml (1 tsp) vanilla flavouring
10 ml (2 tsp) lemon juice
Sift the icing sugar into a bowl and mix in the caster sugar and almonds. Add the egg, vanilla and lemon juice and mix to a stiff dough. Knead lightly, then shape into a ball. Cover until required.
Makes 900 g (2 lb) – enough to cover one 23 cm (9 inch) square or 25.5 cm (10 inch) round cake

ALPESTRA (Alpin) A hard, dry, lightly salted cheese, golden in colour, made at Briançon and Gap in France.

ALPIN (*see* ALPESTRA)

ALPINE STRAWBERRY (*see* STRAWBERRY, WILD)

ALSACIENNE, À L' A French name used to describe a dish with a fairly elaborate garnish, the best known variation probably being smoked sausages, ham and peas.

ALTITUDE This can affect cooking times and temperatures. The higher the altitude, the lower the temperature at which water boils.

ALUMINIUM A strong but light silver-grey metal used widely to make cooking pans, kitchen utensils and food and drink cans. Aluminium conducts heat well and provides even cooking as long as pans remain fairly thick and heavy. Some foods have a tendency to stick to aluminium so many pans sold have a non-stick interior surface.

The surface of aluminium is affected by both alkaline and acid substances; pans will become darker after contact with an alkali, but will lighten again after contact with an acid. Some concern has been expressed over whether acid foods cooked in aluminium pans can become contaminated by the metal. This is part of a general concern about the amount of aluminium consumed both in this way and in drinking water. It has been suggested that high doses of aluminium can lead to premature senility in the form of Alzheimer's Disease.

Aluminium is very expensive to manufacture in terms of the energy it requires. It is therefore one of the most worthwhile metals for recycling and several schemes have been set up for the collection and recycling of aluminium cans.

Aluminium foil has become one of the most popular convenience items in the kitchen. It can be used for food wrapping, particularly for bread, sandwiches and cake, and items to be frozen. Meat and poultry can be roasted in it, keeping the oven clean. It can be used to line tins, is very malleable and does not need greasing. Aluminium foil is also used to make disposable food containers which can be used for freezing and cooking.

AMANDINE The name given to a variety of almond-flavoured French pastries and cakes. It may be applied to a type of tart or tartlet, made with a pastry base and filled with an almond-flavoured mixture, or to an almond-flavoured sponge cake baked in a ring mould and iced with white fondant.

In America, the word may be given to any dish, especially grilled or fried fish or poultry, cooked with chopped almonds.

AMARDINE A Middle Eastern preparation made by pressing dried apricot paste into sheets. It has a concentrated, slightly tart, apricot taste and can be soaked in water and used to flavour desserts or drinks. The sheets can also be torn into pieces and dropped into a hot lamb stew.

AMARETTO DI SARONNO An Italian fruit liqueur, flavoured with apricot kernels, and with an almond-like flavour.

AMBROSIA Mythical food of the gods of Olympus.

AMÉRICAINE, À L' A French term which describes various methods of preparing meat, game, fish, vegetables and eggs, the best known example being *homard a l'américaine*, in which lobster is served with a sauce based on tomato, onion and herbs, cooked in wine or brandy. (*see also* ARMORICAINE, À L')

AMERICAN BLUE POINT (*see* OYSTER)

AMERICAN FROSTING The special feature of this cake icing is that whilst it forms a crust on the outside, it never becomes really hard in texture like royal icing. Although it is mostly used on sponge cakes and on walnut and cherry cakes, it can be applied to any type of cake. Any decorations (such as nuts or crystallized fruit) must be ready to put on immediately, before the icing has time to set.

American Frosting

225 g (8 oz) caster or granulated sugar
60 ml (4 tbsp) water
pinch of cream of tartar
1 egg white

Gently heat the sugar in the water with the cream of tartar, stirring until dissolved. Then, without stirring, boil to 120°C (240°F). Beat the egg white stiffly. Remove the sugar syrup from the heat and immediately the bubbles subside, pour it on to the egg white in a thin stream, beating continuously. When it thickens, shows signs of going dull round the edges and is almost cold, pour it quickly over the cake and spread at once with a palette knife or pull into soft peaks with the back of a spoon. *Makes enough to cover one 18 cm (7 inch) cake*

AMINO ACID Amino acids are the basic constituents of proteins and are essential in a healthy diet. There are about 20 different amino acids in all, most of which can be made within the body, but there are eight 'essential' amino acids which must be supplied by the diet. (For growing infants, the number increases to nine.) Without a complete set of amino acids, the body is unable to make the proteins it needs.

Protein foods which contain the full range of amino acids are egg yolk, fresh milk, liver and kidney. Vegetarian complete sources are brewer's yeast, soya beans and wheatgerm. (*see also* PROTEIN)

AMONTILLADO (*see* SHERRY)

ANATTO (*see* ANNATTO)

ANCHOVY The anchovy is a small round oily fish, which is usually filleted and cured, by salting or brining, and then canned or bottled. As cured anchovies are very salty, they are only used in small amounts in appetizers and cocktail nibbles, as pizza topping and in *salade niçoise*. They can also be used to make anchovy butter (*see* ANCHOVY BUTTER) for use in savouries.

Anchovies are seldom available fresh outside the Mediterranean, but they are easily recognized by their extraordinarily large mouths, which stretch back almost as far as the gills. They have a strong flavour, but are not salty like cured anchovies.

ANCHOVY BUTTER This can be served with grilled fish and meat or as a topping for canapés. Mash six boned anchovies with a fork and cream with 100 g (4 oz) softened butter.

ANCHOVY ESSENCE A strong essence (or extract) made from cured anchovies. It is very salty and should be used sparingly. (*see also* ESSENCE, EXTRACT)

ANCHOVY PASTE This is commercially made by mixing pounded salted anchovies, vinegar, spices and water.

ANCIENNE, À L' Literally, 'old-style', this term usually refers to a dish with a mixed garnish consisting of small sliced onions and button mushrooms.

ANDALOUSE, À L' This French term is applied to a variety of recipes, but most often to those involving the use of tomatoes and rice.

ANDOUILLE A large French black-skinned sausage made from pig stomach and intestines. It may also include other parts of the pig – neck, breast, head or heart. It is usually cut into thin slices and served cold as an hors d'oeuvre, though it may also be poached and served hot. The best *andouille* comes from Vire in Normandy. (*see also* ANDOUILLETTE)

ANDOUILLETTE Although this French sausage is made from similar ingredients to *andouille*, it is much smaller and coarser in texture. It varies in colour, depending on whether or not it has been smoked, and is often sold coated with breadcrumbs, aspic or fat. It is eaten hot, either grilled or fried, and is traditionally served with mustard, fried potatoes and onions, red beans and lentils. (*see also* ANDOUILLE)

ANGEL CAKE (Angel Food Cake) This classic American sponge cake is very light and airy, and very pale in colour, since it is based on egg whites and contains no egg yolk or fat. Its extremely light and delicate texture is the result of thorough whisking of the egg whites and careful folding in of the flour. The traditional American recipe uses a special low-gluten cake flour that is not available in Britain, but good results can be achieved using plain flour. Angel cakes are baked in a special tube tin similar to a ring mould. The finished cake is often iced with American frosting or dusted with icing sugar. (*see also* AMERICAN FROSTING)

ANGEL FISH (Fiddlefish, Shark-ray, Monkfish) A member of the shark family found in warm European waters and tropical seas, this fish has wide pectoral fins which give it its name. Its tail is thick and meaty and contains few bones, while the 'wings' can be treated in the same way as skate wings. (*see also* SKATE)

ANGELICA A tall plant of the parsley family, angelica is chiefly cultivated on the Continent, especially in France, but it can be grown in Britain and was at one time very popular because of its pleasant musk-like scent.

The hollow green stalks are candied and can be cut into shapes and used for decorating cakes and desserts. When buying, look for a really good green colour and a small amount of sugar. To remove sugar, soak briefly in hot water, then drain and dry well.

ANGELS ON HORSEBACK A dish traditionally served as an after-dinner savoury. Oysters are rolled inside strips of bacon, grilled and served hot on crisp fried bread croûtes. (*see also* DEVILS ON HORSEBACK)

ANGLAISE, À L' A French term (meaning, literally, 'in the English style') used to describe food that is plainly cooked, usually boiled in stock or water. It may be applied to vegetables, meat, poultry or fish dishes.

ANGLERFISH (*see* MONKFISH)

ANGOSTURA BITTERS A very bitter, reddish brown liquid made from a secret formula which includes gentian, cloves, cinnamon, nutmeg, citrus peel, prunes, quinine and rum. It was first invented in Venezuela during the nineteenth century and was used for medicinal purposes. Now it is made in Trinidad and is considered a food flavouring. It is used in cocktails (pink gin, for example) and sometimes as a flavouring in casseroles.

ANISEED (Anise) These small seeds come from the sweet cumin plant and have a strong, distinctive flavour thought to aid digestion. They are used mainly to flavour cakes and biscuits, but can also be used in salad dressings, with sugar and butter on carrots and red cabbage, in cheese, fish and shellfish dishes and with baked apples. Aniseed is the main flavouring ingredient in drinks such as Pernod, Ricard, Anisette, Ouzo and Raki.

ANISE PEPPER (Chinese Pepper, Szechuan Pepper) A hot aromatic spice made from the dried red berries of a Chinese tree. It is one of the ingredients of five-spice powder. Anise pepper should be roasted before use. (*see also* FIVE- SPICE POWDER)

ANISETTE A colourless aniseed-flavoured liqueur that comes from France, Spain and Italy. Marie Brizard, from Bordeaux, is the most famous.

ANNATTO (Anatto) A bright yellow-orange food dye derived from the seeds of a South American tree. It is used commercially to colour butter, cheese, smoked fish, potato crisps and sweets. (*see also* COLOURINGS)

ANNONA FRUIT (*see* CUSTARD APPLE)

ANTIBIOTIC The general name for a substance capable of killing living organisms, particularly bacteria. Antibiotics are familiar to us in the form of drugs used to cure a variety of infections, but they are also used to a large extent to prevent illness in cattle and other livestock bred for meat. The continuous use of antibiotics in this way has increased in line with the use of intensive farming methods which bring with them a higher risk of disease.

Some concern has been expressed over the possibility that small amounts of these substances may still be present in meat when it reaches the shops, constituting a health hazard. Farming procedures should ensure, however, that doses of antibiotics are stopped for a given period before animals are slaughtered so that any residue has time to clear from the meat. (*see also* ADDITIVE)

ANTIOXIDANT An organic or synthetic substance added to commercially produced foods to prevent oxidation which leads to deterioration. Common antioxidants include ascorbic acid (vitamin C) and tocopherol (vitamin E). (*see also* ADDITIVE)

ANTIPASTO An Italian name for a selection of hot or cold foods served as an appetizer or starter. Literally, the term means 'before the meal'.

APÉRITIF The French name for a drink served before a meal, differing from a cocktail in that it is fairly mild in character and often bitter in flavour. Patent *apéritifs* are either wine or spirit based; French and Italian vermouths and sherry are amongst the most widely used wine-based *apéritifs*. Others, generically called 'bitters', are made from distilled spirits or wines and are distinctively flavoured (*see* BITTERS).

APPETIZER A name given to hot or cold foods served before or at the beginning of a meal. It can refer to canapés served with an *apéritif* as well as to the first course (starter) or hors d'oeuvre. (*see also* APÉRITIF, CANAPÉ, HORS D'OEUVRE)

APPLE Apples are one of the most familiar and useful of fruits. They are a popular snack and dessert fruit and are used in cooking in countless ways. Nutritionally, they are a useful source of vitamin C and dietary fibre, especially if eaten with the skin on.

The many varieties of apple can be divided into two groups: cooking and dessert (eating). Eating apples often have more flavour than cooking apples, and cooking apples are too tart to eat on their own.

Cooking apples are delicious simply cooked with a little sugar but can also be used in any number of sweet dishes and sometimes in combination with savoury foods. Unlike eating apples, cookers will reduce to a purée when cooked. They can be baked or stewed, or combined with pastry, milk puddings and many other foods. They can also be preserved in the form of jam, jelly, pickles and chutney. Cooking apples are a rich source of pectin and are therefore useful in jam-making to combine with fruits that are poor in pectin (*see* JAM, PECTIN).

Dessert apples should be thoroughly washed or peeled before use. They make good additions to fresh fruit salads, or they can be used in pies, tarts and puddings or served with cheese. Apple slices should be brushed with lemon juice to prevent browning.

To select: When buying apples, choose those that are firm with unblemished skins.

To store: Keep apples cool and dry; those kept at room temperature should be eaten within 2 weeks.

To store large quantities of apples for longer periods, arrange them with the stalks upwards, not touching each other, on slatted wooden shelves in a cool, damp, frost-proof room or shed. They should be looked over once a week and any that show signs of deterioration should be removed and used at once. An alternative method of storing is to wrap apples individually in newspaper, or in unsealed or pierced polythene bags, and then to pack them in boxes in a cool place. Some of the best varieties for keeping are Bramley's Seedling (cookers) and Cox's Orange Pippin (eating).

To stew: Wipe 450 g (1 lb) cooking apples, peel thinly, core and cut into quarters and then into thin slices. Dissolve 100 g (4 oz) sugar in 150 ml (¼ pint) water and boil for 5 minutes. Add the fruit and simmer very gently until the apples are soft but not broken up.

To bake: Wash even-sized cooking apples and cut through the skin round the centre. Remove the cores with an apple corer and stand the apples in an ovenproof dish or baking tin. Pour a little water around, fill up the centre of each apple with demerara sugar and top with a knob of butter. Bake in the oven at 200°C (400°F) mark 6 for 45-60 minutes or until the apples are tender. Serve hot or cold. (Alternatively, the apples may be stuffed with dried fruit or a mixture of chopped dates and nuts, a few shavings of butter being placed on top of the apples before baking. Apples can also be stuffed with a mixture of soft fruits tossed in sugar and complementary spices.)

Apple Varieties
Although many more varieties of apple are grown, only about 50 are commonly available. Those imported from other countries ensure a year-round supply. Below are listed some of the most popular and readily available apple varieties.

Cooking Apples
Bramley's Seedling This is a late season apple produced in the United Kingdom and Ireland. It is generally quite large and green in colour, with dull red patches. Its flesh is firm and solid but tender, with an acid flavour. It is a good keeper and considered the best English cooking apple.
Lord Derby This very large greenish-yellow apple is available in England from September to November. It has soft and tender flesh and is a poor keeper.
McIntosh This is a bright red apple with some russeting. Its flesh is white, juicy and aromatic.
Newton Wonder A large apple with solid, sweet flesh. It is a good keeper.

Eating Apples
Blenheim Orange Produced in the United Kingdom, New Zealand and Nova Scotia, this large apple is orange in colour, streaked with red. Its flesh is crisp, acid and juicy.
Cox's Orange Pippin This small to medium round apple is perhaps the most popular of eating apples. It is greenish-yellow to orange in colour, streaked or shaded with red. Its flesh is tender, crisp and juicy and it has an excellent flavour and aroma. It is a good keeper and is produced in

England, Canada, Australia and New Zealand.

Crispin An apple with Japanese parentage which has recently been introduced in the United Kingdom. It is large, yellowy green in colour and has a good flavour.

Discovery This red-skinned English apple has firm, juicy flesh. It keeps well.

Egremont Russet A medium crisp apple with a russet brown skin and an orange blush. It has a distinct nutty flavour.

Gala A sweet, crisp eating apple with tough orange-red skin.

Golden Delicious Produced in France, South Africa, Australia and New Zealand, this green-yellow apple is available most of the year. It has crisp white flesh and five characteristic 'bumps' at the blossom end.

Granny Smith This bright green apple has white, crisp, juicy flesh with a slightly tart flavour. It is a good keeper and can also be used as a cooker. It is produced in Australia, New Zealand and South Africa.

James Grieve This English apple is pale green to yellow in colour and has thin skin. Its soft flesh bruises rather easily.

Jonagold This dessert apple has yellow or green skin with hints of bright red. Its flesh is white, crisp and juicy.

Jonathan A small yellow apple striped with red. Its flesh is crisp, sweet and juicy and it is an excellent keeper.

Laxton's Fortune This English apple has sweet, crisp aromatic flesh with a red and yellow russeted skin.

Laxton's Superb A medium round apple with yellow-shaded red cheeks. Its flesh is crisp, white and sweet.

Red Delicious This is a shiny red apple with fairly soft yellow flesh and a tough waxy skin.

Royal Gala A quite small, red-skinned apple streaked with yellow.

Spartan A medium dark red apple with crisp, white flesh.

Starking This South African apple has sweet, yellowish, soft and juicy flesh with a thick red skin.

Sturmer Pippin This is a small apple with green to russet-bronze skin. It has good quality flesh that is firm and sweet, and it is an excellent keeper.

Worcester Pearmain A medium apple with a brilliant yellow-green colour flushed with crimson. Its flesh is sweet, aromatic and juicy.

APPLE BRANDY (*see* CALVADOS)

APPLE, DRIED Apples are one of the few fruits which do not lose any vitamin C content in the drying process. They are usually sold as rings and can be eaten as a snack, added to muesli and other breakfast cereals, or they can be soaked and used to make purées or added to other fruits in crumbles, pies or dried fruit salads. (*see also* DRIED FRUIT)

APPLEJACK (*see* CALVADOS)

APPLEWOOD A type of Cheddar cheese which is smoked over apple tree branches and coated with paprika. It is very similar to another British cheese called Charnwood.

APRICOT This fruit is round and about the size of a walnut. The trees grew originally in China but are now cultivated in many warm countries and apricots are available fresh, canned and dried. They have velvety, yellowish-orange skin and fairly soft, juicy flesh of much the same colour. Unripe apricots are hard and sour; over-ripe they are mealy and tasteless.

Apricots are a rich source of vitamin A. Serve them raw or poached as a dessert, or use them in puddings and pies. They also make very good jam which can be used as a glaze or filling (*see* APRICOT GLAZE).

To select: When buying apricots, choose firm, unwrinkled fruit with a deep colour, or leave pale, unripe fruit to ripen at room temperature. Once ripe, apricots should be eaten within 2-3 days.

To prepare: Wash apricots, cut them in half and remove the stones. (The stone contains an almond-like kernel which can be used to flavour apricot jam and apricot liqueur – see ABRICOTINE). To peel apricots, blanch them in boiling water for 30 seconds to loosen the skin, then peel. Sliced apricots should be brushed with lemon juice to prevent browning.

To poach: Wash 900 g (2 lb) apricots. Dissolve 900 g (2 lb) sugar in 600 ml (1 pint) water and boil for 5 minutes. Add the apricots and poach gently for 5-10 minutes or until the fruit is tender. Scoop out the stones as they rise to the surface.

APRICOT BRANDY (*see* ABRICOTINE)

APRICOT, DRIED The flavour of dried apricots is often better than that of the fresh fruit. Some types are specially tenderized so that there is no need to soak them before use, and some are treated with sulphur dioxide (as are other dried fruits) to preserve their colour. Dried apricots that have not been sulphur-treated are a dark brown colour rather than the familiar golden orange.

Hunza apricots grow wild in Afghanistan and Kashmir. They are much smaller than ordinary dried apricots and are pale brown and wrinkled. Their flavour, however, is far superior and is best enjoyed when they are soaked and poached on their own to serve with cream, custard or yogurt.

APRICOT GLAZE A glaze made from apricot jam is commonly used to brush over a rich fruit cake before applying almond paste, and to glaze the top of a fruit flan. It may also be brushed over the surface of a cooked pastry case before filling to protect the pastry and prevent it absorbing fruit juices.

Apricot Glaze

100 g (4 oz) apricot jam

Put the jam and 30 ml (2 tbsp) water in a saucepan and heat gently, stirring, until the jam softens. Bring to the boil and simmer for 1 minute. Sieve and use while still warm.

Makes 150 ml (¹/₄ pint)

AQUAVIT This Scandinavian national drink is made from grain, rye or potato and variously flavoured with caraway, aniseed or dill. It has a high alcohol content and should always be served ice-cold, preferably with open sandwiches or piquant snacks.

ARABICA (*see* COFFEE)

ARACHIDE (*see* OILS)

ARAK (*see* ARRACK)

ARBORIO RICE (*see* RICE)

ARBROATH SMOKIES (*see* SMOKIES)

ARCHIDUC, À L' A French term that is used to describe many dishes, usually those that are seasoned with paprika and blended with fresh cream.

ARCING This occurs when a dish or utensil made of metal, or with any form of metal trim, or gold or silver decoration, is used in a microwave cooker. The metal reflects the microwaves and produces a blue spark. If this happens, the cooker should be switched off immediately as arcing can damage the cooker's magnetron. (*see also* MICROWAVE COOKING)

ARKSHELL (*see* COCKLE)

ARMAGNAC (*see* BRANDY)

ARMORICAINE, À L' A French term used to describe a number of dishes served with a sauce made from shellfish, usually prawns or shrimp. It is also an alternative name for the classic lobster dish known as *homard à l'américaine*. There is some dispute over which is the correct name, some people believing that the dish originated in Armorica, the ancient name for Brittany, where lobsters have long been a particular speciality. (*see also* AMÉRICAINE, À L')

AROMATIC A fragrant plant that is used as a flavouring. The most commonly used aromatics are herbs and vegetables such as garlic, onions, mushrooms, celery and carrots. An aromatic may be added directly to a dish during cooking, or it may be added in the form of a stock, marinade or herb vinegar. The flavour imparted by an aromatic is quite subtle; it gives a dish a particular 'aroma' rather than a distinct flavour. For this reason, many spices are too pungent to be used as aromatics.

ARRACK (Arak, Raki, Rakia) A spirit made in the Near and Far East. It is made from fermented palm sap (toddy) but other bases, such as dates, grapes and milk, are also used. Arrack may be flavoured, particularly with aniseed.

ARRAN CHEESE An individual rindless Dunlop cheese made on the island of Arran and sold in 900 g (2 lb) packs. It is a hard cheese, moist and close-textured. (*see also* DUNLOP CHEESE)

ARROWROOT A pure starch powder (fecula) obtained from the pith of the roots of the maranta plant, which is grown in Bermuda and the West Indies. It is a light, white, odourless powder, which will keep for a considerable time if stored in a dry place.

Arrowroot can be used as an alternative to cornflour as a thickening agent in liquids. It is most useful used in fruit juices to make a sauce or glaze. It gives the sauce a gloss, unlike cornflour which makes a cloudy sauce. Arrowroot should always be blended first with a little cold liquid, then added to the sauce and brought to the boil to thicken. It is usually used in the proportions of 15 ml (3 tsp) arrowroot mixed with 45 ml (3 tbsp) cold water to every 450 ml ($\frac{3}{4}$ pint) liquid, but quantities vary depending on the thickness of sauce or glaze required. (*see also* CORNFLOUR, FECULA)

ARTICHOKE, CHINESE (Chorogi, Crosnes, Japanese Artichoke, Stachys) The small tubers of a plant which grows in Europe as well as in the Far East. Its name comes from its flavour which is similar to that of Jerusalem artichokes. It also looks somewhat like a miniature Jerusalem

artichoke, but is not in fact related to it.

To prepare: Chinese artichokes must be blanched in boiling water before the skins can be removed. Like Jerusalem artichokes, the flesh will discolour when exposed to the air, so they should be dropped straight into acidulated water (*see* ACIDULATE).

To cook: Chinese artichokes may be fried in butter, boiled and served whole or mashed, prepared *au gratin*, or served cold in salads. (*see also* JAPONAISE, À LA)

ARTICHOKE, GLOBE (French Artichoke) A type of thistle native to North Africa but now grown in Europe and America as a vegetable. The edible part is the bud of the flower which is cut off at the point where it joins the stem. The fond or 'heart' of the artichoke is particularly highly prized, while the 'choke', the thistly part, is discarded. Artichoke hearts are available canned. A miniature variety of globe artichoke is now available fresh in many supermarkets.

Snipping off the tips of the remaining artichoke leaves with a pair of kitchen scissors.

To select: When buying globe artichokes, look for heads with a clear green colour and leaves which have no dry edges. Choose heads which are tightly curled rather than wide open.

To prepare: Before cooking, cut the stalks off the artichokes and snip off a few of the rough outer leaves with scissors, so that any brown or dried edges are removed. Trim the tips of the remaining leaves. Miniature artichokes need no preparation other than removing the stalks.

To cook: Cook prepared artichokes whole in boiling salted water for 35 minutes or until a leaf can be pulled out easily.

To serve: Globe artichokes may be served hot with melted butter or hollandaise sauce, or cold with mayonnaise or French dressing. Pull off the leaves, one by one, dip in the dressing, then suck off the fleshy part of each leaf. Once all the leaves are off, slice off or spoon out the hairy choke, which is clearly visible, and use a knife and fork to eat the fond.

Cooked artichokes may also be hollowed out, removing the hairy choke, and stuffed. Miniature varieties or tender young artichokes can be cooked and eaten whole.

Scraping out the choke with a teaspoon after removing the central leaves.

ARTICHOKE, JAPANESE (*see* ARTICHOKE, CHINESE)

ARTICHOKE, JERUSALEM (Root Artichoke, Sunchoke) This is a knobbly tuber with a nut-like taste, which ranges in colour from beige to brownish-red. The plant is a member of the sunflower family that originated in America but is now grown extensively in Europe.

To select: When buying Jerusalem artichokes, choose firm tubers with the smoothest surface available as they are easier to peel. They should be used as soon as possible as they quickly lose their lovely creamy colour and become rather wrinkled and soft.

To prepare: Scrub tubers well and peel thinly. If they are very knobbly and difficult to peel, cook them first and then peel. Like other tubers, Jerusalem artichokes can be cubed, diced, sliced or cut into julienne strips. Put peeled whole tubers or pieces straight into acidulated water (*see* ACIDULATE) to prevent discoloration, if not cooking immediately.

To cook: Jerusalem artichokes may be cooked in boiling salted water for 15-20 minutes or until tender. Add 15 ml (1 tbsp) lemon juice or vinegar to the water to prevent discoloration. They may also be steamed, deep-fried, sautéed or roasted around a joint of meat.

To serve: Cooked Jerusalem artichokes may be served as a vegetable accompaniment. After boiling, drain well and toss in melted butter. Sprinkle with chopped fresh herbs or coat with béchamel, mornay or hollandaise sauce. Alternatively, boiled or steamed artichokes may be mashed with an egg yolk, butter or cream.

ASAFOETIDA A spice derived from the resin of a plant native to Afghanistan and Iran. It can be bought in solid form but as it is very hard it is best bought ground, in powder form. It has a rather strong, unpleasant smell and the flavour is pungent, a little like spicy garlic. It is therefore used in very small quantities, mainly in Indian cooking for pickles, fish and vegetables. It is often used as a substitute for salt in India.

ASCORBIC ACID (*see* VITAMINS)

ASIAN PEAR (*see* NASHI)

ASPARAGUS This is the cultivated form of a plant of the lily family which originally grew near the sea-shore. There are two basic types, blanched (white) asparagus which is cut below the soil when the tips are 5 cm (2 inches) above it, and green asparagus which is cut at soil level. Very thin asparagus stems are called 'sprue' and are excellent for making soups or as garnishes. Asparagus has very little nutritive value, but is prized as a delicious food. It is available fresh and canned.

Asparagus is commonly served as a first course or, if cooked and rolled in thin slices of brown bread and butter, makes a popular buffet party dish.

To select: When buying asparagus, choose stems which look fresh and tender. Avoid wilted stems, those with brown patches, or coarse-looking woody stems.

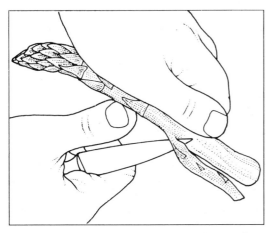

Using a sharp knife to trim tough or woody parts from an asparagus stem.

To prepare: Rinse each asparagus stalk very gently to wash away any loose dirt, then scrape or shave the length of each stalk, starting just below the tip. Cut off any parts that are very tough and woody. Trim the stalks to roughly the same length and tie into neat bundles of six to eight stalks of an even thickness, heads together. Secure each bundle under the tips and near the base.

To cook: If possible, cook asparagus in a special asparagus pan which is taller and narrower than a normal saucepan and allows the stems to be cooked upright. Alternatively, wedge the bundles upright in a deep saucepan. The pan should contain enough boiling water to come three-quarters of the way up the stems. Cover the tips with a cap of kitchen foil and simmer gently for 10-15 minutes or until tender. This way, the stalks are poached while the delicate tips are gently steamed. Drain the water carefully from the pan.

To serve: Untie the bundles and serve with salt and melted butter or hollandaise sauce. To eat asparagus, take one stem at a time, dip the tip into the sauce and eat the tip and soft part of the stem, discarding the remainder. Asparagus may also be served plain as a vegetable accompaniment.

ASPARAGUS BEAN (Cowpea, Yard-long Bean) A bean that is similar in appearance to a French bean, but much longer. Young asparagus beans can be prepared and cooked whole, like French beans. Older beans are tougher, however, and may be left to mature, then the beans removed from the pods and dried. The dried beans of some varieties of asparagus bean have a black area on them and are known as black-eyed beans or black-eyed peas. (*see also* BLACK-EYED BEAN, PULSES)

ASPARTAME A sugar substitute used in low-calorie soft drinks, yogurts, dessert and drink mixes, chewing gum and sweetening tablets. It is 200 times sweeter than sugar and can therefore be used in much smaller quantities. There is some concern about the safety of consuming large amounts of aspartame. (*see also* ADDITIVE, SWEETENERS)

ASPIC An amber-coloured savoury jelly, deriving its name from a herb called 'spike' which was at one time used to flavour it. Aspic is made from clarified meat stock, fortified if necessary with gelatine and flavoured with vegetables, herbs and sometimes sherry. Prepared aspic jelly may be bought ready-made in jars, or in the form of crystals in packets or jars. As a quick alternative, stock (or water) and gelatine may be used.

Aspic jelly is used to set meat, game, fish and vegetables in a mould, and as an exterior coating for decorating cold game, hams, tongues, pâtés, raised pies, galantines, poultry, fish and so on. It may also be chopped or cut into decorative shapes (crescents, triangles and daisies, for example), with aspic cutters, and used for garnishing.

ASSAM TEA (*see* TEA)

ASSIETTE ANGLAISE The French name for a plate of assorted cold meats, usually ham, beef and tongue.

ASTI SPUMANTE A popular Italian sparkling wine that is made by a unique process that combines the champagne method with the *cuve close* (sealed vat) method of producing sparkling wine. (*see also* CHAMPAGNE)

ATEMOYA (*see* CUSTARD APPLE)

ATHOL BROSE (*see* BROSE)

AUBERGINE (Brinjal, Eggplant) The fruit of a plant that is a member of the tomato family and native to South-East Asia. Depending on variety, aubergines range in colour from white and whitish green through dark green to yellowish purple to red-purple to black. They vary also in size, some weighing as much as 450 g (1 lb).

Aubergine is included in many classic dishes, such as moussaka and ratatouille.

To select: When buying aubergines, look for firm, shiny fruit that are free from blemishes. They may be round or oval.

To prepare: Aubergines can contain bitter juices, especially when mature. Salting and draining before cooking helps to remove these juices, and also reduces the aubergine's tendency to absorb large quantities of oil during cooking (*see* DÉGORGER). Before cooking, cut off the stems, trim the ends and halve or slice the aubergines. Place in a colander, sprinkling the layers with salt, and leave for 30-45 minutes. Rinse and dry with absorbent kitchen paper.

To cook: Aubergine slices may be grilled or fried, or halved aubergines may be stuffed and baked. To fry, coat slices in flour and cook in melted butter for about 5 minutes on each side or until golden brown. To grill, coat slices in flour, brush with melted butter and cook under a hot grill for 5-10 minutes or until golden brown, turning once.

To serve: Fried or grilled aubergine slices make a tasty accompaniment to main meat courses, and are particularly good with lamb.

AUDIT ALE A strong ale, originally brewed at Oxford and Cambridge Universities and drunk at the Audit Day festivities.

AURORE, À L' A French name given to dishes served with tomato-flavoured *sauce aurore*, or items of a yellow colour, often dome-shaped, suggesting the rising sun.

AVGOLEMONO A Greek sauce made from egg, lemon and stock. A soup of the same name also contains rice.

AVOCADO (Alligator Pear) The fruit of a tree grown in sub-tropical climates. Originally from Central America and Mexico, the avocado is also widely grown in and exported from Israel. Most avocados are the same shape as pears, though smaller, thinner varieties are sometimes available. They have a shiny smooth green or bumpy purple-brown skin, according to variety. They have a soft, oily, pale green flesh of the consistency of butter, and have a large central stone.

The avocado is a very nourishing fruit, high in protein and rich in vegetable oil, vitamins and minerals. Although it is classed as a fruit, it is usually eaten as a vegetable and has become a very popular starter served simply with a vinaigrette dressing.

To select: A ripe avocado always 'gives' slightly when pressed at the pointed end. A hard, under-ripe fruit will ripen in 1-2 days at room tempera-ture, or in about a week in the refrigerator. Ripe avocados can be stored successfully for 3-4 days on the lower shelf of the refrigerator.

To prepare: To stone an avocado, cut round the fruit lengthways, cutting through to the stone, and twist the two halves in opposite directions until they come apart. Open the halves and remove the stone with the point of a knife. If necessary, an avocado can be peeled with a potato peeler, or if the fruit is ripe, lightly score the skin once or twice and peel it back. Always brush the exposed surfaces of flesh immediately with lemon juice to prevent browning.

To serve: Avocados are usually eaten as a savo-ury, either as a starter or in salads, or they may be made into a dip (such as *guacamole*), soup or mousse.

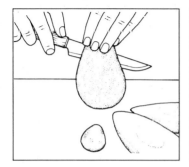

Halving avocados lengthways with a sharp knife, and removing the stones before peeling.

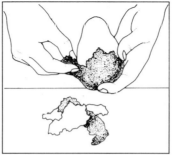

Gently removing the peel from a whole ripe avocado after scoring the peel lightly.

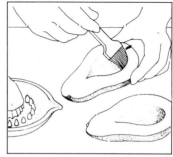

Brushing the exposed surfaces of a halved and stoned avocado with lemon juice to prevent browning.

B

B AND B A drier version of Bénédictine, in which the liqueur is ready-mixed half and half with brandy. (*see* BÉNÉDICTINE)

BABA A rich but light-textured cake made from a sweetened yeast mixture, sometimes containing currants or raisins. Babas are usually baked in individual ring tins or dariole moulds, but can also be baked in one large ring mould. After cooking, babas are usually soaked with a syrup made with rum (*baba au rhum*) or kirsch (*baba au kirsch*). They may be filled with whipped cream and served hot or cold, as a dessert.

BABACO A large tropical fruit, related to the papaya, that has recently become available in Britain. It was first grown in South America but is now cultivated in New Zealand and Guernsey. It is an unusual shape, rather like a long, fat banana with five sides. The colour of its edible skin varies from pale green to dark yellow when ripe. Inside, the flesh is very pale orange, soft and juicy, but its flavour is rather bland on its own. The fruit is best used to add interest to a fresh fruit salad.

BACALAO (*see* COD)

BACILLUS CEREUS (*see* FOOD POISONING)

BACON Bacon is made by curing fresh pork. There are several methods of curing which result in different flavours of bacon. The most common is the 'Wiltshire' cure which involves injecting whole sides of pork, under pressure, with a special 'brine' or 'pickle'. This ensures even distribution of the curing salts throughout the muscles of the carcass. The brine contains permitted additives, which preserve, colour and flavour the meat.

A side of bacon (half a carcass, without the head and feet) may be cured whole, as in the Wiltshire cure, or cuts, such as the middle, may be cured separately, with or without their bones.

Bacon may be smoked after curing – hung over smouldering wood sawdust. Oak chippings or sawdust give the most distinctive flavouring.

Unsmoked bacon is known as 'green', 'pale' or 'plain' bacon. It has white instead of brown rind and a milder flavour than smoked bacon.

Other Curing Methods

Quick Cures Smaller cuts of meat may be cured by modern 'quick' cures. Parts of the side, such as middle and shoulder, are cured separately. The curing solution is injected by machine into the lean and, unlike the Wiltshire method, the bacon is not then immersed in brine. The pieces are simply hung for 2-3 days. Bacon sold in vacuum packs as 'sweet', 'mild' or 'tender cure' has had sugar added to the curing brine.

Traditional Cures As well as new quick methods of curing, developed by modern British curers, there are other traditional methods. In Scotland, the 'Ayrshire' method is as old as the Wiltshire cure. Instead of curing the whole side, the carcass is skinned, jointed, boned and formed into rolls, usually called Ayrshire gigot (hind leg), Ayrshire middle or Ayrshire shoulder. The rolls are injected with brine and then immersed in a brine cure.

Cuts and Methods of Cooking

Bacon is sold sliced (into rashers) and unpacked (loose) or in airtight vacuum packs. Vacuum-packed bacon will remain moist until opened. After being opened, it will gradually dry and deteriorate in a similar way to loose bacon. Fresh loose bacon has moist, lean, firm white fat and smooth rind. Local methods of cutting bacon sides make it difficult to describe all the available joints. Gammon is the name given to a whole hind leg cut from a side of bacon after curing. Joints of gammon and bacon vary in saltiness. Ham, strictly speaking, is the hind leg cut from the whole carcass, then cured and matured separately (*see* HAM). Nowadays, however, cooked gammon is often described as ham.

Prime back is lean and usually sold as rashers or boneless chops (thick rashers), which are grilled or fried. Alternatively, a thick piece can be used for boiling or braising.

Prime streaky rashers combine lean and fat and are best grilled or fried. Streaky bacon is used to line pâté dishes and can be chopped for casseroles, soups and rice dishes, stretched and rolled to make bacon rolls, or crisply fried snippets can be used as a garnish. A joint of streaky bacon is excellent boiled and pressed, to eat cold. Streaky bacon is cut from the belly part of the pig.

Middle or throughcut rashers are the back and streaky cut together, giving a long rasher with a balanced mix of lean and fat – an economical buy. Use them for grilling or have a piece of middle cut rolled and use for boiling or baking – delicious used as a stuffed joint. With the rind removed, this is sometimes called Ayrshire roll, as it is traditionally prepared in Scotland.

Long back lean rashers are best cut fairly thin for frying or grilling. Thick slices cut up well for casseroles, flans or pies.

Middle gammon is a prime, lean, meaty cut for boiling, braising or baking. It is the middle portion of the hind leg. Gammon rashers or steaks, about 1 cm (^{1}/$_2$ inch) thick, are usually cut from this joint. They are excellent grilled or fried.

Corner gammon is a small, economical, triangular cut off the gammon which can be boiled and served hot, with a parsley sauce, then sliced when cold for sandwiches.

Gammon hock gives succulent meat as a small boiling joint or cubed or chopped meat for casseroles, soups and pies.

Prime collar makes a good family joint boiled or braised. The collar joint can also be sliced into rashers. As a joint, it may need to be soaked to reduce its saltiness.

Prime forehock is another joint that is sometimes better soaked. It is a good meaty cut for casseroles or boiled as a joint, and is also suitable for mincing.

Bacon pieces are offcuts that are worth having, when available, for the occasions when small amounts of bacon are required minced or to lard lean joints of meat or poultry (*see* LARDING). Avoid any that look a little dry.

Bacon in the Bag

Joints are sometimes sold ready packed in film bags with special instructions for cooking. They can be cooked without the bags being removed; this has the advantage of keeping the joint a good shape and retaining the natural juices of the meat. Unlike vacuum packs of bacon, the film bag does not extend the keeping qualities of the contents.

Vacuum-Packed Bacon

Bacon is widely sold in vacuum packs, which are hygienic and convenient both for the consumer and the shopkeeper. Mostly rashers come packed in this way, but also small joints and gammon steaks. Vacuum packing extends the keeping qualities of bacon and packets are usually marked with a 'sell-by' or 'best-before' date. Once opened, use and treat as loose bacon.

Using Bacon

To store: Loose bacon should be stored in the refrigerator. Wrap closely in kitchen foil or cling film. Do not use greaseproof paper, which is porous and allows the bacon to dry out. Loose bacon can be kept in the refrigerator for up to a week. Vacuum-packed rashers, chops, steaks and joints keep for about five days without refrigeration, but for about 15 days with refrigeration.

To prepare rashers: If necessary, remove rinds from rashers, using kitchen scissors or a sharp knife. Remove any bone. Thick rashers, steaks or chops should be snipped at intervals along the fat edge to help them remain flat during cooking. If you suspect that chops, collar or gammon steaks are salty, soak them for a short time or poach in water for a few minutes, then drain and discard the water. Pat dry with absorbent kitchen paper before cooking.

For bacon rolls, use thin cut streaky rashers and remove the rind. Stretch the rashers by stroking along their length with the back of a knife. Do this on the work surface or a board. Either roll up the whole rasher or cut each in half crossways before rolling.

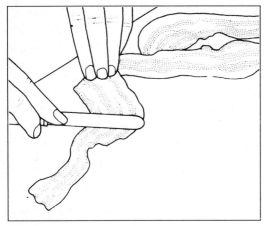

Stretching bacon rashers by stroking along their length with the back of a knife blade.

To fry: Overlap bacon rashers in a frying pan with the lean parts over the fat. Fry gently for 3-5 minutes, turning once.

To grill: Heat the grill pan gently before arranging the rashers on the rack with the fat parts overlapping the lean. Lean rashers are best brushed with a little fat or oil before grilling. Grill under a high heat for 3-5 minutes, reducing the heat and turning the rashers once halfway through cooking. Bacon chops need 12-15 minutes grilling, and steaks 10-15 minutes, depending on thickness.

To boil: Before boiling a bacon joint, weigh it, then put it in a saucepan, cover with cold water and bring to the boil. Drain and discard the water. Cover the joint with fresh water and add flavouring vegetables, such as onions and carrots, a bay leaf and a few black peppercorns. Bring slowly to the boil, cover and simmer for 20 minutes per 450 g (1 lb), plus 20 minutes. (If the joint is over 4.5 kg/10 lb, allow 15-20 minutes per 450 g/1 lb, plus 15 minutes.) When the bacon is cooked, ease off the rind and any excess fat and serve hot, sliced, with parsley or onion sauce.

To braise: Put the bacon joint in a saucepan, cover with cold water and bring to the boil, then drain and discard the water. Weigh the joint and calculate the cooking time, allowing 20 minutes per 450 g (1 lb), plus 20 minutes. Put the joint in a large saucepan, cover with fresh cold water and bring slowly to the boil. Remove any scum, cover, lower the heat and simmer for about half the cooking time.

Meanwhile, prepare vegetables to add to the braise, such as onions, carrots, turnips and celery, and fry gently in a little oil for 3-4 minutes. Drain and place in an ovenproof casserole. Drain the bacon joint and place it on top of the vegetables, add a bouquet garni, salt and pepper and cook in the oven at 180°C (350°F) mark 4 for the remainder of the cooking time. About 30 minutes before the end of the cooking time, remove the bacon from the oven and remove the rind, then continue cooking for the final 30 minutes. Remove the bouquet garni and serve with parsley or onion sauce.

To glaze: Bacon joints may be boiled for half their cooking time (as calculated above) and then baked for the remainder of the cooking time. Weigh and boil the joint as above, then drain and wrap in foil. Place in a roasting tin and bake in the oven at 180°C (350°F) mark 4 until 30 minutes before the cooking time is complete. Increase the oven temperature to 220°C (425°F) mark 7. Remove the foil and rind from the bacon, score the fat in diamond shapes and stud with cloves. Sprinkle the surface with demerara sugar and pat in. Return the joint to the oven for 30 minutes until crisp and golden.

BAGACEIRA (*see* MARC)

BAGEL (Beigel) A traditional Jewish ring-shaped roll, made from a plain or flavoured sweetened yeast dough. After mixing and shaping, the rolls are left to rise, then are boiled briefly before being baked in the oven. They are often brushed with an egg glaze and sprinkled with poppy, sesame or caraway seeds before being baked until golden brown.

BAGNA CAUDA An Italian dip made from anchovies, garlic and olive oil and served hot with fresh vegetable sticks. It is traditionally served in a small flameproof earthenware casserole and kept hot over a table burner, like a fondue (*see* FONDUE).

BAGUETTE The French name for the popular bread sticks commonly known as 'French' bread.

BAILEY'S IRISH CREAM A low-strength coffee-flavoured liqueur made from Irish whiskey and double cream.

BAIN-MARIE A French term used to describe a low-sided container which is half-filled with

Although many types of foods can be cooked in this way, the term is most often used to describe the cooking of breads, cakes, biscuits, and so on.

BAKE BLIND A method used for partially pre-baking the pastry case of a tart or flan before it is filled with fruit that does not need cooking, or with a liquid mixture that might soak into uncooked pastry. Line the dish or tin with pastry, then prick the base all over with a fork. Line with kitchen foil or greaseproof paper and weigh down with special metal baking beans, dried beans, pasta or rice. Bake blind in the oven at 200°C (400°F) mark 6 for about 15 minutes. Lift out the foil and beans and bake for a further 5 minutes or until the pastry base is just firm and lightly coloured.

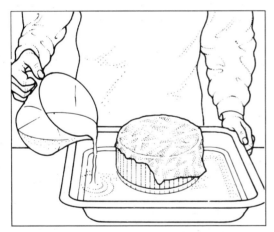

Pouring enough boiling water into a *bain-marie* to come halfway up the sides of a dish.

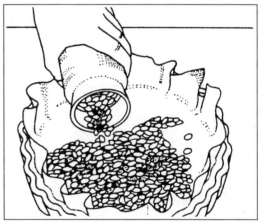

Pouring baking beans into a lined pastry case to weigh down the greaseproof paper for baking blind.

water kept just below boiling point. Containers of food are placed in it to keep warm or cook without overheating. A *bain-marie* is used for cooking custards and other egg dishes and keeping sauces warm. No special container is needed; a roasting tin will do. The term is also sometimes applied to a double saucepan (double boiler).

BAKE In general terms, this is a method of cooking food by dry heat, usually in an oven.

BAKED ALASKA A dessert which consists of ice cream mounted on sponge cake and entirely covered with meringue, which is cooked in a hot oven for so short a time that the meringue is browned but the ice cream is not melted.

BAKEWELL PUDDING Also known as Bakewell tart, this consists of a buttery mixture, flavoured with ground almonds and baked in a light flaky pastry case. It is a traditional Derbyshire recipe, the origin of which is still secret.

BAKING POWDER A commercially prepared chemical raising agent consisting of an acid (usually cream of tartar) and an alkali (bicarbonate of soda) mixed with a dried starch or flour. The mixture dissolves when used in a moist dough and the chemicals react to produce carbon dioxide. This expands during baking and makes cakes and breads rise. 'Double action' baking powder contains two acids – one which begins to react at room temperature, and another which only reacts at oven temperature. The amount of baking powder needed varies from recipe to recipe and it is important to measure the quantity used carefully as too much can upset the balance of ingredients. (*see also* ACID, ALKALI, BICARBONATE OF SODA, CAKE, CREAM OF TARTAR, RAISING AGENT)

BAKING SODA (*see* BICARBONATE OF SODA)

BAKLAVA A rich Greek pastry made of layers of fillo pastry sandwiched with a filling of chopped nuts in a honey syrup. It is cut into diamond shapes and served with coffee or as a dessert. (*see also* PASTRY)

BALLOTTINE A kind of galantine, usually served hot but sometimes cold, made of meat, poultry, game or fish that is boned, stuffed and rolled into a bundle. A ballottine is usually rolled in muslin and poached or braised. Served cold, it may be coated with a chaudfroid sauce or aspic and served in slices. (*see also* GALANTINE)

BALM (*see* LEMON BALM)

BALMORAL LOAF TIN (Ribbed Loaf Tin, Toast Rack Tin) A rounded, fluted metal loaf tin, shaped something like a Nissen hut, and used to bake fruit or plain cakes or bread, or as a mould for mousses or jellies. It produces a ridged loaf which is easy to cut into even slices.

BALSAMIC VINEGAR (*see* VINEGAR)

BAMBOO SHOOT This is the conical-shaped shoot of a bamboo plant native to Asia. The shoots are cut when they are 15 cm (6 inches) long. Fresh bamboo shoots are available from Chinese food shops but they are more widely available precooked and canned. Either variety adds little flavour but a pleasing crunchy texture to stir-fried dishes or salads.
To prepare: Fresh bamboo shoots should be trimmed and peeled before cooking.
To cook: Cook in boiling water for about 40 minutes or until tender.

BANANA A tropical fruit with bright yellow skin and pale, sweet, soft flesh. Bananas grow in most tropical climates and are picked in large bunches called 'hands' when they are still hard and green. They have usually turned yellow by the time they reach the shops.

Bananas can be eaten raw or cooked and make a nutritious snack fruit. They are popular in fruit salads (added at the last minute as they will discolour), sliced on to breakfast cereals, mashed in sandwiches or cooked in cakes and teabreads. They are occasionally used in savoury dishes, such as in the famous American dish, Chicken Maryland, and feature in many Indian and Chinese dishes. They can also be baked or fried in butter or made into fritters. Green bananas are also cooked as vegetables, either by frying, boiling or baking whole in their skins. (*see also* PLANTAIN)
To select: Choose bananas with evenly coloured skins. They are ready to eat when yellow and slightly flecked brown. Black patches on the surface indicate the fruit is over-ripe. Unripe bananas will ripen if kept in the dark (such as in a bag) at room temperature. For cooking, choose slightly under-ripe fruit as they slice better.
To prepare: Once peeled, bananas should be brushed with lemon juice to prevent browning.

BANANA, DRIED Bananas are peeled and dried whole or sliced lengthways. They may be eaten as they are, or soaked and used in compotes, fruit salads or in baking.

BANANA, GREEN (*see* PLANTAIN)

BANANA FLOUR Some cooking varieties of banana (*see* PLANTAIN) are dried and ground into banana flour. This is a highly nutritious flour which can be used to make cakes and biscuits.

BANANA PASSION FRUIT (*see* CURUBA)

BANANA SPLIT An ice-cream dessert consisting of a banana split in two lengthways and arranged in a long boat-shaped dish with scoops of ice-cream in between the pieces of banana. The dessert may be topped with raspberry or chocolate sauce, chopped nuts or glacé cherries and whipped cream.

BANBURY CAKE A flat, oval cake originating from Banbury, Oxfordshire. It is made of flaky pastry filled with dried fruit.

BANNOCK A large round scone made from barley flour, oatmeal or barley meal, baked on a griddle and usually served at breakfast or high tea, particularly in Scotland. There are many variations, including a thin biscuit type and a sweet bannock.

BAP A Scottish type of breakfast roll, eaten hot, which is made from a yeast dough containing a little fat. Baps are usually made in a flat oval shape, brushed over with milk and water, then dusted lightly with flour to give them their characteristic floury finish.

BARA BRITH A Welsh cake made with yeast or baking powder and containing currants and caraway seeds. Bara brith means, literally, 'speckled loaf'. It is very similar to the Irish barm brack (*see* BARM BRACK).

BARBECUE This method of outdoor cooking originated in warmer climates, such as those of California and Australia, but it has become popular in Britain in recent years, especially for informal summer entertaining. Food is cooked over glowing red coals, giving it a delicious 'smoky' flavour.

It is possible to build your own barbecue, using bricks and a metal grid, but many ready-made free-standing models are widely available, some of which are portable. The best fuel to burn is wood charcoal which, when hot, will smoulder, giving off an intense heat. A metal grid, holding the food, is placed over the charcoal at an adjustable height. Some barbecues have a facility for keeping food hot at a greater distance from the coals. Useful barbecue accessories include long-handled tongs, fork and spoon, a poker and oven gloves. (*see also* HIBACHI)

Cooking methods include spit-roasting and grilling, and some of the best foods to barbecue are those that would normally be grilled, such as steaks, chops, sausages, hamburgers, chicken drumsticks and kebabs. Some vegetables (such as potatoes in their jackets) and fruit (such as bananas) can be baked wrapped in foil. Meat is often marinated beforehand (especially if there is any doubt as to its tenderness) and it may be basted during cooking with a piquant sauce.

After lighting the barbecue, the fire should be allowed to burn slowly for about 30 minutes, by which time the coals should have burned to a greyish ash with a red glow. At this point the fire is ready for cooking to begin. If you need to add more fuel, place this round the edge of the fire, gradually drawing it into the centre as it ignites. Keep a sprinkler bottle handy to quench any flames which might char the food.

Food should be prepared as for grilling and may be placed directly on the greased grid (which should be several inches above the coals) or it can be put on kitchen foil or cooked in an old heavy-based frying pan or saucepan. Cooking times are approximately the same as when cooking on a conventional grill.

Accompaniments to serve with barbecued meats and kebabs should be kept simple, such as a variety of salads, ratatouille, jacket potatoes, crisps, crusty bread, rice or pasta salads. One or two flavoursome sauces (including a barbecue sauce) and a choice of salad dressings will add interest.

BARBERRY This thorny shrub grows in the drier, warmer parts of Europe and produces sour red berries that, at one time, were used to make a jelly, or were pickled for use as a garnish. The barberry is far less common than it used to be since it was discovered that the shrub harboured a cereal fungus called black rust. Growth of the shrub was therefore discouraged in many areas.

BARBOT (*see* EELPOUT)

BARCELONA NUT (*see* HAZELNUT)

BARDING Covering the breast of poultry or game birds with pieces of bacon or fat to prevent the flesh drying out during roasting. The name 'bard' is also given to a strip or rasher of streaky bacon used to line a pâté dish or terrine.

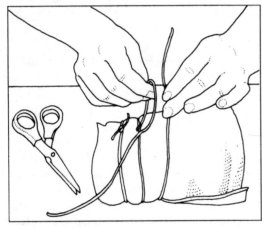

Tying a trimmed sheet of fat (bard) around a lean joint of meat prior to roasting.

BARLEY One of the earliest cereals to be cultivated, barley is now rarely used to make bread since its low gluten content results in a moist, heavy bread. It is used mostly in Scotch whiskies, malt drinks, malt extracts and as an animal food, and is available in a variety of forms for use in savoury dishes. (*see also* GRAINS)

Pot Barley Also known as Scotch barley, this is the most nutritious form as only the outer husk is removed. It requires overnight soaking followed by 2-3 hours' cooking to make it tender, and it is used in soups, stews and salads.

Pearl Barley For this the grain is steamed, rounded and polished in the mill, after the removal of the husk. This form of barley is also used to thicken soups and stews and to add an interesting texture. It needs 1½-2 hours' cooking.

Barley Meal This is a wholemeal flour made by grinding barley coarsely. It is the crudest ground form but is still used in some areas for porridge and gruel, and as an ingredient in a certain kind of bread (*see* BANNOCK).

Barley Flour This is ground and powdered pearl barley. Blended with water, it makes a good thickening for soups and sauces made with milk. It is also used to make bannocks. It has a low gluten content.

Barley Flakes These are pressed and flattened barley grains. They can be used to make milk puddings or in a topping for sweet or savoury foods.

BARLEY SUGAR A hard toffee flavoured with lemon. It was formerly made using barley water (hence its name), but plain water is now used. (*see also* BARLEY WATER)

BARLEY SYRUP (*see* MALT)

BARLEY WATER This is made by infusing pearl barley in boiling water and allowing it to cool before straining off the liquid. Flavoured with lemon, barley water is both refreshing and nourishing and is traditionally served to invalids.

BARM (*see* YEAST)

BARM BRACK A traditional Irish yeast cake which contains dried fruits (raisins, currants, chopped candied peel) which have been soaked overnight in cold tea to make them plump and juicy. It is very similar to the Welsh bara brith (*see* BARA BRITH).

BARON OF BEEF The two sirloins of beef, left uncut at the backbone and roasted, usually on a spit. It is a very large joint that is rarely cooked nowadays. In France, the term 'baron' can also be applied to the same cut of lamb.

BARQUETTE A small, boat-shaped pastry case, used for both savoury and sweet mixtures. Savoury barquettes may be served as canapés, hot or cold, and sweet barquettes, filled with fruit and cream, may be served as a cold dessert or for tea.

BASIL (Sweet Basil) A herb with a distinctive, pungent taste and aromatic scent that is generally used with tomatoes and in Italian cooking. It is also good in salads, with lamb, in basil butter to be served with grilled meats, with green vegetables, in tomato soup and in pesto sauce. Basil grows for a short period in summer and needs plenty of sun. Apart from the familiar sweet basil, there are a number of other varieties, including a plant with deep red leaves, known as purple or opal basil. Other varieties of basil are named after their characteristic aroma, such as lemon-scented basil and cinnamon-scented basil. (*see also* PESTO)

BASMATI (*see* RICE)

BASS (Sea Bass) A round sea fish, similar to salmon in shape, which is a member of a large family of fish that is common in many countries of the world. It can weigh up to 4.5 kg (10 lb), has steel grey or blue scales covering the back and sides and a white or yellowish belly. It has white flesh and is usually sold whole. Large bass, which have a good flavour, may be poached or baked; small fish can be grilled or fried. Bass is generally available from May to September.

BASTING Moistening meat, poultry or game during roasting by repeatedly spooning over it the juices and melted fat from the tin. This prevents the food from drying out, adds extra flavour and improves the appearance. The term is also used to describe spooning over a flavouring liquid, such as a marinade, during cooking.

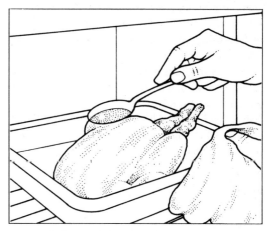

Basting chicken with fat and cooking juices to prevent it becoming too dry during roasting.

BATAVIAN ENDIVE (*see* CHICORY)

BATH BUN A type of yeast bun originally made in the city of Bath around 1700. A distinguishing feature is its topping of coarse sugar crystals.

BATH CHAP (*see* PIG'S CHEEK)

BATH OLIVER A plain flat biscuit created by a Dr. Oliver of Bath around 1700. It is usually served as a cracker, with butter and cheese.

BATTENBERG (Battenburg) A two-coloured oblong sponge cake, usually covered with almond paste.

BATTER A thick, liquid mixture, consisting essentially of flour, milk and eggs, but often combined with other ingredients. As pouring batter, it forms the foundation for pancakes, drop scones and Yorkshire pudding. A thicker coating batter is used for making fritters and *kromeski* and for coating fish for frying.

It used to be the custom to make batters at least 1 hour before cooking, the mixture being beaten or whisked to incorporate air and then allowed to stand in a cool place. Experiments have shown, however, that equally good results are obtained when the batter is beaten just long enough to mix it and does not stand before cooking. Batter can successfully be made in a blender or food processor.

In America, the term is used for a mixture which contains fat and other ingredients, such as cake and biscuit mixtures.

(*see also* CRÊPE, FISH, FRITTER, KROMESKI, PANCAKE, POPOVER, SCONE, WAFFLE, YORKSHIRE PUDDING)

Pouring Batter

100 g (4 oz) plain flour
pinch of salt
1 egg
300 ml (¹/₂ pint) milk

Sift the flour and salt into a bowl and make a well in the centre. Break in the egg and beat well with a wooden spoon, then gradually beat in the milk, drawing in the flour from the sides to make a smooth batter.
Makes 350 ml (10 fl oz)

Coating Batter

100 g (4 oz) plain flour
pinch of salt
1 egg
150 ml (¹/₄ pint) milk, or milk and water mixed

Sift the flour and salt into a bowl and make a well in the centre. Break in the egg and beat well with a wooden spoon, then gradually beat in the liquid, drawing in the flour from the sides to make a smooth batter.
Makes 200 ml (7 fl oz)

BAVARIAN BLUE A rich (70 per cent fat), soft blue cheese made in Germany. It is made from pasteurized whole cows' milk and has a very creamy texture and a slightly sour flavour. It has a moulded white rind and is made in small wheel shapes.

BAVARIAN CREAM (*see* BAVAROIS)

BAVAROIS (Bavarian Cream) A cold dessert consisting of a rich custard made with egg yolks and cream, set with gelatine. It may be flavoured with a fruit purée or juice, a liqueur, coffee or chocolate and set in a jelly or other mould.

BAVAROISE A hot drink, said to have been invented in Bavaria towards the end of the seventeenth century, which used to be served at evening parties. It was made with eggs, sugar, boiling tea and boiling milk, and flavoured with vanilla or a coffee, chocolate or orange liqueur.

BAY (Sweet Bay, Sweet Laurel) A herb with a strong, spicy flavour which can be used fresh or dried (when the flavour is even more pronounced). One or two leaves are all that is needed to flavour a dish. Bay is one of the ingredients in a bouquet garni. Although mainly used in meat and fish casseroles and marinades for fish and poultry, bay is also used in soups and stocks and to flavour infusions of milk for use in sauces, such as béchamel, or milk puddings. Bay trees are very ornamental and can be pruned like hedges to a desired shape. (*see also* BOUQUET GARNI)

BAY SALT (*see* SALT)

BEAN A leguminous plant of which there are many varieties, grown in many parts of the world. The seeds, and sometimes the pods, are used as a vegetable and contain vitamins A and C. The mature seeds of some varieties of bean are suitable for drying (*see* PULSES), while others are eaten fresh.

BEAN, ASPARAGUS (*see* ASPARAGUS BEAN)

BEAN, BOBBY (*see* BEAN, FRENCH)

BEAN, BROAD This bean is also known as Windsor bean, field bean, horse bean, Scotch bean, shell bean and fava (flava) bean. It is thought to be the original bean, first cultivated in prehistoric times and grown in ancient Egypt. The beans are encased in a thick, tough pod with a furry lining. When very young and tender, the pods can be cooked whole, but usually they are shelled. As the plant matures, the beans develop a grey outer skin which gradually becomes tougher. This can be removed before cooking by blanching in boiling water, or the beans can be slipped out of their skins after cooking.

To select: When buying, look for young, small, tender pods. Allow about 225-275 g (8-10 oz) weight of whole beans per person.

To cook: If the pods are less than 5-7.5 cm (2-3 inches) long, both pods and beans can be cooked and eaten. Larger than this, the beans should be removed from the pods. Cook beans in boiling salted water for 15-20 minutes, then drain well.

To serve: Toss whole pods or beans in melted butter and serve sprinkled with freshly chopped parsley or summer savory. Alternatively, stir cooked beans into a creamy white sauce. Old large beans should be cooked, then made into soup or puréed.

BEAN CURD (Tofu, Soya Bean Curd) Bean curd, or tofu, is made from a pressed purée of soya beans. It is available in various forms. Silken tofu is soft, with a texture like firm junket. It is soft enough to mash or to blend with flavourings in a dip or sauce. Firm tofu is a heavily pressed version with a texture rather like firm cheese. It can be diced, cubed or sliced. Soft tofu falls somewhere between the two; its texture is softer than firm tofu, but it is not as soft as silken tofu. All varieties of tofu are available fresh, dried or in cans.

Tofu is a highly nutritious protein food. It contains iron, calcium and B vitamins and is low in saturated fats and cholesterol. It is widely used in vegetarian and oriental cooking, but some find its texture unappealing and its flavour unpleasantly bland. It is best used to add consistency and texture to flavoursome dishes. (*see also* SOYA BEAN)

BEANS, DRIED (*see* PULSES)

BEAN, FRENCH (Common Bean) Varieties of French bean include green beans (*haricots vert*), bobby beans and dwarf beans. They are also known as snap beans. The French bean is an annual plant of South American origin and is a popular home-grown vegetable. The beans are small and thin and available all year round. There is also a Spanish variety known as *monguete*.

To select: When buying, choose slim French beans which break with a crisp snap. Allow 100-175 g (4-6 oz) per person.

To prepare: The beans should be so young that they only need topping and tailing, but if they are a little coarse, remove the stringy sides.

To cook: Steam or cook in boiling salted water for about 10 minutes.

To serve: Drain well and toss in melted butter, or reheat in a clean pan with a little cream. They are also delicious served cold in a salad tossed in French dressing.

BEAN, GREEN (*see* BEAN, FRENCH)

BEAN PASTE (Miso, Bean Sauce) This is produced from fermented soya beans and is used both in cooking and as a condiment, especially in Japanese cookery. Several varieties exist but all are very salty and should be used sparingly. Some varieties combine soya with grains, such as barley and rice, producing pastes with a less strong flavour. In order to conserve the bacteria and enzymes contained in miso, it is often used to flavour a dish at the end of cooking. (*see also* SOYA BEAN, SOY SAUCE)

BEAN, RUNNER This variety of bean was introduced into Europe from Mexico in the mid-seventeenth century. It is also known as scarlet runner, string bean or stick bean. It is a perennial, fast-climbing plant but it is usually grown as an annual. It produces bright orange-red flowers in the summer and is commonly seen growing on tall cane supports in gardens and allotments.

To select: Runner beans are at their best when very young; when they mature they become tough and the outer casing rather stringy. Fresh runner beans should break in two with a crisp snap and the inside should be fresh and juicy. Allow 100-175 g (4-6 oz) per person.

To prepare: Cut off the ends and remove the strings from the sides. Cut diagonally into 2.5 cm (1 inch) lengths, or slice into lengths 5-7.5 cm (2-3 inches) long and cut into thin slithers. (A bean slicer makes this task easier and quicker.)

To cook: Steam or cook in boiling salted water for about 10 minutes.

To serve: Drain well, toss the beans in melted butter, if liked, and serve sprinkled with a little chopped fresh marjoram.

BEAN SAUCE (*see* BEAN PASTE)

BEAN SPROUTS The shoots of germinated dried beans, such as adzuki beans or mung beans. Bean sprouts can be bought fresh from supermarkets and greengrocers as well as from Oriental food shops, but many varieties of bean sprout can be produced easily at home. Bean sprouts are highly nutritious, containing substantial amounts of protein, fibre, vitamins, minerals and starch.

Raw bean sprouts make an interesting addition to salads and sandwiches, adding unusual flavours and a crunchy texture. They can also be used in stir-fried dishes and added to casseroles and are frequently used in Chinese cooking.

To select: Choose crisp, small, fresh sprouts or grow them yourself at home. Allow about 100 g (4 oz) per person.

To cook: Cook as soon as possible after buying or harvesting. Rinse in cold water, then either blanch for 30 seconds in boiling salted water or stir-fry for 1-2 minutes.

Sprouting Beans at Home

Many dried beans are suitable for sprouting at home, including adzuki beans, mung beans and soya beans. Dried peas and seeds are also suitable, though it's important only to use those that are specially produced for eating or sprouting, and not those that are intended for planting, as they may have been treated with preservatives. Seeds for sprouting include alfalfa, fenugreek and mustard and cress. Split peas and lentils will not sprout.

You can buy special bean sprouters, but these are not absolutely necessary. All you need is a jam jar, a piece of muslin, an elastic band, a shallow dish, and a large brown paper bag. Put 15 ml (1 tbsp) of your chosen beans or seeds in the jam jar and cover the jar with the piece of muslin, securing it with the elastic band. Pour warm water into the jar, rinse it round and pour it away. Fill the jar with warm water again and leave it for 24 hours.

Pour away the water and rinse the seeds twice, discarding the water of the final rinse. Put the jar on its side on the dish, put the dish into the paper bag and leave in a warm place. Rinse and drain the seeds every morning and evening and in about 4 days the jar will be full of nutritious sprouts. They will keep in the jar in the refrigerator for up to 4 days.

BEARD The gills of an oyster are known as its 'beard' and can be removed before eating, if liked, though this is not usually necessary. The name is also given to the byssus of a mussel, the whiskery part that protrudes from the shell and which the mussel uses to cling to rocks. This is always removed before cooking (*see* MUSSEL).

BÉARNAISE A classic rich French sauce which uses egg yolks as a thickening agent and is served with grilled meat or fish. The sauce should be served warm, on the meat or fish or in a sauceboat.

Béarnaise Sauce
60 ml (4 tbsp) wine or tarragon vinegar
1 shallot or ¼ onion, skinned and finely chopped
few fresh tarragon sprigs, chopped
2 egg yolks
75 g (3 oz) butter, softened
salt and white pepper

Put the vinegar, shallot and tarragon into a saucepan and boil gently until the liquid has reduced by about one-third. Leave to cool.

Put the egg yolks and reduced vinegar liquid into a double saucepan or bowl standing over a pan of very gently simmering water and whisk until thick and fluffy. Gradually add the butter, a tiny piece at a time. Whisk briskly until each piece has been absorbed and the sauce has thickened. Season with salt and white pepper.
Makes about 200 ml (7 fl oz)

BEATING Incorporating air into an ingredient or mixture by agitating it vigorously with a spoon, fork, whisk or electric mixer. Beating can alter the texture and colour of an ingredient: butter becomes pale and soft; beaten (whisked) egg whites become white and fluffy, then stiff; beaten (whipped) cream becomes thick. (*see also* WHIPPING)

BEAUJOLAIS A light, short-lived, fruity red wine that has come to be one of the most popular of French wines. Most of the grapes used to make Beaujolais are grown in the Lyon region of France, and there are several 'growths' or *crus*, the principal of which are Chiroubles, Brouilly, Côte de Brouilly, Saint-Amour, Fleurie, Juliénas, Chénas, Morgon and Moulin-à-Vent. Beaujolais is popularly drunk as Beaujolais *nouveau*, the young wine that is newly produced and sold each November. It should be drunk by Easter of the following year. Other Beaujolais wines can be kept for up to 7 years.

BÉCHAMEL A classic French white sauce which is used as the basis for a number of dishes as well as other sauces. It can be used for fish, poultry, egg and vegetable dishes, and to make a chaud-froid, Mornay or soubise sauce (*see* CHAUD-FROID, MORNAY, SOUBISE).

Béchamel Sauce
300 ml (¹/₂ pint) milk
1 shallot, skinned and sliced, or a small piece of onion, skinned
1 small carrot, peeled and sliced
¹/₂ celery stick, washed and chopped
1 bay leaf
3 black peppercorns
25 g (1 oz) butter or margarine
25 g (1 oz) flour
salt and white pepper
30 ml (2 tbsp) single cream (optional)

Put the milk, vegetables and flavourings in a saucepan and bring slowly to the boil. Remove from the heat, cover and set aside to infuse for 30 minutes, then strain, reserving the milk.

Melt the butter in a saucepan, stir in the flour and cook gently for 1 minute, stirring. Remove the pan from the heat and gradually stir in the flavoured milk. Bring to the boil and continue to cook, stirring, until the sauce thickens. Simmer very gently for 3 minutes. Remove from the heat and season with salt and pepper. Stir in the cream, if using.
Makes 300 ml (¹/₂ pint)

BEECH NUT A small, triangular nut that grows on various species of beech tree. The nuts are a common sight scattered on country paths in October, when they fall from the trees. They can be removed from their husks, peeled and eaten as they are, but they are often very small, or the husks are found to be empty. Their flavour is similar to that of hazelnut. Gathered and treated commercially, beech nuts can be used to make a fine oil that is excellent on salads.

BEEF The meat of the bullock, cow or even bull, the best (and most expensive) meat being that of a bullock about two years old (*see* VEAL). The quality of beef is very dependent on all sorts of factors, such as the age, breed and sex of the animal and the hanging, storing and cutting up of the joints. It is worth seeking out a butcher who supplies the sort of beef you like. (*see also* MEAT)

Beef should look fresh and moist, but not watery, with small flecks of fat through the lean. This fat (called marbling) helps to keep the meat moist and tender during cooking. Choose meat with little gristle between the fat and the lean. Home-killed beef is the choicest, but imported frozen or chilled beef of good quality comes from South America, Australia, New Zealand and other countries.

Beef, like all meat, is a good source of protein. It also supplies energy, particularly if there is a lot of fat. The amount of fat in different cuts varies considerably and it is impossible to give exact figures for the nutrients. However, it is a good source of B vitamins and a fair source of iron. (*see also* BOVINE SPONGIFORM ENCEPHALOPATHY)

Cuts and Methods of Cooking

Cuts of beef vary from country to country, but the best cuts, for roasting, grilling or frying, always come from the rump of the animal, while the poorer quality meat, for stewing, braising or casseroling, comes from the forequarter. (*see illustration opposite*)

Shin (foreleg) and leg (hindleg) produce lean meat with a high proportion of connective tissue. It is suitable for stews, casseroles, stock, soup and brawn. (**4 and 5**)

Neck and clod are usually cut into pieces and sold as stewing 'steak' or mince. (**6 and 7**)

Silverside is traditionally salted and sold for boiling. Today, it is more often sold for roasting but, because it is lean, needs constant basting. (Uncooked salted beef is grey, but turns pink during cooking.) (**3**)

Fore rib is the traditional cut of roast beef and is sold on the bone or boned and rolled. (**15**)

Wing rib is a popular roasting joint, but is often boned and sliced, then sold as frying or grilling steaks. (**14**)

Sirloin is a tender and delicious cut of beef, sold on the bone or boned and rolled with or without the fillet, for roasting. The fillet is the smaller 'eye' on the inside of the rib bone, which is usually removed. It is sold in slices as fillet steak, or whole for Beef Wellington. Sirloin steaks are slices of the larger 'eye' of the lean. (**12**)

Chuck and blade steak is a large, fairly lean cut of high-quality meat, removed from the bone and sold as 'chuck steak'. Suitable for braising, stewing and pie fillings. (**9 and 10**)

Thick flank (top rump) is a lean cut suitable for roasting, pot roasting and braising or, when sliced, for braising and frying. (**1**)

Thin flank is ideal for braising and stewing. It is often salted or pickled and is frequently sold as mince. (**8**)

Skirt is tasty economical stewing meat which comes from inside the ribs and the flank. (**11**)

Brisket, sold either on the bone or boned and rolled, is suitable for braising or boiling, and is often sold salted. It is good cooked and served cold. (**2**)

Thin ribs and thick ribs, usually sold boned and rolled, are ideal for braising and pot roasting. (**14, 16 and 17**)

Rump is an excellent large lean and tender cut, sold in slices for grilling and frying. (**13**)

Topside, a lean cut of beef, with little or no fat, is often sold with a layer of fat tied around it. It can be roasted or pot roasted. (**18**)

Steaks are slices of the most tender cuts of meat, such as sirloin, fillet, rump, *tournedos*, *châteaubriand*, T-bone, porterhouse, *entrecôte* and *filet mignon*. (*see* STEAK)

'Flash fry' cuts are slices from lean cuts which have been passed between knife-covered rollers. This makes the meat more tender and reduces the cooking so that it can be 'flash' (quickly) fried.

To Roast Beef

Traditionally, beef was roasted at a high temperature to allow the Yorkshire pudding (which is the classic accompaniment) to be cooked at the same time. A lower temperature of 180°C (350°F) mark 4 will produce more succulent meat with less shrinkage. The higher temperature is really only suitable for top-quality meat.

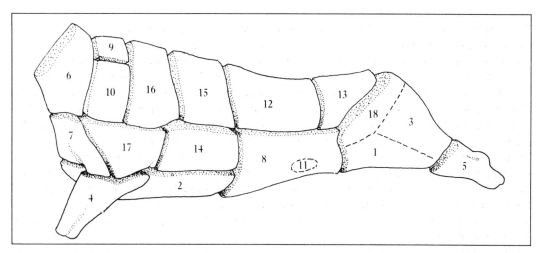

Major cuts of beef to be found at your butcher.

Weigh the joint as it is to be cooked, that is on the bone or boned and rolled or stuffed, as appropriate. Put it in a shallow roasting tin, preferably on a grid, and cook for the following times:

For rare meat, cook for 15 minutes per 450 g (1 lb) plus 15 minutes

For medium meat, cook for 20 minutes per 450 g (1 lb) plus 20 minutes

For well done meat, cook for 25 minutes per 450 g (1 lb) plus 25 minutes

A meat thermometer is useful to determine accurately whether the meat is cooked. Insert it into the thickest part of the joint before cooking, making sure the tip of the thermometer is well clear of the bone. Cook to 60°C (140°F) for rare meat, 70°C (160°F) for medium meat, and 80°C (180°F) for well done meat. These temperatures may vary slightly, depending on taste and the precise oven temperature, so it is worth experimenting to discover which temperature produces the meat exactly as you like it.

Place the cooked joint on a meat dish, wooden board or spiked metal carving dish with recesses to catch the meat juices, and leave to stand for 15 minutes before carving. Roast beef is traditionally served with Yorkshire pudding, roast potatoes, horseradish sauce and cooked fresh vegetables. (*see also* CARVING)

Braised Beef

1.4 kg (3 lb) piece of boned unsalted silverside
2 medium carrots, peeled
2 medium parsnips, peeled
25 g (1 oz) lard or dripping, or 30 ml (2 tbsp)
*   vegetable oil*
75 g (3 oz) streaky bacon rashers, rinded and
*   chopped*
2 medium onions, skinned and thickly sliced
3 celery sticks, washed and thickly sliced
2 small turnips, peeled and thickly sliced
1 bay leaf
salt and pepper
150 ml (¹/₄ pint) beef stock
150 ml (¹/₄ pint) cider
15 ml (1 level tbsp) arrowroot
chopped fresh parsley, to garnish

Tie up the meat to form a neat joint. Cut the carrots and parsnips into slices about 1 cm (¹/₂ inch) thick, halving them if large.

Heat the fat in a 3.4 litre (6 pint) deep flameproof casserole. Add the bacon and fry until it begins to brown. Remove the bacon with a slotted spoon and reserve.

Reheat the fat in the casserole for a few seconds. Brown the meat all over, turning it with long handled spoons. When browned evenly, remove from the casserole and keep warm.

Add the vegetables to the pan and fry over a high heat. Add the bacon pieces and bay leaf to the vegetables and season well. Place the joint in the centre of the bed of vegetables.

Pour the stock and cider into the casserole. Bring to the boil. Fit a piece of kitchen foil over the meat and vegetables to form a 'tent'. Cover the dish with a close-fitting lid.

Cook in the oven at 160-170°C (300-325°F) mark 2-3 for 2-2 ½ hours. Halfway through the cooking time, turn the joint over and re-cover tightly. After 2 hours, test the meat – if done a fine skewer will glide easily and smoothly into the joint.

Lift the joint on to a board and cut into slices no more than 5 mm (¼ inch) thick. Remove the vegetables from the casserole and place on a shallow warmed serving dish. Arrange the meat across the top, cover with foil and keep warm.

Mix the arrowroot to a smooth paste with 45 ml (3 tbsp) water. Skim off excess fat from the juices. Off the heat, stir the paste into the juices, return to the heat, then bring slowly to the boil, stirring. Boil for 1 minute, then adjust the seasoning. Spoon a little gravy over the meat and sprinkle with parsley. Serve the rest of the gravy separately.
Serves 6

Spiced Silverside
1.8 kg (4 lb) piece of boned salted silverside
1 medium onion, skinned and sliced
4 medium carrots, peeled and sliced
1 small turnip, peeled and sliced
1-2 celery sticks, trimmed and chopped
8 cloves
100 g (4 oz) soft brown sugar
2.5 ml (½ level tsp) mustard powder

5 ml (1 level tsp) ground cinnamon
juice of 1 orange
Soak the meat in cold water for several hours or overnight, then rinse and put in a large saucepan with the vegetables. Cover with water and bring slowly to the boil. Remove any scum, cover with a lid and simmer for 3-4 hours or until tender. Allow to cool in the liquid.

Drain well, then put the meat into a roasting tin and stick the cloves into the fat. Mix together the remaining ingredients and spread over the meat. Bake in the oven at 180°C (350°F) mark 4 for 45-60 minutes, basting from time to time. Serve hot or cold.
Serves 6

Classic Beef Stew
50 g (2 oz) lard, or 45 ml (3 tbsp) vegetable oil
700-900 g (1 ½-2 lb) stewing steak, trimmed and cut into 4 cm (1 ½ inch) cubes
4 medium onions, skinned and halved lengthways
350 g (12 oz) carrots, peeled and cut into chunks
30 ml (2 level tbsp) flour
600 ml (1 pint) beef stock
15 ml (1 level tbsp) tomato purée
salt and pepper
2 bay leaves
Melt the lard or heat the oil in a medium flameproof casserole. Increase the heat and when the fat is just beginning to smoke, add the meat about a quarter at a time. Fry each batch until well browned. Remove with a slotted spoon.

Reduce the heat, add the onions and carrots and fry until the vegetables are lightly browned. Remove the casserole from the heat and remove the vegetables.

Sprinkle the flour into the fat remaining in the casserole and stir well until evenly blended. Return the pan to the heat and cook slowly, stirring constantly, until the roux begins to turn a light brown colour.

Add the stock, tomato purée and seasoning and stir until the mixture is quite smooth. Bring slowly to the boil, stirring, then add the meat and vegetables with their juices and the bay leaves.

Cover the casserole tightly and cook in the oven at 170°C (325°F) mark 3 for about 2½ hours. Uncover and stir once during cooking; re-cover and return to the oven. Alternatively, cover and simmer gently on the hob for about 2 hours, stirring occasionally to prevent sticking. Remove the bay leaves before serving.

Serves 4

BEEFBURGER (Hamburger) Although made of beef, these popular minced beef patties are more commonly known as hamburgers, a name that they were first given in America, where it was believed the first hamburgers came from Hamburg. The traditional beefburger is made of lean minced beef, chopped onion and seasoning. Burgers can be bought ready-made from butchers and supermarkets, fresh or frozen, or they can be made at home. They can be grilled, fried, oven-baked or barbecued and they are usually served inside a soft white bread bun with other flavourings, such as cheese, salad and relishes. By law, any beefburger or hamburger sold must contain at least 80 per cent beef. 'Burgers' may also be made from minced lamb or pork; vegetarian 'vege-burgers' are also available.

Hamburgers are a popular 'fast food' or take-away snack, and there are now several restaurant chains, with branches all over the country, all specializing in this food.

BEEF, CORNED Corned beef is beef that has been cooked and preserved in salt. It is imported into this country from the United States, Argentina and other big cattle-producing regions of the world. Corned beef gets its name from the fact that coarse grains, or 'corns' of salt were originally used in the curing process. It is also sometimes known as bully beef or salt beef.

Corned beef can be bought sliced from delicatessens and cooked meat counters in supermarkets, or it is readily available canned. It can be used cold in salads and sandwiches or it can be cooked in a ragoût, stew or casserole, or used to make corned beef fritters or hash.

BEEF OLIVE A British dish of thin slices of beef topside rolled round a flavoursome breadcrumb stuffing and cooked in stock in the oven.

BEER A popular alcoholic beverage produced by the fermentation of malted barley and hops. Beer has been produced from the fermentation of cereals since ancient times. It was originally known as ale but was given the name beer in the thirteenth century when hops were introduced as a flavouring. The name ale is still applied to some pale beers.

Beer can successfully be made at home and there are many preparations and kits on the market to make it an easy task. Commercially produced beers vary according to the types of yeast and malt used. The stronger and more highly 'kilned' (or heated) the malt, the more caramel is produced and the darker the brewed beer.

Lager is made from a lightly kilned malt and a yeast that acts at a low temperature, so the fermentation process is slow, resulting in a pale coloured beer that takes longer to produce. Bitter is also made with a lightly kilned malt, but with a faster-working yeast, resulting in a pale coloured beer that is made quickly but has a rather bitter, dry taste. Bottled bitter and best bitter are known as light ale and pale ale. Mild is also made with a fast-working yeast, but it uses a dark malt, added sugar and caramel, and less hops. It is slightly milder than bitter. Brown ale is bottled mild. The darkest beer of all, stout, is made with a very highly kilned black malt which gives it a strong, almost burnt taste.

Beer is sometimes used in cooking and may replace part of the stock or water used in stews, hot-pots, meat ragoûts, and so on. Classic dishes made with beer include Carbonade of Beef and Welsh Rarebit.

BEESTINGS The first milk drawn from a cow after calving. It is not normally sold.

BEET This name is given to a number of varieties of vegetable which are grown for their fleshy roots. Commercially, the most important beet is sugar beet, which is grown for the distilling and sugar industries. The most familiar domestic beet is a popular salad vegetable, known in the UK as beetroot (*see* BEETROOT).

BEETROOT An easily-grown vegetable cultivated for its swollen bulbous root which is a characteristic dark red in colour. Originally, beetroot was grown for its leaves, as the leaves of the young beetroot plant can be cooked and eaten like spinach. The juice of beetroot can also be used as a red food dye.

There are two types of beetroot generally available: long and globe-shaped. Small, globe-shaped beetroot, available in early summer, are usually sold in bunches; maincrop beetroot, which grow larger, are sold by weight and it is common practice for them to be sold cooked. Golden and white varieties of beetroot are also available. Beetroots sold pre-cooked and packaged are preserved in vinegar.

Beetroot can be grated and eaten raw, or it can be cooked and served hot or cold. A classic use of beetroot is in the colourful beetroot soup, *bortsch*, which is popular in eastern Europe and Russia (*see* BORTSCH).

To select: Choose firm, smallish beetroot with crisp green tops. Allow 100-175 g (4-6 oz) per person.

To prepare: Twist off the stalks about 2.5 cm (1 inch) above the roots and wash the beetroot. Take care not to pierce the skin or juices will 'bleed' into the cooking water.

To cook: Cook in boiling salted water until soft; this may take up to 1¹/₂ hours for large beetroot. Alternatively, bake in the oven at 180°C (350°F) mark 4 for 2-3 hours. To test if beetroot is cooked, remove from the pan or oven, cool slightly and

rub gently; the skin should slide off easily. Beetroot is best peeled while still warm.

To serve: Peel, slice or dice and serve hot with melted butter or a white sauce, or cold in a vinaigrette dressing. To serve in salads, dice or grate large beetroot and thinly slice small ones. Beetroot tends to 'bleed' into salads, so either add at the last minute or serve in a separate dish.

BEIGEL (*see* BAGEL)

BEIGNET A light French doughnut made in the shape of a small ball, deep-fried and served hot, rolled in sugar and eaten with jam or sauce. The name is also given to a small fritter made by stirring pieces of vegetable, poultry or meat into a coating batter and deep-frying. (*see also* FRITTER)

BELGIAN ENDIVE (*see* CHICORY)

BELL PEPPER (*see* PEPPER, SWEET)

BEL PAESE A rich, creamy cheese of mild flavour, made in various parts of Italy, usually from October to June. The whole cheeses weigh about 2.3 kg (5 lb) each and have a yellow waxy rind.

BELUGA (*see* CAVIAR)

BÉNÉDICTINE The most renowned and popular of herb-based liqueurs. The recipe was first created by an Italian Bénédictine monk and was produced commercially as a liqueur in 1863. Bénédictine is now made in Normandy, and the recipe is still a very closely-guarded secret. (*see also* B AND B)

BENTOO NO TOMO A Japanese seasoning mix that is used in Oriental cooking. It is made from coarsely ground dried fish, salt, soy sauce, seaweed and monosodium glutamate.

BERGAMOT A small citrus fruit, similar to a tiny bitter orange, from a tree grown mostly in Sicily and Calabria. Oil is extracted from its rind and used in perfumery and confectionery. Candied, the fruit can also used as a decoration. (*see also* ORANGE)

Bergamot is also the name of a lemon-scented herb which comes from the same family as mint. Its flowers can be crystallized and used as a decoration, and its leaves can be added to salads or used to make a soothing herb tea.

BESAN FLOUR (*see* GRAM FLOUR)

BETEL LEAF The leaf of the betel vine (closely related to the black pepper vine) which grows in various tropical areas. It is used in Indian cooking as a wrapping for *pan* (*see* PAN).

BETEL NUT A hard nut that grows on trees resembling the coconut palm. The small nut in its untreated state is slightly poisonous. As the nut is a stimulant, it is often added to Indian *pan* to be chewed after a meal (*see* PAN).

BEURRE, AU A French expression used to describe a dish that is cooked in or served with butter.

BEURRE DE NOISETTE (*see* BEURRE NOISETTE)

BEURRE MANIÉ A liaison of butter and flour, kneaded together to a paste, and used for thickening soups, stews or casseroles after cooking is complete. Whisk a little of the paste into the hot liquid and bring back to the boil, whisking until the liquid thickens slightly. Add more *beurre manié* in small amounts, whisking each piece into the liquid before adding more, until the required thickness is reached.

BEURRE NOIR Translated literally, this means 'black butter', and it is the name given to a sauce which is made by cooking butter until it turns a dark brown and mixing it with a little warmed vinegar and flavourings such as parsley or capers. It is traditionally served with poached skate, but can also be poured over other fish, eggs and some vegetables.

BEURRE NOISETTE A French butter sauce made by cooking butter until it turns a golden brown and produces a nutty aroma (*noisette* is French for hazelnut). The butter can be flavoured with lemon juice and seasonings and poured over cooked fish, eggs or vegetables.

Rather confusingly, *beurre de noisette* is the name of a flavoured butter made by combining crushed toasted hazelnuts with softened butter.

BEVERAGE Any liquid, other than water, that is consumed as a drink. (*see* ALCOHOL, ALE, APÉRITIF, BEER, etc.)

BHAJI An Indian vegetable dish served as a starter or as an accompaniment to a curry.

BICARBONATE OF SODA (Sodium Bicarbonate, Baking Soda) A commercially produced white powder which can be used as a raising agent. Bicarbonate of soda is an alkaline substance which gives off carbon dioxide when mixed with an acid, such as lemon juice, cream of tartar or buttermilk, in a cake or soda bread recipe. It is one of the ingredients of baking powder. (*see also* ALKALI, BAKING POWDER)

BIERWURST A German dried sausage made from spiced pork and sometimes flavoured with garlic. Its name comes from the fact that it was once made with ham that had been marinated in beer. It is a rather coarse-textured sausage that can be sliced and served cold as part of a platter of cold meats.

BIGARADE, À LA A French term used to describe a dish cooked or served with orange or orange sauce.

BILBERRY (Blaeberry, Huckleberry, Whortleberry) This small dark blue or mauve berry is the fruit of a bush which grows wild on open moorland and is also cultivated. Bilberries may also be sold as whortleberries or huckleberries. They can be eaten raw, though they have a distinctly acid taste, or they can be stewed with sugar, cooked in pies or made into jam. They should be cooked or eaten soon after picking as they do not keep well. (*see also* BLUEBERRY, CRANBERRY)

To prepare: Remove the stalks and any leaves, rinse well under cold running water and dry thoroughly.

BILTONG (Jerky) Strips of meat dried by a method developed in South Africa which enables it to be kept for years. The strips can be grated or sliced and eaten raw, though they can be very chewy. (*see also* CHARQUI, DRIED MEAT)

BINDING Adding a liquid, gelatine, egg or melted fat to a mixture to hold it together.

BIOTIN (*see* VITAMINS)

BIRD Most of the birds killed for human consumption these days are domesticated (poultry) or game birds that have mostly been bred for the purpose. (*see* CHICKEN, DUCK, PHEASANT, TURKEY, etc.)

In the past, however, a number of wild birds were caught and cooked in this country and still are in many other countries. Favoured species in the past included tits, warblers, herons, gulls, blackbirds, crows, robins and sparrows.

In some cases, the hunting of wild birds has resulted in species being in danger of extinction, and protection orders now exist to prevent the catching and killing of so many wild birds. In most regions of France, all birds smaller than the thrush are protected, but thrush itself is frequently on the menu, cooked in pâtés, pies or terrines. In England, the thrush is a protected species.

BIRD'S NEST SOUP This Chinese speciality is made from part of the nest of a small species of swallow found on the coasts of Eastern countries, such as Java, Thailand and the Philippines. The birds construct their nests high on the walls and ceilings of huge caverns and collecting them is a very dangerous business. The nests are not made of the usual mud, twigs and moss, but are constructed from gelatinous saliva that the birds produce and secrete as a result of eating seaweed.

The nests are cleaned and soaked before they are used to make the soup, which has a somewhat sticky texture. The nests can also be used in stews. Dried birds' nests are available from Chinese food stores in Britain.

BIRYANI An Indian dish, the main ingredients of which are Basmati rice and meat or fish. It is similar to a *pilau* but is always brightly coloured with turmeric or saffron and flavoured with cumin, cardamom, coriander and other spices. There are many kinds of *biryani*, some using cooked rice, others using par-boiled or uncooked rice.

BISCUIT Originally, as the name implies, biscuit dough was baked twice (*bis* is French for twice, *cuit* is French for cooked). This resulted in the characteristic biscuit texture, which is crisp and dry. The name, 'biscuit', is given to small, round or shaped, flat, baked, sweet or savoury cakes. There are six main types of biscuit: rolled, shaped, drop, piped, bar and refrigerator, with dozens of versions to be made from each basic recipe.

Rolled biscuits are the traditional basic biscuits. The dough is rolled out very thinly, then cut into rounds or shapes with biscuit cutters. Examples of rolled biscuits are Shrewsbury biscuits and gingerbread men.

Shaped biscuits are made from soft doughs that need quick and deft handling. They can be moulded with the palms of the hands into small balls or barrels, then rolled in crushed nuts or cornflakes. This type of biscuit dough can also be cooked in a mould. Examples of shaped biscuits are melting moments and madeleines.

Drop biscuits are made from a soft dough and are usually spooned directly on to the baking sheet. The term 'drop' is misleading, since the mixture must be stiff enough to need pushing from the spoon. The baked texture is variable; it can be soft and cake-like, crisp or even brittle. Drop biscuits are often irregular in shape as they tend to spread as they bake. They can be shaped while still hot.

Examples of drop biscuits are florentines and brandy snaps.

Piped biscuits look very impressive but do not take any more time to make than other biscuits; the mixture is simply put into a piping bag and piped in fingers or rings. They are the ideal choice when cooking for large numbers. They have a crisp yet melt-in-the-mouth texture, and can be served plain or sandwiched together with a filling. Examples of piped biscuits are Viennese fingers and *langues de chats*.

Bar biscuits are especially easy and quick to prepare. The mixture is pressed into a large tin and cut into bars when cooked. Some bars need to cool on a wire rack, others in the tin. Often bar biscuits cannot be stored for as long as other types of home-made biscuits. Examples of bar biscuits are flapjacks and date bars.

Refrigerator biscuits are very handy as the dough can be kept in the refrigerator and baked when required, providing oven-fresh biscuits on demand. The biscuits made by this method are always crisp and flavourful, their individual taste and finish depending on the extra ingredients added to the basic recipe. The dough must always be chilled until firm, so that it can be sliced as thinly and evenly as possible. Examples of refrigerator biscuits are ginger refrigerator cookies and honey jumbles.

(*see also* BRANDY SNAP, COOKIE, FLAP-JACK, FLORENTINE, JUMBLE, LANGUES DE CHATS, PETIT FOUR, RUSK, SHREWSBURY BISCUIT, etc.)

BISHOP A favourite drink during the Middle Ages, composed of wine (usually port), sweetened, spiced and flavoured with orange or lemon. It is still a popular hot beverage in northern European countries. Bishop can also be prepared with champagne or any other wine.

BISMARCK (*see* HERRING)

BISQUE Nowadays, this is the name given to a rich creamy soup, the main ingredient of which is a thick purée made of shellfish, game or (very occasionally) vegetables. Correctly speaking, however, the 'bisque' is the purée on which the soup is based, not the finished soup. The most famous bisques are those made from lobster, crayfish or shrimp.

BITTERS The name given to a group of aperitifs made from distilled spirits flavoured with roots, herbs and barks. Campari, the best known Italian bitters, is usually mixed with soda, as is the French Amer Picon. Campari mixed with red Italian vermouth, a splash of soda and a slice of lemon makes the popular drink called Americano. Suze is a very bitter, yellow, gentian-based apéritif, good as a restorative. Fernet-Branca and Underberg are ferocious-looking-and-tasting medicinal bitters. (*see also* APÉRITIF)

BIVALVE Any shellfish in the mollusc family with two shells that are hinged together and which must be opened in order to extract the edible portion. Most bivalves are edible, the most common being oysters, mussels, cockles, clams and scallops. Bivalves, such as mussels and clams, are usually sold while still alive, and the two shells should be tightly shut before cooking. Open uncooked bivalves should be discarded. (*see also* CLAM, COCKLE, MUSSEL, OYSTER, SCALLOP, etc.)

BLACK BEAN (Black Kidney Bean, Mexican Bean) These dried beans are oval in shape with a shiny black casing and white flesh. They are used mainly in soups but can also be used as a substitute for red kidney beans in several dishes. (*see also* PULSES)

BLACK BEAN, CHINESE The Chinese black bean is a type of soya bean that has been fermented and salted. It is used as a flavouring in meat and vegetable dishes. (*see also* SOYA BEAN)

BLACKBERRY (Bramble) This small soft fruit, dark red to black in colour, is available wild and cultivated. The cultivated varieties tend to be larger and juicier.

Once picked, blackberries lose their flavour rapidly and should be eaten on the day of purchase. They can be eaten raw, stewed (they are especially good cooked with apple), included in fruit puddings and pies or made into jams and jellies.

To select: Pick or buy firm fruit that is black all over, with no red or green patches.

To prepare: Wash blackberries thoroughly and remove any stalks.

To stew: Put blackberries in a saucepan with a little water and sugar to taste and cook for about 10 minutes or until soft.

BLACK BUN (Scotch Bun) A spiced plum cake with a pastry case that is eaten at Hogmanay, the Scottish New Year's Eve. It is made several months (sometimes even a year) beforehand, so that it has time to mature.

BLACK BUTTER (*see* BEURRE NOIR)

BLACK CUMIN (*see* CUMIN)

BLACKCURRANT (*see* CURRANTS)

BLACK-EYED BEAN (Black-eyed Pea, Cow-pea) A cream-coloured dried bean with a black spot. It has an earthy taste and goes well with pork and in casseroles. (*see also* ASPARAGUS BEAN, PULSES)

BLACK FOREST GÂEAU A luxurious rich layered chocolate cake, made from layers of sponge soaked in a kirsch-flavoured syrup and filled with whipped double cream mixed with black cherries. The top of the gâteau is usually decorated with more whipped cream, cherries and chocolate caraque (*see* CHOCOLATE).

BLACK GAME (*see* GROUSE)

BLACK GRAM BEAN (Urd Bean, Mash) This dried bean usually has a black outer casing, but it can sometimes be green, and is therefore often confused with the mung bean. However, the flesh of the black gram bean is white, while the flesh of the mung bean is yellow. It is about half the size of a pea and is available whole or split. The black gram bean is very important in Indian cooking and is grown all over India. Unlike most beans, it is best cooked without pre-soaking, but it needs longer cooking. (*see also* PULSES)

BLACK KIDNEY BEAN (*see* BLACK BEAN)

BLACK PEPPER (*see* PEPPER)

BLACK PUDDING (Blood Pudding) A kind of sausage, popular in the Midlands and North of England, which is made of pig's blood, suet, breadcrumbs, oatmeal, onions and seasonings. In Scotland, black pudding is made using sheep's blood. It is usually sold ready boiled, but is then sliced, fried and served with mashed potatoes or bacon. (*see also* BLUTWURST, BOUDIN NOIR)

BLACK SALSIFY (*see* SCORZONERA)

BLACKSTRAP (*see* MOLASSES)

BLACK TREACLE (*see* MOLASSES)

BLACK TRUMPET (*see* MUSHROOM)

BLADDER CHERRY (*see* CHINESE LANTERN)

BLAEBERRY (*see* BILBERRY)

BLANC, AU A French term used to describe a dish (often chicken or veal) that is white in colour, or is cooked in a white stock.

BLANCHING Immersing food briefly in boiling water to whiten it, as in sweetbreads, or to remove the skin of such foods as peaches and tomatoes. Vegetables which are to be frozen and kept for a certain length of time are blanched to destroy enzymes and preserve the colour, flavour and texture.

BLANCMANGE Blancmange is one of the oldest desserts, thought to be popular in the Middle Ages. Traditionally almond flavoured, a blancmange may now be one of any number of flavours, including chocolate, strawberry or vanilla. It is a sweet dessert, usually made these days with milk and cornflour, although some versions are set with gelatine. A blancmange may be set in a jelly mould, then turned out to serve. Packets of commercially prepared flavoured blancmange powder are readily available from supermarkets.

BLANQUETTE A stew usually made from white meat, such as veal or poultry, cooked in a white sauce enriched with cream and egg yolk. It can also be made with fish or vegetables. (*see also* FRICASSÉE)

BLEAK A small European river fish of the carp family, which may be cooked like the sprat (*see* SPRAT).

BLENDER (Liquidizer) An electric machine usually consisting of a goblet with rotating blades in the base. It can be used to purée wet mixtures and to grind dry ingredients. It is ideal for making milk shakes, soups, pâtés, sauces, dips and baby meals, as well as for producing fresh breadcrumbs, chopped nuts, ground coffee, crushed biscuits and fruit or vegetable purées.

Smaller, hand-held electric blenders are also now available. They are long and narrow, with the rotating blades at one end, and can be used to blend a mixture in the bowl in which it has been prepared.

BLENDING Mixing flour, cornflour, rice flour and similar ground cereals to a smooth paste with a cold liquid (usually milk, water or stock), before being added to a boiling liquid, in the preparation of soups, stews, puddings, gravy, etc., to prevent the cereal from forming lumps when added to the hot dish. Use a wooden spoon and add the liquid gradually, stirring all the time. Experience will soon show the right amount of liquid to use – too little makes hard lumps which are almost impossible to disperse, and too much causes smaller, softer lumps which are also difficult to smooth out completely.

BLENNY A small European and American sea fish that may be prepared like whitebait (*see* WHITEBAIT). A species of blenny is also commonly found in rivers in the south of France.

BLEU, AU A French term used to describe a method of cooking fish, such as trout, cooked immediately after they are caught by simmering in white wine with herbs, or in water containing salt and vinegar.

BLEU DE BRESSE (Bresse Bleu) A soft and creamy blue cheese from France with a rich, subtle flavour. It has a grey-coloured rind and should not be allowed to over-ripen as it develops a strong, unpleasant flavour.

BLEWIT A variety of edible fungus. It has a lilac stem and grows wild in Britain. (*see also* FUNGUS)

BLINI A small Russian yeast pancake made of buckwheat flour. It is often served with smoked salmon or caviar.

BLOATER (*see* HERRING)

BLOOD Blood has long been used as an enriching and thickening agent in traditional British country cooking, though its use is rare today. It is still often used in classic French dishes, such as *coq au vin*, which uses chicken's blood. Pig's blood is the main ingredient of black pudding.

BLOOD ORANGE (*see* ORANGE)

BLOOD PUDDING (*see* BLACK PUDDING)

BLOODY MARY A cocktail made from vodka and tomato juice, flavoured with Worcestershire or Tabasco sauce, and served over crushed ice.

BLUEBERRY This fruit is a member of the bilberry family. Its berries are small, round and black, like the bilberry, but it is larger and juicier. It can be used in dishes instead of bilberries. Blueberries grow wild in the United States and are very popular as a topping for cheesecakes, as a pancake filling, or in blueberry pie. (*see also* BILBERRY)

BLUE CASTELLO A Danish blue cheese with a soft creamy texture, made from cows' milk.

BLUE DORSET (Dorset Blue, Blue Vinny, Blue Vinney) A white and crumbly blue cheese that is made in Dorset. It is made from locally produced skimmed milk and, nowadays, is quite hard to obtain. It has a brown, crusty rind, rather like Stilton, and a strong, sharp flavour.

BLUEFISH A medium-sized fish caught in the North Atlantic and the Mediterranean. As its name suggests, it is an attractive blue-coloured fish with firm white flesh. It is best baked or poached.

BLUE SHROPSHIRE The name of this blue cheese is somewhat misleading, since the cheese is in fact made in Leicestershire. It is made by a similar method to Stilton, but is orange in colour. It has a brown rind and a mild flavour. (*see also* STILTON)

BLUTWURST A German blood sausage made from pig's blood and pork and bacon fat, and flavoured with herbs, spices and onion. It can be poached, sliced and eaten cold, or fried and eaten hot. (*see also* BLACK PUDDING, BOUDIN NOIR)

BOAR (Wild Boar) This species of wild pig is now extinct in Britain but used to be a popular animal for hunting and roasting. It survives in parts of Europe, including France, and Asia, often growing to enormous proportions. In France, a young boar is known as a *marcassin* and is prized for its tender meat. Wild boar is not bled before cooking, as pork is, so the meat, when cooked, is much darker. It can be dry and tough unless prepared and cooked carefully, but it has a good flavour which increases in strength with the age of the animal.

BOCKWURST (*see* FRANKFURTER)

BOEUF The French word for beef, and used in the names of such recipes as *boeuf bourguignonne*, *boeuf Stroganov* and *carbonnade de boeuf*.

BOG MYRTLE (Sweet Gale) Although not often used these days, this plant was once a popular aromatic herb. It grows in abundance on the northern moors of Britain. Its flavour is something like that of bay.

BOILED SWEETS A wide variety of hard-textured sweets is made commercially by boiling sugar, glucose, an acid and a fruit or other flavouring to 149°C (300°F) and putting the mixture through a 'drop machine' so that round or fancy shapes are obtained. (*see also* SUGAR BOILING, SWEETS)

BOILING Cooking in liquid (usually water) at 100°C (212°F), which is the boiling point of water. The main foods that are boiled are vegetables, rice and pasta. Syrups and glazes that need reducing and thickening are also boiled, as are some sauces. Other foods, such as meat, are often said to be 'boiled' but in fact should be cooked slowly, or simmered, at a temperature just below boiling point. Fast boiling for a long period causes meat or other foods to shrink, lose flavour and become tough. (*see also* SIMMERING)

BOILING FOWL (*see* CHICKEN)

BOK CHOY (*see* PAK CHOLI)

BOLETUS A genus of fungi, including both poisonous and edible mushrooms, which can be distinguished from other mushrooms by the fact that it has tube-shaped features under its cap rather than the usual gills. The best-known member of the boletus family is the edible Bordeaux cep, which is much esteemed in France. (*see also* FUNGUS, MUSHROOM)

BOLOGNA SAUSAGE (Bolony, Polony) This finely ground smoked pork sausage is modelled on the original mortadella sausage from the Italian town of Bologna. It is known as polony in Britain, and bolony in the United States. It is sold ready for slicing and eating cold. (*see also* MORTADELLA)

BOLOGNESE An Italian beef and vegetable sauce that is typical of a style of cooking that originated in Bologna. It is traditionally served with spaghetti (*see* PASTA).

BOLONY (*see* BOLOGNA SAUSAGE)

BOMBAY DUCK Rather incongruously, this name is given to dried pieces of the bummaloe fish which is found in Indian waters. The fish is dried in the sun, then cut into strips or chunks to be baked or fried and served with curry. It has a strong fishy smell and is very nutritious.

BOMBE The name (originally French) given to a metal mould, usually copper, with a tightly fitting lid, which is mostly used for shaping different flavours of ice cream and sometimes fruits. The ice cream itself, when turned out, is also known as a bombe. A basic bombe mixture is usually very rich, containing egg yolks and double cream, and can be flavoured with fruit purée, candied fruit, chocolate, nuts, coffee, liqueur, chocolate, etc. The bombe mould is often first lined with layers of contrasting colours of ordinary ice cream, then the bombe mixture spooned into the centre, creating an attractive effect when the bombe is turned out, cut and served. (*see also* CASSATA, ICE CREAM, PARFAIT)

BONBONS A general name, especially in France, for various kinds of sugar confectionery.

BONDON (Bondard, Bondart, Bonde) A group of small, soft, whole-milk French cheeses made in Normandy. They are shaped in the form of a bun.

BONES Bones, both raw and from cooked meat, are used to make stock to use in any number of sauces, gravies, soups and other cooked dishes. When meat is cooked on the bone, such as in soups, stews and casseroles, the collagen contained in the bone is dissolved to form gelatine and enriches the dish. Bones from young animals contain the most collagen, but older bones enhance flavour. The soluble contents of bones are more easily released during cooking if the bones are roughly broken up first.

Large tubular limb bones contain a nutritious fatty substance known as marrow, which can be extracted from the bone and poached, or can be left inside the bone during cooking, as in the Italian dish, *osso buco*. Bone marrow is also used to enrich dishes, such as *risotto alla milanese*. (*see also* OSSO BUCO, STOCK)

BONING Removing the bones from meat or poultry, cutting the flesh as little as possible, so that it can be rolled or stuffed. Special boning knives are usually used. (*see also* POULTRY)

BONITO The name of various species of sea fish, found in the Atlantic, Pacific and Mediterranean. They are oily fish, related to the tuna (*see* TUNA).

BONNE-BOUCHES Canapés or other small items of savoury food served as an appetizer or as a savoury course at the end of a meal.

BONNE FEMME A French term used to describe a dish that is prepared in a simple, homely way and often served from the casserole or tin in which it has been cooked. Any garnish on such a dish would also be very simple, such as fresh herbs or vegetables.

BOQUERONES A Spanish dish of anchovy fillets pickled in salt and vinegar.

BORAGE This herb has slightly hairy leaves and bright blue flowers, both of which have a flavour of salt and cucumber. The herb is mainly used in drinks, such as claret cup and Pimm's, but young, hair-free leaves can also be used in salads. The flowers can be candied and used as decorations for cakes and desserts, and the herb can also be used to make an infused tea. Borage is easy to grow and is not sold dried.

BORDEAUX The Bordeaux region of France produces the complete range of quality wines, from light, quick-maturing reds to the greatest clarets, and from modest dry whites to the world's greatest sweet whites. It is the largest wine-growing region in France and there are many hundreds of châteaux making and bottling excellent wines. The main Bordeaux 'rouge' (red) districts are Médoc, St. Émilion, Pomérol and Graves (*see* GRAVES, MÉDOC).

Bordeaux white wines are usually medium-sweet or sweet and are generally best served as dessert wines. The sweetest are the Barsacs, whereas some Graves are quite dry. The best white Bordeaux wines are considered to be the Sauternes.

BORDELAISE, À LA A French term used to describe a dish that incorporates a wine sauce, bone marrow, ceps, or a garnish of artichokes and potatoes.

BORDURE (Border, Ring) A mixture or group of ingredients (especially cooked vegetables) arranged in a ring or border around the edge of a dish, either to enhance the appearance of the dish or to contain other ingredients in the centre.

BORECOLE (*see* KALE)

BORLOTTO BEAN This attractive speckled-pinkish dried bean is a member of the same family as the kidney bean. It is an Italian bean and is excellent used in many Italian dishes. (*see also* PULSES)

BORRIDE (*see* BOURRIDE)

BORTSCH (Borsch, Borshch, Borscht) This eastern European soup is well known for its brilliant red colour, which it gets from one of its main ingredients, beetroot. It also contains other vegetables and sometimes diced meat, and can be served hot or cold, traditionally with soured cream.

BOSTON BAKED BEANS (*see* NAVY BEAN)

BOTARGO (Poutarg) The salted, pressed and dried roe from the female tuna fish or grey mullet. This is a popular delicacy in Italy, Greece and Egypt and is very similar to Greek *tarama* which is used to make *taramasalata*. In Britain, tuna fish

botargo can be bought from shops specializing in Italian foods, but it is expensive. It is best served as an hors d'oeuvre, or with drinks. (*see also* TARAMA)

BOTTLE GOURD (*see* DUDI)

BOTTLING (Canning) The term used for preserving food or preserves in glass jars under sterile conditions. It is an economical way of using windfall fruit or produce which is in season and plentiful. Yeasts and moulds already present in the food are killed by heating the jars of fruit in the oven, in a water bath on top of the cooker, or in a pressure cooker, and then sealing the jars when hot.

It is not possible to use bottling as a method of preserving meat, fish, poultry or vegetables in the home. In order to kill the bacteria which can lead to food poisoning, the food must be preserved in acid conditions (which is why most fruits can be bottled successfully) or heated to extremely high temperatures. Heat processing carried out at home, even when using a pressure cooker, is inadequate and cannot ensure that bottled vegetables are free from bacteria. Extra acid needs to be added when bottling tomatoes but almost any type of fruit can be bottled, providing the general rules for preparing and processing are followed. As with any other preserving process, the fruit must be fresh, sound, clean and properly ripe – neither too soft, nor too hard.

Bottling Jars

These are wide-necked jars with glass caps or metal discs, secured by screw-bands or clips or a polypropylene screw-band. These all fit the jars. These bands can be used in a pressure cooker but are not really suitable for prolonged heating in the oven. If the cap or disc has no integral rubber gasket, a thin rubber ring is inserted between it and the top of the bottle. Neither the rubber rings nor the metal discs with fitted seals should be used more than once. Jars can be obtained in different sizes ranging from 450 g (1 lb) upwards.

Packing Jars

Fruit may be preserved in either syrup or water, but syrup imparts a much better flavour and colour.

Fruit should be packed as tightly as possible in the jars. Syrup or water is added before or after processing.

Processing

Filled jars can be sterilized in the oven, in a water bath or in a pressure cooker. The water bath method is the most exact, but needs special equipment a large vessel that will allow the jars to be completely immersed in water. The oven method is more convenient as all the jars can be processed at once, but it is less exact. The pressure cooker method shortens the time and also ensures that the temperature is controlled exactly.

After processing, the screw-bands on the jars are tightened immediately. After cooling, it is necessary to test the jars for a good seal. If the bottling process has been carried out correctly and the seals are good, the jars can be stored in a cool, dark place until required.

(For more detailed instructions for home bottling, refer to a reliable book on preserving.)

BOTULISM (*see* FOOD POISONING)

BOUCHÉE A small round piece of cooked puff pastry served hot with a savoury filling on top or inside. It should be no more than 4 cm (1½ inches) in diameter so that it can be eaten in one mouthful (*bouchée*).

Petits fours of the same name consist of small pieces of sponge cake, cut in various shapes, filled with a rich cream or jam filling, then sandwiched together and coated in fondant icing.

BOUDIN BLANC A French sausage that is creamy white in colour, containing finely minced veal, pork, rabbit or chicken meat mixed with cream, egg, onions and flavourings. They are sold cooked and ready for eating but are best served hot, grilled, fried or poached. There are many regional variations of this sausage, some of which contain truffles. It is a very popular Christmastime speciality all over France.

BOUDIN NOIR This is a French blood sausage made from pig's blood, pork fat, cream, onion and spices. It is usually served hot, sliced and lightly fried or grilled. There are many regional variations of this sausage, containing additional flavourings. (*see also* BLACK PUDDING, BLUTWURST)

BOUILLABAISSE A famous fish stew which came, originally, from the south of France. It is made of various kinds of Mediterranean fish, cooked with olive oil, spices and herbs. Saffron is usually included as a flavouring. An authentic *bouillabaisse* can only be made in the south of France as some of the fish used are only available there. However, there are many regional variations, made using which ever types of fish are locally available. After cooking, the fish is removed from the soup and served on a separate dish; the soup may be served poured over chunks of crusty bread.

BOUILLON Plain, unclarified meat or vegetable stock that is strained, flavoured and served as a soup or used as a basis for a sauce or other dish. (*see also* BROTH, COURT BOUILLON, STOCK)

BOUQUET GARNI A small bunch of herbs tied together and used to give flavour to stews, casseroles, soups and stocks. A simple bouquet garni consists of a sprig each of parsley and thyme, a bay leaf, two cloves and a few peppercorns, but the herbs included vary from dish to dish and region to region. Other aromatic vegetables, such as celery or leek, may also be included. The bouquet garni can be enclosed in a small piece of muslin, if preferred, and should be removed from a dish before serving. A bouquet garni may be made from dried herbs, and ready-made bouquets are produced commercially and are readily available, but the best flavour is produced

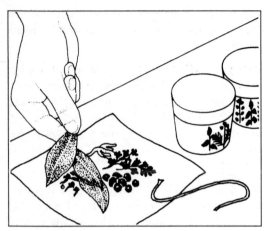

Laying herbs on a square of muslin prior to tying into a bouquet garni.

from a bouquet garni made from a selection of fresh herbs.

BOURBON This American whiskey is named after Bourbon County in Kentucky, where it was first made. It is more full flavoured, robust and fruity than Scotch, but with less finesse. It is distilled from maize, flavoured with malted barley and rye, and matured for at least two years before it is drunk. Its flavour varies, depending on the manufacturer, and it may be drunk with ice, water or soda. (*see also* WHISKY)

BOURGEOISE, À LA A French term used to describe a style of cooking that is homely but appetizing. It includes dishes, usually meat, that are normally cooked for a family meal and which may not have a set recipe. Such dishes are often garnished with carrots, onions and bacon.

BOURGUIGNONNE (Bourguignon) A French term applied to dishes in which burgundy red wine and small braised button onions are used, for example *boeuf bourguignon*.

BOURRIDE (Borride) A fish soup that originated in Provence. It is traditionally made using monkfish, but other fish can be used. The soup is strongly flavoured with garlic.

BOURSIN The brand name of a fresh cream cheese made in France and usually flavoured with garlic or herbs, or rolled in crushed peppercorns.

BOVINE SOMATOTROPIN (*see* MILK)

BOVINE SPONGIFORM ENCEPHALOPATHY (BSE) Often referred to as the 'mad cow disease', this is a disease that many British cattle have become infected with following, it is thought, their being given feed containing ground-up sheep carcass which was infected with a similar disease, scrapie. Although the chance that the disease could be transferred to humans is remote, at the time of going to press, scientists are still unable to state categorically that there is no risk. As a precaution, all cattle suspected of having BSE are slaughtered and incinerated, so that no part can enter the food chain. As an additional safeguard, tissues that might contain the agent which causes the disease (brain, spinal cord, spleen, thymus, tonsils and intestines) in healthy cattle are also banned from use in human food.

BOYSENBERRY One of several hybrids of the raspberry, in this instance in combination with the strawberry, dewberry and loganberry. It is similar to a blackberry in appearance, but longer and plumper. It is dark red in colour and has a rather acid taste. Boysenberries should be treated in the same way as raspberries. (*see also* DEWBERRY, LOGANBERRY, RASPBERRY)

BRAIN The brains of various animals have long been sold as offal to be cooked in a number of ways. They are very nutritious, containing protein, minerals and vitamins. However, since June 1989, certain bovine offal, including brain, has been banned for use as food for human consumption as a precaution against Bovine Spongiform Encephalopathy, or BSE (see above). Lamb's brains are available, however, and are usually sold in sets. One set of lamb's brains is sufficient for one portion.

To select: Fresh brains should look shiny, pinkish-grey, plump and moist.

To prepare: Soak brains for 1-2 hours in cold water to remove all traces of blood. Drain and discard the soaking water. Remove arteries and membranes with a sharp, pointed knife.

To cook: Put brains in a saucepan, cover with water and parboil for 5-15 minutes, depending on size. Vinegar or lemon juice can be added to the cooking water to help retain the pale colour. Add other ingredients for flavour, such as a whole onion or a bay leaf, if required. After par-boiling, plunge into cold water or allow to cool in the cooking liquid to firm the meat. Discard the water and any loose particles of meat which will have solidified.

After par-boiling and cooling, brains can simply be sliced and fried in a little butter or oil, or used in various recipes. They have a very creamy texture and delicate flavour.

BRAISING Braising is a slow method of cooking cuts of meat, poultry and game which are too tough to roast. It is also good for some vegetables. A pan or casserole with a tightly fitting lid should be used so that little liquid is lost through evaporation. The meat is first fried, then cooked on a bed of chopped vegetables (called a *mirepoix*), with just enough liquid (water, stock or wine) added to cover the vegetables. A braise may be cooked on the hob or in the oven. (*see also* MIREPOIX)

BRAMBLE (*see* BLACKBERRY)

BRAN The name given to the outer layer of cereal grains, usually wheat or oats. Bran is a rich source of dietary fibre and because of the current interest in healthy eating, bran is now added to many foods in order to increase the fibre content. Oat bran is particularly rich in soluble fibre which is thought to be important in helping to reduce blood cholesterol levels. (*see also* CHOLESTEROL, FIBRE)

BRANDADE A dish based on salt cod and flavoured with garlic, which is popular in southern France.

BRANDY A spirit distilled from wine. There are many grape brandies; the finest in France come from Cognac, and from southern Bordeaux comes Armagnac, where it is proudly called 'D'Artagnan's Brandy'. It has a distinctive herby, sometimes smoky, flavour and aroma. Brandy is popular as an after-dinner drink, and is believed to have certain medicinal qualities. In cooking, it is often used to flambé or flame a dish (*see* FLAMBÉING).

The name, 'brandy', is also given to a number of fruit liqueurs, such as cherry brandy and apricot brandy, which are not distilled from wine, but from fruit juice, although brandy may be added. (*see also* EAU-DE-VIE, GRAPPA, MARC)

BRANDY BUTTER (Hard Sauce) A butter sauce made from softened butter combined with icing or caster sugar and brandy. It is left to harden before serving. Brandy butter is traditionally served with Christmas pudding or mince pies, but may be served with other hot puddings. Rum butter is a variation made with soft brown sugar and flavoured with lemon.

BRANDY SNAP A crisp biscuit made by the drop method of biscuit making (*see* BISCUITS). The syrupy mixture is flavoured with lemon rind, ginger and brandy and cooked for only a short time. As the biscuits are removed from the oven, they are rolled round greased wooden spoon handles and left to cool and set in a cylindrical shape. Before serving, brandy snaps are usually filled with whipped or Chantilly cream.

BRATWURST A pale coloured German sausage made of finely minced pork or veal. It should be grilled or fried before serving. Smoked varieties of *bratwurst* need only a little cooking.

BRAWN (Fromage de Tête, Head Cheese) True brawn is a preparation of boned meat made from pig's head and is eaten cold. Sheep's head, veal and other meats may be used to make an economical brawn.

The meat is stewed with spices and seasoning until very soft, then picked from the bone and finely chopped. It is then set in moulds with some of the stock which is reduced sufficiently for the mixture to set to a jelly. Brawn is served cold and thinly sliced.

BRAZIL NUT (Cream Nut) This is a large, oval, creamy-coloured nut with a high percentage of fat. The nuts grow, grouped together in their individual shells, inside the round fruit of a South American tree.

Brazil nuts are eaten raw, used in sweet-making or added to vegetarian dishes, such as nut roasts and rissoles. They have a very hard brown shell which is not easy to crack and remove by hand, but the nuts are available shelled from most supermarkets.

BREAD One of the world's staple foodstuffs, found in various forms in every country. Bread is a cereal-based food, made mostly from wheat flour combined with yeast, salt and liquid (water or milk). Fat is sometimes added to enrich the bread and to improve its keeping qualities. The shape of bread varies from country to country. In Britain, it is traditionally baked in rectangular, round or oval loaves, while French bread is traditionally shaped into a long stick (*see* BAGUETTE). Many of the world's breads are unleavened, such as pitta bread, chapattis and matzos. Bread is also available in any number of different shaped rolls. (*see also* CHAPPATI, MATZO, NAN, PITTA BREAD, etc.)

The process of bread-making has changed very little over the years. Most leavened (or risen) bread is made with yeast and the dough is kneaded, left to rise, and shaped before baking. A few breads are made with other raising agents and do not have to be left to rise – these are known as 'quick' breads.

Ingredients for Bread Making
Raising Agents
Yeast is a living plant available fresh or dried. When mixed with flour and liquid it gives off carbon dioxide, which expands, making the dough rise.

Fresh yeast is rather like putty in colour and texture, and should have a faint 'winey' smell. There should be no discoloration and it should crumble easily when broken. Although it will store for up to a month in a screw-topped jar, the best results are obtained when it is absolutely fresh, so buy it in small quantities when required.

Fresh yeast is usually blended with a liquid and then added to the flour all at once. It can also be rubbed directly into the flour or added as a batter. The batter method is known as the 'sponge dough process'; some ingredients are mixed to form a sponge, which is allowed to ferment, then mixed with other ingredients to form a dough.

Fresh yeast is most easily measured by weight. The amount of yeast required varies according to the richness of the dough and the type of flour used.

Dried yeast is sold in granular form and is very convenient as it can be stored in an airtight container in a cool place for up to six months. Ordinary dried yeast requires sugar to activate it; the yeast granules are sprinkled over tepid liquid with the sugar and the mixture is then left to froth for about 15 minutes before using. The sugar used to activate the yeast loses its sweetness in the frothing process so dried yeast can be used in savoury recipes. However, there are now several new varieties of dried yeast available, often known as 'easy-blend'. Some require only one rising of the dough, while others can be added directly to the flour without having to be mixed with water and sugar first.

Dried yeast is most easily measured in 5 ml (1 level tsp) or 15 ml (1 level tbsp) quantities. As it is more concentrated than fresh yeast, generally half the amount of dried yeast is required, so that

15 ml (1 level tbsp) dried yeast has the same effect as 25 g (1 oz) fresh yeast.

Bicarbonate of soda is the main raising agent for quick breads. When added to liquid and heated, it gives off carbon dioxide which expands and makes the dough rise.

Cream of tartar is often used with bicarbonate of soda as it reacts with it to help produce carbon dioxide. It also helps to neutralize the slightly soapy taste of bicarbonate of soda.

Baking powder is a ready-made mixture of bicarbonate of soda and acid (often cream of tartar) which produces carbon dioxide when it comes into contact with moisture. It is also used for quick breads.

Flour

Wheat is either hard or soft, depending on its gluten content. When hard wheat is milled it produces a strong flour, rich in protein, containing a sticky, rubber-like substance called gluten. In bread making, the gluten stretches like elastic and as it is heated, it expands and traps in the dough the carbon dioxide released by the yeast. The gluten then sets and forms the 'frame' of the bread. It is the gluten content in a strong flour that gives the volume and open texture of bread and best results are obtained by using this flour. (*see also* GLUTEN)

When soft wheats are milled they produce a flour with different gluten properties, more suited to the making of cakes or pastries where a smaller rise and closer, finer texture are required. This ordinary soft flour, which is either plain or self raising, can be used for bread but it will give a smaller rise and closer crumbly texture with a pale, hard crust, and a disappointing result. Self raising flour (that is, plain flour with raising agents already added) can be used in recipes for quick breads.

Generally, bread made with wholemeal flour has a closer texture and a stronger, more distinctive taste than white bread.

Wholemeal (or wholewheat) flour contains 100 per cent of the wheat (that is, the entire grain is milled). Bread made with this flour is coarse-textured, has a nutty taste, and is brown in colour. Strong, plain and self raising types of wholemeal flour are available.

Brown (wheatmeal) flour contains 80-90 per cent of the wheat (that is, some of the bran is removed) and it is more absorbent than white flour, giving a denser-textured bread than white, but not as coarse as wholemeal. It is available in strong, plain and self raising forms.

White flour contains 72-74 per cent of the wheat. The bran and wheatgerm which give wholemeal and brown flours their brown colour are removed, resulting in the white flour which is used to make fine-textured 'white' bread. Much is bleached chemically; look for the word 'unbleached' for untreated flour. White flour is available in strong, plain and self raising forms.

Stoneground flour takes its name from the specific process of grinding which heats the flour and gives it a slightly roasted, nutty flavour. Both wholemeal and brown flours can be stoneground.

Granary flour is a strong brown flour with added malted wheat flakes, giving a nutty flavour. The name is actually the brand name of a flour manufactured by Rank Hovis McDougall plc, but it has fallen into general use and is frequently applied to similar flours and to bread made from them.

If you wish to eat a bread high in fibre, choose a flour with a high percentage of the wheat grain. Extra fibre can be added to bread recipes in the form of bran, bran flakes or oatmeal. Add in small quantities and use a little extra liquid for mixing.

Salt

Salt improves the flavour of bread. It should be measured accurately, as too little causes the dough to rise too quickly and too much kills the yeast and gives the bread an uneven texture. Salt is used in the proportions of 5-10 ml (1-2 level tsp) to 450 g (1 lb) flour. Low sodium salts may also be used.

Fat

Adding fat to the dough enriches it and gives a moist, close-textured loaf with a soft crust. It also helps keep the bread fresh and soft for longer. It is often rubbed into the flour and salt or, if a large quantity is used, it is melted and added with the liquid ingredients. If using margarine, block margarine is better than soft tub as it is easier to rub in. Oil may be used instead of fat.

Liquid

Water is suitable for plain bread, producing a loaf with an even texture and a crisp crust. Milk and water, or milk alone, will give a softer golden crust and the loaf will stay softer and fresher for a longer period.

The amount of liquid used will vary according to the absorbency of the flour. Too much will give the bread a spongy and open texture. Wholemeal and brown flours are usually more absorbent than white.

The liquid is generally added to the yeast at a tepid temperature, that is 43°C (110°F). Boiling water will kill the yeast.

Glazes and Finishes

If a crusty finish is desired, bread or rolls can be brushed before baking with a glaze made by dissolving 10 ml (2 level tsp) salt in 30 ml (2 tbsp) water.

For a shiny finish, the surface should be brushed with beaten egg or beaten egg and milk.

For a soft finish, dust the bread or rolls with flour before baking. Some breads and yeast buns are glazed after baking to give them a sticky finish. To do this, brush the bread with warmed honey or a syrup made by dissolving 30 ml (2 level tbsp) sugar in 30 ml (2 tbsp) water and bringing to the boil.

There are many ways of adding interest, variety and extra fibre and vitamins to bread and rolls. After glazing and before baking, lightly sprinkle the surface with one of the following:

* Poppy, caraway, celery or fennel seeds
* Sesame seeds – particularly good sprinkled on to the soft baps used with hamburgers
* Cracked wheat, barley or wheat flakes, wheat germ, oatmeal or crushed cornflakes. Sprinkle them on top of wholemeal bread or baps.

Making Bread

Mixing the Dough Warmed ingredients and bowl will help to speed up the first rising process. Measure all the ingredients carefully into a large bowl. Add the yeast liquid and mix with the dry ingredients, using a wooden spoon or fork, until blended. Work the dough, using your hands, until the mixture is smooth and leaves the sides of the bowl clean.

Kneading the Dough

Kneading is essential to strengthen the gluten in the flour, thus making the dough elastic in texture and enabling it to rise more easily.

Turn the dough on to a floured work surface and knead the dough by folding it towards you and quickly and firmly pushing down and away from you with the heel of the hand. Give the dough a quarter turn and continue kneading for about 10 minutes, until it is firm, elastic and no longer sticky.

Using a dough hook If you have a mixer with a dough hook attachment, it can take the hard work out of kneading. Follow manufacturer's instructions; working with small amounts of dough is more successful than attempting a large batch all at once. Place the yeast dissolved in the liquid in the bowl, add the dry ingredients, begin at the lowest speed and mix to form the dough. Increase the speed for the recommended time.

Using a food processor A food processor also takes the hard work out of yeast mixtures. Follow the manufacturer's instructions on quantities as it is important that the bowl is not over-filled. You may need to halve the recipe and prepare two batches of dough.

Rising

The kneaded dough is now ready for rising. Unless otherwise stated in a recipe, place the dough in a bowl and cover with a clean tea towel. This will prevent a skin forming during rising. Rising times vary with temperature. Allow 1½-2 hours at room temperature for the dough to rise. After rising, the dough should have doubled in size and should spring back when gently pressed with a lightly floured finger.

Good results are obtained by allowing the covered dough to rise in the refrigerator overnight or for up to 24 hours. The dough must be allowed to return to room temperature (taking several hours) before it is shaped.

The dough can be made to rise in about 45-60 minutes in a warm place such as an airing cupboard or above a warm cooker.

Preparing Tins

While the dough is rising, grease the tins or baking sheets. Where reference is made to a 450 g (1 lb) loaf tin, capacity 900 ml (1½ pints), the approximate size to use is 16.5 × 10.5 cm (6 ½ × 4 inch) top measurements, and for a 900 g (2 lb) loaf tin, capacity 1.7 litres (3 pints), use one with 20 × 13 cm (8 × 5 inch) top measurements.

Knocking Back

The best texture is obtained by kneading the dough for a second time after rising. Turn the risen dough on to a lightly floured work surface and knead for 2-3 minutes to 'knock' out any large bubbles and ensure an even texture. The dough is then shaped as required (see right), placed in the prepared tins or on baking sheets, covered with a clean tea towel and left in a warm place to rise again.

Proving or Second Rise

This is the last process before baking. The shaped dough should be allowed to 'prove', that is left at room temperature until it has doubled in size and will spring back when lightly pressed with a floured finger. After proving, the dough is ready for glazing and baking.

Baking

Basic breads are baked in the oven at 230°C (450°F) mark 8. When cooked, the bread should be well risen and golden brown, and it should sound hollow when tapped underneath with the knuckles. Larger loaves may need to be turned out of the tin and returned to the oven upside down for the last 10-15 minutes of the cooking time to ensure they are cooked through. Allow to cool on wire racks.

Traditional Bread and Roll Shapes

Baton Shape the dough into a long roll with tapering ends, about 20.5 cm (8 inches) long.

Bloomer Flatten the dough and roll up like a Swiss roll. Tuck the ends under and place on a baking sheet. When proved to double its size, make diagonal slits on top with a sharp knife. Glaze the top with beaten egg or salt water before baking.

Cob Knead the dough into a ball by drawing the sides down and tucking them underneath to make a smooth top.

Cottage Cut one-third off the dough. Knead both pieces well and shape into rounds, place the smaller round on top of the larger one, and place on a baking sheet. Make a hole down through the middle of both pieces using the handle of a wooden spoon. Glaze with salt water before baking.

Crown Divide the dough into 50 g (2 oz) pieces. Knead, shape into rounds and place in a greased round sandwich tin. The crown is usually pulled apart into rolls when served.

Knots Divide the dough into three, shape each piece into a thin roll and tie into a knot.

Loaf Only fill the tin two-thirds full for a perfect shape. Fold the dough in three, smooth over the top and tuck in the ends, then place in the tin.

Plait Divide the dough into three and shape into long rolls about 30.5 cm (12 inches) long. Pinch the ends together and plait loosely, then pinch the other ends together. Before baking, glaze with beaten egg and sprinkle with poppy seeds.

Rings Divide the dough into three, shape each piece into a thin roll and bend it round to form a ring; dampen the ends and mould them together.
Rounds Divide the dough into three, place the pieces on a very lightly floured surface and roll each into a ball. To do this, hold the hand flat almost at table level and move it round in a circular movement, gradually lifting the palm to get a good round shape.
Tin Roll out the dough to an oblong and roll up like a Swiss roll. Tuck the ends under and place in the prepared tin. Before baking, score the top of the loaf with a sharp knife if wished.
Trefoil Divide the dough into three and divide each piece into three smaller pieces. Roll each into a ball. Place the three balls grouped together on a baking sheet.
Twist Divide the dough into three and divide each piece into two. Shape into thin rolls. Hold one end of the two pieces of dough together and twist. Dampen the ends and tuck under.

Bread in Cooking Bread is used in cooking in a number of ways. In the form of breadcrumbs it is used in stuffings and home-made sausages, and to coat foods for frying. Breadcrumbs also form the basis of a bread sauce, and can be used as a thickening agent in other sauces. Sprinkled on top of cooked dishes and browned under the grill, breadcrumbs form a crisp topping to many dishes. In desserts, bread is the main ingredient in bread and butter pudding, and it forms the outer shell of a summer pudding, filled with fresh soft fruits and soaked in their juice. Bread is also served as an accompaniment to many dishes, either plain or as herb or garlic bread. As crisply fried cubes, or *croûtons*, bread adds texture and flavour to soups. (*see also* BREAD AND BUTTER PUDDING, BREADCRUMBS, BREAD SAUCE, CABINET PUDDING, CROÛTONS, GARLIC BUTTER, SUMMER PUDDING)

BREAD AND BUTTER PICKLE Somewhat confusingly named, this is a cucumber pickle that is best served with bread and butter – hence its name. (*see also* PICKLE)

BREAD AND BUTTER PUDDING A hot pudding made using stale bread, spread with butter and layered in a pie dish with mixed dried fruit and sugar. A custard mixture is then poured over and the pudding is baked until set and golden brown. Bread and butter pudding is a great family favourite.

Osborne pudding is a variation of bread and butter pudding made with brown bread and butter spread with marmalade. The mixed dried fruit is omitted.

BREADCRUMBS Both fresh white crumbs and browned dried crumbs (raspings) are used in cookery, as an ingredient in puddings and savoury dishes and as a topping or coating. Fried crumbs are traditionally served with game. Ready-prepared crumbs can be frozen, and they can also be bought.

To make fresh breadcrumbs, use bread that is one or two days old, remove the crusts, break into pieces and process in a blender or food processor. Alternatively, rub the bread through a wire sieve, or use a grater.

Dried breadcrumbs are used for coating ham, topping scalloped dishes, coating the inside of a mould used for *réchauffés*, and coating fish and other foods before frying. To make dried breadcrumbs, put stale pieces of bread on a baking sheet and put in the bottom of the oven with the oven set at the lowest temperature. Leave them for several hours or until they are quite crisp and pale golden brown. Cool, then break into pieces and crush in a blender or food processor, or use a rolling pin. Store in an airtight container.

To fry breadcrumbs, mix 100 g (4 oz) crumbs with 15 g (1/2 oz) melted butter and fry over a gentle heat until golden brown, stirring constantly or they will brown unevenly and burn. Serve with roast game.

BREADFRUIT The fruit of a large tree that grows in tropical regions. The fruit is eaten as a vegetable in South-East Asia, the Pacific Islands and the West Indies. It is a large, round fruit, about the size of a small football, and it has a rough, green skin that turns brown as the fruit ripens. The fruit should be peeled, sliced and the pips discarded, before being baked, fried, roasted or boiled. The flesh is creamy-yellow in colour and its flavour is not unlike bread or potatoes. It can be served in place of potatoes as a vegetable accompaniment, or it can be cooked in a stew or soup. It can also be sliced and made into chips or crisps.

BREAD PUDDING A traditional English baked pudding, made by soaking stale white bread in milk and mixing it with mixed dried fruit, candied peel, suet, sugar and egg. The mixture is flavoured with mixed spice and softened with a little milk before being baked in the oven.

BREAD SAUCE An English sauce made from breadcrumbs and milk, flavoured with onion, cloves, bay and pepper. It is traditionally served with roast poultry and game.

Bread Sauce

2 cloves
1 medium onion, skinned
1 small bay leaf
450 ml (³/₄ pint) milk
75 g (3 oz) breadcrumbs
salt and white pepper
15 g (¹/₂ oz) butter or margarine
30 ml (2 tbsp) single cream

Stick the cloves into the onion and place in a heavy saucepan with the bay leaf and milk. Bring slowly to the boil, remove from the heat, cover and leave to infuse for 10 minutes, then remove the onion and bay leaf.

Add the breadcrumbs and seasoning, return to the heat, cover and simmer gently for 10-15 minutes, stirring occasionally. Stir in the butter and cream.

Serves 4

BREAD STICKS (*see* GRISSINI)

BREAKFAST CEREALS Cereals form the basis of many popular breakfast foods. Apart from porridge, made from oats, there is a huge range of commercially produced breakfast cereals to choose from, and the range is constantly growing as new products are brought on to the market in line with revised ideas about nutrition.

Most breakfast cereals are based on maize, rice, wheat or oats which are modified to make them immediately ready to eat. Some varieties are aimed specifically at children, with cartoon characters pictured on the packet, free toys inside the pack, and the cereals themselves coated in sugar or even a chocolate flavouring. Others are marketed at the health-conscious and are advertised as being high in fibre or low in calories. Vitamins and iron may be added to some cereals artificially. Only a few are made from 100 per cent pure cereal, although manufacturers are slowly responding to an increased demand for more healthy breakfast cereals.

For those who prefer to mix their own cereals, muesli is a good choice. Commercial brands of muesli are available, but it is easy to mix your own version at home (*see* MUESLI). (*see also* GRAINS, PORRIDGE)

BREAM (Sea Bream, Red Bream) Bream is a round, red-backed fish with a silvery belly and red fins. It has firm white flesh which has a mild flavour. It is usually sold whole and can be stuffed and baked, poached, fried or grilled. A freshwater species of bream also exists, but it is less good for eating. Another species, found in the United States, is known as porgy or red porgy.

BRESAOLA The name given to tender strips of beef which have been air-dried and left to mature for several months. It comes from Italy, where it is marinated in olive oil, lemon juice and black pepper and served as an appetizer. (*see also* BUNDERFLEISCH, DRIED MEAT)

BRESSE BLEU (*see* BLEU DE BRESSE)

BRETONNE, À LA A French term used to describe a dish garnished with haricot beans or bean purée. The name is also given to eggs or fish coated with Breton sauce, which does not contain haricot beans.

BREWER'S YEAST (*see* YEAST)

BRICK An American cheese, of medium firm texture, with many small holes. It is made from cows' milk, has a somewhat sweet taste and may be either mild or strong. Brick may be eaten raw or used in cooking.

BRIDGE ROLL A small, slim roll made from a bread dough enriched with egg. Bridge rolls have a soft crust, and are most often filled and served as part of a buffet, as picnic food, or as an accompaniment to a meal.

BRIE A soft-textured farm cheese, produced from cows' milk in the north of France. It is made from whole milk and is mould-inoculated (*see* CHEESE). A Brie is flat and round, usually 35 cm (14 inches) in diameter and about 2.7 kg (6 lb) in weight; it has a white floury crust instead of the more usual hard rind. Brie should be eaten fresh when soft all through and it does not keep well. There are several types of Brie, varying from region to region. One of the best known is *Brie de Meaux* which comes from the area of Meaux, south-east of Paris. It has a less smooth crust and a darker colour than the ordinary Brie. Some Brie cheeses have added flavourings of herbs or peppercorns.

Brie is readily available from supermarkets and delicatessens. A Brie can be bought whole, but is more usually sold in wedge-shaped portions.

BRILL This is a flat sea fish with a good flavour and texture, resembling turbot. The flesh is firm and slightly yellowish; any with a bluish tinge should be avoided. Brill is sold whole or as fillets and may be grilled, baked or poached and served cold with mayonnaise. It can also be cooked by any method suitable for turbot (*see* TURBOT).

BRINE A salt and water solution in which food is immersed for the purposes of preservation. Nowadays, brining is mostly only done on a commercial scale, although it is possible to preserve small items in brine at home. Always consult a good recipe book before attempting to brine any foods at home.

A brine has the effect of slowing down the deterioration of foods as some bacteria cannot function in such a salty environment. A brine that contains 20 per cent salt is usually sufficiently strong. Modern industrial methods of curing meat include injecting a brine solution into the meat before it is immersed, a more reliable method than just soaking. (*see also* SALTING)

BRINJAL (*see* AUBERGINE)

BRIOCHE An enriched yeast dough baked in the shape of a cottage loaf. It is French in origin and usually eaten warm as a dessert or for breakfast. Both large and small *brioches* are made in France, their shape varying from region to region. Raisins are sometimes added to the dough, and small *brioches* may be filled with various sweet or savoury fillings.

BRISKET One of the less tender, rather fatty cuts of beef, cut from the lower part of the shoulder. It is sold on or off the bone and is suitable for braising, stewing or pot-roasting. It can sometimes be bought salted and spiced and can then be treated as salted silverside (*see* BEEF). After boiling, brisket is delicious served cold and thinly sliced.

BRISLING (*see* SPRAT)

BROAD BEAN (*see* BEAN, BROAD)

BROCCOLI (Calabrese) A green vegetable of which there are several types. Some are 'sprouting' varieties, producing many purple, white or green shoots; others, known as calabrese, produce just one large close head, like cauliflower. In fact, all varieties of broccoli are from the same family as cauliflower. Broccoli originally came from Italy, but it is now widely available most of the year. It can also be bought frozen.

To select: Choose firm, tightly packed heads with strong stalks. The purple and green varieties have a more delicate flavour than the white. Allow 100-175 g (4-6 oz) per person.

To prepare: Varieties of broccoli with a single head should be trimmed and broken into florets, or cooked whole. For sprouting varieties, simply trim the stalks and leaves and halve the shoots if large.

To cook: Sprouting broccoli is best steamed or boiled in the same way as asparagus. Tie the shoots in bundles of four or five and stand upright in a pan of boiling salted water. The stalks are thus boiled, while the heads are gently steamed. Cook, covered, for 10-15 minutes, then drain.

Whole heads of broccoli should also be cooked upright. Florets need only about 5 minutes boiling or steaming, or they can be stir-fried or added to casseroles.

To serve: Toss hot drained broccoli in melted butter and sprinkle with toasted flaked almonds, or coat with hollandaise or mornay sauce. Broccoli can also be served cold with mayonnaise or a vinaigrette dressing.

BROCHETTE Similar to a kebab, this name is given to a dish of meat or fish that has been cooked on a skewer or spit, either on a rotisserie, under the grill or over hot coals on a barbecue. The ingredients are often marinated before cooking. *Brochette* is actually the French name for the special type of skewer used for this purpose. Small *brochettes* may be served as an hors d'oeuvre; larger *brochettes* make a good main course, accompanied by rice and salad.

BROILER (*see* CHICKEN)

BROILING (*see* GRILLING)

BROSE A Scottish dish, somewhat resembling gruel, made by pouring boiling water over oatmeal or barley, stirring well and adding salt. A richer version contains additional milk and butter or cream. Fish, meat or vegetables may be added to make mussel, beef or kale brose, etc. When made with whisky and honey, it is called athol brose.

BROTH (Bouillon) Also sometimes called stock, broth is the liquid produced after boiling meat or fish bones for a long time in water. Unlike stock, however, a broth may be strained and flavoured to serve as a soup. A stock, on the other hand, is always used as the basis of another dish, such as a soup or stew. (*see also* BOUILLON, FUMET, STOCK)

BROWNING Giving a dish (usually already cooked) an appetizing golden-brown colour by placing it under the grill or in a hot oven for a short time.

BROWNING DISH (Browning Griddle) Used in microwave cooking, a browning dish or griddle is made of a special material which absorbs microwave energy. It is heated empty in the microwave cooker for 8-10 minutes, or according to the manufacturer's instructions, during which time it becomes very hot. The food is then placed on the hot surface and is immediately seared and browned. (*see also* MICROWAVE COOKING)

BROWNING ELEMENT (Grill) When buying a microwave cooker, it is worth considering buying one that has a browning element or grill built in. It works in the same way as a conventional grill, either on its own or in combination with microwave energy. It is especially useful when the microwave cooker is the main cooking appliance since there is no need to transfer a cooked dish to a conventional grill for browning. (*see also* MICROWAVE COOKING)

BROWNING, GRAVY A dark liquid, used to colour gravy, soups or stews. There are many proprietary brands on the market, but a home-made browning can also be made by boiling sugar until it turns brown, then adding water (*see* CARAMEL). (*see also* GRAVY)

BROWN SAUCE A brown sauce is made by cooking a roux until it is brown, thus giving the sauce its colour. Brown sauces range from simple gravies made with meat juices, to the classic *sauce espagnole* and sauces based on it. (*see also* SAUCE)

BRÛLÉE A French word (meaning, literally, 'burnt') applied to a dish with a crisp topping or coating of burnt or caramelized sugar. (*see also* CARAMEL, CRÈME BRÛLÉE)

BRUNCH Originating in America, this meal is a combination of breakfast and lunch (as its name suggests). It usually consists of both hot and cold dishes served late in the morning, often on a Sunday. Brunch is always very informal, although Sunday brunch is increasingly served in restaurants.

BRUNOISE A mixture of finely diced or shredded vegetables used as a base for a soup or sauce, or as a garnish.

BRUSSELS SPROUTS A member of the cabbage family, Brussels sprouts are about the size of small walnuts and a good source of vitamins. They are a popular winter vegetable, grown all over Europe, but originating in Belgium. They are usually cooked and served hot as a vegetable accompaniment, but very young Brussels sprouts can be shredded and served raw in a salad. Brussels sprout 'tops', that is the leafy part of the sprout plant, can be cooked like spring greens.
To select: Choose small, round, even-sized sprouts with tightly packed, firm heads and no wilted or yellow leaves. Allow 100-175 g (4-6 oz) per person.
To prepare: Remove any damaged or wilted leaves and cut off the stems. If the sprouts are large, cut a cross in the stump to allow the thick part to cook as quickly as the leaves. This is not necessary for small, young sprouts. Wash the sprouts well and drain.

To cook: Brussels sprouts may be steamed for about 15 minutes, or cooked in boiling salted water for 8-10 minutes, until just tender.
To serve: Serve Brussels sprouts hot, tossed in melted butter or butter-fried breadcrumbs, or coat in Mornay sauce.

BRUT Meaning unsweetened, this French word is used to describe champagne or dry wine.

BSE (*see* BOVINE SPONGIFORM ENCEPHALOPATHY)

BST (*see* MILK)

BUAL (*see* MADEIRA)

BUBBLE AND SQUEAK A traditional English dish, originally made from cold boiled beef (thinly sliced, diced or minced), mixed with cold cooked potatoes and finely chopped cabbage, or other greens, and then fried. It derived its name from the noises made while it was frying. The cooked dish was sometimes sprinkled with vinegar. In the modern version of bubble and squeak, the meat is usually omitted and the dish is made from cooked vegetables only, often leftover Brussels sprouts and potatoes.

BUCATINI (*see* PASTA)

BÛCHE DE CHÈVRE A soft French goats' milk cheese. (*see also* CHÈVRE)

BÛCHE DE NOËL The French name for a type of Swiss roll known as a Yule log in Britain.

BUCKLING (*see* HERRING)

BUCK RAREBIT (*see* WELSH RAREBIT)

Opposite: Globe artichoke
Overleaf: Left, Avocados; **Right**, Bagna cauda
Centre Pages: (clockwise from top) Marmalade teabread, Cheese and chive scones, Chelsea buns, Marbled chocolate teabread, Herbed granary bread stick, Cottage loaf

BUCK'S FIZZ A refreshing chilled cocktail made by mixing two parts champagne with one part orange juice, often served at brunch.

BUCKWHEAT (Saracen Corn) Although cooked and eaten as a cereal grain, buckwheat is actually the fruit of a plant related to rhubarb. The grain is a triangular shape, rather like a beech nut. It is widely used in Russia to make porridge known as *kasha*, and in Japan to make noodles called *soba*. It is often sold lightly roasted, which enhances the mild flavour, and can then be used without further preparation. Buckwheat is a rich source of vitamins A and B, and also contains calcium.

Buckwheat is made into a rather coarse flour which lacks gluten but gives an interesting texture to white flour doughs when mixed with them. Buckwheat flour is also used to make *blinis*, traditional Russian pancakes (*see* BLINI).

BULGAR (Bulghur, Bulgur, Burghul, Burgul) Bulgar is produced from whole wheat grains which are steamed, then spread out to dry. Finally, they are broken into pieces. Bulgar wheat can be used in salads or it can be used as a stuffing mixture. It is the main ingredient of the traditional Lebanese salad, *tabbouleh*. It can also be served as an accompaniment to roast or grilled meats, especially kebabs. (*see also* CRACKED WHEAT, TABBOULEH)

BULLACE (*see* PLUM)

BULLOCK'S HEART (*see* CUSTARD APPLE)

BULLY BEEF (*see* BEEF, CORNED)

BUMMALOE (*see* BOMBAY DUCK)

BUN Strictly speaking, buns are small, sweet cakes made from a mixture containing yeast. They are similar in texture to bread, but containing sweetening and some kind of fat, currants and spice. Typical examples are currant buns, Chelsea buns, Bath buns and hot cross buns. However, the term is also very often applied to small cakes made of a sponge mixture, such as rock buns. (*see also* BATH BUN, CHELSEA BUN, HOT CROSS BUN)

BUNDERFLEISCH (Bundenfleisch, Bundnerfleisch) A Swiss variety of cured and dried beef. Similar to *bresaola*, the beef is cut in thin slices and is considered a great delicacy. It is often served as an hors d'oeuvre (*see also* BRESAOLA, DRIED MEAT)

BURGER (*see* BEEFBURGER)

BURGHUL (*see* BULGAR)

BURGUL (*see* BULGAR)

BURGUNDY A French province famous for the fine wines produced by its vineyards. The most important area in Burgundy, for red and white wines, is the Côte d'Or, which includes the Côte de Nuits and the Côte de Beaune. Other areas are Chablis, Beaujolais and Mâconnais.

The greatest reds come from Côte de Nuits. *Grands crus* need 10 years' maturity; *premiers crus* up to 12; village wines (such as Gevrey-Chambertin or Vosne-Romanée) about six. The big wines from the Côte de Beaune are the *premiers crus* prefixed Corton, and the reds of Pommard, slightly weightier than Volnay. Great whites are the *premiers crus* of the Montrachet family and of Meursault.

In cooking, red burgundy is most famous as an important ingredient of *boeuf bourguignon* (*see* BOURGUIGNONNE).

BURNET (Salad Burnet) A herb that has a slightly nutty flavour with a hint of cucumber. It is good in salads, especially in winter when it continues to flourish, though it is becoming increasingly rare in Britain. It can also be used in sauces, soups and stews.

Previous Pages: Left, Aubergines; **Right**, Braised beef
Opposite: Blueberries

BURRIDA An Italian fish soup or stew made from local seafood. It is a classic Sardinian dish, made from tuna, dogfish (huss) or skate, often served cold in summer. (*see also* BOURRIDE)

BUTTER A solid fat substance made by churning cream in special conditions of temperature. The cream must first be separated from the milk, then it is pasteurized, that is heated to a high enough temperature to destroy enzymes and bacteria, then rapidly cooled before churning begins. 'Churning' involves rapidly agitating the cream until the fat it contains forms a solid mass that can be gathered, washed and shaped to make butter. The remaining liquid (buttermilk) can be drained off and used separately.

The composition of butter must be at least 78 per cent milk fat, 20 per cent other milk solids (whey) and not more than 16 per cent water. Countries that produce butter have national schemes of quality control. Butter may also contain salt and lactic acid cultures. If kept cold, butter remains a solid fat, but softens when warmed and melts when heated. Although most butter is made from cows' milk, it can also be made from the milk of goats, sheep, yak and water buffalo.

There are two main types of butter: sweet cream butter and lactic butter. Sweet cream butter is left to age for 12 hours after the initial heating and before churning. To make lactic butter, the cream is heated again after the initial heating, to allow lactic bacteria to develop; this produces diactyl, a flavouring substance. After ripening, the cream is then churned. Most continental butters are lactic butters, traditionally made in Denmark and Holland.

Butter is available salted, slightly salted or unsalted. Salt was originally added to butter as a preservative, especially if it had to travel long distances, such as the butter from New Zealand, but salt is now also used as a flavouring. Butter is labelled as salted when it contains 1½-2 per cent salt. Most butter-producing countries produce both salted and unsalted butters. Unsalted butter is a paler yellow than salted butter, almost cream-coloured.

Butter is perishable and therefore needs to be stored in the refrigerator, where it will keep for two to three weeks. It can also be frozen. Being an animal fat, a high consumption of butter is not nowadays recommended as part of a healthy diet as it is a saturated fat which is thought to contribute to cholesterol levels and therefore to heart disease. It is also very high in calories, but does contain vitamins A and D and calcium. There are many supposedly healthier butter substitutes on the market these days. Some of these are made by mixing animal fat with vegetable fat, while others have quantities of water whipped into them. Some are designed to look and taste like butter, others are nothing like it.

Butter in Cooking
Despite its unhealthy reputation, butter is used for countless tasks in the kitchen. Nothing can replace it for flavour and richness in cakes, pastry, biscuits and sauces. Butter is also used for frying, especially to achieve a browned effect, and is used to enrich casseroles, stews and soups. It is also used, in the form of *beurre manié*, to thicken and enrich stews towards the end of cooking (*see* BEURRE MANIÉ).

A knob of butter makes all the difference to a dish of hot vegetables, and some vegetables, such as asparagus and corn on the cob, are served with melted butter. Butter is also added to creamed potatoes, and baked jacket potatoes are served split and topped with a knob of butter. Flavoured butters are also popular and can easily be made by mixing the chosen herb, garlic or other flavouring into softened butter. After chilling, herb butters can be sliced and used to top hot steaks, fish or vegetables. Other flavourings to mix with butter include ground nuts, anchovies, mustard, chives and watercress.

Apart from its many uses in cooking, butter is popular for spreading on bread, scones, hot toast, toasted teacakes and crumpets. (*see also* BEURRE NOIR, BEURRE NOISETTE, GARLIC BUTTER)

Clarified Butter

The purpose of clarifying butter is to separate the pure butter from the water, salt and other milk solids (whey) contained in the butter. Pure butter can be heated to a much higher temperature without burning, so is more suitable for frying. Clarified butter is also used in Genoese sponge and other cake mixtures. To clarify butter, simply heat it to boiling, then leave it to stand until the sediment has settled to the bottom of the pan. The pure butter can then be strained off. (*see also* CLARIFYING, GHEE)

Concentrated Butter

This is rather like commercially-made clarified butter, with a high percentage of butterfat (about 96 per cent). Like clarified butter, it can be heated to a higher temperature without burning so is very useful for shallow-frying. It is also very economical used in baking as less concentrated butter is needed in a recipe than ordinary butter. However, it may be necessary to adapt baking recipes by adding more liquid when using concentrated butter which contains less liquid than ordinary butter.

BUTTER BEAN (Lima Bean, Madagascar Bean) This dried bean is large, oval, flat and white and, when cooked, has a rather floury texture and a buttery flavour. Butter beans need gentle cooking so they do not break up and are excellent added to stews or casseroles. (*see also* PULSES)

BUTTER CREAM ICING A soft, creamy cake icing, made with softened butter and icing sugar, mixed with a little warm water or milk. The basic icing is usually flavoured with vanilla, but it can also be coloured and flavoured with chocolate, coffee, orange, lemon or almond. Butter cream icing can be used as a filling or a covering for sponge cakes. (*see also* CRÈME AU BEURRE)

Butter Cream Icing
75 g (3 oz) butter, softened
175 g (6 oz) icing sugar
few drops vanilla flavouring
15-30 ml (1-2 tbsp) milk or warm water

Put the butter in a bowl and cream until soft. Gradually sift and beat in the icing sugar, then add the vanilla flavouring and milk or water.
Makes about 250 g (9 oz)

Variations

Orange or lemon Replace the vanilla flavouring with a little finely grated orange or lemon rind. Add a little juice from the fruit instead of the milk, beating well to avoid curdling the mixture.

Chocolate Dissolve 15 ml (1 level tbsp) cocoa powder in a little hot water and cool before adding to the mixture.

Coffee Replace the vanilla flavouring with 10 ml (2 tsp) instant coffee blended with some of the liquid, or replace 15 ml (1 tbsp) of the liquid with the same amount of coffee essence.

Mocha Dissolve 5 ml (1 level tsp) cocoa powder and 10 ml (2 level tsp) instant coffee in a little warm water taken from the measured amount. Cool before adding to the mixture.

Almond Add 30 ml (2 level tbsp) finely chopped toasted almonds and mix.

To use Butter Cream Icing

Spread butter cream over the top only, or over the top and sides of a cake. Decorate by making swirl marks or mark with the prongs of a fork. For more elaborate decoration, butter cream pipes well.

BUTTER, FRUIT Similar to a fruit cheese, this is a soft, butter-like preserve which can be used like jam. A fruit butter does not keep very well so should only be made in small quantities and used up fairly quickly. Common fruits used to make butters include apricots, oranges, plums and apples. Black butter (*nier beurre*) is a thick, dark, spicy butter traditionally made in the Channel Islands from apples, cider, lemons, cinnamon and nutmeg. (*see also* CHEESE, FRUIT)

BUTTERMILK The liquid left over after cream has been turned into butter by churning. It is composed of water, mineral salts, protein and milk sugar, and has a sour flavour. Since it does not contain the fat of the cream, it is currently considered a healthy sour milk substitute. Buttermilk can also be made artificially by adding a culture to skimmed milk, and it is this 'cultured buttermilk' that is usually to be found in the supermarket.

Buttermilk is often used to make scones. It contains lactic acid and, combined with bicarbonate of soda, acts as a raising agent as well as adding flavour. It can also be made into refreshing drinks, popular in Scandinavia.

BUTTERNUT A type of nut very similar to the walnut. It is a mild flavoured nut, rich in oil, and can be used like the common walnut. (*see also* WALNUT)

BUTTERNUT SQUASH A North American winter squash, one of a number of new vegetables now occasionally available in Britain. It is a large, club-shaped vegetable with a smooth, pale yellow skin and deep yellow flesh. It should be peeled and the seeds removed before or after cooking. It can be cut in half lengthways, stuffed and baked, or sliced or diced and braised, boiled or fried. (*see also* NARA NUT, SQUASH)

BUTTERSCOTCH A variety of hard toffee, made from butter, sugar and water. Butterscotch can be bought or made at home. (*see also* SWEETS)

C

CABBAGE The cabbage is one of the oldest vegetables, introduced into Britain by the Romans. All cabbages are members of the brassica family, along with cauliflower, broccoli, kohlrabi, kale, Brussels sprouts and many Oriental green leafy vegetables. Cabbage is a good source of vitamins, especially if eaten raw but, unfortunately, it loses its goodness quickly during preparation and cooking. Gentle cooking methods, such as steaming, are therefore recommended.

Cabbage is also available pickled. Pickled red cabbage is particularly delicious served with cold meats and baked jacket potatoes. Pickled white cabbage forms the basis of German or Austrian *sauerkraut* (see SAUERKRAUT).

CABBAGE, CHINESE (*see* CHINESE CABBAGE)

CABBAGE, DUTCH (*see* CABBAGE, SAVOY)

CABBAGE, RED AND WHITE Apart from their colour, red and white cabbages are very similar. They are both round and firm, with shiny leaves.

Red cabbages are in season from November to March. They can be cooked like other cabbage varieties, but are often casseroled, pickled or served raw in salads.

White cabbages are usually available all the year round, although their main season is from October to February. White cabbage is usually finely shredded and used in coleslaw-type salads (*see* COLESLAW), but it can also be cooked and served tossed in butter or a little single cream and sprinkled with nutmeg.

To select: Choose those with either a deep, bright red or pale yellowish white colour, that are round, heavy for their size and firmly packed. Allow 175–225 g (6–8 oz) per person.

To prepare: Cabbage can be shredded for using raw in salads or, for cooking briefly, cut into thick wedges, or the centre can be removed and the cabbage stuffed.

To cook: Cook white cabbage in boiling salted water for 2–3 minutes (shredded), 10 minutes (wedges), or steam for the same length of time. Shredded red cabbage is best braised.

To serve: Cooked cabbage should be drained and served immediately after cooking. Braised red cabbage is traditionally served with game dishes and roast pork.

CABBAGE, SAVOY (Dutch Cabbage) These firm, dark green cabbages are easily recognized by their very crinkly leaves. They are available in Britain from November to spring and are the hardiest of all the cabbage varieties, withstanding harsh winter frosts. They are best served as a vegetable accompaniment, stuffed or braised. A dwarf variety of Savoy cabbage is also sometimes available.

To select: Look for a cabbage that is a good fresh green colour and heavy for its size, with few wilted outer leaves. Allow 175–225 g (6–8 oz) per person.

To prepare: Remove the coarse outer leaves and cut the cabbage in half. Cut out the centre stalk, wash and cut the remaining cabbage into fine shreds or wedges.

To cook: Cook in boiling salted water for 2–3 minutes (shredded), 10 minutes (wedges), or steam for the same length of time. To braise, pour boiling water over shredded cabbage to wilt it. Drain and cook in a covered pan with about 25 g (1 oz) butter for 15–20 minutes.

To serve: Boiled or steamed cabbage should be drained well, then served hot, tossed in melted butter, if liked, and sprinkled with freshly grated nutmeg and ground black pepper.

CABBAGE, SEASONAL There are many different varieties of green cabbage, available at different times of year.

Spring cabbages are available from March to May. They tend to be pointed in shape, bright green in colour and much more tender than the winter varieties. The full flavour of this cabbage is fully appreciated if cooked lightly and served in wedges rather than shredded.

Spring greens are early spring cabbages that have not yet formed a heart. They should be shredded before quickly cooking to retain their flavour.

Summer cabbages are in season from June onwards. This sweet cabbage should be cut into wedges or coarsely shredded and used in salads or gently steamed.

Winter cabbages are in season from September to December. They are coarser in texture and stronger in flavour, making them suitable for braising, stuffing whole or as separate leaves, as well as using in salads or cooking as an accompanying vegetable. Varieties of winter cabbage include the January King, which can be recognized by its purple-ribbed bluish-green leaves. *To select:* Choose fresh looking cabbage with no wilted leaves. Allow 175–225 g (6–8 oz) per person.

To prepare, cook and serve: Follow the directions for Savoy cabbage (*see* CABBAGE, SAVOY).

CABINET PUDDING A simple moulded pudding made from bread and butter. A richer version is made with sponge cake and glacé cherries, with an extra egg added.

CABOC A very rich, soft, double cream cheese that originated in the Western Highlands of Scotland in the fifteenth century. The recipe is believed to have been handed down from mother to daughter through the centuries. It can easily be recognized by its coating of fine oatmeal.

CABRALES A semi-hard cheese from northern Spain, with a strong flavour. It is traditionally made from goats' milk but may also be made from cows' or ewes' milk. Some varieties of Cabrales have a blue veining similar to Roquefort; others are a deep yellow colour with a mottled black coating.

CACAO (*see* COCOA)

CACCIO-CAVALLO (Caciocavallo) An Italian semi-hard cheese made from skimmed cows' milk. It is pale yellow in colour, with a shiny yellow rind, and is usually moulded into large pear shapes. It has a mild flavour, and is similar to another, smaller Italian cheese called Cacietto.

CACIETTO (*see* CACCIO-CAVALLO)

CACTUS PEAR (*see* PRICKLY PEAR)

CAERPHILLY Originally a Welsh cheese, this is now made also in Somerset, Wiltshire, Devon and Dorset. It is made from whole cows' milk, pressed only lightly and eaten in its 'green' state, when only about ten days old. Caerphilly is soft and white, with a creamy mild flavour, and is best served uncooked.

CAFETIÈRE (*see* COFFEE)

CAFFEINE An alkaline substance present in varying amounts in coffee, tea and cola nuts (used to make cola drinks). Caffeine has stimulating and diuretic properties and can be toxic if consumed in large quantities. Some types of coffee bean and tea leaf contain more caffeine than others. Nowadays, it is possible to buy decaffeinated coffees, teas and cola drinks.

CAJUN A style of cooking popular in the southern United States, especially Louisiana. It was brought to the area by the Cajuns – French Canadians who settled in the Louisiana tree swamps during the mid-eighteenth century. The area is famous for such dishes as gumbo (a soup-like stew containing okra), jambalaya (the Louisiana version of paella) and numerous other rice dishes. Crayfish features strongly in Cajun cooking as the small lobster-like shellfish is caught in abundance in Louisiana waters. (*see also* CRAYFISH, CREOLE, JAMBALAYA, OKRA)

CAKE This name is given to a variety of baked sweet items, often served as a dessert or at tea or coffee time, usually made from a mixture of flour, sugar, fat and eggs. Cakes are most often round or square but can also be made in all sorts of other shapes and sizes, for example for a children's birthday tea. They are frequently used to celebrate a family occasion or religious festival, for example Christmas cake, Wedding cake, Christening cakes, etc. Most cakes are decorated to some extent, varying from a simple dusting of icing sugar to elaborate designs piped in royal icing or moulded in fondant sugarpaste. Some cakes, such as Dundee and Simnel cakes, are associated with traditional kinds of decoration. (*see* DUNDEE CAKE, SIMNEL CAKE)

There are three main types of cake, classified according to the proportion of ingredients they contain, and the method by which they are made. The three main types are plain, rich and sponge. Other smaller categories include 'quick-mix' (one-stage) cakes and those made by a method which involves warming the sugar, fat and a liquid sweetener (syrup or treacle) together before they are added to the dry ingredients.

(*see also* BUN, GÂTEAU, SCONE, TEABREAD)

Ingredients for Cake Making

Flour
A wide range of different types of flour is available and the difference between them is largely due to the varying gluten content. Gluten is an elastic, sticky substance formed when the flour is moistened. It sets when heated, trapping air in the mixture and giving it a light texture. (*see also* GLUTEN)

For cake making, soft flour with a low gluten content is best. It is starchy and absorbs fat well to give a light, soft texture. Self raising flour may be used for cakes made by the rubbing-in method, but for richer cakes and sponges, which need varying quantities of raising agent, or none, it is better to use plain flour. Flour should always be sifted before use. Wholemeal flour can be used in some recipes but it gives a denser texture. Alternatively, use a mixture of plain white and wholemeal flour.

Sugar and other Sweeteners
Sugar is an important ingredient in all cakes and is essential in sponges. Granulated sugar is suitable for plain cakes, but it is better to use fine caster sugar for creamed and sponge mixtures to give a better texture. Brown sugars and other kinds of sweeteners, such as golden syrup, treacle or honey, can be used to add variety and extra flavour. Dark sugars are particularly good in gingerbreads as they give a rich, treacly flavour. (*see also* SUGAR)

Fat
Butter and margarine are the commonest fats used, but lard, blended white vegetable fat, dripping and oil may be used. Butter and block margarine are usually interchangeable, though butter gives a special flavour. Soft tub margarines are best suited to 'quick-mix' recipes but it is possible to experiment with using them in other recipes, though the texture will be different. Oil is being used more often these days, but specially proportioned recipes are needed.

Eggs
These may be used as a raising agent or to bind the mixture. Size three or four eggs should be used unless otherwise stated in a recipe.

Liquid
Moisture is required for the raising agents to work. Milk or water are the most usual liquids used but brewed tea, cider, fruit juice and beer are included in certain specific recipes. Buttermilk is used in certain kinds of bread and scones.

Raising Agents
Baking powder is the most commonly used. It usually consists of bicarbonate of soda and an acid-reacting chemical such as cream of tartar, and, when moistened, these react together to give off carbon dioxide. Flour contains gluten (see left) which holds this gas in the form of tiny bubbles when it is wet.

Since all gases expand when heated, these tiny bubbles formed throughout the mixture become larger during baking, and thus the cake rises. The heat dries and sets the gluten and so the bubbles are held, giving the cake its characteristic light texture.

However, cake mixtures are capable of holding only a certain amount of gas, and if too much raising agent is used the cake rises very well at first, but then collapses, and a heavy, close texture is the final result. It is therefore important to measure baking powder carefully and to use only the amount specified in a recipe.

Bicarbonate of soda and cream of tartar combined may be used in some recipes to replace baking powder. It is usually in the proportion of one part bicarbonate of soda to two parts cream of tartar.

Eggs By including whisked egg in a cake mixture, air is used as a raising agent, instead of carbon dioxide. When a high proportion of egg is used and the mixture is whisked, as in sponge cakes, very little, if any, other raising agent is needed to obtain the desired result.

In creamed mixtures also, the eggs are beaten in and, as long as the correct proportion of egg is used and the mixture is well beaten, little additional raising agent is needed. In plain cakes, where beaten egg is added together with the liquid, the egg helps to bind the mixture, but it does not act as the main raising agent.

Spices and Flavourings

Ready-mixed spices are useful for general flavouring, since they are carefully blended, but for some recipes it is better to have individual spices, such as cinnamon, mace and nutmeg.

Cake flavourings are available in a variety of flavours, such as coffee, rum, almond and vanilla. They are usually concentrated and should be used sparingly.

Natural flavourings, like lemon or orange, are the most pleasant to use whenever practical. Remember, when using the rind of any citrus fruit, to grate only lightly, so as to remove just the zest – the white pith imparts a bitter flavour.

Fruit, Nuts and Peel

Fruit Use good quality dried fruits; if necessary, leave them to plump up in hot water, drain and dry off. They can be bought ready-washed, but it is wise to give them a good looking over. Any excess syrup should be rinsed off glacé cherries before use and the cherries thoroughly dried.

Peel Buy 'caps' of candied orange and lemon peel and cut to the required size or use ready-mixed chopped peel. Ready-cut peel may need chopping into smaller pieces.

Nuts All types of nuts are used in cake making and can usually be bought in the state they are required, that is whole, blanched, flaked, chopped, ground, etc.

Cake Making Methods

Rubbing-in Method

Plain cakes are made by the 'rubbing-in' method – the fat is 'rubbed' or 'worked' into the flour with the fingers until the mixture resembles fine breadcrumbs. Some air is incorporated during this process, but the main raising agents in plain cakes are chemical. The proportion of fat to flour is half or less. Examples of plain cakes are rock cakes, scones and raspberry buns.

Creaming Method

Rich cakes are made by the creaming method. The fat and sugar are beaten together until as pale and fluffy as whipped cream, the eggs are beaten in and the flour is then folded in. In some recipes, the egg whites are whisked separately and folded in with the flour. The best known cake made by this method is the Victoria sandwich.

Whisking Method

Sponge cakes are made by the whisking method which produces the lightest of all cakes. The classic sponge is light and feathery and is made by whisking together eggs and caster sugar, then folding in the flour. There is no fat in the mixture, and the cake rises simply because of the air incorporated during whisking. For an even lighter cake, the egg yolks and sugar can be whisked together, with the whites whisked separately and folded in afterwards. As sponge cakes are made without fat they always need a filling, and do not keep well.

A moister version of the whisked sponge is a Genoese sponge. This is also made by the whisking method, but melted butter is added with the flour. This gives a delicate sponge, lighter than a Victoria sandwich, but with a moister texture than the plain whisked sponge, and a more delicious rich and buttery taste. A Genoese sponge keeps better than a plain whisked sponge.

To make a really good sponge, the eggs and sugar must be whisked until thick enough to leave a trail when the whisk is lifted from the surface. This thickening process is speeded up if the bowl is placed over a saucepan of hot water while whisking with a rotary whisk or hand-held electric mixer.

One-stage Method

'Quick-mix' cakes are made by the one-stage method which is based on soft tub margarine. This type of cake is wonderfully quick and easy to prepare. There is no need for any creaming or rubbing in: all the ingredients are simply beaten together with a wooden spoon for 2–3 minutes, until well blended and slightly glossy. This method is also ideal for making cakes in an electric mixer, though care should be taken not to over-beat the mixture.

Self raising flour is invariably used in one-stage mixtures, often with the addition of a little extra baking powder to boost the rise. Either caster or soft brown sugar can be used because their fine crystals dissolve easily.

These cakes are similar to those made by the creaming method, but their texture is more open and they do not keep so well.

Melting Method

Gingerbreads and other cakes made by the melting method have a deliciously moist and sticky texture and a rich dark colour. This is due to the high proportion of sugary ingredients, including liquid sweeteners, such as syrup or black treacle, used. To ensure the liquid sweetener is easily incorporated, it is warmed with the fat and sugar until blended and then added to the dry ingredients together with any eggs and the liquid.

Bicarbonate of soda is often used to raise these cakes – it reacts with natural acids present in liquid sweeteners. Spices are frequently added to enhance the flavour and also to counteract the faintly bitter taste of bicarbonate of soda.

Most cakes made by the melting method should be stored for a day or so before cutting, to allow the crust to soften and give the flavour time to mellow.

Cakes Made Using Oil

Cakes made using oil (corn oil, for example) are very easy to mix and very successful. When using oil for making sandwich cakes, it is essential to add an extra raising agent or to whisk the egg whites until stiff and fold them into the mixture just before baking. This counteracts the heaviness of the cake that sometimes occurs when oil is used.

Cake Tins

Choose good-quality, strong cake tins in a variety of shapes and sizes. Non-stick surfaces clean most easily and are particularly useful in small awkwardly-shaped tins. Some cake tins have a loose bottom or a loosening device to make it easier to remove the cake.

Always use the size of tin specified in a recipe. Using too large a tin will tend to give a pale, flat and shrunken-looking cake; cakes baked in too small a tin will bulge over and lose their contours. If you do not have the tin specified, choose a slightly larger one. The mixture will be shallower and will take less time to cook, so test for doneness 5–10 minutes early.

Flan rings and tins come in many forms. Round tins with plain or fluted sides and removable bases are primarily for pastry flan cases. For sponge flans, use a special flan tin with a raised base.

Loaf tins are used for cakes as well as bread. The most useful sizes are 900 ml (1½ pint)/450 g (1 lb) and 1.7 litre (3 pint)/900 g (2 lb).

Sandwich tins are shallower round tins with straight sides for making sandwich and layer cakes, in sizes 18–25 cm (7–10 inches).

A *moule à manqué* tin is a deep sandwich tin with sloping sides.

Small cake tins and moulds come in sheets of six, nine or 12 or individually. There are shapes for buns, sponge fingers, madeleines, etc.

Spring-release or springform tins come complete with separate loose bottoms.

Standard cake tins For everyday use, 15 cm (6 inch), 18 cm (7 inch) and 20.5 cm (8 inch) square or round tins are adequate; for celebration cakes you may need larger sizes that are available in a variety of shapes and sizes.

Preparing Cake Tins

Follow the manufacturer's special directions regarding non-stick (silicone-finished) tins, which do not usually require greasing or lining.

Greasing

When greasing cake tins, brush lightly with melted margarine or butter (preferably unsalted). They may also be dredged with flour as an additional safeguard against sticking; sprinkle a little flour in the tin and shake until coated, then shake out any surplus.

For fatless sponges, use a half-and-half mixture of flour and caster sugar. You can do the same to a sponge flan tin to produce a crisper crust.

Lining

For most cakes it is necessary to line the tins with greaseproof paper, which is usually greased before the mixture is put in, or with non-stick paper, which does not require greasing, and can be used several times.

For a Victoria sandwich cake mixture, it is sufficient to line just the base of the tin. For rich mixtures and fruit cakes, line the whole tin. The paper is usually doubled to prevent the outside of the cake from over-browning and drying out. With the extra rich fruit mixtures used for wedding and other formal cakes, which require a long cooking time, it is also advisable to pin a double strip of thick brown paper or newspaper around the outside of the tin, to help prevent the outside of the cake overcooking.

To line a deep tin Cut a piece (or two pieces, if necessary) of greaseproof paper long enough to reach around the tin and overlap slightly, and high enough to extend about 2.5 cm (1 inch) above the top edge. Fold up the bottom edge of the strip about 2.5 cm (1 inch), creasing it firmly, then open out and snip into this folded portion with scissors; this snipped edge enables the paper band to fit a square, oblong, round or oval tin neatly.

Grease the inside of the paper. Place the strip in position in the greased tin, with the cut edge flat against the base. In a rectangular or square tin, make sure the paper fits snugly into the corners.

Cut a double round of paper to fit inside the base of the tin. (Stand the tin on the paper, draw round it and then cut out.) Put the rounds in place – they will keep the snipped edge of the band in position and make a neat lining. Brush the base of the lining with melted butter or margarine.

To line a sandwich tin Cut a round of greaseproof paper to fit the bottom of the tin exactly. If the tin's sides are shallow and you want to raise them, fit a band of paper inside the tin, coming about 2.5 cm (1 inch) above the rim.

To line a Swiss roll tin Cut a piece of paper about 5 cm (2 inches) larger all round than the tin. Place the tin on it and in each corner make a cut from the corner of the paper as far as the corner of the tin. Grease the tin and put in the paper so that it fits closely, overlapping at the corners. Grease the paper and dust with a half-and-half mixture of flour and sugar sifted together. Non-stick paper is very satisfactory for lining this type of tin, but greaseproof paper can also be used.

To line a loaf tin It is not usually necessary to line a loaf tin fully. Grease the inside, line the base only with an oblong of greaseproof paper and grease the paper.

To line a sponge flan tin Grease the inside well, and place a round of greased greaseproof paper over the raised part only of the tin.

Baking Cakes

Preparing the Oven

Preheat the oven before starting to make cakes so that it will be at the correct temperature by the time the cake is ready to go in. Check that the shelves are in the correct position – cakes should be baked in the centre of the oven whenever possible.

To maintain a correct temperature, avoid opening the oven door too often or too suddenly while the cake is cooking.

To Test Whether a Cake is Cooked

Small cakes should be well risen, golden brown in colour and firm to the touch – both on top and underneath – and they should begin to shrink from the sides of the tin on being taken out of the oven.

Larger cakes present more difficulty, especially for beginners. The oven heat and time of cooking give a reasonable indication, but the following tests are a guide:

* Press the centre top of the cake very lightly with a fingertip. The cake should be spongy and should give only very slightly to the pressure, then rise again immediately, retaining no impression.

* In the case of a fruit cake, lift it gently from the oven and listen to it, putting it close to your ear. A continued sizzling sound indicates that the cake is not cooked through.

* Insert a warmed long fine skewer (never use a cold knife) into the centre of the cake. If any mixture is sticking to it when you pull the skewer out, the cake requires longer cooking.

Cooling

Allow a cake a few minutes to cool before turning it out of the tin; it will shrink away from the sides and is more easily removed. Turn out on to a wire rack and leave to cool. Allow fruit cakes to cool completely in the tin.

Filling and Decorating Cakes

Plain sponge cakes may be made in layers, or deep cakes may be split horizontally to create two or more layers. The layers can then be sandwiched together with a variety of fillings, such as butter cream icing, jam, lemon curd or whipped cream.

Decorations for informal cakes may be anything from a light dusting of caster sugar or a smooth coating of glacé icing, to whirls of butter cream interspersed with nuts or coloured sweets. Popular decorations include crystallized flowers, angelica, chocolate vermicelli, silver dragees (balls), hundreds and thousands, chocolate scrolls and curls, chocolate caraque, and shapes made from melted chocolate.

For formal cakes, you need to master piping techniques and the method of flat icing with royal icing. (*see also* ALMOND PASTE, BUTTER CREAM ICING, CRÈME AU BEURRE, FROSTING, GLACÉ ICING, ICING, PIPING, ROYAL ICING)

To Store Cakes

Store cakes in a tin with a tightly fitting lid. Most cakes are most delicious when eaten quite fresh, but gingerbread and some rich fruit cakes are improved by keeping. Rich fruit cakes which are to be kept for any length of time should be wrapped in double greaseproof paper before being put in the tin and left to mature.

Most types of cake can be frozen successfully, including sponge flans, Swiss rolls, layer cakes, large gâteaux and fruit cakes. Plain cakes should be wrapped separately, or together with cling film or waxed paper between the layers. Decorated cream cakes should be open frozen, then packed in rigid boxes to protect them. All cakes should be thoroughly thawed at room temperature before serving.

CALABASH (*see* DUDI)

CALABRESE (*see* BROCCOLI)

CALAMARE (*see* SQUID)

CALCIUM One of a number of naturally-occurring minerals that are essential to the healthy development and functioning of the human body, and particularly important for growing and maintaining strong teeth and bones. Calcium cannot be produced by the body so it must be supplied in the diet. The current daily calcium requirement for adults is at least 0.5 g. For women, this requirement increases during pregnancy to 1 g, and to 2 g when breast-feeding.

The prime sources of calcium are milk and dairy products, such as cheese and yogurt, but it is also present in eggs and some vegetables (particularly pulses) and cereals. It is essential to have sufficient vitamin D to permit both the absorption and use of the calcium in the body. Without it, little is absorbed, whereas 20–30 per cent can be absorbed with adequate vitamin D. (*see also* DIET, MINERALS, NUTRITION, VITAMINS)

CALDO VERDE A Portuguese vegetable soup made of olive oil, potatoes and finely shredded dark green cabbage.

CALF'S FOOT JELLY A jelly that was at one time often served to invalids. It has little food value but is easily digested. It takes two days to make, as the stock must be made the first day and the jelly finished the second. The stock is made by boiling pieces of calf's foot for several hours in water, until the liquid is very reduced and will set when left to cool.

To clarify the jelly, it is boiled up with flavourings, such as sugar, sherry, cinnamon, cloves and lemon, and with egg shells. It is whisked while heating, then, when it comes to the boil, the mixture is strained through a jelly bag or muslin until it is clear. A ready-made preparation can now be bought. (*see also* CLARIFYING)

CALLALOO (Calaloo, Calalou, Callalo, Callilu, Chinese Spinach) The West Indian and Creole name given to the leafy green tops of a number of varieties of yam, including the dasheen and eddoe. The leaves can be cooked like spinach, but in the Caribbean they are used to make a soup, also called callaloo. (*see also* DASHEEN, EDDOE, YAM)

CALORIE Although this word has now come into common use, it is in fact a scientific term used in dietetics to measure the heat- and energy-producing quality of foods. One Calorie (with a capital 'C') is defined as the amount of heat needed to raise the temperature of 1,000 grams of water by 1 degree Celsius. Heat and energy are produced when food is 'burned up' by the body, and the amount produced can be measured in Calories; thus a food can be said to 'contain' a certain number of Calories, that is it has the power to produce that many when it is digested by the body.

Spelt with a small 'c', a calorie is a term used in physics to denote the amount of heat needed to raise the temperature of 1 gram of water by 1 degree Celsius. This sort of calorie is in fact 1,000 times smaller than a Calorie, and much too small to be used as a measurement of energy. What is commonly known as a Calorie, is in fact a kilocalorie, made up of 1,000 calories.

The term 'Calorie' has become all too familiar to anyone who has ever tried to lose weight. Many slimming diets are based on 'counting Calories', that is being aware of the number of Calories contained in foods and limiting the number consumed. Since excess energy leads to weight gain, it is logical to eat less of the foods that provide most energy in order to lose weight. It sounds simple but, in fact, the success of such a regime is based on many other factors, including how active a person is and on normal metabolic rate. This is the rate at which energy is used by the body simply in order to exist – in keeping warm, breathing, walking, etc. This rate varies from person to person. Large, active men or breast-feeding women have much higher metabolic rates than a small sedentary person, and therefore have a higher daily requirement of Calories. Dietitians are able to calculate roughly the amount of Calories a person might need daily and many slimmers base their diets on such average figures, aiming to consume less Calories than their average daily requirement.

Foods vary very much in their calorific value; fats yield about 250 Calories per 25 g (1 oz), but vegetables and fresh fruit yield only about 5–10 Calories. In general, fats, proteins and carbohydrates (sugars and starches) provide the most Calories, but these are all nutrients needed by the body in some quantity. It is very important, therefore, that a slimming diet based on counting Calories be properly balanced.

Although the term Calorie will continue to be used for some time, it is in fact being replaced by the standard international unit of measuring energy production, the joule, or kilojoule. One kilojoule is equal to 1.24 Calories. (*see also* DIET, JOULE, METABOLISM, NUTRITION)

CALVADOS (Applejack) An apple brandy that takes its name from Calvados, the centre of the Normandy apple orchards. Applejack is its American equivalent, though it is not, strictly speaking, Calvados. Calvados may be served as an apéritif or as a liqueur, but it is a harsh brandy and is most often used in cooking, imparting a distinctive apple flavour.

CALZONE A type of filled and folded over pizza which is very popular in southern Italy. Fillings vary enormously but, unlike pizzas, they never contain tomatoes. They are baked in the oven and served hot, sometimes with a sauce. *Calzoncelli*

are miniature versions, made from pizzas only about 7.5 cm (3 inches) in diameter. They are stuffed and fried and may be served hot or cold as savoury snacks or canapés. (*see also* PIZZA)

CAMBAZOLA A full-fat soft German cheese with a white Camembert-like mould on the rind and a blue Gorgonzola-like mould internally. It is very creamy in texture, with a light bite coming from the blue.

CAMBRIDGE SAUSAGE A very lean English pork sausage, flavoured with herbs and spices. It may be grilled or fried.

CAMEMBERT A French soft cheese, made of cows' milk, the curd being inoculated with a white mould. The cheese was made originally in Normandy, but is now also made in other parts of France. Camembert is at its best when it begins to get soft; if allowed to become over-ripe, it develops a smell which many people find unpleasant.

CAMOMILE (Chamomile) There are many varieties of this daisy-like plant which grows wild over much of Europe and in America. It has an aromatic scent and bitter flavour. The dried flower heads of some varieties are used to make camomile tea by infusing them in boiling water. The tea is said to have a calming effect. Dried camomile is also used in some hair shampoos and rinses which claim to enhance blondness.

CAMPARI (*see* BITTERS)

CANAPÉ A small item of food served hot or cold as an appetizer, usually with drinks, and often consisting of a bread or pastry base with a savoury topping.

CANDLE NUT (Candlenut) These round cream-coloured nuts come from Indonesia and are often used in Malaysian and Indonesian cooking, usually roasted, ground and added to sauces, soups and stews. Like bitter almonds, candle nuts are mildly poisonous when raw, so should always be eaten cooked.

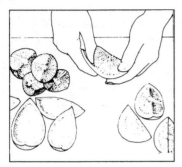  

Removing the fruit from segments of orange peel prior to candying in sugar syrup.

Straining off the liquid after cooking the peel segments for 1-2 hours in simmering water.

Placing the segments on a wire rack to dry after cooking and soaking in a heavy sugar syrup.

CANDY Strictly speaking, a candy is a sweet made from crystallized sugar, but in America the term is used with reference to all confectionery. (*see also* SWEETS)

CANDYING Candying is a method of impregnating pieces of fruit or peel with sugar to preserve them. Candied fruits may be served as a dessert or eaten as sweets. The peel of such citrus fruits as oranges, lemons and citrons can be candied and is widely used in making cakes, puddings and mincemeats.

Candying essentially consists of soaking the fruit or peel in a syrup, the sugar content of which is increased daily over a stated period of time, until the fruit or peel is completely impregnated with sugar. Candied fruits may be left plain, glazed with a final coating of caramel, or given a crystallized finish by dipping them first in boiling water, then in caster sugar. (*see also* GLACÉ FRUIT)

CANELLE KNIFE A kitchen tool used to crimp, that is cut V-shaped grooves into, the surface of fruit or vegetables, for decorative effect. The fruit or vegetable, such as lemon or cucumber, may be sliced after it has been canelled, producing slices with 'frilly' edges that can be used as a garnish or decoration.

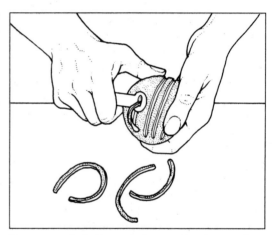

Using a canelle knife to cut thin matchstick strips from the rind of an orange.

CANNELLINO BEAN (Canellino Bean) This creamy-white dried kidney bean is very popular in Italian cooking. Cannellini beans belong to the same family as haricot beans, though they are much larger. Like haricot beans, they have a floury texture when cooked. (*see also* PULSES)

CANNELLONI (*see* PASTA)

CANNING The preservation of food by canning is now only carried out on a commercial scale. Home canning is not recommended because of the risk of inefficient sterilization, resulting in food poisoning.

Canning was first used as a form of preservation in the early nineteenth century. Canned foods did not reach the shops until 1830, but sales were slow, mainly because of the high prices. However, by the end of the century, certain canned foods were becoming an accepted part of the British national diet.

Traditionally, the canning process was carried out by placing the food in the can, sealing it and heating it to a high temperature to sterilize it. Nowadays, canning is done by what is known as the 'aseptic' method. The food is sterilized by heating it to a higher temperature for a few seconds before it is placed in a sterilized can and sealed with a sterilized lid. Food canned in this way has a better flavour and a higher nutritional value. The higher, shorter heat treatment also means that food is sterilized without being overcooked.

Preserving foods in cans serves the double purpose of making seasonal fruits and vegetables available all the year round, and allows food to be kept for long periods of time. To some extent, however, canning has been replaced in recent years by freezing. In America, 'canning' is the name given to what we in Britain call bottling.

CANTAL A hard, strong, French cheese, made in the Auvergne for more than 2,000 years. It is a yellow cheese with a grey rind and is available as a farmhouse cheese, made only in summer from unpasteurized milk, and as a dairy cheese, made all the year round from pasteurized milk. It is often served as a dessert cheese, with wine and fruit, but can also be used in cooking.

CANTALOUPE (*see* MELON)

CAPE GOOSEBERRY (Goldenberry, Physalis) This tropical fruit belongs to the same family as the tomato, as does the Chinese lantern which the cape gooseberry slightly resembles. It has recently become more readily available in Britain, imported from such countries as South Africa. The small golden berries are encased in a papery husk which is easily peeled away so that the fruit can be eaten. The flavour is similar to that of a gooseberry. Cape gooseberries may be eaten raw or made into a delicious jam They also make attractive cake decorations if the calyx is bent back to reveal the berry within.

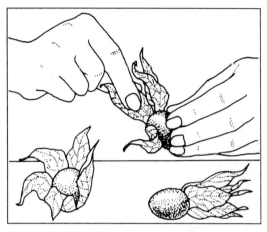

Bending back the calyx of a cape gooseberry to form a petal around the berry for use as a decoration.

CAPER The pickled flower buds of a low-growing deciduous shrub native to the south of Europe. The fresh buds are picked each day during the flowering season, left to dry for 24 hours, then put into a cask of pickling brine. Once their flavour has fully developed, the capers are bottled in brine, and they should be kept submerged in brine until they are used. Capers are used to flavour a sauce which is traditionally served with boiled mutton, and are also added to mayonnaise to make a variety of other sauces.

CAPERCAILZIE (Capercaillie, Cock o' the Wood, Wood Grouse) The largest member of the grouse family, this game bird has a distinctive flavour. Its habitat is the hilly coniferous woodlands of Scotland, where it feeds on the shoots of pine trees, which gives its flesh a somewhat resinous flavour. It can be cooked in the same way as grouse and is most often roasted. (*see also* GROUSE)

CAPILLAIRE An infusion of maidenhair fern syrup with orange-flower water, used as a flavouring for punches and cocktails. It can also be made from water, eggs and orange-flower water or lemon essence, though it is quite rare today. (*see also* MAIDENHAIR FERN)

CAPPELLETTI (*see* PASTA)

CAPPUCCINO (*see* COFFEE)

CAPSICUM The family name for a number of varieties of pepper. There are two main types: hot, such as the chilli, and sweet, such as those eaten as a vegetable. Capsicums can be green, black, purple, red, yellow (almost white) or orange, and vary considerably in shape – sometimes being rounded and plump, sometimes long and thin. All capsicums have a glossy skin with a bright colour. (*see also* CHILLI PEPPER, PEPPER)

CARAMBOLA (*see* STAR FRUIT)

CARAMEL (Burnt Sugar) A syrupy substance obtained by heating sugar very slowly until a rich brown colour. It quickly sets hard on cooling, unless water is added to produce a dark brown liquid which is used commercially as a colouring (E150), but has a rather bitter flavour. Sugar usually begins to caramelize at about 150°C (300°F).

If the syrup is heated for a shorter time, it will retain its sweet sugary flavour and can be used as a flavouring for cakes, puddings, custards and sauces. Light caramel is also used for making spun sugar, and for dipping in fruits, such as grapes, orange segments and strawberries. The caramel sets around the fruit into a brittle sugary coating.

Caramel is also used in sweet-making, not only to make caramels, but also to make nougat, praline, toffee and other sweets. (*see also* BRÛLÉE, SUGAR BOILING, SWEETS)

CARAMEL (Toffee) A type of sweet made in much the same way as toffee, but not boiled to such a high temperature. Caramels may be either soft or hard in texture, according to the temperature to which they have been boiled, and the mixture is usually enriched with butter, cream or condensed milk, which necessitates stirring during cooking. Caramels may be flavoured with nuts, honey, vanilla or dried fruits, and are usually shaped into small rounds, squares or rectangles. They may also be coated in chocolate.

CARAQUE (*see* CHOCOLATE)

CARAWAY A biennial, umbelliferous plant which grows in many parts of Europe and Asia, the seeds of which are used as a spice. The small, brown seeds, with tapering ends, have a pleasant, sharp, liquorice-like taste. They are widely used in central European and Jewish cookery, mainly for flavouring cakes, biscuits and bread, but also in soups, salads, *sauerkraut*, with vegetables, in cheese dishes, omelettes and pork dishes. Caraway is also an ingredient of the liqueur Kümmel. Like aniseed, caraway is thought to aid digestion.

CARBOHYDRATE Carbohydrates consist of carbon, hydrogen and oxygen and exist in food as sugars, starches and cellulose, providing most of the energy of the human diet.

Carbohydrate sugars include glucose, fructose, sucrose, lactose, maltose and others. These are not of any nutritional value, except as the best source of energy. They are very easily digested.

Starchy foods include cereals and their products (bread, pasta, semolina, etc.), and some vegetables, especially pulses, potatoes and other root vegetables. Most starch foods contain other important nutrients, such as protein and minerals, besides carbohydrates, and are therefore more valuable nutritionally than sugars.

Cellulose forms the cell structure of fruits, vegetables and grains. Unlike the sugars and starches, cellulose does not provide energy; it is most useful as a source of fibre.

Carbohydrates are converted by the body into glucose, which is absorbed by the blood stream and used as energy. Excess carbohydrate is stored by the body as fat. Some carbohydrate should be eaten at the same time as protein, or some of the valuable protein will be used to produce energy instead of body-building. The habit of eating such combinations as bread and cheese, and meat and potatoes, is therefore nutritionally sound. A certain amount of the vitamin, thiamin, is required to make use of carbohydrates. Thiamin is found in cereals.

(*see also* CALORIE, DIET, FIBRE, NUTRITION, PROTEIN, VITAMINS)

CARBONADE (Carbonnade) A rich stew or braise of meat which includes beer.

CARBONATED WATER (*see* SODA WATER)

CARDAMOM A member of the ginger family, cardamom is sold both whole, either green or black, or ground. Black cardamom pods are much larger than green, and are very whiskery. Faded green cardamom pods should not be mistaken for genuine white cardamoms, which can sometimes be found in Asian food stores, though they are increasingly rare. Cardamom consists of small husks containing tiny black seeds that are almost impossible to grind at home, so buy *freshly* ground cardamom whenever possible and use it immediately as it quickly loses its aromatic qualities. Alternatively, the whole husks can be roughly crushed, before use, then removed from the dish after cooking.

Cardamom has a strong, bitter-sweet, slightly lemony flavour and should be used sparingly. It is widely used in Indian, Eastern and continental European cooking. It is an expensive spice (only saffron is more expensive) as the seed pods have to be snipped individually from the plant by hand. It is an ingredient of most curry powders and can also be used in pickles, soups, beef and pork dishes, with sweet potato, pumpkin and apples and in bread, buns, biscuits and cakes, with iced melon and in custard and rice puddings. It is also added to Turkish coffee (*see* COFFEE).

CARDINAL A French name given to dishes with a scarlet effect, as when a fish dish is served with a coral (shellfish roe) or lobster sauce dusted with paprika or cayenne. The name is also given to iced desserts made with red fruits or served with a red fruit sauce.

CARDOON An edible thistle, related to the globe artichoke, which grows in Mediterranean countries. Its stalks are like celery and it can be eaten in the same way. Its flavour faintly resembles the globe artichoke.

To select: When buying cardoons, look for firm, plump, creamy-white stalks. Allow 225–275 g (8-10 oz) per person.

To prepare: To eat raw, separate the stalks and remove the strings and inner white skin. Cut the stalks into lengths and thinly slice the heart. Leave in cold water acidulated with lemon juice to prevent browning until ready to serve. To prepare for cooking, separate the heart and stalks and slice or cut into short lengths.

To cook: Cook in boiling salted water with added lemon juice for 30–40 minutes or until tender, then peel away the strings and skin. Serve hot. Cardoon may also be braised or sautéed.

To serve: Serve hot with melted butter or a cheese or tomato sauce, or serve cold with a vinaigrette dressing.

CARMINE A carnation-red food colouring derived from cochineal (*see* COCHINEAL).

CARMOISINE A red food colouring (E122) used to colour jams and preserves.

CAROB (Locust Bean) The large, dark brown beans of the carob tree that grows in Mediterranean regions contain a sugary pulp which can be dried and ground and is available for use as a flavouring. It has become fashionable as a substitute for chocolate, especially from a nutritional point of view, as it contains less fat than chocolate and no caffeine. It is also available in bars and chips, and can be bought from most health food shops.

Carob powder can be used to make a hot drink, or as a substitute for cocoa powder in cakes and biscuits, but neither the flavour nor the texture of the finished dish will be the same as when made with real chocolate. Cakes and biscuits made with carob powder are also much darker in colour. As carob powder is much sweeter than cocoa, only half as much carob powder is needed in a recipe. Carob bars and chips can be melted and used to decorate cakes, or to make a carob sauce.

CAROTENE The yellow-orange pigment present in yellow and green vegetables and fruit. It is the precursor of vitamin A, being converted into that substance in the body. Derivatives of carotene, namely alpha-carotene, beta-carotene and gamma-carotene, are used as colouring (E160a) in margarines and soft drinks. (*see also* VITAMINS)

CARP There are several varieties of this freshwater fish, found in ponds, lakes and rivers in most parts of the world, and also artificially bred on fish farms. The finest species of carp is the mirror carp, so called because it has just a very few large scales.

Carp feed on vegetation in the mud on the riverbed, and its flesh tends to have a slightly 'muddy' flavour. This can be improved by soaking the fish in salted water for 3–4 hours, then rinsing thoroughly before cooking. Some carp are very scaly and need careful scaling before use. Carp have sweet, firm flesh with few bones and are therefore ideal for cooking whole. They can be stuffed and baked, poached or braised over vegetables.

CARRAGEEN (Carragheen, Irish Moss, Seamoss, Pearl Moss) A dark purple or green seaweed found on many coasts of northern Europe. When dried and bleached it can be used as a substitute for gelatine, similar to agar-agar. Commercially, it is used as a thickening agent. It can also be cooked and eaten as a vegetable (*see* SEA VEGETABLES). (*see also* AGAR-AGAR)

CARRÉ DE L'EST A small, soft, square-shaped cheese made from pasteurized cows' milk in the Champagne and Lorraine regions of France. It has a mild flavour and a soft white rind. A stronger version with an orange rind has the same name.

CARROT Known since Elizabethan times, this root vegetable is probably the most familiar and popular of all vegetables. Carrots are available all the year round and come in a variety of shapes, sizes and shades of orange. Some, such as the Parisienne carrot, are short, round and stumpy, while others, such as the Chatenay or Nantaise carrot, are longer and conical or slender in shape. Carrots are an invaluable flavouring ingredient for soups, stocks, casseroles and stews, as well as a versatile vegetable in their own right.

New sweet baby carrots, sold complete with their greenery, are available in bunches in early summer. They are a great delicacy when gently steamed or simmered until tender, served with butter and sprinkled with chopped fresh parsley or chives. As carrots get older and larger, the skin becomes thicker and they will need scraping or even thinly peeling. Carrots are a rich source of vitamin A (in the form of carotene) and also contain small amounts of the B vitamins and some calcium. When peeling, remember that most of the vitamin content is only skin deep and the more that is peeled away, the greater the vitamin loss.

Carrots make a delicious salad ingredient – simply grate them raw and add to summer or winter salads, giving colour and flavour. Blanched slices or cubes of carrot make a refreshing salad when tossed in French dressing, soured cream or yogurt and sprinkled with chopped fresh herbs.

Raw grated carrot may also be added to a variety of dishes to add extra moisture and sweetness – grate a small carrot into the Christmas pudding mixture or add to minced beef when making meatballs, hamburgers, kebabs or meat sauce for spaghetti. Grated carrot is also used as an ingredient in a popular carrot cake. Carrots can also be liquidized and pressed to produce a nutritious and refreshing juice for drinking.

To select: When buying carrots, choose those which are brightly coloured, firm, well shaped and with smooth skins. Allow 100–175 g (4–6 oz) per person.

To prepare: Small new carrots should have their stalks removed and simply be well scrubbed. Pare the skins as thinly as possible from older carrots and cut lengthways or slice.

To cook: Cook in boiling salted water for 10–15 minutes, or steam for about 20 minutes or until just tender. Carrots may also be cooked with a little water in a casserole in the oven at 150°C (300°F) mark 2 for about 45 minutes, then served with a knob of butter and a sprinkling of chopped fresh parsley. (*see also* VICHY CARROTS)

To serve: Serve hot as an accompaniment, topped with a knob of butter and sprinkled with chopped fresh herbs. Very old carrots are best made into a purée or soup.

CARVING Cutting a joint of cooked meat, or a whole poultry or game bird into even slices or portions for serving. Skilful carving makes the most of food, enabling one to obtain the maximum number of neat, appetizing portions and, if possible, leaving the joint or bird looking attractive enough to serve cold.

Carving Tools
Carving is made much easier if good tools are used. You need a large carving knife, usually with a plain cutting edge, although knives with serrated edges are often used. Whatever knife you choose, it should be very sharp.

A carving fork has two prongs and a guard to prevent your hand being cut should the knife slip up the fork.

Carving Meat
Boned and rolled joints are just sliced through. The backbone of rib or loin cuts of lamb or pork helps to keep the joint in shape during cooking. Get the butcher to 'chine' it (partially chop through the bone lengthways) when you buy it so you can then remove the bone just before serving, for easier carving.

Place the cooked joint on a meat dish, wooden board or spiked metal carving dish with recesses to catch the meat juices, and leave to stand for 15 minutes before carving. Always carve on a non-slip surface. Before starting to carve, loosen the cooked meat from any exposed bones. Take off all or at least some of the crackling before carving pork.

Aim to cut across the grain of the lean in order to shorten the muscle fibres. This makes the meat more tender. This procedure will usually mean cutting at right angles to the bone.

Beef
Fore rib Ask the butcher to chine the backbone. After cooking, remove the backbone and run a sharp knife between meat and bone. Carve the meat downwards, on to and between the rib bones.

Sirloin Sirloin of beef comprises the fillet and sirloin muscles, with a T-shaped bone between, and a portion of flank. Sometimes the fillet is removed and sold separately. When carving, gradually loosen the meat from the bones with a sharp knife as you carve along the joint. Carve slices of meat down to the bone, first on one side, then the other. If the entire joint is to be carved at one time, it may be easier to remove the three pieces of meat first.

Lamb
Leg With the meatier side of the leg uppermost, carve a narrow, wedge-shaped piece of meat from

the middle of the leg right down to the bone. Then carve slices from either side of the cut, slanting the knife to obtain larger slices. The underside of the joint can be carved, after removing any excess fat, by slicing along the length of the leg.

Shoulder Secure the joint at the shank end, with the crisp skin uppermost. Cut a wedge-shaped slice through the middle of the joint in the angle between the shoulder blade and the leg bone. Carve slices from each side of the first cut until the shoulder blade and shank bones are reached. Turn the joint over and carve horizontal slices from the underside.

Best end of neck Get the butcher to chine the joint.

After cooking, remove the chined bone and cut the meat into cutlets between the rib bones.

Pork

Loin Ask the butcher to chine the bone. After cooking, remove it and cut through the fat just beneath the crackling and remove a section or all of it before carving thinly, downwards to the bone.

Leg (shank end) Remove some of the crackling. Cut thin slices down to and around the bone as far as possible. When the shank bone is reached, carve slanting slices over the top of the bone. Turn the whole joint over and cut slanting slices down towards the thin end of the bone.

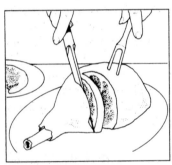

Cutting a second slice from a leg of lamb, after removing the first wedge-shaped slice.

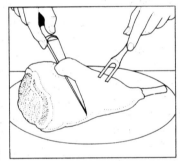

Carving horizontal slices along the length of the second side of a leg of lamb.

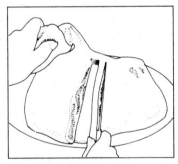

Holding the shank end of a shoulder of lamb while carving a slice from one side of the first cut.

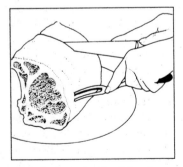

Carving a loin of pork, slicing downwards toward the bone, having removed the crackling.

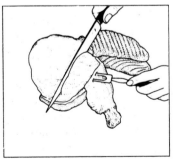

Carving a leg of pork (shank end). Remove the crackling and carve at an angle over the bone.

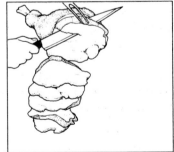

Carving a leg of pork (fillet end). Remove the crackling and carve slices through to the bone.

Leg (fillet end) Carve slices through to the bone, on either side of it.

Carving Poultry or Game Birds
Remove the trussing string and place the bird so that one wing is towards your left hand, with the breast diagonally towards you. Prize the leg outwards with the fork. Sever the leg. Repeat with the other leg.

Divide the thigh from the drumstick by cutting through the joint; in a big bird the thigh is further divided. Hold a wing with the fork and cut through the outer layer of breast and wing joint Ease the wing away from the body. Repeat with the other wing.

Slice the breast, cutting parallel with the bone. Slice stuffed birds from the front of the breast.

Small game birds, like partridges and pigeons, are usually cut in half. If very small, the whole bird may be served as one portion; guinea fowl, snipe and quail are among the birds which are served whole, on the toast or fried bread on which they were cooked. Special poultry shears are for cutting birds in half, or use a game carver or a short, pointed knife. Insert the point of the knife in the neck end of the breast and cut firmly through in the direction of the breast bone and tail.

CASEIN A substance produced from milk by precipitation. It results from the action of rennin on the milk protein caseinogen. This reaction takes place in the stomach as a part of normal digestion; it also occurs in the making of junket when rennet is added to warm milk. The milk sets but, when cut, a liquid (whey) separates from the solids (curd); the casein is contained in the curd. The precipitation also takes place when an acid is added to milk, although a less firm curd is formed.

The fermentation of casein is the origin of all cheese-making as the milk is always clotted with rennet and/or acids. The casein clot traps the fat, leaving much of the water to be drained off.

Cheese is therefore a concentrated form of milk nutrients.

Casein has a high nutritional value as a protein, which is one reason why milk and cheese are so important in the diet.
(*see also* CHEESE, JUNKET, RENNET)

CASHEL BLUE A semi-soft blue cheese made in Ireland from unpasteurized cows' milk. It is a comparatively new cheese with a sharp flavour and a creamy texture.

CASHEW NUT These whitish-coloured nuts come from the tropical cashew tree. The tree bears reddish pear-shaped fruit (cashew 'apples') and one kidney-shaped nut grows in its shell from the base of each fruit. As there is toxic oil in the shells of cashews, they are always sold shelled.

They can be bought whole (often salted), in pieces, or roasted. They have a slightly crumbly texture and delicate sweet flavour. They are often served with drinks or used in stir-fried dishes.

CASSAREEP (*see* CASSAVA)

CASSATA Generally, this is the name given to an Italian frozen dessert, consisting of ice cream shaped around a bombe mixture containing chopped nuts, candied fruit and candied peel. However, a Sicilian cassata is more like a cheese-cake, consisting of layers of Genoese sponge soaked with a liqueur and sandwiched together with Ricotta cheese. The cake is topped with chocolate and crystallized fruits. Sicilian cassata is traditionally served at Easter time. (*see also* BOMBE)

CASSAVA (Manioc, Yucca Root) A long, brown-skinned tuber with white starchy flesh, shaped rather like a very large carrot. It is cultivated in the Caribbean, where there are two main varieties: the sweet cassava and the bitter cassava. Bitter cassava is poisonous unless specially prepared. Only the sweet variety is available in Britain.

Cassava may be cooked and eaten as a vegetable, but it is also used to produce cassava flour, cassava meal (*garri*), tapioca and a syrup called *cassareep*. Cassava flour can be made into bread and cakes, and *cassareep* is used in Caribbean cookery. (*see also* GARRI)

To select: Look for firm cassava roots with a smooth skin. Allow 100–175 g (4–6 oz) per person.

To prepare: Peel well and cut into slices.

To cook: Cook in boiling salted water for 20 minutes or until tender.

To serve: After cooking, cassava can be served as a vegetable accompaniment instead of potatoes.

CASSEROLE Strictly speaking, an ovenproof dish with a tightly fitting lid used for cooking meat and vegetables slowly in the oven. A flameproof casserole is one that can also be used on the hob. The term 'casserole' is now also applied to the method of cooking and to the food cooked by this method. (*see also* COCOTTE)

CASSEROLE, ELECTRIC (*see* ELECTRIC CASSEROLE)

CASSIA The inner bark of a type of cinnamon tree grown in the East, particularly in China. Cassia resembles cinnamon in flavour, colour and aroma, but is coarser and less expensive. It may be used in many of the ways in which cinnamon is used, but is less suitable for sweet dishes. Cassia sticks very much resemble what they are – pieces of bark – whereas cinnamon sticks are usually formed into neat scrolls. Cassia is also available in powder form. (*see also* CINNAMON)

CASSIS (Crème de Cassis) A blackcurrant-flavoured liqueur from Dijon. It is often added to dry white wine to make a pretty, cooling summer drink called Kir.

CASSOLETTE An individual heatproof china, glass or metal dish, made to hold one portion of a savoury mixture (such as creamed chicken or mushrooms, game in sauce, etc.) which is to be served as an hors d'oeuvre, entrée or after-dinner savoury. The container is sometimes lined with duchess potato or puff pastry before the mixture is put in. Occasionally, a sweet mixture is served in the same way.

CASSOULET A classic haricot bean stew originating in the Languedoc region of France. It is prepared from pork, lamb and goose (or duck) and is traditionally made in an earthenware utensil known as a *cassole*; this word has evolved into the name 'cassoulet'. In France, the cassoulet recipe varies from region to region. (*see also* HARICOT BEAN)

CASTLE PUDDING An English pudding which consists of a rich sponge mixture, baked or steamed in small dariole moulds or cups, and served with jam sauce.

CATALANE, À LA A French term used to describe a dish garnished according to a Spanish style of cooking, usually with aubergine and rice, tomatoes, olives or artichokes.

CATFISH A sea fish which gets its name from its long, cat-like whiskers. It is also known as wolf-fish, distinguishing it from freshwater varieties of catfish (see below). The flesh of this fish is firm and white with a pinkish tinge and a strong flavour. It is ideal for casseroles or stews. It can also be grilled or cooked as for cod. It is sold as fillets, portions or cutlets, sometimes under the name of rock salmon or rock turbot. (*see also* COD)

Freshwater varieties of catfish are also found in Europe and in the southern United States, where they are an important ingredient in Cajun cooking (*see* CAJUN).

CATMINT (Catnip) Best known as a garden plant loved by cats, this plant has strongly aromatic leaves that can be used as a herb, though it is less popular nowadays. It is also available dried from health food shops and can be used to make a herbal tea.

CATSUP (*see* KETCHUP)

CAUDLE A hot spiced wine drink, resembling mulled wine, which was popular in earlier centuries as a cure for a cold. It was sometimes made with water in which oatmeal had been soaked, or with gruel.

CAUL (Caul Fat) A thin lace-like membrane covering the lower portion of an animal's intestines. At one time it was always used commercially for sausage-making and it is still used for home-made sausages and faggots. Pork caul is the best and most readily available type; it can be bought from the butcher and is usually soaked before use.

CAULIFLOWER This familiar vegetable is a member of the brassica family and is characterized by its compact, creamy white flower head, often called the curd, surrounded by green leaves, many of which have been removed by the time the cauliflower reaches the shop. It is available all year round, though at its best (and cheapest) during the summer months. Cauliflower is a good source of vitamins, iron and calcium.

Recently, green- and purple-headed varieties of cauliflower have appeared in the shops, as has a dwarf white-headed variety. Purple cauliflower is often called cape broccoli.

Whole or broken into florets, cauliflower makes a delicately flavoured vegetable accompaniment for roast meats, or can be made into cauliflower cheese, soup or a soufflé. Small florets can be served raw in salads or dipped in batter and deep-fried. (*see also* CAULIFLOWER CHEESE)

To select: Look for a cauliflower with fresh green leaves surrounding a firm white curd or head, with no blemishes or bruises. If the curd has been exposed to sunlight, rain or frost it will turn a yellowish shade – this only affects the appearance, not the flavour. Cook cauliflower soon after buying or cutting as it will lose flavour if stored for more than a few days. A medium cauliflower will serve about four people.

To prepare: Cut away the outer leaves and chop off the stem. Cut a cross in the stump to help the thick part cook more quickly. Wash and drain.

To cook: Cook in boiling salted water for 10–15 minutes, keeping the stem immersed, but the florets out of the water. Cover the pan so that the florets cook in the steam. Cook separated florets in boiling salted water for about 5 minutes, or steam for about 10 minutes. Drain well.

To serve: Cauliflower can be served plain or with melted butter, white, béchamel or cheese sauce.

CAULIFLOWER CHEESE (Cauliflower au Gratin) A popular supper dish made by covering lightly cooked cauliflower (either whole or broken into florets) with a cheese sauce. The top is sprinkled with grated cheese and browned under the grill.

CAVEACH A method of preserving fish by pickling in vinegar. The better-known Spanish version of caveach is *escabèche*. Most fish can be preserved in this way, including cod, salmon, mackerel, whiting, red mullet, anchovies and sardines. The fish is fried before it is pickled. (*see also* ESCABÈCHE)

CAVIAR (Caviare) True caviar is the salted roe (or eggs) of the female sturgeon fish, considered a great delicacy because of its rare flavour, though it is an acquired taste and not appreciated by everyone. Most prized are the Russian varieties – the processed roe of the sterlet (the smallest sturgeon) from the Caspian Sea. It consists of a mass of black eggs, each about the size of a pinhead. Caviar is also imported into Britain from Germany and America, the latter type being less expensive. Caviar has poor keeping qualities and therefore is often pasteurized. A pressed variety of caviar is also available, made by pressing together immature or damaged sturgeon eggs, resulting in a rather jam-like texture.

One of the best known caviars is beluga, which comes from the beluga sturgeon, the largest of the sturgeon family. The eggs are a light grey in colour and comparatively large. More readily available and less expensive is sevruga caviar, which is taken from a smaller member of the sturgeon family. Its eggs are smaller than beluga, but similar in colour. Another variety is known as mandarin caviar, coming from the large, white Chinese sturgeon.

Caviar should be kept very cold, preferably on ice. Once opened, a can or jar of caviar should be eaten as soon as possible. It is served either from its jar or from a small bowl nestling in crushed ice, and is accompanied by crisp toast, crackers or brown bread and butter. It may be sprinkled with lemon juice, if liked. Caviar may also be made into canapés, included in hors d'oeuvre, spread on croûtes of fried bread, or served in blinis (small Russian pancakes).

Mock Caviar
Roe from a number of other fish is sold as 'mock caviar'. It is less expensive than real caviar and the eggs may be coloured orange, red, white or black. Lumpfish roe is the best known and is available black, red or orange. It is a useful garnish. Other types of mock caviar include the roe of salmon, whitefish and salmon trout.

CAYENNE (Cayenne Pepper) This spice comes from the red pepper (capsicum) family and is prepared from the smallest, hottest chillies. It is always sold ground and is sweet, pungent and very hot. It should be used sparingly to flavour meats and sauces, especially barbecue and 'devilled' recipes, eggs, fish, vegetables, cheese sauces and pastry, chicken croquettes, cheese and vegetable soups. Unlike paprika, it cannot be used for colouring as it is far too strong. (*see also* CAPSICUM, CHILLI PEPPER, PAPRIKA)

CEBICHE (*see* CEVICHE)

CELERIAC (Celery Root, Knob Celery) Also sometimes known as turnip-rooted celery, celeriac is a large, knobbly swollen root with a pronounced celery flavour. It is a versatile winter vegetable to add to soups, stocks, casseroles and stews, as well as to grate and serve raw as an hors d'oeuvre or in salads. Strips or slices may be blanched and served in a salad. Celeriac is also good served hot, especially when made into fritters.

To select: Choose bulbs which are firm, heavy and free from blemishes. Avoid very large bulbs, which may be too tough. Allow 100–225 g (4–8 oz) per person.

To prepare: Scrub well, cut off the roots and peel thickly. Leave whole, grate or slice into julienne strips. Leave in cold water acidulated with a little lemon juice until required.

To cook: Cook in boiling salted water for about 20 minutes (slices and strips), 35–45 minutes (whole). Drain well.

To serve: Serve hot with melted butter or a sauce. Cooked celeriac may also be mashed and served like potatoes.

CELERY A vegetable of the carrot family widely grown in temperate regions. There are two main varieties of celery – the self-blanching variety available from July to October, and the maincrop non-self-blanching variety which is available from October through to the following year. Self-blanching celery is easily recognized by its clean green or golden stalks, consistent good quality throughout the season, and its subtle flavour. The maincrop celery is covered with earth to keep the stalks white. Therefore, it is often dirty when bought and needs a good wash before using. These days, however, celery is most often sold ready washed, trimmed and packed in polythene. Celery hearts are also available.

Celery is often used as a flavouring ingredient in soups, stews and casseroles, or it can be boiled or braised and served hot with a sauce as an accompanying vegetable. It is also very popular served raw, with salt, cheese and bread or crackers. It adds extra crunch and flavour to salads. Both the leaves and the stalks make useful garnishes; the stalks can be cut and made into celery frills, the leaves can be chopped and sprinkled over soups and stews like parsley. Short lengths of celery can be filled with cream cheese and served as canapés or as part of a buffet spread. (*see also* CELERY SEED)

To select: Choose celery with thick unblemished stalks and fresh leafy tops. The stalks should break crisply. Allow 3–4 sticks per person.

To prepare: Separate the stalks and scrub well to remove any dirt. Remove any stringy fibres from outside stalks. Leave whole or cut into slices or lengths.

To cook: Boil or steam pieces for about 20 minutes. To braise, cook 2.5 cm (1 inch) lengths of celery in butter for 5 minutes. Add sufficient stock to cover and simmer gently for 15–20 minutes or until tender.

To serve: Serve boiled or braised celery hot as a vegetable accompaniment for fish or grilled meats.

CELERY CABBAGE (*see* CHINESE CABBAGE)

CELERY ROOT (*see* CELERIAC)

CELERY SALT A commercially prepared flavouring made by combining ground celery seeds with salt. It may be used to flavour egg dishes, and in any other dish requiring the flavour of celery.

CELERY SEED These spice seeds do not come from the same variety of celery as the one used in salads, though they have a strong taste that resembles the vegetable. They are sold whole or ground and can be used sparingly in pickles and chutney, meat and fish dishes, salads, bread, marinades, dressings and dips.

CELLOPHANE NOODLES (*see* NOODLES)

CELSIUS (Centigrade) A scale for measuring temperature, in which the freezing point of water is 0° and the boiling point is 100°. The oven settings on modern electric cookers are given in degrees Celsius (°C), replacing the Fahrenheit scale which is gradually becoming obsolete in Europe.

CENTIGRADE (*see* CELSIUS)

CEP (*see* MUSHROOM)

CEPHALOPODS A group of sea creatures found all over the world and belonging to the mollusc family. It includes squid, octopus and cuttlefish, all of which have no external shell, unlike other molluscs, but they do have an internal bone of sorts. Cephalopods are also characterized by the fact that they all have tentacles with suckers and ink sacs, and their internal organs are all contained in a muscular bag which, once emptied, is ideal for stuffing. (*see also* CUTTLEFISH, OCTOPUS, SQUID)

CEREAL Cereals are grasses cultivated for food. They grow all over the world, even in the Arctic Circle, and the seeds, or grains, of these grasses generally form the staple food of the population, being a cheap source of energy (in the form of carbohydrate), protein, some vitamins and minerals.

The most common cereals are barley, maize, oats, rye, rice and wheat; others, such as buckwheat and millet, are not true cereals, although they are treated as such. Many of these cereals are processed into flour but, until recently, such refining has resulted in the loss of most of the nutritional value of the original grain. New health food and vegetarian trends favour using whole grains in the diet, and it is possible to buy whole barley (pot or pearl), oats, wheat, rye, millet and buckwheat. Some cereals are also available as flakes or 'meals'.

Amongst other things, cereals are eaten in the form of bread, cakes, biscuits, pasta, rice, oatcakes, porridge, breakfast cereals, popcorn, corn on the cob, semolina and many others. (*see also* BARLEY, BREAKFAST CEREAL, BUCKWHEAT, BULGAR, CORN, GRAINS, MILLET, OATS, RICE, RYE, WHEAT, etc.)

CERVELAS A short, fat French pork sausage, often flavoured with garlic. It is usually poached in water and served hot.

CERVELAT A large, smoked German sausage made from pork and beef. It can be sliced and eaten cold.

CERVELLATA Made in northern Italy, this pork sausage is flavoured with spices, Parmesan cheese and saffron.

CEVICHE (Cebiche, Seviche) A South American method of preparing white fish by marinating in lime or lemon juice for several hours. Flavourings, such as onion and garlic, are added to the marinade, and the fish is served with slices of tomato, pepper and sweetcorn.

CHABICHOU (Chabi) A small, soft goats' milk cheese made in Poitou, France. The farmhouse variety has a grey rind with red streaks, while the dairy variety has a white rind. Both are small, cylindrical cheeses, with a strong 'goaty' smell and flavour.

CHABLIS A light but distinctive, very dry white Burgundy wine, from the vineyards around Chablis. It is pale yellow in colour and is served slightly chilled with fish or white meat.

CHAFING DISH This is a heatproof dish that can be used at the table to cook foods, such as a flambé, or to keep foods warm. It is usually positioned over a small table burner or hot plate, or is stood in a larger container of hot water.

CHAMBÉRY (*see* VERMOUTH)

CHAMBÉRYZETTE (*see* VERMOUTH)

CHAMPAGNE A sparkling wine made from grapes grown within the boundaries of the ancient French province of Champagne. Champagne is always blended, firstly because the wines from different vineyards, although similar in type, are different in style, and it is only by judicious blending that the individual wines are improved, the special qualities being merged into a harmonious whole; secondly, because the quantity of wine made each year from individual vineyards is so small that shippers must blend the wine of a number of vineyards in order to have sufficient champagne of uniform style to meet the demands of their customers.

Unlike other wines, champagne is bottled before fermentation is finished, so that the carbonic acid gas remains in solution and escapes when the cork is removed, giving a sparkling effect. This method is known as *cuve close*. A vintage champagne is one bearing the date of an outstanding year. These are not sold until five years old but the best will improve for another five years.

Considered the world's greatest sparkling wine, champagne is often reserved for special occasions or celebrations, such as weddings and anniversaries. It should be served chilled but not iced.

CHAMOMILE (*see* CAMOMILE)

CHAMPIGNON The French name for the button mushroom.

CHANNA (Channa Dal, Chana Dal, Chana Dhal, Cholla) Yellow in colour, this pulse is often mistaken for the yellow split pea. In fact it is the husked, split, black chick pea. It is a high protein pulse with an irregular surface and a slightly nutty flavour. Widely cultivated in India, channa is used in many Indian dishes and is also ground into a flour known as besan or gram flour. (*see also* CHICK PEA, GRAM FLOUR)

CHANTERELLE (*see* MUSHROOM)

CHANTILLY CREAM The name given to a sweetened version of whipped cream which may be flavoured with vanilla or brandy. It is a classic French preparation which may be used as a filling for pastries, cakes and meringues, or served as a luxurious accompaniment instead of plain whipped cream. It can also be used as the basis for a Bavarian cream dessert or a charlotte, or made into a sauce. In French cooking, dishes that have been made using whipped cream are often given the name *à la chantilly*. (*see also* BAVAROIS, CHARLOTTE)

CHAPATTI (Chapati, Chappati, Phulka, Roti) An Indian unleavened bread or pancake, made from a mixture of wholemeal flour, ghee and water, sometimes flavoured with salt. The paste is rolled out thinly into rounds, then browned on a griddle. Chapattis are then toasted directly over the flame, causing them to swell slightly. They may be served hot, brushed with melted butter or ghee. (*see also* GHEE)

CHAR A freshwater fish that is a member of the salmon family. Unfortunately, it is becoming increasingly rare, though it is still to be found in clean lakes and rivers in Britain and Europe. It has firm white-to-pink flesh and is similar in flavour to salmon and trout. It can be cooked like trout. Potted char is an old English delicacy, popular as a breakfast dish in the nineteenth century, and still made in parts of the country, such as the Lake District, where char is available freshly caught. (*see also* TROUT)

CHARCUTERIE The French name traditionally given to cooked pork products, such as ham, sausages, pâtés and terrines. Nowadays, however, it may include other items, such as raised pies and pâtés containing meats other than pork. In France, *charcuterie* is also the name given to the pork butcher's shop.

CHARD (*see* SWISS CHARD)

CHARENTAIS (*see* MELON)

CHARLOTTE A hot or cold moulded dessert. For a hot charlotte the mould is lined with bread and for a cold charlotte it is lined with home-made or bought sponge fingers. For one recipe, known as *charlotte royale*, the mould is lined with slices of jam-filled Swiss roll.

A charlotte mould is deep and bucket-shaped and may be made of aluminium or ovenproof glass. The sloping sides help to keep the bread or sponge in position until the filling is poured in.

The filling mixture for a cold charlotte may be a thick fruit purée or a very rich mixture, based on egg custard and lightened with plain whipped or Chantilly cream. It may be flavoured with citrus or soft fruit, chocolate or coffee, and a liqueur, such as Kirsch, is often added. The most famous cold charlotte is *charlotte russe* (see below).

The classic hot fruit charlotte is lined with slices of bread soaked in melted butter and filled with a purée of blackberry and apple, or just apple. Savoury charlottes, made with fish or vegetable purées, can also be made. (*see also* CHANTILLY CREAM, CHARLOTTE RUSSE)

CHARLOTTE RUSSE A classic chilled dessert thought to have been invented by the great French chef, Antonin Carême (1783–1833). It became popular at the Russian court during the nineteenth century, hence its name.

Based on the traditional charlotte recipe, a *charlotte russe* is lined with sponge fingers soaked in liqueur, and filled with a rich mixture of Bavarian or Chantilly cream, coffee or chocolate mousse, or a bombe mixture, sometimes containing candied fruits. After chilling and setting, the charlotte is turned out of the mould and may be dusted with icing sugar or decorated with piped whipped cream. (*see also* BAVAROIS, BOMBE, CHANTILLY CREAM, CHARLOTTE)

CHARNWOOD A smoked type of English Cheddar cheese, similar to Applewood (*see* APPLEWOOD, CHEDDAR)

CHARQUI (Jerky) The original Spanish-American name for an American version of biltong, that is strips of beef that are preserved by drying in the sun (*see* BILTONG). The beef is occasionally salted or soaked in brine before drying. *Charqui* is now commonly known as jerky, and is still a popular snack food.

CHARTREUSE One of the most famous herb-flavoured liqueurs originally compounded by the

Carthusian monks at Chartreuse, near Grenoble. It is a brandy-based liqueur, flavoured with a secret combination of plants and herbs, including hyssop. Yellow Chartreuse is sweeter, while green (the original) Chartreuse has a higher alcohol content. It may be used in cocktails, baking, desserts and confectionery.

Chartreuse is also the name given to a famous French recipe which combines vegetables (especially braised cabbage) with meat or game (especially partridge), arranged in layers in a mould and turned out when cooked.

CHASOBA (*see* NOODLES)

CHASSEUR A French term, meaning literally 'hunter'. Before the days of cultivation, mushrooms were 'hunted' by dogs, much as truffles are today by pigs, and this word has come to be applied to dishes cooked with mushrooms or served with a sauce made from mushrooms, shallots and white wine.

CHÂTEAUBRIAND A large thick steak cut from the tender fillet of beef and traditionally grilled and served with *maître d'hôtel* butter or *sauce béarnaise*. It is large enough to serve two people. (*see also* STEAK)

CHAUDFROID (Chaud-froid) A French name given to a cold dish of cooked fish, meat, poultry or game that is coated in a thick jellied white béchamel-based or brown sauce set under a layer of aspic. The sauce is also known as a chaudfroid sauce.

A chaudfroid is a very decorative dish, being garnished with shaped pieces of vegetable, egg white, herb leaves, anchovies, etc., before being glazed with the clear aspic. It makes a very impressive dish.

Chaudfroid Sauce

28.35 g (1 oz) packet aspic jelly powder
300 ml (¹/₂ pint) Béchamel Sauce (see BÉCHAMEL)
150 ml (¹/₄ pint) single cream
salt and pepper

Sprinkle the aspic powder in 150 ml (¹/₄ pint) water. Place the bowl over a pan of simmering water and stir until dissolved, taking care not to overheat the mixture.

Add to the Béchamel Sauce, beating well, then stir in the cream and extra seasoning, if necessary.

Strain the sauce and leave to cool, stirring frequently, so it remains smooth and glossy. When at the consistency of thick cream, use as a coating sauce.
Makes about 450 ml (³/₄ pint)

CHAYOTE (Christophine, Choko, Chow-chow, Custard Marrow, Pepinello) A pear-shaped member of the squash family grown in the Caribbean, California and Africa, and widely used as a vegetable in West Indian and Creole cooking. It has a smooth or ridged dark green skin and white to green flesh with a high water content. The central seed is edible.

Chayotes have a delicate flavour which becomes more insipid as they become larger, and are best cooked in combination with other strongly flavoured vegetables, or stuffed with a good flavoured stuffing. In this country, they are available from West Indian shops and some supermarkets.

To serve chayote as a vegetable main dish, it is best stuffed and baked, like a marrow, but can also be peeled, sliced and boiled or fried, like courgettes, and served as an accompaniment. It can be made into chutney. (*see also* COURGETTE, MARROW, SQUASH)

To select: Choose small, firm chayotes with no blemishes or soft spots. Allow 2–3 small chayotes per person, 175–225 g (6–8 oz) per person for larger ones.

To prepare: Large chayotes should be peeled and sliced, though they should not be peeled if they are to be stuffed and baked. Small chayotes do not need peeling.

To cook: Small chayotes can be cooked like courgettes, larger peeled ones should be cooked in boiling salted water for 15–20 minutes or until tender.

To serve: Stuffed and baked, chayotes may be served as a main dish. Sliced and boiled or sautéed, they may be served as a vegetable accompaniment, with a tomato sauce if liked.

CHEDDAR Perhaps the best known and most widely used of all the English cheeses. The name was first given to a cheese made by a method used in the Cheddar region of England in the Middle Ages. Now, the name 'Cheddar' is given to any cheese which undergoes the 'cheddaring' process, regardless of where it is made. Cheddar is now produced in various other parts of England and also in Scotland, Ireland, Canada, Australia and New Zealand.

Cheddar is made from pasteurized cows' milk and has a hard, sometimes crumbly, texture and a yellow colour which deepens with age. The process used to make Cheddar involves cutting the drained curds into blocks and squeezing them together to extract still more of the whey, resulting in a very hard cheese. Flavours vary from mild to quite strong, depending on how long the cheese is left to mature before it is eaten.

English Farmhouse Cheddar is made with whole milk from a single herd of cows. The process is the same as ordinary Cheddar but Farmhouse is allowed to mature longer to produce a richer and more mellow flavour.

Cheddar cheese is equally good cooked or uncooked. It makes an excellent 'ploughmans' lunch', served with crusty bread and pickles or can be made into sandwiches. In cooking, it has any number of uses and has particularly good melting qualities. It is often grated and sprinkled on top of a dish before browning under the grill.

The mellow, slightly salty Cheddar made in Canada is similar to Farmhouse Cheddar. Its strong, mature flavour makes it excellent for cooking. Australian and New Zealand Cheddars are also widely available and are of a mild quality.

Cheddar cheese is also available smoked (*see* APPLEWOOD, CHARNWOOD).

CHEESE Cheese is a solid derivative of milk. It is produced by coagulating the protein (casein) in milk so that it forms curds – usually by adding rennet (or a vegetarian equivalent) – and draining off the liquid (whey). Cheese then undergoes a ripening process, during which it changes in taste, texture and appearance and each variety takes on its own particular characteristics. Some cheeses develop veining during ripening, while others form holes or 'eyes'. Veining is caused by a bacteria in the cheese, which may occur naturally, or may be introduced. All cheeses develop a rind or crust of some sort, or are given one artificially, such as the red wax rind of Edam. Some cheeses, such as Brie and Camembert, develop a mould on the outside surface which produces enzymes which help ripen the cheese from the outside towards the centre.

Most cheese is made from cows' milk with a small amount made from ewes' or goats' milk. The type of milk and the different techniques used to separate the curds and whey and ripen the cheese result in the many different types of cheese. Climate, vegetation and seasonal changes can also influence the finished cheese, which means that some varieties can only be produced in a certain area and cannot be produced in large quantities or under factory conditions. Cheddar, however, lends itself well to factory techniques.

Although casein makes up 78 per cent of the milk protein, there are other proteins present in smaller quantities, but they are soluble and are drained out with the whey. (They are known as whey proteins.) The whey may then be processed to curdle the remaining protein and used to make low fat cheese such as Ricotta – a moist, unsalted Italian cheese.

Much of the cheese bought in this country is factory produced but increasingly cheese is being made by the traditional methods on farms using unpasteurized milk. Traditional Cheddar, Single and Double Gloucester, Cheshire, Lancashire, Leicester, Wensleydale and Caerphilly are all being produced as 'farmhouse' cheeses.

(For descriptions of particular cheeses, see individual entries.)

Types of Cheese

Semi-hard and Hard Cheeses

A semi-hard cheese is produced by removing as much of the whey as possible from the curd, often by mechanical pressing, before moulding and ripening. Hard cheeses undergo a further process which involves heating the curd so that it shrinks and hardens, making it possible to extract even more of the whey. These cheeses are left to mature much longer than the softer cheeses. Semi-hard cheeses include Cheddar and Edam, while the most familiar hard cheeses are Parmesan and Pecorino.

Fresh and Soft Cheeses

A true soft cheese is made by coagulating unpasteurized milk with rennet. The addition of a 'starter' just before rennet is added ensures a clean acid flavour. The majority of soft cheeses, such as Camembert, are foreign in origin. English soft cheeses include York and Colwick.

The British cheeses are usually marketed in a fresh or unripened state, whilst the better known of those made abroad, such as Brie and Camembert, are consumed when fully mature. This requires the growth of specific bacteria and moulds to produce the desired ripening action. These are the cheeses that have been involved in recent scares about listeria bacteria, and are best avoided by small children, pregnant women, the elderly and anyone not in the best of health (*see* FOOD POISONING). The British varieties of unripened soft cheese are usually made from cows' milk, but goats' milk can equally well be used.

Today, many soft cheeses are made from skimmed milk, which means they are lower in calories and fat. Varieties of soft cheese are defined and labelled according to the amount of milk fat and water they contain. Skimmed milk soft cheese must by law contain less than 2 per cent milk fat and not more than 80 per cent water. They are generally low in calories, soft and smooth with a bland or slightly acid taste. Examples include *fromage frais*.

Those labelled as low fat soft cheese have 2-10 per cent milk fat and up to 80 per cent water. Textures may vary from smooth and yogurt-like to lumpy-textured cottage cheese (see below).

Medium fat soft cheese must contain 10–20 per cent milk fat and not more than 70 per cent water. It is white with a smooth but slightly granular texture and lightly acid flavour.

Full fat soft cheeses are often called 'creamy' and are frequently confused with the higher fat cream cheeses. Full fat means they must contain at least 20 per cent milk fat and not more than 60 per cent water.

The higher fat cream cheeses are often referred to as double cream cheese (see below). One example is Caboc.

Cream cheese can be classified as a soft cheese. Its manufacture is very similar to that described above, but it is made from cream rather than milk. A typical cream cheese is a soft-bodied, unripened cheese with a rich, full and mildly acid flavour. It has a rather granular texture, buttery consistency and a high content of milk fat which gives it a creamy appearance. It is usually moulded into small cylindrical, square, rectangular or round shapes of varying sizes. There are two recognized varieties of cream cheese – single or double cream cheese.

Single cream cheese is made from single cream with an optimum fat content of 20–25 per cent. About 1.2 litres (2 pints) of this cream will yield about six cheeses weighing 100–125 g (about 4 oz) each. Carefully prepared, it will keep for a week in a refrigerator, after which it deteriorates quickly both in flavour and appearance.

Double cream cheese is produced from cream containing about 50–55 per cent butter fat. Usually 1.2 litres (2 pints) of this cream will yield eight double cream cheeses weighing 100–125 g (about 4 oz) each. This cheese does not keep quite as long as single cream cheese.

Acid Curd Cheeses

Acid curd cheese is frequently classed as a soft cheese, but is fundamentally different. The curds are formed solely by the action of lactic acid upon the casein. Acid curdling is a completely different action from rennet coagulation and yields a curd of high acidity, quick drainage properties and somewhat granular texture. The cheese has a clean, acid flavour, and a slightly granular, soft, spreadable flavour. It has a short shelf-life and must be eaten in a fresh state.

Cottage cheese is an acid curd cheese, but is made from pasteurized, skimmed milk. The curd is cut into small cubes and slowly heated to develop the right body and texture. The whey is drained off, and the curd washed several times and cooled. The washing of the curd produces the familiar lumpy appearance of cottage cheese. Salt and single cream are then added and the cheese is packaged in cartons. The addition of the cream gives the cottage cheese a final fat content of 4 per cent. This, combined with the high moisture content, gives the cheese its soft velvety texture. Cottage cheese has poor keeping qualities and should be eaten while fresh.

Low Fat Cheeses

Low fat hard cheeses, such as Cheddar and Cheshire, have been produced in response to the needs of people who want to reduce the amount of fat in their diet. They are made in a similar way to traditional hard cheeses but with half their fat content and a consequent reduction in calories. Low fat cheeses tend to be mild flavoured. For use in cooking where a stronger flavour is required, either add a pinch of mustard or keep the cheese in the refrigerator for 2–3 weeks to allow the flavour to mature and develop.

Processed Cheese

This is made by combining cheese with a number of other ingredients, such as flavourings and cream, and melting it down. A processed cheese contains at least 50 per cent dry matter and 40 per cent fat. A cheese spread contains less dry matter. Processed cheeses are sold in portions wrapped in foil, often shaped in triangles, cubes and very thin slices. They can be used to make sandwiches, in hamburgers or in appetizers.

Buying and Storing Cheese

At specialist cheese shops, cheese is kept in exactly the right conditions for each type and you can often taste a sliver of a particular cheese before you buy it. If buying pre-packed cheese, check that it does not look sweaty or excessively runny and that it is within the life of its date stamp: if the date is many weeks ahead it may mean that the cheese is immature.

Store cheese in a covered, ventilated china dish or in a bowl with a plate on top, or wrap in foil (avoid using cling film) and store in the refrigerator. Keep it in the door, dairy compartment or bottom of the refrigerator so that it does not get too cold. Leave cheese at room temperature, still in its paper or other wrappings to prevent drying out, for about 30 minutes before serving.

If you want cheese to become hard and dry for grating, leave it exposed to the air in a cool, dry place for a couple of days, turning it from time to time. Grated cheese can be stored in a polythene bag in the refrigerator for several weeks.

Cheese can be frozen, though some varieties freeze better than others, especially the higher fat varieties. Once thawed, all cheese should be eaten as soon as possible as it deteriorates quickly.

Serving Cheese

Cheese may be served at the end of a meal, or it may form the main course for a light lunch. When planning a cheese board, serve some of the following accompaniments with it:

* Biscuits which may be savoury or salty, plain or semi-sweet. Rolls or bread (French, granary-style, wholemeal or rye), cut into chunks and put into a separate bowl or basket. Fruit bread is also delicious with cheese.

* Butter, margarine which is low in saturated fats or a low-fat spread.

* Salad vegetables, such as lettuce, celery, chicory, tomato wedges, small whole radishes, watercress, carrot sticks and spring onions.

* Fresh fruit, such as apples or grapes.

Cheese and wine have a natural affinity; they can be served together for informal parties, lunches or dinner parties. For a dinner party, the cheese can either be served French-style between the main course and the dessert (in which case it is eaten with the wine served with the main course) or at the end of the meal. As a general rule for serving wine with cheese, serve richer cheeses with full-bodied wines and lighter, creamier cheeses with lighter red or white wine.

Cooking with Cheese

Cheese goes well with many other ingredients, such as eggs and pasta, and is a flavouring for many sauces and toppings. When cooking cheese, remember that too fierce a heat can make it stringy. It should melt rather than bubble fiercely and, when added to a sauce, it should not be allowed to boil. Hard cheese can be grated for cooking, but softer cheeses are best sliced, shredded or crumbled before adding to a dish.

It is important to think carefully about what cheese you use in which dish. If a recipe specifies a particular type of cheese, it is usually because of its individual flavour and texture, and substituting another variety may alter the taste of the dish. However, some cheeses can be used as substitutes for each other.

Well matured cheese gives the best flavour; if using a mild Cheddar, add a little mustard for extra flavour if wished – adding an extra quantity of a mild cheese will not give a greater depth of flavour. Cheddar is good in baking; use Lancashire, Cheshire or Leicester for toasting; Mozzarella for pizzas, while crumbly cheeses, such as Feta or Roquefort are best for mixing into salads and dressings.

CHEESECAKE Traditionally, a cheesecake was a mixture of local soft cheese, eggs and sugar baked in a pastry case. The term now covers a wide variety of flan-like recipes which always include a soft cheese in the filling. The cheese used may be full fat soft cheese, curd cheese or Ricotta, and the filling may be flavoured with lemon rind and juice or raisins.

It is usual for a cheesecake to have a base of pastry, biscuit crust or sponge cake and a topping of fruit, nuts or another layer of the base. Continental-type cheesecakes have a rich, creamy, smooth texture which is contrasted by the sharpness of a fruit topping. Chilled cheesecakes (originally from America) are usually set with gelatine and have a lighter texture.

Cheesecakes may be served as a dessert or as an indulgent snack at coffee-time.

CHEESE, FRUIT A type of jam- or jelly-like preserve, made by boiling a fruit purée with sugar to make a stiff mixture that can be set in a mould, then turned out to serve. A good cheese should be firm enough to cut with a knife.

Cheeses are a particularly good method of preserving fruits that contain a lot of pips or stones, such as blackcurrants or damsons. Other popular cheeses are made from quinces, cranberries, gooseberries, blackberries (often in combination with damsons), apples (often with other fruit) and medlars.

Some fruit cheeses are eaten like jam, with scones or bread and butter, while others are excellent served as an accompaniment to cold meats, cheese and other savoury foods.

A similar but softer preserve is known as a fruit butter (*see* BUTTER, FRUIT).

CHELSEA BUN A small, sweet yeast cake that was an eighteenth century speciality of the Old Chelsea Bun House in Pimlico, which was then in the Borough of Chelsea. After rising, the yeast dough is rolled out and filled with a mixture of dried fruit, chopped candied peel and brown sugar, then rolled up Swiss-roll-style. The roll is then sliced and the pieces are fitted, close together, cut-sides up, into a baking tin. After proving and baking, the buns are glazed with honey while still warm, then turned out and broken apart to serve.

CHERIMOYA (*see* CUSTARD APPLE)

CHERRY There are many varieties of this popular fruit which is grown all over the world. It is a small, round fruit with a central stone, and it varies in colour from white, through red to a very dark red, almost black. Cherries are mainly eaten raw but some varieties have sour flesh and may be poached or used to make pies and jams, amongst other things. Popular varieties of sweet cherries are Napoleon Bigarreau, Frogmore Early, Merton Heart and White Heart. The best variety for cooking is Morello.

Cherries are used all over the world in a number of classic dishes, including the Russian dessert, *kissel*, and in the French batter pudding, *clafoutis*. They are also used to make the liqueurs Kirsch, Maraschino and cherry brandy.

Glacé cherries are candied versions of the fruit that may be used in baking or as a decoration for desserts. They are available in many colours, including yellow, red and green.

Maraschino cherries are coloured and preserved in a sweet syrup (not the liqueur) flavoured with almond oil. They are a popular addition to some cocktails.

To select: Avoid split, diseased or immature fruit. Look for large soft berries with fresh green stalks, if possible, for eating raw.

To prepare: Remove the stalks and rinse the fruit in a colander. The stones can be removed with a

cherry stoner or the fruit can be split with the point of a knife and the stones prized out.

To cook: Poach in a little water for 5–10 minutes or until tender.

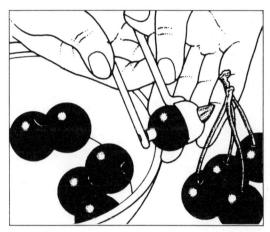

Removing stones from whole cherries using a special cherry stoner.

CHERRY BRANDY (*see* BRANDY)

CHERVIL This green leafy herb has a sweet, delicate flavour with a hint of aniseed. It looks a little like coriander or flat-leaved parsley and can be used in a similar way to parsley. It grows mostly in France, where it is used in many dishes as one of the classic *fines herbes*. Fresh chervil is good in salads, as a garnish, with a variety of vegetables (especially new potatoes), and as a flavouring for sauces such as hollandaise. It also blends well with egg, cheese and chicken dishes. (*see also* FINES HERBES)

CHESHIRE CHEESE This well known cheese is said to be the oldest of all English cheeses, dating back possibly to the eleventh century. Like Cheddar, it is a hard cheese, but rather more crumbly in texture, with a mild yet mellow flavour and a natural oily rind.

There are two main varieties – the red, which is coloured by the addition of a vegetable dye (annatto), and the white. There is no significant difference in the flavour. Unlike Cheddar, however, Cheshire cheese is unique to that county, as its characteristic flavour can only be produced from milk from cows grazed on grass growing on its salty soils.

A blue Cheshire is also made but is less widely available. Farmhouse Cheshire, which is made from a single herd of cows, is also available. Cheshire is good in cooking too.

CHESTNUT This is the fruit of the sweet chestnut tree, which grows mainly in southern European countries. Chestnuts are sold in their skins, dried, cooked and canned or as a purée (sweetened or unsweetened) in cans or tubes. Chestnuts in their skins must be peeled and cooked before eating.

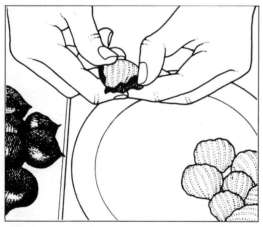

Peeling off both the outer and inner skins from chestnuts after soaking in boiling water.

Chestnuts have a rich flavour and are used to make soups and stuffings, served with vegetables such as Brussels sprouts and cabbage, or preserved in sugar to make *marrons glacés*. Chestnut purée is used in gâteaux and desserts. Dried chestnuts should be soaked in hot water for 30 minutes, then cooked and used as for fresh chestnuts. Chestnuts may also be ground into a flour and used to make cakes, bread and biscuits, though it is increasingly difficult to find.

To peel: Make a tiny slit in the skin near the pointed end, then cover with boiling water and leave for 5 minutes. Remove from the water, one at a time, and peel off the thick outer skin and thin inner skin while still warm.

To cook: Simmer the peeled nuts in water for 30-40 minutes. Alternatively, bake the nuts in their skins in the oven at 200°C (400°F) mark 6 for 20 minutes, then peel. Chestnuts are also delicious roasted over an open fire. The skins should first be slit to prevent them exploding, then they should be held over the flame, turning, until blackened. Skins can easily be removed after roasting.

CHEVIOT CHEESE A type of Cheddar cheese flavoured with chopped chives.

CHÈVRE The French name for various types of cheese made from goats' milk. Cheese given this name should be made from 100 per cent goats' milk, whilst those made from a mixture of goats' and cows' milk are often labelled *mi-chèvre*, containing a minimum of 25 per cent goats' milk. French goat cheeses are usually small and rounded or cylindrical in shape. The cheese itself is soft, white and somewhat sour in flavour. Various regional goats' cheeses exist, including *chevret*, *chevreton*, *chevrette* and *chevrotin*.

CHIANTI The best-known Italian red wine, light and fairly dry. It is produced in the Tuscany region of Italy and is traditionally sold in bottles surrounded by a woven straw or cane covering. There is also a white Chianti of good quality.

CHICKEN A domestic fowl that is classified as poultry and bred for its meat and eggs (*see* EGGS). It is extremely popular and very widely available. Modern methods of breeding and rearing have led to chicken being reasonably cheap and plentiful; it is available fresh or frozen and is used in dishes all over the world.

Most chickens bought in the shops have been produced by intensive methods, that is they have been reared under battery conditions and fed in a particular way designed to fatten them ready for slaughter as quickly as possible. The birds are therefore slaughtered very young – too young, some people think, to produce birds with the best flavour.

In response to some public concern about the cruelty of intensive farming methods, and in an attempt to produce better-flavoured birds, more farmers have started to rear chickens under free-range conditions. These chickens are fed less intensively and slaughtered when they are older. Although free-range chickens are more expensive, and sometimes hard to find, many people feel they are a great improvement on intensively reared birds. It is unlikely, however, that the amount of free-range birds available will ever be able to meet the demand for cheap, plentiful chicken.

Whether bought fresh or frozen, whole chickens in the shops are nearly always 'oven-ready', that is they have been plucked and drawn, and had their heads and feet removed. The giblets (the edible innards of the bird – usually the gizzard, heart, liver and kidneys) are very often sold in a small plastic bag inside the bird and can be used to make delicious stock and gravy. A chicken therefore needs very little preparation before cooking, unless it is to be stuffed, boned or jointed. A freshly bought chicken can simply be washed thoroughly inside and out, then cooked. It is very important, however, that a frozen bird be thoroughly thawed before cooking to ensure it is cooked through before eating.

Chicken, like all meat, is a good source of protein, iron and B vitamins. It contains very little fat. Chicken can be grilled, fried, roasted, boiled (poached) or casseroled. Classic chicken dishes include *coq au vin*, chicken Maryland, chicken Marengo, chicken Kiev and chaudfroid of chicken.

Buying Chicken

As well as the standard whole bird, chicken can be bought in a number of other forms in the shops, including a variety of smaller or larger birds that are best treated in particular ways, and various ready-cut chicken portions.

It is usually cheaper to buy a whole chicken and cut it up yourself. This way you also get the whole carcass, and sometimes the giblets, which can be used to make a good stock for use in soups, sauces and casseroles (*see* STOCK). Chicken pieces are ideal to use if you are short of time. All weights given are for oven-ready birds.

Poussins are very small chickens, 450–575 g (1–1¼ lb) 4–8 weeks old; one serves 1–2 people.

Spring chickens (broilers) are small birds, 1.1 kg (2½ lb) 12 weeks old; one serves 2–3 people.

Roasters are generally young cockerels or hens. They are 1.8–2.3 kg (4–5 lb) and one serves 5–6 people.

Boiling fowls are older, tougher birds; 1.8–3.2 kg (4–7 lb). They should be 18 months old, but may in some cases be older. They are usually served in casseroles. A 2.3–3.2 kg (5–7 lb) boiling fowl will serve 6–8 people.

Corn-fed chickens are yellow in colour because of their diet of sweetcorn (maize) and cost more than chickens fed on standard feed.

Halves and quarters are available and can be used instead of jointing a whole chicken.

Breasts are usually bought with the skin and some bones attached. They are also sold as fillets and escalopes. They vary considerably in size.

Suprêmes are a French cut of breast sold with the wing bone attached.

Thighs and drumsticks are dark meat portions which can be baked, fried, grilled or casseroled.

Wings are available in packs from some supermarkets. They are best casseroled.

Preparing Chicken

For boning, jointing, stuffing and trussing instructions, see POULTRY.

Roast Chicken

1.4–1.8 kg (3–4 lb) oven-ready chicken
stuffing
1 onion, skinned
1 lemon wedge
butter, melted, or vegetable oil
salt and pepper
streaky bacon rashers (optional)

Wash the bird, dry thoroughly and stuff with the chosen stuffing at the neck end before folding the neck skin over. Put the onion and lemon wedge in the body cavity.

Truss the bird and weigh it. Place it in a deep roasting tin, brush with melted butter or oil and sprinkle with salt and pepper. A few strips of streaky bacon may be laid over the breast to prevent it from becoming dry. Roast in the oven at 200°C (400°F) mark 6, basting from time to time, allowing 20 minutes per 450 g (1 lb) plus 20 minutes.

Put a piece of foil over the breast if it shows signs of becoming too brown.
Serves 4–6

Traditional accompaniments for roast chicken include stuffing balls, bread sauce and thin gravy.

Poached Chicken

1.4 kg (3 lb) oven-ready chicken
½ lemon
salt
1 medium onion, skinned and stuck with 3–4 cloves
1 medium carrot, peeled
6 black peppercorns
bouquet garni

Rub the bird with the cut side of the lemon half. Put it in a large saucepan and just cover with water. Add the salt, onion, carrot, peppercorns and bouquet garni.

Bring to the boil, cover and simmer for about 50 minutes or until tender. Remove from the stock and cool.

Remove the meat from the bones, dice and use for fricassées, curries or salads. Strain the cooking liquid and use to make a gravy, sauce or chicken soup.
Serves 4

Fried Chicken

When frying chicken, to ensure that the pieces remain moist, the surface should be browned at a high temperature to seal in the juices and give a good colour, then the heat reduced for the remaining cooking time.

4 chicken joints or pieces
salt and pepper
45 ml (3 level tbsp) flour
50 g (2 oz) butter or margarine, or 45 ml (3 tbsp) vegetable oil

Wipe the chicken joints or pieces and pat dry with absorbent kitchen paper. Season to taste with salt and pepper. Toss the chicken in the flour until completely coated.

Heat the butter in a frying pan or flameproof casserole and add the chicken pieces. Cook until golden brown on both sides, then lower the heat and cook for 30–40 minutes or until tender. Drain on absorbent kitchen paper.
Serves 4

Grilled Chicken or Poussin

4 chicken joints or whole poussins
salt and pepper
50–75 g (2–3 oz) butter or margarine, melted, or 45–60 ml (3–4 tbsp) vegetable oil

If using chicken joints, season and brush with melted butter, margarine or oil and grill under a medium heat for 20 minutes.

To prepare poussins for grilling, place them, breast sides down, on a board. Cut through the backbone, open the bird out and flatten. Brush all over with melted butter or oil and season lightly. Place in the grill pan.

Grill under a medium heat, turning once or twice, for about 30 minutes or until tender.
Serves 4

Chicken Casserole (Poulet en Cocotte)

1.4 kg (3 lb) oven-ready chicken

50 g (2 oz) butter or margarine
225 g (8 oz) lean back bacon in one slice
450 g (1 lb) potatoes, peeled and cut into 2.5 cm
(1 inch) dice
3 celery sticks, trimmed and sliced
450 g (1 lb) small new carrots, peeled
50 g (2 oz) button mushrooms, wiped
25 g (1 oz) shelled walnuts
chopped fresh parsley, to garnish
FOR THE STUFFING
100 g (4 oz) sausagemeat
30 ml (2 level tbsp) fresh breadcrumbs
1 chicken liver, chopped
30 ml (2 tbsp) chopped fresh parsley
salt and pepper

To make the stuffing, mix all the ingredients together in a bowl until well blended. Season well.

Stuff the chicken at the neck end, then truss the bird as for roasting (*see* POULTRY). Season well.

Melt the butter in a large frying pan, add the chicken and fry, turning it until well browned all over. Place the chicken and butter in a large ovenproof casserole.

Rind the bacon and cut into 2 cm (³/₄ inch) cubes. Add to the casserole, cover, and cook in the oven at 180°C (350°F) mark 4 for 15 minutes.

Remove the casserole from the oven and baste the chicken. Surround it with the vegetables and walnuts, turning them in the fat. Return the casserole to the oven and cook for a further 1¹/₂ hours. Transfer the chicken to a warmed serving plate and garnish with chopped parsley. Serve the vegetables and juices straight from the casserole.
Serves 4

CHICKEN BRICK An unglazed earthenware cooking utensil shaped to take a whole chicken. The brick separates into two halves and the chicken is put inside and cooked at a high temperature without fat or liquid, giving a cooking result comparable to that done in clay. The

brick should be soaked in cold water for at least 10 minutes before use.

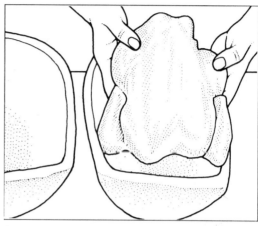

Placing a whole chicken into a soaked chicken brick ready for cooking.

CHICKEN LIVER The liver of a chicken is edible and is included in the giblets sold with a whole chicken, or can be bought separately, often frozen. Chicken livers should be carefully washed and trimmed, if necessary, before being lightly cooked. It is important not to overcook them as they will become dry and coarse. They may be fried and served on toast as an after-dinner savoury, used to make a pâté, or finely chopped and included in a stuffing.

CHICK PEA (Channe, Garbanzo, Ram's-head Pea) This is a round, beige-coloured pulse that looks a little like a pale hazelnut. It is the seed of a bush that is cultivated in southern Europe. Chick peas are used in many ways all over the world, most famously to make the Greek dip, *hummus*. In India, both white chick peas (*kabli channe*) and black chick peas (*kale channe*) are used in a number of dishes, including salads, sauces and stews. Chick peas can also be ground into a flour, known as besan or gram flour.

Chick peas are a rich source of carbohydrate and protein, calcium and iron, and also have a high calorie content. Like most pulses, chick peas need soaking before lengthy cooking; it is virtually impossible to cook them for too long. (*see also* CHANNA, GRAM FLOUR, HUMMUS, PULSES)

CHICORY (Witloof) What is known as chicory in Britain is a spear-shaped vegetable with tightly-packed white fleshy leaves. The plant belongs to the same family as a vegetable known in Britain as endive (or curly endive) or *frisée*, a curly-leaved dark green lettuce-like plant. In France and the United States, the plant we call chicory is called endive (or Belgian endive in the States), while what we know as endive is called chicory (or *chicorée frisée* in France).

An Italian red variety of chicory is known as *radicchio* or red chicory. Types of red chicory, from Italy or Holland, are becoming more commonly available in Britain and can be used in salads. Another variety of chicory, though not easily recognized as such, is the Batavian endive, or *escarole*, a green- or red-leaved salad vegetable that looks more like a round lettuce. It, too, is an attractive vegetable to use in salads as a substitute for lettuce.

The roots of another variety of chicory, which is not eaten as a vegetable, are roasted and ground and used to blend with coffee, producing a slightly bitter flavour.

Chicory is grown in darkness to produce its crisp white leaves. Its flavour can become somewhat bitter in older plants. It can be used as a salad ingredient or braised and served as a vegetable accompaniment.

To select: Choose heads with crisp white leaves. Too much green on them indicates a bitter flavour, though any suspected bitterness can be partially removed by blanching the 'chicons' (heads) before cooking. Allow half a head per person for use in salads, and one head per person for cooking.

To prepare: Remove any damaged outer leaves, scoop out the core and cut off the root end. Chop into pieces or leave whole.

To cook: Plunge the heads into boiling salted water and cook for 5 minutes, then drain and cook in about 60 ml (4 tbsp) water and a little lemon juice for about 25 minutes or until tender but still slightly crisp.

To serve: Serve hot with a cheese sauce, or sprinkle with chopped parsley or paprika. As a salad ingredient, chicory may be sliced or quartered, or the separated leaves may be used whole.

CHIFFONNADE (Chiffonade) A French name given to lettuce, spinach and other salad vegetables that are coarsely shredded and used as a garnish for soups or cold hors d'oeuvre.

CHILL To cool foods quickly, either by placing them in the refrigerator, or by surrounding them with ice. Many dishes made with gelatine or melted butter need to be chilled in order to set. Some foods are always served chilled, that is straight from the refrigerator and/or in a bowl surrounded with crushed ice, for example fresh oysters and caviar.

Many drinks are also served chilled. Cocktails and liqueurs may be mixed with crushed ice or poured over ice in the glass, while champagne and many white wines are always served from a bottle that is kept in a bucket full of ice.

CHILLED FOOD Chilled foods are kept at a low temperature, usually in a refrigerator, without freezing. The temperature must be sufficiently low to prevent bacteria, mould and enzymes (called micro-organisms) developing in the food, leading to deterioration. The average domestic refrigerator maintains a temperature of 2–7°C (35–45°F), which is not low enough to destroy any micro-organisms already present in the food, but will inhibit their further growth, except in the case of listeria (*see* FOOD POISONING).

All perishable foods, that is meat, fish, dairy products, fruit and vegetables, are best kept under chilled conditions. If this is not possible, these foods should be bought daily to ensure safe eating. In general, it is best to buy perishable foods as you need them, and in small quantities, to ensure that surplus does not sit around too long, even if chilled, before being eaten.

Chilled ready-prepared meals (cook-chill foods) are very popular. These are dishes, such as lasagne, shepherds' pie, chilli con carne and moussaka, which have been cooked and are packed in portions ready to be reheated and served. They are the ideal convenience food since they need no preparation and can be ready to eat in minutes. It is very important, however, that these foods be reheated thoroughly.

Although they have been stored under chilled conditions, ready-cooked foods will contain micro-organisms which will begin to multiply as the temperature rises during reheating. If the food is heated to a sufficiently high temperature, such micro-organisms will be destroyed and the food will be safe to eat. If not, eating it could result in food poisoning. It is important, therefore, to follow the food manufacturers' instructions carefully, especially if reheating a meal in a microwave cooker. If microwave cooking instructions are not given on the pack, it is best to assume that it is not safe to reheat that particular item in a microwave, and to use a conventional oven. When using a microwave cooker, pay particular attention to the centre of the food, which is the last area to become hot. Do not remove the food from the microwave cooker before the recommended time is up, even if the food appears to be bubbling. As a rough guideline, reheated chilled foods should be too hot to eat when they are removed from the cooker.

(*see also* FOOD POISONING, FOOD STORAGE, FREEZING, MICROWAVE COOKING, REFRIGERATION)

CHILLI CON CARNE A meat dish that is a speciality of Mexico but which has become popular in the United States and in Britain. Opinion varies as to what constitutes the authentic dish but its two main ingredients are beef and chilli peppers. The beef may be minced or cubed, and other spices may be added, such as cumin, cinnamon and sesame seeds, along with onions and tomatoes. In Britain, chilli con carne usually also contains red kidney beans, but these are not thought to be an authentic ingredient. Chilli con carne can be served with plain boiled rice or baked jacket potatoes.

CHILLI PEPPER These small but powerful peppers are from a plant that is a member of the capsicum family, as are sweet peppers. There are many varieties of chilli pepper, varying enormously in size, shape and colour, but the flesh and seeds of all of them have a very potent hot flavour.

Most chilli peppers start green and ripen to a deep red, but others are yellow or even black; some are very small and thin, others are large and rounded. The largest varieties come from the West Indies and Mexico and are rarely seen in Britain. The fresh chilli peppers most familiar here are imported from Africa.

Chilli peppers are also available dried in Britain, or ground in the form of chilli flakes, chilli powder, chilli seasoning, chilli sauce or cayenne. They are also used to make Tabasco sauce and are included in commercially produced spice mixes.

Chillies are used in countless dishes all over the world but should be used with caution if they are unfamiliar. The volatile oils in the flesh and seeds of the chilli can make your skin tingle, so treat with care. Wear rubber gloves when preparing them, or wash your hands thoroughly afterwards, and never allow chillies near your eyes. They are sometimes eaten on their own in Indian and Far Eastern countries but otherwise they are added in small quantities to soups and casseroles for flavour. Discard the seeds for a less hot flavour.

(*see also* CAPSICUM, CAYENNE, CHILLI POWDER, CHILLI SAUCE, PAPRIKA, PEPPER)

CHILLI POWDER Chilli powder is pure ground chilli peppers, and a very hot spice indeed. It can be used extremely sparingly in Mexican dishes, pickles, chutneys, ketchups, soup, tomato dishes, casseroles, spaghetti and meat sauces.

Some pre-mixed commercial chilli powders, often called mild chilli powder or chilli seasoning, contain a mixture of chilli and other spices such as cumin, oregano, salt and garlic, and are less hot. It is important to check the label carefully, so that you know whether what you are using is very hot pure chilli powder or mild chilli seasoning, before adding some to a dish. Recipes should also state which type is required.

CHILLI SAUCE A number of hot chilli sauces and relishes are produced commercially from red chillies, many combining them with tomatoes and other spices. Some are a thick paste, while others are quite thin sauces. They can all be used as a condiment or added to marinades, sauces, soups or stews during cooking.

The best known chilli sauce is Tabasco, a very hot, thin red sauce produced in Louisiana. It is made by combining fermented chillies with spirit vinegar and salt, and is named after the region of Mexico where the chillies first originated. It should be used sparingly in meat dishes, with shellfish and in sauces, salad dressings and some cocktails, such as a Bloody Mary. Usually, only a few drops are required.

CHINE Applied to joints of meat, this means to sever the rib bones from the backbone by sawing through the ribs close to the spine. Joints such as loin or neck of lamb, veal or pork are best chined so that the backbone can be removed after cooking, making it easier to carve the joint into chops or cutlets ready to serve. Chining is usually done by the butcher.

CHINE BONE A joint of meat, usually pork but also beef or lamb, consisting of part of the backbone of the animal, and some of the surrounding flesh. It is an uneconomical joint, owing to the quantity of bone, and is difficult to carve. It is best jointed and stewed or braised with vegetables.

CHINESE ARTICHOKE (*see* ARTICHOKE, CHINESE)

CHINESE BROCCOLI (*see* CHINESE KALE)

CHINESE CABBAGE (Celery Cabbage, Chinese Leaves) A type of Asian cabbage that has become popular in Britain in recent years. It looks rather like a very long cos lettuce, with wide white ribs and elongated leaves. Its Chinese name is *po tsai* (or *pe-tsai*). Although it originated in China, it is now grown in Spain, Holland, Israel and in Britain, ensuring a year-round supply. It may be eaten raw or cooked. (*see also* PAK CHOI)

To select: Choose heads that are heavy and look fresh. Allow 100–175 g (4–6 oz) per person.

To prepare: Cut off the stem and cut the leaves widthways into about eight thin slices. Wash thoroughly.

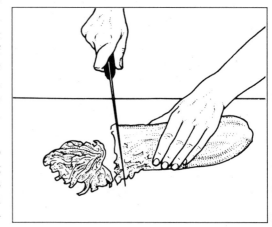

Cutting Chinese cabbage (Chinese leaves) into about eight thin slices.

To cook: Cook as for cabbage (*see* CABBAGE), or stir-fry.

To serve: Serve raw in salads, or serve hot as a vegetable accompaniment.

CHINESE CHIVE (Flowering Chive, Garlic Chive, Kuchai) This is a long, thin dark green variety of the onion family, looking very similar to the common chive but with flat rather than hollow leaves. Chinese chives produce white flower buds and have a strong onion-garlic flavour. They may be bought with or without flowers. Chinese chives can be used in many of the same ways as ordinary chives, but are also excellent cut up and stir-fried with other vegetables. (*see also* CHIVE)

CHINESE FIVE-SPICE POWDER (*see* FIVE-SPICE POWDER)

CHINESE FLOWERING CABBAGE Known in Chinese as *choy sum*, this variety of Oriental cabbage has smooth dark green leaves and firm white stems. It produces dark yellow flowers. It can be steamed or shredded and stir-fried, and is frequently served in Chinese restaurants.

CHINESE GOOSEBERRY (*see* KIWI FRUIT)

CHINESE KALE (Chinese Broccoli) This Oriental vegetable has large soft green leaves and green stems which can be cooked and eaten like the stems of broccoli. Its Chinese name is *gaai laan* and it produces white flowers, which should be in bud when the vegetable is best for eating. Chinese kale can be steamed or shredded and stir-fried.

CHINESE KEYS The name of this root vegetable comes from the fact that it looks like a small bunch of oddly-shaped keys. It is reddish-brown in colour and a member of the ginger family. It is more often used in Thai and Indonesian curries and pickles than in Chinese cooking.

CHINESE LANTERN (Bladder Cherry) This plant comes from the same family (Physallis) as the cape gooseberry but is grown more for its decorative red, papery husks than for its berries. (*see also* CAPE GOOSEBERRY)

CHINESE LEAVES (*see* CHINESE CABBAGE)

CHINESE MUSTARD CABBAGE This slender Oriental vegetable has long green stalks topped by comparatively small dark green leaves. Its Chinese name is *gai choy* and it is often used as a soup ingredient or made into a pickle, rather like *sauerkraut*. It has a strong mustard-like flavour.

CHINESE PARSLEY (*see* CORIANDER)

CHINESE PEPPER (*see* ANISE PEPPER)

CHINESE SPINACH (*see* CALLALOO)

CHINESE WATER SPINACH This small-leaved, dark green vegetable does faintly resemble spinach, but it has much firmer stems that stay firm when cooked. Its Chinese name is *ung choy* and it is available fresh from Chinese greengrocers.

CHIPOLATA A very small British pork sausage, made of ordinary pork sausagemeat in a narrow casing. Chipolatas are used to garnish meat dishes and to serve with roast chicken and turkey. They are also served on sticks as part of a buffet spread or as cocktail savouries. They may be baked, fried or grilled.

CHIPS (*see* POTATO)

CHIRONGI NUT A small rounded nut that resembles a large whole Egyptian lentil, both in colour and size. Chirongi nuts have a musky flavour and are used as a flavouring in Hyderabadi cooking.

CHITTERLINGS The name given to small sausages made by the butcher from scraps of pig intestines, or the name of the intestines themselves, from which they are made. They may be grilled or fried.

CHIVE This common herb is a member of the onion family and can be grown easily in most parts of the world. It produces purple flowers and has long, narrow, tubular green stems which can be used raw to flavour salads and dressings and as a garnish for soups and savoury dishes. Chives are also included in the *fines herbes* of classic French cooking. For the best flavour, the plant should be cut back regularly and should not be allowed to produce its flowers. The stems should be snipped into short lengths before use. (*see also* CHINESE CHIVE, FINES HERBES)

CHOCOLATE Chocolate is derived from the bean of the cacao tree which was first discovered in tropical America but is now cultivated mostly in Africa and Brazil. It was originally used only as a drink, and was introduced to Europe as such by the Spaniards in 1524. It is now familiar to us all as a deliciously rich, smooth, sweet and irresistible confection, as an important ingredient in desserts, cakes, biscuits and sweets, and as a warming drink. It is also used to enrich some savoury dishes, especially in Mexican cooking.

The fruit of the cacao tree consists of a large pod (ranging in colour from purple to yellow, according to variety) containing the seeds or beans. To produce chocolate, cocoa beans are first left to ferment until the pulp drops off, then they are dried and the hard outer skin is removed. The beans are then roasted and shelled, leaving the kernels or 'nibs'. These are ground into a thick paste called cocoa paste (or chocolate liquor) which consists of cocoa solids and a fat called cocoa butter. The next stage in the process is known as 'conching'. The hardened chocolate liquor is compressed by heavy rollers, giving it a smooth texture and mellow flavour. Conching can take as long as seven days; the longer conching continues, the finer the chocolate produced.

Chocolate is available in many different forms, from plain cocoa powder to the best dark chocolate. The type of chocolate produced depends on the blend of the original beans, the methods of roasting and conching used, and the proportion of cocoa butter contained in the final product. Other ingredients may also be added, such as condensed milk, cream, sugar, extra cocoa butter or dried fruit and nuts, producing a variety of different chocolates.

Types of Chocolate

Chocolate is available in bars or blocks, often with flavourings added, or in powder or 'chip' form. For cooking and baking, it is important to choose the right type of chocolate for the recipe, to ensure the correct flavour is achieved.

Cocoa powder is a rather bitter-flavoured powder that is used in baking. It is made by removing most of the cocoa butter from cocoa paste, leaving a dry cake that is ground to a fine powder, then sifted and blended to become the cocoa powder of commerce. Cocoa powder is widely available and is mainly used to make chocolate-flavoured desserts, cakes and biscuits. Its bitter flavour makes it rather unpalatable as a drink without the addition of sugar.

Drinking chocolate is also a powder, made in the same way as cocoa powder, but it is sweetened with sugar and blended with powdered milk. It is mixed with hot milk, or milk and water, to make it into a drink.

Eating chocolate comes in a variety of shapes and sizes and varies enormously in flavour. Its rich, smooth texture is the result of adding more cocoa butter, increasing the fat content to about 35 per cent. Flavourings such as vanilla, almond, cinnamon, cloves and cardamom are added in varying proportions.

Eating chocolate described as 'plain', 'bittersweet' or 'semi-sweet' contains just enough sugar to make it enjoyable to eat alone, but it may also be used in cooking. Some varieties of bittersweet chocolate contain cream.

'Milk' chocolate, as its name suggests, is made by adding condensed or powdered milk or cream and a larger amount of sugar, making it the sweetest, least bitter, most palatable type of chocolate. It is rarely used in cooking but is a very popular snack food.

'White' chocolate is made from cocoa butter, but no cocoa solids. It is similar in texture to other forms of chocolate, but its flavour is distinctly different. It can be used in cooking to some extent, but it is very sweet and has inferior setting qualities.

Cooking chocolate is usually available in block form but can also be bought as chocolate 'chips' or 'polka dots'. It is unsweetened and can be used in baking. Block chocolate is usually melted for use in recipes, but chocolate 'chips' (available in semi-sweet and milk varieties, too) are often simply stirred into a mixture. Cooking chocolate can be replaced by plain eating chocolate, if a richer flavour is preferred.

Couverture is often called 'covering' or 'dipping' chocolate, since its primary use is for dipping and coating sweets. It is a high quality chocolate, used by the makers of expensive, hand-made chocolates. It has a very high cocoa butter content, making it excellent for melting and it sets with a smooth, glossy finish. It is also the best chocolate to use for making chocolate caraque or curls to use as decorations (see right). It is available in bittersweet, semi-sweet, white and milk varieties; the best *couverture* comes from Belgium, Switzerland and France.

Chocolate-flavoured cake covering is readily available for home use, but it is not of the quality of *couverture*. It is useful for making scrolls and curls (see below), and for melting.

Using Chocolate

For flavouring cakes and biscuits, cocoa powder is most frequently used. It is sifted with the dry ingredients before being added to the mixture. Cocoa powder may also be used for coating chocolate truffles. Block chocolate may be grated or made into curls to use as decoration for cakes or desserts, but for most purposes, block chocolate is melted.

To melt Chocolate

Break chocolate into pieces and place in a small heatproof bowl over a pan of hot (not boiling) water. It is important that the bottom of the bowl does not touch the hot water as the chocolate will get too hot and the texture will be spoiled, becoming granular. Heat gently until the chocolate has just melted, then remove from the heat and stir until smooth and glossy. Do not allow any water or steam to come into contact with the chocolate.

Chocolate Cake Decorations

'Instant' chocolate cake decorations can be bought in the form of chocolate vermicelli (*see* VERMICELLI), crumbled chocolate flake or moulded chocolate shapes (such as leaves and flowers), or quick decorations can be made by making chocolate curls or finely grating or chopping plain chocolate. Chocolate flavoured cake covering can be used, but a good plain chocolate gives a better flavour. Melted chocolate can also be piped on to the surface of a cake, usually with a small greaseproof paper piping bag.

To make Chocolate Curls

Using a potato peeler, pare thin layers of chocolate straight from the sides of the block. For the best curls, the chocolate should be at room temperature; if chilled, the curls will break into 'shavings', which can also be used as a cake decoration.

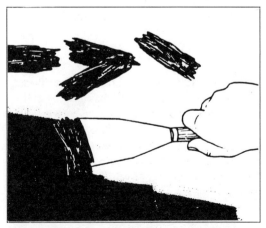

Pushing the blade of a scraper across the surface of solidified chocolate to make caraque. (*see overleaf*)

To make Chocolate Caraque

Melt 100 g (4 oz) chocolate in a bowl over a pan of hot water. Pour it in a thin layer on to a marble slab or cold baking tray and leave to set until it no longer sticks to your hand when you touch it. Holding a large knife or scraper, push the blade across the surface of the chocolate to roll pieces off in long curls. Adjust the angle of the knife blade to get the best curls.

To make Chocolate Shapes

Make a sheet of chocolate as above and cut into neat triangles or squares with a sharp knife, or stamp out circles or other shapes with small cutters.

Stamping out shapes from solidified chocolate, using a petit four cutter.

CHOCOLATES Any form of confectionery made using chocolate. The term is usually applied to a selection of high-quality sweets, often expensively packaged, and consisting of a variety of fudges, toffees, fondants, nougats, etc., coated in plain, milk or white chocolate. Chocolates can be bought as a pre-packaged selection, or they can be chosen individually from specialist shops. Liqueur chocolates are chocolates containing a light liqueur-flavoured syrup.

Chocolates can also be made at home by dipping home-made fondants, nuts, crystallized or fresh fruits, toffees, fudges and almond paste sweets into melted chocolate. The best type of chocolate to use for this is *couverture* (*see* CHOCOLATE), though ordinary plain and milk chocolates can be used. Filled chocolates can also be made with the help of special moulds which are first lined with melted chocolate which is allowed to set before being filled with a soft fondant or cream. Special moulds can also be bought for making hollow chocolate Easter eggs or other shapes.

CHOCOLATE TRUFFLE (*see* TRUFFLE)

CHOKO (*see* CHAYOTE)

CHOLESTEROL Much discussed by dietitians over the years, cholesterol is a fatty substance which occurs naturally in the cells of all animals, including humans. It is manufactured in the liver and used to transport fatty acids around the body in the blood. The more fat and, in particular, saturated (usually animal) fats, are eaten, the more cholesterol the liver produces to enable the fatty acids to be transported, stored or burned up as energy. Having delivered the fatty acids to the body organs, the cholesterol is left – a fatty, sludgy substance which often ends up on the inner walls of the arteries, where it forms a main component of atheroma which, if allowed to build up on the coronary arteries, leads to atherosclerosis – a blocked artery causing a heart attack.

Cholesterol, therefore, forms the link between saturated fats and heart disease, and it is because of the problems caused by excess cholesterol that dietitians recommend limiting the amount of fat, particularly saturated fats, consumed. (*see also* DIET, FATS, NUTRITION)

CHOLLA (*see* CHANNA)

CHOP A slice of meat 2.5 cm (1 inch) to 3.5 cm (1½ inches) thick, usually mutton, lamb, pork or veal. A chop generally includes a rib, but may also be cut from the chump or tail end of the loin, and is then known as a chump chop. Neck chops are usually referred to as cutlets. Chops may be roasted, casseroled, grilled or fried. (*see also* LAMB, PORK, VEAL)

CHOPPING Cutting food into small neat pieces without damaging the tissues. This may be done before or after cooking, with a very sharp knife and a chopping board, in a food processor or in any of several other gadgets specially designed for the purpose.

CHOP SUEY This Chinese dish originated in the United States and is the Chinese method of dealing with leftovers. Chop suey can be made of thin strips of raw chicken, pork or beef, cooked with onions in a little oil, with bean sprouts, mushrooms and other vegetables. Chicken stock, soy sauce, sugar and salt are added to taste and the whole is thickened, if necessary, with cornflour. It should be served in a shallow bowl with a flat omelette on top. This omelette is intended as a cover to keep the food hot. (To eat the chop suey, you lift back this 'lid', help yourself to chop suey, then replace the 'lid'.) Chop suey is usually served with rice or noodles.

CHORIZO There are many varieties of this famous Spanish sausage, all containing pork and pimiento. Some varieties are sold ready-cooked, while others may be sliced and fried before eating. It is used in the classic Spanish dish, *paella*.

CHOROGI (*see* ARTICHOKE, CHINESE)

CHOUX (*see* PASTRY)

CHOW-CHOW (*see* CHAYOTE)

CHOWDER An American stew-like soup that originated in New England. Its main ingredient is usually shellfish, e.g. clam chowder. The name is thought to have derived from the French *chaudière*, meaning stew pot.

CHRISTMAS CAKE A large cake traditionally made in Britain to celebrate Christmas. A Christmas cake is usually a rich fruit cake flavoured with spices and brandy, covered in almond paste and decorated (sometimes elaborately) with royal icing. Seasonal cake decorations may include sprigs of holly and miniature Christmas trees, Santa Claus, reindeer and snowmen. The fruit cake itself may be made several months in advance to allow the flavours to mellow.

CHRISTMAS PUDDING (Plum Pudding) A steamed pudding traditionally served in Britain after the turkey on Christmas day. It is made from a very rich mixture of dried fruit, candied peel, nuts, suet, breadcrumbs, eggs, flour, sugar and spices, packed into a pudding basin and steamed very slowly. A Christmas pudding improves with keeping and is often made up to a year in advance.

In days gone by, Christmas puddings were always shaped like a large ball and steamed wrapped in a cloth. Silver sixpences or charms were dropped into the mixture before cooking, to be discovered in portions at the table. This tradition is decreasing, since sixpences no longer exist and coins are no longer made of pure silver. (It is recommended that any modern coins used should be wrapped in several layers of aluminium foil before they are added to the pudding mixture before cooking, or stuck into the cooked pudding just before serving.) A Christmas pudding is still served in a traditional way, however. After being turned out, the pudding is usually topped with a sprig of holly, soaked in brandy or rum and carried flaming to the table. Traditional accompaniments include brandy or rum butter (*see* BRANDY BUTTER) and sherry sauce.

CHRISTOPHINE (*see* CHAYOTE)

CHUB A freshwater fish of the carp family that is found in most European rivers. It has little flavour and lots of bones, so is not particularly popular for cooking and eating. However, it can be prepared and cooked like carp (*see* CARP).

CHUCK STEAK (*see* BEEF)

CHUFA (Tiger Nut, Earth Almond, Earthnut, Rush Nut, Galingale, Pignut) A small, wrinkled brown tuber that is produced by a plant that grows mainly in Mediterranean Europe and Portugal. Chufas have crisp white flesh with a sweet, nutty flavour and can be eaten as nuts or used to flavour ice cream. Their most important use, however, is to make *horchata de chufa*, a popular milky drink that is served all over Spain.

CHUMP The name given to the rear end of a loin of lamb, mutton or pork. It is often cut into chump chops which are less tender than loin chops and are therefore a more economical buy. (*see also* LAMB, PORK)

CHUTNEY A chutney is a thick piquant purée of fruit and/or vegetables which is usually served as a condiment. Chutneys were first made in India and introduced to Britain in colonial times. However, what is known as a chutney in Britain today is very different from the original Indian chutney.

Chutneys are often used as a method of preserving fresh fruit or vegetables, or of using up excess produce, such as tomatoes, which need not be in the best condition. A mixture of finely chopped or minced fresh fruit and/or vegetables is cooked to a pulp with vinegar, sugar, spices and salt, then packed into clean hot jars and sealed with vinegar-proof lids. Chutneys should be allowed to mature for 2–3 months before eating. They are delicious served with cold meats or cheese; mango chutney is commonly served with curry. Commercially-produced chutneys are readily available. (*see also* RELISH)

CIDER An alcoholic drink made from the fermented juice of apples. Special 'cider' apples are grown in parts of England (especially the southwest), Normandy and northern Spain, from which cider is produced. The flavour of cider varies from region to region but there are generally two types – sweet and dry (or 'champagne') cider.

Most cider is made from a blend of apple varieties. The fruit is crushed to a pulp, then the juice is extracted and left for about a month to ferment naturally. Dry cider is left until all the sugar has fermented before it is strained and bottled, while sweet cider is strained before all the sugar has fermented. Dry cider is therefore more alcoholic than sweet cider. Both still and sparkling ciders are made.

Cider can be used in cooking, and is a characteristic of recipes from south-west England, Normandy and Brittany. It also makes a very refreshing drink.

CILANTRO (*see* CORIANDER)

CINNAMON This is a popular spice with a sweet, pungent flavour. It is, in fact, the inner bark of a small evergreen tree which is grown mostly in Sri Lanka. It is available ground to a powder or in fine scrolled sticks or 'quills', as well as in rough pieces of bark, its more natural state. Cinnamon is widely used in all sweet, spicy baking, as a flavouring for chocolate dishes, on cheesecakes, in pork dishes, pickles and chutneys, and to flavour hot drinks, mulled wines and punches. (*see also* CASSIA)

CINZANO (*see* VERMOUTH)

CITRANGE A hybrid citrus fruit developed in America from the sweet orange and the trifoliate orange. It has a strong orange flavour but is more acid than the common orange. (*see also* CITRUS FRUIT)

CITRIC ACID A mild acid which occurs naturally in lemons and other citrus fruits. It is produced commercially and can be bought, usually from a chemist, in powdered form. It is used mainly in preserving (it helps to draw the natural pectin out of fruit), in soft drinks and in home wine making.

CITRON A fruit which resembles a lemon but is larger, longer and greener. The rind is used in candied form in cookery, being chopped and added to cakes, puddings and biscuits; a slice of candied citron peel is the traditional decoration for a Madeira cake. The flesh of the citron is too sour to eat raw but the fruit can be used to make marmalade. In Corsica, it is also used to make a liqueur known as *cedratine*.

CITRUS FRUIT The generic name for a group of fruits, all of which grow on trees or shrubs of the genus *Citrus*, found mostly in tropical or warm temperate regions. They are widely cultivated in Mediterranean countries and in the United States (particularly Florida and California).

The fruits vary from very sour to quite sweet, but all have a slightly acid flavour and are high in pectin and vitamin C, making them ideal for making marmalade. All citrus fruits are covered in a thick skin consisting of a layer of white pith and an outer, brightly coloured coating known as the rind. The group includes oranges, lemons, limes, grapefruit, tangerines, bergamots, ugli fruit, kumquats and citrons, as well as various hybrids, such as the clementine, tangelo, citrange and limequat.

Sweeter varieties of citrus fruits may be eaten fresh as a dessert or included in fresh fruit salads. Tangerines and clementines, in particular, are very popular snack fruits. Whole lemons, lemon juice and lemon rind have countless uses in cooking. Lemons and limes may be sliced and served in drinks. Grapefruit are commonly served for breakfast. All citrus fruits may be used in preserves.

(*see also* CITRANGE, CITRON, GRAPEFRUIT, LEMON, LIME, ORANGE, TANGERINE, etc.)

CLAFOUTIS A French dessert consisting of fresh fruit (usually cherries) baked in a batter. The pudding is served warm, sometimes sprinkled with brandy and dusted with icing sugar.

CLAM This is a shellfish of the mollusc variety. It is known as a bivalve because it lives within a pair of hinged shells. Clams can be found along the coast of both sides of the North Atlantic and are also cultivated in special clam beds in parts of France.

There are many different species of clam, varying considerably in size. These are some of the most common:

Carpet shell clams are whitish, yellow or light brown in colour, sometimes with darker brown markings. They grow up to about 7.5 cm (3 inches) in diameter.

Common otter shell clams are white, fawn-coloured or light yellow. They have a longer-shaped shell than other clams and grow up to 12.5 cm (5 inches).

Quahog clams are also known as 'little-neck' or 'hard-shell' clams. They are dirty white, greyish or brown in colour and grow up to about 12.5 cm (5 inches).

Rayed-trough shell clams are cream-coloured with purplish markings. They grow up to about 12.5 cm (5 inches).

Soft-shelled clams are also known as 'long-neck' or 'steamer' clams and are a dirty white or fawn colour. They grow up to 15 cm (6 inches).

Venus shell clams are shiny red or pink and look as if they have been varnished. They grow up to about 7.5 cm (3 inches).

Warty venus clams are dirty white or brownish coloured. Their shells are quite plump with ridges that develop into wart-line spines. They grow up to about 7.5 cm (3 inches).

Wedge shell clams are also known as 'bean' clams and are one of the smallest clams, generally under 4 cm (1 ½ inches). Their colour varies from white or yellow to brown or purple.

Clams are sold live in their shells and smaller ones can be eaten raw. As with all shellfish, it is important to buy them from a reputable source as they can be infected with bacteria. Large clams can be cooked and served as for mussels (*see* MUSSEL). They are famous as the main ingredient of a North American soup, clam chowder. Also popular in America are 'clambakes', beach picnics at which clams, as well as other shellfish, are cooked and eaten.

Clams are in season all year, but best in autumn. They are also available frozen, canned and smoked from supermarkets throughout the year.

To prepare raw clams: Scrub the clams with a stiff scrubbing brush. Hold each clam in a cloth or glove in the palm of one hand and prize open the shells at the hinge. (A special clam knife is available for doing this.) Alternatively, if they are to be cooked, clams can be heated for a minute or two in a covered saucepan or in the oven to encourage them to open. Loosen the clams and serve them in one half-shell.

CLARET In England, this is the name given to the red wine from the Bordeaux district of France. The term may also be used for other red wines, but in this case the country of origin should be given, for example Australian claret. The Bordeaux wines were first given this name in the Middle Ages to distinguish them from other wines that were also shipped out from Bordeaux. The Bordeaux wines are a paler shade of red (*plus clair*) than the other wines.

Claret jelly, made with half claret and half water, flavoured with lemon and suitably coloured, makes a good party dessert. (*see also* BORDEAUX)

CLARIFIED BUTTER (*see* BUTTER)

CLARIFYING Clearing or purifying. The term is used mainly to denote the releasing of fat from water, meat juices, salt, etc., so that it may be used for frying, pastry-making and so on.

The process of clearing jellies and consommés is also sometimes called clarifying. This is usually done by adding egg whites which, during boiling, rise to the surface of the consommé or jelly in a grey froth that coagulates and forms a filter which traps all impurities, leaving a crystal clear liquid beneath. (*see also* BUTTER, CONSOMMÉ, FATS, GHEE)

CLARY A herb from the same family as sage, and grown in southern Europe. It has tall pink, white and mauve flowering spikes and smells a little like grapefruit, with a bitter flavour. It was once quite popular in cooking but is little used today.

CLEMENTINE A hybrid citrus fruit, developed from the tangerine and the bitter (Seville) orange. The fruit was first grown accidentally in Algeria in 1902, when it was discovered in the garden of a priest, Father Pierre Clément, hence its name.

Clementines are imported to Britain from Spain, Morocco and South Africa and are most plentiful in the winter months. They are small, round and juicy, with a sweet flavour, thin bright orange skin and few pips, making them a very popular snack fruit. They make a good addition to a mixed fruit marmalade. (*see also* CITRUS FRUIT, ORANGE, TANGERINE)

CLOTTING The name given to the process of applying a gentle heat to cream, producing the thick clotted cream of the south-west of England. (*see also* CREAM)

CLOUDBERRY This soft berry slightly resembles a raspberry, varying in colour from pale golden to blush pink, with a very sweet flavour. It can sometimes be found in hilly areas in the north of Britain, but it grows mostly in Scandinavia and Finland. Unfortunately, it is so delicate that it is rarely cultivated.

CLOVE When whole, this spice resembles small nails, and it gets its name from the Latin word for nail, *clavus*. It is in fact the tiny dried flower bud of a large evergreen tree that grows best near the sea in tropical regions. The main clove growing area is now the island of Zanzibar, although the tree originated in the 'spice islands' of South-East Asia.

Cloves are frequently used whole, either added directly to a dish or pushed into an onion or other fruit or vegetable that is to be used as a flavouring, but they are also available ground. Cloves have a distinctive pungent flavour and are used mainly to flavour apple dishes, Christmas pudding, mincemeat, bread sauce, and to stud ham and pork. They are also good with pumpkin and in mulled wine. Whole cloves are best removed from a dish before serving.

Cloves contain a powerful oil with antiseptic and anaesthetic qualities which can be used to relieve toothache.

COALFISH (*see* COLEY)

COATING A term used in cooking to describe covering foods with flour, batter, egg and breadcrumbs, egg white or some other mixture before frying. Coating is done in order to protect the food during cooking or to improve its flavour or appearance. A coating batter should be thick enough to adhere to the food, yet not so thick that it will be stodgy when cooked. When coating with egg and breadcrumbs, excess breadcrumbs should always be shaken off, as should excess flour. Foods most often coated include fish, meat and a variety of fruit and vegetables. (*see also* BATTER, FRITTER)

The term is also used to describe the covering of sweet items or cakes with chocolate, icing or caramel.

COB (*see* HAZELNUT)

COBBLER A sweetened cooling drink, usually made of a mixture of fruit and wine or liqueur, with ice.

The name also applies to meat or fruit dishes which have a topping of scone rounds. The scones may be flavoured with herbs, cheese, spices or dried fruits to add additional flavours that complement the other ingredients in the dish. The rounds of scone dough are usually arranged and cooked on top of the meat or fruit. (*see also* SCONE)

COB NUT (*see* HAZELNUT)

COBURG CAKES (Coburg Buns) Small sponge cakes containing syrup and usually flavoured with spices.

COCHINEAL A red colouring matter obtained from the female of a small species of beetle found in Mexico. The beetle is dried and ground to produce the pigment. Carmine is also derived from cochineal.

Cochineal is available in small bottles and can be used to give various shades of pink and red to sweetmeats, cakes, buns, biscuits, cold desserts and so on, and also to improve the colour of jams and bottled fruits. Commercially, cochineal is used as a colouring (E120) in alcoholic drinks, but it is used less these days than it used to be. It is very expensive and many people, including vegetarians, object to the use of this colouring when other colourings, not derived from animals, are available. It has been replaced in manufacturing to some extent by a synthetic coal tar dye known as Ponceau (E124).

COCK-A-LEEKIE A thick soup that is a Scottish speciality, the ingredients of which include chicken, leeks and barley.

COCKLE (Arkshell) A small bivalve mollusc shellfish. There are numerous varieties of cockle, commonly found around the coasts of Britain and Europe, as well as in other parts of the world. The colour of their shells varies from beige, pale pink and cream to a dark blue, but they can all be recognized by the deep ridges radiating from the hinge side of their shells.

These days, cockles are usually sold cooked and shelled, ready to be added to a cooked dish or sauce. They are also sold pickled and bottled and, in this state, can be eaten straight from the jar as an appetizer. If you do come across live cockles, they can be treated as clams and mussels (*see* MUSSELS), then eaten plain with vinegar or used in dishes in place of mussels or oysters.

Cockles are available most of the year, but at their best from September to April. Be sure that any live cockles you buy have been gathered from absolutely clean, unpolluted waters, and in any case, they should always be left to soak in clean water for several hours, or overnight, before cooking.

To prepare: Scrub well under cold running water, then leave to soak for several hours, or overnight, before cooking.

To cook: Place the cockles in a saucepan with a little water and heat gently, shaking the pan, for about 5 minutes or until the shells open. Remove the cockles from their shells and cook for a further 4 minutes. Overcooking will make them tough.

To serve: Freshly cooked cockles should be served plain, seasoned with a little vinegar and black pepper, and accompanied by brown bread and butter.

COCKTAIL A short or long alcoholic drink, consisting of a variety of ingredients so well blended together (by thorough stirring or shaking in a cocktail shaker, usually with crushed ice) that no one flavour predominates. Cocktails first became popular in America and are still very much associated with the American way of life.

A cocktail may be based on a spirit or on a blend of drinks, such as Pimm's, mixed with soda or lemonade. Very often, cocktails have been given names which reflect their place of origin, the name of their inventor or their contents, such as Manhattan, Tom Collins or Black Velvet.

Cocktails, which traditionally are offered before lunch or dinner, may be served in short or tall glasses and are often decorated with a stuffed olive, a curl of lemon peel or a Maraschino cherry; they should be served very cold.

Following an American trend, cocktails have enjoyed a revival in popularity in Britain recently, both for serving at home and in cocktail bars, clubs and restaurants. Cocktail-making equipment (shakers, stirrers, measures, etc.) can be bought quite easily, as can books containing cocktail recipes, although the precise content of a cocktail varies enormously according to taste. Some of the most famous alcoholic cocktails include Martini (sweet and dry), Daiquiri, Harvey Wallbanger, Bloody Mary and Tequila Sunrise Non-alcoholic cocktails, based on fruit and vegetable juices, have also become popular in recent years.

In cookery, the word 'cocktail' is also used to describe a cold hors d'oeuvre which consists of a mixture of ingredients, for example prawn cocktail, melon and grape cocktail, etc. It is also sometimes applied to a mixture of fruit (sometimes canned) to be served as a dessert on its own or with ice cream.

COCOA (*see* CHOCOLATE)

COCONUT The fruit of the coconut palm, a tree native to South-East Asia but which now grows in all tropical areas. In the countries where they grow, coconuts are harvested when young and green, and their watery juice is served as a refreshing drink. It is the mature fruit that is most familiar in Britain. It has a hard, hairy brown shell containing sweet white flesh and a thicker liquid known as coconut milk which also makes a delicious drink. Coconut features strongly in the cooking of the Caribbean, India, Sri Lanka and South-East Asia, where it is used in soups, stews, curries and drinks.

Coconuts are a rich source of vitamins, protein and natural oils, but unlike other vegetable oils, coconut oil is a saturated fat and high in cholesterol. The flesh of a coconut can be eaten raw, puréed in a blender with the milk to make coconut cream, or it can be shredded and used as an ingredient in baking or Oriental cooking. Freshly grated coconut can be toasted in the oven and stored for up to four days. Fresh coconut milk can be kept, covered, in the refrigerator for up to two days. Coconut flesh is also available flaked or shredded and dried (desiccated).

A version of coconut milk can be made by soaking grated fresh or desiccated coconut in boiling water. Leave until cool, then strain and squeeze through muslin. 'Creamed coconut' is sold in blocks and can be sliced and used in the same way to make coconut milk to use in curries or other dishes.

To select: When choosing, look for a coconut that is heavy for its size and test it for freshness by shaking it to make sure it contains liquid. There should be no signs of mould around the three indentations (eyes) at the top of the coconut.

To prepare: Puncture two of the eyes with a hammer and screwdriver and drain out the milk. Open the coconut by cracking the shell all around at the widest part. Separate the halves and prize the flesh from the shell with a small sharp knife.

To toast: Spread freshly grated coconut on a baking sheet and toast in the oven at 180°C (350°F) mark 4 until golden brown.

COCONUT ICE A confection made by mixing desiccated coconut into a boiled mixture of sugar and milk. It is often coloured pink, or half pink and half white, and left to set in a tin before being cut into bars. (*see also* SWEETS)

COCONUT MILK (*see* COCONUT)

COCOTTE The French name for the type of lidded cooking pot known in England as a casserole. The term is also used, however, to describe dishes cooked in small individual soufflé or ramekin dishes, such as eggs *en cocotte*. (*see also* CASSEROLE, RAMEKIN)

COCUM (*see* KOKUM)

COD Perhaps the most common fish eaten in Europe and America, cod is a large round sea fish found in the cold waters of the North Atlantic. Once plentiful around English shores, fishing for cod now takes place further afield, particularly around Iceland.

Cod is the largest of a fish family which includes coley, haddock and whiting. Small cod are known as codling. Cod may be sold whole when young and small, or as fillets or steaks when large. Cod has close, white flesh and it can be grilled, baked, fried in batter or used in various cooked dishes. It is available all year but at its best from October to May. Cod fillets and steaks are also available frozen.

Cod's roe is available either fresh, canned or smoked. Smoked cod's roe does not need cooking and can be used to make the Greek dish, *taramasalata*, although traditionally this should be made from the roe of grey mullet (*see* TARAMA).

Salt cod fillets are sold in some ethnic shops. Most salt cod sold in Britain is imported from Spain where it is known as *bacalao*. Look for fillets that are thick and have white flesh; when not fresh, salt cod takes on a yellow appearance. Soak for 24 hours in cold water, changing the water several times, before use. Drain and remove any skin and bones before cooking. Salt cod tends to be uninteresting cooked alone, but is good made up with other well-flavoured ingredients.

Smoked cod fillets are taken from large fish, skinned and cold-smoked. They are dyed, often to a bright orange yellow, though manufacturers are responding to public demand for uncoloured fish. To cook, poach the fillets in milk, water or *court bouillon* for 10–15 minutes. (*see also* SMOKED FISH)

Dried cod is also known as stockfish and has been dried, usually whole, in the sun. It needs long soaking before cooking and is used mostly in Scandinavian recipes.

COD LIVER OIL An oil which is extracted from the fresh liver of cod by heating. It is then cooled and processed. When sold, it is pale yellow in colour. The oil can be relatively tasteless if it is prepared from the fish liver when this is absolutely fresh, and if it is kept from contact with the air; for this reason the plants for extracting the oil are now sited at or near to ports so that processing can take place as soon as fish are brought ashore.

Cod liver oil contains large, though varying, amounts of vitamins A and D, and the oil used to be given to small children as a vitamin supplement. Nowadays, commercially prepared vitamin drops are used instead.

CODDLING A method of soft-boiling eggs. The eggs are put into boiling water, then the pan is removed from the heat and left to stand for 8–10 minutes. Coddled eggs were particularly popular in the Victorian era, when they were cooked in special containers or egg coddlers. Shaped like egg cups with a lid, these were often made of china. The egg was cracked into the cup and butter, salt, pepper and sometimes cream were added. The cup was then covered, placed in a pan of boiling water and cooked as above. The egg was served straight from the cup. (*see also* EGGS)

COD'S ROE (*see* COD)

COEUR À LA CRÈME (Fromage à la crème) A French cheese made from sour milk. The curd is drained, mixed with cream and again drained in special heart-shaped moulds lined with muslin. It is usually turned out and served as a dessert with fresh cream and sugar or salt. It can also be served with fresh strawberries or raspberries and sugar. The cheese can also be made from a fresh cheese, such as curd cheese or *fromage frais*, and whisked egg whites are sometimes folded into the mixture before it is put in the moulds.

COFFEE A popular beverage all over the world, coffee has been imported into Britain for the past 300 years. It is derived from the berries of the coffee tree which is grown in a number of tropical countries. As they ripen, the berries turn first green, then red to reddish-black. Coffee beans are extracted from bright red berries, each of which contains two small oval green seeds encased in a fine silvery skin which is protected by a tough outer husk.

Once the seeds are ripe, they are picked and the red pulp is removed. They then undergo a wet or dry process to remove all traces of the pulp, are dried in the sun and finally have the skins removed by machine. After this, the beans are graded according to size and quality.

The flavour of coffee beans varies enormously, depending on climate, soil, picking, processing, storing and transport. The buyers of the beans and, where appropriate, the blenders, are the people who aim for consistency of taste, particularly if the beans are destined to become instant coffee. The best, most finely flavoured varieties are known as *arabicas* and grow at altitudes of 2000 to 6500 feet above sea level. *Robusta* varieties are coarser, with a poorer flavour, and grow between sea level and 2000 feet.

Buying Coffee

You can buy green beans and roast them yourself either in the oven or in a special electric roaster, but it is more reliable to buy them ready-roasted in small quantities from a specialist coffee merchant, good grocer or supermarket. For best flavour, the beans should be freshly roasted and used within a few days, at most a week. If you do not have regular access to a good supplier, buy larger quantities periodically and store them in the freezer. The beans will keep for six months frozen with virtually no loss of flavour.

Coffee is also sold ready ground in vacuum sealed containers which often specify the method which should be used for making the coffee (e.g. filter). Instant coffees come in powder or freeze-dried granule form, the latter being better flavoured and more expensive. There is also coffee essence (usually mixed with chicory) which has a sweet flavour. The essence is best used in cooking or for making quick iced coffee.

All coffee beans naturally contain caffeine but, for those who want to avoid this, decaffeinated coffee is available in beans, ground and instant forms, with only marginal loss of flavour.

Types of Coffee

The subtle variations of flavour of individual coffees are endless. It is worth trying them separately and in a blend until you find the one you like best. Among the types of coffee available are:

Brazilian The flavour is very smooth and mild and has no bitterness or acidity.

Chagga Chagga coffee is produced by the Wa-Chagga tribe living on the slopes of Mount Kilimanjaro in Tanzania. The beans are picked and washed in the mountain streams from the Kibo Glacier and then dried in the mountain air. This is a full bodied and usually medium to dark roast.

Colombian Colombian coffee is from South America and has a smooth, strong flavour with very little acidity.

Continental Blend A blend of dark roasted coffees with a strong flavour. Popular for drinking at breakfast.

Java A mature coffee from the East Indies with a subtle, mellow flavour. It is most suitable for drinking 'black' (without milk or cream) as an after-dinner coffee.

Kenya A very aromatic coffee with a pleasant sharpness. At its best when served 'black' as an after-dinner coffee.

Mocha Mocha is the traditional Turkish coffee. The flavour, traditionally described as 'gamey', is strong and subtle.

Mysore This coffee is a rich, full flavoured coffee from southern India.

Vienna This coffee is often sold already blended to give a smooth, subtly strong flavour.

The best way to discover which kinds of coffee you like best is to talk to a specialist coffee merchant and to buy small quantities of different types to try.

Making Coffee

If you buy coffee beans you need a coffee grinder, either electric or manual. You may also need special equipment for making the coffee unless you use the time-honoured method of pouring boiling water on to grounds in a jug, then straining.

Electric filter coffee machines work by heating the water and then pouring it through ground coffee in a filter into a glass jug on a heated plate. You can also buy plastic filter cones for use with filter papers on jugs, but this does not keep the coffee hot.

Espresso machines work by forcing water through coffee grounds under pressure. They may be electric or for use on a hob.

Other methods include the *cafetière* (a heatproof glass jug with a fine wire mesh plunger which is used to push the coffee grounds to the bottom before serving the coffee), glass vacuum machines (Cona), drip pots and electric percolators. For authentic Turkish and Greek coffee you need a special small, long-handled pan (known as an *ibrik*) which is wider at the bottom than the top.

Coffee Grinding Grades

The various methods for making coffee work best if the correct grade of ground coffee is used. The most suitable grinds for some common methods of brewing coffee are as follows:

Method	Grinding Grade
Filter/drip	Fine to medium
Jug	Coarse
Turkish	Fine
Cafetière (plunger)	Medium
Glass balloon/vacuum (Cona)	Medium fine or fine
Espresso	Very fine
Percolator	Medium or coarse

Serving Coffee

Allow 50 g (2 oz) coffee per 600 ml (1 pint) water. Coffee may be drunk black (without milk) or white with the addition of milk – allow one part hot milk to two parts coffee – or cream. Some people like to sweeten their coffee with sugar or honey, and some add alcohol (see below). Coffee should be served hot but not boiling and should not be kept hot for too long after making or the flavour will be spoiled.

Iced coffee is also a popular way to drink coffee. Hot strong black coffee is sweetened with sugar and left to chill, then poured over ice cubes in a glass and topped with whipped cream.

Cappuccino is an Italian version of coffee made by adding frothy cream or milk to strong black coffee. It is often served with a sprinkling of powdered chocolate on top. Turkish coffee is served strong and black, flavoured with cardamom.

Liqueur Coffee
Coffee served with alcohol added is known as liqueur coffee. The most famous of these is Irish or Gaelic coffee which is made by adding one part Irish whiskey to three or four parts very strong coffee, sweetened with sugar and topped with double cream. The cream is carefully poured over the back of a spoon on to the surface of the coffee so that it stays in a thick layer on top. Liqueur coffee is usually served in a glass.

Other popular liqueur coffees include Cointreau coffee, Caribbean coffee (made with rum), German coffee (made with kirsch), Normandy coffee (made with Calvados), Russian coffee (made with vodka), Calypso coffee (made with Tia Maria), Witch's coffee (made with strega and topped with a little grated lemon rind) and Curaçao coffee (made with curaçao and stirred with a stick of cinnamon).

Cooking with Coffee
Coffee is frequently used as a flavouring for ice creams, desserts, cakes and biscuits, sometimes combined with chocolate to produce a 'mocha' flavour. At one time, coffee essence was usually used to flavour a dish, but many recipes now use instant coffee dissolved in a little water. (*see also* COFFEE ESSENCE)

Coffee Substitutes
In recent years, concern has been expressed about the amount of coffee drunk by some people, particularly in relation to its caffeine content. Some varieties of instant coffee contain a substance produced from chicory root, which blends with the coffee and reduces the amount of caffeine each cup contains. Although this alters the flavour, many people have come to prefer a blend of coffee and chicory.

Decaffeinated coffee is widely available, and various coffee substitutes exist, including a drink made from roasted barley and another made from dandelion root and called 'dandelion coffee'. Although these substitutes do not taste very much like coffee, they are a useful alternative for those who prefer not to drink real coffee. (*see also* CAFFEINE)

COFFEE ESSENCE Bottled coffee concentrate (often mixed with chicory), which is used to impart flavour to both sweet and savoury dishes, and also for making quick iced coffee.

COGNAC (*see* BRANDY)

COING (*see* EAU-DE-VIE)

COINTREAU A popular French orange-flavoured liqueur, one of a number of different types of curaçao (*see* CURAÇAO).

COLA (Kola) A tropical African tree, the seeds or 'nuts' of which contain caffeine and have stimulating properties. Cola nuts are best known as an ingredient in many popular fizzy soft drinks. (*see also* CAFFEINE)

COLANDER A perforated metal or plastic (or occasionally earthenware) draining basket. Larger than a sieve, a colander can be used to drain vegetables or pasta after cooking, or to rinse fruit or vegetables before cooking. If you have not got a proper steamer, a colander can also be used to steam vegetables over a pan of boiling water.

COLBERT A French name given to a number of dishes, including *sole colbert*, which is coated in egg and breadcrumbs and fried, and *consommé à la colbert*, which is garnished with small poached eggs. Colbert butter is flavoured with tarragon and served with grilled or fried fish or meats. Colbert sauce, flavoured with spices, lemon, parsley and Madeira is also served with vegetables.

COLBY A mild, semi-hard American cheese, produced in Colby, Wisconsin. It is similar to a

Cheddar cheese, and easily recognized by its deep yellow colour and dark brown rind. It is a 'washed-curd' cheese, that is its curds are washed frequently, encouraging it to mature rapidly. It is popular served as a snack or in a salad.

COLCANNON A popular Irish dish made from a mixture of cooked vegetables, including potato and cabbage, flavoured with herbs and sometimes fried.

COLESLAW A salad with a base of finely shredded raw white cabbage dressed with cream or mayonnaise. Other ingredients that may be added include grated carrot, chopped apple, chopped onion, nuts, dried fruit, cooked sweetcorn, chopped celery and chopped green pepper. Coleslaw may be served with any savoury dish but usually accompanies cold meats and quiches. Ready-made coleslaws can be bought in delicatessens or supermarkets.

COLEY (Coalfish, Pollock, Saithe) A member of the cod family, this round sea fish has bluish-black skin. It is usually sold as fillets or cutlets, but may be sold whole. The well-flavoured meaty flesh is pinkish-grey, turning to white when cooked. Coley can be cooked in the same way as cod (*see* COD), but as it is inclined to be dry, it is improved if extra moisture is added during cooking. It is a good fish to use in soups, stews and pies. Coley is at its best from September to February.

COLLAR (*see* BACON)

COLLARD (*see* KALE)

COLLARED Pickled or salted meat which is rolled, boiled with suitable seasonings and served cold.

COLLEGE PUDDING An English suet pudding flavoured with dried fruits and spices. It may be steamed or baked in one large pudding basin or in individual dariole moulds (*see* DARIOLE).

COLLOP A term derived from the French *escalope*. It is used (chiefly in Scotland) to describe a small boneless piece of meat, but may also be applied to a savoury dish made of finely minced meat.

COLOCASSI Belonging to the same family as dasheen and eddoe, this is a root vegetable which can be used in many of the ways potato is used. It looks rather like a large, rough-skinned parsnip but has a thick white stalk. Colocassi features quite strongly in Greek Cypriot cooking.

COLOURINGS Edible food colourings or dyes have been added to foods since ancient times, in both home and factory. Commercially, their use has greatly increased over recent decades in line with a demand for more processed foods, because such processing often results in a loss of the natural colour preferred by the consumer. For example, we like canned peas to be an appetizing fresh green colour, but peas lose much of their natural colour when subjected to high temperatures in preparation for canning. The manufacturer may therefore choose to add a colouring to improve the colour of the peas, making them more appealing to the consumer, and therefore more likely to sell.

In the home, food colourings are mostly used to improve the appearance of a finished dish, for example green colouring may be added to a gooseberry fool or pistachio ice cream, and colourings of many shades are commonly used to colour icing for cake decorating. Spices, such as saffron and turmeric, are used to colour rice dishes and curries, as well as to add flavour.

Commercially, colourings are also used to ensure the same food is consistently the same colour, particularly if the customer is able to compare the colour of one jar of a particular food with another jar of the same food (jam, for instance). In the case of foods such as yogurt and soft drinks, additional colour may be added to meet the expectations of the consumer. For example, we expect a strawberry yogurt to be pink coloured, but the amount of real strawberries in the yogurt may not be sufficient to give the final product any colour at all, so the manufacturer may add some red food colouring to enhance the colour, thereby making the yogurt appear, and possibly even appear to taste, better.

Food dyes in common use include those that occur naturally as well as those that are produced synthetically. Natural colourings, such as cochineal, riboflavin, chlorophyll and carotene, tend to be less stable than synthetic dyes, and often fade more quickly. Synthetic colourings are chemically produced and include a number of dyes, known as 'coal tar' dyes, which at one time were made from coal tar but are now produced industrially. Commonly used coal tar dyes include amaranth, carmoisine and tartrazine. Among the coal tar dyes are a number of dyes known as 'azo dyes', so called because of their particular chemical structure. The most frequently used colouring is caramel, which gives a brown colour to beer, soft drinks, sauces, gravy browning, biscuits and sweets, amongst other foods.

Although the use of colourings was generally accepted for a great number of years, they became a common cause for concern during the nineteen eighties, when they were linked with a number of allergic reactions, including hyperactivity in children. Research into the possible side effects of consuming large quantities of colourings (particularly the azo dyes and caramel) led to public demand for a reduction in the use of colourings in processed foods. Manufacturers have responded to this demand by removing colourings from many foods, or by switching from synthetic to natural dyes. It is now common to see 'No artificial colouring' printed on a label as an added incentive to the consumer to buy the product.

In common with other additives, such as preservatives and sweeteners, the use of all food colourings is now strictly regulated in most countries, and the 'E' code, introduced in Britain in 1984, made it possible for consumers to identify the additives, including colourings, present in some foods. Since 1986, all packaged foods have had to carry a label which lists their ingredients, including all additives, in descending order by weight. Food colourings are numbered E100 to E199. However, these food regulations do not at present extend to foods that are sold loose, or to certain 'hidden' additives which are used in the production processes of some foods, though they may not appear in the food itself. For example, there are no regulations governing the use of colourings in the feed given to battery hens, which help produce eggs with deep yellow yolks, similar to the yolks of free-range eggs.

(*see also* ADDITIVE, ALKANNA, AMARANTH, ASPARTAME, ANNATTO, CARMOISINE, COCHINEAL, TARTRAZINE)

COLWICK CHEESE A traditional English cheese made from cows' milk. It is usually sold unsalted to be served as a dessert, but is also available salted.

COMBINATION OVEN A comparatively recent development, a combination oven is a versatile piece of kitchen equipment which provides a choice of cooking methods in one appliance. It can be used as a microwave cooker or a conventional oven, or the two cooking methods can be used at the same time.

When the oven is used to cook food by the conventional method, the oven usually operates as a convection (fan-assisted) oven, that is the food is heated by continuously circulating hot air. When it is used as a microwave cooker, the food is cooked by microwaves and the oven functions in the same way as any other microwave cooker. Some combination ovens are available that use halogen heat as a method of cooking instead of the convection method. Halogen heat can also be used in combination with microwaves. Some combination ovens also incorporate a grill, which can be used on its own or in combination with microwaves.

Combination ovens are available in table-top models, like the standard microwave cooker, or in full-size, built-in models. Controls vary from high-tech electronic digital touch-controls to push buttons and dials. Various additional features and accessories are available, such as cooking by autosensor and a pre-programmed roasting control.

Apart from its versatility, the main advantage of a combination oven is its ability to cook food almost as fast as a microwave cooker, while at the same time producing cooked food with the appetizing brown colour that is usually only achieved in a conventional oven. A combination oven is ideal for cooking roast meats, pastry, bread, cakes and biscuits.

COMFREY A member of the borage family, comfrey is now one of the less common herbs. Its leaves and flowers can be used fresh in salads, or it is used dried to make a tisane. The dried root may also be used as a flavouring.

COMMON BEAN (*see* BEAN, FRENCH)

COMMON EEL (*see* EEL)

COMPOTE A dish of fresh or dried fruit stewed in sugar syrup. A compote may be made from one fruit or from a mixture of fruits, and is sometimes flavoured with spices, lemon, orange, almonds, red wine or a liqueur. A compote may be served hot or cold as a dessert or for breakfast, or if the fruit is cooked until very soft, it may be puréed and used as a filling for turnovers or pies.

The name compote is also sometimes given to stews made from game birds, such as pigeon or partridge, which are cooked until the meat is very tender.

COMPOTIER A large shallow dish, usually made of glass, on a raised base. It may be used to serve compotes or other desserts, or simply as a fruit bowl.

CONCASSER A French term used to describe food that is finely or roughly chopped. It is most often applied to tomatoes which have been skinned, seeded and chopped, but may also describe roughly chopped herbs, or even crushed ice.

CONCHIGLIE (*see* PASTA)

CONDÉ This French name is most often given to a dessert consisting of a thick moulded rice pudding served with stewed fruit, but it is also the name of a pastry coated with almond-flavoured royal icing. It may also be given to savoury dishes which contain a purée of red kidney beans.

CONDENSED MILK (*see* MILK)

CONDIMENT The general name for a number of strongly-flavoured sauces, pickles, relishes, vinegars and other items, including salt, pepper and mustard, which are served at table as an accompaniment to other foods. A condiment should complement and heighten the flavour of the food it is served with, while adding extra interest and stimulating the appetite. Some condiments are traditionally served with certain foods, such as horseradish with roast beef, mayonnaise with salad, mustard with sausages, and pickles and chutneys with cold meats and cheese.

CONE (*see* CORNET)

CONFECTIONERS' CUSTARD (Crème Pâtissière, French Pastry Cream) A rich cream mixture made from a thick custard, usually flavoured with vanilla, though other flavourings, such as chocolate, can be added. Whisked egg whites, whipped cream or butter cream icing may also be added to lighten the mixture. As confectioners' custard is so thick, it can be used as a filling for pastry without making the pastry soggy. It is mainly used as a filling for profiteroles, éclairs, *mille-feuilles* and Danish pastries, but may also be used in tarts and other desserts.

Confectioners' Custard

2 eggs
50 g (2 oz) caster sugar
30 ml (2 level tbsp) plain flour
30 ml (2 level tbsp) cornflour
300 ml (¹/₂ pint) milk
a few drops of vanilla essence

Beat the eggs and sugar together until really thick and pale in colour. Sift and beat in the flour and cornflour and a little cold milk to make a smooth paste. Heat the rest of the milk in a saucepan until almost boiling and pour on to the egg mixture, stirring well all the time. Return the mixture to the saucepan and stir over a low heat until the mixture boils. Add vanilla essence to taste and cook for a further 2–3 minutes. Cover and allow to cool before using as required.

Makes 300 ml (¹/₂ pint)

CONFIT The French name for a preserve, usually made with portions of duck, goose or pork, which undergo lengthy cooking and are then sealed in their own cooking fat. It is one of the oldest methods of preserving and is a speciality of south-western France, where pieces of duck confit are traditionally used to make *cassoulet* (*see* CASSOULET).

CONGER EEL (*see* EEL)

CONGRESS TART This is a small pastry tart spread with jam and filled with a mixture of ground almonds, sugar and egg. Congress tarts are often decorated with a cross made of pastry strips or topped with glacé icing. They can be made at home, but are usually bought ready-made.

CONSERVE A conserve consists of whole, sometimes chopped, fruits suspended in a thick syrup. In most cases, the fruit is layered with an equal quantity of sugar and left for 24 hours to extract the juices, before boiling for a short time. Fruits which make good conserves are strawberries, raspberries and loganberries. Conserves are potted and stored in the same way as jam, though they do not have the same keeping qualities. However, they have a flavour which is very much closer to the flavour of the fresh fruit, and they make excellent desserts when served with cream or custard.

The name, conserve, is also sometimes given to jam, especially strawberry jam, which is made using whole fruit.

CONSISTENCY A term used to describe the texture of a mixture, for example the consistency of a cake mixture or bread dough may be said to be firm, stiff, dropping or soft.

CONSOMMÉ A concentrated and clarified stock. Consommé is made by boiling strained veal, beef or poultry stock until it is reduced and concentrated, then clarifying it by cooking again with egg whites. A consommé may be served as a soup, with other flavourings added, or may be used as the basis of another dish. A consommé can become gelatinous when chilled and extra gelatine is sometimes added so that it will set to a jelly that can be chopped and used as a garnish. Consommé is also available canned. (*see also* CLARIFYING, SOUP, STOCK)

CONTACT GRILL (Infra-red Grill) This piece of kitchen equipment consists of a hinged pair of non-stick heated plates between which you can cook any flat food (chops, burgers, steaks), cooking both sides simultaneously. They can also cook foil-wrapped vegetables and fish.

Some contact grills come supplied with a baking tin, which increases the versatility of the grill by producing what is, in effect, a mini-oven between the heated plates. You can buy a separate baking tin of a suitable size if your grill is not supplied with one.

Contact grills run off a 13-amp socket outlet, so are cheap to run and are a useful buy for anyone who does not need to cook food in large quantities. They are also good buys for people with built-under continental ovens who find the grilling position inconvenient.

CONTRE-FILET (*see* STEAK)

COOKIE Originally the American word for sweet biscuits, cookie is also the name given in Britain to some types of biscuits, especially those, such as brownies, that have a softer texture than the traditional crisp English biscuit.

In Scotland, the name cookie is also given to a glazed bread roll made from an enriched yeast dough with dried fruit added.

COPPA An Italian ham cut from the shoulder. It is more fatty than *prosciutto*, but in its cured form, *coppa cruda*, it is frequently served as part of a classic Italian *antipasto* (hors d'oeuvre). *Coppa di Corse* is a similar smoked ham produced in Corsica. *Coppa cotta* is a cooked version typical of central Italy, made from the pressed cooked meat of pig's head and tongue. (*see also* HAM, PANCETTA, PROSCIUTTO)

COPPER A red-coloured metal that is an excellent conductor of heat, making it a popular but expensive metal for making cooking utensils. Copper also heats up and cools down very quickly, so it is much easier to control the cooking of foods in copper saucepans. Unfortunately, however, unless copper pans are used frequently and kept scrupulously clean and dry, a green coating known as *verdigris* is likely to develop on them, and this can prove toxic if allowed into contact with food. For this reason, copper pans are often lined with tin (or 'tinned').

Tinned copper pans are ideal for cooking most foods, and the tin lining can be renewed when it becomes worn, but it is not possible to boil sugar or make jam in a tinned copper pan as the high temperatures required will melt the tin. Some stainless steel saucepans have a copper base, to help conduct heat more efficiently.

Many chefs insist on using nothing but a solid copper bowl for whisking egg whites. This is because a chemical reaction takes place between copper and raw egg white, strengthening the protein in the egg and enabling it to stretch further and increase in volume. Special round-bottomed solid copper bowls are available specifically for whisking egg whites.

Copper is also one of the elements present in very small quantities in the human body, and is important to the formation of red blood cells, amongst other things. Good dietary sources of copper include oysters, yeast, liver and chocolate.

COQ AU VIN A famous French dish consisting of chicken cooked in red wine, flavoured with brandy, onion, carrot, garlic and herbs, served with button onions and mushrooms, and garnished with fried bread croûtons.

COQUILLE, EN This French term is used to describe dishes (usually shellfish) that are served in the shell, or made to resemble a shell.

COQUILLES ST. JACQUES (*see* SCALLOP)

CORDIAL Originally, a cordial was a spirit sweetened and infused with fruit or other agent to add flavour and scent. It was supposed to have some stimulating effect on the heart, hence the name, which means of or belonging to the heart. This product is now more often called a liqueur and the word 'cordial' is applied to a sweet fruit drink with no alcoholic content, or to a concentrated fruit drink (as in lime juice cordial).

CORE To remove the hard, indigestible centre of certain foods, particularly fruits, such as apples, pears and pineapples. The term is also used to describe removing the centre of kidneys.

CORIANDER (Chinese Parsley, Cilantro) A herb plant grown both for its leaves and its seeds. Native to southern Europe, coriander is used in Chinese, Japanese, Indian, Middle Eastern and Mexican cooking. Its chopped leaves add an unusual flavour to salads and chilled soups; used whole the leaves make an alternative garnish to parsley.

Coriander seeds (also known as *dhania*) have a mild, sweet, orangey flavour and are sold whole or ground. Coriander is an ingredient of most curry powders and pickling spice and is also used in chutney, meat dishes (especially pork), casseroles, Greek-style dishes, apple pies, pea soup and baked goods.

The root of the coriander plant may also be used, either as a vegetable in casseroles and curries, or as a flavouring, as in Thai cooking.

CORN (Maize) A general term which used to be applied in England to all kinds of grain, such as wheat, rye, oats, barley, maize, etc., but is now applied only to maize or sweetcorn. In Scotland, the word sometimes denotes oats, while in America it mostly refers to maize.

Maize originated in Central America, where it was first used by the American Indians. It is now widely grown and used all over the world. The grains grow on the plant around a central cob and are surrounded by large fibrous leaves with tasselled tops. There are two main varieties – sweetcorn (*see* SWEETCORN), which is grown and used as a vegetable, and grain corn, which has smaller, harder kernels that are difficult to cook whole. Grain corn is often ground to a meal or flour.

Cornmeal may be yellow or white, coarse or fine; Italian yellow cornmeal is called *polenta*. In the southern United States, cornmeal is widely used to make corn cakes and cornbread, though as corn lacks gluten, it must be mixed with other flours to make leavened bread. One variety of corn produces blue-black, rather than yellow, grains. When ground, this is known as blue cornmeal and is popular in the United States.

Masa harina (Tamale flour) is a specially processed cornflour which is used for making Mexican tortillas.

Hominy is whole dried corn without the yellow husk. It needs to be softened by boiling in water or milk before being fried, baked or added to a casserole.

Grits are coarsely ground dried corn and may be yellow or white, depending on whether the outer husk has been removed. Grits without the husks are called hominy grits (see above). Grits are cooked in water until soft, then traditionally served in America with bacon and eggs for breakfast. Hominy grits may also be used to make a type of porridge.

Cornflour, or cornstarch, is a finely ground white powder produced from corn kernels. It is lighter than wheat flour and is mainly used as a thickening agent in sauces, soups and stews, but it may also be used in some biscuits and cakes, such as shortbread, to give a lighter, shorter texture.

Popcorn is a variety of corn which is sold as kernels of 'popping' corn or as 'popped' corn. When heated in a covered container with a little oil, the moisture and air inside the kernels expands until the kernels explode, or 'pop', turning them into soft, white balls. Popcorn can be sprinkled lightly with salt and eaten as a savoury high-fibre snack, or it can be sweetened, dipped in honey or syrup, or coated in melted butter.

Corn is also used to make corn syrup and corn oil, which provides a subtle flavour for salad dressing. (*see also* CORN SYRUP, OILS, POLENTA)

CORNED BEEF (*see* BEEF, CORNED)

CORNET (Cone) A hollow conical biscuit, made of thin, crisp wafer, and used to hold scoops of soft ice cream. (*see also* CREAM HORN)

CORNFLOUR (*see* CORN)

CORNISH CREAM (*see* CREAM)

CORNISH PASTY (*see* PASTY)

CORNMEAL (*see* CORN)

CORN OIL (*see* OILS)

CORN ON THE COB (*see* SWEETCORN)

CORN SALAD (*see* LAMB'S LETTUCE)

CORNSTARCH (*see* CORN)

CORN SYRUP This product, which varies in colour from clear white to amber, is manufactured from cornstarch by treatment with an acid. The darker varieties of corn syrup have a stronger flavour.

Corn syrup may be used as a table syrup or as a sweetening agent, but is not as sweet as ordinary cane sugar. For this reason, corn syrup is often mixed with other sweeter syrups, such as golden syrup or maple syrup. It is also possible to use corn syrup in preserving, brewing and cake making, but some additional sugar is needed for some of these purposes and less liquid should be used, as corn syrup is 20 per cent water. (*see also* CORN)

CORONATION CHICKEN A well known cold chicken dish that is often served as part of a buffet spread. It is made from diced cooked chicken meat combined with mayonnaise flavoured with curry, tomato, wine, onion, lemon, bay and apricot, and lightened with whipped cream.

COS (*see* LETTUCE)

COSTMARY (Alecost) Once used in beer-making, costmary is now quite a rare herb that is mostly only available dried. It has an overpowering minty scent and flavour which can be rather bitter, so it should only be used in very small quantities in soups and stews.

COTECHINO A large Italian pork sausage flavoured with white wine, garlic and spices. It is available fresh, or uncooked, in Italy and must be cooked for several hours before serving. In Britain, it is available part-cured and part-cooked and needs only short cooking before serving hot with mashed potatoes, cooked beans or lentils, or it can be used in a stew.

COTHERSTONE CHEESE An English farmhouse cheese made in the Yorkshire Dales from unpasteurized cows' milk. It is a yellow crumbly cheese with a soft crust and a mild, slightly sharp flavour. A blue variety of Cotherstone is also available.

COTSWOLD CHEESE This is a type of Double Gloucester cheese which is flavoured with chives and chopped onion. (*see also* GLOUCESTER CHEESES)

COTTAGE CHEESE (*see* CHEESE)

COTTAGE PIE A homely dish usually made with leftover cooked meat, often thought to be identical to shepherd's pie (*see* SHEPHERD'S PIE). Some people, however, assert that while cottage pie may be made with any meat, only lamb or mutton should be used for shepherd's pie. Other people say that whereas cottage pie is made with minced meat, that used for shepherd's pie should be sliced.

COTTONSEED OIL (*see* OILS)

COULIBIAC (Coulibiaca, Koulibiac, Koulibiaca) A classic Russian fish pie consisting of layers of sturgeon (or salmon), mushrooms, buckwheat and hard-boiled eggs wrapped in brioche or puff pastry.

COULIS (Cullis) Originally, this meant the juices that ran out of meat in the natural way while it was cooking. It then came to mean various sauces, but especially a rich gravy or concentrate made from meat and/or poultry, used in making sauces, soups and stews, etc. Veal stock is also sometimes called by this name.

In French cooking, *coulis* is also the name given to a thickened type of soup made with a purée of game, poultry, fish or shellfish (though some authorities say that the last-named should be called a bisque). It is also the name given to a thin purée of cooked vegetables, especially tomatoes, used as a sauce. A fruit *coulis* is a purée of fresh or cooked fruits served as a sauce with hot or cold desserts or ice cream.

COULOMMIER A soft and creamy French cows' milk cheese which is very like Brie, with a similar white rind. It is made in smaller rounds, however, and has a milder flavour than Brie. It is a popular dessert cheese.

COUPE The French name for a rounded glass or stainless steel cup or goblet in which various cold desserts may be served. The dessert itself may also be known as a *coupe*. Ice cream sundaes are known as *coupes glacées* in France.

COURGETTE (Zucchini) Although this member of the squash family is usually grown as a separate vegetable, it is in fact the baby fruit cut from a variety of marrow plant before fully developed, while the yellow flower head is still attached. Most courgettes are dark green, streaked with paler green, and they have a smooth, shiny skin. They vary in size from about 7.5 cm (3 inches) to about 20.5 cm (8 inches) long, and they are available all year round, either grown in this country or imported. Less common varieties of courgette include a yellow variety and a round variety.

Tender young courgettes taste best when cooked in the simplest of ways – steamed whole, sliced and sautéed in butter, or lightly cooked and served cold with French dressing. They should never be peeled as most of the flavour is in the skin. If courgettes are on the large side, they can either be treated as a marrow and stuffed; sliced, coated in batter and deep-fried; made into a soup, or casseroled.

Courgettes are a traditional ingredient of *ratatouille*, and may also be sliced thinly lengthways and served, either raw or blanched, with a dip. Courgette flowers may also be eaten and, in Italy and France, are stuffed and deep-fried in batter.

To select: Choose small, tender courgettes with skins that are free from blemishes. Large ones tend to be tough. Allow 2–3 courgettes, 100–175 g (4–6 oz) per person.

To prepare: Slice off both ends, wash or wipe the skin and slice or dice, if liked. Larger courgettes may need salting to draw out some of the moisture before cooking. Sprinkle sliced courgettes with a little salt and leave to drain in a colander for 30 minutes. Rinse well and pat dry before cooking. (*see also* DÉGORGER)

To cook: Steam whole small courgettes for 5–8 minutes or until tender but still crisp. Cook sliced courgettes in boiling salted water for about 5 minutes, steam for 5 minutes, coat in batter and deep-fry for 2–3 minutes, or sauté in butter for about 5 minutes.

To serve: Drain well and serve hot sprinkled with fresh herbs, such as basil, marjoram, mint or thyme.

COURT BOUILLON (Court-bouillon) Any seasoned and flavoured liquid in which meat, poultry, fish or vegetables are boiled or poached in order to give them greater flavour. Flavourings used to make a *court bouillon* vary according to what it is to be used for, but they usually include aromatics, such as herbs, vegetables, spices, and sometimes lemon juice, white wine or vinegar. The flavourings are boiled up in the liquid before the food is added, so a *court bouillon* is particularly useful for food which needs only brief cooking, such as fish and shellfish.

Court Bouillon

1 litre (1³/₄ pints) water or dry white wine and water mixed
1 small carrot, scrubbed and sliced
1 small onion, skinned and sliced
1 small celery stick, washed and chopped (optional)
15 ml (1 tbsp) wine vinegar or lemon juice
few fresh parsley sprigs
1 bay leaf
3–4 black peppercorns
10 ml (2 level tsp) salt

Place all the ingredients in a saucepan and simmer for about 30 minutes. Allow to cool and strain the liquid before using, if wished.

Makes about 900 ml (1 ¹/₂ pints)

COUSCOUS (Cous-cous) Couscous is produced by moistening grains of semolina and forming them into tiny pellets coated with fine wheat flour. It is a staple food in North African countries where it is treated like a grain and is traditionally served with a meat or vegetable stew known as a *tagine*. A manufactured version of couscous is readily available in packets, with cooking instructions given. The name couscous also refers to the complete dish of stew and couscous served together.

Couscous is usually steamed in a steamer, sieve or *couscousière* which can be placed over the pan in which the stew is cooking, so that the couscous cooks at the same time, absorbing flavour from the stew below. Pre-cooked couscous is also

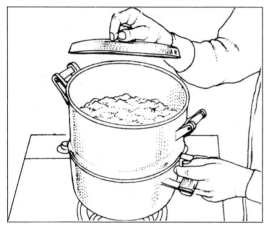

Cooking couscous in a steamer placed over a saucepan in which a stew is simmering.

available in packets; to serve, follow the manufacturer's instructions. Cooked couscous can also be combined with onions and other ingredients and served cold as a salad.

COWBERRY (Lingonberry, Mountain Cranberry) This member of the cranberry family grows in cold mountainous regions of Europe and North America and has quite large dark red berries with a very tart flavour. It is popular in Scandinavian countries and Germany and can be used to make compotes, sauces and jellies, especially to serve with savoury dishes.

COW-HEEL The name given to the foot of a cow, which can be hard to come by these days. At one time, cow-heel was stewed until the meat could be removed from the bone, then served with a white sauce, and in the north of England, jellied cow-heel was cooked with bacon to make a popular brawn. Nowadays, if used at all, cow-heels are split, scalded and used to make a soup, stew or casserole, giving it a rich, gelatinous consistency. (*see also* CALF'S FOOT JELLY)

COWPEA (*see* ASPARAGUS BEAN)

CRAB A shellfish of the decapod crustacean type, belonging to the same family as the lobster, crayfish, prawn and shrimp. It has a wide flat body encased in a hard shell (or carapace) which is shed periodically to allow the crab to grow. Crabs have five pairs of legs, the first of which is the largest and bears strong claws. Unlike other decapod crustaceans, the crab has a very small tail which is tucked underneath its body. There are many edible species of crab, found all over the world.

Blue (Atlantic blue) crabs get their name from their blue claws. They have the finest flavour of all the crabs. They are extremely popular in America, where they are eaten in the soft-shell state when they have shed their shells and before they grow new ones. The blue crab is also found in the Mediterranean. It grows to a maximum width of about 20.5 cm (8 inches).

Common crabs have brownish-red shells and can grow to a width of about 20.5 cm (8 inches).

Rock crabs have yellowish shells marked with purple or brown spots and can grow to a width of about 10 cm (4 inches).

Shore (green) crabs have green shells, sometimes with yellow spots, and they can grow up to a width of about 7.5 cm (3 inches). In Venice, the shore crab is very popular in its soft-shell state. *Southern stone crabs* have greyish shells and claws that are enormous in proportion to their body size; one claw is bigger than the other. The southern stone crab grows to a width of about 12.5 cm (5 inches).

Spider (spiny) crabs have shells which vary in colour from brown to reddish-orange and are covered with prickly spines. They have round bodies and long legs – hence their name. Spider crabs grow up to a width of about 20.5 cm (8 inches).

Crabs are sometimes sold alive, but more often they are ready-cooked. Some fishmongers will also dress a crab for you. The crab's edible part consists of white meat in the claws and legs and brown meat in the shell. Crab meat can be eaten on its own straight from the shell or with salad, or used to flavour a fish soup. Fresh crabs are at their best from May to November but crab meat is also available canned and frozen throughout the year. (*see also* SHELFISH)

To select: When buying a cooked crab, look for one that is plump and heavy for its size, with a fresh smell. When buying a live crab, look for one that is active and not already half dead. When shaken, there should be no sound of water inside the shell of a live crab. A male crab has larger claws and therefore contains more white meat than a female crab. A male crab has a narrower, more pointed, tail than a female.

To cook: Place an uncooked crab in a large saucepan and cover with cold, salted water. Add a bay leaf and 15 ml (1 tbsp) lemon juice and bring slowly to the boil. Cover and boil fairly rapidly for 10–20 minutes, then remove from the heat and leave the crab to cool in the water.

To dress: Drain the crab and place it on its back on a large chopping board. Take a claw firmly in one hand, holding it as close to the body of the crab as possible. Twist it off, steadying the body with the other hand. Remove the other claw and the legs in the same way. Snap the claws in half by bending them backwards at the joint.

Hold the claws at the top end and, with a hammer or heavy weight, tap the shell smartly on the rounded edge to crack the claws open. Try not to shatter the shell. Repeat with the second claw. Using a blunt knife, ease the white meat out of the claws. Keep the blade as close to the edges of the shell as possible. Using a teaspoon handle or skewer, reach well into the crevices to make sure all the white meat is removed. Discard any membrane.

Crack the larger legs open and scrape out the white meat. Keep the small legs for decoration. Reserve all the white meat in one bowl.

Place the crab on its back with the tail flap towards you, head away from you. Hold the shell firmly and press the body section upwards from beneath the tail flap, easing it out with your thumbs until the body is detached.

Pull off the inedible, grey feather-like gills (known as dead men's fingers) from the body section and discard them.

Use a spoon to remove the stomach bag and mouth which are attached to the back shell. If the bag breaks, make sure you remove all the greenish or grey-white matter.

Opposite: British and Continental Cheeses: 1. Double Gloucester; 2. Farmhouse Cheddar; 3. Blue Stilton; 4. Blue Shropshire; 5. Edam; 6. Caerphilly; 7. Sage Derby; 8. Emmenthal; 9. Huntsman; 10. Fourme d'Ambert; 11. Smoked German; 12. Rutland Cheddar; 13. Torta San Gaudenzio; 14. Tomme du Raisin; 15. Roulé (garlic and herbs); 16. Bel Paese; 17. Walnut Crédioux; 18. Roulé (peppers and chives); 19. Bûche de Chèvre; 20. Mozzarella; 21. Cambazola; 22. Camembert

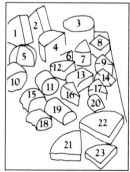

Overleaf: Left, Chayote; **Right**, Dressed crab
Centre Pages: Peking duck

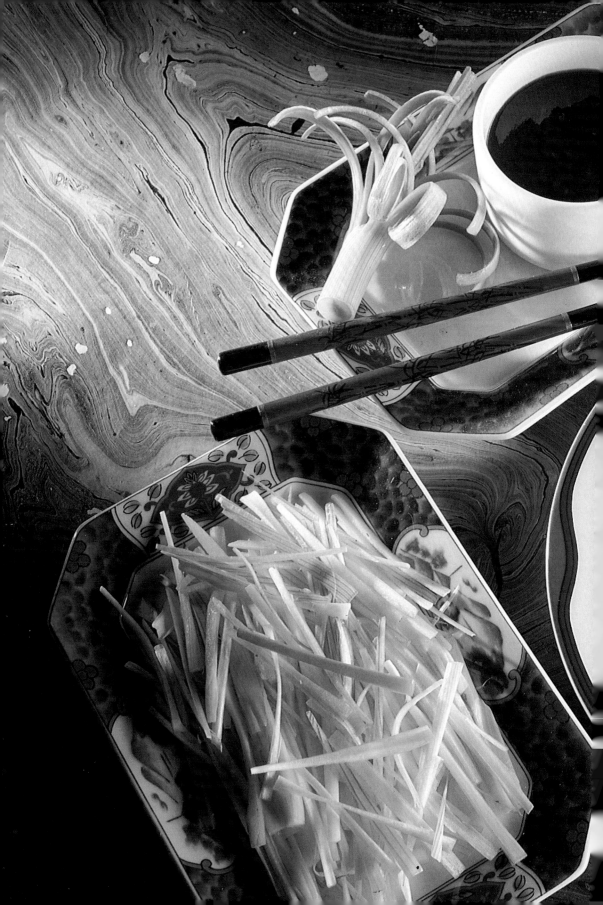

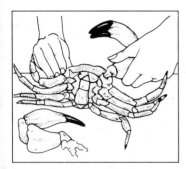

Twisting off the claws of the crab, holding them as close to the body as possible.

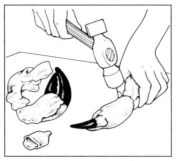

Using a hammer to tap the shell smartly on the rounded edge to crack open the claws.

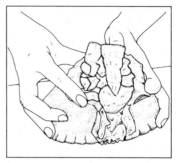

Easing the body of the crab out of its shell by pushing it upwards from beneath the tail flap.

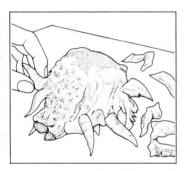

Pulling off the inedible, grey, feather-like gills from the body section, and discarding them.

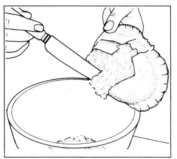

Running a knife around the edge of the body shell to ease out the brown meat.

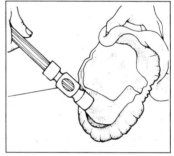

Tapping with a hammer just inside the natural line of the shell to break away the inner shell.

Ease the brown meat out of the shell, running a knife around the edge to bring it out smoothly. Put it in a separate bowl. Discard any membrane and scrape out the corners of the shell with the handle of a teaspoon.

Protecting your hand with a cloth, hold the shell firmly and, with the other hand, tap with a hammer just inside the natural line of the shell until the inner shell breaks smoothly away. Scrub the shell well under cold running water, then dry on absorbent kitchen paper and rub the outside lightly with oil.

Place the body on its back on the board. Cut through the body to divide it in two. Spoon any creamy brown meat out into the bowl with the rest. Discard the body pieces.

Using two forks, flake all the white meat, removing any shell or membrane. Season and add about 5 ml (1 tsp) lemon juice.

Pound the brown meat and work in about 30 ml (2 level tbsp) fresh breadcrumbs with about 10 ml (2 tsp) lemon juice and salt and pepper to taste.

Using a small spoon, place the white meat in both ends of the crab's empty shell, making sure

Previous Pages: Left, Christmas pudding; **Right**, Croquembouche
Opposite: Coeur à la Crème

that it is well piled up into the shell. Keep the inside edges neat. Spoon the brown meat in a neat line down the centre, between the two sections of white crab meat.

Hold a blunt knife between the white and brown crab meat and carefully spoon lines of chopped fresh parsley, sieved egg yolk and chopped egg white across the crab, moving the knife as you go to keep a neat edge.

To serve, place the shell on a bed of lettuce or endive, surrounded by the small crab legs.

CRAB APPLE The common European crab apple is probably the original wild apple. The trees are found growing all over Europe, with an abundance of fruit in early Autumn. The small fruits have a shiny red or yellow skin and firm flesh, which is usually very sour. They are chiefly used to make a beautiful delicate pink, crystal-clear jelly and other preserves.

CRACKED WHEAT To produce cracked wheat, whole uncooked grains of wheat are crushed under light pressure. It is often mistaken for 'kibbled' wheat, which is pricked by machine and split into small pieces. Cracked wheat cooks more quickly than whole wheat grains. (*see also* WHEAT)

CRACKER The name given, especially in America, to any type of plain or salted, hard biscuit that is suitable for eating with cheese.

CRACKLING The crisp skin on a joint of roast pork. To produce good crackling, score the rind of the joint and rub with salt before putting it in the oven, and avoid basting with fat during roasting. (*see also* PORK)

CRACKNEL A type of plain biscuit made of paste which is boiled before being baked, causing it to puff up.

CRAKEBERRY (*see* CROWBERRY)

CRANBERRY This small American fruit is similar to the bilberry, but its skin is coloured pink to dark red. The fruit is hard and sharp-tasting, with a high pectin content, making it excellent for making jams and jellies. However, cranberries are mostly used for sauces and jellies to serve with poultry (especially roast turkey) and game or in tarts and puddings. Fresh cranberries are only available in the winter months in Britain, but they are available frozen all year round. Cranberry juice is becoming more widely available too.

To select: Look for shiny, plump berries, avoiding any that are squashed. Tradition has it that a good, ripe cranberry will bounce if dropped.

To prepare: Remove all the stalks and any leaves, if necessary, then rinse well under cold running water.

CRAWFISH (Langouste, Rock Lobster, Southern Lobster, Spiny Lobster) Crawfish is the British name for a variety of lobster, known in France as *langouste*. In America, the name crawfish is given to what, in Britain, is known as crayfish (see below). In America, crawfish are known as rock lobsters.

Crawfish are large crustaceans, found in most temperate coastal waters. They have no claws and most of their flesh is contained in their tails. They can be used in any recipe suitable for lobster, and are delicious in casseroles and stews. They are often used in Creole-style cooking. Crawfish are available fresh from May to October, but can occasionally be bought canned or frozen throughout the year.

CRAYFISH (Écrevisse) This freshwater crustacean is known as crawfish in America. It looks like a miniature lobster and varies in colour from dark purple to red. Crayfish are found mostly in the rivers and lakes of northern Europe, especially France, though they are also very popular in Scandinavian countries.

Small crayfish can be used for soups and garnishes, larger ones can be served hot in a cream sauce, or cold with salad and brown bread and butter.

To prepare: Rinse well, then remove the intestinal tube under the tail, using a pointed knife.

To cook: Put the fish in a saucepan of cold, salted water, bring to the boil and cook for about 10 minutes.

CREAM If whole cows' milk is left to stand, the richest part of it, consisting of larger but lighter fat globules, rises to the top to form the cream. At one time, cream was separated from milk simply by leaving the milk to stand and 'creaming off' the cream; nowadays separation is carried out mechanically. Most cream available today is pasteurized before it is sold, and may also undergo other treatment, depending on what type of cream it is to become. All creams are perishable and should be kept refrigerated.

A wide variety of types of cream is available, each one with specific uses. The different types are classified according to their fat content. In order to whip successfully, cream must have a fat content of at least 35 per cent.

Half cream is the thinnest, least rich cream available and is best used for pouring over desserts or for adding to coffee. It is usually homogenized to prevent separation, but is also available in pasteurized form. The fat content of half cream is 12 per cent.

Single cream is a popular pouring cream, delicious served with fresh strawberries or fruit salad. It is usually homogenized to prevent separation, and may also be pasteurized. Single cream can also be added to coffee or poured over breakfast cereals, or used to enrich soups and other savoury dishes. Its fat content is 18 per cent.

Whipping cream has not been homogenized and is therefore suitable for whipping. It has a higher fat content than single cream but is less rich (and less expensive) than double cream. If whipped correctly, it will double in volume and is ideal for piping in decorative shapes on cakes and cold desserts, or for folding into mousses and fools. Unwhipped, the cream can be used as a pouring cream or to enrich soups and sauces. Its fat content is between 35 and 40 per cent.

It is also possible to buy ready-whipped whipping cream in frozen form or chilled. It is often sweetened with quite a large amount of sugar and can be served with desserts.

Double cream is most frequently used for whipping and serving with desserts, or folding into mousses or fools. It will whip to slightly less volume than whipping cream, but adding 15 ml (1 tbsp) milk for every 150 ml (5 fl oz) cream will help it achieve greater volume. Double cream is a vital ingredient in many cream desserts, such as *crème brûlée*, and ice creams. Its fat content is 48 per cent.

Extra-thick double cream also has a fat content of 48 per cent and is a rich spooning cream, though it cannot be whipped because it has been homogenized. It can be served with desserts and fruit salads.

Clotted cream is the richest cream of all. It is a speciality of south-west England and is often called Cornish or Devonshire cream. Clotted cream is the main constituent of a 'cream tea', served with scones and jam. It is produced commercially by scalding and cooking cream until it forms a thick yellow crust which is skimmed off. Its fat content is 55 per cent.

Soured (sour) cream is made by adding a 'souring' culture to homogenized single cream. It is used in a number of sweet and savoury dishes and is delicious mixed with snipped chives or spring onions and served with baked jacket potatoes. It has the same fat content as single cream.

UHT cream has been heated to a high temperature to destroy all micro-organisms that may be present in the cream and which might otherwise cause the cream to deteriorate. The treatment slightly alters the flavour of the cream, which is subsequently homogenized and packed and sealed under sterile conditions. UHT forms of half, single, double and whipping cream are all available.

Crème fraîche is an important ingredient in French cooking. It is fresh cream that has matured and fermented to the point where it has thickened slightly and has a faintly acid taste. It adds a slight tang to savoury dishes and acts as a very good thickener. It is possible to make a home-made version by gently heating together double cream and soured cream or buttermilk, then leaving the mixture in a warm place until thick. *Crème fraîche* keeps better than fresh cream – 10-14 days in the refrigerator – though it will become thicker as time goes on.

Frozen single, double or whipping cream is available in chip or stick form. Only double and whipping creams can be frozen at home successfully. Both creams benefit from being semi-whipped before freezing, then whipped to the desired consistency after thawing.

Aerosol cream is a fairly recent development. Whipped UHT cream is packed into aerosol containers with up to 13 per cent added sugar, stabilizers and a propellant to make it flow from its container. Although it is convenient for topping desserts, it cannot be used for decoration as it does not hold its shape for long periods.

Sterilized cream is available in cans and has been heat-treated and homogenized. The sterilization process gives it a distinctive caramel flavour. It will not whip.

Extended life cream is packed in vacuum-sealed bottles and keeps in the refrigerator, unopened, for 2–3 weeks. It is spoonable double cream and can be whipped.

CREAM BUN (Cream Puff) A popular confection made of choux pastry with a filling of whipped cream or confectioners' custard.

CREAM CHEESE (*see* CHEESE)

CREAM, DESSERT There are three main types of cream dessert: 'whole', in which cream is the main ingredient; custard, made from a combination of cream and custard; and fruit, made from fruit purée and cream and sometimes including custard. Gelatine is frequently used to set a dessert cream. All dessert creams have a rich, smooth texture reminiscent of cream itself.

Dessert creams are used as desserts or as the basis for a dessert, or they can be used as fillings, toppings or accompaniments for pastries, cakes, etc. They are a major constituent of *bavarois*, charlottes and other puddings. Set cream desserts include caramel custard, baked custard and blancmange.

CREAM HORN A pastry, made by wrapping a strip of puff pastry in a spiral round a cone-shaped tin, often called a cream horn tin or mould. The pastry is baked and cooled slightly while wrapped round the tin, then the tin is gently removed, leaving a horn-shaped pastry which is usually filled with jam and whipped cream. To finish, cream horns may be dusted with icing sugar.

CREAMING Beating together fat and sugar until the mixture resembles whipped cream in texture and colour (pale and fluffy). It is a method frequently used when making cake mixtures which contain a high proportion of fat and require the incorporation of a lot of air.

CREAM NUT (*see* BRAZIL NUT)

CREAM OF TARTAR (Tartaric Acid) A raising agent which is an ingredient of baking powder and self raising flour. (*see also* ACID, BAKING POWDER, BREAD, FLOUR, RAISING AGENT)

CRÉCY A French name used to describe a dish made or garnished with carrots.

CRÉDIOUX A processed cheese shaped either as a small cake or round log. It is creamy with a highly refined flavour, and is coated with walnuts.

CRÈME ANGLAISE (*see* CUSTARD)

CRÈME AU BEURRE (Rich Butter Cream) A French butter cream icing made with butter, sugar, egg yolks and flavouring, used to fill or coat sponge cakes. Alternative flavourings include chocolate, coffee or fruit such as crushed strawberries, orange or lemon.

Crème au Beurre

Crème au beurre can be made a day in advance and stored in a cool place. If it separates out, place it in a slightly warmed bowl and beat until smooth.

75 g (3 oz) caster sugar
2 egg yolks, beaten
175 g (6 oz) butter, softened

Place the sugar in a heavy-based saucepan, add 60 ml (4 tbsp) water and heat very gently to dissolve the sugar, without boiling. When completely dissolved, bring to boiling point and boil steadily for 2–3 minutes, to reach a temperature of 107°C (225°F). Pour the syrup in a thin stream on to the egg yolks in a deep bowl, whisking all the time. Continue to whisk until the mixture is thick and cold. In another bowl, cream the butter until very soft and beat in the egg yolk mixture.

Makes about 275 g (10 oz)

Variations

Chocolate Melt 50 g (2 oz) plain chocolate with 15 ml (1 tbsp) water. Cool slightly and beat into the *crème au beurre* mixture.

Fruit Crush 225 g (8 oz) fresh strawberries, raspberries, etc., or thaw, drain and crush frozen fruit. Beat into the *crème au beurre* mixture.

Orange or lemon Add freshly grated rind and juice to taste to the *crème au beurre* mixture.

Coffee Beat 15–30 ml (1–2 tbsp) coffee essence into the *crème au beurre* mixture.

To use Crème au Beurre

Use as butter cream icing on more elaborate cakes (*see* BUTTER CREAM ICING).

CRÈME BRÛLÉE A rich cream dessert made with double cream and egg yolks and flavoured with vanilla. Crème brûlée may be made in one large dish, or in individual ramekin dishes.

The dessert is baked in the oven in a *bain-marie* until just set. When cold, it is topped with a layer of sugar which is heated under the grill until caramelized. After further chilling, the caramel sets hard and forms a crunchy topping which contrasts deliciously with the smooth rich cream beneath.

Crème brûlée may be served on its own or with a selection of fruit, such as sliced fresh strawberries and peaches and stoned cherries.

CRÈME CARAMEL (*see* CUSTARD)

CRÈME CHANTILLY (*see* CHANTILLY)

CRÈME DE CASSIS (*see* CASSIS)

CRÈME DE CACAO A very sweet chocolate-coloured and cocoa-flavoured liqueur from the West Indies, sometimes drunk through a layer of cream.

CRÈME DE MENTHE A green coloured liqueur with a pronounced peppermint flavour. It is often served poured over crushed ice.

CRÈME FRAÎCHE (*see* CREAM)

CRÈME PÂTISSIÈRE (*see* CONFECTIONERS' CUSTARD)

CRÉOLE, À LA A French term used to describe dishes which have been inspired by a West Indian style of cooking. They usually include rice and, in the case of savoury dishes, a garnish or sauce of red peppers and tomatoes. For sweet dishes, orange, banana, pineapple or rum are often included.

CREOLE A style of cooking that combines many of the characteristics of West Indian, French, African and Spanish cooking. Creole cookery is popular in many parts of the world including, most famously, the southern United States, especially Louisiana.

Creole recipes are based on rice mixed with a variety of local ingredients, such as filé powder (*see* FILÉ POWDER), shellfish (especially crayfish) and 'gumbo' (okra). Gumbo is also the name of one of the most famous Creole dishes, a rich soup-like stew of which there are many versions, all of them based on shellfish, smoked sausage and okra, amongst other vegetables. Another famous Creole dish is jambalaya, a rice-based dish similar to a Spanish paella.

CRÊPE The French name for a thin pancake which may be served plain or filled with a sweet or savoury mixture. Crêpes are made from a thin pouring batter (*see* BATTER). (*see also* PANCAKE)

CRÊPE SUZETTE A French sweet pancake. The pancake is very thin, traditionally made from an orange-flavoured batter and reheated in a mixture of butter, orange juice, sugar, orange liqueur and lemon juice and flambéed with orange liqueur or brandy just before serving.

CRÉPINETTE A small, flat French sausage usually made from sausagemeat flavoured with parsley and wrapped in pig's caul (*see* CAUL). They may also be made from other minced meats, such as lamb, veal, liver or poultry. *Crépinettes* are occasionally sold ready-cooked, but usually need to be grilled, sautéed or baked before serving. They are traditionally served with a potato or lentil purée. (*see also* GAYETTE)

CRESS (Garden Cress, Mustard and Cress, Salad Cress) This popular salad plant is native to Britain. It grows very quickly and easily on any damp patch of ground, and is harvested and eaten as a seedling when it has a fine white stem with just two small dark green leaves. It is usually bought, still growing, in small plastic punnets and can be kept fresh by frequent watering before cutting. The seedlings in a punnet are usually a mixture of cress with rape or mustard, though as mustard seeds germinate more quickly than cress, it is often just mustard growing in the punnet when you buy it. It is possible to sprout mustard and cress seeds quite easily at home (*see* BEAN SPROUTS).

Cress should be washed very carefully to remove loose seed pods, grit and soil. Apart from using it in a salad, cress can be used as a garnish for roast game and poultry, hot and cold entrées, meat, cheese, fish, etc., and in sandwiches. Cress appears to be a fairly rich source of vitamins A and C, but the amount consumed at a serving is too small to contribute much of value to the diet.

(*see also* LAND CRESS, WATERCRESS)

CRIMPING Decorating the edges of a pie, tart or shortbread by pinching it at regular intervals to give a fluted effect. The term may also refer to trimming cucumber, lemons, etc., with a canelle knife (*see* CANELLE KNIFE) or fork.

CRISPBREAD (Flatbread) Bread made from crushed whole grains, such as rye and wheat, and prepared in large, thin, brittle biscuits.

Crispbread is often served at breakfast instead of toast, offered with the cheese course and used as a base for cocktail savouries. Crispbreads are very popular in Scandinavia, where they originated, and always appear on the Smörgasbord; they may also form the base of Smörrebröd (*see* SMÖRGASBORD and SMÖRREBRÖD).

CROISSANT A French crescent-shaped roll made from a special leavened dough that is folded and rolled with butter many times, producing a rich and flaky layered pastry. (Less authentic croissants are made with puff pastry.) The dough is rolled and cut into strips, then cut into triangles which are rolled up from one side, then curled round into crescent shapes.

Croissants are very popular and are usually served warm for breakfast, with butter and jam, or for dunking, French-style, in hot milky coffee (*café au lait*). Croissants may also be filled with a sweet or savoury filling.

CROQUE-MADAME (*see* CROQUE-MONSIEUR)

CROQUEMBOUCHE A large impressive pyramid-shaped French 'cake' usually made of small choux buns filled with cream or confectioners' custard, then dipped in sugar syrup and stuck

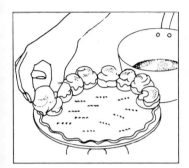

Arranging caramel-glazed choux buns around the edge of the pâte sucrée base of a croquembouche.

Continuing to pack layers of choux buns loosely together, building them up into a cone shape.

Drizzling hot caramel over the outside of the croquembouche for a decorative finish.

together. A *croquembouche* is sometimes constructed inside a conical stainless steel mould of the same name, which is removed when the sugar syrup has set and will hold the buns together, though the shape can be achieved without the use of a special mould (see below).

The finished cake usually stands on a base of *pâte sucrée* or nougat and may be decorated with sugar almonds, almond paste flowers, whipped cream or, more traditionally, a 'veil' of spun sugar. A *croquembouche* is traditionally served in France as part of the buffet at a wedding, anniversary, birthday or christening celebration.

Croquembouches may also be constructed using small meringues, candied fruits, roasted chestnuts or brandy snaps instead of choux buns.

CROQUE-MONSIEUR A hot French sandwich consisting of two thin slices of crustless bread with slices of Gruyère cheese and ham between. The sandwich is brushed with melted butter and fried until lightly browned, or toasted under the grill, before serving hot. Variations include replacing the Gruyère cheese with Cheddar and using sliced cooked chicken instead of ham. If the sandwich is served with a poached egg on top, it is known as a *croque-madame*.

CROQUETTE A cooked mixture of meat, fish, poultry or vegetables (especially potatoes) bound together with beaten egg or a thick sauce and formed into small roll or cork shapes. Croquettes are then coated with egg and breadcrumbs and shallow- or deep-fried. Fish or meat croquettes may be served as an hors d'oeuvre or main course, while vegetable croquettes may also be served as an accompaniment.

CROSNES (*see* ARTICHOKE, CHINESE)

CROUSTADE The French name for a case, usually small, made of fried bread, pastry, duchess potato, etc., and used to hold a savoury or sweet mixture. Filled *croustades* are most often served hot as an hors d'oeuvre.

CROÛTE A circle or rectangle of fried or toasted bread on which game and other main dishes and savouries are served. The name is also given to a small pastry crust, usually crescent shaped, served with savoury dishes.

In French cookery, the term may also refer to small pastry cases (such as individual *vols-au-vent*) that are similar to *croustades*.

CROÛTE, EN A French term used to describe game, entrées and savouries, etc., served on a shaped slice of bread or pastry, which is toasted, fried or baked. It may also be used to describe a dish of meat, poultry or pâté cooked inside a pastry case, such as *filet de boeuf en croûte*.

CROÛTONS Small pieces of fried or toasted bread which are served as an accompaniment to salads and soups, or as a garnish. Croûtons are most often cube-shaped, but may also be cut with small cutters into hearts, diamonds or rounds. (*see also* SOUP)

CROWBERRY (Crakeberry) A European heath-like wild plant bearing black berries, which may be used like cranberries.

CROWDY (Crowdie) The Scottish name for oatmeal gruel or a traditional Scottish farmhouse soft cheese similar to cottage cheese (*see* HIGHLAND CROWDIE).

CROWN OF LAMB OR PORK (Crown Roast) A crown of lamb or pork is an impressive roast to serve at a dinner party. A crown of lamb consists of two best end necks (sometimes called racks of lamb) joined together and curved round, bones outwards, and secured with string to form a crown shape. A crown of pork is formed in a similar way from two fore loins of pork.

In both cases, before cooking, the joints are chined, the cutlets partially separated, and the tips of the cutlet bones neatly trimmed and scraped clean of fat and meat. The joints may be stuffed and are cut into cutlets to serve. (*see also* GUARD OF HONOUR, LAMB, PORK)

CROWN ROAST (*see* CROWN OF LAMB OR PORK)

CRUDITÉS The French name for a dish of raw vegetables, including carrots, celery, cauliflower, peppers, radishes, etc., usually cut into sticks and served with one or more dips or sauces as an appetizer or cocktail snack.

CRULLER Similar to a doughnut, this is an American fancy-shaped bun. It is made from a spiced yeast or baking powder dough and deep-fried in fat.

CRUMBLE A rubbed-in plain cake mixture, usually sweetened and used instead of pastry as a topping for a fruit pie. A savoury mixture can be made to top meat or vegetable dishes by omitting the sugar and adding cheese and other flavourings. Crumble toppings may also contain chopped nuts, sesame or sunflower seeds, rolled oats, wheat flakes and other grains.

CRUMBS (*see* BREADCRUMBS)

CRUMPET A small round soft yeast cake, baked on a griddle in a special metal ring. The underneath of a crumpet is smooth and brown and the top is full of small holes. Crumpets are toasted and served hot, spread with butter and honey. (*see also* PIKELET)

CRUSHING Breaking down food into smaller particles either, as in the case of spices, in a pestle and mortar, or garlic through a garlic press, to release the flavour in cooking or to make a crumb-like texture, as with biscuits, for mixing with other ingredients.

CRUST The most common meaning of this term is the crisp or outer part of a loaf, pie or other baked dish. As applied to wine, crust means the deposit of organic salts which wines throw off as they age.

CRUSTACEAN The name given to several species of shellfish, all of which have a hard external skeleton which is segmented to allow for movement. The most common crustaceans are crabs, lobsters and prawns. All crustaceans are sea fish, except crayfish. (*see also* CRAB, CRAWFISH, CRAYFISH, LOBSTER, PRAWN, etc.)

CRYSTALLIZED FRUIT (*see* CANDYING)

CUBEB A kind of pepper, native to Indonesia. The grey berries, when dried, somewhat resemble peppercorns. They have a pungent, spicy flavour like camphor and are used in Eastern cookery and also in some medicines.

CUCUMBER This familiar long green vegetable is in fact the fruit of a climbing member of the gourd family that was first cultivated in India more than 3000 years ago. It was brought to Britain by the Romans, though it did not become established until the sixteenth century. Inside its dark green skin it has firm watery flesh (cucumbers are 96 per cent water) and flat edible seeds. Its flavour is slightly bitter but mild and refreshing.

There are two main types of cucumber – the long, smooth-skinned greenhouse or frame cucumber and the ridge cucumber which is less perfect in shape and has a thicker, uneven skin. The ridge cucumber is only sometimes found in supermarkets or on vegetable stalls, as it is the variety more easily grown at home. Other varieties of outdoor cucumber worth searching for or growing are burpless, which lives up to its name, and the little round apple cucumber. Some small varieties of cucumber are grown for pickling (*see* GHERKIN).

Although cucumbers are available all the year round, they are at their best in the summer. Cucumbers are usually eaten raw but may also be boiled, steamed or sautéed and eaten hot. They may be cut in a variety of ways and used as a decorative garnish.

To select: Choose smallish firm cucumbers with skins that are free from blemishes. Allow 100-175 g (4–6 oz) per person if serving as a hot vegetable, 50–100 g (2–4 oz) per person in salads.

To prepare: When using small young tender cucumbers in salads, leave the skin on and cut into thin slices, dice or chunks. Larger cucumbers and ridge cucumbers should be peeled thinly. If cucumbers are bitter, peel and slice or dice and place in a colander. Sprinkle with salt and leave to stand for about 45 minutes. Drain off the juice, rinse thoroughly and pat dry. (*see also* DÉG-ORGER)

To cook: Steam, cook in boiling salted water or sauté in melted butter for 5–10 minutes.

To serve: Drain steamed or boiled cucumber thoroughly and toss in a little melted butter, or coat in hollandaise or béchamel sauce. Stir a squeeze of lemon juice into sautéed cucumber and serve sprinkled with fresh herbs.

CULATELLA (Culatella di Parma, Culatello di Zibello) An Italian smoked raw ham that is made only from lean pork cut from the rump and is cured in a similar way to *prosciutto*, then sometimes soaked in wine before being left to mature. It is a speciality of the Parma region of Italy, is considered one of the best Italian hams and is therefore very expensive. It may be sliced thinly and served as *antipasto*.

CULLIS (*see* COULIS)

CUMBERLAND SAUCE A traditional English sauce made from redcurrant jelly, orange, lemon and port and served with ham, venison and lamb. It usually contains fine strips of softened orange and lemon rind.

CUMBERLAND SAUSAGE An English pork sausage flavoured with black pepper and herbs and formed into one continuous coil, not linked as other sausages are. It is usually baked.

CUMIN (Jeera, Zeera) The seeds of a plant related to parsley that are used as a spice. Cumin is mostly cultivated in Mediterranean countries and is occasionally confused with caraway, though their flavours are in no way similar. Cumin has a strong, slightly bitter taste and the seeds are sold whole or ground. Black and white varieties of cumin are available in Asia, where cumin is used more frequently than in the West, where brown cumin is the most common variety. 'Sweet cumin' is in fact anise (*see* ANISEED).

Cumin is an ingredient of curry powders and some chilli powder mixtures, and the seeds are also used in pickles, chutney, cheese dishes, soups, with cabbage and rice dishes, in Mexican and Eastern dishes, meat loaves, marinades and fruit pies.

CUP A type of drink usually made from claret or light white wine diluted with ice or soda water, and with sprigs of herbs, fruit and flavourings added. Pimm's is a well known commercial cup base.

CUP MEASURE A special cup used for measuring ingredients in cookery. It is the standard method of measuring in the United States, Canada and Australia, whereas in Britain, these days, most recipes use measuring spoons and weights.

The standard American and Commonwealth cup contains 250 ml (8 fl oz) of a liquid ingredient, but the amount it holds varies for dry ingredients. For example, 1 cup holds approximately 150 g (5 oz) plain flour but 200 g (7 oz) caster sugar. Some old British cookery books do give quantities of ingredients in cups; the British standard cup measure was equivalent to 300 ml (10 fl oz/^{1}/$_2$ pint). It is therefore important to use just one set of standard measuring cups when measuring ingredients, and to check whether the recipe you are using refers to American or British standard cup sizes.

CURAÇAO An orange-flavoured liqueur, the original of which was made from the dried peel of citrus fruit from the island of Curaçao, off the west coast of Venezuela. The term is now generic and is used for various orange-flavoured liqueurs, such as Cointreau and Grand Marnier. Curaçao is usually colourless or amber-coloured, but may also be pink, green or even blue.

In cookery, curaçao is often used to impart an orange flavour in cakes and desserts, most notably *crêpes Suzette* (*see* CRÊPE SUZETTE).

CURD CHEESE (*see* CHEESE)

CURDS The parts of milk which coagulate when natural fermentation takes place, or when a curdling agent, such as rennet or an acid, is added. When coagulated, the curds can be separated from the remaining liquid, known as the 'whey'. Curds consist of the milk protein (casein) plus fat and other constituents trapped with them. The coagulating and separating process is known as 'curdling' and is the first stage of cheese-making.

Curd is also the name given to a creamy-textured preserve made from fruit (usually lemon or orange) and sugar, eggs and butter. The white head of a cauliflower is also sometimes known as the curd.

CURING Preserving fish, meat or poultry by salting, drying or smoking.

CURRANTS Currants are the small, round berry fruits of a variety of shrubs that originated in northern Europe, North Africa and Siberia. Depending on their variety, they may be black, red or white. All currants contain soft flesh and edible pips. Blackcurrants are more common than red or white currants. Currants are normally sold still on their strings or stalks and are more expensive when not. Avoid withered or dusty currants; choose only those with a distinct gloss. To remove currants from their stalks, use a fork to rake them off.

Blackcurrants have a rich flavour but tend to be slightly sour; they are best known for their use in making the liqueur *crème de cassis* and other drinks, but can also be used in puddings, pies and jams. They are particularly rich in vitamin C.

'Stringing' blackcurrants by raking them off their stalks with a fork.

Redcurrants are sweeter than blackcurrants and can be eaten raw, but are mainly used in preserves, syrups and puddings, or as a pretty garnish. Redcurrant jelly is an essential ingredient of Cumberland sauce (*see* CUMBERLAND SAUCE) and an accompaniment to roast lamb. *White currants* are a less common variety of redcurrant. They are similar in flavour, although slightly less acid, and can be used in the same ways.

CURRANTS, DRIED (*see* VINE FRUITS)

CURRY The name given to a number of Indian and Far Eastern savoury dishes that may be based on meat, poultry, fish or vegetables, but which are all flavoured with a varying mixture of crushed spices and herbs. In countries where curries are eaten every day, spices are always dried and ground fresh, but in western countries the tendency is to use a ready-mixed curry powder, or canned or bottled curry paste, or to buy ready-ground spices to mix at home. For this reason, curries that are cooked in Britain, other than those served in Indian restaurants, seldom bear any real resemblance to a true curry.

The flavour of a curry is often described as 'hot', because an essential ingredient is chilli. The 'heat' of a curry varies according to how much chilli is included; some curries may be quite mild. (*see also* CURRY PASTE, CURRY POWDER)

CURRY LEAF This looks similar to a bay leaf and comes from a plant that is native to south-west Asia. When used in Indian or Asian dishes, curry leaves impart a strong curry flavour. The leaves may be used fresh or dried and are usually chopped and fried in oil until crisp before the remaining ingredients are added. Fresh curry leaves are sometimes available from Indian food stores.

CURRY PASTE A ready-made mixture of dried spices, fresh chillies, onion, ginger and oil for using in curries. It is usually sold in jars or bottles. (*see also* CURRY, CURRY POWDER)

CURRY PLANT The silver-grey, spiky leaves of this shrubby perennial give off a strong curry aroma when touched. It is an attractive plant that adds colour to a herb garden in the form of clusters of yellow flowers. Although not used in Indian curries, the fresh or dried leaves may be used sparingly in soups and stews.

CURRY POWDER The flavourings for authentic Indian curries are made up of different mixtures of ground spices which usually include cumin, coriander, turmeric, pepper, chilli powder and other spices, which are ground or crushed just before use. However, such mixtures can be bought in bottles ready-prepared, the proportions of each spice used varying from one manufacturer to another. Curry powders are usually described as mild, medium or hot, depending on how much chilli is included in the mixture. Although bought curry powders are convenient, the best flavour is achieved by grinding and mixing your own spices just before using.

Apart from its use in ethnic dishes, curry powder can add spice to many other types of dish, though it is usually best if lightly cooked first to remove any harsh flavours. Add it to salad dressings, sprinkle it into sauces and casseroles, and rub it into chicken skin before poaching. (*see also* CURRY, CURRY LEAF, CURRY PASTE)

CURUBA (Banana Passion Fruit) A type of elongated passion fruit that grows in South America and can occasionally be bought in Britain. It has a yellow-green skin and flesh that is full of seeds, like the passion fruit. It tastes similar to the passion fruit, if slightly more sour. (*see also* PASSION FRUIT)

CUSHION The cut of meat nearest the udder in lamb or beef.

CUSTARD Traditionally, a custard is a sweet mixture made from egg yolks (or whole eggs) and milk, which is used as a sauce or cold dessert. Custards vary in thickness, depending on the amount of egg in the mixture. A thin custard may be used as a sauce, while some custards are baked and left to set in a mould until thick enough to turn out.

Custard is also the name of a sweet sauce made by mixing cornflour or a commercially prepared powder with hot milk. Custard powder is also made from cornflour, but usually includes some colouring agent to make the custard a dark yellow colour. Ready-made custard, to use as a sauce or for topping a trifle, is now available in cans or cartons.

A good egg custard should be smooth and creamy and special care is needed to heat the mixture only sufficiently to cook the eggs, as boiling results in curdling. The use of a double saucepan helps to control the temperature; baked egg custards are cooked in the oven in a *bain-marie*. Flavourings may be as simple as nutmeg or vanilla, but a smooth custard is also the perfect foil for stronger flavours, such as a very sweet caramel. The classic French version of custard is known as *crème anglaise*.

Sweet custards can be served alone or as an accompaniment to other dishes, and often form part of cold desserts, such as trifles, fruit fools, custard tarts and *crème caramels*. A custard is also the basis of desserts like bread and butter pudding.

The most familiar use of a savoury custard is in a quiche or savoury flan, where it is poured over other ingredients, such as bacon, vegetables or fish, in a pastry case, then baked until golden brown and the custard has set firm enough for the quiche to be sliced. A savoury custard is some-times used to make a vegetable terrine that is to be unmoulded.

CUSTARD APPLE This is the name of a group of tropical fruits also known as annona fruit. The group includes atemoyas, cherimoyas, sweet sops (sugar apples), sour sops and bullocks' hearts (so called because of their colour and shape).

Most custard apples look similar to apples with green, purple-green or yellow-brown scaly skin and flesh that varies from sweet to acid. The best known variety is cherimoya, which has a pat-terned skin and pineapple flavoured flesh the colour and texture of custard. Most of the custard apples in Britain's supermarkets have been imported from Spain or Israel.

To select: A ripe custard apple will give when gently squeezed. Slightly unripe fruit can be left to ripen in the dark for a few days. They are delicate fruit which need careful handling to prevent piercing their skin.

To prepare: Cut off the top and remove the flesh, discarding the shiny black seeds.

To serve: Use in fruit salads, ice cream and creamy desserts. Alternatively, the fruit can be cut in half lengthways and the flesh eaten straight out of the skin with a spoon.

CUSTARD MARROW (Custard Squash, Cymling, Patty Pan Squash, Scallop Squash) A summer squash that is flat rather than round, with an attractive scalloped edge. It may be pale green, white or yellow in colour and can be sliced and cooked like courgettes, or stuffed and baked like marrow. (*see also* COURGETTE, MARROW, SQUASH)

CUSTARD POWDER (*see* CUSTARD)

CUTLET A term applied to a chop cut from the best end of neck of lamb, veal or pork. Cutlets may be grilled, fried or braised. (*see also* CHOP, ESCALOPE, LAMB, PORK, VEAL)

CUTTING AND FOLDING (*see* FOLDING IN)

CUTTING IN To combine one ingredient (usu-ally fat) with others, by means of a knife used with a repeated downward cutting motion, or with a pastry blender. (*see also* RUBBING IN)

CUTTLEFISH One of a small group of sea creatures known as cephalopods. Others in the group include squid and octopus.

Cuttlefish are found in the Mediterranean and are very popular in Spain and Italy. They have soft bag-like bodies with eight 'arms' and two tentacles which they use to catch their prey. Internally, they have one long bone (the cuttlebone) which is easily removed by cutting a slit in the body. The guts, including the ink sac, are also removed from inside the body before cooking, as are the head and parrot-like beak.

Cuttlefish are rarely sold fresh in Britain but are available frozen. They can be cooked and eaten like squid, and are frequently stuffed or cooked in their own ink. In Japan and other eastern countries, cuttlefish are available dried and are a popular snack. (*see also* CEPHALOPOD, OCTOPUS, SQUID)

CYCLAMATE A chemical substance once used as an artificial sweetener, particularly in soft drinks. It is thirty times sweeter than sugar, is not fattening, and leaves no after-taste. However, in 1970, it was removed from the list of permitted additives in many countries as a result of research in America which linked the consumption of a mixture of cyclamates and saccharine with bladder cancer. (*see also* SACCHARIN, SWEETENERS)

CYMLING (*see* CUSTARD MARROW)

D

DAB A small, flat sea fish belonging to the plaice family, dab is found in north European waters and the Atlantic. It has a distinctive rough skin and white flesh and is excellent fried or baked. It may be sold whole or as fillets and is at its best from August to December.

DACE (Dare, Dart) A small freshwater fish of the carp family found in rivers in Britain and Europe. It is not often used as food as it does not grow to any size and has coarse, rather muddy-flavoured flesh. It can, however, be fried, grilled or baked whole, with or without a stuffing.

DAIKON (*see* RADISH)

DAIQUIRI Originally the name of a Cuban rum and of a cocktail made by mixing it with fresh lime juice, a daiquiri may now be flavoured with a variety of fruit syrups. A daiquiri is often served in a glass frosted with fruit juice and caster sugar. A frozen daiquiri is made in a blender with crushed ice.

DAKTYLA A Greek bread usually made in a long loaf made up of several sections which are pulled apart to eat. The tops of the sections are usually sprinkled with sesame seeds. *Daktyla* bread is available from delicatessens and some supermarkets.

DAL (Dhal) The collective name for a variety of lentils, peas and other pulses which are a very important ingredient in Indian cooking and a good source of protein. There are many different types available. A large selection can be found in Indian shops, and larger supermarkets and health food stores stock a good range.

Among the most frequently used dals are *channa dal* (*see* CHANNA) and *moong dal* (*see* MUNG BEAN). Most dals are cooked in spiced water with various other flavourings added. They may also be ground to a flour (*see* GRAM FLOUR) and used to make pancakes or a purée. (*see also* PULSES)

DALLE The French name for a small slice or escalope of fish, usually cut from a salmon, hake or tuna. A *dalle* may be grilled, poached, braised or sautéed. (*see also* DARNE)

DAMSON (*see* PLUM)

DANABLU (*see* DANISH BLUE CHEESE)

DANDELION The dark yellow flowers of this wild plant may be used for making wine, while the leaves may be eaten raw in salads or boiled and served as a vegetable. It is one of the most nutritious of green leafy vegetables, containing vitamins A and C, calcium and iron. A variety cultivated in France and Belgium has larger leaves that are paler in colour and milder in flavour than the wild variety.

If picking your own dandelion leaves, select plants that are growing in a clean area; they should be picked when young and tender, before the flower heads develop. Trim the roots from the leaves and wash them well, then serve in a salad or cook like spinach until tender. Drain well, then purée, season well and serve with a knob of butter. A popular way to serve dandelion leaves is to mix freshly shredded leaves with crisply fried bacon and hot bacon fat.

The roasted dried root of dandelion is used as a coffee substitute (*see* COFFEE).

DANISH BLUE CHEESE (Danablu) A white softish cheese made in Denmark from pasteurized cows' milk. Its white paste has a blue mould veining and a sharp, salty taste. It is often used in dips and dressings.

DARE (*see* DACE)

DARIOLE Originally the name of a small cake, dariole now means a small, narrow mould with sloping sides used for making madeleines, babas and individual desserts and savouries.

DARNE The French name for a thick slice of raw fish, either on the bone or filleted, usually cut from a salmon, hake or tuna. A *darne* may be grilled, poached or braised. (*see also* DALLE)

DART (*see* DACE)

DARTOIS A small, light pastry, made from two strips of puff pastry sandwiched together with a sweet or savoury filling. A savoury dartois is usually served as an hors d'oeuvre, while a sweet dartois is served as a dessert. Popular savoury fillings include anchovies, sardines and chicken; a sweet filling may be confectioners' custard, jam or a fruit purée.

In French cooking, the name *dartois* is also given to certain meat dishes garnished with cooked carrots, turnips and celery.

DASHEEN A West Indian root vegetable similar to a potato with a dark, bark-like skin. It comes from the same family as the taro, colocassi and eddoe, and its leaves can be used as callaloo (*see* CALLALOO). It should be treated like potatoes and boiled or baked.

DASHI A Japanese stock made from dried fish (usually bonito), seaweed and various flavourings. Like other stocks, it is used as a basis for sauces and soups, and for cooking meat, fish, rice or vegetables. It can be bought as a paste or powder to be made up with boiling water.

DATE The fruit of the date palm tree with firm sweet flesh and a long inedible central stone. Dates are usually about 4 cm ($1^{1}/_{2}$ inches) long and grow in clusters on either side of a long stalk hanging down from the tree. Originating in the Persian Gulf, dates are now mainly cultivated in Tunisia, Israel and southern Algeria.

Fresh dates are now commonly available in Britain and are especially abundant in the winter months. They should be plump and shiny, with smooth golden brown skins. Squeeze the stem end to remove the tough skin, then slit open and remove the stone. Dates have a deliciously sweet, honey-like flavour and can be eaten raw, used in salads or desserts, or may be stuffed with cream cheese to serve as canapés or almond paste to serve as petits fours. (*see also* DATE, DRIED)

DATE, DRIED Dried dates are available whole, with or without stones, or as pressed blocks of stoned fruit. Whole dates can be stoned, if necessary, and used without soaking for teabreads. The pressed blocks need to be soaked overnight and are best used for puddings, breads and cakes. Chopped dates rolled in sugar are also available and these can be used in baking without the need for soaking.

'Semi-dry' dates are also available in presentation boxes, especially popular at Christmas time. They are usually arranged in the box on either side of a real or plastic stalk, as it still attached to it.

Unlike many dried fruits, dried dates have not been treated with sulphur, but their skins are sometimes treated with mineral oil to make them glossy. Untreated dates are available from health food shops.

DATE MARKING Most of the pre-packed foods on sale in supermarkets today are marked with a 'sell-by' or 'best-before' date. At present, food intended for consumption within six weeks of packing has a 'sell-by' date, often accompanied by an instruction to eat or use the food on the day of purchase, or within two to three days. However, by the end of 1992, this will be replaced by a 'use-by' date. Food which has a life of six weeks to three months will have a 'best-before' date, showing both the day and the month. If a food is likely to stay in good condition for a longer period (from three to 18 months), then the date may be expressed as a 'best-before-end' date, and only the month and year are given.

With certain exceptions, such as canned and frozen foods, date marking is now mandatory for any pre-packed food with a 'shelf-life' of less than 18 months. Very often, however, food with a longer shelf-life is also marked. Storage instructions are also given where necessary. Packed foods from some food shops are also marked with a 'display-until' date, but this is simply an instruction to the shop that the food should be taken off the shelves on or before that date if it has not been sold.

Assuming shop storage conditions are satisfactory, food can be relied upon to remain in good condition until the dates given. To be sure the food you eat is in prime condition, fresh and safe, it is always best to follow the manufacturers' recommendations.

DATE MUSSEL (*see* SEA DATE)

DAUBE The French name given to a method of braising meat or vegetables in stock, often with wine and herbs.

DECANTING Pouring wine carefully from a bottle into a wine jug or decanter, leaving any sediment in the bottle. It is only necessary to decant fine wines which have been long aged in the bottle, such as old clarets and ports. However, younger wines can also benefit from being exposed to the air before serving, and decanting may also be done for aesthetic reasons.

DEEP-FAT FRYER, ELECTRIC (*see* ELECTRIC DEEP-FAT FRYER)

DEEP FRYING (*see* FRYING)

DEGLAZING Heating stock, wine or other liquids with the cooking juices and other sediment left in the pan after roasting or sautéing meat, game or poultry, in order to make gravy or a sauce. As the liquid is heated, it is stirred to dissolve the sediment, then may be cooked for a longer period in order to darken it and reduce it to a thicker consistency.

DÉGORGER The French name for a process which uses salt to draw moisture out of foods, especially vegetables, before cooking. It may be necessary to remove excess moisture because it will make the finished dish too liquid, or because, as in the case of aubergines, it has a bitter flavour. Other vegetables which may be treated in this way include courgettes and cucumber.

In French cookery, the term is also used to describe the soaking of meat, poultry, fish or offal

in water to remove impurities before cooking. (*see also* AUBERGINE)

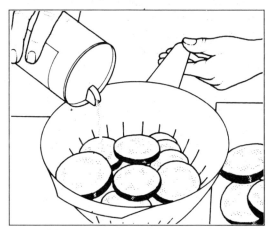

Sprinkling salt over slices of aubergine in a colander, before leaving to *dégorge*.

DEHYDRATED FOODS Dehydration, or the removal of most or all of the moisture from food, is the modern name for drying, one of the oldest methods of preserving, carried out on a commercial basis. Although dehydration is the result of drying all foods, the term 'dehydrated foods' usually refers to a variety of dried individual or mixed foods that undergo total dehydration by a variety of methods before being packed in foil sachets or cans and sold as 'convenience foods'.

Concentrated foods, such as fruit juice and canned soups, have been partially dehydrated in order to reduce their volume, making transportation and storage easier. The dehydrated convenience foods most commonly used are packet soups and sauces, instant coffee, dried milk, instant mashed potato, stock cubes and baby foods. They are all reconstituted simply by adding hot or cold water or milk. (*see also* DRIED FISH, DRIED FRUIT, DRIED HERBS, DRIED MEAT, DRYING, PULSES, VINE FRUITS)

DELICATESSEN A German word, meaning 'delicacies', which has been adopted in many other countries as the name of a variety of ready-to-eat foods, such as cold meats, pâtés, continental sausages, poultry, pickled and smoked fish, potato salad, coleslaw and other salads, olives, etc., and to the shop or supermarket department in which such foods are sold. A delicatessen is also likely to sell other more unusual and specialist foods.

DEMERARA SUGAR (*see* SUGAR)

DEMI-GLACE SAUCE This very rich classic French brown sauce is based on espagnole sauce and is usually served with red meat or game. A liquid meat glaze, meat extract or, if preferred, brown or white stock or clear soup is added to espagnole sauce, then the mixture is boiled for about 20 minutes or until well reduced, skimming frequently to remove fat. Finally, sherry or Madeira may be added to flavour the sauce. (*see also* ESPAGNOLE SAUCE)

DEMI-SEL A fresh cream cheese with a 40 per cent fat content, usually sold in small squares wrapped in foil. It is lightly salted and has a mild flavour, though sometimes herbs, paprika or pepper may be added. It is made in France, mainly in Normandy, from pasteurized cows' milk.

DERBY CHEESE A hard, close-textured British cheese made from cows' milk. Though mild in flavour when young, it develops a fuller flavour as it matures and is at its best when it is six months old.

Sage Derby is probably more popular than plain Derby cheese and was originally made by layering the plain cheese with sage leaves to give a pleasant, sharp, tangy flavour. It must be eaten fresh or the flavour becomes very sharp. Nowadays, sage oil is used in place of the leaves.

DESSERT The last course of a formal dinner, which originally consisted of fresh, dried and crystallized fruit and nuts of various kinds and sometimes, in addition, ices, petits fours or fancy biscuits. Nowadays, the term is used with reference to any sweet course which may include hot or cold tarts, mousses, pies, trifles, cheesecakes, fruit compotes, meringues, pancakes and profiteroles. Cheese may also be served as part of the dessert course, or may replace the dessert altogether.

The choice of dessert served at a meal depends very much on what has been served before it and on whether or not a cheese course will be served after it. Fruit desserts often reflect the time of year, being based on soft fruits in the summer and, perhaps, dried fruits in the winter. A rich main course is best followed by something light, such as a sorbet or a fresh fruit salad, whereas if the rest of the meal has been light, a fruit pie, trifle, cheesecake or pancakes may be served. Desserts are often served with fresh cream, yogurt or a sweet sauce. (*see also* PUDDING)

DEVILLING The process of applying a highly flavoured paste, or a mixture of dry condiments, to legs of poultry, game, fish roes, etc., and then grilling them, or coating them with breadcrumbs and frying them. Various mixtures of condiments are used, but they usually include some very hot ingredients and something piquant; mustard is often used. Turkey legs and similar foods are slashed in several places so that the mixture may be inserted or rubbed in; roes, etc., are simply brushed over with the devilling mixture.

DEVILS ON HORSEBACK Similar to angels on horseback, these small savouries are made with prunes stuffed with fried, salted almonds. Each prune is wrapped in half a rasher of streaky bacon, secured with a cocktail stick or small skewer, and grilled until the bacon is golden brown. Devils on horseback are served on croûtes of fried bread. (*see also* ANGELS ON HORSEBACK)

DEVONSHIRE CREAM (*see* CREAM)

DEVONSHIRE SPLIT (*see* SPLIT)

DEWBERRY A trailing, less prickly variety of blackberry that can be found growing in Britain and the United States. The fruit is bluish-grey in colour and smaller than the blackberry, with a more delicate flavour. Dewberries may be used for making jam and desserts in the same way as blackberries.

DEXTRIN (British Gum) A white or yellowish powder which is produced from starch. It is dissolved in hot water to form a glaze for brushing on bread and rolls.

DHAL (*see* DAL)

DIABETIC FOODS Specially prepared foods containing reduced amounts of carbohydrate. Diabetic squashes, jams and marmalades, biscuits, chocolates and sweets may be bought. Saccharin is also available to replace sugar. Although these foods may be useful in certain circumstances, it is generally considered better for people with diabetes to get accustomed to doing without sweet foods and to build their diets around the foods they are allowed, rather than to perpetuate a sweet tooth by buying expensive substitutes.

DIABLE The French name for an unglazed earthenware cooking pot consisting of two parts like two individual bowls, one being placed upside-down on top of the other. Both parts have long handles which form one handle when the two parts are put together, and both parts have a flat base so that the pot may stand on either side and can be turned during cooking. A *diable* is used, either on the hob or in the oven, for cooking chestnuts, potatoes and other vegetables without any water. A *diable* should never be washed as the tenderness of the vegetables depends on the pot being dry.

DIABLE, À LA A French word used to describe foods that are devilled or highly spiced. (*see also* DEVILLING)

DIBS A syrup derived in the Middle East from the natural sugars found in raisins, grapes or carob beans. It is used as a sweetener.

DICE To cut food, such as vegetables, into small cubes. The small cubes may also be called dice.

DIEPPOISE, À LA A French term used to describe a number of dishes made from sea fish, such as sole, whiting or brill, garnished with shrimps, mussels and sometimes mushrooms, and served with a white wine sauce.

DIET In general terms, diet refers to the food eaten regularly by one person or a group of people, or to a regular pattern of eating. More specifically, diet may also mean a strict regime of eating, that must be followed, perhaps for medical reasons.

The normal healthy diet should provide sufficient protein, carbohydrate, fat, vitamins, minerals, fibre and water, without providing excess energy which can be converted and stored as body fat, leading to obesity, or too much fat, especially saturated fat, which can lead to raised blood cholesterol levels. Actual requirements of nutrients are difficult to assess and can at best only be a rough estimate, for individual needs vary enormously.

Specific diets include weight-reducing diets, which are based on the basic principle that energy expenditure should exceed energy input, thereby encouraging the body to utilize surplus body fat. They may be based on calories, carbohydrates, fibre or fat, or may rely on commercially produced meal substitutes. For the last twenty years or so, slimming has been a profitable business for the manufacturers of special slimming foods and for those running slimming clubs. There are countless different diets to choose from but few people successfully achieve and maintain the weight loss they had hoped for, and it seems that a normal healthy diet, balanced by sufficient exercise, is a more sensible plan.

Diet is particularly important for a number of people with specific diseases, such as coeliac disease or diabetes, or for those who suffer food allergy problems. In most cases, such diets are based on the need to avoid certain types of food. People with coeliac disease, for example, are unable to eat wheat and other cereals which contain gluten. A diabetic diet is based on the need to maintain a normal blood sugar level from day to day. Cholesterol-lowering diets have become more common in recent years, in line with the increasing incidence of heart disease. A number of disorders are blamed on an allergy to certain foods, or to something contained in some processed foods. Allergic reactions to chocolate, cereals, dairy products and certain additives are not uncommon.

A vegetarian diet is one that does not include any meat, though it may include fish and dairy products. A vegan diet excludes all food of animal origin, including dairy products. (*see also* ADDITIVE, CALORIE, CARBOHYDRATE, CHOLESTEROL, DIABETIC FOODS, FATS, FIBRE, MINERALS, NUTRIENT, NUTRITION, TRACE ELEMENTS, VEGAN, VEGETARIANISM, VITAMINS)

DIJON MUSTARD (*see* MUSTARD)

DILL The feathery leaves of this European plant (known as dill weed) are used as a herb, and the dried seeds as a spice. Dill weed has a mild, sweet, caraway-like flavour and needs to be used in fairly large quantities. The dried dill seeds are more pungent. Dill is used in salads, as a garnish, in scrambled eggs, white meat dishes and, classically, with salmon in the Scandinavian dish *gravad lax* (*see* GRAVAD LAX). Dill is also used to make an aromatic vinegar and to flavour dill pickles (*see* GHERKIN).

DIM SUM The name given to a variety of popular small Chinese savoury and sweet snacks which are a speciality of Cantonese cooking. They may be eaten individually as a snack at any time, or several dishes may be eaten together for a light lunch.

DIP A fairly soft, well-flavoured mixture, often served with cocktails or drinks as an appetizer. A dip is usually accompanied by a variety of small savoury biscuits, crisps and crudités which are dipped into the mixture, then eaten. Dips may be based on cheese, soft cheese, whipped cream or yogurt and can have a variety of flavours, including onion, cheese, garlic and mustard. Well known dips include the Greek *hummus*, made from chick peas, and the Mexican *guacamole*, made from avocado.

DITALINI (*see* PASTA)

DOGFISH (*see* HUSS)

DOLCELATTE A mild, blue Italian cheese made from cows' milk. It is similar to Gorgonzola, but slightly softer and creamier.

DOLMAS (Dolmades) A Turkish or Arabian dish prepared by stuffing vine, fig, cabbage or other edible leaves with a savoury mixture, usually minced lamb and cooked rice, then braising the rolled-up leaves. Dolmas are usually served cold as an hors d'oeuvre.

The term is sometimes applied in the Middle East to stuffed aubergines, courgettes, etc. Dolmades is the name given to stuffed vine leaves in Greece.

DORSET BLUE (*see* BLUE DORSET)

DOSA A traditional dish from southern India, consisting of pancakes made from ground rice and *urad dal*. The dish has become a favourite teatime snack throughout India. The rice and *dal* are both soaked overnight, then ground into a smooth, thick pouring batter which is left to ferment for a few hours. The pancakes are then made by frying the batter on a flat griddle. (*see also* URAD DAL)

DOUBLE GLOUCESTER CHEESE (*see* GLOUCESTER CHEESES)

DOUGH A thick mixture of uncooked flour and liquid, usually combined with other ingredients. The term is used to refer to mixtures such as pastry, scones and biscuits as well as those made with yeast. A dough is usually thick enough to knead and roll out or shape, as opposed to batters or cake mixtures which are much softer, even liquid. (*see also* BATTER, BISCUIT, BREAD, PASTRY, SCONE)

DOUGHNUT A small cake made of slightly sweetened dough cooked in hot fat and dredged with sugar. Doughnuts can be made using either yeast or baking powder as a raising agent. Ring-shaped doughnuts are usually sold simply dusted with icing sugar; spherical doughnuts are filled with jam; éclair-shaped doughnuts are filled with whipped cream.

DOVER SOLE (*see* SOLE)

DRAGÉE A French sweet, usually consisting of a fruit or nut coated with a hard sugar icing; sugar almonds are the best known example. In Greece, it is traditional to serve sugar almonds at weddings, festive occasions (such as Christenings) and parties. In British cooking the name most often referes to small silver or coloured balls used to decorate iced cakes.

DRAGON'S EYES A fruit, found in the Far East, which resembles the lychee (*see* LYCHEE).

DRAINING Removing surplus liquid or fat from foods. The two main methods of doing this are by means of a sieve or colander (for liquid), or by placing the food on absorbent paper (for fat).

DRAMBUIE A golden-coloured Scottish liqueur, with the flavour of whisky and heather honey.

DRAWING Removing the entrails from poultry or game birds. Most birds on sale in supermarkets or from butchers have already been drawn, and the giblets may or may not be sold with the bird.

Drawing is usually done after a bird has been hung (in the case of game) and plucked. Usually the feet are removed, the sinews in the legs drawn, the head and neck cut off, and the gullet and windpipe loosened before removing the internal organs. The entrails are removed through the enlarged tail end vent of the bird.

After drawing, the bird should be thoroughly wiped out before stuffing and trussing. The gizzard, heart and liver (with yellow gall bladder removed) can be kept and used for stock. (*see also* GAME, GIBLETS, POULTRY)

DRAWN BUTTER Melted butter, used as a dressing for cooked vegetables, etc. Water or vinegar is sometimes added and the mixture beaten until thick.

DREDGING (Dusting) Sprinkling food lightly with flour, sugar or other powdered coating. Fish and meat are often dredged with flour before frying, while cakes, biscuits and pancakes may be sprinkled with caster or icing sugar after cooking.

DRESSING A term used to describe the plucking, drawing and trussing of poultry and game in preparation for cooking. A cooked crab is also 'dressed', that is the meat is removed from its body and legs and arranged decoratively, usually in the shell, prior to serving. Dressing can also mean garnishing a dish or coating a salad. (*see also* CRAB, GARNISH, SALAD DRESSING)

DRESSING, FRENCH (*see* SALAD DRESSING)

DRESSING, SALAD (*see* SALAD DRESSING)

DRIED BEANS (*see* PULSES)

DRIED FISH As a method of preserving fish, drying is usually used in combination with smoking, dry salting or soaking in brine. A few fish are simply dried and may be used as they are or reconstituted by lengthy soaking in water, then cooked as fresh fish.

Although dried fish is not used a great deal in Britain, it features strongly in many other cuisines of the world. Bombay duck is a well known accompaniment to Indian food and consists of pieces of dried bummaloe fish. It may be cooked and eaten without soaking. Dried cod, sometimes called stockfish, is much used in Scandinavia and Portugal. Dried cuttlefish are a popular snack in Japan, while dried grey mullet fillets are used in Thai cooking, and dried grey mullet roes are used in France and Italy. Dried scallops feature in Chinese cooking.

Although fish was originally dried on a domestic basis, home drying of fish is not now recommended. (*see also* DRYING, DRY SALTING)

DRIED FRUIT Drying fruit is one of the oldest methods of preserving, and although the methods have changed – much fruit is now dried by artificial heat rather than the sun – the principle is the same. The water content is drawn out, preventing the growth of mould and bacteria and leaving the natural sugar in the fruit to act as a preservative.

Dried fruits are a useful source of concentrated nutrients as they are high in fibre, natural sugars, protein, vitamins A, B and C, iron, calcium and other minerals. However, the drying process can alter their appearance quite dramatically, making some fruits, such as dried bananas and peaches, particularly unattractive. Many dried fruits have to be sliced or cut before drying, and the fruit is sometimes treated (usually by fumigating with sulphur dioxide) to prevent discoloration. Mineral oils may be sprayed on fruits after drying to give them a glossy appearance and to prevent them sticking together. These oils can be washed off with warm water but it is preferable to buy fruit treated with vegetable oils instead. Fruits that have not been treated with sulphur or mineral oils can be bought from health food shops.

Although some dried fruits, such as apricots, dates and figs are delicious eaten just as they are, most need soaking for at least 3 hours, preferably overnight, before using. They may be soaked in water, wine or cider. Dried fruits can be used to make jam, desserts, sauces, fruit salads and compotes, or can simply be chopped and added to muesli or baked in cakes, teabreads, biscuits and scones.

(*see also* DEHYDRATED FOODS, DRYING, VINE FRUITS and individual dried fruit entries)

DRIED HERBS Most herbs are available in dried form, usually 'rubbed' or chopped into fine pieces. When buying dried herbs, look for those that are bright in colour, rather than faded and dull. They should be stored in sealed containers in a dry place and, despite the fact that they are often sold in glass jars, they should also be stored in the dark. The flavour of a dried herb is much stronger than that of the fresh version, so only about a third as much should be used in a recipe if substituting dried for fresh.

Placing fresh herbs on a wire rack covered with muslin prior to drying.

Herbs may be dried at home very successfully. Pick them on a dry day, when the dew has lifted, before the sun dispels the volatile oils. The best time of year is shortly before they flower – usually June or July – when they contain the maximum amount of oil. Pick off any damaged leaves and rinse dusty stems and leaves quickly in cold water.

Herbs can be dried in the sun over a period of 4-5 days. However, this method tends to result in loss of the colour and aromatic properties of some herbs. It is much quicker and better to dry them in an airing cupboard or the oven on the lowest possible setting, both with the door left slightly ajar to allow air to circulate. The oven temperature should not exceed 32°C (90°F). Place the herbs on wire racks covered with muslin or cheesecloth which will let the air through. Herbs will dry in an airing cupboard in 3–5 days and in 2–3 hours in the oven. Turn the herbs gently from time to time during drying to ensure they dry evenly.

For even quicker drying, use a microwave cooker. Place herbs on a sheet of absorbent kitchen paper in a single layer and place in the centre of the cooker floor or turntable. Microwave on HIGH for 2–3 minutes, depending on the quantity.

Herbs are dry when the stem and leaves become brittle but remain green and will crumble easily when rubbed between the fingers. Once dried, you can strip the leaves from the stems and crumble them for storage. The exception is bay, whose leaves should be left whole as they contain large amounts of oil and, if crushed, they will release it before it is required. (*see also* DRYING)

DRIED MEAT Drying has long been used as a method of preserving meat, but these days is seldom used as the sole method. Its purpose, as with all curing, is to draw the moisture out of the meat, so that micro-organisms that cause deterioration cannot multiply.

Most preserved meats are cured commercially by a combination of drying, smoking and brining, such as *bündnerfleisch* from Switzerland and *bresaola* from northern Italy. Both are lean, tender cuts of beef which are brined, air-dried and matured, then cut into wafer-thin slices and served in an oil and vinegar dressing as an hors d'oeuvre. Both are very expensive delicacies. *Biltong* is a South African version that may be dried, salted or smoked. *Charqui* (jerky) is also preserved beef traditionally cured by drying, though it may also be smoked or soaked in brine before drying.

Although originally done on a domestic basis, home drying of meat is not recommended. (*see also* BILTONG, BRESAOLA, CHARQUI)

DRIED PEAS (*see* PULSES)

DRIED VEGETABLES The most frequently used dried vegetables are the pulses which include many varieties of beans, peas and lentils. Other vegetables, such as garlic and onion are dried commercially and included in a variety of dehydrated soup and sauce mixes. It is also possible to buy dried onion and garlic flakes for using as flavourings. Few vegetables, other than onions, mushrooms, French beans and chilli peppers, are suitable for drying at home. Vegetables are usually blanched before drying. (*see also* DEHYDRATED FOODS, DRYING, PULSES)

DRIPPING Fat obtained from roasting meat, or from pieces of fat which are rendered down deliberately. Dripping can be collected and stored in the refrigerator, where it solidifies in a white block, often with a little brown jellied meat juice (or meat extract) underneath. Dripping can be used for frying or for roasting the next joint of the same meat. (*see also* EXTRACT, RENDERING)

DROPPING CONSISTENCY A term used to describe the correct texture of a cake or pudding mixture just before cooking. To test for dropping consistency, scoop up a spoonful of the mixture and hold the spoon on its side above the bowl. The mixture should fall off the spoon of its own accord within 5 seconds.

DRUMSTICK The most familiar use of this term is as the name of the lower part of the legs of chicken, turkey and other birds (*see* CHICKEN, TURKEY, etc.). However, it is also the name of a tree that grows mostly in India, but is also found in the southern United States and the West

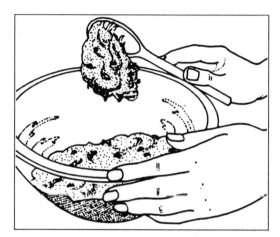

Testing a mixture for dropping consistency by holding a spoonful above the bowl until it drops.

Indies. It may also be called horseradish tree (because of the flavour of its roots) and ben tree. (Its seeds are known as ben nuts and an oil is extracted from them for commercial use.)

The flowers, leaves, seed pods and even the twigs of the drumstick tree are used as a vegetable in Indian cooking, often being added to vegetable curries. The drumsticks that can be found in Indian food shops in Britain are the unripe seed pods, looking rather like long ridged green beans. They taste a little like asparagus and can be cooked and eaten in the same way, though they need longer cooking and can be very fibrous.

DRY FRYING (*see* FRYING)

DRYING Preserving food by dehydration. Since ancient times, food has been hung in the air or left in the sun to dry because, without moisture, the micro-organisms that lead to deterioration cannot thrive in the food.

Some fresh foods can be dried successfully under quite simple conditions, but most these days are dried commercially by a variety of reliable, high-speed methods, including drying under pressure, spray drying and freeze drying. Fruits, vegetables, fish and meat can all be dried

successfully, either whole or in pieces. Dried grains, such as rice, are familiar to us all, as are dried pulses and dried fruits.

The flavour of dried foods is altered by drying but is not necessarily impaired. Sultanas and raisins, for example, do not taste very much like fresh grapes, but they have a delicious sweet flavour of their own which is put to good use in baking, dried fruit salads and other desserts. Most dried foods need lengthy soaking before they can be used.

(*see also* DEHYDRATED FOODS, DRIED FISH, DRIED FRUIT, DRIED HERBS, DRIED MEAT, DRIED VEGETABLES, PULSES, VINE FRUITS)

DRY SALTING A method of curing food using salt. Salt is rubbed very thoroughly into food and left to produce a brine by drawing out moisture from the food. It is a slower method of salting than soaking in a brine, but produces a better flavour. On a commercial level, dry salting is used for ham, bacon and other cured meats, sometimes combined with drying or smoking.

Dry salting can be carried out at home for small items of food, such as nuts, sliced vegetables or small fish, such as anchovies or sprats. It is important to use a coarse salt, such as rock, sea or block salt, rather than free-running table salt. The prepared food should be packed in a large glass or earthenware container between layers of salt and left until a brine is produced. (For more detailed information, look in a reputable cookery book before attempting dry salting at home.)

Dry salting is particularly associated with *sauerkraut*, a German speciality made from dry-salted cabbage, and *gravad lax*, a Swedish dish made by dry salting salmon.

(*see also* DRIED FISH, DRIED VEGETABLES, DRYING, GRAVAD LAX, SAUERKRAUT)

DU BARRY, À LA The French name given to a rich cauliflower soup, or to other dishes garnished with cauliflower.

DUBLIN BAY PRAWN (*see* SCAMPI)

DUBONNET The brand name of a well-known and popular quinine-flavoured French apéritif which may be drunk neat, with ice and lemon, made into a cocktail with vodka or gin, or mixed with soda or lemonade.

DUCHESSE, À LA The French name given to any dish garnished or served with the rich creamed potato mixture known as duchess potatoes. It also refers to a dish of tongue and mushrooms in a béchamel sauce, and to various pastries containing an almond mixture.

DUCHESS POTATOES (*see* POTATO)

DUCK (Duckling) Although not as popular or readily available as chicken, duck is a flavoursome bird that is delicious roasted and served with its traditional accompaniment, orange sauce. Originally a game bird, duck is now domesticated and several breeds are bred for eating all over the world.

Nearly all breeds of domestic duck are descended from just two species of wild duck, the mallard and the South American Muscovy duck. The best breeds are considered to be the British Aylesbury, the American Long Island and the French Rouen and Nantes ducks. A true Aylesbury duck is seldom found these days; most of those on sale are a species of common duck descended from the wild mallard in Lincolnshire or Norfolk. Some breeds of duck are fattier than others and need longer cooking, but all have a layer of fat under the skin intended to keep the live duck warm. Barbary ducks are a species descended from the Muscovy and bred mostly in France. They are not slaughtered until at least three months old and can weigh as much as 3.2 kg (7 lb). Barbary ducks are less fatty than other breeds and have a stronger flavour.

Duck is sold both fresh and frozen, ready for the oven. Commercially-produced birds are nearly all ducklings, that is they are usually killed before the second feather stage, at about 7–8 weeks. A smaller number are also sold 'New York dressed' or 'rough-plucked' (with heads and feet on and not drawn). When choosing a rough-plucked bird, check that the beak and feet are pliable and the breast plump.

Oven-ready weights range from 1.4–2.7 kg (3–6 lb) and you should allow a minimum of 450 g (1 lb) dressed weight per person. Portions of fresh or frozen duckling are also available and can be used when a recipe calls for a jointed duck.

Roast Duckling

Only young ducklings should be used for roasting and older birds reserved for slower cooking methods, such as braising, or for using in pâtés.

Roast duckling may be served with sage and onion stuffing and accompanied by apple sauce and thin brown gravy.

1 oven-ready duckling
salt and pepper

If frozen, thaw the duckling completely. Leave it in its bag and thaw at room temperature. Remove the giblets as soon as possible. Wash and pat the bird dry both inside and out.

Rub the skin with salt and prick it all over with a sharp skewer or fork to allow the fat to run during cooking. Weigh the bird.

Place the duckling on a wire rack over a roasting tin and roast in the oven at 180°C (350°F) mark 4, allowing 30–35 minutes per 450 g (1 lb).

DUCK EGGS (*see* EGGS)

DUDI (Bottle Gourd, Calabash) The dudi is a club-shaped member of the gourd family and can be treated much like any summer squash. It grows up to 60 cm (2 feet) long and is thinner at the stalk end, becoming wider at the other end. It has a yellowy-green skin and a creamy taste. Dudi can be cooked in the same way as marrow and served as a vegetable accompaniment or included in a ratatouille. It can also be stuffed and baked and served as a main course. (*see also* MARROW, SQUASH)

To select: Choose smooth-skinned dudis with no bruising. One dudi will serve four people.

To prepare: Top and tail and cut into thick slices, leaving the seeds in. (There is no need to peel.)
To cook: Cook in boiling salted water for 10–20 minutes, until tender, or shallow fry.
To serve: Drain well and serve with melted butter as a vegetable accompaniment.

DULSE (*see* SEA VEGETABLES)

DUMPLING A ball or outer casing of sweet or savoury dough, usually boiled but occasionally baked. The dough may be a suetcrust or yeast mixture, or shortcrust pastry may be used, especially in making apple dumplings (whole apples wrapped in pastry). Breadcrumbs are sometimes used to make a type of dumpling; for Sussex (or hard) dumplings, flour, salt and water only are used; Norfolk dumplings are sometimes made of a milk, egg and flour batter, sometimes of a yeast mixture. Savoury dumplings may be flavoured with herbs or cheese and are usually served with a soup or stew.

DUNDEE CAKE A fairly rich Scottish fruit cake, decorated with split almonds.

DUNLOP CHEESE A Scottish cheese, made originally in Dunlop, Ayrshire, but now fairly general throughout Scotland. It is made from cows' milk and is not unlike Cheddar, but is whiter, moister and of a closer texture. (*see also* ARRAN CHEESE)

DURIAN A very large Asian tree fruit that can weigh up to 9 kg (20 lb). Durians have a thick dull yellow skin covered with rough spines, and a cream coloured flesh which has an unpleasant smell but delicious taste. Durian flesh can be eaten raw or added to Indonesian rice and meat dishes. The large brown seeds can be lightly roasted and eaten like nuts.
To prepare: Slit the fruit at the segment joints with a sharp knife and prize open, protecting your hands from the sharp spines.
To serve: The creamy flesh can be scooped out with a spoon and eaten raw as an hors d'oeuvre or dessert.

DURUM WHEAT (*see* WHEAT)

DUSTING (*see* DREDGING)

DUTCH CABBAGE (*see* CABBAGE, SAVOY)

DUXELLES (*see* MUSHROOM)

DWARF BEAN (*see* BEAN, FRENCH)

E

EARL GREY TEA (*see* TEA)

EARTH ALMOND (*see* CHUFA NUT)

EARTHNUT (*see* CHUFA NUT)

EASTER BISCUITS These small, soft biscuits were at one time a popular Easter tradition. They are made with fruit and spices, are sometimes flavoured with brandy and have a sugary topping.

EASTER CAKE (*see* SIMNEL CAKE)

EASTER EGGS Eggs are the symbol of Easter and the tradition of giving decorated hard-boiled or novelty eggs at Easter is centuries old. In Britain today, an Easter egg has come to be a hollow chocolate egg of varying size, made in two separate halves and filled with loose sweets or a cream filling. Hundreds of different types of chocolate egg are on sale in supermarkets and confectionery shops every Easter, but it is possible to make Easter eggs at home using plastic or tin moulds.

EAU DE COLOGNE MINT (*see* MINT)

EAU-DE-VIE Meaning, literally, 'water of life', this is the French name given to a number of fruit brandies. The best known are *kirsch* (cherry), *framboise* (raspberry), *fraise* (strawberry), *myrtille* (bilberry), *mirabelle* (golden plum), *quetsch* (Switzen plum), *prunelle* (sloe), *poire Williams* (pear), *houx* (holly berry), *coing* (quince), *alisier* (rowanberry), and in Germany and Switzerland *enzian* (gentian).

Eaux-de-vie are distilled from various wines and may be drunk as an aperitif or a liqueur. Some, such as *kirsch*, are used in cooking.

ECCLES CAKE A small English pastry with a filling of dried fruit moistened with melted butter and sugar.

ÉCLAIR A small, finger-shaped cake made from choux pastry and filled with whipped cream or confectioners' custard. The top is usually iced with chocolate or coffee glacé icing.

Small éclairs made in the same way, but with a cream cheese or other savoury filling, are delicious served with drinks or as part of a buffet. (*see also* PASTRY, GLACÉ ICING)

EDAM CHEESE A popular Dutch ball-shaped cheese, with a distinctive bright red wax coating and deep yellow paste. The average Edam weighs about 2.3 kg (5 lb) but it is usually sold in small wedge-shaped portions. A smaller 'baby' Edam is also available. Made from pasteurized skimmed cows' milk, Edam is a firm, smooth-textured cheese that is comparatively low in calories. It has a mild flavour and is best served as a snack, as part of the cheese course at the end of a meal, or used in sandwiches.

EDDOE (Eddo) The West Indian name of a small tropical root vegetable from the same family as dasheen and colocassi. It has a small central bulb surrounded by tuberous growths. Its white mealy flesh can be prepared, cooked and used very much like potatoes; it even tastes quite like potato.

To select: Choose vegetables that are firm. Allow 175–225 g (6–8 oz) per person.

To prepare: Peel and cut into sections.

To cook: Eddoes can be boiled, baked or chopped and fried.

To serve: Serve hot as a vegetable accompaniment, like potatoes, or add to a vegetable stew or curry.

EEL The common or freshwater eel is a long, snake-like fish with shiny, dark green to black skin and dense, fatty flesh which is enhanced by strong flavoured sauces. As eels must be fresh, whole eels are sold alive and should be cooked soon after killing. The fishmonger will usually kill and prepare them for you.

Eels can be jellied, fried, stewed or made into pies. Their bones are rich in gelatine and can be used to make a rich jellied stock in which jellied eels are sold, or to give soups and stews a rich consistency. Young eels, called elvers, are best eaten stewed in garlic, sautéed or deep-fried. They are considered a great delicacy in France, Spain and Portugal. Eels are also sold jellied, whole or as fillets.

Smoked eel is not widely available, but may be found either whole or as chunks of fillet in some delicatessens and fishmongers. It is ready to eat and can be served as a starter with cayenne pepper, lemon wedges and brown bread and butter.

Conger eel is a sea fish that is commonly found in the Atlantic and the Mediterranean. It is a greying brown colour on top and silver underneath, with a dorsal fin running almost the entire length of its body. It is usually sold in steaks or cutlets. The full-flavoured flesh is white and firm; larger eels have a coarser texture than small ones. The conger eel is larger than the common freshwater eel, but it can be prepared and cooked in the same way, though it is most frequently used in soups. Conger eel is usually available fresh from March to October. Smoked conger eel is also available.

EEL POUT (Barbot, Burbot, Lote) A freshwater fish of the cod family. It resembles eel and can be prepared and cooked in the same ways (*see* EEL).

EGG CUSTARD (*see* CUSTARD)

EGGPLANT (*see* AUBERGINE)

EGGS Eggs are versatile, good value food and have a tremendous number of uses in all kinds of cooking. They are an essential ingredient of most cakes and of many other dishes, such as sauces and hot and cold puddings. Nutritionally, they are rich in protein (one egg contains about the same amount of protein as 50 g/2 oz meat) and fat and also contain vitamin A, vitamins of the B complex and useful amounts of iron and calcium.

Although the eggs of many different types of bird can be eaten, the one most widely available is that of the hen or female chicken. Hens are domestic fowls, usually kept, under various conditions, for the sole purpose of producing eggs. Over 90 per cent of egg producers keep hens under 'battery' conditions, that is they are crowded into small cages, row upon row in huge barns. The hens never leave their cages and are automatically watered and fed a precise diet. Although this sort of intensive farming produces a huge quantity of eggs, the cramped conditions can be unhealthy, both for the hens and for the people who eventually consume their eggs.

There are a number of alternative ways of keeping hens for egg production and many farmers are changing their methods in response to public demand for healthier eggs. Today, on supermarket shelves, it is common to see a variety of eggs bearing different labels.

Free range eggs are produced by birds that have continuous daytime access to open-air runs mainly covered with vegetation, and with a maximum number of 1,000 hens per hectare (405 per acre). Eggs from hens that are truly allowed to range freely, to pick and choose whatever they like to eat, are less easily found but can often be bought directly from the farm.

Semi-intensive egg production involves housing hens so that they have continuous daytime access to open-air runs mainly covered with vegetation and with a maximum number of 4,000 hens per hectare (1,619 per acre).

Deep-litter eggs come from hens that are kept in hen houses with a maximum number of seven hens per square metre of floor space.

Perchery eggs are also sometimes called by the somewhat misleading name of 'barn' eggs. Hens producing these eggs are also kept in hen houses, but under much more crowded conditions than under the deep-litter system – up to 25 hens per square metre of floor space.

Buying and Storing Eggs

Egg Sizes
Eggs are usually sold in boxes of six or 12. Under

EC regulations, they are graded for size as follows:

Size 1 over 70 g
Size 2 65–70 g
Size 3 60–65 g
Size 4 55–60 g
Size 5 50–55 g
Size 6 45–50 g
Size 7 below 45 g

Unless a particular egg size is specified in a recipe, use Size 3 or 4 eggs. It does not matter if they are white or brown, there is no difference in taste or nutritional value; the simple explanation is that varying breeds of hen produce different coloured eggs. The colour of the yolk also varies, depending on what the hen eats.

When buying pre-packed eggs in shops you can get some idea of how old they are by checking the week number given on the box. Week 1 falls at the end of December or beginning of January. If the eggs are fresh, they can be stored for 2–3 weeks in the refrigerator.

The small air space inside every egg increases in size with age and it is possible to carry out a simple test at home to see if an egg is fresh. Place an uncooked egg in a bowl of water; if it lies on the bottom it is fresh; if it tilts it is older (and should be used for frying or scrambling rather than boiling) and if it floats it is likely to be bad. However, this test should only be done just before using the egg as immersing it in water makes the shell porous and open to bacteria.

Storing Eggs

Eggs are best kept in a rack in a cool, dry place preferably under refrigeration. If you store them in a refrigerator, keep them well away from the ice compartment (there is often a special egg storage rack, perhaps in the door) and away from foods like cheese, fish or onions whose smells may transfer to the eggs.

Store eggs pointed end down and use them at room temperature; eggs that are too cold will crack when put into boiling water and are also difficult to whisk.

If you buy free range eggs which have dirty shells, do not attempt to wash them with water, as this could transfer any organisms present to the raw egg inside.

Since eggs are usually in plentiful supply all year round, there is little point in preserving them unless you keep your own hens and have a sudden glut. Pickled eggs, however, are quite popular as a snack, and can be bought in delicatessens or sometimes in pubs.

If eggs have been separated and only one part used, the remaining part can be stored in the refrigerator; yolks will keep for 2–3 days covered with water, whites for up to 7 days in a covered container, or whites may be frozen. If freezing, label the container with the number of whites it holds. If you forget, an egg white measures about 25 ml (1 fl oz).

Using Eggs in Cooking

Eggs have three main functions in cooking:

Emulsifying The yolk only is used as an emulsifying agent in mixtures like mayonnaise.

Thickening and binding Beaten eggs will thicken sauces and custard mixtures. They will also bind

Testing an uncooked egg for freshness by placing it in a bowl of water.

flaky ingredients like fish for fish cakes, and coat foods which are likely to disintegrate during cooking, such as fish for frying, fritters and croquettes.

Raising Eggs are used as a raising agent for batters and for many cakes.

Where an extra light mixture is needed, whisk the egg whites separately before incorporating them. Whisked egg whites are also used for making meringues, soufflé omelettes, soufflés and light foamy desserts and icings.

Eggs should be cooked thoroughly but gently, except when hard-boiling. Cooking them at too high a temperature or for too long makes them tough. Custards and mousses containing eggs should be cooked very slowly, preferably in a double saucepan or *bain-marie*.

How to Separate an Egg

Tap the egg sharply once on the side of a bowl or cup and break the shell in half. Tapping it gently two or three times is liable to crush the shell instead of breaking it cleanly, and may cause the yolk to break and mingle with the white. Egg whites will not whisk well if any yolk is present.

Collect all the egg in one half of the shell, then pass the yolk back and forth between the two

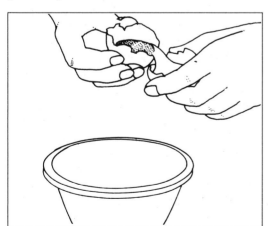

Separating an egg by breaking it and passing the yolk between the two halves of shell.

halves, allowing the white to drop into a bowl below. Put the completely separated yolk into another container.

When separating more than one egg, use a third container and crack each egg over this, so that if you do break a yolk you will only spoil one white. As the eggs are successfully separated you can add the white and yolk to the two separate bowls.

Cooking Eggs

Boiled Eggs

Although called 'boiled' eggs, eggs cooked this way should in fact be simmered rather than boiled. Using a spoon, lower the eggs into boiling water, reduce the heat and simmer for 3½ minutes for a light set and up to 5 minutes for a firm set. Alternatively, put them in cold water and bring them slowly to the boil, then cook for 3–4 minutes for a light set. The water in each case should be just sufficient to cover the eggs.

If the egg cracks in the pan, quickly add a little salt or vinegar to the water to prevent a stream of egg escaping from the shell.

Hard-boiled Eggs

Put the eggs into boiling water, bring back to the boil and simmer gently for 10–12 minutes.

Once they are cooked, hard-boiled eggs should be placed under cold running water, then tap the shells and leave them until cold. (This prevents a discoloured rim forming round the outside of the yolk and enables the shell to be removed easily.) When cold, crack the shell all over and peel off the shell.

Soft-boiled Eggs (Oeufs Mollets)

Soft-boiled eggs can be served hot or cold. Cold, they are ideal for eggs in aspic; hot they can be served in a savoury sauce. They can also be used as an alternative to poached eggs.

Put the eggs into a pan of boiling water, reduce the heat and simmer gently, allowing 6 minutes from the time the water comes back to the boil.

Small eggs take 3–4 minutes. Plunge at once into cold water, leave for about 8 minutes, then crack and carefully peel away the shell from the centre, remembering that the egg is only lightly set and will easily break.

Coddled Eggs

Place the eggs in boiling water, cover, remove from the heat and keep in a warm place for 8–10 minutes; they will then be lightly set. Alternatively, the eggs can be cooked in a china egg coddler. (*see also* CODDLING)

Poached Eggs

The eggs may be cooked in a poaching pan or in water or in a frying pan.

To use an egg poacher, half-fill the lower container with water, place a small knob of butter in each cup and heat. When the water boils, break the eggs into the cups, season and cover the pan. Simmer gently until the eggs are set, then loosen them with a knife before turning out.

To use a frying pan, half-fill it with water and add a pinch of salt or a little vinegar to help the eggs keep their shape and give added flavour. Swirl the water with a spoon and slip the eggs into the water. Cook gently until lightly set, then lift out with a slotted spoon or fish slice. Serve on buttered toast.

Fried Eggs

Melt a little butter or oil in a frying pan. Break each egg separately into a cup and slide them into the hot fat. Cook gently, basting with the fat, so the eggs cook evenly on top and underneath. When just set, remove from the pan with a fish slice or broad palette knife.

Baked Eggs

Place the required number of ramekin or other individual ovenproof dishes on a baking sheet, with a knob of butter in each dish. Put them in the oven until the butter has melted. Break an egg into each dish, season, and cook at 180°C (350°F) mark 4 for 8–10 minutes or until the eggs are just set. Serve at once.

Scrambled Eggs

Melt a knob of butter in a small saucepan. Whisk 2 eggs with 30 ml (2 tbsp) milk or water and season. Pour into the saucepan and stir slowly over a gentle heat until the mixture begins to thicken. Remove from the heat and stir until creamy. Pile on to hot buttered toast and serve immediately. *Serves 1*

Salmonella in Eggs

Egg shells are porous so, although eggs may seem to be sealed, it is possible for bacteria to enter, especially if eggs are dirty or wet. If hens are kept in unhygienic conditions, whether battery or free range, they can become diseased and infected with bacteria, such as salmonella, and this can be passed on to their eggs.

Bacteria in eggs are destroyed when the eggs are heated to a high enough temperature, so as long as eggs are thoroughly cooked they are quite safe to eat. Unfortunately, however, many of our favourite foods, such as mousses, cheesecakes, cold soufflés, meringues, mayonnaise, lemon curd and royal icing, use either raw or very lightly cooked eggs. Even lightly cooked scrambled egg or a very soft boiled egg or runny omelette can carry some risk of salmonella poisoning. It is advised that 'at risk' groups, such as the elderly, the sick, babies and pregnant women, should only consume eggs that have been cooked until the white and the yolk are solid, whilst avoiding any raw egg products, such as home-made mayonnaise or ice cream at least until farmers have eradicated salmonella and other bacteria from their hens and eggs. In the meantime, it is possible to buy dried or frozen pasteurized egg, either whole or separated into yolks and whites. These products can be used in some, but not all, of the ways in which normal raw eggs are used. (*see also* ALBUMEN POWDER, FOOD POISONING)

Other Birds' Eggs

Duck eggs are larger and richer than hens' eggs. They must be thoroughly cooked to ensure that all bacteria are killed; allow at least 10 minutes for boiling. Duck eggs can be included in cakes and puddings, but should not be used in meringues or any dessert which is cooked for only a short time or at a low temperature. They should only be stored for up to four days.

Turkey and goose eggs taste similar to hens' eggs but are much larger. They can be cooked by any of the methods given for hens' eggs and can be used in all cakes and puddings. Allow about 7 minutes for a soft boil. They can be stored for up to four days.

Quails' eggs are much smaller than hens' eggs; boil for 1 minute.

ELDERBERRY The fruit of the elder tree which grows wild in hedgerows and similar places. The berries are small, round and shiny, almost black in colour. They grow in clusters, ripening in late summer. Elderberries have a rather bitter flavour and are used to make elderberry wine or preserves.

Elder flowers are also edible and have a strong perfume. They can be stirred into jams, wines and stewed fruits to add extra flavour, or they can be infused in water to make a tea.

ELDER FLOWER (*see* ELDERBERRY)

ELECTRIC CASSEROLE Sometimes known as a slow cooker or crockpot, an electric casserole is used for cooking dishes that can be cooked very slowly, at an even, low heat. Electric casseroles are particularly useful for people who are out all day, as food can be left to cook in the casserole without risk of burning or boiling dry – most dishes will keep in perfect condition for a few hours longer than is needed to cook them. Electric casseroles provide controlled gentle cooking at about a third of the cost of heating a large conventional oven.

Electric casseroles come in a variety of sizes. Some have removable inner pots which can be taken out of the casing and used to serve from at the table. Some have automatic timers and can be set to turn themselves from the high to the low setting. Most models need to be pre-heated before the prepared food is put into the casserole.

Electric casseroles must not be used to reheat either frozen or refrigerated cooked food as the food will not be heated to a high enough temperature to destroy bacteria. If you are adding red kidney or soya beans to a dish cooked in an electric casserole, always boil them in a separate pan for at least 10 minutes before adding them to the casserole. This is to destroy a particular toxic enzyme which will not be destroyed by the heat of the appliance. (This is not necessary for canned kidney beans.)

ELECTRIC DEEP-FAT FRYER This is a separate electric appliance that can be used instead of a chip pan for deep-fat frying. It is much the safest method of deep-fat frying since an electric fryer is thermostatically controlled, so the risk of fat overheating and catching fire is eliminated. (Deep frying on hobs is one of the biggest single causes of accidents in the home.)

Capacities of deep-fat fryers range from 1–4 litres (2–7 pints) of oil, so consider your needs carefully when purchasing; the larger models can take up a lot of space. Some models have a filter in the lid which helps cut down cooking odours. The oil in a deep-fat fryer can be re-used a number of times. (*see also* FRYING)

ELVER (*see* EEL)

EMBUCHADO DE LOMO A Spanish ham made from cured loin of pork enclosed in a skin like a long, straight sausage. It is very highly thought of in Spain and very expensive. It is eaten cold, sliced into chunks.

ÉMINCÉ A French term used to describe foods, such as vegetables, fruit or meat, that are cut into thin slices or shredded. This may be done by hand with a sharp knife or mandolin, or in a food processor. (*see also* MANDOLIN)

EMMENTHAL (Emmental) A Swiss cheese similar to Gruyère but larger and slightly softer in texture, with larger 'eyes'. Made from unpasteurized cows' milk, it is a deep yellow in colour with a mild, slightly nutty flavour. Emmenthal may be served as part of the cheese course at the end of a meal or may be used in cooking. It is traditionally used to make a Swiss fondue (*see* FONDUE).

EMULSION A mixture of two liquids which do not automatically dissolve into each other, e.g. oil and water. They can be made to emulsify by vigorous beating or shaking together, as when combining oil and vinegar in a French dressing. Another 'emulsifying' substance may be added to an emulsion to prevent it separating, as when adding egg yolk to mayonnaise.

ENCHILADA A Mexican dish made by softening corn tortillas in oil or sauce, then rolling and stuffing them with cheese, chicken, meat or beans. They may be topped with cheese or a hot sauce. (*see also* TACOS, TORTILLA)

ENDIVE (*see* CHICORY)

ENRICHMENT Commercially-produced foods may be enriched by the addition of certain nutrients which have otherwise been removed during processing. Other foods may be enriched with nutrients to make them comparable with similar types of food, for example certain vitamins and minerals may be added to margarine to make its food value comparable with that of butter. Occasionally the enrichment is to ensure a constant level of a particular nutrient in an otherwise variable food (as when vitamin C is added to fruit juice).

The term may also be applied to the addition of eggs, cream or butter to a dish, thereby enriching itss flavour.

ENTRECÔTE A steak cut from the middle part of the sirloin of beef; in France it means a steak taken from between two ribs. (*see also* STEAK)

ENTRÉE A dressed savoury dish, consisting of meat, poultry, game, fish, eggs or vegetables, either hot or cold, complete with sauce and garnish, and usually these days forming the main course of a meal. If there are two entrées, the hot one should be served first and the two should be quite different in both flavour and general appearance.

An entrée was originally a dish forming a complete course in itself and was served without accompaniments. In the days of long dinner menus, the entrée followed the fish course and preceded the roast.

ENTREMET At one time, this French name was given to all the dishes served after the main course, but is now more generally applied to the dessert course which, in France, is served after the cheese. (*see also* DESSERT)

ENZIAN (*see* EAU-DE-VIE)

ENZYME Enzymes exist in all foods which have not been subjected to processing. They work within foods continuously, and are responsible for the ways in which the condition of food changes. Their action can be prevented by substances such as salt and vinegar, and most enzymes are killed if subjected to high temperatures (*see* BLANCHING).

EPAZOTE (Mexican Tea, Wormseed) A strong-flavoured herb that grows in America and some parts of Europe. It is most used as a herb in Mexican cooking, but can also be used to make an infused tea.

ÉPOISSES A soft French cows' milk cheese made in the Burgundy region of France. It has a scored orange crust and is sometimes sold wrapped in vine leaves. In France, it is eaten fresh in the summer months but is also available mature from June onwards. It has a strong flavour and may sometimes also be flavoured with black pepper, cloves, fennel or wine.

ESCABÈCHE A Spanish dish consisting of cooked whole small fish, such as anchovies, sardines or mullet, marinated in a spiced oil and vinegar marinade (also known as *escabèche*). The fish are served in the marinade as a cold hors d'oeuvre. (*see also* CAVEACH)

ESCALOPE A thin slice of meat, especially veal or pork, which is cut from the top of the leg. Turkey escalopes are thin slices carved from the breast of the bird. Escalopes are usually grilled or coated in egg and breadcrumbs and fried.(*see also* WIENER SCHNITZEL)

ESCARGOT (*see* SNAIL)

ESCAROLE (*see* CHICORY)

ESPAGNOLE SAUCE A classic French brown sauce that is used as the basis for a number of other sauces, though it may also be served as it is, usually with red meats and game. (*see also* DEMI-GLACE SAUCE, ROBERT SAUCE, REFORM SAUCE)

Espagnole Sauce

25 g (1 oz) butter or margarine
1 rasher streaky bacon, rinded and chopped
1 shallot, skinned and chopped, or a small piece of
  onion, skinned and chopped
60 ml (4 tbsp) mushroom stalks, wiped and
  chopped
1 small carrot, peeled and chopped
30–45 ml (2–3 level tbsp) flour
450 ml (³/₄ pint) beef stock
bouquet garni
30 ml (2 level tbsp) tomato purée
salt and pepper
15 ml (1 tbsp) sherry (optional)

Melt the butter in a saucepan, add the bacon and fry for 2–3 minutes. Add the vegetables and fry for a further 3–5 minutes, until lightly browned. Stir in the flour, mix well and continue cooking until it turns brown.

Remove from the heat and gradually add the stock, stirring after each addition.

Bring to the boil slowly and continue to cook, stirring, until the sauce thickens. Add the bouquet garni, tomato purée, salt and pepper.

Reduce the heat and allow to simmer very gently for 1 hour, stirring from time to time to prevent sticking. Alternatively, cook in the oven at 170°C (325°F) mark 3 for 1 ¹/₂–2 hours.

Strain the sauce, reheat and skim off any fat, using a metal spoon. Adjust the seasoning and add the sherry, if using, just before serving.
Makes about 300 ml (¹/₂ pint)

ESROM A semi-hard slab-shaped cheese made in Denmark from pasteurized cows' milk. Its pale yellow paste contains many irregular holes and it has a soft darker yellow rind. Esrom has a pleasant, mild flavour when young but becomes stronger and spicier as it matures.

ESSENCE An essence is a liquid used to add a particular flavour (vanilla, lemon, coffee, almond, etc.) to a recipe. Essences are usually very strong and only a tiny amount is needed to impart sufficient flavour. The most frequently used essence is vanilla, which is used in countless cake, biscuit and dessert recipes.

True natural essences are made by extracting (usually by distillation) the essential oils from foods, such as lemon, orange or bitter almond. Essences can be quite hard to come by, these days, as they have been replaced to some extent by a wide range of artificial flavourings which are much cheaper to buy, but lack the delicacy and richness of the true essence.

The term essence is also sometimes applied, especially in the French kitchen, to extracts of meat, poultry or fish, which may be used for flavouring. Anchovy essence is an example of an extract which is given the name essence. (*see also* EXTRACT)

ESTOUFFADE (Estouffat) The French name given to a dish, usually of meat and vegetables, that has been cooked very slowly in very little liquid, such as a stew or casserole.

EVAPORATED MILK (*see* MILK)

EVERTON TOFFEE A brittle sweet similar to butterscotch, but containing cream or evaporated milk. (*see also* SWEETS)

EVE'S PUDDING An English dessert pudding made by arranging slices of cooking apple in an ovenproof dish, with a little grated lemon rind and sugar, and covering with a sponge cake mixture. The pudding is baked and served hot.

EXTRACT A concentrated flavouring used in small quantities. Examples include meat extract and yeast extract; soya sauce is a vegetable extract. A meat extract may be made by boiling down a clarified stock, or the juices produced by cooking, until a very concentrated liquid remains. This can then be used as a flavouring for gravies or sauces. Such extracts are also available ready-made in small black jars. (*see also* ESSENCE)

EYEBALLS Eyeballs (especially sheeps' eyeballs) are considered a great delicacy in some Middle Eastern countries. They are usually removed from the head after it has been cooked, then eaten absolutely plain.

F

FAGGOT Faggots are a traditional north of England and Welsh dish and are made from a mixture of pork offal, onion and breadcrumbs, usually shaped into balls or small squares and sometimes wrapped in caul. Faggots may be fried or baked and are usually eaten hot with gravy. The mixture is sometimes baked in one large tin, then cut into squares to serve. Faggots may also be eaten cold with salad.

The name faggot may also be given to a small bunch of herbs tied and wrapped in two pieces of celery stick, like a miniature faggot of wood, such as a bouquet garni.

FAHRENHEIT A system of measuring temperature, named after the German physicist, Gabriel Daniel Fahrenheit (1686–1736). On the Fahrenheit scale, the freezing point of water is 32° and its boiling point 212°. Although the Fahrenheit scale is still the main system of measuring temperature in the United States, in Europe it is being phased out in favour of the Celsius (Centigrade) scale. Most cookery books give oven and other temperatures in both Fahrenheit and Celsius. (*see also* CELSIUS)

FALAFEL A Middle Eastern dish made from bulgar wheat and chick peas, flavoured with garlic, cumin and coriander. The mixture is usually shaped into small balls or patties, baked or fried and served hot with salad or as a filling for pitta bread.

FANCHETTE (Fanchonnette) A tiny French tart made of puff pastry, filled with confectioners' custard and covered with meringue. The name is also given to certain types of petits fours.

FARCE The French word for forcemeat or stuffing.

FARINA The name given to various fine flours made from wheat, nuts or root vegetables. Examples include chestnut flour, cassava flour and potato flour. (*see also* FECULA)

FARINACEOUS FOODS Foodstuffs which consist very largely of starch, for example bread (which is 50 per cent starch), oatmeal, flour, pasta and semolina (which are 70-75 per cent starch). Pulses may also be described as farinaceous foods.

FARL A Scottish oatmeal cake, similar to a bannock and triangular in shape. It is usually a quarter of a whole round loaf.

FARMHOUSE CHEESES (*see* CHEESE)

FATS Although a small amount of fat is essential for good health, most people in Britain (as in most developed countries) eat for more than they need and there is a substantial amount of evidence to show that this is responsible for a number of diseases, such as coronary heart disease, obesity and even some types of cancer.

Fats are either of animal or vegetable origin. Animal fats include butter, margarine, lard, dripping and suet, while vegetable fats include vegetable margarines (such as those based on sunflower oil), and any of the many oils derived from seeds or nuts, such as sesame or rapeseed oil, or walnut oil. In general terms, fats are solid at room temperature, whereas oils are liquid, though oils can be turned into solid substances by processing. (*see also* OILS)

All fats and oils are made of fatty acids which are the basic building blocks of fats. There are more than 20 fatty acids, all with different names and chemical structures, and with different properties. Some fatty acids are said to be 'saturated', some 'monounsaturated', and some 'polyunsaturated'. The difference relates to their chemistry. All fats and oils contain both saturated and polyunsaturated fatty acids and it is the relative proportion or balance between different fatty acids that makes a fat or oil solid or liquid, smelly or odourless, easily stored or prone to rancidity.

Fats and Health

Some types of fat are essential for life. These essential fats are the building blocks of nerves, brain cells and cell walls throughout the body; they also provide the essential fat-soluble vitamins A, D and E. Fat also provides the body with fuel needed for warmth, work, growth and repair. In fact, our consumption of fat only becomes a problem when there is an excess of fat in our diet. Too much of any kind of fat is harmful, though the balance of saturated fats and unsaturated fats is important.

Too much fat is harmful for a number of reasons. Firstly, fats are very high in calories and can contribute to some extent to a weight problem. Secondly, fats (particularly saturated fats) stimulate the body to produce excessive amounts of cholesterol which causes clogging or furring of the coronary arteries, leading to coronary heart disease.

There are three main types of fat which are frequently discussed with regard to health. These are saturated fats, polyunsaturated fats and monounsaturated fats.

Saturated fats contain a high proportion of saturated fatty acids which encourage the body to produce cholesterol. They tend to be solid at room temperature and have a good keeping quality. Most saturated fats are of animal origin – meat, butter, lard, dripping, hard margarine, cheese and egg yolks, but there are some vegetable fats that are high in saturated fatty acids, such as cocoa butter, coconut oil and palm oil and so-called 'hydrolyzed' vegetable oils.

Polyunsaturated fats contain a high proportion of polyunsaturated fatty acid, which are thought to reduce cholesterol. They tend to be liquid at room temperature. Polyunsaturated fatty acids are sometimes called essential fatty acids because they cannot be made by the body. Good sources are nuts, seeds, and the oils and margarines made from them. Fish oils are also high in polyunsaturated fatty acids. In oily fish such as mackerel and herring, the oil is distributed throughout the flesh but in white fish, such as cod and haddock, it is only found in the liver.

Monounsaturated fats were, until quite recently, generally considered to be neutral, that is it was thought they neither contributed to the amount of cholesterol in the blood nor reduced it. However, some recent research indicates that these fats may in fact be beneficial and may behave rather like polyunsaturated fats. The oil with the highest proportion of monounsaturated fat is olive oil. Peanuts and avocados are also good sources of monounsaturated fats.

Using Fats in Cooking

Fats are used for many basic cooking techniques. At one time, butter was used more than anything else, and its unique richness and flavour is still an essential ingredient in many classic sauces, cakes and pastries. Polyunsaturated vegetable margarines or oils now often replace butter for frying and baking, and a number of low-fat spreads now on the market can be used instead of butter in sandwiches and on crackers and toast. All fats should be treated as perishable and stored in the refrigerator.

Pastry

Flavour and shortening power are the most important factors in pastry making. Butter or margarine provides flavour whereas lard has more shortening properties, hence for some pastries a mixture of the two fats is used. Block margarine is more suitable for pastry than soft margarine. Whipped vegetable fats and oil can also be used for pastry, but these are usually added to the flour with the water and mixed with a fork, rather than by the usual 'rubbing in' method.

Cakes

Butter is considered to give the best flavour although margarine is usually easier to cream. Soft margarines are often preferred for cake making and certainly give a better result in the 'one-stage' method. Oils can also be used in cake making.

Puddings

Many of these include pastry or cake mixture but the term also applies to suet puddings. Suet can be bought ready shredded or it can be obtained from the butcher and prepared at home. Shredded vegetarian suet is also readily available from supermarkets.

Frying

A good frying fat should be free from moisture, which makes it spatter when heated. This is why low-fat spreads, which contain a high proportion of water, are not suitable for frying. A fat used for frying should also have a high 'smoking temperature', that is it should be capable of being heated to high temperatures before it smokes and burns. Butter is not suitable for general frying because its smoking temperature is too low. Clarified butter or ghee has a higher smoking temperature and is therefore more suitable for frying. Ordinary butter is good, however, for cooking omelettes and certain vegetables, and a mixture of butter and oil is sometimes used to give flavour and enable the use of a higher temperature. The best fats for frying are olive oil, vegetable oil, lard and clarified dripping.

Fat Substitutes

In recent years, a number of companies have been working towards the development of an artificial fat substitute which would have the creamy taste and texture of fat but not the calories and cholesterol. To date, only one of these products has been approved for use in Britain. Simplesse is a protein-based fat substitute which is made primarily from egg white and/or milk proteins. It has approximately 40 calories per 25 g (1 oz) compared with butter at 210 per 25 g (1 oz). It can be used to replace some or all of the fat in certain manufactured foods, thereby reducing both the fat and calorie content. For example, a tablespoon of mayonnaise made in the traditional way would contain approximately 100 calories; made with Simplesse, it would only contain 25 calories.

Simplesse will only be available for use by food manufacturers.

(*see also* BUTTER, CHOLESTEROL, CLARIFYING, DIET, DRIPPING, GHEE, LARD, MARGARINE, NUTRITION, OILS, RENDERING)

FAVA BEAN (*see* BEAN, BROAD)

FECULA The name given to any of the starchy powders obtained from potatoes, rice, corn, arrowroot, etc. A fecula is similar to a farina, but the starch is separated from the source by washing with water. Arrowroot and cornflour are two familiar feculas. (*see also* FARINA)

FEIJOA (Pineapple Guava) These are large berries native to Brazil but now grown mainly in New Zealand. They have a tough reddish-green skin, white, rather coarse, scented flesh and a soft centre containing edible seeds. Feijoas taste like a combination of pineapple, strawberry and guava. They are ripe when they are slightly soft and sweet smelling. The thin outer skin, which can be bitter, should be peeled off, but the rest of the fruit can be eaten, either raw, sliced into fruit salads, or made into jams or jellies.

FENNEL There are two types of fennel plant, both of which are common in Mediterranean countries and in many other parts of the world. The feathery leaves of one type are used as a herb, while the bulbous root of the other type, often called Florence fennel, is eaten as a vegetable. The seeds of both types are used as a spice and are considered an aid to digestion. They may also be used to make a herb tea.

Herb or sweet fennel has a slightly aniseed flavour. It is a classical flavouring for fish – especially oily fish where it counteracts the richness – and in marinades, soups and sauces. Dried sweet fennel root is also available.

Florence fennel, or fennel root, is a white bulbous vegetable topped with green feathery leaves. The bulb looks somewhat like and is similar in texture to celery but has a strong aniseed flavour. Blanched, or left raw and grated or chopped, fennel makes an interesting addition to winter salads and is delicious eaten raw with cheese. Fennel is also good braised.

To select: Choose heads with white or pale green bulbs. A dark green bulb indicates a sharp bitterness. Allow 100–175 g (4–6 oz) per person.

To prepare: Trim both root and stalk ends. Chop or grate if it is to be eaten raw. (Keep any feathery leaves to use as a garnish.)

To cook: Quarter the bulb and cook in boiling salted water for about 30 minutes, then drain and slice. If liked, the slices can then be sautéed in butter.

To serve: Fennel may be served raw in salads or as a hot vegetable accompaniment.

FENUGREEK (Methi) The fenugreek plant originated in the Middle East and now grows throughout the Mediterranean area. The plant belongs to the pea family and produces long pods containing a number of irregularly shaped brown seeds. These seeds are roasted and dried, then ground for use as a spice.

Fenugreek is rarely used on its own; its major use is as an ingredient in curry powder. Fenugreek leaves are important in Indian cooking where they are used in any number of curries. It may also be used to add flavour to chutneys, pickles and sauces. The seeds are suitable for sprouting at home (*see* BEAN SPROUTS).

FERMENTATION This term is used to denote chemical changes deliberately or accidentally brought about by fermenting agents, such as bacteria or yeast – for example, the decomposition of carbohydrates, with the production of alcohol and carbon dioxide, caused by the action of yeast. This process is utilized in the making of breads, wines, etc. (*see also* YEAST)

Malt and wine vinegars are produced by a ferment action which converts alcohol (wine) into acetic acid. The souring of milk, with the formation of lactic acid, is another well-known example (used to make yogurt), and there are many more.

Jams sometimes show signs of fermentation when they are stored, if they have not been carefully made and covered. Fresh fruit, for example cherries, sometimes ferments when kept and develops a slight alcoholic flavour. The change is entirely harmless and the fruit can be eaten with perfect safety. If, however, fermentation occurs in bottled or canned fruit, it denotes incomplete sterilization and it is unwise to eat the fruit, since other undesirable changes may also have occurred.

FETA CHEESE (Fetta) A ewes' milk cheese originally from Greece but now made in many other countries, and sometimes also made (less successfully) from goats' or cows' milk. True Greek feta is not easy to come by outside Greece.

Feta is often stored in barrels of brine which may account for its salty flavour. It is a fairly hard white cheese that crumbles easily for use in salads and other raw dishes. It can also be sprinkled on to stews, or used in pastries and vegetable stuffings.

FETTUCINE (*see* PASTA)

FERNET-BRANCA (*see* BITTERS)

FEUILLE DE CHÊNE (*see* LETTUCE)

FIBRE This is now the popular name for what used to be called 'roughage', and has been much discussed in recent years in connection with health. Fibre is present in varying amounts in all our diets, but the quantity we eat has decreased over recent decades in line with an increased consumption of refined foods. Research has shown that many people could benefit from eating more fibre.

Dietary fibre is found only in plant foods, where it gives structure to plant cell walls. It is indigestible and remains in the intestine after the nutrients have been absorbed. Although, in itself, it is of no nutritional value, it plays a vital role in keeping the body healthy. It prevents constipation and may also prevent certain diseases of the intestine, such as diverticular disease, cancer of the large bowel and possibly other disorders like varicose veins and heart disease, although this has yet to be proved.

The health-promoting properties of dietary fibre are a direct result of its ability to absorb fluids. The more fibre that is eaten, the more moisture is absorbed and it becomes easy for the intestine to push the soft, bulky waste matter along without pressure or straining. It also means that any potentially harmful substances are diluted and eliminated quickly from the body, spending little time in contact with the wall of the intestine.

The fibre found in cereals is particularly effective at absorbing moisture, but the fibre in vegetable foods may have other roles in preventing disease, so it is sensible to eat fibre from a variety of sources.

There is no recommended daily intake for dietary fibre, but experts agree that at least 30 g (1 oz) a day, rather than the average 20 g (¾ oz) would be beneficial. In parts of Africa, where so-called diseases of civilization, such as cancer of the colon, are rare, the average intake of fibre is around 150 g (5 oz) a day, proving to a large extent the type of damage lack of fibre in the diet can do.

Increasing fibre intake doesn't mean adding bran (the fibrous part of grains that is usually removed during the refining process) to everything. It is much better to eat more foods that are naturally high in fibre, like whole grain cereals (including wholemeal bread), whole grain breakfast cereals, muesli, wholewheat pasta and rice, fruit, vegetables and pulses. There is little danger of eating too much fibre, but an excess of uncooked bran can reduce the absorption of zinc and certain other minerals, though an adult would have to eat quite a large quantity for this to happen. Children under the age of two, however, should not be given uncooked bran. (*see also* BRAN)

FIDDLEFISH (*see* ANGEL FISH)

FIELD BEAN (*see* BEAN, BROAD)

FIELD MUSHROOM (*see* MUSHROOM)

FIG Native to the Middle East and the Mediterranean coast, fig trees are now grown in many parts of Europe and the United States. There are green, white, purple or black varieties of fig, all with sweet, juicy flesh full of tiny edible seeds. Most figs have thin skins which are also edible.

Figs are available fresh or dried (see below). Fresh ripe fruit should be soft to the touch and have skins with a distinct bloom. To prepare, rinse and remove the stalk, then eat as it is or poach in syrup. Like melon, figs are also delicious served with Parma ham as an hors d'oeuvre.

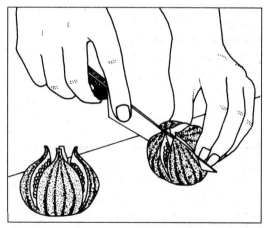

Slicing fresh figs and opening them up like flowers for serving.

FIG, DRIED Dried figs may be sold loose or in pressed blocks. Unlike most dried fruits, figs are not usually treated with sulphur. Dried figs have a very high sugar content and are also a rich source of protein, B vitamins and calcium. They should not be too sticky and make a delicious snack just as they are. They may also be soaked overnight, then drained and used to make compotes, fruit salads or hot puddings. They can also be used without soaking in biscuits, cakes or teabreads.

FILBERT (*see* HAZELNUT)

FILÉ POWDER (Filet Powder) This flavouring powder is produced from the dried leaves of the sassafras tree which grows in the United States. Filé powder gives a spicy flavour to savoury dishes and is particularly associated with the Creole style of cooking. (*see also* CREOLE, SASSAFRAS)

FILET MIGNON (*see* STEAK)

FILLET The undercut of a loin of beef, pork, etc., or the boned breast of a bird or the boned side of a fish. (*see also* FISH)

FILLETING (*see* FISH)

FILLING (*see* STUFFING)

FILLO PASTRY (*see* PASTRY)

FILTERING Straining a liquid through a special fine filter, as when making coffee, or through a cloth, as when making jelly preserves.

FINANCIÈRE, À LA A French term used to describe a dish of meat or poultry in a rich brown Madeira sauce containing mushrooms and truffles, or with a garnish of cocks' combs, cocks' kidneys, truffles, olives and whole or sliced mushrooms.

FINES HERBES A classic French herb mixture, traditionally consisting of finely chopped fresh chives, chervil, parsley and tarragon. The herbs included may vary according to taste and use. *Fines herbes* may be used in omelettes, with fish, poultry and salads. A ready-mixed dried version is available.

FINNAN HADDOCK (*see* HADDOCK)

FINO (*see* SHERRY)

FIOCHETTI (*see* PASTA)

FISH A staple food all over the world, fish come in a variety of shapes, sizes and colours. Broadly speaking, however, they may be divided into two distinct groups – those that live in the sea and those that live in freshwater rivers and lakes – although some migratory species, such as salmon and eels, spend part of their time in the sea and part in rivers. Included in these groups are the many types of shellfish (*see* SHELLFISH).

Sea fish are also sometimes categorized according to their shape, and preparation techniques vary according to whether a fish is round or flat. The shape of the round fish is generally considered the classic fish shape – a rounded tapering body with one eye on each side of the head. Types of round fish include many common varieties, such as cod, haddock, herring and mackerel, as well as other less familiar species, such as red mullet, sturgeon and bream. The flat sea fish group includes some of the most highly rated fish, such as Dover and lemon sole, plaice, turbot and halibut. Flat fish have both eyes on one side and, in fact, swim on their sides, though they spend much of their time lying flat on the seabed.

Fish are an excellent source of protein and are low in saturated fats and carbohydrates. Most of the fat they do contain is polyunsaturated (unlike animal fat which is saturated). White fish have a more delicate flavour than oily fish. They have less than 2 per cent fat and contain approximately 80 calories per 100 g (4 oz). Oily fish, such as mackerel, generally have darker, richer flesh. They have 8–20 per cent fat and contain approximately 160 calories per 100 g (4 oz).

Fresh fish is widely available from supermarkets and fishmongers, though the number of fishmongers has decreased in recent years, due to competition from supermarkets and the greater convenience and availability of frozen fish. Fish is also available dried, smoked and canned or made up into convenience foods, such as fish fingers, fish cakes and ready-made meals. (*see also* DRIED FISH, SMOKED FISH)

(For information about particular species of fish, see individual entries.)

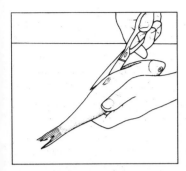 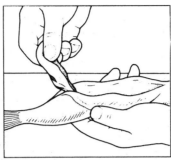 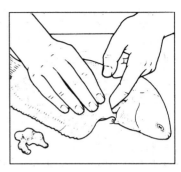

Using scissors to cut a slit along the abdomen of a round fish in order to remove the entrails.

Drawing out the insides of a round fish before rinsing thoroughly until completely clean.

Removing the insides of a flat fish by drawing them out through a slit under the gills.

Buying Fresh Fish

Look for fish that are as fresh as possible and preferably cook on the day they are bought. Whole fish should have clear, bright eyes, bright red or pink gills, shiny bodies and close-fitting scales. Fillets, steaks and cutlets should not show signs of dryness or discoloration, nor should they be wet and shiny. All fresh fish should have a mild, clean smell; do not buy any strong-smelling fish.

Buying Frozen Fish

Frozen fish are sold in a variety of ways – whole, filleted, as cutlets or as fingers or as cakes. Use frozen fish like fresh, but be sure to follow the manufacturer's instructions concerning the storage, thawing and cooking times.

Cleaning Fresh Fish

The fishmonger will nearly always prepare fish for you, but you can do it yourself if you follow these instructions:

Using the back of a knife, remove any scales, scraping from tail to head (the opposite way to the direction in which the scales lie). Rinse frequently under cold running water.

To remove the entrails from round fish, such as herrings or trout, make a slit along the abdomen from the gills to the tail vent. Draw out the insides and clean away any blood. Rub with a little salt to remove the black skin and blood. Rinse under cold running water and pat dry with absorbent kitchen paper.

To remove the entrails from flat fish, such as sole and plaice, open the cavity which lies in the upper part of the body under the gills and clean out the entrails in the same way as for round fish. Rinse under cold running water.

Cut off the fins and gills, if wished, if the fish is to be served whole. The head and tail may also be cut off, if wished. Rinse the fish under cold running water and pat dry with absorbent kitchen paper.

Fillets and cutlets should also be rinsed under cold running water, then patted dry with absorbent kitchen paper.

Skinning Fish

Whole Flat Fish

Rinse the fish and cut off the fins, if not already removed. Make an incision across the tail, slip the thumb between the skin and the flesh and loosen the dark skin around the sides of the fish. Salt your fingers, then hold the fish down firmly with one hand and hold the skin with the other hand. Then pull the skin upwards towards the head. The white skin can be removed in the same way, but unless the fish is particularly large, this layer of skin is usually left on.

 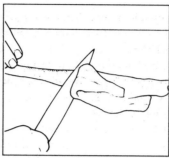 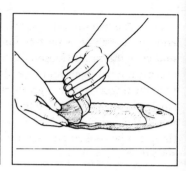

Skinning a whole flat fish by pulling the cut skin upwards towards the head, using salted fingers.

Skinning a flat fish fillet by sawing between flesh and skin with a sharp knife, working from head to tail.

Skinning one side of an uncooked round fish by pulling the cut skin off towards the tail.

Fillets of Flat Fish

Lay the fillet on a board, skin side down. Salt your fingers and hold the tail end of the skin firmly. Insert a sharp knife between the flesh and the skin and work from head to tail, sawing with the knife from side to side and pressing the flat side of the blade against the skin. Keep the edges of the blade close to the skin while cutting, but do not press it down at too sharp an angle or you will slice through the fish's skin.

Round Fish

These are usually cooked with the skin on, but may be skinned if wished.

Using a sharp knife, cut along the spine and across the skin just below the head. Loosen the skin under the head with the point of the knife. Salt your fingers, then gently pull the skin down towards the tail, working carefully to avoid breaking the flesh. Skin the other side of the fish in the same way.

Filleting Fish

Flat Fish

Four fillets are taken from flat fish, two from each side.

Using a small, sharp, pointed knife, make an incision straight down the back of the fish, following the line of the bone and keeping the fish flat on the board. Insert the knife between the flesh and the bone and carefully remove the flesh with long, clean strokes, cutting the first fillet from the left-hand side of the fish, carefully working from the head to the tail.

Turn the fish and cut off the second fillet from tail to head. Fillet the other side using the same method. There should not be any flesh left on the fish's bones.

Round Fish

Two fillets are taken from round fish.

Keeping the fish flat on the board, cut along the centre of the back to the bone, using a sharp knife. Then cut along the length of the abdomen of the fish.

Remove the flesh cleanly from the bones, working from the head down, pressing the knife against the bones and working with short, sharp strokes. Remove the fillet from the other side in the same way. If the fish is large, cut the fillets into serving-size pieces.

Cleaning and Boning Small Round Fish

Small fish, such as herring and mackerel, are often cooked whole rather than being divided into fillets. This is how to remove the bones:

Cut off the head, tail and fins. Split the fish along the underside and remove the entrails. Salt your fingers and rub off the black inner skin and blood.

Open the fish out on a board, cut side down, and press lightly with the fingers down the middle of the back to loosen the backbone.

Turn the fish over and ease the backbone up with the fingers, removing with it as many of the smaller bones as possible. If the fish contains roes, remove these before easing out the backbone (they can be cooked and served with the fish or served separately).

Cooking Fish

Poached Fish

Fish can be poached very gently, so that it does not break up and the texture is not spoilt by overcooking. It can be poached on the hob in a fish kettle or saucepan, or in the oven. The poaching liquid may be wine, milk or salted water, flavoured with parsley sprigs, a small piece of onion and/or carrot, a few mushroom stalks, a squeeze of lemon juice, a bay leaf and some peppercorns. Alternatively, poach in a *court bouillon* (*see* COURT BOUILLON).

Fillets, steaks or whole fish, such as halibut, turbot, brill, haddock, flounder, salmon, sea trout, smoked haddock and kippers, can be poached.

Heat the liquid in a fish kettle or saucepan until simmering, then add the fish. Cover and simmer very gently until tender, allowing 10–15 minutes per 450 g (1 lb), according to the thickness of the cut, or about 20 minutes in all for a small piece.

Drain the fish, transfer to a warmed serving dish and serve with a sauce made from the cooking liquid. Alternatively, serve the fish cold, in aspic or with mayonnaise.

Steamed Fish

Fillets, such as sole, trout and monkfish, can be steamed. If you do not have a steamer, the fish can be placed between two greased plates over a saucepan of simmering water.

Season the prepared fish with salt and pepper. Heat the water in the base of a steamer to simmering point (line the top of the steamer with buttered foil to keep in the flavour, if wished).

Put the fish into the steamer and cover with a tight fitting lid. Steam for 10–15 minutes or until the fish is firm to the touch and just flaking from the bones.

Grilled Fish

Small fish, thin fillets and thicker cuts, such as sole, plaice, halibut, turbot, hake, brill, cod, haddock, flounder, salmon, sea trout, trout, herring, mackerel, kippers, red mullet and monkfish, can be grilled.

Put the prepared fish in the grill pan, season and make two or three diagonal cuts in the body on each side, to allow the heat to penetrate the flesh.

Brush with melted butter, oil or margarine and cook under a moderate heat, allowing 4–5 minutes for thin fillets, 10–15 minutes for thicker fillets, steaks and small whole fish, adjusting times according to size and thickness.

Barbecued Fish

Many types of fish can be barbecued – trout, bass, red mullet, mackerel and sardines. Use a special grilling basket or wrap in foil to prevent the fish breaking up. Alternatively, thread the fish on to long skewers. Cooking times should be roughly the same as for grilled fish.

Shallow-fried Fish

Fillets, steaks and whole fish, such as sole, plaice, dab, bass, monkfish, bream, cod, haddock, mackerel, herring, trout, perch and pike, can be shallow-fried.

Coat the prepared fish with either a coating of seasoned flour, or egg and breadcrumbs.

Heat either clarified butter (*see* BUTTER), vegetable oil, or oil and butter until fairly hot.

Add the fish and fry for 3–4 minutes for small fillets, steaks or whole fish, and 8–10 minutes for larger cuts, turning once.

Drain well on crumpled absorbent kitchen paper and serve with lemon and parsley or maître d'hôtel butter.

Deep-fried Fish

Fillets from large fish coated with batter or egg and breadcrumbs, small whole fish, such as cod, haddock, hake, whiting, coley, monkfish and skate, can be deep-fried.

Heat vegetable oil in a deep-fat fryer to 190°C (375°F). Coat the fish with flour, egg and breadcrumbs or coating batter (*see* BATTER).

Lower the fish gently into the oil, using a basket for egg-and-crumbed pieces, and deep-fry for 4–5 minutes or until golden brown and crisp. (Take care when cooking small fish like whitebait, as they will cook in little more than a minute.)

Drain well on absorbent kitchen paper before serving.

Baked Fish

Fillets, steaks, whole fish and cuts from large fish, such as cod, haddock, hake, whiting, sole, plaice, trout, halibut, salmon, herring and monkfish, can be baked.

Place the prepared fish in an ovenproof dish, season, add a knob of butter or margarine and pour over a little water, milk, lemon juice, stock or wine.

Cover with foil and bake in the oven at 180°C (350°F) mark 4 for whole fish, allowing 25–30 minutes, and at 200°C (400°F) mark 6 for smaller fish or fillets, allowing 15–20 minutes or until tender. (Never allow the liquid to boil as this results in the flesh flaking and a dry texture.)

Alternatively, wrap the prepared fish in greased foil and add a squeeze of lemon juice and a sprinkling of salt and pepper.

Place the fish on a baking sheet and bake in the oven at 180°C (350°F) mark 4, allowing 20 minutes for steaks and 8 minutes per 450 g (1 lb) plus 10 minutes extra for whole fish, according to size, unless otherwise directed in a particular recipe.

FISH, DRIED (*see* DRIED FISH)

FISH KETTLE A long, deep, narrow pan specially made for poaching large whole fish. Fish kettles usually have a lid, a handle at each end and an internal perforated grid on which a whole fish may be lowered into the liquid. The cooked fish can be lifted out on the grid, reducing the risk of it breaking up. Fish kettles can often be hired from kitchen shops. Square-shaped versions are also available for cooking large flat fish, such as turbot.

FISH, SMOKED (*see* SMOKED FISH)

FIVE-SPICE POWDER A mixture of ground spices used as a flavouring in authentic Chinese cooking. Five-spice powder usually consists of ground star anise, anise pepper, fennel seeds, cloves and cinnamon or cassia. The powder is cocoa-coloured and very pungent and should be used sparingly. Five-spice powder is used to season Chinese red-cooked meats (meats simmered in soy sauce) and roast meats and poultry. It can also be added to marinades and sprinkled over whole steamed fish and vegetable dishes.

FLAGEOLET BEAN A type of dried bean that may be white or pale green. Flageolet beans are small and oval, with a delicate flavour. They may be served hot as a vegetable accompaniment or cold in salads. (*see also* PULSES)

FLAIR FAT The layer of fat found on the inside of a loin of pork, and also covering the kidneys.

FLAKE To separate cooked fish into individual flakes, usually with a fork, or to cut hard foodstuffs, such as almonds, into thin slivers.

FLAKY PASTRY (*see* PASTRY)

FLAMANDE, À LA The French name for a number of dishes based on a Flemish style of cooking, including dishes served with a garnish of braised vegetables and bacon or small pork sausages. The name is also given to certain dishes consisting of large cuts of meat coated in a demi-glace sauce, and to asparagus served with melted butter and sieved hard-boiled egg yolks.

FLAMBÉING (Flaming) The French name for a method of flavouring a dish with alcohol, usually brandy, whisky or rum. The spirit may be

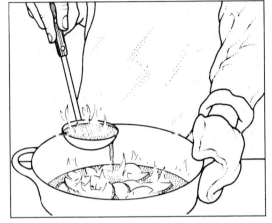

Adding flavour to a dish by pouring flaming spirit over the hot food.

warmed in a ladle or spoon, then ignited and poured flaming over the food, or the warmed spirit is poured over the food, then ignited. The actual alcohol is burned off, but the flavour remains.

Flaming may be done as part of the cooking process, or it may be done to the finished dish just prior to serving, so that the dish is carried flaming to the table. Dishes that are traditionally flambéed include Christmas pudding, *coq au vin* and *crêpes Suzette.*

FLAN The name given to a number of deep sweet or savoury tarts which may have a pastry, sponge or biscuit crumb base. Savoury flans include quiches of all types.

A sweet flan traditionally has a sponge base that is cooked separately in a flan tin, then filled with a cold fruit mixture, often glazed with jelly. The flan tin used for sponge flan bases is similar to a sandwich cake tin, but with a raised base. Sponge flan bases can be bought ready-made.

Pastry flan bases may be made in plain or fluted flan rings which are placed on a baking sheet, lined and baked, or in loose-bottomed plain or fluted flan tins, or in fluted porcelain dishes. Larger rectangular flan forms are also available. Flan rings or loose-bottomed tins make removing the fragile pastry case from the tin much easier. Flans made in porcelain dishes are usually served straight from the dish. Traditionally, a savoury flan is made in a plain tin or dish, while sweet flans are made in fluted tins or dishes.

Pastry flan cases may be made from shortcrust pastry or rich shortcrust pastry (often called 'flan' pastry). They are usually baked blind before being filled as most fillings require little or no cooking.

Flan bases made from biscuit crumbs are usually formed in fluted loose-bottomed tins or in porcelain flan dishes. They are usually filled with sweet mixtures that need no cooking.

Sweet flan fillings may be as simple as an arrangement of fresh fruit, or may involve cooking a custard or sponge mixture which is poured into the flan, then topped with fruit or nuts. The classic French apple flan is filled with sweetened apple purée or confectioners' custard, then topped with beautifully arranged slices of apple. (*see also* PASTRY, QUICHE, TART)

FLAPJACK A popular biscuit made from a mixture of fat, sugar, rolled oats and usually golden syrup.

FLATBREAD The collective name for a variety of unleavened breads made without yeast, including the Middle Eastern pitta bread, the Indian *chappati, paratha* and *nan,* the Jewish matzo, the Mexican tortilla and Scandinavian crispbreads.

FLAT FISH (*see* FISH)

FLAVA BEAN (*see* BEAN, BROAD)

FLAVOURINGS Almost as old as the art of cookery itself is the practice of adding or enhancing taste, or disguising a poor flavour, by adding extra ingredients, by cooking food in a flavoured *court bouillon* or by marinating in a flavoured marinade before cooking. Herbs and spices are added to innumerable dishes during cooking to give flavour, and flavouring essences and extracts are also very widely used. Wines, spirits, liqueurs and beers are also used to add flavour to a variety of sweet and savoury dishes. Salt is probably the most widely used flavouring of all and is added to vegetable cooking water and most savoury dishes, as well as being served as a condiment, usually with pepper.

Some flavourings are added to a dish at the very beginning of cooking, such as aromatic vegetables and herbs to a casserole, while others are added at the end of cooking, such as pepper and some fragile herbs which are best not heated for too long.

Many flavouring substances are produced commercially, such as soy sauce, meat and yeast extracts, Worcestershire sauce, Tabasco sauce and tomato purée, essences and extracts. They are widely available and can be used in small amounts as and when required.

Both natural and synthetic flavourings are widely used in processed foods and, at present, manufacturers are under no legal obligation to declare the exact nature of the flavourings included in their products, although it is common for a food label to declare that it contains no artificial flavouring. However, the European Community is currently working towards some sort of control over the use of flavourings which, hopefully, will result in the drawing up of a list of approved artificial and natural flavourings, as well as flavourings being included in statutory food labelling.

The names of certain foods do give some clue as to the source of its flavour. A 'strawberry flavour' yogurt, for example, need contain no strawberries or natural strawberry flavour whatsoever, but a 'strawberry-flavoured' yogurt must be flavoured to a significant degree by real strawberries. A 'strawberry' yogurt should contain whole strawberries from which its flavour is derived. The same distinctions apply to other foods, such as orange drinks, orange-flavoured drinks and orange flavour drinks.

Substances known as flavour enhancers or modifiers are also used in commercially processed foods. These should be neutral substances, with no flavour of their own, and are used to enhance or reduce the taste or smell of a food. Monosodium glutamate is a typical flavour enhancer that is frequently listed on food labels. (*see also* ADDITIVE, COURT BOUILLON, ESSENCE, EXTRACT, MARINADE)

FLEURON A small, fancy-shaped piece of pastry (usually puff, flaky or rough puff) used for garnishing entrées, ragoûts, mince, etc.

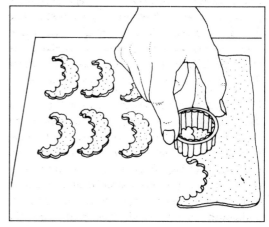

Stamping out pastry fleurons using a small, round, fluted pastry cutter.

FLIP A drink made with beaten egg and milk, wine, spirit or beer and sugar. Various flavourings may also be added.

FLITCH A side of pork, salted and cured. In Great Dunmow, Essex, the 'Dunmow flitch' is awarded annually to any married couple who can prove they have not quarrelled for a whole year.

FLOATING ISLANDS A cold French dessert consisting of an egg custard topped with spoonfuls of poached meringue mixture. The dessert is often finished with a sprinkling of crushed praline or with caramel dribbled over it.

FLORENCE FENNEL (*see* FENNEL)

FLORENTINE A very thin sweet biscuit made from a mixture of chopped nuts, candied peel, glacé cherries and dried fruit combined in melted butter, sugar and cream or milk. After baking and cooling, the biscuits are usually coated with melted plain chocolate which is marked with a fork into wavy ridges before it sets.

FLORENTINE, À LA The French name given to dishes of fish or eggs served with spinach.

FLOUNDER A flat sea fish which resembles plaice, but does not have such a good texture and flavour. It is available all the year round and is sold whole or as fillets. It can be cooked like plaice (*see* PLAICE). In the United States, the name flounder is given to several species of flat fish.

FLOUR A staple foodstuff all over the world, flour is produced from finely ground cereal grains (such as wheat and rye), root vegetables (such as potato and cassava), and pulses (such as chick peas and soya beans). Flour is now commercially produced in enormous quantities and is used to make bread, cakes, biscuits, scones, pastry, pasta and countless other foods. The most frequently used types of flour are those produced from wheat grain, to the extent that 'flour' has come to mean wheat flour more than any other.

Flour has been produced since prehistoric times, but the processes involved in making it have changed drastically over the years. Up until comparatively recently, flour producers aimed to produce flour that was highly refined. Public demand was for white flour that produced soft white bread and cakes. Refined white flour is produced only from the starchy part of the wheat grain, the endosperm, and contains none of the bran (or husk), which is a source of fibre and vitamins, nor the germ, which is rich in vitamins

and minerals. Although British white flour producers are compelled by law to add certain supplements to their flour to compensate for the loss of nutrients, white flour is not as healthy as wholemeal flour which contains all the nutrients of the natural grain without any additives. The varying proportions of the wheat grain contained in a type of flour is known as the 'extraction rate' and is often expressed by a percentage number on the bag. In line with greater public awareness of what constitutes a healthy diet, much more wholemeal flour of various types is produced these days.

Types of Wheat Flour
Wholemeal (or wholewheat) flour contains 100 per cent of the wheat grain (i.e. the entire grain is milled). However, much of the wholemeal flour sold in Britain is produced by the steel roller process which automatically removes the bran and germ from the flour. Wholemeal flour can only be produced in this way by returning the bran and germ to the milled flour after processing, which has already destroyed many of the nutrients they contain. Strong, plain and self raising types of wholemeal flour are available.
Brown (wheatmeal) flour contains 80–90 per cent of the wheat (i.e. some of the bran is removed) and it is more absorbent than white flour. It is available in strong, plain and self raising forms.
White flour contains 72–74 per cent of the wheat grain. The bran and wheatgerm which give wholemeal and brown flours their brown colour are removed, resulting in the white flour which is used to make fine-textured 'white' bread. Much white bread is bleached chemically; look for the word 'unbleached' for untreated flour. White flour is available in strong, plain and self raising forms. Self raising flour has a raising agent already blended with it.
Stoneground flour takes its name from the specific process of grinding used to produce it. The whole wheat grain is ground between two stones, one of

which remains fixed, while the other moves over it with the grain in between. The process heats the flour slightly, giving it a slightly roasted, nutty flavour. Both wholemeal and brown flours can be stoneground.

Granary-style flour is strong brown flour with added malted wheat flakes giving a nutty flavour. 'Granary flour' is in fact the brand name of a particular type of flour produced by Rank Hovis McDougall plc, but the name is often used to describe other granary-style flours and the bread made from them.

Organic flour is produced from wheat grown to strict standards of organic husbandry, in soil which has not been treated with artificial fertilizers for at least two years. No chemical pesticides, herbicides or artificial fertilizers are used, and the flour contains no additives. Both white and wholemeal types of organic flour are available.

Food Value of Wheat Flour

Flour is a cheap and valuable food. It supplies energy, protein, calcium, iron and vitamins of the B group. White flour has only about half the minerals and B vitamins contained in wholemeal flour, although it has much the same amount of protein and energy value. White bread contains no fibre, since the bran has been removed, and for this reason, many people prefer to use wholemeal flour and to eat wholemeal bread. (*see also* BRAN, FIBRE)

Gluten Content or 'Strength' of Flour

Wheat is said to be either hard or soft, depending on its gluten content. When hard wheat is milled it produces a strong flour, rich in protein, containing a sticky, rubber-like substance called gluten. In bread making, the gluten stretches like elastic and, as it is heated, it expands and traps in the dough the carbon dioxide released by the yeast. The gluten then sets and forms the 'frame' of the bread.(*see also* BREAD)

When soft wheats are milled they produce a flour with different gluten properties, more suited to the making of cakes or pastries where a smaller rise and closer, finer texture are required. (*see also* GLUTEN)

Other Types of Flour

Various other grains can be milled to produce flour, such as barley, rye, maize (corn), buckwheat, millet and rice. (See individual entries for detailed information about these flours and their uses.)

Chick peas are ground to produce gram or besan flour (*see* GRAM FLOUR), and soya beans are ground to produce soya flour (*see* SOYA BEAN). Some root vegetables, such as potatoes and cassava are also ground to produce flours (*see* FARINA, FECULA, POTATO FLOUR), as are some nuts (*see* CHESTNUT).

FLOURING To dredge flour over the surface of food in order to dry it or coat it for frying, to dust the inside of a greased cake tin with flour, or to sprinkle flour over a pastry board before use.

FLOWERING CHIVE (*see* CHINESE CHIVE)

FLUMMERY An old English cold dessert made of a cereal (originally oatmeal), set in a mould and turned out. Other types seldom made these days include Dutch Flummery, made with gelatine or isinglass, egg yolks and flavourings, and Spanish Flummery, made of cream, rice flour, cinnamon and sugar.

FLUORINE A naturally occurring trace element that has received attention in recent years in connection with dental health. Fluorine is believed to help prevent tooth decay by strengthening tooth enamel. Most drinking water naturally contains fluorine, but some water authorities artificially increase levels by adding fluorine salts (sodium fluoride) to their drinking water in an attempt to improve dental health, particularly in young children. It is also possible to give extra fluoride to children of all ages in the form of tablets or drops.

FOIE GRAS The abnormally large liver of a goose or duck that has been specially fed and fattened with maize. The most famous *foie gras* comes from Toulouse, but it is also produced in Austria, Hungary, Israel, Czechoslovakia and Luxembourg. These very large livers are esteemed a great delicacy in France and are cooked in various more or less elaborate ways. They may be served hot or cold, as a savoury or hors d'oeuvre.

Fatted goose livers are also combined with pork, truffles and other ingredients to make the smooth, rich paste known as *pâté de foie gras*, which is exported to Britain from France in small earthenware terrines. This pâté is often eaten as an hors d'oeuvre and may be served straight from the terrine or cut into thin slices and garnished with chopped parsley and sliced lemon. Puréed *foie gras* may be served as a savoury dish and the pâté may also be used in making sandwiches, canapés and small savouries.

FOIL, ALUMINIUM (*see* ALUMINIUM)

FOLDING IN (Cutting and Folding) A method of combining a whisked or creamed mixture with other ingredients so that it retains its lightness. It

Using a metal spoon to combine a whisked or creamed mixture with other ingredients by folding in.

involves a careful cutting through and turning over of the mixture to incorporate other ingredients without breaking down the air bubbles held in the mixture. It is very important not to beat or stir when folding in.

Folding in is mainly used for meringues (sugar is folded into whisked egg white), soufflés (whisked egg white is folded into a thick sauce), mousses (whisked egg white or whipped cream is folded into a flavoured egg mixture) and certain cake mixtures (flour is folded into a whisked sponge or creamed mixture). Folding in is best done with a metal spoon and cannot be done with an electric mixer.

FOND (*see* FUMET)

FONDANT This forms the basis of a large number of sweets and is also used for chocolate centres and for icing cakes, etc. True fondant is made by boiling sugar syrup to a temperature of 116°C (240°F) to 118°C (245°F), but an unboiled version may be used for making simple sweets (*see* SWEETS).

For icing cakes, boiled fondant must be diluted and used at a precise temperature. It can be quite difficult to use and quickly becomes brittle and unworkable. It is really only suitable for pouring over a cake to flat ice it. Nowadays, however, it is possible to buy a ready-made fondant to use for icing cakes. It is also sometimes called sugarpaste, fondant paste or moulding icing, and can be coloured, rolled, cut out and shaped. It can also be used to make the most delicate flowers and other decorations for cakes. It usually contains tragacanth gum or gum arabic, which gives it its malleable properties.

FONDUE This popular style of informal eating involves cooking at the table. A pan of oil is kept hot over a fondue burner in the centre of the table and diners dip pieces of lean beef, speared on long pronged fondue forks, into the oil to cook it. This type of fondue is usually known as a *fondue bourguignonne* and should be accompanied by a variety of dips and sauces, such as barbecue, tomato and horseradish, and other condiments.

A Swiss fondue does not involve any cooking. The fondue pot is filled with a delicious mixture of melted Gruyère cheese, wine and other flavourings and pieces of bread are dipped into it and eaten hot. For a Chinese fondue, pieces of meat, fish and vegetables are cooked in boiling chicken stock. A chocolate fondue may be used for dipping pieces of fruit, cake and biscuits in a mixture of melted chocolate and cream.

FONDUE DU RAISIN A mild French cheese covered with grape pips which comes from the Province of Savoy. This cheese tends to lack flavour but it adds colour to a cheese board.

FONDUTA A famous dish from Piedmont in Italy. Similar to a Swiss fondue, *fonduta* is made with Fontina cheese and truffles.

FONTAINEBLEAU A fresh French cows' milk cheese with a soft, creamy texture. It is made in the country round Fontainebleau, mostly in the summer, and is generally eaten as a dessert cheese.

FONTAL A cows' milk cheese produced both in France and Italy. It is similar to Fontina (see below) but is produced commercially in areas other than the Aosta Valley, where true Fontina is made. Fontal has a smooth, orange-coloured rind and the cheese is very even textured and mild flavoured. It is a good cheese to use in cooking, in fondues and toasted cheese sandwiches.

FONTINA One of Italy's great cheeses, Fontina is made from unpasteurized cows' milk in the Aosta Valley. Similar cheeses made commercially in other areas of Italy, and in France, are known as Fontal (see above). Fontina is a mild flavoured dark yellow cheese with a tough brown rind. Its soft texture is slightly rubbery, with numerous small holes. It is best served as a dessert cheese or used to make *fonduta* (see above).

FOOD In very general terms, food consists of all the substances needed by all living things to support life. Plants can make their own food from minerals, water and the gases in the air, but animals (including humans) must obtain their food ready-made. We need food to provide us with energy and to maintain our health by supplying all the nutrients our bodies need to function efficiently.

Basically, all animals get their food from plants, although many of them obtain it indirectly by eating other animals. The water, minerals and gases thus used are eventually returned to their original state through breathing, excretion and decay after death, and are then once more available to build new plants. This is the so-called 'food chain' and is a continuous cycle.

No single food eaten by humans supplies all nutritional needs, although milk comes very near to doing so. Each food supplies nutrients of some kind in varying amounts, so a combination of foods is required to obtain all the necessary nutrients. The wider the choice of food, the more likely it is that all the necessary food factors will be obtained. Many nutritionists believe that variety is the key to a healthy diet and that the important thing is not to allow one or two foods to dominate to the exclusion of others. (*see also* DIET, NUTRITION)

FOOD IRRADIATION (*see* IRRADIATION)

FOOD POISONING The general name given to a group of illnesses caused by the consumption of food contaminated with bacteria, bacterial toxins or chemicals. It is a sad fact that, even in these days of increased knowledge and advanced technology, it is not possible to have complete confidence in the safety of the food we eat. Despite the use of food processing methods such as pasteurization and ultra-heat treatment (UHT), it is still possible for contaminated foods to reach the consumer.

In recent years the number of reported cases of food poisoning has increased dramatically. Food poisoning is a notifiable illness, but because attacks are so often blamed on just a 'tummy bug', it is likely that the number of cases of food poisoning is actually far higher than the number notified. Some recent outbreaks of food poisoning have caused particular concern to the public and have led to Government intervention in methods of food production. They include Salmonella in eggs and poultry, Listeria in cheese and chilled ready-made meals and Botulism caused by eating contaminated yogurt.

The symptoms of food poisoning are severe stomach pains, vomiting and diarrhoea. An attack can occur anything up to 24 hours after consuming the contaminated food, depending on the type of poisoning. The illness usually lasts no longer than a few days and sufferers rarely need to go into hospital. However, some cases can be very severe and there are possible side-effects, such as dehydration, which can be dangerous for young children and elderly people.

Types of Food Poisoning

Bacterial Poisoning

Nearly all the food we eat is contaminated to some extent by harmless numbers of bacteria. In some cases, however, the bacteria present in a food can multiply to such an extent that, when consumed, the body's natural defences are unable to cope and food poisoning results. Types of bacteria that can cause food poisoning, either directly or by producing poisonous toxins, include *Salmonella, Clostridium botulinum, Listeria* and *Staphylococcus*.

Food can become contaminated with bacteria at a very early stage. As recent cases have shown, an egg produced by a Salmonella-infected hen can become contaminated even before it is laid, and many edible bivalve molluscs, such as mussels, become contaminated as a result of their habit of flushing themselves through with water that is dirty and polluted. (*see also* SHELLFISH)

Some soft continental cheeses made from unpasteurized milk can contain high numbers of Listeria which can cause food poisoning. These cheeses are best avoided by pregnant women, babies and people in poor health.

However, food can also become contaminated by bacteria at a later stage, due to unhygienic handling, storage or processing. Fortunately, salmonella and other similar bacteria can be destroyed by high temperatures.

Bacterial Toxin Poisoning

In some cases, it is not the bacteria themselves that cause food poisoning, but the toxins, or spores, that they produce. Staphylococci are germs that are often present in infected wounds or boils, and can be transferred to food during handling. Once in the food, and if warmth, moisture and the right nutrients are present, the germs will multiply and produce 'staphylococci toxin'. When the food is subsequently eaten, the toxin rapidly causes food poisoning. Staphylococci toxin can not be destroyed by boiling under normal conditions.

Botulism is a rare but very dangerous form of food poisoning that is caused by the germ *Clostridium botulinum*. This type of bacteria cannot multiply if oxygen is present, so the most likely places to find it are in canned or bottled foods. It forms spores that are almost impossible to destroy by boiling under domestic conditions (except perhaps in a pressure cooker), but can be destroyed under factory conditions when temperatures are pushed up beyond boiling point. However, the poison produced by the botulism bacteria *can* be destroyed by boiling for only a very short time, so botulism cannot result from eating hot, thoroughly cooked food. It is because of the risk of botulism that home bottling of most fruits and vegetables is no longer recommended, although botulism-causing spores cannot develop in very acid or salty conditions.

Another type of toxin-producing bacteria is

Bacillus cereus, a germ that thrives in cooked rice. The toxin it produces cannot be destroyed by reheating, even to a high temperature. It is essential, therefore, to keep cooked rice in the refrigerator.

Poisoning from Chemicals

Some foods, such as certain types of fungi, naturally contain chemicals that are poisonous if consumed, even in small quantities. Other foods, such as bitter almonds and green potatoes, contain chemicals that are harmless in small quantities but poisonous if eaten in large quantities.

It is also possible for food to become contaminated with chemicals intended for use as pesticides or insecticides, but this is rare. Fruits and vegetables should be washed thoroughly to avoid this risk. Poisonous chemicals can also be produced by the action of some acidic foods on metal pans or containers, so it is important to remove such foods to non-metallic containers.

Avoiding Food Poisoning

It is possible to safeguard yourself and your family against food poisoning by habitually following some very simple guidelines.

* Always wash your hands thoroughly before handling food. Raw food can contaminate cooked food, so wash your hands and any utensils between handling raw and cooked foods. (Your butcher should do the same if he sells both raw and cooked meats.)

* Keep your kitchen and utensils scrupulously clean. Use a separate board for preparing raw meat.

* Always buy food in good condition from a reputable shop or supermarket with high standards of hygiene. Never buy food that looks unfresh, is not packed properly or has a broken seal.

* Check the 'sell-by', 'use-by' or 'best-before' date on packaged food and be guided by recommendations about storage times and conditions given on food labels.

* After buying chilled or frozen foods, get them into the refrigerator or freezer as soon as possible. It is unwise to leave food in a warm car while doing further shopping.

* Store foods at the correct temperature. Food labels usually state whether a food needs to be refrigerated after opening, such as long-life milk, tomato ketchup, mayonnaise and fruit juices. All perishable foods should be stored in the refrigerator.

* Wash all fresh fruit and vegetables thoroughly before eating them.

* Do not buy rusty, leaking, badly dented or 'blown' cans, and throw away any you find in your store-cupboard. If you have canned food left over, transfer it to a clean bowl and store it in the refrigerator.

* Never eat food that looks or smells 'off', or which may have been exposed to insects or mice.

* Never eat unknown wild plants or berries.

* Only buy shellfish from a reputable source. If you ever gather your own, be sure they come from clean waters. Healthy live mussels are tightly shut before cooking, but they open when boiled. Discard mussels that are open before boiling and never eat any that do not open after boiling.(*see also* SHELLFISH)

* Food cooked in advance should be cooled as quickly as possible, then covered and stored in the refrigerator until required. If reheating, make sure the food is piping hot before it is served, and never reheat food more than once.

* Take particular care when reheating bought ready-cooked meals, which may be infected with bacteria such as Listeria so it's essential to reheat them really thoroughly until piping hot. Take extra care when using a microwave cooker.

* Keep your refrigerator clean and run it on the lowest setting. The temperature should not be higher than 5°C.

* Make sure frozen foods are completely thawed before cooking, especially meat and poultry. Never re-freeze foods that have thawed (such as

meat) unless they are cooked first, or melted (such as ice cream).

(*see also* CHILLED FOODS, FOOD STORAGE, FREEZING, MICROWAVE COOKING, PASTEURIZE, REFRIGERATION)

FOOD PROCESSOR An electric kitchen appliance that can help with many everyday cooking tasks, such as chopping, slicing and grating vegetables and cheese, and creaming, kneading and beating mixtures. Food processors consist of a bowl that is fitted on to a motor housing. You select the appropriate blade or cutting disc for the task in hand, fit it inside the bowl, put the ingredients inside the bowl, secure the lid and switch on. The ingredients are processed in seconds. In fact, you will need to practise for a while before experience can tell you how long it takes to process different types of food. Just a few seconds too long can mean the difference between chopping meat and turning it into a paste.

A food processor can be used to make soups, pâtés, purées, pastry and baby foods, although you may be reluctant to use a food processor for very small quantities. When puréeing, processors do not always achieve such a smooth texture as a blender. Some food processors cannot whip cream or whisk egg whites, but they do, on the whole, make perfectly acceptable cakes, although sponges do not turn out as fluffy and well risen as when mixed by hand or with electric beaters. If you use your food processor a great deal it is a good idea, storage permitting, to buy one or two extra bowls to save frequent washing up.

FOOD STORAGE It is extremely important that food be stored correctly, both at home and in the shop or supermarket. Fresh foods need clean, hygienic conditions where the temperature is appropriate to maintain it at its best. Some foods are best stored in airy places, while others keep better in an airtight container. You will need to allocate space in your kitchen both for foods that you use everyday and for those which spend longer in the cupboard as they are used only in small quantities or for emergency meals.

Storage for perishable foods, e.g. meat, fish, dairy products, fruit and vegetables, is of vital importance since these, if kept too long, will develop bacteria, mould and enzymes (called micro-organisms) whose activity will cause these foods to go off. The best place to keep them is in a refrigerator (*see* REFRIGERATION), failing this a ventilated food cupboard or cool larder. If you have neither, these products should be bought daily when needed, to ensure safe eating. In general, it is advisable to buy perishable foods as you need them and in small quantities to ensure that surplus does not sit around too long before being eaten. Perishable foods intended for long-term storage can be kept in a freezer (*see* FREEZING). (*see also* FOOD POISONING)

The Larder or Food Cupboard
Ideally, the temperature in a larder or food cupboard should not exceed 10°C (50°F) and there should be some ventilation. Any outlet or window should be covered with gauze or perforated zinc to keep out insects and it is also wise to draughtproof the door to prevent heat from the kitchen getting into the larder, and to reduce condensation.

If you are fitting out your larder from scratch, it is a good idea to vary the height between shelves. The shelves should be covered with easily cleaned materials such as self-adhesive plastic, laminated plastic, ceramic tiles or spongeable shelf paper, and all spills should be wiped up immediately.

Perishable foods should be checked daily and store-cupboard cans and packets should be used in rotation. A good way to keep a check on them is to date each one as you buy it. Packaged dry ingredients can be kept quite safely in the original packets until opened, after which the contents should be transferred to a storage jar with a well fitting lid. Really airtight lids are essential only for strong-smelling foods like coffee, herbs and spices, which lose their aroma when exposed to the air, and for things like salt and baking powder which absorb moisture and easily become caked.

Cereal products, such as flour and semolina, keep well but should be watched for insect infestation. Affected foods should be thrown out at once and stocks checked to ensure that damage has not spread. The high fat content of wholemeal flour and oatmeal may cause rancidity so buy in fairly small quantities and use up quickly.

Canned fruit is best used within a year as the contents may deteriorate in colour after this time even though the food value is not altered. Condensed milk will begin to discolour after 6–9 months. Dried full-cream milk will keep for a few weeks after opening, but then tends to go rancid.

Always discard any cans that have 'blown', recognizable by bulging ends and leaking or rusty seams. Bacteria can penetrate them so the contents are no longer sterile.

Larder and Food Cupboard Storage Times

Food	Storage life
Flour, white	Up to 6 months
wheatmeal	Up to 3 months
wholemeal	Up to 1 month
Baking powder, bicarbonate of soda, cream of tartar	2–3 months
Dried yeast	Up to 6 months
Cornflour, custard powder	Keep well
Pasta, all types	Keep well
Rice, all types	Keep well
Sugar, loaf, caster, granulated	Keep well
Sugar, icing, brown	Limited life
Tea	Limited life
Instant and ground coffee in sealed can or jar	Up to 1 year
Coffee beans, loose ground coffee	Very limited life
Instant low-fat skimmed milk	Up to 3 months
Breakfast cereals	Limited life
Dehydrated foods	Up to 1 year
Herbs, spices, seasonings	Up to 6–8 months
Nuts	Limited life
Dried fruits	Up to 2–3 months
Jams, etc.	Keep well
Honey, clear or thick	Keep well
Golden syrup, treacle	Keep well
Evaporated milk	Up to 6–8 months
Canned fruit	Up to 1 year
Canned vegetables	Up to 2 years
Canned fish in tomato sauce	Up to 1 year
Canned meat	Up to 5 years
Canned ham	Up to 6 months
Pickles, sauces	Keep quite well
Chutneys	Limited life
Oils, olive, corn	Up to 18 months

FOOL A cold dessert consisting of puréed fruit with whipped cream or custard blended into it. Popular fools are made with rhubarb and gooseberry.

FORCEMEAT (*see* STUFFING)

FORESTIÈRE, À LA A French term used to describe a dish of meat or poultry with a garnish of mushrooms, ham or bacon and fried potatoes.

FORTIFIED WINE A type of wine with extra spirit added during the fermentation process, resulting in a higher alcohol content. Examples of fortified wine include port, sherry and Madeira.

FOUR, AU A French term meaning 'cooked in the oven'.

FOURME D'AMBERT A firm but soft French blue cheese produced in the Auvergne from cows' milk. It has been made since the seventh century and is a highly regarded cheese with a creamy texture and a rich, full-bodied flavour. It has a dark crust and is produced in tall cylinder-shaped cheeses.

FOWL An edible bird, especially the domestic cock or hen. As a general term, the word can apply to a bird of any age, but it is often applied more particularly to an older tougher bird, suitable for boiling, steaming or casseroling. (*see also* POULTRY)

FRAISE (*see* EAU-DE-VIE)

FRAMBOISE (*see* EAU-DE-VIE)

FRANGIPANE (Franzipan) Originally, frangipane was a jasmine-scented perfume, which gave its name to an almond cream which was flavoured with the perfume and used to fill various types of pastry. The term is now usually applied to a flan filled with an almond-flavoured mixture.

In classic cookery, frangipane is also the name of a type of thickening mixture, or panada, rather like choux pastry, which may be used in stuffings and forcemeats.

FRANKFURTER A German smoked sausage made traditionally from minced pork and salted bacon fat, but various versions may be made from pork only or beef and pork. In the United States, and to an increasing extent in Britain, frankfurters are the type of sausage normally used to make hot dogs. Unless otherwise stated in a particular recipe, frankfurters are usually poached gently for a few minutes before being used. (*see also* HOT DOG)

Bockwurst is a similar German sausage that looks very like a long frankfurter, but may be made from a highly spiced mixture of veal and pork or beef and pork. *Knackwurst* is yet another variation, but is short and fat, made from lean pork, beef and fresh fat pork, and flavoured with spices and garlic.

FRAPPÉ A French word used to describe dishes or drinks that are served iced, frozen or chilled.

FREEZING A method of preserving fresh or cooked foods by storing them in a frozen state. Freezing is done both on a commercial scale, so that it is possible to buy ready-frozen foods, and on a domestic scale. Owning a freezer means you can buy food (such as meat) in bulk, shop less often, have a store of pre-cooked dishes or produce readily available, and preserve produce straight from the garden or when it is cheap at the height of the season. It also means that meals for unexpected guests are no longer a problem and you can spread the work required for catering for a large party over a period of weeks.

Freezing is the easiest method of preserving food and, as long as the simple basic rules are followed, the food retains its colour, texture, taste and nutrients.

Most foods are largely made up of water; even something like lean meat contains about 70 per cent water. Freezing converts this water to ice crystals. Freezing the food quickly results in tiny ice crystals, retained within the cell structure, so that when thawed, the structure is undamaged and the food value remains unchanged. However, slow freezing results in the formation of large ice crystals, which damage the cell structure and cause loss of nutrients. As this damage is irreversible, slow-frozen food shows loss of texture, colour and flavour when thawed.

Foods like cucumber and strawberries, which have a high water content and delicate structure, never freeze successfully because the tiniest crystal formation breaks down their cell structure.

The success of freezing as a method of food preservation depends on the fact that low temperatures destroy some micro-organisms and prevent the growth of others. However, enzymes (chemicals naturally present in food which cause the destruction of vitamins, texture and colour) are not destroyed by freezing, but are slowed down.

Buying a Freezer
There are various types of freezer to choose from and it is largely a matter of personal choice.
Upright freezers These range in size from small, table-top models to large upright ones. They have front opening doors (large freezers sometimes

have two doors), take up less floor space than chest freezers and are less obtrusive.

Upright freezers, fitted with shelves and/or pull-out baskets, are easy to load and unload. In some models, each shelf or basket is fronted by its own flap which shuts out warm air when the door is opened. Upright freezers need defrosting more often than the chest type – although frost-free models are available, they are more expensive both to buy and to run.

Chest freezers Size for size, chest freezers are cheaper than upright models, and running costs are lower. They have an additional advantage too: more food will fit into the same amount of space, since large items can be accommodated with small ones tucked round them, unrestricted by shelves and baskets. However, they take up considerably more floor space, are more difficult to keep organized, and small people and those with bad backs find it difficult to reach down to the bottom of the cabinet.

Fridge/freezers These units incorporate a refrigerator and a freezer, one built above the other, and are popular in kitchens with little space. The refrigeration and freezing capacities are roughly equal in many models, although it is also possible to buy units which have bigger freezers than refrigerators, and vice versa.

What size freezer? The size of freezer you need depends on a number of factors: how often you shop, whether you plan to freeze pre-cooked dishes or merely to store basic ingredients, how many people there are in the household, and whether or not you will be freezing your own produce.

Freezer capacity is quoted either in cubic litres or feet. To make a rough comparison, divide the number of litres by 30 to give the number of cubic feet (1 cubic foot is equal to 28.3 litres and will hold 9–11 kg/20–25 lb food).

As a general rule, allow 56 litres (2 cubic feet) per person, plus an extra 56 litres (2 cubic feet), but do think carefully about your particular needs

before deciding. Talk to friends who own freezers to see whether they are satisfied with the size they have. If in doubt, buy a model that is 28–56 litres (1–2 cubic feet) larger than you think you need – it is better to have more space than you need than not enough.

Star symbols All freezers must carry a four-star symbol which indicates that they are capable of freezing fresh food. An appliance with three stars or less is suitable only for storing ready-frozen food as follows:

    *   for 1 week
    ** for 1 month
    *** for 3 months

Defrosting

Upright freezers need defrosting two or three times a year; chest freezers once, or at the most twice, a year. As a general guide, defrost your freezer when the frost on the shelves reaches a thickness of 0.5 cm (1/4 inch). Follow the manufacturer's instructions for your particular freezer as the procedure varies with different models.

Try to defrost when stocks are low or when it is a cold day. Put the contents of the freezer into the refrigerator or wrap in newspapers or blankets.

You will need a plastic spatula to tap the frost loose as it melts, some old towels to mop up with, and bowls of hot water to speed up the process. When the freezer is free of frost, wash it out with a solution of 15 ml (1 level tbsp) bicarbonate of soda in 1 litre (1 3/4 pints) warm water, then dry it thoroughly before switching on again.

Power Cuts

Most power cuts do not last for long and the food in your freezer should be safe.

If there is advance warning of a power cut, turn on the fast-freeze switch, but before you do make sure the freezer is as full as possible. Fill any gaps with rolled up newspaper, old towels or plastic boxes filled with cold water.

Cover the freezer with a blanket or rug to increase its insulation, but make sure you leave the condenser and pipes on the back uncovered. Do not open the door during a power cut as this lets warm air into the freezer.

After the power has been restored, leave the fast-freeze on for at least 2 hours. Food in a chest freezer will be undamaged for about 48 hours if you have had advance warning, and 30–35 hours if there has been no warning. An upright freezer will keep its contents safe for about 36 hours with advance warning, 30 hours without.

Moving House

It is best to move a freezer when it is empty, although some removal firms have the facility to plug a loaded unit into an electrical supply in their van. Bear in mind that a freezer full of food is very heavy and might be damaged during transportation. It is better to use its contents and transport it empty.

When moving a freezer, it should be kept as upright as possible and never tipped to an angle of more than 30°, as this could cause an airlock in the cooling system. When it is unloaded and installed in your new home, switch on the freezer to check that all the lights are working.

Twenty Freezing Tips

1. Freeze only good quality foods – what comes out is only as good as what went in.
2. Handle food as little as possible.
3. Pack food for freezing in small quantities. It will thaw more quickly and you only need to thaw what you need.
4. Pack and seal food carefully. Food that is exposed to air or moisture will deteriorate and there is a risk of cross flavouring.
5. Never put anything hot or even warm into a freezer. It will raise the temperature of other items in the freezer and may cause deterioration. Once food has been cooked or blanched, cool it rapidly in a bowl of iced water.
6. Freeze food as quickly as possible so that it retains its texture.
7. Follow the manufacturer's instructions on use

of the fast-freeze switch and where in the cabinet to freeze down food.
8. Do not pack food too closely together; spread it out until it is frozen.
9. Move newly-frozen items from the fast-freeze area, if your freezer has one, once they are frozen.
10. Remember to switch the fast-freeze control back to normal setting once food has been frozen.
11. Do not keep opening the door of your freezer; it raises the temperature inside the cabinet. Decide what you want to get out and remove it quickly.
12. Use a freezer thermometer to help you maintain a steady storage temperature of -18°C (0°F). Move it around within the freezer to check that the temperature is maintained throughout the cabinet.
13. Label and date food so that you can rotate stock efficiently. Consider keeping a freezer log book to stop you going through the contents to see what you have stored.
14. Defrost the freezer when stocks are low and preferably on a cold day. Do the job as fast as you can so that the contents can be put back into the freezer quickly.
15. Tape the address of the service organization to an inconspicuous spot on the freezer casing or inside the adjacent kitchen cupboard door.
16. Know what to do in emergencies such as a power cut or freezer breakdown (see left).
17. If you are storing a large quantity of food, particularly expensive items, consider taking out special freezer insurance to cover you against loss.
18. If your freezer is in a garage or outhouse, fit a freezer alarm to it so that you have immediate warning if anything goes wrong, and fit a lock.
19. Plug in a built-in alarm on the freezer to warn you if the fuse blows.
20. Keep your freezer full to reduce the running costs. Fill gaps with basics like bread, or if you are running down your stock to defrost, fill the gaps with old towels or crumpled newspaper.

How to Freeze

Never freeze more than one tenth of your freezer's capacity in any 24 hours, otherwise heat will be absorbed by the freezer's refrigeration system and also by the food already frozen. If, for instance, you have a 50 kg (110 lb) freezer (approximately 170 litres/6 cubic feet), you should only freeze about 5 kg (11 lb) food at a time.

Using the fast-freeze switch The fast-freeze switch works by over-riding the thermostat. It allows the temperature in the freezer to fall well below -18°C (0°F) – the normal storage temperature (which is controlled by the thermostat). The food freezes faster in the colder temperature, forming smaller ice crystals, so that the texture of the food will be better when thawed. Reducing the temperature means, too, that the food already in the freezer gets colder and will be less affected by the higher temperature of the fresh food. Turn on the fast-freeze switch about 6 hours before you plan to put in food to be frozen, then leave it on for 12–24 hours to freeze the food.

It is possible to freeze food without using the fast-freeze switch, but the faster the food is frozen the better the texture when thawed.

Freezing Solids

Package solids tightly, so that you expel as much air as possible, wrapping them in foil or freezer wrap, which fits where it touches. If filling a rigid container and the food only comes halfway up, fill up the vacant space with crumpled foil or non-stick paper. However, if possible, avoid half-empty containers as they waste valuable freezer space.

Freezing Liquids

Liquid expands one tenth when frozen, so it is essential to leave at least 1 cm (1/2 inch) of 'headspace' in a container holding about 300 ml (1/2 pint) and about 2.5 cm (1 inch) for a container holding 600 ml (1 pint). Unless you leave room for expansion, items such as soups, sauces and fruits packed in syrup will push off their lids.

If you use a glass container, make sure it has straight sides, as it is easier to get the frozen contents out again.

Freezing Solids Plus Liquids

Combinations of solids and liquids, such as stews and casseroles or fruit in syrup, should, if possible, have a layer of liquid on the top with no pieces of food sticking out. Leave 1 cm (1/2 inch) of headspace. Solids which rise above the surface of the liquid, such as fruit salad, need an inner covering of crumpled non-stick paper before wrapping.

Pre-forming

This is ideal for storing liquid foods such as fruit purées, casseroles and stocks in a polythene bag, rather than a rigid container. The food is placed in a polythene bag-lined container, frozen until solid, then removed from the container. The food is then in a neat, regular shape for storing in the freezer, and the container can be used for other things.

Storage Times

Bacteria cannot multiply in or on frozen food, so there is no danger of the food becoming a health hazard, no matter how long it is stored. However, freezing does not kill bacteria and food contaminated before freezing will still be contaminated after it has been thawed. As with all perishable foods, if frozen food is thawed and then kept at room temperature, bacteria will develop and it will become a health hazard. (*see also* FOOD POISONING)

Different foods have different recommended storage times. These are determined by the length of time they can be stored frozen without any detectable change in food value, taste, colour and texture. They can be stored longer than the recommended times without becoming harmful to health, but the flavour and texture will not be as good.

Packaging

Good packaging is vital if frozen food is to remain in good condition. Freezing converts the water content of the food to ice crystals which must be retained, as they are converted back to moisture when the food is thawed. Badly packed food will dry out, causing white patches known as 'freezer burn'. There is also the risk that strong-smelling foods will transfer their odours to other foods. Although it is important to store all frozen food correctly, any food which is to be stored for a long time must be extremely well wrapped, since it will tend to get pushed around when other items are put into and removed from the freezer. When choosing packaging materials, it is worth considering whether or not you will want to thaw or reheat the food in a microwave cooker. Anything wrapped or packed in foil will need to be transferred to another container before it can be put in a microwave cooker. (*see also* MICROWAVE COOKING)

Polythene bags and sheeting These should be of fairly heavy gauge polythene unless they are to be used for overwrapping, when a thinner gauge will do. Exclude as much air as possible before sealing. They must be sealed by twist ties or by heat-sealing. Have an assortment of sizes to hand. A self-sealing bag is obtainable.

Cling film/freezer wrap Plastic film is very useful when wrapping food for the freezer. Use it as a lining if you want to pack acidic fruits in foil and also for wrapping individual portions of foods which can then be stored together in a polythene bag and removed one at a time.

Foil This is ideal for wrapping awkward shaped items and can be moulded closely around the food to ensure air does not get in. Use a single layer of the standard thickness or a double layer if you are using thin kitchen foil.

Foil should not be used for wrapping acidic fruits which may react with it. If you think the foil is likely to become punctured in the freezer, overwrap large items with a polythene bag.

Foil is also useful for lining casserole dishes when preparing food. Once the dish has been cooked and frozen, the foil lining containing the food can be removed from the casserole. Overwrap the parcel and store in the freezer until needed, then unwrap and return the solid food to the casserole to reheat and serve.

Foil dishes Foil dishes come in a range of sizes and shapes and you can cook, freeze and reheat food in them.

Plastic containers These are more expensive than other types of freezer packaging, but will last for years. Some varieties may lose their airtight seal after a while and need sealing with freezer tape to prevent air affecting the contents. While you may want special plastic shapes for some food, ice cream bombes for instance, square and rectangular containers make better use of freezer space than round ones.

Other packaging Packaging containers from some bought foods are useful in the freezer. Good examples are soft margarine and cottage cheese tubs, ice cream cartons, yogurt and cream pots and foil dishes. Make sure they are scrupulously clean and do not expect to use them more than two or three times. Use freezer tape for an airtight seal.

Specially toughened glass dishes are handy for mousses and desserts which are to be served in the dish, but they must be freezer-proof.

In addition to wraps, bags and boxes, you will also need sheets of waxed or non-stick paper; plastic or paper-covered wire twist ties, which can be bought ready-cut or on a roll; freezer tape; labels; a chinagraph pencil or waterproof felt-tipped pen.

Labelling

It is essential to label everything that goes into your freezer, stating what it is and the date it went into the freezer, unless it is a commercial packet which clearly states what the contents are, in which case just label with the date. Use a chinagraph pencil or waterproof felt-tipped pen for labelling.

You can buy freezer labels in different colours

so that you can code things for easier finding – for example, red for meat, green for vegetables, and so on.

Freezing Vegetables
Vegetables should be frozen really fresh, not more than 12 hours after harvesting. All vegetables will keep better if they are blanched before freezing. Blanching means immersing food in boiling water for a short time to inactivate enzymes that would otherwise cause deterioration of flavour, texture, colour and nutritional value.

Blanching also kills many micro-organisms that spoil food and forces out air from inside the vegetables. Air trapped inside the cell walls expands on cooking and ruptures them, so that they leak and give off scum. Although some vitamin C is destroyed during blanching, more is lost with unblanched vegetables, as destructive enzymes remain active when the vegetables are frozen. The vitamin loss can be minimized by blanching in fast boiling water for the precise time recommended for each type of vegetable (see below).

Vegetables should be prepared as for cooking (see individual entries). Have ready a large bowl of ice-cold water. Using a saucepan large enough to hold a wire basket or colander, add about 4 litres (7 pints) water and 10 ml (2 level tsp) salt for every 450 g (1 lb) vegetables and bring to the boil. Place the vegetables in the wire basket and immerse in the boiling water. Bring back to the boil quickly and blanch for the time required. Blanching times vary from vegetable to vegetable but, as a rough guide, all types of bean should be blanched for 2–3 minutes; peas and cabbage for 1–2 minutes; carrots for 3–5 minutes; courgettes and mange-tout for 1 minute; broccoli, cauliflower and Brussels sprouts for 3-4 minutes; onions, spinach, fennel, parsnips and turnips for 2 minutes; corn on the cob for 4 minutes (small), 6 minutes (medium) or 8 minutes (large).

Remove the basket and plunge into the ice-cold water. Drain well and pack immediately in polythene bags or rigid containers; seal and label. The blanching water can be used six or seven times, then should be replaced with fresh water.

Unblanched vegetables Some people prefer not to blanch vegetables and the following can be frozen without blanching and kept for the times stated:

Brussels sprouts	3 days	Peppers	3 months
Broad beans	3 weeks	Peas	6–9 months
Runner beans	1 month	Carrots	12 months
Sweetcorn	1 month	Spinach	12 months

Some vegetables are unsuitable for freezing (except as soups and purées), including chicory, cucumber, endive, kale, lettuce, radishes and Jerusalem artichokes. Potatoes are best frozen cooked as croquettes or duchess potatoes, or as partially-cooked chips. Tomatoes are most useful if frozen as purée, though small whole tomatoes packed in bags and frozen can be used in cooked dishes. Mushrooms and sliced leeks are best lightly sautéed in butter or oil before being frozen; they may then be used in casseroles, soups and other cooked dishes. Avocados should be frozen as a purée, with a little lemon juice added to preserve the colour. After freezing, celery is only suitable for use in cooked dishes.

Storage Times
The maximum recommended storage time for vegetables is 10–12 months; 6–8 months for vegetable purées.

Cooking Frozen Vegetables
Blanching partially cooks the vegetables, so they need shorter cooking times when taken from the freezer. Cook all vegetables from frozen.

Freezing Fruit
Fruit for freezing should be just ripe and free from blemishes. It should be prepared as for eating or cooking (see individual entries). The various ways of freezing fruit are as follows:

Dry pack Fruits like blackberries, gooseberries, blackcurrants and raspberries can be frozen just as they are. Spread the fruit on baking trays or sheets lined with non-stick or greaseproof paper and put into the freezer until frozen. This is known as 'open' freezing. When frozen, pack the fruit in polythene bags. The fruit will stay separate in the bag so that small amounts can be removed as needed without having to thaw all of it.

Dry sugar pack If preterred, fruits like the above can be sprinkled with sugar before freezing, then as they thaw the fruit and sugar make a syrup. Spread the fruit in a shallow dish, sprinkle over caster sugar, allowing 100 g (4 oz) sugar to each 450 g (1 lb) fruit. Mix together gently until evenly coated, then pack in rigid containers, leaving 1–2 cm ($^1/_2$–$^3/_4$ inch) headspace.

Cold syrup Firm-textured fruits like apples, peaches and apricots are best frozen in a sugar syrup. Fruits that discolour, such as apples and pears, should also be soaked in a solution of lemon juice first. Use the juice of one lemon to each 1 litre (1 $^3/_4$ pints) water used. When preparing large quantities of fruit, make the syrup the day before and leave to chill overnight, as it has to be used cold.

As a rough guide, for every 450 g (1 lb) fruit, allow 300 ml ($^1/_2$ pint) syrup. For most fruits the syrup should be made with 450 g (l lb) sugar to 1 litre (1 $^3/_4$ pints) water, but for some acid fruits (such as gooseberries, blueberries and bilberries), the syrup should be made with 900 g (1 lb) sugar to 1 litre (1 $^3/_4$ pints) water.

Dissolve the sugar in the water, bring to the boil, remove from the heat, add lemon juice if necessary, cover and leave to cool. Pour the syrup over the prepared fruit or place the fruit in a container with the syrup. Light-weight fruits which tend to rise in liquids can be held below the surface by placing a dampened and crumpled piece of non-absorbent paper on top of the mixture. Leave 1–2 cm ($^1/_2$–$^3/_4$ inch) headspace for expansion.

Purée Over-ripe fruit can be puréed and frozen to make good stand-by sauces and desserts.

Some fruits are not suitable for freezing, including bananas, pomegranates and kiwi fruit. Only cantaloup and honeydew melons are worth freezing, though they lose their crispness when thawed. Whole frozen strawberries can be a disappointment and are best frozen as a purée.

Storage Times
The maximum recommended storage time for most fruits is 9–12 months; 6–8 months for dry pack fruits and purées; 4–6 months for fruit juices.

Thawing and Cooking Fruit
If the fruit is to be served raw, thaw it slowly in the unopened container and eat while still slightly chilled; turn it into a dish only just before serving. Fruits which tend to discolour, such as peaches, should be thawed more rapidly and kept submerged in the syrup while thawing. Allow 6–8 hours per 450 g (1 lb) fruit in the refrigerator or 2–4 hours at room temperature. Dry sugar packs thaw rather more quickly than fruit in syrup. For quick thawing, place the container in slightly warm water for 30 minutes to 1 hour.

If the fruit is to be cooked, thaw it until the pieces are just loosened. Cook as for fresh fruit, but do not forget that it will already be sweet if it has been packed in dry sugar or syrup.

Freezing Meat, Poultry and Game

Freezing Meat
Many butchers will supply bulk meat at a good discount on normal retail prices, and will cut it into usable-sized joints. Sometimes butchers will also blast-freeze the meat, so that you get it ready frozen. Alternatively, ready-frozen meat is sold as whole carcasses, halves or quarters, or in bulk packs. Fresh meat needs very little preparation; trim off excess fat and, whenever possible, remove any bones as well. These only take up freezer space and are better used for making stocks for soups, which are much more economical to store.

It is essential to package meat well, excluding as much air as possible to prevent the fat going rancid and the meat drying out. Use heavy duty polythene bags. Separate chops and steaks with layers of greaseproof or non-stick paper.

Meat and Meat Products Storage Times

Food	Recommended storage time	Food	Recommended storage time
Beef	8 months	Curry	4 months
Lamb	6 months	Ham	2 months
Mince	3 months	Meat pies	3 months
Offal	3 months	Pâté	1 month
Pork	6 months	Sliced meat -	
Sausages	3 months	with gravy	3 months
Veal	6 months	without gravy	2 months
Casseroles –		Cottage pie	3 months
with bacon	2 months	Soup	3 months
without bacon	3 months	Stock	6 months

Freezing Poultry

Commercial quick-frozen raw poultry is so readily available that it is only an advantage to freeze at home if the price is favourable.

A chicken takes up less freezer space if it is jointed first (*see* POULTRY). Use the carcass for making stock, then freeze the stock.

Wrap chicken quarters or joints individually in foil or polythene bags, label, then combine into a larger package to save time hunting for individual packs.

Cold roast or poached chicken should be cooled as quickly as possible after cooking. Wrap small amounts in foil, with any stuffing packed separately, and freeze at once. To avoid excessive drying, freeze it with gravy or stock.

A turkey takes up valuable freezer space, so it is not good planning to store one for too long. Turkeys can be jointed and stored like chicken. Cooked turkey can also be frozen like chicken; cut the meat off the bone and discard the fat.

Choose young duckling and geese for freezing. Look for ones without too much fat, though very lean birds may be dry. Freeze as for chicken, packing the giblets separately.

Poultry Storage Times

The recommended storage time for chicken, duckling and geese is 12 months; turkey 6 months; giblets 2–3 months and cold cuts of meat 2–3 months.

Freezing Game

Venison must be hung before freezing, then frozen in usable joints as for meat. Hares and rabbits should also be prepared as for cooking fresh. As most recipes call for portions, it is sensible to pack them this way, discarding the more bony parts. Pack and freeze game as for meat.

Game birds actually improve with freezing. Hang, undrawn, until sufficiently high, then pluck, draw, wash well and dry thoroughly. Pack in foil or freezer bags and freeze.

Game Storage Times

The maximum recommended storage time for venison is 12 months; hares and rabbits 6 months; game birds 9 months.

Freezing Bacon

Only very fresh bacon should be frozen; the longer bacon has been cut or kept in the shop, the shorter its storage life in the freezer.

Commercial vacuum-packed bacon is good for freezing as the maximum amount of air has already been extracted from inside the wrapping. Alternatively, freeze top-quality bacon, closely wrapped in freezer cling film or foil and over-wrapped in polythene bags. If wished, rashers can be interleaved with waxed or non-stick paper. Wrap bacon chops individually in foil, then pack together in a polythene bag. Joints up to 1.5–2 kg (3–4 lb) should be wrapped in foil, then over-wrapped in a polythene bag.

Bacon Storage Times

The recommended storage times for bacon are: vacuum-packed bacon 3 months; smoked rashers, chops, gammon steaks and joints 2 months; unsmoked rashers, chops, gammon steaks and joints 1 month.

Freezing Fish

Whole fish may be frozen uncooked but must be really fresh. Wash and scale the fish, gut and wash thoroughly under cold running water. Drain and dry on absorbent kitchen paper. For best results, place the whole fish unwrapped in the freezer and freeze until solid. Remove from the freezer and dip in cold water. This will form a layer of thin ice over the fish. Return the fish to the freezer and repeat the process until the ice glaze is 0.5 cm (¼ inch) thick. Lay the fish on a thin board and wrap in freezer wrap.

Fish steaks should be separated with a double layer of cling film, then overwrapped in foil or freezer wrap.

Allow whole uncooked fish to thaw for 24 hours in a cool place before cooking. Once thawed, use promptly. Fish steaks should be cooked from frozen.

Fish Storage Times

Whole salmon, other freshwater and oily fish can be stored in the freezer for 2 months. White fish and steaks can be stored for 2–3 months.

Thawing and Cooking from Frozen

Some foods can be cooked from frozen, others need to be thawed. Foods can be thawed slowly or quickly; those thawed slowly have a slightly better texture.

Meat Small cuts of meat, such as chops, steaks, mince, sausages and liver, can be cooked gently from frozen, if there is no time for thawing. When cooking, you will need to cook for almost twice as long as usual. Start cooking at a low temperature and increase the temperature halfway through the cooking time. Some whole joints of meat can also be cooked from frozen, provided you use a meat thermometer to check that they are cooked right through. Cooking times for frozen joints over 2.8 kg (6 lb) are very difficult to calculate. To prevent the outside being overcooked before the inside is thawed, it is better to thaw large joints before cooking.

Rolled joints, such as breast of lamb, whether stuffed or not, must be thawed before cooking. This is because all the surfaces of the meat have been handled and rolled up, so it is important to ensure thorough cooking to destroy any bacteria which might be present in the meat.

Bacon Must be thawed before cooking.

Stews, pre-cooked pies and casseroles There is a danger that these will not heat through properly if they are cooked from frozen. Thaw at cool room temperature.

Fish Whole large fish should be thawed out as slowly as possible to retain moisture and texture. Small fish and cuts are best cooked from frozen.

Vegetables These should be cooked from frozen. Try slow-cooking them in a heavy saucepan with a knob of butter or margarine instead of water, to preserve the vitamins.

Fruit If it is going to be eaten without further preparation, fruit needs very gentle thawing to prevent it from going too soft and mushy. If wished, it can be eaten while it is still a little icy.

Bread and rolls Thawing in a warm oven makes them crisp and smell like newly baked bread.

Slow Thawing

The slowest way of thawing is in the refrigerator or at cool room temperature. Always leave food in its original wrapping, otherwise meat will bleed and lose some of its quality and colour; fruit will lose its juice and suffer in texture; fish will dry out. Allow plenty of time; as little as 450 g (1 lb) of food can take anything up to 6 hours to thaw.

Quick Thawing

Food thawed at normal room temperature takes about half the time. In an emergency, submerge the package in a bowl of cold water or hold it under running cold water. Once thawed, treat as fresh.

Cooking and Reheating from Frozen

In general, foods that can be cooked or reheated from frozen should be heated as rapidly as possible, as this preserves the flavour and texture. As the food thaws, gently separate the pieces.

Thawing Meat

Meat can be thawed at room temperature, but there is less risk of contamination if it is thawed in the refrigerator. If the juices which have come from the meat during thawing are used in cooking, they should be cooked as soon as possible. Thawed meat can be cooked and then re-frozen, if wished.

Approximate Thawing Times for Meat

	Time per 450 g (1 lb)	
Type of cut	In a refrigerator	At room temperature
Joints		
1.4 kg (3 lb) or more	6–7 hours	2–3 hours
less than 1.4 kg (3 lb)	3–4 hours	1–2 hours
Steaks, chops,		
stewing steak	5–6 hours	2–4 hours

Thawing Poultry

All frozen poultry must be completely thawed before cooking, so leave plenty of time. A large turkey can take a few days. Thaw poultry weighing up to 2.7 kg (6 lb) in the refrigerator and poultry weighing over that at cool room temperature. If the giblets are inside the body cavity, remove them as soon as possible.

The bird is completely thawed when no ice crystals remain in the body cavity and the limbs are flexible. Once thawed, poultry should be cooked as soon as possible and should not be stored for more than two days.

Freezing Miscellaneous Foods

Sauces, soups and stocks make very useful standbys to keep in the freezer. After cooking, cool, then pour into rigid containers, leaving headspace. Seal well, label and freeze. Sauces and soups may be stored for 3 months, stock for 6 months. Either thaw for 1–2 hours at room temperature, or heat gently from frozen until boiling.

Double or whipping cream can be frozen, but single cream does not freeze well. Whipped cream may be piped in rosettes on to non-stick paper and frozen. Transfer to a suitable container and seal, leaving space for expansion. Fresh cream frozen at home can be stored for 3 months, commercially-frozen cream for up to 1 year. Thaw at room temperature for 45–60 minutes. Put rosettes in position as decoration before thawing; they will be thawed in 30 minutes.

Cakes of all sorts can be frozen – sponge flans, Swiss rolls, layer cakes and large gâteaux, as well as light fruit cakes, though it is a waste of freezer space to freeze rich fruit cakes as they keep so well anyway. Bake cakes in the usual way and cool on

---

Opposite: Fish: 1. Cod; 2. Grey mullet; 3. Monkfish; 4. Turbot; 5. Dover sole; 6. Sea bass; 7. Whiting; 8. Red mullet; 9. Skate; 10. Halibut; 11. Plaice; 12. Mackerel; 13. Herring; 14. Sardine; 15. Whitebait; 16. Conger eel; 17. Salmon; 18. Salmon cutlets; 19. Trout

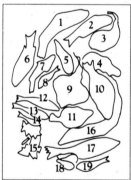

Overleaf: Left, Gravad lax; **Right**, Roast grouse
Centre Pages: Shellfish: 1. Crab; 2. Great scallops; 3. Queen scallops; 4. Prawns; 5. Lobster; 6. Crayfish; 7. Jumbo prawns; 8. Brown shrimps; 9. Oysters; 10. Clams; 11. Mussels; 12. Raw jumbo prawns; 13. Scampi (Dublin Bay prawns)

a wire rack. Do not spread or layer sponge cakes with jam. Wrap plain cake layers separately, or together with cling film or waxed paper between layers. Pack decorated cream cakes in rigid boxes to protect them. All types of cake may be stored in the freezer for 3 months.

Thaw smaller cakes for 1–2 hours at room temperature; larger gâteaux for 3–4 hours. Cream cakes may be sliced while frozen for a better shape and quicker thawing. Light fruit cakes need 4–5 hours to thaw.

Bread is another useful standby to keep in the freezer. Freshly-baked bread, both bought and home-made, can be frozen. Crisp, crusty bread stores well for up to 1 week, then the crust begins to flake off. Freeze bought bread in its original wrapper for up to 1 week; for longer periods, seal in foil or polythene. Freeze home-made bread in foil or polythene. The maximum recommended storage time for frozen bread is 1–2 months.

Thaw bread in the sealed polythene bag or wrapper at room temperature for 3–6 hours. Sliced bread can be toasted from frozen.

Previous Pages: Left, Gâteau Saint-Honoré; **Right**, Mangosteens, Lychees, Rambutans
Opposite: Tropical Fruits:1. Pineapple; 2. Papayas; 3. Custard apples; 4. Mangoes (yellow and green); 5. Green bananas and Plantain; 6. Guavas; 7. Pomegranates; 8. Kiwi fruit; 9. Persimmons; 10. Prickly pears; 11. Tamarillos; 12. Medlars; 13. Figs; 14. Dates; 15. Kumquats; 16. Cape gooseberries; 17. Passion fruit

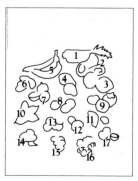

Herbs can be frozen in small bunches in a rigid foil container or bag. Wash and trim if necessary and dry thoroughly before freezing. Herbs can be stored in the freezer for up to 6 months. They can be crumbled and added to dishes while still frozen.

Cheese should be wrapped in freezer film or a polythene bag for freezing. Full fat soft cheeses and cream cheeses are the most suitable; hard cheeses become crumbly if stored too long, but are fine grated for cooking. Cottage cheese and low fat soft cheeses are not suitable for freezing. The maximum recommended storage time for frozen cheese is 3–6 months. Thaw cheese for 24 hours in the refrigerator, then allow to come to room temperature before serving. Use grated cheese straight from frozen.

FRENCH ARTICHOKE (*see* ARTICHOKE, GLOBE)

FRENCH BEAN (*see* BEAN, FRENCH)

FRENCH BREAD (*see* BREAD)

FRENCH DRESSING (*see* SALAD DRESSING)

FRENCH TOAST (Pain Perdu) There are both sweet and savoury versions of this popular dish. In France, French toast is served as a dessert and is made by soaking pieces of stale bread in a sweet vanilla-flavoured custard mixture before frying them in butter until crisp and golden. In America, French toast is a popular breakfast dish. It may be served topped with maple syrup, fruit or jam, sprinkled with cinnamon and sugar.

The savoury version of French toast is made by omitting the sugar and vanilla and dipping the bread simply in a mixture of beaten egg and milk. It may be served as a snack or light supper dish.

FRESHWATER EEL (*see* EEL)

FRESHWATER SHARK (*see* PIKE)

FRIANDISES The French name for a selection of small sweets, preserved fruits, etc., served as petits fours or with tea or coffee.

FRICASSÉE The French name for a white stew of chicken, rabbit, veal or vegetables, finished with cream and egg yolks. (*see also* BLANQUETTE)

FRIKADELLER (Fricadelle) A north European dish, popular in Germany, Belgium and Denmark, consisting of small meatballs or burgers made of minced pork. Frikadeller may be deep- or shallow-fried and are served hot, usually with a tomato sauce.

FRISÉE (*see* CHICORY)

FRIT (Frite) A French word meaning fried, as in *pommes de terre frites* (fried potatoes).

FRITTATA An Italian dish that is similar to an omelette, but is flat and round, not folded. It is also firmer than a French omelette because the eggs are cooked over a low heat for at least 10 minutes. Like a French omelette, a *frittata* may be cooked with various fillings, such as Parmesan cheese, onions, Mozzarella cheese and Mortadella.

FRITTER A portion of sweet or savoury food, coated with batter or (less often) egg and breadcrumbs, then deep- or shallow-fried. Apple, banana, orange, cheese, corned beef and prawns are among the many fillings that may be used. If desired, mixed spice or ground cinnamon may be added to the batter used to coat a fruit filling such as apple or pineapple. Sweet fritters are served hot, sprinkled with sugar, as a dessert, and savoury fritters may be served as an hors d'oeuvre or light supper dish. (*see also* BATTER)

A type of fritter may also be made from flavoured choux pastry (*see* PASTRY) or from a sweetened yeast dough (*see* BEIGNET).

FRITTO MISTO An Italian dish consisting of a variety of small, thin pieces of meat, poultry, liver, or vegetables, which are coated with batter or egg and breadcrumbs and deep-fried. *Fritto misto di mare* consists of small pieces of various sea fish and shellfish coated with flour or batter and deep-fried.

FROG Although it has never been generally accepted in Britain, the edible frog (*grenouille* in French) is of real gastronomic merit. Since frogs do not count as meat, they are regarded as a useful supplement to the diet during Lent. Only the hind legs are used, being either fried in butter or cut up, stewed and served in a white sauce containing mushrooms. The meat is delicate in flavour, resembling the flesh of a young rabbit or chicken. Frogs' legs are usually thought of as a French speciality, but they are also popular in Italy and Germany, and most of the frogs eaten in France today are imported from central Europe and Yugoslavia, and even from as far afield as Cuba and the United States.

FROMAGE À LA CRÈME (*see* COEUR À LA CRÈME)

FROMAGE BLANC A very low fat soft French cheese with a light, fresh, clean taste and a smooth texture. (*see also* FROMAGE FRAIS)

FROMAGE DE MONSIEUR A soft French cheese made from cows' milk. It is similar to Camembert, but milder.

FROMAGE DE TÊTE (*see* BRAWN)

FROMAGE FRAIS Similar to *fromage blanc*, this is a soft cheese that originated in France but is now made in many other countries and is widely available in Britain. It is sometimes enriched with cream, increasing its fat content, and it is often sold flavoured with fruit. Depending on its fat content, the consistency of *fromage frais* varies from quite runny to very thick. Some varieties are quite rich and are sold in very small pots. Fruit flavoured *fromage frais* may be served as a dessert, while plain varieties are often used in cooking. (*see also* FROMAGE BLANC)

FROSTED FRUIT Soft, juicy fruit, such as grapes and redcurrants, may be given a crisp, sparkling coating, or frosting, of fine sugar and served as a dessert or used to decorate puddings or cakes. The fruits are dipped, one at a time, in

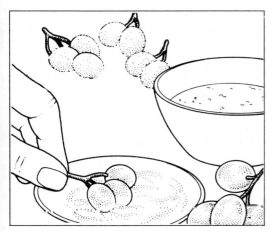

Frosting grapes by dipping first in egg white, then in caster sugar.

very lightly whisked egg white, then in caster sugar, and are then left to dry.

FROSTING An American expression referring to the icing of cakes and, more specifically, to a particular type of icing (*see* AMERICAN FROST-ING). It also refers to the decorating of fruits, flowers and the rims of cocktail glasses by coating with a fine layer of sugar (*see* FROSTED FRUIT).

FROTHING The name given to a method of browning roast meat, especially game, by dredg-ing the surface with flour and heating to a brown colour in a hot oven.

FROZEN FOODS The process of deep freezing foods in order to preserve them was first put into commercial use in 1924 by the American, Clarence Birdseye, and frozen foods first appeared in American food stores in the late 1930s. They did not become generally available in Britain, however, until the late 1940s. Today, the range of frozen foods available is vast, including prepared dishes and complete meals as well as most types of uncooked food. The present high degree of technical skill results in the supply of excellent products that have an important part to play in the diet of every household.

The three great assets of frozen foods are that they retain a high proportion of their vitamins and other nutrients, as well as their flavour, colour and good general appearance; they require very little preparation and entail no waste; they enable the consumer to enjoy out-of-season foods. Com-mercially-frozen foods are frozen very quickly to an extremely low temperature that cannot be achieved in the home freezer, so bought frozen foods are generally of a superior quality.

Once bought, frozen foods should be got home and into the freezer as soon as possible. Thawed items cannot be re-frozen unless they are cooked first. Any four-star-rated home freezer can be used for storing frozen foods, but storage times are limited if using the ice-making or frozen food compartment of a refrigerator.

Pre-packed frozen foods usually carry detailed instructions about storage, thawing and cooking. It is important to follow these precisely. (*see also* FREEZING)

FRUCTOSE (*see* SUGAR)

FRUIT Botanically speaking, a fruit is the ovary or seed-bearing part of any growing plant. Many varieties of fruit are edible and are eaten all over the world, either raw or cooked in any number of ways. The range of fruits available in Britain is expanding all the time, with new varieties of tropical fruits being imported each year. As well as apples, pears, bananas, grapes and citrus fruits, we can now choose between kiwi fruit, passion fruit, guavas, lychees and mangoes, amongst many others. Many of the soft fruits, such as strawberries, traditionally associated with the warmer months of the year, can now also be bought in the winter months, thanks to improved methods of growing and transportation.

Nutritionally, fruit is very important as it is a rich source of fibre (especially if the skin is eaten), and energy in the form of natural fruit sugar (fructose). Many fruits also contain vitamins and minerals. It is a popular snack food as many varieties can conveniently be eaten with no preparation at all, and nearly all fruit is comparatively low in calories.

Buying and Storing Fruit

Most fruits should be bought when ripe and eaten as soon as possible, but some, such as bananas, can be bought when unripe and safely left to ripen for a few days at home. Hard fruits, such as apples and pears, will not ripen after picking and should be bought ready to eat. Soft fruits, such as raspberries, strawberries and redcurrants have very poor keeping qualities and should be eaten soon after buying. Peaches, nectarines and other stone fruits should be firm but ripe when bought and will not ripen further.

Choose fruit that looks and smells fresh and ripe, with no bruises or damaged skin. Stone fruit should yield only slightly when gently squeezed. Berries and other soft fruits should be plump and dry; check that punnets are not stained with juice and that the underneath fruit is not squashed.

Many fruits will keep well at room temperature and it is common to see a fruit bowl in the kitchen or living room containing a ready supply of apples, pears, bananas and citrus fruits. Bananas will quickly become over-ripe if left for too long, and the skins of citrus fruits will become dry and wrinkled after a few days, although the fruit will remain edible for up to two weeks. Fruit stored in the refrigerator will keep for a longer period but may lose flavour. Most fruits can successfully be frozen (*see* FREEZING).

Serving and Cooking Fruit

One of the beauties of fruit is that it needs little preparation and is often at its best when eaten raw. However, in these days of chemical farming, it is likely that the fruit you buy has been sprayed with pesticides or other chemicals, so all fruit should be thoroughly washed or peeled before it is eaten. This is also true of citrus fruits which may be treated with preservative and glazing substances before transportation, so it is important to wash the peel thoroughly if it is to be included in a recipe.

Fruit can be served at any meal, and may be included in any course. Simple starters include fruit cocktails and Parma ham served with fresh figs or slices of melon; meat, poultry and game are often served with a fruit accompaniment, such as pork with apple, gammon with pineapple and turkey with cranberries; lemon wedges are served with any number of fish and meat dishes, as well as with many desserts; countless desserts, such as mousses, soufflés, fools, trifles, ice creams, sorbets, tarts, cheesecakes and pavlovas, are made with fruit; grapes are often served with the cheese board at the end of a meal.

Basic methods of cooking fruit include stewing or poaching and baking. It can also be used in countless other ways, either singly or in combination, to make any number of desserts, from the simplest fruit salad or compote, to the most elaborate gâteaux and pastries. Fruit is also used to make preserves, such as jams, jellies, marmalades and fruit butters and cheeses. It is also a main ingredient in many drinks and frequently forms part of a garnish or decoration.

(See individual entries for information about particular fruits.)

FRUIT BUTTER (*see* BUTTER, FRUIT)

FRUIT BRANDY (*see* EAU-DE-VIE)

FRUIT CHEESE (*see* CHEESE, FRUIT)

FRUIT, DRIED (*see* DRIED FRUIT)

FRUIT SALAD A popular dessert dish consisting of a mixture of sliced or diced fresh fruits served in natural fruit juice or in a plain or flavoured sugar syrup. Popular flavourings include liqueurs, such as kirsch, or white wine. The fruits used vary according to season and availability, but any combination of up to four or five fruits may be used. Variations include dried fruit salad, made from a mixture of pre-soaked dried fruits, and tropical fruit salad, made from a variety of tropical fruits, such as kiwi fruit, mango and pineapple.

A fruit salad may be served with cream, custard, ice cream or natural yogurt.

FRUMENTY A traditional Harvest Home dish, which used to be made from the new wheat. The grains were steeped in water and left in a warm place for hours, then husked and boiled with milk to make a kind of porridge, which was spiced and sweetened. It was sometimes enriched with cream or egg yolks.

FRYING A method of cooking food in hot fat or oil. There are various methods of frying, using different quantities of fat or oil.

Frying is not as popular as it once was because many people are trying to cut down the amount of fat in their diets. However, the newer methods of frying, such as dry-frying and stir-frying, are healthier methods that, in many cases, can be used instead of more traditional shallow- and deep-frying. (*see also* FATS, OILS)

Shallow-frying

This is the most frequently used type of frying and is a quick method of cooking many different types of food. Shallow-frying is frequently used prior to further cooking, for example when browning and sealing in the flavour of meat or poultry before cooking in a casserole, or as the main method of cooking, such as when frying eggs, steak, bacon, etc. Only a small quantity of fat is used, in a shallow frying pan. Shallow-frying is used for steaks, chops, sausages, fish steaks or white fish (such as sole) and pancakes, which need only sufficient fat to prevent them from sticking to the pan. Made-up dishes, such as fish cakes or hamburgers, require enough fat to come halfway up the food.

Most oils are suitable for shallow-frying. Butter is not suitable as it burns and smokes at too low a temperature, but clarified butter and ghee can be used (*see* GHEE), as can a combination of oil and butter. Low fat spreads cannot be used as they contain a high proportion of water.

The fat or oil should be heated until a faint haze rises from it before the food is added; take care not to overheat it – it should *not* be smoking. It is important that the oil is hot before the food is added, otherwise oil will be absorbed by the food, making it soggy. Sometimes the food is coated with a suitable covering, such as egg and breadcrumbs, which helps to prevent oil being absorbed, but the coating itself can become soggy if the oil is not hot enough. Cook the food quickly for a few minutes or until the surface is browned and crisp on both sides, then reduce the heat and complete the cooking slowly. Turn the food carefully to avoid breaking up the coating, if used. When the food is cooked, lift it from the pan and drain on absorbent kitchen paper to remove surplus fat. Serve at once.

(*see also* SAUTÉING)

Deep-frying

This method of frying is suitable for made-up dishes such as croquettes and fritters, and also for fish coated with batter and for whitebait, chipped potatoes, doughnuts, etc. It involves immersing the food completely in hot oil or fat, usually in a deep frying pan, which is a saucepan with a wire basket that fits inside it in which the food is placed for frying.

Most types of oil are suitable for deep-frying. Corn oil is popular as it can be heated to a very high temperature (about 425°C/220°F) before it reaches its 'smoking point'. The oil should be pure and free from moisture, to avoid any spurting or boiling over. It must be heated to the correct temperature (see overleaf) before any food is added; if there is a haze over the oil, it is too hot and the food will burn. If it is not hot enough, it will become sodden with oil.

Most food to be deep-fried (except potatoes, pastry, doughnuts, etc.) is covered with a coating of batter or egg and breadcrumbs. This helps stop oil entering the food, and prevents the food flavouring the oil, so that it can be used again. Place the food in the wire basket and lower the basket slowly into the oil. When a large quantity of food is to be fried, cook it a little at a time to avoid lowering the temperature of the oil. As soon as the food is golden brown, lift it out and drain on absorbent kitchen paper. Serve at once.

After use, strain the frying oil into a clean bowl and keep it for further use. With care, the oil can be used many times and can be kept for several months. (*see also* ELECTRIC DEEP-FAT FRYER)

Temperatures for Deep-frying

The temperature the oil should be heated to depends on the food to be cooked in it. For doughnuts, fritters and fish, the temperature should be from 175°C (350°F) to 188°C (370°F). For croquettes and potato chips, the temperature should be about 190°C (375°F). For Scotch egg and chicken Kiev, the temperature should be about 160°C (325°F).

If you do not have a thermometer, the temperature may be tested as follows: Put one or two 2.5 cm (1 inch) cubes of bread into the hot oil. If they take 60 seconds to brown, the temperature of the oil is between 175°C (350°F) and 188°C (370°F); if they take 40 seconds, it is between 188°C (370°F) and 190°C (375°F).

Safety Precautions

Hot oil ignites when overheated so care should be taken to avoid this happening when deep-frying. Never fill the pan more than one-third full and watch carefully to be sure the fat does not become too hot. Make sure food is dry when it is put into the hot oil and never leave a deep-frying pan unattended.

If the oil does ignite, *never never* carry the pan to the sink or garden. Immediately cover your hands with a thick cloth and place either the saucepan lid, a metal baking sheet or, best of all, a kitchen fire blanket over the fire. Turn off the heat. Leave until cool enough to handle.

Stir-frying

Originally Chinese, this is a method of cooking foods quickly in very hot oil. Stir-frying is done in a large frying pan or wok (*see* WOK). A little oil is heated to a very high temperature before the food is added in small batches. During the short cooking time, the food is constantly stirred with a spatula so that it cooks evenly. Stir-frying is a very healthy method of frying since it uses very little oil, and foods such as vegetables are cooked in a very short time and lose less nutrients than when cooked by longer methods.

Stir-frying is ideal for thinly sliced meats, poultry, fish and vegetables. Stir-fried vegetables are cooked until only just tender.

Dry-frying (Pan-grilling)

This is a method of frying that does not involve the use of extra fat or oil. It is used for fatty foods, such as bacon and sausages, which are placed in a cold, often non-stick, pan. As the food is heated, fat is released and excess can be poured off, leaving just enough to cook the food. As no extra fat is added to the food, this is obviously a very healthy method of frying. It is also used for 'roasting' spices.

FUDGE A sweet made from sugar, butter, milk and cream, in varying proportions. By using different flavourings and such additions as chopped nuts and glacé or dried fruit, many varieties of fudge can be made, including chocolate, vanilla, honey, etc. The mixture is heated to a temperature of about 116°C (240°F) and then it is 'grained', that is it is stirred until minute crystals are formed. The mixture is also stirred during cooking to prevent burning. While it is still liquid, the fudge is poured into an oiled tin and left to set. It is usually cut into squares as soon as it is firm. (*see also* SWEETS)

FUL MEDAMES (Foule Medames) This rounded oval-shaped brown bean is a member of the broad bean family and is the basic ingredient of an Egyptian dish of the same name. The beans are available dried in this country and need overnight soaking followed by long slow cooking before they can be used, usually in a mixed bean salad, soup or casserole. (*see also* PULSES)

FUMET The French name generally given to a liquid used to add flavour and body to soups and sauces. It is prepared by cooking fish, meat, game or vegetables in stock or wine until reduced to a syrupy consistency, then straining off the liquid. In classic French cookery, the name *fumet* may only be given to concentrated fish or mushroom stocks; for meat, poultry or game stocks, the word *fond* is used.

FUNGHI PORCINI (*see* MUSHROOM)

FUNGUS The general name of a particular type of plant that lives off other living, dead or decaying organic matter. Included in the group are mushrooms, toadstools and other similar plants that can be found growing in fields, woods and parks all over the country.

There are thousands of different types of fungus and only a comparatively small number of them are edible. Since some types are poisonous, it is essential to be able to distinguish between them or to buy only from a reliable source. A number of well-illustrated books on the subject have been published and will help one to recognize the main edible fungi, but it must be emphasized that if there is any doubt about a particular type, it should be rejected. All fungi should look fresh, not dried up or slimy, when picked or bought.

Mushrooms, blewits, morels and some species of boletus (ceps) are the chief edible fungi. The field mushroom is the most widely known. This grows wild, as its name suggests, but is also cultivated to an increasing extent and indeed most of the mushrooms on sale in shops are in fact cultivated field mushrooms.

The food value of fungi is negligible, apart from a little thiamin, and they are eaten for their excellent flavour. They may be used in many ways, either as the main ingredient of a dish or as a flavouring, accompaniment or garnish, particularly with fried foods. (*see also* AGARIC, MUSHROOM)

FUSILLI (*see* PASTA)

G

GAGE (*see* PLUM)

GALANGAL (Laos, Leuqkuas) There are two varieties of this spice plant, lesser galangal and greater galangal, both of them related to ginger. Like ginger, the spice is derived from the root-like underground stem (or rhizome) of the plant which looks very like ginger root, and indeed the flavour of galangal is very similar to that of ginger. The plants are native to South-East Asia and the spice is an important ingredient in the food of Malaysia, Indonesia and Singapore. It is available in Britain in fresh, dried and ground forms and can be used in many of the same ways as ginger, especially as a curry ingredient.

GALANTINE A dish of white meat (such as poultry, veal or pork) which has been boned, sometimes stuffed, rolled, cooked, pressed into a symmetrical shape and glazed with aspic to be served as a cold main dish. A galantine is some-times formed into a cylindrical shape and wrapped in muslin for cooking, very like a *ballottine* (*see* BALLOTTINE).

GALETTE The French name for a variety of sweet or savoury flat round cakes or biscuits. A galette may be large or small and may be made from puff pastry, shortbread, almond paste, various cereals and even potatoes, the ingredients depending on which region of France the recipe has come from. One of the most famous French galettes is the Twelfth Night cake (*galette des rois*) which is made from puff pastry. Traditionally, a bean, symbolizing the baby Jesus, is hidden in the pastry before it is baked for one lucky person to find when the galette is served.

GALINGALE (*see* CHUFA)

GALLIANO A golden, spicy, herbal Italian liqueur, famous as an ingredient of a Harvey Wallbanger cocktail, in which it is mixed with vodka and orange juice.

GALLIMAUFRY Originally a hash or ragoût of poultry or meat, this term may now be applied to any poorly presented and unappetizing dish made from a mixture of ingredients.

GALLON An imperial measure used for liquids, containing 4 quarts (8 pints). The standard UK gallon contains about 277 cubic inches and its weight is equal to 4.5 kg (10 lb) of distilled water. Its metric equivalent is 4.55 litres.

An American gallon is smaller than a UK gallon, being equivalent to 0.83 of a UK gallon, or 3.78 litres.

GAME The name given to wild birds and animals which are hunted for food, but which at certain times of the year are protected by law (see opposite). Also included in this category are pigeons (though, strictly speaking, only wood or wild pigeons count as game), quail, which are farmed, rabbits, which are also farmed but are cooked in the same way as hares, and venison. Game feeds on food not available to farm-reared animals which gives it its distinctive gamey flavour.

For information about individual types of game, see CAPERCAILZIE, DUCK, GOOSE, GROUSE, PARTRIDGE, PHEASANT, PIGEON, PTARMIGAN, QUAIL, RABBIT, SNIPE, VENISON and WOODCOCK.

Game Birds

Game birds are best eaten young. The plumage is a guide as all young birds have soft, even feathers. With pheasant and partridge, the long wing feathers are V-shaped in a young bird, as distinct from the rounded ones of an older bird. Smooth, pliable legs, short spurs and a firm, plump breast are other points to look for. Most game birds need to be hung so ask the butcher or poulterer if the bird has been hung and for how long. If it is not hung, the flesh will be tough and tasteless.

Alternatively, order game from your butcher or poulterer and he will hang the bird for the specified time and supply it ready plucked and drawn on the required day. If you are given game, you can hang it yourself in a cold, dry, airy place for the time specified opposite. The birds should be hung by the neck without being plucked or drawn, except in the case of wild duck, which may be drawn before hanging.

If you are given a bird that has been damaged by shot or is wet, it will not keep as long as a bird in good condition. Check it frequently and cook it as soon as the tail feathers will pluck out easily.

Hanging Times for Game Birds

Bird	Hanging time (days)
Black game (black grouse)	3–10
Capercailzie	7–14
Grouse	2–4
Partridge (Grey and Red-legged)	3–5
Pheasant	3–10
Ptarmigan	2–4
Snipe	3–4
Wild duck (Mallard, Teal and Widgeon)	2–3
Wild geese (Pink-footed and Greylag)	2–9
Woodcock	3–5
Wood pigeon	Requires no hanging

Open Seasons for Game Birds

Bird	Shooting Season
Black game (black grouse)	20 Aug-10 Dec
Capercailzie	1 Oct-31 Jan
Grouse	12 Aug-10 Dec
Partridge (Grey and Red-legged)	1 Sept-1 Feb
Pheasant	1 Oct-1 Feb (10 Dec in Scotland)
Ptarmigan	12 Aug-10 Dec
Snipe	12 Aug-31 Jan
Wild duck (Mallard, Teal and Widgeon)	1 Sept-31 Jan
Wild goose (Pink-footed and Greylag)	1 Sept-31 Jan
Woodcock	1 Oct-31 Jan (1 Sept-31 Jan in Scotland)
Wood pigeon	No close season (best May-Oct)

Storing Game Birds

A bird that has been hung and is ready for cooking can be stored for 1–2 days in the refrigerator or it can be frozen. If necessary, a bird can be frozen for a short time with its feathers on, and plucked after thawing, but it is best to pluck and draw first.

Cooking and Serving

The more simply game is cooked, the better. For a young bird, there is no better way than roasting, but for older birds, which are likely to be tough if plainly roasted, braising or casseroling are better methods.

Game birds lack fat, so it is usual to cover (or 'bard') the breast before roasting with pieces of fat bacon and to baste frequently with butter or margarine during cooking. When the bird is nearly cooked, the bacon can be removed in order to brown the meat.

See individual game bird entries for detailed cooking instructions.

(*see also* BARDING, CARVING)

Accompaniments

Thin gravy can be served with any roast game bird. Add 150 ml (¼ pint) water or meat stock to the roasting tin and, with a spoon, work in any cooking juices left in the tin. Bring to the boil and boil for 2–3 minutes. Remove all grease from the surface with a metal spoon, season to taste and strain before serving.

Fried crumbs are another popular accompaniment. Fry 50–100 g (2–4 oz) fresh breadcrumbs in 25 g (1 oz) butter or margarine until golden brown. Stir from time to time to ensure even browning.

Game chips can be made by cutting potatoes into very thin slices and deep-frying them until golden (*see* POTATO). Alternatively, serve potato crisps that have been warmed in the oven.

Bread sauce is traditionally served with pheasant, but may also accompany other game birds (*see* BREAD SAUCE).

Small birds, such as grouse, are often roasted on a slice of toast or bread. The bird is then served on the toast or bread on which it is roasted.

GAMMON (*see* BACON)

GANACHE A French chocolate-flavoured cream mixture used as a filling or topping for cakes, pastries, chocolates and biscuits. The basic ingredients are fresh cream and plain, milk or white chocolate, though butter is sometimes added and other flavourings, such as coffee and liqueurs, are occasionally used. The texture of *ganache* varies according to the type of chocolate used, a chocolate with a high cocoa butter content producing a firm mixture (*see* CHOCOLATE).

GANCIA (*see* VERMOUTH)

GAR (Garfish, Garpike) A slender sea fish, found off most European coasts, its main characteristic being that it has green bones. Gar is usually skinned and may then be cooked in any way desired.

GARAM MASALA A mixture of ground spices used in Indian cooking. The ingredients of a *garam masala* vary according to the dish in which it is to be used. A basic all-purpose version can be made by grinding together four black cardamom pods or 10 green cardamom pods, 15 ml (1 level tbsp) black peppercorns and 10 ml (2 level tsp) cumin seeds. The amounts can be increased or decreased according to taste, and spices such as dried red chillies or whole coriander seeds may be added. Other versions of the mixture may include cinnamon, cloves or even nutmeg. The spices may be lightly roasted or dry-fried before being ground. *Garam masala* is usually added to a dish towards the end of the cooking time, and can even be used as a condiment and sprinkled on food after serving. Commercially mixed and ground *garam masala* can be bought ready for use.

GARBANZO (*see* CHICK PEA)

GARLIC Although often used like a herb or spice, garlic in fact belongs to a group of plants known as *alliums*. Also included in the group are onions, leeks and chives. A garlic bulb is made up of a cluster of small curved segments called 'cloves' around a central stem. The cloves vary considerably in size according to variety and season. Usually, only one or two cloves are needed in any one dish to provide a subtle garlic flavour. Three varieties of garlic are available – white, red and pink or purple. The pink or purple variety is generally considered to be superior. Most of the garlic available in Britain has been imported from France, Italy or Spain.

Garlic has been mentioned in medical and herbal literature for well over 700 years as a vital food, if taken regularly and in small doses, to improve and maintain good general health. It is also recognized as an aid to digestion.

The flavour of garlic can change an ordinary salad into something quite special. If a crushed clove of garlic is too strong to include in a salad, rub it in a crust of bread, or a slice of French bread, and place the bread in the salad bowl. This crust is then tossed with the salad ingredients and dressing just before serving, and pushed to the bottom of the bowl out of sight. In France this crust is called a *chapan* and is not really intended to be eaten, though it is considered a great delicacy by enthusiastic garlic eaters. Alternatively, for a subtle garlic flavour, simply rub the inside of the salad bowl with a cut clove of garlic. Garlic is also widely used in hot savoury dishes and to make garlic butter (see opposite). A *subtle* flavour of garlic can be added to any dish or sauce by heating a skinned clove of garlic in the oil or butter used to fry the vegetables or meat. The clove is discarded before the other ingredients are added. To enhance the flavour of any meat or vegetable dish, sauté the crushed garlic in butter or oil at the beginning of the preparation.

The strong taste of garlic is held in its oil and is passed through the lungs on the breath and, if enough is eaten, through the pores of the skin. The traditional cure for garlicky breath is to chew a sprig of fresh parsley.

To select: When choosing garlic, look for bulbs that are hard and firm. The less papery the skin, the more moist the cloves will be.

To prepare: In most dishes, garlic is used finely chopped or crushed. Peel the clove of its outer papery skin and chop finely or crush, using a garlic press. If you do not have a garlic press, cut the clove into two or three pieces and place on a plate or board. Sprinkle with a little salt and crush to a smooth paste with a round-bladed knife.

The strong garlic flavour can be lessened by removing the very centre of the garlic clove before crushing. Cut the clove in half lengthways and ease out the yellow or pale green centre.

GARLIC BREAD (*see* GARLIC BUTTER)

GARLIC BUTTER A savoury butter made by combining crushed garlic with butter, salt and chopped parsley. Garlic butter may be added to sauces or used as a garnish for meat, fish and vegetable dishes. It can also be used to make garlic bread to serve as an accompaniment to soups, salads and casseroles.

Garlic Butter

100–175 g (4–6 oz) butter
2 garlic cloves, skinned and crushed
5–10 ml (1–2 tsp) chopped fresh parsley (optional)
salt and pepper

Soften the butter and cream until smooth. Beat the garlic and parsley, if using, into the butter with salt and pepper to taste. Shape into a neat block and chill slightly before using.

For garlic bread, partially cut through a large French loaf at 5 cm (2 inch) intervals. Place a pat of garlic butter in each incision. Wrap the whole loaf in foil and heat in the oven at 180°C (350°F) mark 4 for about 15 minutes or until the butter has melted and flavoured the bread. For a crisp finish, unwrap the bread 5 minutes before removing it from the oven.

Serves 8–10

GARLIC CHIVE (*see* CHINESE CHIVE)

GARLIC SALT A ready-made seasoning consisting of pounded and dried garlic mixed with refined salt crystals. It can be used in a variety of savoury dishes.

GARNISH A decoration, usually edible, which is added to a savoury dish to enhance its appearance. Popular simple garnishes include sprigs of, or chopped, fresh parsley or other herbs, watercress sprigs, cucumber or lemon slices or 'twists', radish 'roses', spring onion 'tassels', tomato wedges, gherkin fans, carrot curls, etc.

In classic French cookery, garnishes are often very elaborate and may consist of a number of ingredients that are prepared and cooked separately, then arranged around the meat, fish, poultry or game. The garnish forms an important part of the whole dish and is composed of ingredients which blend well with each other and with the main food. The name of a dish is often an indication of the garnish served with it, which, in turn, often reflects the origin of the dish, such as *allemande* or *bordelaise*.

GARRI (Gari) A product of the cassava plant, this is a type of meal that is a staple food in many parts of Africa and the Caribbean, although it is deficient in protein and vitamin B. It is available from many Indian and West Indian food shops in 450 g (1 lb) packets. Garri may be cooked in boiling water and used to make a classic West African dish known as *eba*, a type of porridge that is served with soups and stews. (*see also* CASSAVA)

GASTROPOD (Univalve) The name given to any member of a group of molluscs with a single coiled shell. Included in the group are snails, winkles, whelks, limpets and abalones, although not all these still have a coiled shell. Less common edible gastropods include the top shells and horn shells of the Mediterranean.

Gastropods are nearly always cooked before they are shelled, and most of them are eaten whole. (*see also* ABALONE, SNAIL, WHELK, WINKLE)

GÂTEAU A term applied to various fairly elaborate cakes or desserts which are made by using a sponge, biscuit or pastry base and adding fruit, jelly, cream, etc., as filling and decoration. Some of the best known gâteaux, especially those that are professionally made, are of French, Austrian or Swiss origin.

GÂTEAU SAINT-HONORÉ A French pastry consisting of a base of *pâte sucrée* (*see* PASTRY) around the edge of which is piped a ring of choux pastry. After baking, the choux ring is topped with a crown of baked choux buns glazed with caramel. The choux buns are filled with plain whipped or Chantilly cream and the centre of the gâteau is filled with confectioners' custard. The gâteau may be further decorated with piped whipped cream, crystallized videts, cherries and angelica.

GAUR (*see* GUAR)

GAYETTE A small flat French sausage, similar to a *crépinette*, but usually made of pig's liver, kidney and lung, flavoured with garlic and parsley. *Gayettes* are traditionally made in Provence and are usually baked in the oven and served hot or cold. (*see also* CRÉPINETTE)

GAZPACHO A famous Spanish soup which is served cold. In its simplest form, it is a puréed mixture of raw salad ingredients, such as cucumber, tomato, green pepper and onions, combined with oil and vinegar and flavoured with garlic and tomato purée, but the recipe varies throughout Spain. A few ice cubes, and a garnish of finely chopped green pepper and croûtons, are often added to the soup just before serving.

GELATINE (Gelatin) A gelling agent usually sold in powdered form in packets of small sachets, each one conveniently containing 11 g (1/3 oz) gelatine, roughly enough to set 600 ml (1 pint) liquid. It is also available in sheet form. Gelatine is produced commercially from boiled beef bones and is therefore not suitable for vegetarian use. Alternatives include agar-agar

and carrageen (*see* AGAR-AGAR, CARRAGEEN).

Gelatine is virtually colourless and tasteless and can be used in sweet and savoury dishes. The amount used varies depending on the required texture of the finished dish, so it is advisable to follow a recipe closely to be sure the correct amount is used. Soft mousses or cheesecakes require less than a firm jelly.

Clear instructions for the use of commercial gelatine are given on the packet and should be followed carefully. Before adding gelatine to a mixture, it is first sprinkled into a small amount of cold liquid (usually water or fruit juice) and left to soften, then dissolved by gently heating the liquid, usually by standing the bowl in a pan of hot water. After dissolving, the gelatine solution is left to cool slightly before it is added to the mixture, which should be warm enough to prevent the gelatine setting immediately. The gelatine should be thoroughly stirred in to ensure it is evenly distributed in the mixture before it is poured into the mould. A gelatine mixture can be set in the refrigerator or by standing the mould in a bowl full of ice. Whipped ingredients, such as cream or egg whites, are usually added after the mixture has set slightly, to avoid the risk of separation.

Gelatine can be used with most ingredients, but some fruits, notably raw (but not canned) pineapple, contain an enzyme that prevents gelatine setting. (*see also* JELLY)

GENDARME In France, this is the popular name of a type of herring also known as *hareng saur* (*see* HERRING). However, *gendarme* is also the name of a small flat rectangular smoked sausage usually made in Switzerland.

GENOA CAKE A popular fruit cake, generally decorated with almonds or brazil nuts.

GENOESE (Génoise) A light sponge cake made with a whisked egg mixture enriched with melted butter. (*see also* CAKE)

GENTIAN A yellow-flowering plant that grows in the mountains of Europe, the roots of which are used to produce a bitter-flavoured essence that is an ingredient of many apéritifs, such as the French *suze* and the Austrian *enzian*.

GERANIUM (Pelargonium) There are many varieties of this popular flowering plant, frequently seen in gardens, hanging baskets and window boxes all over Britain, although the plant in fact originated in South Africa. Some varieties have bright orange or pretty pink blooms; others, such as the lemon geranium, have only small insignificant flowers and are grown for their attractive perfumed leaves. Other varieties smell of rose, pine, orange, apple, peppermint and nutmeg. The leaves can be used to flavour creams, custards, jams and jellies by infusing them in the liquid before it is used in the recipe.

GERMAN POUND CAKE This is similar to Genoa cake, but contains less fruit and no almonds (*see* GENOA CAKE).

GERMAN SAUSAGE The general name given to many different varieties of sausage that originated in Germany. They may be made of pork, veal, beef, liver, bacon or blood, often containing a mixture of two or more of these ingredients, suitably salted and spiced; garlic is a favourite addition. German sausages are often smoked and, in fact, all those imported into Britain are so treated. They are usually eaten cold. (*see also* BIERWURST, BLUTWURST, FRANKFURTER, SAUSAGE)

GERVAIS A small, soft, delicately flavoured cream cheese made in France. It is generally sold in boxes containing six individual foil-wrapped portions.

GHEE A type of clarified butter originally made in India but now produced elsewhere. It has a better flavour than ordinary clarified butter because it is cooked a little longer during the clarifying process. It is particularly useful for frying and is much used in Indian cookery. Commercially-produced varieties of ordinary and vegetarian ghee (made from hydrogenated vegetable oil) are available. (*see also* BUTTER, CLARIFYING)

GHERKIN The pickled fruit of a small variety of cucumber. The best gherkins are small and dark green and have a rough skin; large quantities are imported from France and Holland and are sold bottled in brine. In the United States, some pickled gherkins are known as dill pickles as they are preserved in a dill-flavoured vinegar.

Gherkins are used as one of the ingredients in mixed pickles, as an accompaniment to cold meats and in savouries, sauces, etc., and they also make an attractive garnish for dishes of cocktail canapés and other cold savoury dishes. (*see also* CUCUMBER)

GIBLETS The edible parts of the entrails of birds, consisting of the gizzard, liver, heart and also the neck. Giblets are largely used in making gravy or soup, but the liver is often rolled in bacon and served with the bird or as a savoury. When buying an oven-ready fresh or frozen bird, the giblets may or may not be included. If they are, they are usually in a small plastic bag inside the cavity of the bird and should be removed before cooking. (*see also* POULTRY)

To make giblet stock for gravy, put the giblets in a large saucepan and cover with stock or water. Bring to the boil, then reduce the heat and simmer for at least 1 hour.

GIGOT A French cut of lamb or mutton taken from the leg. It is best roasted.

GILL A liquid measurement equivalent to 150 ml ($^1/_4$ pint).

GIN A colourless spirit distilled from rye and barley or maize and flavoured with juniper berries. Gin is the purest of all spirits, being distilled at a high strength. It does not improve with keeping in the same way as brandy.

Two popular types of English gin are Dry or London gin and Old Tom or Plymouth gin, the former being dry and the latter slightly sweetened. Schnapps is a type of gin popular in Holland.

Gin is used as the basis of many cocktails, such as Martini, Gin Sling, Pink Gin and Bronx. It is also used for various other long and short drinks, diluted to the required strength with water, tonic water, fruit juice or bitter lemon.

(*see also* SLOE)

GINGER A plant that is native to South-East Asia but is now grown in warm climates all over the world. The plant is grown for its root-like underground stem (or rhizome) which has a hot, sweetish taste and is sold in various forms. Root ginger is available fresh or dried, or it may be dried and ground. Stem (green) ginger is available preserved in syrup or crystallized.

Root ginger needs to be cooked to release the true flavour; peel and slice or grate and use in marinades, curries, sauces, chutneys and Chinese and Indian cooking. Ground ginger is used in curries, sauces, preserves, cakes and sprinkled on to melon. Preserved ginger is used in sweet dishes.

GINGER ALE A soft drink or 'mixer' commercially made from water aerated with carbon dioxide and flavoured with ginger. It is used in punches and in place of soda to dilute spirits such as whisky and brandy.

GINGER BEER A slightly alcoholic effervescent beverage with a flavour of ginger. Ginger, cream of tartar and sugar are fermented with yeast, water is added and the liquid bottled before fermentation is complete. The legal limit is two per cent alcohol, but most ginger beers contain much less.

GINGERBREAD This is a moist brown cake flavoured with ginger and containing treacle or golden syrup; it is usually served cut into squares, which may be decorated with preserved ginger.

There are many different forms of gingerbread, varying in colour from light brown to a very dark shade, according to the amount of bicarbonate of soda and the type of treacle used. (*see also* PARKIN)

GINGER WINE A commercially produced drink made from water, ginger, yeast, sugar, lemon, raisins, pepper, and sometimes alcohol. It may be mixed with whisky to make Whisky Mac.

GINKGO NUT The kernel from the fruit of the ginkgo (or maidenhair) tree which originated in China but also grows in Japan and some Mediterranean countries. The ginkgo fruit is like a small green plum, but it has foul-smelling flesh that is not edible. The nuts, however, are an important ingredient in Japanese cooking and may be roasted and used in sweet and savoury dishes, as a garnish, or simply eaten as a snack.

GIROLLE (*see* MUSHROOM)

GIZZARD Part of a bird's digestive system, the gizzard is a thick muscular organ that acts as a second stomach. It is one of the giblets removed from a bird before cooking. (*see also* GIBLETS)

GJETÖST (*see* MYSÖST)

GLACÉ A French word meaning iced or glossy, such as glacé cherries and glacé icing.

GLACÉ FRUIT Fruit which has been preserved by impregnation with a concentrated sugar syrup, giving a fairly firm texture and shiny, moist and sticky surface. This process is usually carried out commercially, the commonest glacé fruit being cherries, although almost any good quality eating fruit can be treated in this way. Glacé fruits are used in cakes and sweet dishes, as a cake decoration and as a dessert to serve at the end of a formal meal. (*see also* CANDYING)

GLACÉ ICING A simple glossy icing, made from icing sugar and water, which can be used to ice sponge cakes, small buns and biscuits. It can be coloured and flavoured as required.

Glacé Icing

100 g (4 oz) icing sugar
few drops of vanilla or almond flavouring (optional)
colouring (optional)

Sift the icing sugar into a bowl. Add a few drops of vanilla or almond flavouring if wished. Gradually add 15 ml (1 tbsp) warm water. The icing should be thick enough to coat the back of a spoon. If necessary, add more water or sugar to adjust the consistency. Add colouring, if liked, and use at once.

Makes about 100 g (4 oz)

Variations

Orange or lemon Replace the water with 15 ml (1 tbsp) strained orange or lemon juice.

Mocha Dissolve 5 ml (1 level tsp) cocoa powder and 10 ml (2 level tsp) instant coffee in a little hot water and use instead of the same amount of water.

Liqueur Replace 10–15 ml (2–3 tsp) water with the same amount of any liqueur.

Chocolate Dissolve 10 ml (2 level tsp) cocoa powder in a little hot water and use instead of the same amount of water.

Coffee Flavour with 5 ml (1 tsp) coffee essence or dissolve 10 ml (2 level tsp) instant coffee in a little hot water and use instead of the same amount of water.

Rosewater Use 10 ml (2 tsp) rosewater instead of the same amount of water.

To use Glacé Icing

If coating both the top and sides of a cake, stand it on a wire rack with a tray underneath to catch the drips. As soon as the icing reaches a coating consistency and looks smooth and glossy, pour it from the bowl on to the centre of the cake. Allow the icing to run down the sides, guiding it with a palette knife. Keep a little icing back to fill the gaps. Scrape up any icing which falls underneath the rack and use this also. Make sure there are no cake crumbs or it will ruin the appearance of the finished cake.

If the sides are decorated and only the top is to be iced with glacé icing, pour the icing on to the centre of the cake and spread it with a palette knife, stopping just inside the edges to prevent it dripping down the sides.

If the top is to be iced and the sides left plain, protect them with a band of greaseproof paper tied around the cake and projecting a little above it. Pour on the icing and let it find its own level. Peel off the paper when the icing is hard.

Small cakes can be coated in the same way or may be dipped one at a time into a bowl of icing, the cakes being held in tongs or between thumb and forefinger. This method is excellent for éclairs, when only a strip of icing is required on top.

Arrange any ready-made decorations, such as nuts, cherries, sweets, silver balls, etc., in position as soon as the icing has thickened and formed a skin. Unless planning to 'feather ice' the cake, leave the icing until quite dry before applying piped decorations.

To Feather Ice a Cake

Make a quantity of glacé icing and mix to a coating consistency. Make up a second batch of icing using half the quantity of sugar and enough warm water to mix it to a thick piping consistency.

Tint the second batch of icing with food colouring and spoon into a greaseproof paper piping bag.

Coat the top of the cake with the larger quantity of icing. Working quickly, before it has time to form a skin, snip the end off the piping bag and pipe parallel lines of coloured icing about 1–2 cm (^{1}/$_2$–^{3}/$_4$ inch) apart, over the surface. Quickly draw the point of a skewer or a sharp knife across the piped lines, first in one direction, then in the other, spacing them evenly apart.

GLASGOW PALE (*see* HADDOCK)

GLASSWORT (*see* SAMPHIRE)

GLAYVA A Scottish whisky-based liqueur flavoured with honey and herbs.

GLAZE The name given to any food used to give a glossy coating to sweet and savoury dishes to improve their appearance and sometimes flavour. (*see also* GLAZING)

GLAZING Giving sweet and savoury foods a glossy coating, usually to create a decorative finish. Glazing ingredients include beaten egg, egg white, butter, milk and syrup.

Cold foods may be glazed by brushing with or dipping into an aspic jelly or sugar syrup. Fruit tarts and flans may be coated with a fruit glaze made from melted jam or redcurrant jelly (*see* APRICOT GLAZE). Some foods are brushed with a glaze before they are baked, giving them a golden brown finish after baking. Loaves of bread, scones and pastry may be brushed with water, beaten egg or milk. Vegetables, such as carrots, are sometimes glazed by cooking in a very little liquid with butter and sugar, or may be tossed in melted butter after cooking.

The term may also be used to describe browning food under a hot grill or in the oven, especially if the surface is sprinkled with sugar, creating a caramelized effect.

GLOBE ARTICHOKE (*see* ARTICHOKE, GLOBE)

GLOUCESTER CHEESES Genuine Gloucester-shire cheeses are traditionally made from the now rare Gloucester cattle. Originally there were 'double' and 'single' Gloucesters, one being twice the size of the other, but Single Gloucester cheese is now very hard to find. It is a mild, pale-coloured cheese which was originally considered an inferior, 'thin' cheese, because it was made from the lower fat milk produced at the morning milking.

Double Gloucester is called 'double' Gloucester because the original cheese was made from milk from the morning milking combined with the previous evening's richer milk. Double Gloucester is an orange-yellow, hard cheese with a close, crumbly texture and a good rich flavour, rather similar to that of a mature Cheddar. Its dark colour is the result of adding a natural food colouring, annatto.

Gloucester cheese was originally made with a very tough rind, which enabled it to withstand the annual cheese-rolling ceremony, an ancient custom originally carried out to protect grazing rights. These still take place, although today the cheese is wrapped in hessian to protect it on its downhill journey.

GLOUCESTER PUDDING A type of steamed suet pudding in which 100 g (4 oz) finely chopped raw apple and 50 g (2 oz) mixed peel are added to a standard pudding mixture containing an egg. (*see also* SUET PUDDING)

GLUCOSE (*see* SUGAR)

GLUTEN A protein substance that is a constituent of wheat and other cereals. The amount of gluten present varies from cereal to cereal, and even different types of the same cereal contain varying amounts. Wheat that is high in protein is known as 'hard' wheat and is grown mainly in Canada and the United States. 'Soft' wheats are grown mainly in western Europe. The flours produced from these wheats obviously vary in the same way as the wheat itself. Some are hard or 'strong' flours, containing a high proportion of protein, others are soft, containing less protein. It is this difference in the flours used that creates the varying textures of cakes and breads.

When flour is mixed with water, gluten develops in long elastic strands, turning the mixture into a soft, stretchy dough that can be kneaded and shaped. If a raising agent, such as yeast, is also used, bubbles of carbon dioxide are formed within the dough and are held there by the gluten structure. When the dough is baked, the air bubbles expand, stretching the structure still further until it sets. A hard flour contains more gluten and produces a tougher structure that is able to trap larger bubbles of carbon dioxide, producing the characteristic texture of bread. Soft flours contain less gluten and are therefore more suited to making light cakes and pastries. Most all-purpose flours labelled simply 'plain' or 'selfraising' are made from a blend of hard and soft wheats, but some flours, called 'bread' flour or 'strong plain' flour, are specially produced for bread making.

The strength, or 'toughness', of the gluten in a dough is increased by water, by kneading and mixing and by very acid or alkaline conditions. Thus, pastry becomes tough if the fat is not rubbed in sufficiently to prevent the water having access to the particles of flour; over-mixing of a cake or pastry makes it tough because it causes the gluten to develop too much; again, a cake mixture containing an excess of lemon juice or acid may be tough.

Some people suffer from a condition known as coeliac disease, which is an inability to digest gluten, and must therefore eat a gluten-free diet. Gluten-free flours and other products are available. (*see also* BREAD, FLOUR)

GLYCERINE (Glycerin, Glycerol) A sweet, colourless, oily liquid that is a compound of carbon, hydrogen and oxygen, formed by the breaking down of fats and produced chiefly as a by-product of the manufacture of soap. Glycerine is occasionally added to royal icing to keep it moist and can usually be bought from chemists. (*see also* ROYAL ICING)

GNOCCHI This name is given to several different dishes. Italian in origin, *gnocchi* are small dumplings which are cooked in boiling water and served like pasta with a sauce. The *gnocchi* mixture may also be spread in a dish, cooked and cut into rounds or squares. These are arranged in a dish, sprinkled with cheese and browned under the grill, then served with a sauce.

Gnocchi are sometimes made with flour, water and egg, or some or all of the flour can be replaced with semolina, cornmeal, cooked potato or grated raw potato. They may also be made from choux pastry (*see* PASTRY).

GOA BEAN A green bean grown in tropical Asia and West Africa. It can be recognized by its characteristic angular pods which are cooked whole and served as a vegetable. The roots of the plant are also edible.

GOAT Although the goat is closely related to the sheep, its meat has never been appreciated in Britain in the same way as lamb. However, it is often eaten in some Mediterranean countries, and in Italy and France young kid is considered a delicacy reserved for spring festivals. In Britain today, goats are mostly kept for their milk.

GOATFISH (*see* MULLET, RED)

GOATS' MILK Goats' milk has a higher percentage of fat and protein than some varieties of cows' milk and it has a somewhat stronger flavour. It is widely used for making cheeses (for example, Sainte-Maure) which are produced from May to November; in Scandinavia it is used for such cheeses as *Gjetöst* (*see* MYSÖST). Goats' milk yogurts are also available. These taste richer and more acid than cows' milk yogurts, but can be used in the same ways.

Goats' milk can also be used for ordinary household purposes and in making milk puddings and similar dishes. It is useful for feeding babies who are allergic to cows' milk, though it must be adjusted to their particular needs. (*see also* CHÈVRE)

GOFIO A flour that is a speciality of the Canary Islands and sold as a health food in Spain. *Gofio* is made from a variety of toasted cereals, such as wheat, maize or barley, and has a nutty flavour. It may be used to make a type of gruel or can be formed into cakes that are fried and used as bread.

GOOD KING HENRY (*see* SPINACH)

GOLDENBERRY (*see* CAPE GOOSEBERRY)

GOLDEN CUTLETS (*see* HADDOCK)

GOLDEN NUGGET SQUASH (*see* SQUASH, VEGETABLE)

GOLDEN SYRUP A light-coloured syrup that is produced by further refining a by-product of the sugar refining process. It contains various sugars (glucose, sucrose and fructose), with some flavouring and colouring matter; it thus supplies energy but nothing else of nutritional value. Syrup is not quite as sweet as sugar, since it contains more water and glucose.

Golden syrup is used to sweeten and flavour cakes and puddings, to make sauces, as a filling for tarts and in gingerbreads. (*see also* SUGAR, SYRUP)

GOLD LEAF (*see* VARAK)

GOLDWASSER A German aniseed-flavoured liqueur. It is colourless but has little gold particles in it.

GOMASHIO (Sesame Salt) This is a seasoning powder made by grinding roasted sesame seeds and combining them with a little sea salt. It has a light, nutty flavour and is much used in Japan as a condiment instead of salt. It makes a delicious addition to many savoury dishes.

GOOSE Originally a game bird, a species of goose descended from the wild Greylag goose is now domesticated and bred for the table. However, geese do not adapt to modern intensive farming methods in the same way as hens or ducks, and they are not so readily available. Wild geese are sometimes shot, but they are not so highly prized as other game birds (*see* GAME).

A goose for the table should be young – not more than a year old. A 'green goose' is a bird up to the age of three to four months, a gosling one up to six months. When choosing a goose, see that the bill is yellow and free from hair and the feet supple; young geese have yellow feet, but these gradually turn red, so that the colour is some indication of age. Deep yellow fat indicates an old goose. Fresh geese are sold dressed or 'rough plucked' (with head and feet on and not drawn).

The season for home-killed geese lasts from September to February, but goslings are in season all the year round and foreign birds are available at most times, especially at Easter. Frozen oven-ready birds are also available. The traditional time for eating geese in Britain is Michaelmas (29th September), but they are also popular at Easter and as an alternative to the roast turkey at Christmas.

It is advisable to order a goose in advance as butchers, poulterers and supermarkets tend not to keep extensive stocks. Geese range in weight from about 3 kg (7 lb) to as much as 6.75 kg (15 lb), with the most popular size being 3.6–5.5 kg (8–12 lb). A 4.5 kg (10 lb) goose will serve six to eight people.

Geese are rather fatty and when they are cooked the flesh is dark, with a rich, meaty flavour, therefore accompaniments should counteract this. Traditional accompaniments include sage and onion stuffing and apple or gooseberry sauce.

Roast Goose
It is important to remember that the breast meat will cook faster than the leg and underside and care must be taken that it does not dry out so cover it with foil. The legs are cooked if the juices run clear when a skewer is inserted.

4–5 kg (9–11 lb) oven-ready goose
salt
Sage and Onion Stuffing (see STUFFING)

Prick the skin of the goose in several places with a fork. Pull the inside fat out of the bird. Rub salt over the skin.

Spoon the stuffing into the neck end of the goose, skewer the neck skin to the back of the bird, then truss (*see* POULTRY) or tie up the goose with string. Weigh the bird.

Put the goose on a rack placed over a roasting tin. Cover the breast with foil. Roast in the oven at 200°C (400°F) mark 6 for 15 minutes per 450 g (1 lb) plus 15 minutes, basting frequently.

Remove the foil for the last 20 minutes to brown the bird.

Serve the goose with apple sauce and thin gravy.

Serves 8

GOOSEBERRY There are many varieties of this berry fruit which belongs to the same family as the currant; they may be round or long, hairy or smooth, cooking or dessert. Gooseberries grow on thorny bushes and are available from May to August. They are native to Europe and are cultivated in Britain, Germany and France.

Cooking gooseberries are usually small and green with very sour, firm flesh and a fairly large number of edible seeds. Dessert gooseberries can be green, yellow-white or russet coloured, often with hairy skin and usually with sweet pulpy flesh and large seeds. The flavour of dessert gooseberries is less good when cooked.

Gooseberries are rarely eaten raw but can be cooked in pies, tarts, crumbles and fools. They have a high pectin content which makes them ideal for making preserves. Gooseberry preserve is traditionally served with smoked mackerel or deep-fried Camembert portions.

To select: Choose evenly-coloured, firm, unbruised gooseberries. They may be stored in the refrigerator for up to 3 days.

To prepare: Wash the berries and snip off the stem and flower ends (top and tail). This is not necessary if the fruit is to be strained after cooking, such as when making jelly.

To cook: Dessert varieties of gooseberry may be eaten raw, though they can be very sour; cooking varieties can be stewed and used in pies, puddings, fools and preserves.

GOOSE EGGS (*see* EGGS)

GOOSE LIVER (*see* FOIE GRAS)

GORGONZOLA A semi-hard, blue-veined, sharp-flavoured cheese made from pasteurized cows' milk in Italy, near Milan. It should be a creamy-textured cheese and is produced in cylindrical shapes wrapped in silver paper.

Gorgonzola may be eaten as a dessert cheese and is often served with pears, or may be served as part of a cheese board. It can also be used to make a delicious sauce for pasta.

GOTA A brightly coloured mixture of spices served in India at the end of a meal as an aid to digestion.

GOUDA An important Dutch wheel-shaped cows'-milk cheese, not unlike Edam in taste and texture, but flatter in shape, with a yellow skin, and very much larger, weighing about 5 kg (9 lb). There are also small Gouda cheeses, about 450 g (1 lb) in weight, known as 'midget' Goudas. The flavour of most Gouda is rich but mild, since it has only been ripened for two to four months. Mature Gouda has a stronger, more distinctive flavour and a black coating. Gouda is an excellent cheese for cooking, but can also be eaten as a snack or dessert cheese.

GOUGELHOPF (*see* KUGELHOPF)

GOUGÈRE A French pastry, usually made by piping choux pastry (often flavoured with Gruyère or Emmenthal cheese) in a ring on a baking sheet or in an ovenproof dish and baking it. The pastry ring may then be filled with a savoury mixture, such as fish, kidneys, chicken or ham. Individual *gougères* may also be made and served as canapés or as an hors d'oeuvre. Large or individual *gougères* may also be served warm as a main course.

GOUJON (*see* GOUJONETTE)

GOUJONETTE The French name for a small diagonally-cut strip of firm white fish, such as sole fillet, which is tossed in flour or coated in batter and deep-fried. *Goujonettes* may be served like whitebait or used as a garnish. The name is derived from *goujon*, the French name for gudgeon, which are also cooked and served in this way. *Goujonettes* are so called because they resemble deep-fried gudgeon. (*see also* GUDGEON)

GOULASH A rich beef stew, flavoured with paprika, that is Hungarian in origin, but found in several European countries. Soured cream can be stirred in or served as a separate accompaniment.

GOURD This vegetable belongs to the same family as the marrow, pumpkin and squash. There are over 500 varieties of gourd, some of which are edible and in certain parts of the world form an important food. The skins of gourds may be dried and used as containers or simple decorations.

The best gourds to eat are the Turk's Cap and the Turban; the flesh, which is yellow, sweet and floury, is used in the same way as that of the pumpkin. Among other edible gourds are the Dudi (or Calabash), Towel and Snake.

GRAHAM FLOUR An American flour named after the nutritionist Sylvester Graham (1794–1851) who led a movement against unhealthy eating habits and promoted the use of wholemeal flour for making bread. He developed his own brand of flour that included all the wheat bran and was known as Graham flour. From it were made the first Graham bread and Graham crackers. Today in America, the name may be given to any food made with wholemeal (or wholewheat) flour.

GRAINS Grains are the edible seeds of different grasses. They are high in vitamins and minerals and, though widely used in the form of flour, they can also be used whole, cracked or flaked to add interest and nutrients to a wide range of dishes. Most of the grains commonly used are cereal grains, that is they come from cultivated members of the grass family. The most commonly used cereal grains are wheat, durum wheat, rice, maize (corn), millet, barley, oats and rye. Some other non-cereal foods are used in the same way as grains, though they are not true grains. These are buckwheat, tapioca, soya and sago.

All cereal grains can be cooked and eaten whole, but are also available in a variety of other forms. The whole cereal grain (seed) is made up of three main parts: the outer protective layer or bran; the central germ from which the new shoot grows; the endosperm, which is the remaining starchy part of the grain, providing food for the seed when it starts to grow. Different grain products use all or part of the grain; highly refined white flours remove all but the endosperm, while 100 per cent wholemeal flours contain every part of the grain. Wheat germ and bran, the by-products of the manufacture of white flour, can be bought separately.

Whole grains can be stored for some time in dry conditions in an airtight container, but they do become tougher and take longer to cook as they get older. Flakes, meals and flours are best used within 3–6 months, while wheatgerm should be used within 2–3 weeks.

Whole Grains
Most whole grains have nothing but the inedible husk removed so no valuable nutrients are lost. Wheat, rice, corn, barley, oats, rye, millet and buckwheat are all available as whole grains and may be cooked and used in a variety of stews and salads. Softer grains may be used to make savoury croquettes and stuffings, while some are good for sweet puddings.

Whole grains are usually boiled for about 10-20 minutes, depending on the variety, but the flavour of some (barley, buckwheat and millet in particular) is improved by toasting or lightly frying the grains before boiling. Spices and vegetables can be added for flavour and different grains can be mixed to vary the taste and texture.

Flakes
Flakes are made by flattening whole grains between large rollers, making them easier to cook and easier to digest when eaten raw, such as in muesli. Some flakes are lightly steamed or toasted in advance. Flakes can be used to make porridge

or muesli, or combined with other ingredients to make a crumble topping.

Cracked Grains
These are whole grains that have been cut or broken into pieces. Some varieties, such as couscous and bulgar are cooked before they are broken up. Cracked grains are easier to cook than whole grains and are often used in stews, porridge and bread. 'Kibbled' wheat is pricked by a machine and split into small pieces.

Meals and Flours
A huge range of flours is available, some more refined than others. Meals are less finely ground than flours.

(*see also* BARLEY, BRAN, BUCKWHEAT, BULGAR, CORN, COUSCOUS, CRACKED WHEAT, MILLET, OATS, QUINOA, RICE, RYE, SEMOLINA, SAGO, SOYA BEAN, TAPIOCA, WHEAT, WHEATGERM)

GRAM FLOUR (Besan Flour) This fine, yellow flour is made by grinding the pulse known in India as *channa dal*, a type of chick pea. Gram flour can be used to thicken various dishes and sauces or to make a coating batter. In Indian cookery, it is used to make samosas, bhajis and chapattis. (*see also* CHANNA, CHICK PEA)

GRANA (*see* PARMESAN)

GRANADILLA (*see* PASSION FRUIT)

GRAND MARNIER The best known French brand of orange-flavoured liqueur in the curaçao family. It is often used to flavour desserts, such as *crêpes Suzette*. (*see also* CURAÇAO)

GRANITA Similar to a sorbet, a *granita* is an Italian half-frozen water ice made of large ice crystals which give it a coarser texture. *Granitas* are made from a sugar syrup which may be flavoured with coffee, liqueurs or various fruits. They are usually served as a refreshing dessert. (*see also* SORBET)

GRANOLA A breakfast dish, similar to muesli, and made from a varying mixture, usually including oats, wheat flakes, rye flakes, seeds and nuts, sometimes with wheatgerm and bran added. Flavourings such as honey, raisins and desiccated coconut may also be added. The mixture is usually baked until lightly toasted, then cooled and stored in an airtight container ready to serve. Granola may be served with milk, yogurt, fruit juice or fresh fruit.

GRAPE One of the oldest and best loved of all fruits, grapes are grown on vines all over the world. Wine-producing varieties of grape are cultivated on a massive scale in areas of France, Italy, Germany and many other countries, and dessert varieties are available in Britain all year round. Some varieties of grape are cultivated for drying and selling as raisins, currants and sultanas (*see* VINE FRUITS).

Dessert varieties can range from pale amber to a deep blue colour. Popular dessert varieties include Muscat with white or golden coloured berries, Almeria with golden-yellow or pale green berries, and Alicante with purple-black berries. Dessert grapes have sweet succulent flesh surrounding two or three small inedible pips, but seedless varieties, such as the American Thompson (now grown in other countries, including Greece and Israel), are also readily available.

Grapes can be used in fruit salads and other raw fruit dishes. They can be arranged decoratively on a layer of confectioners' custard in a cooked flan case, or simply served as a refreshing accompaniment to cheese at the end of a meal. Grapes are rarely cooked, but do appear in one or two classic dishes, such as *sole Véronique*. They can also be frosted and used to make a very attractive decoration (*see* FROSTED FRUIT).

(*see also* VINE LEAVES)

To select: Choose plump, unbruised grapes with a distinct bloom to them; where possible buy in bunches and avoid any with shrivelled or squashed berries or any with signs of mould near the stem. Keep grapes refrigerated and use within three days. They should be left unwashed until ready to serve.

To prepare: Grapes should be washed thoroughly before eating, or they may be peeled by dipping them briefly in boiling water, then carefully peeling back the skin with the fingers. Pips can be removed from inside grapes before serving. Halve the fruit with a knife and flick out the pips with the point of the knife. To remove pips from whole grapes, push the tip of a skewer into the grape and push out the pips.

GRAPE, DRIED (*see* VINE FRUITS)

GRAPEFRUIT These large citrus fruits grow in clusters, rather like grapes (hence their name), and are cultivated in the United States, South America and some Mediterranean countries. They have thick yellow skins with either yellow or pink flesh. The pink fleshed varieties are sweeter than the yellow. A green-skinned variety, known as Sweetie, is particularly sweet. (*see also* CITRUS FRUIT, POMELO)

Grapefruit may be eaten raw on their own or with other fruits or used to make mixed fruit marmalades. Halved grapefruit are often served as a starter, either simply sprinkled with sugar or sprinkled with sherry or vermouth and grilled until bubbling. Grapefruit segments are sometimes served at breakfast.

To select: Choose grapefruit that have a shiny skin and no soft spots. Fruits that feel heavy for their size are more likely to be juicy. Grapefruit will keep for four days at room temperature or two weeks in the refrigerator.

To prepare: Grapefruit may simply be peeled and segmented in the same way as oranges. To prepare for serving as a starter, cut in half and separate the flesh from the skin with a serrated knife, then cut between the segments of fruit and

their surrounding membranes so that the segments can easily be removed with a spoon. Serve prepared grapefruit halves in special glass dishes.

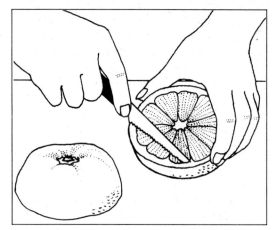

Preparing grapefruit halves by separating the flesh from the skin with a serrated knife.

GRAPESEED OIL (*see* OILS)

GRAPPA An Italian spirit, rather like a brandy, which, like the French *marc*, is distilled from the remains of grapes that have been pressed to produce wine. It has a strong flavour, sometimes enhanced by the addition of rue, and is used in some Italian recipes. (*see also* MARC)

GRAS, AU A French term used to describe dishes cooked and dressed with a rich gravy or sauce.

GRAS DOUBLE (*see* TRIPE)

GRATIN, AU A French term which describes a dish which has been coated with sauce, sprinkled with breadcrumbs or grated cheese and finished by browning under the grill or in the oven. This type of dish is often cooked in a low-sided dish known as a *gratin* dish. Dishes finished in this way are often known as *gratins*.

GRATING The name given to a method of shredding cheese, carrots and other foods with a grater or food processor attachment. A grater is a flat or box-shaped metal utensil perforated with rows of small holes of varying size. The edges of the holes are sharp so that when food is rubbed across them they shave off coarse or fine threads. The large holes are usually used for cheese and vegetables, while the small holes are reserved for grating lemon rind or Parmesan cheese. Some graters consist of a perforated round drum which is turned with a handle, grating the food as it turns. The smallest graters are nutmeg graters, specially designed for grating fresh nutmeg.

GRAVAD LAX (Gravlax) A famous Swedish dish made by drysalting raw salmon fillets. The cut sides of the fillets are coated with coarse salt and sugar and the two are sandwiched together, with chopped fresh dill in between. A weight is put on top and the salmon is then left in the refrigerator for about two days, during which time it is basted occasionally with the juices drawn out by the salt. *Gravad lax* is usually served thinly sliced as an hors d'oeuvre. (*see also* DRY SALTING)

GRAVES The name given to the wines produced from the vineyards of the Graves district of France, west and south of Bordeaux. Both red and white wines are made, the red being the better of the two. The parishes which produce the best wines are Leognan, Martillac, Villenave d'Ornon and Mérignac. There are many famous château names for Graves: Château Haut-Brion is considered the best, followed by La Mission Haut-Brion, Pape Clément, etc. White Graves wines are usually sold under the name Graves and are often blended. The wine is medium-dry and may be served with fish, poultry, veal, etc.

GRAVLAX (*see* GRAVAD LAX)

GRAVY A type of brown sauce made from the juices and extracts which run out from meat during cooking. These juices are sometimes served as they are, but they can be thickened, diluted or concentrated; a little extra flavouring may be added but too much tends to mask the true meat flavour.

A rich brown gravy is served with all roast joints – thin with roast beef and thick with other meats. If the gravy is made in the roasting tin, there should be no need to use colouring. (A commercially produced gravy browning made from caramel is available in bottles – see BROWNING, GRAVY.) Remove the joint from the tin and keep it hot while making the gravy.

Thin Gravy
Pour the fat very slowly from the roasting tin, draining it off carefully from one corner and leaving the sediment behind. Season well with salt and pepper and add 300 ml (½ pint) hot vegetable cooking water or stock. Stir thoroughly until all the sediment is scraped from the tin and the gravy is a rich brown. Return the tin to the heat and boil for 2–3 minutes to reduce. Serve very hot.

You may prefer to make a slightly thickened version, using half the amount of flour used for thick gravy (see below).
Makes about 300 ml (½ pint)

Thick Gravy
Pour off most of the fat from the roasting tin, leaving about 30 ml (2 tbsp) of the sediment. Stir in about 15 ml (1 level tbsp) flour, blend well and cook over the heat until it turns brown, stirring. Slowly stir in 300 ml (½ pint) beef stock or hot vegetable cooking water and boil for 2–3 minutes. Season well, strain and serve very hot. A little gravy browning may be added.
Makes about 300 ml (½ pint)

GRAYLING
A silvery freshwater fish belonging to the salmon family. It has a thyme-like scent and firm white flesh, similar to trout. It can be cooked like trout (*see* TROUT).

GRECQUE, À LA Strictly speaking, this term should only be applied to dishes of Greek origin, but this is seldom the case and it more often refers to dishes cooked in a generally Mediterranean style, with olive oil, lemon and spices. Vegetables cooked *à la grecque* are often served cold as an hors d'oeuvre.

GREEN ALMOND (*see* PISTACHIO NUT)

GREEN BEAN (*see* BEAN, FRENCH)

GREENGAGE (*see* PLUM)

GREEN GODDESS DRESSING A popular dressing consisting of thick mayonnaise thinned with soured cream and flavoured with garlic, anchovy, parsley and lemon juice. It is usually served with fish or shellfish.

GREEN GRAM (*see* MUNG BEAN)

GREEN LAVER (*see* SEA VEGETABLES)

GREENS (*see* CABBAGE)

GRENADIN The French name for a small slice of fillet of veal. A *grenadin* is usually larded (*see* LARDING) and braised, then served with a vegetable garnish, such as braised celery, chicory, or lettuce, or buttered carrots.

GRENADINE A French syrup made from pomegranate juice. Grenadine is red in colour and is used as a sweetening and colouring agent in cocktails (notably Tequila Sunrise), fruit drinks and desserts.

GREY MULLET (*see* MULLET, GREY)

GRIDDLE (Girdle) A flat, heavy, metal plate used to cook scones, teacakes, crumpets, soda bread, pancakes and other foods. The griddle is first heated on the hob, then greased, before the dough or batter is added. A heavy, thick-based frying pan may be used instead of a griddle.

GRILLING (Broiling) A method of cooking food by direct heat under a grill or over a hot fire (*see* BARBECUE). Grilling is most often used for cooking small cuts of meat (steaks, chops and bacon rashers), poultry (chicken portions), fish (whole or steaks), kebabs, sausages and hamburgers. Most vegetables are unsuitable for grilling, but tomatoes and mushrooms are suitable.

Grilling is a fast method of cooking that produces a crisp brown finish. It is also useful for browning the tops of cooked dishes. It is a healthier method of cooking than frying as the food is cooked on a rack in the grill pan, so that excess fat can drip away during cooking.

The grill should be thoroughly heated and sometimes greased before use. The distance between the food and the heat source can usually be adjusted, and the heat itself can be reduced or increased. Food is usually brushed with oil or a marinade before cooking, and must be turned at least once during cooking.

(*see also* CONTACT GRILL)

GRILSE (*see* SALMON)

GRIND To reduce hard foods to small particles in a food mill, pestle and mortar, electric grinder or food processor. The most frequently ground foods are coffee beans, nuts and spices.

GRISSINI Long, thin, crunchy Italian bread sticks, commonly served as appetizers in Italian restaurants. They can also be bought in packets in most supermarkets.

GRISTLE A tough inedible substance that forms part of the connective tissue of all animals and is sometimes found in poorly trimmed meat. The principal constituent of gristle is collagen, which is converted into gelatine by prolonged cooking.

GRITS (*see* CORN)

GROATS (*see* OATS)

GROG A drink made with spirits, sugar and hot water, traditionally served as a warming drink in winter. The spirit used may be rum, brandy or whisky.

GROUND CHERRY (Dwarf Cape Gooseberry, Strawberry Tomato) One of a group of tropical fruits known as the Physalis fruits, along with the Cape gooseberry and the Chinese lantern. The ground cherry originated in America and is a popular wild fruit in Hawaii. Like the Cape gooseberry, it has a papery calyx surrounding a small round fruit. It can be cooked in pies or used to make preserves.

GROUND MEAT (*see* MINCE)

GROUNDNUT (*see* PEANUT)

GROUNDNUT OIL (*see* OILS)

GROUND RICE (*see* RICE)

GROUND TOMATO (*see* TOMATILLO)

GROUPER A large family of sea fish found in warm waters all over the world, especially the Mediterranean and the Caribbean. Groupers vary in size and colour and are often identified by their Creole names, such as *vieille maconde* or *vieille rouge*. Small groupers are sold whole, while larger fish are usually sold cut into steaks. It may be baked, steamed, poached, grilled or fried and served hot or cold. They have firm white flesh.

GROUSE (Moor Fowl) There are several varieties of this game bird, but the name generally refers to the red or Scotch grouse, which is at its best from August to October; the shooting season is from 12th August (the Glorious Twelfth) to 10th December.

The young birds make the best eating; they may be distinguished by downy feathers under the wings, which have pointed flight feathers; the feathers on head and neck are of a rich brown colour.

Ptarmigan, which turns white in winter but is otherwise similar to grouse, is often called 'white grouse', while blackcock (or black game) is called 'black grouse'. (*see also* CAPERCAILZIE, HAZEL HEN)

Grouse should be hung for 2–4 days before drawing and plucking (*see* GAME). It is usually cooked by roasting, but may also be made into a pie or removed from the bone and used for made-up dishes, though this is not recommended, as the distinctive flavour of the grouse is to some extent lost. As grouse is a small bird, serve one per person. (*see also* CARVING)

Roast Grouse

4 oven-ready grouse
salt and pepper
8 rashers streaky bacon
50 g (2 oz) butter
4 slices toasted bread
flour for dredging

Season the birds inside and out with salt and pepper and lay two bacon rashers over the breast of each one. Put a knob of butter inside each bird and place each one on a slice of toast in a roasting tin.

Roast in the oven at 200°C (400°F) mark 6 for 40 minutes, basting frequently. After 30 minutes, remove the bacon, dredge the breast with flour and baste well.

Remove the trussing strings before serving the birds on the pieces of toast on which they were roasted. Garnish with watercress and serve with thin gravy (*see* GRAVY), bread sauce (*see* BREAD SAUCE), fried crumbs and matchstick potatoes (*see* ALLUMETTES).
Serves 4

GRUEL A drink or thin porridge, sometimes given to invalids or children, which is made by boiling fine oatmeal or barley meal in water, milk or stock.

GRUYÈRE A hard, large cheese, weighing anything up to 45 kg (100 lb), made from unpasteurized cows' milk. Originally, Gruyère came exclusively from Switzerland, but it is now made in France, Italy and other parts of Europe. It is pale yellow in colour and is sparsely scattered with 'eyes' or holes, caused by the rapid fermentation of the curd; it has a distinctive and fairly sweet taste. Gruyère is served uncooked, but is also used in such classic cooked dishes as fondue (*see* FONDUE).

GUACAMOLE A Mexican speciality that has become popular in many other countries, including Britain and the United States. It consists of a purée of ripe avocados flavoured with tomato, onion, parsley and chilli, usually served as a dip with fingers of toast, raw vegetables or corn chips. It may also be used as a filling for Mexican *tacos* or *tortillas*.

GUANCIALE A cured cut of bacon taken from the jaw of the pig. It is an Italian speciality and is the bacon traditionally used to make *spaghetti alla carbonara*. (*see also* PIG'S CHEEK)

GUAR (Cluster Bean, Gaur) A variety of green bean that has long, thin pods. It is mainly grown in India where it is used as a vegetable or in curries, but it is also grown in the south-western United States as cattle fodder. The beans are not usually dried for use as a pulse.

The beans are also the source of a gum which is used commercially as a thickening agent or stabilizer (E412) in a variety of foods, including packet soups, salad dressings, meringue mixes, horseradish cream, yogurt and ice cream. (*see also* ADDITIVE)

GUARD OF HONOUR The name given to a roast consisting of two racks (or best ends of neck) of lamb arranged back to back, fat side outwards, to form an arch with bones interlinking. The cavity between the racks may be filled with a stuffing. The racks must first be prepared in the same way as for a crown roast (*see* CROWN OF LAMB OR PORK).

GUAVA A tropical fruit of South American and Indian origin, the guava is now also grown in many other tropical and sub-tropical countries, including Australia, Thailand, the West Indies and Africa. It is one of many tropical fruits becoming more readily available in Britain and can be found in some shops from November to March.

Guavas may be round or pear-shaped, with whitish-yellow to red skins and musky smelling white or pale pink flesh containing edible seeds. A less common variety, known as the strawberry or purple guava, is smaller and sweeter, with dark red skin. Guavas have one of the highest vitamin

C contents of all fruit. Canned guava is also available.

Guavas can be eaten raw, in a fruit salad or puréed to make a sauce. They can be cooked in crumbles, stewed in a compote or stuffed and baked like apples. They can also be used to make sorbets, jams, jellies and fruit cheeses.

To select: Choose firm, unblemished fruit. A yellow skin speckled with tiny black spots indicates the fruit is ripe.

To prepare: Cut the fruit in half and peel. The whole fruit is edible, but large seeds are best removed before eating or cooking.

GUDGEON A freshwater fish belonging to the carp family, found in European rivers. It grows to about 20.5 cm (8 inches) in length and has barbels at each corner of its mouth and black spots along the side of its body. Like all freshwater fish, gudgeon need soaking in salted water before cooking to remove impurities. It is best fried or grilled; small fish may be dipped in flour or batter and deep-fried, like whitebait. (*see also* GOUJONETTE)

GUINEA FOWL Originally a game bird, guinea fowl is now farmed and classified as poultry rather than game. It is usually about the same size as a pheasant (about 1 kg/2 lb) but can be as large as a small chicken. It has grey plumage with white spots. Guinea fowl are available all year round but the birds are at their best from February to June. When in good condition they have a plump breast and smooth-skinned legs.

All recipes for cooking chicken or pheasant are suitable for guinea fowl, especially braising or casseroling, but take care to use plenty of fat when roasting, otherwise the flesh will be dry. For this reason, guinea fowl are often barded with bacon rashers or pork fat before roasting (*see* BARDING). An average-sized bird will serve about four people. Guinea fowl are not usually available jointed. (*see also* POULTRY)

Roast Guinea Fowl

Singe, draw and wipe the bird, then truss it for roasting (*see* POULTRY). Bard the bird, then roast in the oven at 200°C (400°F) mark 6 for 45-60 minutes, or longer according to size, basting frequently with butter or dripping. Garnish with watercress and serve with thin gravy (*see* GRAVY) and an orange or mixed green salad, or with bread sauce (*see* BREAD SAUCE).

GUITAR FISH (*see* SHARK)

GUM A sticky substance, which hardens somewhat on exposure to the air, obtained from various trees and plants. The two chief types used in cookery are gum arabic and gum tragacanth. The former, which is derived from Arabian and Indian species of acacia, is used in the manufacture of chewing gum, marshmallow and pastilles, and as a glaze that can be painted on cake decorations.

Gum tragacanth, which is obtained from a spiny shrub grown in western Asia, is used commercially for thickening creams, jellies and pastes, particularly the special stiff royal icing (*pastillage*) formerly employed to make ornaments for wedding cakes, etc. Gum tragacanth is also added to ice creams and jams to prevent crystallization. (*see also* GUAR)

GUMBO (*see* OKRA)

GUNGA PEA (*see* PIGEON PEA)

GUR (*see* JAGGERY)

GURNARD (Gurnet, Sea Robin) A small round sea fish with a large, distinctive, bony head and three rays of the pectoral fins extending downwards. There are three types of gurnard (the grey, yellow and red), found mostly in the north-eastern Atlantic and the Mediterranean. The red gurnard is considered the best, but all types have firm white flesh and can be baked, grilled or poached. Gurnard is especially good for fish soups.

GUT To clean out the inside of a fish, removing all the entrails.

H

HACHÉ A French word meaning minced or chopped. It is applied to various dishes, including an ancient sauce (*sauce hachée*) traditionally served with roast red meat or venison. It is usually made from a mixture of chopped vegetables, herbs, spices, gherkins and capers, combined with espagnole sauce.

HACHIS (Hash) The French name for any dish that is made from very finely chopped foods. It can also refer to a garnish of chopped parsley, garlic and ham. (*see also* HASH)

HADDOCK This round sea fish is a slightly smaller cousin of the cod and is distinguished from it by a dark streak which runs down its back, and two black 'thumb marks' above the gills. It is mainly fished on both sides of the Atlantic and in the North Sea. It is a popular fish that is in danger of becoming scarce; prices are already much higher than they were.

Haddock has firm, white flesh and may be cooked by any method suitable for white fish (*see* FISH); it is particularly useful for cooked dishes such as fish pie. It is sold as fillets or cutlets and is available all year round, though it is at its best from May to February. Haddock does not take salt as well as cod does, and it is traditionally cured by smoking.

Smoked Haddock
Smoked fillets are taken from large fish and cold-smoked with the skin on. They are dyed, often to a bright orange yellow. To cook, poach the fillets in milk, water or *court bouillon* (*see* COURT BOUILLON) for 10–15 minutes.
Finnan haddock is named after the village of Findon, near Aberdeen in Scotland. Before smoking, the fish are split and lightly brined, but not usually dyed. They are a light straw colour, but darken during cooking. Cook as for smoked fillets. Smaller smoked haddock are known as Glasgow Pales.
Golden cutlets are small haddock with the heads removed, which are split and boned before smok-

ing. Cook as for smoked haddock fillets. (*see also* SMOKIES)

HAGGIS A type of sausage that is the Scottish national dish. It is made from oatmeal, suet, onions, herbs and the internal organs of a sheep, the stomach of the sheep being cleaned and used as a 'skin' to contain the mixture. A simpler type of haggis can be made at home with liver and cooked in a basin. Haggis is available fresh or canned and is usually cooked by gentle poaching, though it can also be wrapped in foil and baked in the oven. It is traditionally served with mashed potato and mashed swede (neeps), with pure malt whisky to drink.

HAKE This round sea fish belongs to the same family as cod and haddock; varieties of hake are found all over the world, particularly in the North and South Atlantic. It is similar in shape to cod and haddock, but has a firmer white flesh and a better flavour. Small hake are sold whole; large ones are sold as fillets, steaks or cutlets. Fresh hake is available from June to January. It can be grilled, baked, fried in batter or used in various cooked dishes.

HALIBUT A very large, flat sea fish that, like turbot, is regarded as one of the best flavoured of all fish. It is found in the North Atlantic and the northern Pacific.

Halibut has firm white flesh and is sold as fillets or steaks. It is usually baked or grilled, though it may also be cooked by any recipe suitable for turbot (*see* TURBOT) or cod (*see* COD). The flavour of halibut is slightly milder than turbot, and the flesh can be drier. Halibut is available all year round but is at its best from June to March.

Smoked Halibut
This is not widely available, but may be found as slices of fillet. It does not need cooking.

HALIBUT LIVER OIL This is a very good source of vitamins A and D (containing a higher proportion than cod liver oil) and can be taken as a supplement in capsule form.

HALOUMI (Halloumi) A semi-hard cheese made in Cyprus, mostly from goats' milk. It has quite a mild, salty flavour and a slightly rubbery texture. Slices of *haloumi* may be grilled and served hot.

HALVA (Halvah) An Eastern sweetmeat, popular in Greece and Turkey. It is made from crushed sesame seeds or almonds combined with a boiled sugar syrup, sometimes with cream or crystallized fruits added. In Britain, *halva* can be bought in delicatessens and is often served as a petit four in Greek restaurants.

HAM Strictly speaking, a ham is the hind leg of a pig cut from the whole carcass, then cured and matured separately. Nowadays, cooked gammon (*see* BACON) is often described as ham. When selecting a ham, choose a short, thick leg without too much fat and a thin rind. More often than not, hams are cooked prior to purchase but, if not, cook as for bacon (*see* BACON).

Ham can be bought ready-sliced from delicatessens or in vacuum packs from supermarkets. Sliced cooked ham does not keep well and should be kept in the refrigerator. Once opened, it should be used within a day or so. Ham may be served with other cold meats and salad or used to make sandwiches. Sliced cooked ham is occasionally used in cooked dishes.

Types of Ham

There are many types of ham, produced mostly in Spain, Italy, France, the United States and Britain. The characteristics of a ham depend firstly on the breed and age of the pig and on what it has been fed on. Secondly, methods of curing vary enormously, though all are based on salt. Some cures incorporate a dry salting method, while others involve soaking the ham in brine. Most often, these days, commercially cured ham is injected with a brine solution before other curing processes begin. After curing, a ham may simply be hung up and left to dry, or it may be smoked with any of a variety of smokes, including oak, beech, juniper, sage and peat. Finally, the flavour of a ham is also affected by the length of time and the conditions under which it is left to mature. The maturing period can be anything from two months to two years, during which time the distinctive flavour of a ham develops.

Some of the best known hams are listed below.

York ham is cured with dry salt and lightly smoked before being boiled. York ham is cut from the side near the oyster bone, which makes it a long shape. It is then rounded off. The meat is pale with a mild, delicate flavour. The average weight of a York ham is 7–11 kg (16–24 lb).

Bradenham ham is rarely found today and is expensive. It is cured in a similar way to York ham and then pickled in molasses for a month. The cure turns the skin black and the meat rather red with a slightly sweet flavour. To cook, soak for 48–72 hours, drain and put in fresh cold water. Boil as for bacon.

Suffolk ham is sweet cured and has a rich red-brown meat with a 'blue' bloom. This ham, cured in beer and sugar or black molasses, has a deep golden, toasted look to the skin. It is not widely available today.

Cumberland ham is dry salted, with the addition of brown sugar.

Belfast ham is now almost entirely found in the west of Scotland. These hams are dry salted and traditionally smoked over peat.

Honey-baked ham is baked with a coating of honey, or honey and brown sugar.

Virginia ham is an American ham. A true Virginia ham comes from pigs fed on peanuts and peaches.

Kentucky ham is an American ham from pigs fattened on acorns, beans and cloves.

Raw Hams

All English hams need to be cooked, but there are several hams from other countries produced specially for eating raw. The most famous is *prosciutto* from Parma in Italy. Bayonne in France and Westphalia in Germany also produce notable raw hams.

HAMBURGER (*see* BEEFBURGER)

HAND A joint of meat taken from the forequarter of a pig (*see* PORK).

HANGING Leaving meat or game suspended in a cool, dry place to allow air to circulate around it to tenderize the flesh and develop the flavour. Meat and oven-ready game bought from a butcher or supermarket have already been hung and are ready for cooking. Hanging times for different species of game birds vary enormously (*see* GAME).

HARD SAUCE (*see* BRANDY BUTTER)

HARE (*see* RABBIT)

HARENG SAUR (*see* HERRING)

HARICOT BEAN (Kidney Bean) Strictly speaking, haricot bean is the generic name for a family of beans that includes the French bean and the dried beans known as kidney, cannellini, navy and flageolet beans. However, in general use, it is the name of a small, white oval-shaped dried bean that is a member of the same family. Haricot beans have a bland flavour and are mainly used to add texture and protein to casseroles, stews and soups. They are a traditional ingredient of cassoulets (*see* CASSOULET). They may also be used in a mixed bean salad. (*see also* PULSES)

HARICOT VERT (*see* BEAN, FRENCH)

HARISSA A hot mixture of chilli and other spices that is used in Middle Eastern cooking. It can be bought in powder and paste form and may contain up to 20 spices. *Harissa* is often served with couscous and other North African dishes: it is put in a separate bowl, stock from the main dish is poured in to dilute it and it is spooned back over the dish to taste. *Harissa* can be stored, covered with olive oil, in a jar in the refrigerator for up to two months.

HARUSAME (*see* NOODLES)

HASH A dish of diced cooked meat reheated in a highly flavoured sauce. Hash provides a good way of serving the last of the joint (the bones can be used to make stock as a basis for the sauce). It can be served with a border of creamed potatoes or savoury rice.

A hash may also consist of diced cooked meat, poultry or fish combined with mashed potato and fried in oil or butter until browned and crisp.

HASLET (*see* PIG'S FRY)

HAVARTI A Danish semi-hard cheese with a good full flavour. It is made from pasteurized cows' milk and has a yellow paste with many irregular holes, giving it a soft, loose texture. It is usually sold foil-wrapped.

HAZEL HEN (Hazel Grouse) A game bird that used to be imported into this country in a chilled or frozen state, mainly from Scandinavia and Russia. The birds have white tender flesh of excellent flavour and are best roasted or prepared as for grouse (*see* GROUSE).

HAZELNUT (Barcelona Nut, Cob Nut, Filbert) Hazelnuts, filberts and cob nuts are all fruits of different varieties of hazel tree. Cobs are not as common as the other two. Filberts are considered one of the best types of hazelnut and are cultivated in Kent as well as being imported from Italy and Spain. Rather confusingly, these filberts are usually sold fresh under the name of Kentish cobs. They may be recognized by their long fringed green husks and elongated form. They are in season from September to March, though in England they are best left until October, when they will fall if the trees are shaken. After drying, they will keep for a long time.

Dried hazelnuts are available in their shells, as shelled whole nuts (plain or roasted), chopped, flaked or ground. They have a tough but edible skin under their shells which can be removed by roasting, then rubbing off the skins, or by blanching in the same way as almonds (*see* ALMOND).

Hazelnuts have a distinct flavour which goes well with chocolate; they are often used in sweet making or to make desserts, biscuits, cakes and pastries, as well as being served as a dessert nut. They may also be used to make a flavoured butter (*see* BEURRE NOISETTE) and an oil is extracted from them.

HEAD Pigs' and sheep's heads are the most commonly seen and are usually sold whole or split in half. The best brawn is made from boiled pig's head, although some is made from calf's head. Head meat can also be used for pie fillings. On gala occasions, a pig's head is sometimes roasted whole, glazed and decorated as a boar's head. Ask the butcher to prepare the head as for roasting. Cook and remove the meat for brawns or pies. (*see also* BRAWN)

HEAD CHEESE (*see* BRAWN)

HEART The heart of various animals is classified as offal and is a nutritious food, although it has never been as popular in Britain as other types of

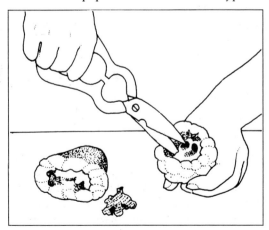

Snipping out fat, arteries, tendons and cavity walls from inside a heart.

offal. Lamb's and pig's hearts are the most commonly available. They are sold whole and one per portion is usually sufficient. Since the heart is a muscular organ and tends to be tough, best results are achieved by pot roasting, braising or casseroling. An ox heart weighs up to 1.8 kg (4 lb) and is best cut into cubes for stews and casseroles.

Whole hearts are frequently stuffed. Wash thoroughly in cold water, trim away fat and tubes and snip the cavity walls. Leave to soak for an hour in clean salt water. Rinse and drain. When slicing, cut across an ox heart and thus across the grain to increase tenderness.

HEMLOCK (*see* SPRUCE)

HERBS This name generally refers to a group of aromatic plants grown specifically for use in cooking, though many are also attributed with medicinal properties. Along with spices, herbs have been used with food since time immemorial. Originally, one of their main purposes was to disguise the flavour of perishable foods which were past their best, or even starting to rot. Today, they are appreciated for the distinctive tastes they add to heighten or improve the flavour of meat, fish and vegetable dishes.

Herbs are sold fresh or dried; fresh have a better appearance than dried and are essential for adding to salads, but many dried herbs have a good flavour and it is virtually impossible to detect the difference in cooked dishes such as casseroles. Dried herbs have a stronger flavour than fresh and should be used more sparingly; as a rule, you need about one third the amount specified for fresh herbs if substituting dried.

The flavour of fresh herbs is contained in essential oils found in their leaves and stems, which are released when herbs are heated, crushed or chopped. Some herbs are chopped before being added to a dish; others, such as bay, are added whole. The more delicate herbs, such as parsley and tarragon, should be added towards the end of cooking, while the tougher varieties may be added at the beginning. A bouquet garni can be used to impart the flavours of a mixture of herbs to a dish during cooking, and enables the herbs to be removed before serving (*see* BOUQUET GARNI). Other classic herb mixtures include the French *fines herbes* (*see* FINES HERBES) and *herbes de Provence*, which may be made from a variety of herbs, but usually includes bay, basil, rosemary, savory and thyme.

The majority of herbs, even if they do not originate in this country, can be grown successfully, either outdoors or under glass. Some are annuals and need to be sown each year, others are perennial.

Ideally, fresh herbs should be picked just before using, but if necessary they can be stored in the refrigerator in a plastic box or glass jar with a top for 1–2 days. Herbs can be dried very easily (*see* DRIED HERBS) or they can be frozen and used in soups or casseroles.

Dried herbs keep best in airtight jars away from the light. Choose wood, earthenware or dark-coloured glass. In a cool place, dried herbs will keep their flavour for 6–8 months. After that, any left can be scattered around the herb garden or sprinkled round pot plants to keep away various insects.

(*see also* ANGELICA, BASIL, BAY, BORAGE, BOUQUET GARNI, etc.)

HERRING A fairly small, round, oily sea fish with creamy-coloured flesh and a distinctive flavour, found in the Atlantic and Pacific Oceans as well as the North Sea. There are many varieties of herring, one of the most common being known as alewife. Unfortunately, due to pollution and intensive fishing, herring is less abundant than it used to be. Fresh herring are available all year round and are generally sold whole, though the fishmonger will fillet them for you on request. They may be grilled, fried, sautéed or stuffed and baked. (*see also* FISH)

Herrings are also sold ready-prepared in various ways:

Salt herrings are gutted and preserved in wooden casks between layers of salt. They are usually sold in delicatessens.

Matjes herrings are herrings cured in salt, sugar and a little saltpetre. They are sold whole or as fillets and have a better flavour than salt herrings.

Rollmops and bismarcks are boned herrings marinated in spiced vinegar. Rollmops are rolled with chopped onions, gherkins and peppercorns. Bismarcks are flat fillets covered with sliced onion.

Canned herrings are most popular in tomato sauce. Canned kippers and bloaters are available too, as are herring roes.

Smoked Herring

Bloaters are lightly smoked, dry salted herrings with bones, heads and tails removed. They should be eaten within 24 hours of buying and can be lightly grilled or fried.

Buckling are whole smoked herrings that are ready to eat.

Kippers are herrings that have been split, lightly brined, then cold-smoked. To cook, grill or poach for about 5 minutes, or place in a jug of boiling water and leave in a warm place for 5-10 minutes, or wrap in foil and bake in the oven at 190°C (375°F) mark 5 for 10–15 minutes.

Red herrings are heavily smoked and highly salted. They are rarely available in Britain but can be lightly grilled or fried. A French version of red herring, known as *hareng saur* or *gendarme*, is very popular and often served as part of an hors d'oeuvre.

HIBACHI This Japanese word, meaning 'fire bowl', has been adopted as the name of a small type of barbecue, consisting of a container, usually of cast iron, with a metal grilling rack over it. The coals are placed in the container for lighting in the same way as for a standard-sized barbecue, and the food is cooked on the grill rack. The beauty of a *hibachi* is that it is easily transportable and can be taken on picnics or moved from place to place in the garden. Some models have a detachable stand or legs. (*see also* BARBECUE)

HICKORY NUT The name of various types of walnut grown in North America, the best known being the pecan nut (*see* PECAN NUT).

HIGHLAND CROWDIE This Scottish farmhouse cheese is similar to cottage cheese but more finely ground. It is made from cows' milk, although at one time it was also made from goats' milk. Crowdie is high in protein and low in fat with a light, fresh flavour. (*see also* CHEESE)

HIPPOCRAS A mediaeval drink, consisting of wine heavily sweetened with honey and flavoured with herbs and spices. It is likely that soured wine was used up in this way.

HIZIKI (*see* SEA VEGETABLES)

HOCK The name given to white wines from the Rhine Palatinate and other parts of Germany. The original name, Hochheimer, was given to the wine made in the vineyards close to the town of Hochheim and this region still produces the best Hock, which is sold under a number of well known names, such as Johannisberger, Steinberger, Liebfraumilch, Marcobrunner, Hochheimer.

A traditional Hock or Rhine wine glass is tall, with a stout knobbled stem of brown or green glass which is intended to reflect the colour of the wine. All classic German wines are contained in slim-necked bottles, brown for Rhine wines and green for Moselle.

Hock is served with white fish, white meats and desserts, while the sparkling variety is used in place of champagne. It is also a good wine for making a cold refreshing cup to serve at buffet parties, etc.

The term hock also applies to meat taken from just above the foot of a pig, bullock or sheep.

HOG PUDDING A kind of sausage made from pork.

HOISIN SAUCE (Hoi Hsien Chiang) A sweet, reddish-brown, rather spicy sauce made from garlic, soya beans, sugar and spices. It is sold in Chinese and health food shops and will keep for a long time. It is often used as a dip for batter-coated, deep-fried vegetables.

HOLLANDAISE A classic white sauce that uses eggs rather than flour as a thickening agent. It may be served with fish, egg, chicken and vegetable dishes. When making hollandaise sauce, it is important to cook the sauce very slowly and gently. The water in the double saucepan should be barely simmering; a fierce heat will produce a granular texture and, if overcooked, the eggs will scramble.

Hollandaise Sauce
If not serving immediately, remove the sauce from the heat and keep warm over warm (not hot) water.
30 ml (2 tbsp) wine or tarragon vinegar
15 ml (1 tbsp) water
2 egg yolks
225 g (8 oz) unsalted butter, softened
salt and white pepper
Put the vinegar and water into a saucepan. Boil gently until the liquid has reduced by half. Set aside until cool.

Put the egg yolks and reduced vinegar liquid into a double saucepan or bowl standing over a pan of very gently simmering water and whisk until the mixture is thick and fluffy.

Gradually add the butter, a tiny piece at a time. Whisk briskly until each piece has been absorbed by the sauce and the sauce itself is the consistency of mayonnaise. Season with salt and pepper. If the sauce is too sharp add a little more butter – it should be slightly piquant, and warm rather than hot when served.
Makes about 300 ml (¹/₂ pint)

Variation
Mousseline sauce This is a richer version of hollandaise which is suitable for asparagus and

broccoli, and poached fish, egg and chicken dishes. Simply stir 45 ml (3 tbsp) whipped double cream into the sauce just before serving.

HOLLANDS A type of gin distilled in Holland and highly prized by the Dutch. It is made from barley, malt, rye and juniper berries. The best-known type is Schnapps. (*see also* GIN)

HOMINY (*see* CORN)

HOMOGENIZE To process milk commercially in order to break down the fat (cream) globules into particles of a uniform size to prevent the cream separating out. The process involves forcing the milk through a tiny valve. Homogenized milk is more digestible, but cream made from homogenized milk cannot be whipped.

HONEY One of our oldest and most natural foods, honey is a sweet syrupy liquid made by bees from the nectar of flowers. It has been highly thought of since ancient times, both for its medicinal properties and its sweet flavour. Bees are kept all over the world, producing a vast range of different honeys.

Honey is a nutritious food that is very easily assimilated by the body, due to the way it is naturally processed by the bees. As nectar is collected, it is stored in a bee's 'honey stomach', where it undergoes a sort of pre-digestion before it is secreted as a sugary solution in the hive. This transforming process continues after the nectar has been deposited in the honeycomb of the hive and moisture is evaporated off. Only when the honey is completely transformed do the bees coat it with wax.

To produce honey on a commercial scale, the honeycombs are removed from the hives and the honey is extracted by centrifugal force. The honey is then filtered and purified before being packed in jars. Honey produced in this way is known as 'cast' honey. An alternative method of production is to crush the honeycombs, producing 'pressed' honey. Some honeys are sold in the honeycomb or with chunks of honeycomb in the jar. In both cases, the honeycomb is edible.

Honeys vary in colour, flavour and texture, depending on the flowers visited by the bees, the time of year the honey is collected, and on the country of production; jars are usually labelled accordingly. Other non-specific honeys are the result of blending several different types. Some honeys crystallize more quickly than others, due to the balance of natural sugars they contain. However, most clear honeys will crystallize in time and many types of honey are sold in clear and crystallized forms.

Popular honeys produced from particular flowers include lavender, clover, heather, rosemary, acacia and orange blossom. Jars labelled simply 'honey', 'Australian honey' or 'wild-flower honey' contain blended honeys which are popular but do not have such excellent flavours or appealing aromas. Lavender honey, for example, really does smell of lavender. There are some very rare honeys that are seldom seen in the shops, such as the pohutakawa honey from New Zealand.

Honey is delicious spread on bread and butter or toast, but is also used in a number of ways in cooking. It can be used as a sweetener in cakes and desserts, and is an important ingredient in sweet-making. Clear (runny) honey is generally recommended for cooking as it dissolves more easily. If honey is used as a substitute for sugar in a recipe, it is important to reduce the amount of other liquids used accordingly. Honey is also delicious served as a sweet condiment, either for pouring over ice cream or pancakes, or as a dip for popcorn. A delicious healthy dessert can be made simply by combining honey with natural yogurt. Honey is also used in savoury dishes, as a glaze on a roast gammon joint, for example, or in marinades.

HONEYCOMB MOULD The name of a light dessert consisting of an egg jelly with whisked egg white folded in. As it sets, it separates into a jelly layer topped by a fluffy mousse-like layer with the appearance of a honeycomb – hence the name.

HONGROISE, À L' A French name given to a number of dishes consisting of meat, fish, poultry, eggs or vegetables cooked in a sauce seasoned with paprika.

HOPS The ripened catkins or flowers of a climbing vine, the hop plant, which are used to impart a bitter flavour to beer. The tender shoots are eaten as a vegetable in France and Belgium.

HORN OF PLENTY (*see* MUSHROOM)

HORS D'OEUVRE This French term is often used as a general name for any dish served as the first course of a meal. Strictly speaking, however, it is the name of a selection of cold foods served together as an appetizer.

HORSE Horse meat is not used for human consumption in Britain, but is still eaten in some European countries, including France and Belgium. In fact, horse meat is said to have quite a sweet flavour and it is a safer meat to eat than beef since horses are not prone to some of the diseases that can be passed from cows to people. In France, horse meat is used in many recipes that are also used for beef. In Britain, however, horse meat is reserved for dogs.

HORSE BEAN (*see* BEAN, BROAD)

HORSERADISH A plant of the mustard family, horseradish originated in eastern Europe and is cultivated for its root. Horseradish is used raw, grated into dressings of cream and vinegar and is classically served with roast beef. It has a hot, biting, pungent taste and should be used sparingly. Horseradish is also good with some fish, particularly smoked mackerel, and as a flavouring for sandwich fillings. Commercially prepared horseradish cream or relish is available in bottles. Dried flaked horseradish is also available and can be used as a substitute for fresh if necessary.

HOTCH-POTCH (Hotchpotch) A thick soup or stew made of meat and vegetables.

HOT CROSS BUN A yeast bun traditionally eaten on Good Friday and around Easter time. The buns contain currants and chopped peel and are flavoured with a mixture of spices. They have glazed dark brown tops and are characterized by a cross marked on top either by cutting the buns with a knife before they are left to prove, by marking a cross with trimmings of pastry before cooking, or by forming a cross with candied peel. (*see also* BUN)

HOT DOG A popular snack food that originated in America in the 1930s. It consists of a long thin sausage, usually a poached frankfurter, served hot inside a similarly-shaped soft bread roll. Fried chopped onions, mustard, ketchup or relish may also be added. (*see also* FRANKFURTER)

HOT-POT A baked stew or casserole made with meat, fish or vegetables and finished on top with a layer of sliced potatoes or a savoury crumble mixture. The best known hot-pot is Lancashire hot-pot, which consists of a stew of lamb chops and kidneys, leeks and carrots topped with a layer of potato slices.

HOT WATER CRUST PASTRY (*see* PASTRY)

HOUX (*see* EAU-DE-VIE)

HOWTOWDIE A Scottish dish consisting of boiled chicken with poached eggs and spinach.

HRAMSA CHEESE A soft Scottish cheese made from Caboc cheese, mixed with fresh double cream, delicately flavoured with chopped wild garlic leaves. Its name is derived from the Celtic word for wild garlic. Although not widely available outside Scotland, it is excellent served on savoury crackers or made into a dip.

HUCKLEBERRY (*see* BILBERRY)

HUILE, À L' A French term used to describe dishes served with olive oil or with a dressing made from olive oil.

HULLING Removing the calyx from soft fruits such as strawberries.

HUMBUG A cushion-shaped boiled sweet, hard in texture and usually flavoured with peppermint, though other flavours may be used. (*see also* SWEETS)

HUMMUS (*Hummus bi Tahina*) A Middle Eastern dip made from a purée of cooked chick peas and olive oil flavoured with *tahini* (sesame seed paste), garlic and lemon juice. It is usually served as a snack or starter with pitta bread or crudités.

HUNDREDS AND THOUSANDS (Sprinkles) A quick and simple decoration for desserts and cakes, these tiny coloured sugar strands or balls can be bought in cartons or tubes. In France, they are known as *nonpareille*.

HUNGRY RICE (*see* MILLET)

HUNTSMAN CHEESE The brand name of an attractive British processed cheese made by a dairy in Melton Mowbray, Leicestershire. It consists of two layers of Double Gloucester with a layer of Stilton in between.

HUNZA APRICOT (*see* APRICOT, DRIED)

HUSS (Dogfish) A long, pointed sea fish with light brown skin and a cream-coloured belly. It is also known as dogfish and used to be known as rock salmon. The firm flesh is white with a tinge of pink and is excellent fried. Huss is usually sold as fillets or cutlets; it is available all year but at its best from September to January.

HYDROGENATION (*see* MARGARINE)

HYDROLYZED PROTEIN Familiar to anyone who reads labels on processed foods, these substances are produced by breaking down proteins by adding hydrogen and oxygen atoms, a process known as hydrolysis. The transformation creates a new, different-flavoured substance which can be used as a flavouring in processed foods. Hydrolyzed vegetable protein, for example, is produced from wheat, maize or soya beans, but has a taste not unlike meat. It is used as a flavouring in meat extracts and stock cubes.

HYDROMEL An ancient drink, known to be enjoyed by the Romans and popular until the eighteenth century. It was made from honey and water, flavoured with herbs and spices. When fermented, it became mead.

HYGIENE The function of hygiene is to promote good health, and the term covers many processes carried out in order to prevent the development and spread of disease, including cleanliness. Kitchen hygiene is, of course, vitally important in order to avoid food poisoning, but of more importance is the use of hygienic practices wherever food is produced, stored and handled before it reaches the consumer, including farms, shops and supermarkets. Recent concern about the risk of food poisoning from contaminated eggs, cheese, pâté and dressed salads has shaken public confidence in the hygiene of the British food industry, leading in some cases to Government intervention. (*see also* FOOD POISONING)

HYSSOP A plant of the mint family with dark green leaves and deep blue flowers. Its pungent, aromatic leaves may be used in salads and soups. Honey made from hyssop flower nectar is said to be particularly good. An oil distilled from the leaves is used in liqueurs, such as Chartreuse.

I

ICE Water begins to turn to ice when its temperature is reduced to freezing point or below (0°C/32°F), but it takes some time for a quantity of water to freeze to a solid block of ice. In cookery, ice is used for chilling purposes and can be made in ice cube trays or bags in a domestic freezer or the ice-making compartment of a refrigerator. Larger quantities of ice can also be bought from specialist suppliers.

Ice is commonly added to fruit and alcoholic drinks and cocktails to chill them, either as ice cubes or crushed ice, and foods, such as oysters and caviar, may be served in a bowl surrounded by crushed ice. Chilled soups are sometimes served with an ice cube or two floating in them, and a bottle of wine or champagne is usually kept chilled at the table in an ice 'bucket'. Cold desserts made with gelatine may be placed over ice instead of in the refrigerator to set. Ice is also used in shops to chill food on display; fish is the most common food seen displayed on or surrounded by ice.

ICEBERG LETTUCE (*see* LETTUCE)

ICE CREAM A very popular frozen confection made from a mixture based on milk or cream but to which may be added a variety of flavourings and colourings. Nowadays, a vast range of ready-made ice creams are available, many of which contain no creams but are instead based on vegetable fat. In 1984, the Milk Marketing Board launched the 'Ice Cream made with Dairy Cream' campaign, which aims to promote premium quality ice cream containing double cream. It uses a trade mark featuring two cows standing nose to nose beneath an ice cream sundae, which only features on products which meet standards specified by the Milk Marketing Board. UK legislation states that all ice cream must contain at least 5 per cent milk fat and 7.5 per cent milk solids.

By combining ice cream with sweet sauces and other ingredients, such as fresh fruit, chopped nuts, chocolate and cream, it is easy to make simple yet delicious desserts, such as banana split, peach Melba and pears *belle-Hélène*. A number of famous classic desserts are based on ice cream or other frozen mixtures, such as baked Alaska, cassata and bombes, *parfaits* and *coupes*.

Home-made ice creams are richer and creamier than bought varieties and have more flavour. They are seldom made entirely from cream, but are usually a mixture of equal parts of cream and custard (the best being egg custard made with yolks only), cream and fruit purée or cream and egg whites. If wished, the cream may be replaced by evaporated milk or a commercial cream substitute. Flavourings and colourings are then added.

Making Ice Cream

Equipment
Ice cream can be made with everyday kitchen equipment or with a specially designed machine.
Large bowl, flat whisk or fork are needed for beating if not using an ice cream maker.
Bombe mould or freezerproof bowl for bombes.
Rigid freezer containers for freezing the mixture if not using a machine. The mixture will set more quickly in a shallow one, but transfer to a deeper container if you want to serve in scoops.
Manually operated ice cream maker has an inner and outer container. The space between is filled with salt or ice while beating the mixture.
Electric ice cream makers are available in two types; a small one that fits into the freezer or one that has its own freezing unit. They produce smoother, creamier ice with a greater volume.

Beating and Freezing
When making ice cream, the smoothest texture is achieved if the mixture is continuously beaten while it freezes, as in a hand operated or electric machine. If making ice cream without a machine, it is necessary partially to freeze the mixture, then to return it to a bowl for further beating to break down the ice crystals. Additional ingredients,

such as whipped cream or egg yolks may also be added at this stage and further beating after a second freezing may be necessary to prevent separation.

For freezing, use maximum freezing power; the quicker the mixture freezes, the better the texture. If using the ice-making compartment of a refrigerator, set the dial to maximum about 1 hour before required. If using a freezer, set to fast-freeze 1 hour ahead. Home-made ice cream stored in a freezer will be very hard and should be removed to the refrigerator to soften slightly at least 30 minutes before serving.

(*see also* BOMBE, COUPE, GRANITA, SORBET, WATER ICE)

ICELAND MOSS A lichen closely resembling carrageen, but darker in colour, which grows on barren mountains in Iceland and other northern regions. It grows to about 1.2 metres (4 feet) in height and has branched and flattened mycelium, with a dried appearance.

Iceland moss is sometimes used in cooking in the same way as carrageen. The rather bitter flavour of the moss is removed by soaking it for 15 minutes in boiling water, to which a pinch of bicarbonate of soda has been added, repeating this once or twice and finally pouring on more boiling water and leaving it to soak overnight. (*see also* CARRAGEEN, SEA VEGETABLES)

ICING A sweet coating or covering for cakes, biscuits, pastries, etc., which improves their flavour and appearance and forms a good background for other decorations, while also helping to keep a cake moist. The art of making and applying simple icing is easily learned. Some icings may also be piped or moulded into decorations. (*see also* ALMOND PASTE, AMERICAN FROSTING, BUTTER CREAM ICING, CRÈME AU BEURRE, GLACÉ ICING, FONDANT, PIPING, ROYAL ICING, TRANSPARENT ICING)

ICING SUGAR (*see* SUGAR)

ILCHESTER CHEESE An English cheese made by flavouring Double Gloucester with mustard pickle. (*see also* GLOUCESTER CHEESES)

IMPÉRATRICE, À L' A French name given to various rich dishes and cakes, the best known being *riz* (rice) *à l'impératrice*.

IMPÉRIALE, À L' A French name given to dishes served with a rich garnish of *foie gras*, truffles, cocks' combs or kidneys.

INDIAN CORN (*see* CORN)

INDIAN CRESS (*see* NASTURTIUM)

INDIAN DATE (*see* TAMARIND)

INDIAN FIG (*see* PRICKLY PEAR)

INDIAN NUT (*see* PINE NUT)

INDIAN RICE (*see* RICE)

INDIAN TEA (*see* TEA)

INDIENNE, À L' A French term generally applied to dishes influenced by Indian styles of cooking, including curries and chutneys, and to dishes served with rice.

INFRA-RED GRILL (*see* CONTACT GRILL)

INFUSING A method of imparting flavour to a liquid. Flavourings, such as aromatic vegetables, herbs, spices or coffee beans are added to milk or water, sometimes brought to the boil, then left to soak. The liquid is then strained and used to make a sauce, dessert or drink. Tea is an infusion of tea leaves or herbs in boiling water.

INJERA An East African bread, shaped rather like a large pancake and made from millet flour and yeast. It is used in much the same way as pitta bread.

INSECTS Although insects are not generally used for food in European countries or the United States, they are considered a worthwhile source of protein in other parts of the world, such as Australia, Africa, Japan and South-East Asia.

Insects and insect larvae that may be eaten include locusts, termites, witchity grubs, caterpillars and scorpions. Although, in western countries, insects are not eaten, they are exploited in other ways, in the use of cochineal and honey.

IODINE A naturally-occurring element, small amounts of which are essential to the human body; iodine deficiency can result in a condition known as goitre (enlargement of the thyroid gland). Most people's diets contain enough iodine as it is usually present in drinking water, milk and bread and in vegetables grown in soil containing the element. Rich sources of iodine include sea fish, shellfish and sea vegetables. If a deficiency is suspected, iodized salt can be used instead of other cooking or table salts.

IRISH COFFEE (*see* COFFEE)

IRISH MIST A liqueur made from Irish whiskey and heather honey.

IRISH MOSS (*see* CARRAGEEN)

IRON One of several minerals that are vital to health, iron is used to make the haemoglobin in red blood cells and is stored in the muscles and liver. Haemoglobin carries oxygen to supply all the body's cells and a shortage leads to a condition known as anaemia.

Like other minerals, iron cannot be manufactured by the body and must be obtained from food. Iron deficiency is fairly common in Britain, particularly in women of child-bearing age since iron requirements are increased by menstrual loss and pregnancy. The body can adapt to increased needs by increasing its absorption of iron from the intestine, but some women still need to be prescribed iron tablets or supplements. Iron is found in meat and offal (particularly liver), some fish, cereals, pulses and vegetables. The iron in vegetable foods is less well absorbed than the iron in animal foods, but vitamin C increases the absorption of iron from all foods.

IRRADIATION The subject of considerable controversy, irradiation is a method of preserving food by exposing it to gamma rays which destroy micro-organisms which would otherwise lead to deterioration. Irradiation can be used to extend the shelf-life of many fresh foods by delaying ripening processes or by inhibiting the sprouting of potatoes and onions, and may reduce the amount of preservatives and other additives currently in use.

Although irradiated foods have been on sale in many other countries for some time, at the time of going to press, irradiation is not legalized in Britain and irradiated foods are not generally available. There is substantial consumer resistance to the use of irradiation, since it can adversely affect the flavour of some foods and, although it may efficiently destroy some bacteria, it may leave others (or their toxins) unaffected so that food which appears fresh and safe may actually be stale and contaminated. There is also very little information available on the real effects irradiation might have on the nutritional content of foods, or on how it might alter the nature of pesticide residues and other chemicals that might be present in foods. Of prime importance to consumers, however, is that irradiated foods should be correctly labelled as such so that they can be avoided if preferred. There is no sure way to test whether food has been irradiated or not, which has also led to considerable concern amongst both the food industry and the general public.

ISINGLASS A substance produced from fish that was formerly used as a setting agent. It has been almost completely replaced by gelatine, though it is still used to clarify wine.

ISLAY CHEESE A miniature Dunlop cheese which is excellent for melting and is best eaten when fairly mature. (*see also* DUNLOP CHEESE)

ITALIENNE, À L' A French term usually applied to dishes made partly or wholly from pasta, often flavoured with cheese or tomato, but which may also be applied to other dishes of Italian origin, or to those served with or cooked in an 'Italian' sauce made from mushrooms, ham, tomato and herbs.

IZARRA The name of various green and yellow herbal liqueurs based on armagnac and with a bouquet of mimosa honey, from the Basque country.

J

JACKET POTATO (*see* POTATO)

JACKFRUIT Widely cultivated in the tropical lowlands of Asia, Africa and America, jackfruit can grow up to 31.75 kg (70 lb) in weight. They have a rough, spiky green skin and yellow fibrous flesh which contains pockets of juicy pulp surrounding walnut-sized white seeds. The pulp tastes like a cross between banana and pineapple, with the texture of lychee. Jackfruit can be eaten raw or cooked and served as an accompaniment to savoury dishes.

To prepare: Remove the skin and cut out the sections of tender pulp, discarding the fibrous flesh and white seeds.

JAGGERY (Gur) The name of a crude brown Indian sugar made from palm juice, or of brown cane sugar.

JALOUSIE A French pastry that is made by spreading a sweet filling on a strip of puff pastry, then covering it with a second strip of pastry. The top strip is slashed horizontally and the effect is said to resemble a Venetian blind (*jalousie* in French).

JAM Jam-making is a method of preserving fresh fruits and sometimes vegetables by cooking them with sugar. The high concentration of sugar used in jam prevents the growth of micro-organisms and allows the jam to be kept for many months. Jam is a sweet, thick spread which is produced by cooking the fruit and sugar until the mixture reaches 'setting point', at which stage the hot jam is poured into jars and covered. When cool, the jars can be stored in a cool, dark place until required.

Jam can be used as a filling for sandwiches, sponge cakes and tarts or a topping for scones, toast and crumpets. Apricot jam is melted and used for making apricot glaze and various jams can be spooned into a bowl of hot rice pudding or used to make a sauce for ice creams, waffles, pancakes and other desserts.

Jam-making is probably the most popular of all methods of preserving, since it allows you to make the most of fresh fruits when they are in season and to enjoy their wonderful flavours at times when they are not. As you need quite large quantities of fruit to make jam, you can take advantage of a glut of fruit on the market or from your garden, or you might be able to pick quantities of wild fruits, such as blackberries or bilberries, in the countryside.

Equipment for Jam-making

Some special utensils and tools, though by no means essential, make jam-making easier.

Preserving pans Also known as maslin pans, these are deep, wide pans that are wider at the top than at the bottom; they usually have a handle on each side, or one curved handle over the top. Choose a preserving pan made from a heavy metal, such as aluminium or stainless steel. There is some concern over the possible link between aluminium and Alzheimer's Disease, but evidence at present is inconclusive. However, it is advisable that people with kidney problems, who are less able to expel aluminium from their systems, should avoid cooking acidic foods in plain, uncoated aluminium pans, and this includes making jams and preserves in unlined aluminium preserving pans.

A good preserving pan should have a fairly thick base to prevent the jam burning, and should be wide enough to allow the jam to boil rapidly without splashing all over the hob. The best size for you will depend on how much jam you want to make at one time – preferably, the jam should come no more than halfway up the pan.

Old-style preserving pans made from unlined copper or brass can be used for jams, providing they are perfectly clean. Any discoloration or tarnish should be removed with a patent cleaner and the pan should be thoroughly washed before use. Tin-lined copper pans cannot be used as the tin lining is likely to be melted by the hot jam.

Jams made in copper or brass pans will contain less vitamin C than those made in aluminium or stainless steel pans so any preserve must not be left standing in a copper or brass pan for any length of time.

If a preserving pan is not available, a large thick-based saucepan can be used, remembering that, since most saucepans are not as wide as a preserving pan, a longer simmering and boiling period for the fruit may be necessary.

Jam jars Jars should be thoroughly clean and free from cracks, chips or other flaws. Those holding 450 g or 1 kg (1 or 2 lb) are the most useful sizes as covers are available for these sizes. Waxed discs, cellophane covers, rubber bands and labels for covering and labelling jars can be bought in packets from most stationery shops and some chemists.

Other equipment The following items are also useful when making jam:

* A large, long-handled wooden spoon for stirring.

* A slotted spoon for skimming off any scum or fruit stones from the surface of jam.

* A sugar thermometer, though not essential, is very helpful when testing for a set.

* A funnel with a wide tube for filling jars is useful. Failing this, a large heatproof cup or jug can be used.

* A cherry stoner saves time and prevents hands becoming stained with cherry juice.

* Any sieve used in jam-making should be made of nylon, not metal which may discolour the fruit mixture.

Fruit for Jam-making

Fruit should be sound and just ripe. It is better to use slightly under- rather than over-ripe fruit as the pectin (see below) is most readily available at this stage.

Pectin and acid content of fruit Pectin is a substance derived from carbohydrate which is naturally present in fruit. Like gelatine, it has natural setting properties and works best when combined with acid and sugar. Jam will only set if there are sufficient quantities of pectin, acid and sugar present. Some fruits are rich in pectin and acid and give a good set, while others do not contain so much.

The fruits which contain most pectin are the more acid varieties, such as citrus fruits, damsons, currants (red and black), cranberries, crab apples and cooking apples. Some varieties of plum are also rich in pectin. Most of the other fruits used for making jam have a medium pectin content, the exceptions being strawberries and cherries which are low in pectin.

Test for pectin content If you are not sure of the setting qualities of the fruit you are using, the following test can be carried out: When the fruit has been cooked until soft and before adding the sugar, take 5 ml (1 tsp) juice, as free as possible from seeds and skin, put it in a glass and, when cool, add 15 ml (1 tbsp) methylated spirits. Shake the glass and then leave for 1 minute. If the mixture forms a jelly-like clot, the fruit has a good pectin content. If it does not form a single, firm clot, the pectin content is low and some form of extra pectin will be needed.

Fruits that lack acid and pectin require the addition of a fruit or fruit juice that is rich in these substances. Lemon juice is most often used for this purpose, since it aids the set and often brings out the flavour of the fruit. Allow 30 ml (2 tbsp) lemon juice to 2 kg (4 lb) of a fruit with poor setting properties. Alternatively, it is possible to make home-made pectin extract from sour apples, or a commercially bottled pectin is available. This is usually available from supermarkets or chemists.

Sometimes an acid only is added, such as citric or tartaric acid. These contain no pectin but help to extract the natural pectin from the tissues of the fruit and improve the flavour of fruits lacking in acid. Allow 2.5 ml ($\frac{1}{2}$ level tsp) to 2 kg (4 lb) of a fruit with poor setting properties.

Sugar

The presence of sugar in jam is very important as it acts as a preservative and affects the setting quality. The exact amount of sugar to be used depends on the pectin strength of the fruit so it is important to use the amount suggested in a recipe. Too little sugar will result in a poor set and the jam may go mouldy on storing. Too much sugar will produce a dark and sticky jam, the flavour will be lost and it may crystallize. Granulated sugar is suitable and the most economical for jam-making but less scum is formed when lump sugar or preserving sugar crystals are used. The finished preserve will also be slightly clearer and brighter. Caster sugar or brown sugar can also be used, but brown sugar produces much darker jam with a changed flavour. It is also possible to buy preserving sugar crystals with added pectin, specially produced for use with fruits low in pectin.

There is no completely satisfactory substitute for sugar in jam-making. If honey or treacle is used, its flavour is usually distinctly noticeable and the jam will not set easily. Glucose and glycerine do not have the same sweetening power as cane sugar. If one of these alternatives must be used, not more than half the amount of sugar specified in the recipe should be replaced.

Preparing the Fruit and Cooking the Jam

Fruit should be thoroughly checked and washed before use, then prepared according to variety. The first stage of jam-making is to put the fruit in a preserving pan with some water and to simmer it gently until it is quite tender. The time will vary according to the fruit – tough-skinned fruit, such as gooseberries, blackcurrants or plums, will take 30–45 minutes. This simmering process releases the pection and acid. If extra acid or pectin is needed, it is added at this stage. Adequate reduction of the fruit before adding the sugar is necessary for a good set. The sugar should only be added when the fruit has been sufficiently soft-ened and reduced as sugar has a hardening effect on the fruit and, once added, the fruit will not soften.

The next stage is to add the sugar. The pan is removed from the heat and the sugar stirred in until dissolved. (The sugar dissolves more easily if warmed in the oven before it is added.) A knob of butter may be added at this stage to reduce foaming. The pan is then returned to the heat and the jam is boiled rapidly until it sets when tested. (see below)

Testing for a Set

There are several ways of testing a preserve for setting point, some of which are less accurate than others or require special equipment. The following are the simplest and most accurate methods:

Temperature test This is the most accurate method of testing for a set. A sugar thermometer is placed in the jam and when the temperature reaches 105°C (221°F), a set should be obtained. Some fruits may need a degree lower or higher than this, so it is a good idea to combine this test with one of the following.

Saucer test A very little jam should be put on a cold saucer or plate and left to cool. If the surface of the jam wrinkles when a finger is pushed gently through it, setting point has been reached. (The pan should be removed from the heat during the test or the jam may be over-boiled, which weakens the setting property.)

Flake test This test is carried out by lifting a little jam out of the pan on a wooden spoon. After it has cooled, the jam is then allowed to drop back into the pan. If it has been boiled long enough, drops of jam will run together along the edge of the spoon and form flakes which will break off sharply.

Potting, Covering and Storing

As soon as a set has been reached, the pan should be removed from the heat and the surface of the jam should be skimmed to remove any scum. It may then be poured or ladled into warm jars, filling right to the tops. Exceptions are strawberry and other whole-fruit jams which should be allowed to cool for about 15 minutes before being potted, to prevent the fruit rising in the jars.

While the jam is still hot, the surfaces are covered with waxed discs, waxed-side down, then the jars are covered with dampened cellophane rounds secured with rubber bands or string. This may be done immediately, or the jam may be left until quite cold before the cellophane covers are put on.

Most preserves keep well for over a year if properly covered and stored, but their flavour deteriorates if they are kept for too long. The best idea, therefore, is to use them within the year, thus making room in the store-cupboard for next year's batch of preserves.

Jam-making Problems

Mould This is most often caused by failure to cover the jam with a waxed disc while it is still very hot – this should be done immediately the jam is potted, or it may become infected with mould spores from the air. Alternatively, the pots may have been damp or cold when used, or insufficiently filled, or they may have been stored in a damp or warm place. Other possible causes are insufficient evaporation of water while the fruit is being 'broken down' by the preliminary cooking, and/or too short a period of boiling after the sugar has been added. It is important not to eat jam that has mould growth on it as it produces toxins. Throw away the whole jar if you find any mould on the top surface.

Bubbles in the jam Bubbles indicate fermentation, which is usually the result of too small a proportion of sugar in relation to fruit; accurate weighing of fruit and sugar is very important. This problem can also occur, however, when jam is not reduced sufficiently, because this too affects the proportion of sugar in the preserve. Fermentation is harmless enough but it is apt to spoil both flavour and colour. Fermented jam can be boiled up again but the boiling should only be continued for a short time if the preserve was not reduced enough in the first instance. The jam can then be re-potted and sealed in clean, preheated jars and used for cooking purposes.

Peel or fruit rising in the jam Strawberry jam is particularly susceptible to this trouble. It helps if the jam is allowed to cool for 15–20 minutes and then given a stir before potting (despite the fact that it is normally advisable to pot all preserves as hot as possible).

Crystallized jam This is usually caused by lack of sufficient acid. You should either use a fruit rich in acid, or make sure that acid is added to the fruit during the preliminary softening process. Under- or over-boiling jam after the sugar has been added can also cause crystallization, as it will upset the proportion of sugar in the finished jam.

Setting problems One cause is the use of over-ripe fruit in which the pectin has deteriorated. Another reason is under-boiling of the fruit, so that the pectin is not fully extracted; there may also be insufficient evaporation of the water before the sugar is added (this can be remedied by further boiling); or over-cooking after adding the sugar, for which there is no remedy.

To ensure a set with fruits deficient in pectin, such as strawberries, it is helpful to add an acid such as lemon juice or citric acid; alternatively, mix with a pectin-rich fruit such as redcurrants, or a pectin extract.

Shrinkage of jam on storage This is caused by inadequate covering, or failure to store the jam in a cool, dark, dry place.

JAMAICA FLOWER (Flor de Jamaica, Jamaica Sorrel, Red Sorrel, Rosella) The red flower of a type of hibiscus plant which originated in Mexico and is now found in the West Indies and India. It is used to flavour a syrup that forms the basis of a popular drink, but may also be cooked and used as a vegetable or to make a savoury sauce. The red fruits of the same plant may be used to make jam.

JAMAICAN PEPPER (*see* ALLSPICE)

JAMBALAYA A popular Creole dish based on rice and similar to a Spanish *paella*. Other ingredients may include chicken, ham, sausage, prawns, crayfish and tomatoes. (*see also* CREOLE)

JAMBERRY (*see* TOMATILLO)

JAMBON BLANC (Jambon glacé, Jambon de Paris) This French cooking ham is available unsmoked or lightly smoked. It is usually boiled, but can be cooked in other ways. (*see also* HAM)

JAMBON D'ARDENNES A type of cured ham produced in Belgium. It is usually thinly sliced and eaten raw. (*see also* HAM)

JAMBON DE BAYONNE This dry-cured and lightly smoked ham is produced in France. It should be thinly sliced and eaten raw. (*see also* HAM)

JAMBON DE TOULOUSE An unsmoked variety of French ham that is salted and dried. It is eaten raw or cooked. (*see also* HAM)

JAMBONS DE CAMPAGNE A general name given to a number of French hams prepared according to local recipes. They are usually sweet-cured and smoked and are intended for cooking, though some varieties may be eaten raw. (*see also* HAM)

JAMÓN SERRANO (Mountain Ham) A high quality Spanish ham which is salted and air-dried. It is eaten raw as an hors d'oeuvre or in sandwiches.

JAPANESE ARTICHOKE (*see* ARTICHOKE, CHINESE)

JAPANESE GELATINE (*see* AGAR-AGAR)

JAPANESE MEDLAR (*see* LOQUAT)

JAPONAISE, À LA A French term used to describe various dishes containing or garnished with Chinese artichokes (called Japanese artichokes in France).

JAPONICA (Japanese Quince) The fruit of the japonica tree is the ornamental version of the quince. They do not always ripen on the tree but can be picked whilst green and stored for about a month until they begin to turn slightly yellow. They have a distinctive flavour and are often mixed with apples in a pie or when stewed, or can be made into a jelly. They cannot be eaten raw. (*see also* QUINCE)

JARDINIÈRE A French term which refers to dishes garnished with mixed fresh spring vegetables or green peas and sprigs of cauliflower.

JARLSBERG A wheel-shaped semi-hard Norwegian cheese with a yellow wax rind. The cheese is made from pasteurized cows' milk and is usually sold in wedges. It has a sweet, nutty flavour like Emmenthal, and also has similar holes in it.

JELLY (DESSERT) The basic method for making a dessert jelly is simply a matter of combining a flavoured liquid, such as fruit juice, with a setting agent, such as gelatine, and allowing it to set in a mould, then turning it out to serve. Home-made jellies containing fresh fruit and fruit juice are very simple to prepare and the flavour is much better than jellies made with commercial jelly tablets and crystals which contain mostly sugar, flavouring and colouring.

Jellies can also be made with other liquids, such as milk, or combinations of liquids, and may be added to other ingredients, such as whipped cream to make a mousse, or fruit purée and soft cheese to make a cheesecake. Jelly also forms a traditional constituent of trifle and a lightly set jelly may be used to glaze a fruit flan.

Most jellies are made with gelatine, a colourless, tasteless animal substance which sets liquid. It may be used in powdered or sheet (leaf) form. Agar-agar may also be used as a vegetarian alternative. (*see also* AGAR-AGAR, GELATINE)

Making a Jelly

When making fruit jellies, warm the liquid, sweeten and flavour it, then quickly stir in the dissolved gelatine. The more closely the two are to the same temperature, the more easily the gelatine can be evenly blended with the liquid. To hasten the set, heat half the liquid, add the gelatine, then combine with the remaining cold liquid. For the best flavour, allow jellied desserts to come to room temperature for about 1 hour before serving.

To Set Fruit in Jelly

Use fresh fruits such as black grapes, bananas, raspberries or orange segments. Do not use fresh pineapple and kiwi fruit as they contain an enzyme which breaks down gelatine and destroys its setting powers. Boil fresh pineapple juice for 2–3 minutes before using.

Pour about 2.5 cm (1 inch) clear jelly into a mould and arrange a little of the fruit in this. Allow the jelly to set. Add more jelly and fruit and allow to set; continue until the mould is filled.

To Line or Mask a Mould with Jelly

First prepare any decorations (such as sliced glacé cherries and pistachio nuts and cut angelica). Fill a large bowl with crushed ice and rest the wetted mould in it. Pour 30–45 ml (2–3 tbsp) cold but liquid jelly into the mould and rotate this slowly until the inside is evenly coated. Continue pouring in and setting cold liquid jelly until the whole surface is lined with a layer about 0.3 cm (¹/₈ inch) thick. Using two fine skewers, dip the decoration pieces into liquid jelly and place in position in the mould, allowing each piece to set firmly. Pour a thin coating over the decorations and allow to set before adding the cream mixture or other filling.

To Unmould a Jelly

Draw the tip of a knife or your finger around the rim of the mould to loosen the edge of the jelly. Immerse the mould in hot water for 2–3 seconds and place a wetted serving plate upside-down on top of the mould. Hold in position with both hands, then quickly invert plate and mould together, giving sharp shakes until the jelly drops on to the plate.

JELLY (PRESERVE) Jelly preserves are made in very much the same way as jams, but with an additional straining stage which produces a clear jelly made only from the juice and containing no pieces of fruit. Jellies take longer to make than jams and the yield from the fruit is not as high as with jams, but they are well worth the extra trouble. The most popular jellies include redcurrant (traditionally served with roast lamb) and crab apple, a beautiful pink sparkling sweet jelly which is delicious on bread and butter.

The equipment and method used for making jellies is similar to that used for jams (*see* JAM).

The Fruit

Only fruits giving a good set, that is those with a high pectin content (*see* JAM) are really suitable for jelly-making. Fruits with poor setting qualities can be combined with others with a higher pectin content.

Preparing the Fruit

Fruit for jelly-making needs very little preparation, though any damaged fruits should not be used. It is not necessary to peel or core fruit; just wash and roughly chop it. Any skin, core, stones or pips will be extracted when the pulp is strained.

Jelly-making

Cooking the Fruit

The first stage in jelly-making is to cook the fruit in water. The amount of water needed depends on how juicy the fruit is. Hard fruits should be covered with water. The cooking must be very slow and thorough to extract as much juice as possible, so only simmer the fruit gently until very tender. This takes from 30–60 minutes, depending on the softness of the fruit. To save time, particularly when using hard fruits, this stage of jelly-making can be done in a pressure cooker.

Straining off the Juice

After cooking, the fruit pulp is transferred to a jelly bag and left to drip until all the juice has been strained off. If a jelly bag is not available, a large piece of muslin or a double thickness of fine cloth (such as a tea towel or cotton sheet) can be used. Whatever is used should first be scalded in boiling water. Suspend the bag or cloth between the legs of an upturned chair or stool with a large bowl placed underneath to catch the dripping juice. Leave until the dripping has stopped (overnight if necessary) and do not be tempted to squeeze or poke the bag or the finished jelly will be cloudy.

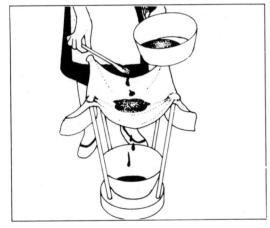

Spooning fruit pulp into a cloth attached to an upturned stool to strain off the juice.

Double Extraction

If a fruit that is very high in pectin is being used, a double extraction can be made to increase the final yield. After the first straining, the pulp should be cooked again in a little water and then strained again. The two juices are then combined.

Adding the Sugar

The next stage in jelly-making is to add the sugar to the juice. If necessary, the pectin test (*see* JAM) can be carried out beforehand. If the result is poor, put the juice in a pan, boil, then test again.

Measure the strained juice (known as the extract), put it in a preserving pan and add the sugar. About 600 ml (1 pint) extract rich in pectin will set with 450 g (1 lb) sugar, and 600 ml (1 pint) juice with a medium pectin content will set with 375 g (12 oz) sugar. Granulated sugar is suitable, though lump sugar or preserving crystals will cause less scum to be formed and will result in a clearer jelly. Stir the sugar into the juice, return the pan to the heat and bring to the boil, stirring until the sugar has dissolved. Continue boiling until setting point is reached, stirring occasionally. Test for setting point in the same way as for jam (*see* JAM). When setting point is reached (usually after boiling the jelly for about 10 minutes), remove any scum with a slotted spoon before quickly potting and covering as for jam (*see* JAM).

JELLY (SWEET) Under this heading come various popular sweets, including fruit jellies, *crèmes de menthe*, Turkish delight, marshmallows and jujubes, some of which are quite simple to make at home. There are several methods of stiffening the sugar syrup which is used for making them – by adding gelatine, gum arabic, blended cornflour or arrowroot; by reducing the syrup by fast boiling, or by boiling an acid with cornflour to hydrolize it.

The sweets may be set in small moulds, in sweet rings or in tins. The more experienced sweet-maker can use starch trays or moulds, the liquid syrup being poured into the impressions.

Fruit jellies are usually tossed in caster or icing sugar. Turkish delight and marshmallows are both tossed and packed in a mixture of cornflour and icing sugar, while other sweets are tossed in icing sugar alone.

(*see also* SWEETS)

JERKED BEEF (*see* CHARQUI)

JERKY (*see* CHARQUI)

JEROBOAM A bottle of wine, equivalent to four normal-sized bottles. For champagne, a jeroboam is equivalent to a double magnum.

JERUSALEM ARTICHOKE (*see* ARTICHOKE, JERUSALEM)

JICAMA (Jicana, Yam Bean) A root vegetable that is native to Central America and used a great deal in Oriental cooking. It has a thin brown skin and crisp, juicy white flesh and can be cooked and used like potato. It can also be thinly sliced and eaten raw in salads or dipped in lime juice and chilli pepper. In Oriental cooking, it is often stir-fried and used like water chestnuts.

JOHN DORY This ugly flat sea fish has very large jaws and a body that is nearly oval in shape, and olive-brown skin with a black 'thumb mark' on each side just behind the head. In France, the fish is known as *Saint-Pierre* and tradition has it that the thumb marks on the fish are those of Saint Peter who picked up the fish and threw it back into the water when fishing on the Sea of Galilee (which, in fact, could never have contained this sea fish). The name John Dory is derived from one of its French nicknames, *jean-doré*.

John Dory has firm, white flesh with a delicate flavour. The head and fins can be removed and the fish poached or baked whole, but it is more usually filleted and cooked like sole. John Dory is fished on both sides of the Atlantic and in the Mediterranean, and is available fresh in Britain from June to September. (*see also* SOLE)

JOINT The carcasses of animals intended for human consumption are cut up into different parts, known as joints or cuts. The names of these joints and the methods of cutting the carcasses vary in different parts of Britain, and still more so in other countries, but there is a fair amount of similarity between the general methods of cutting them up. (*see also* BEEF, LAMB, PORK, VEAL)

JOULE The name given to a unit of energy that is used to measure the amount of energy provided by different foods. The joule is now gradually replacing the calorie as the most appropriate unit for this use since the calorie is, strictly speaking, a unit of heat, not energy. A joule is also a smaller unit than a calorie and enables tests to be carried out to a greater degree of accuracy. Like the calorie, however, a joule is an extremely small measurement, too small for the purpose of measuring the energy values of foods, so they are used by the thousand and referred to as kilojoules. A unit known as a megajoule is also used – this is a thousand kilojoules. Calories can be approximately converted to kilojoules by multiplying by 4.2. (*see also* CALORIE)

JUGGED A traditional method of cooking hare in a tall covered pot. The hare is cut into portions and cooked until very tender and a rich dark brown in colour. The blood of the hare is added at the end of the cooking time. These days, jugged hare is usually cooked in the oven in a covered flameproof casserole. (*see also* RABBIT)

JUICE The liquid content of fruits and vegetables which can be extracted by hand or in an electric juice extractor. Small quantities of juice, from a lemon or orange for example, are extracted by using a lemon squeezer, while larger quantities from tough vegetables, such as carrots, are best produced by machine. A liquidizer can be used to reduce a fruit or vegetable to a pulp which can then be strained to separate the juice. Tomato juice can be produced by rubbing canned or very ripe peeled tomatoes through a sieve.

Fruit juices are frequently used in cooking. Lemon juice is often added to both sweet and savoury dishes, to provide flavour or acidity. Fruit juices also make refreshing and healthy drinks; some of them are particularly rich in vitamin C. Natural juices can also be used to make jellies, ice creams and water ices.

Many types of fruit juice can be bought in cartons, bottles and cans. As well as orange, apple and grapefruit juices, it is now possible to buy tropical fruit juices, either individually or mixed. The most expensive are pure natural 100 per cent fruit juices which must be kept chilled and used within a limited period. Other varieties, usually sold in waxed cartons, have been heat treated and have a longer shelf-life. These varieties do not need to be kept in the refrigerator before opening, but must be kept chilled and used within two to three days after opening. Bottles of concentrated fruit juice are available and need diluting before use. Apple juice concentrate can also be used as a sweetening substitute for sugar. Cans of concentrated fruit juice are available frozen, and must be thawed and diluted with water before use. There are also a confusing number of fruit juice *drinks* and *squashes* on the market. These are made up from varying amounts of real fruit juice and water and usually contain sugar as well as other colourings, flavourings and preservatives. When selecting commercially produced fruit juices, especially for young children and babies, it is important to read the labels to discover exactly what you are buying.

JUJUBE Originally the name of a shrub of the buckthorn family growing in the East, the fruit of

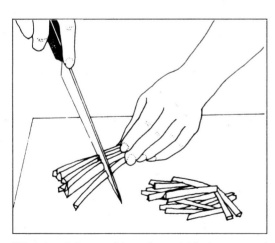

Trimming julienne strips of vegetable to an equal length.

which is eaten candied or made into jelly. The name is also applied to a sweet made of gelatine or gum arabic, water, sugar and flavourings. Jujubes are sometimes medicated or scented.

JULIENNE The French name given to vegetables or fruit rind cut into very fine strips of equal length. Vegetable *julienne* may be used raw as *crudités* or as a garnish or salad ingredient, or may be cooked. Fruit rinds cut in this way are often caramelized or simply cooked until soft and used as a garnish.

JULEP A drink which was popular in England, but is now better known in America. It is based on whisky or fruit brandy and is often flavoured with fresh mint. It is served with ice and a slice of lemon.

JUMBLE A small rich biscuit flavoured with lemon or almond. It is usually baked in the shape of an 'S' or in tiny rock-like heaps.

JUNIPER The name of a tree which grows in northern climates and produces small purple-black berries with an aromatic scent and a tang of pine. Juniper berries may be used fresh or dried, the dried berries having a stronger flavour than the fresh. They should be crushed before being added to a dish to release maximum flavour. They may be used with game, venison, pork and mutton, in marinades and casseroles with these ingredients, and in pâtés and *sauerkraut*. Juniper is also used as a flavouring agent in the manufacture of gin.

JUNKET An old-fashioned English milk pudding made by adding rennet to pasteurized milk, causing it to set. It is important not to use homogenized or UHT milk or the junket will not set properly. Do not overheat the milk, or cool the junket too rapidly as this may kill the rennet enzyme. Flavourings, including sugar, may be added, and the surface of the pudding may be sprinkled with grated nutmeg. Junket should not be disturbed until it is served as once it is cut it separates into curds and whey. (*see also* RENNET)

JUS, AU A French term used to describe meat that is served with the natural juices or gravy.

K

KABOCHA A round, medium-sized squash with a dark green ridged skin, similar to a small green pumpkin. This winter squash has recently appeared in the shops and can be baked or boiled and mashed like swede, or stuffed and baked, like marrow.

KAFFIR CORN (*see* MILLET)

KAHLUA A Mexican coffee liqueur which is based on rum, though it is quite different from Tia Maria (*see* TIA MARIA).

KAKI (*see* PERSIMMON)

KALE (Borecole, Collard Greens) There are many varieties of this leafy winter vegetable, both flat and curly. It is a member of the cabbage family but, like spring greens, does not form a heart. The most common variety is curly kale; borecole is a flat-leaved variety. Kale has a tough texture and a stronger flavour than other cabbages, but it is a good source of vitamins in the winter.
To select: Choose kale that is firm and green with no wilted yellow leaves. Allow 175–225 g (6–8 oz) per person.
To prepare: Trim off all but the small, tender stalks and discard any wilted or damaged leaves. Wash thoroughly in cold salted water and drain.
To cook: Cook in boiling salted water for 8–10 minutes or until tender but still crisp. Drain well and shred finely.
To serve: Serve hot with a knob of butter.

KANTEN (*see* AGAR-AGAR)

KANTOLA (Balsam Apple, Ucche) A small variety of bitter gourd that is much used in the cooking of China, India and the Far East. Kantolas have a thick, green, knobbly skin and contain seeds that are edible when the vegetable is young, but harden as it ripens. Kantolas can be sliced and made into soups or used in vegetable curries, or they can be stir-fried, or cooked in other ways suitable for courgettes (*see* COURGETTE). They have a bitter flavour and should be blanched or *dégorged* before cooking.

To select: Choose firm, bright green vegetables. Allow 100 g (4 oz) per person.
To prepare: Trim and scrub thoroughly. Slice the vegetables and place in a colander. Sprinkle with salt and leave to drain for about 1 hour, then rinse and dry with absorbent kitchen paper.
To cook: Prepared slices may be boiled, steamed, fried or stir-fried.
To serve: Serve as a vegetable accompaniment or in a mixed vegetable curry or stir-fry.

KARELLA (Balsam Pear, Bitter Gourd, Karela) This long pod-like vegetable is a member of the gourd family and is much used in Indian and Chinese cooking. It is closely related to the kantola (above) and looks something like a large okra with knobbly skin and edible red seeds. Its flavour is rather bitter and it is usually *dégorged* before being cooked.
To select: Choose firm, green pods, avoiding any that are brown or withered. Allow 100 g (4 oz) per person.
To prepare: Top and tail and scrape off the knobs. Slice the pods, place in a colander, sprinkle with salt and leave for 1 hour. Wash, drain and pat dry with absorbent kitchen paper.
To cook: Fry slices of karella gently in butter or oil.
To serve: Sprinkle with a little sugar and serve as a side dish with curry.

KASHA (*see* BUCKWHEAT)

KATSUOBUSHI The Japanese name for boned and dried bonito fish. Along with *kombu*, it is one of the main ingredients of *dashi*, a stock used in Japanese cooking. (*see also* BONITO, DASHI, KOMBU)

KEBAB This is the general name for a dish consisting of cubes of meat, fish, shellfish, fruit and vegetables which are cooked on metal or wooden skewers under a grill or on a barbecue. Kebabs are a speciality of Middle Eastern cookery, particularly when made with lamb or mutton. A true *doner kebab* is marinated boned leg of lamb roasted on a vertical spit. Thin slices are cut from the meat and served in pitta bread with salad. A *shish kebab* is made from cubes of lamb, tomato, onion and pepper threaded on to skewers and grilled or barbecued. The meat is often marinated before it is used to make kebabs. Meats other than lamb may also be used.

Kebabs may be served on their skewers, or the meat and vegetables may be removed for serving. Kebabs are usually served with rice and salad and accompanied by wedges of lemon. (*see also* BROCHETTE)

Threading cubes of meat on to kebab skewers prior to grilling.

KEDGEREE An English dish, traditionally served for breakfast, and consisting of rice mixed with flaked cooked or smoked fish (usually smoked haddock) and hard-boiled eggs. The dish is based on an Indian dish called *khichri* and first became popular in England in the eighteenth century. Nowadays, kedgeree may also be served as a light lunch or supper dish, accompanied by salad.

KEFIR A cultured milk product which originated in Russia and Poland. It is made from whole or skimmed cows' milk to which kefir grain is added. It differs from yogurt in that additional cultures are introduced which produce alcohol. Kefir is a milky white, slightly greasy, homogenous product resembling liquid cream. It has a lactic flavour and usually no additional flavour is introduced. It should be kept in a glass container which is resistant to pressure as carbon chloride is produced during storage. To allow a slight escape of gas, the jars usually have spring-loaded clip closures. (*see also* KOUMISS)

KELP (*see* SEA VEGETABLES)

KENTJOER (*see* ZEDOARY)

KETCHUP (Catsup) A type of table sauce with one predominating flavour, such as tomato, mushroom, cucumber or walnut. Ketchup is made by extracting the juice, boiling it down to a very concentrated form and seasoning it well.

KEWRA (Screwpine) Kewra trees grow in the swampy, humid areas of Kerala in southern India and produce flowers with a beautiful scent that is similar to that of roses. The flowers are used to make a flavouring that is used to flavour and perfume both sweet and savoury dishes.

KHAS-KHAS (Vetiver) An aromatic grass that is used in Indian cooking as a flavouring. *Khas-khas* is grown in India and in the southern United States and it is available in other countries in the form of *khas* water and *khas* syrup.

KHORESH An Iranian dish, similar to a soup or stew, served with rice. A *khoresh* usually consists of a combination of meat, fruit and nuts, often walnuts.

KIBBLED WHEAT (*see* CRACKED WHEAT)

KIBBLING This term generally means to grind or chop coarsely, but 'kibbled' wheat is treated in a slightly different way (*see* CRACKED WHEAT).

KID A young goat. Kid is seldom eaten in this country, but is popular in some Mediterranean regions. The flesh is sweet and tender if properly prepared, but inclined to be dry and a little lacking in flavour, so it is either marinated in a mixture of vinegar, oil and seasonings before cooking, or is stuck with slices of onion or sprigs of herbs.

Kid is usually roasted whole, like sucking pig. It should be thoroughly cleaned, then marinated for a few hours before being hung for a day or two. It is best larded (*see* LARDING) before cooking, seasoned and dredged with flour. It should be roasted as for lamb and served with mint sauce, fruit chutney or redcurrant jelly, as liked. (*see also* LAMB)

KIDNEY Classified as offal, kidney is a nutritious and economical meat that is a popular partner for steak in traditional steak and kidney pies and puddings. At one time, kidneys were a popular breakfast dish, served with grilled bacon, but are now most often served as a light supper dish or savoury.

Calf's kidney is light in colour, delicately flavoured and considered the best. Lamb's kidney is darker than calf's, smaller and with a good flavour. Pig and ox kidneys have a much stronger flavour; ox kidney needs slow moist cooking and is traditionally used in casseroles, puddings and pies.

Calf and lamb kidneys should be cooked quickly to be tender and are most frequently

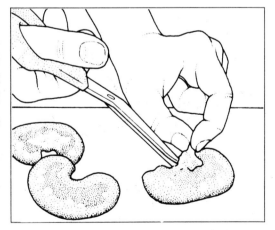

Using scissors to remove the white cores and tubes from halved kidneys.

grilled or fried. To prepare, remove the outer membrane, split in half lengthways and, using scissors, remove the white core tubes.

Grilled Kidneys

550–700 g (1¼–1½ lb) lamb's kidneys, washed, skinned and cored
45 ml (3 tbsp) vegetable oil
salt and pepper
grilled bacon, to serve

Thread the kidneys on to four skewers, cut-side uppermost. Brush with oil and sprinkle with salt and pepper. Cook under a hot grill for 3 minutes, uncut-side uppermost, then turn over to allow the juices to gather in the cut side and grill for a further 3 minutes. Serve immediately with grilled bacon.
Serves 4

KIDNEY BEAN (Haricot Bean) In common use, this name usually refers to the type of dried red bean that is added to *chilli con carne*. In fact, the original kidney bean, was a red, kidney-shaped type of French (haricot) bean, which was eaten fresh in its pod when still immature. The common green French bean we know today is descended from this first 'kidney' bean, as are several types of bean which are cultivated for use as dried beans. The group includes beans such as the flageolet, cannellino, haricot, borlotto and butter bean, as well as the red, black and white kidney beans. (For detailed information about individual beans, see separate entries.)

The common red kidney bean is dark red with white flesh and a full, strong flavour. Like other dried beans, red kidney beans should be soaked, preferably overnight, before cooking, then it is essential to boil them for at least 10 minutes at the start of the cooking time to kill the toxic haemoglutinens. They should not be included in a slow cooking casserole unless they have been pre-boiled. (*see also* PULSES)

KILOJOULE (*see* JOULE)

KIMCHI A Korean relish made from finely shredded vegetables, such as cabbage, onions, garlic and chillies, pickled in brine and flavoured with spices.

KING, À LA An expression used to describe dishes served in a rich cream sauce (often flavoured with sherry) and including mushrooms and green peppers.

KIPPER (*see* HERRING)

KIR (*see* CASSIS)

KIRSCH (Kirschwasser) Classified as an *eau-de-vie* rather than a liqueur, this is a stone fruit brandy, in which the crushed kernels are included with the fruit juice – in this instance, cherry. It is made in north-eastern parts of France, such as Alsace, and in the Black Forest region of Germany. It is often used as a flavouring in fruit compotes and other desserts. (*see also* EAU-DE-VIE)

KISHK A Lebanese and Syrian staple food made from a fermented mixture of bulgar, milk and yogurt. After drying, the mixture is turned to a fine powder and used to make a type of porridge.

KISSEL (Kisel) A classic eastern-European dessert made from puréed red berries or fruit juice thickened with arrowroot, cornflour or gelatine and sometimes flavoured with white wine. It is usually served cold with cream, but may also be served warm and is sometimes used as a sauce for savoury dishes.

KIWANO (Horned Melon) This small but striking-looking fruit has recently become available in Britain. It originated in Africa but is imported to Britain mostly from New Zealand. It has a tough, reddish-orange skin covered in spines similar to those on a horse chestnut. Inside, it has bright green watery flesh which contains large, flat, edible seeds, rather like those in a cucumber. The flesh is so soft it is best scooped out and eaten with a spoon.

KIWI FRUIT (Chinese Gooseberry, Kiwi) This is an egg-shaped fruit with brown hairy skin and bright green flesh pitted with edible black seeds. Kiwi fruit are native to China, but are now grown mainly in New Zealand.

Kiwi fruit are usually eaten raw but can be poached. They may be peeled and sliced and added to a fruit or savoury salad, or they are very often used as an attractive decoration. They have a very high vitamin C content.

To select: Choose firm fruit with no blemishes. A ripe kiwi fruit feels just soft to the touch.

To prepare: Cut in half and eat with a teaspoon, or peel and slice thinly.

KNACKWURST (*see* FRANKFURTER)

KNEADING A method used to combine the ingredients of a mixture (or dough) which is too stiff to stir. Kneading can be carried out by machine but is more usually done by hand. The mixture is gathered into a ball and placed on a board or work surface. If it is inclined to stick, the board should first be dusted with flour. It may also be necessary to dust hands with flour.

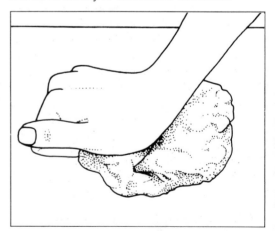

Kneading bread or pasta dough, folding it inwards, then pushing it away with the heel of the hand.

Pastry and scone doughs are kneaded lightly, the outside edges being brought into the centre of the mixture with the fingertips. Bread dough, which must be kneaded to distribute the yeast and gas evenly throughout the mixture and to strengthen the gluten for a good rise, needs firmer treatment. The easiest way to deal with it is to pull out the dough with the right hand, then fold it back over itself and push it away with the heel of the hand; give a quarter-turn and repeat the process.

KNICKERBOCKER GLORY An ice cream sundae which was very popular in the nineteen sixties. It consists of jelly, fruit, ice cream and whipped cream arranged in layers in a tall sundae glass.

KNOB CELERY (*see* CELERIAC)

KNOCK BACK To knead a yeast dough for a second time on a lightly floured surface for 2–3 minutes after rising. This knocks out any large air bubbles and ensures an even texture.

KNUCKLE A joint of pork or veal which consists of the lower part of the leg. Knuckle end (or hock) of pork is a popular roasting joint. The knuckle end (or shin) of veal is traditionally used to make the classic Italian dish *osso buco*, for which the joint is cut into 5 cm (2 inch) pieces. Ready-prepared *osso buco* pieces are available from the butcher. The hind knuckle of veal is usually meatier and tastier than the fore. A knuckle of lamb is the lower part of the shoulder. (*see also* LAMB, PORK, VEAL)

KOFTA The name given to various types of Middle Eastern meatballs, usually made from minced lamb, onion, garlic and spices.

KOHLRABI (Kohl Rabi, Turnip-Cabbage) This is a rather unusual-looking vegetable, belonging to the cabbage family and similar in size to a turnip. It is a swollen stalk, not a root, with leaves growing out from the surface. It can be white or purple skinned. Kohlrabi may be cooked and served hot as a vegetable accompaniment, or it may be grated or sliced very thinly and eaten raw.
To select: Choose small kohlrabi, no more than 5 cm (2 inches) in diameter, as larger ones can be very tough. Do not buy any with decaying leaves. Allow 100–175 g (4–6 oz) per person.
To prepare: Trim the base, cut off the leaves and stalks and peel the globe thinly. Alternatively, the vegetable can be cooked and peeled after cooking.
To cook: Cook in boiling salted water for 20–30 minutes, steam for 30–40 minutes, braise or fry. Cooked sliced kohlrabi is also delicious sautéed in melted butter for 5–10 minutes or until golden.
To serve: Grated raw kohlrabi adds a sweetness to a winter salad. Cooked kohlrabi should be served hot with a knob of butter and a sprinkling of parsley, or coated in a cheese sauce.

KOKUM (Cocum) The fruit of a tree that grows in India and belongs to the same family as the mangosteen (*see* MANGOSTEEN). The fruit contains large seeds from which kokum butter is made, and the flesh is dried and used in cooking, particularly in southern India. The dried fruits resemble prunes but have a more pronounced, sour flavour.

KOLA (*see* COLA)

KOMBU (*see* SEA VEGETABLES)

KORMA An Indian method of cooking that is similar to braising. The technique is used in cooking all over north and central India and is especially important in Mughlai dishes. Each region of India presents a different korma – there is a story of a grand chef who claimed to be able to cook a different version for every day of the month. Meat and poultry are often marinated in yogurt and spices, then cooked very slowly with some spices in the marinade. The finished dish is mild-flavoured and creamy. Kormas have now become popular all over the world – wherever there is an Indian restaurant.

KOSHER (Kasher) A name used to describe food prepared according to orthodox Jewish laws.

KOULIBIAC (*see* COULIBIAC)

KOUMISS (Kumiss) A sour-tasting weak alcoholic beverage similar to *kefir* (*see* KEFIR). *Koumiss* is made from mares' milk which has a fat content of 1.7 per cent. A culture and yeast are added to give the sour taste. It is a milky white mixture with a grey tinge; the texture is similar to that of cream except that it is permeated by small gas bubbles. A characteristic odour reflects the alcoholic content and sour taste.

Koumiss originated in Russia where it was at one time widely used in the treatment of tuberculosis as, like other cultured milk products, it was thought to have therapeutic value.

KROMESKI (Kromesky) A Russian and Polish dish, consisting of a mixture of minced poultry, game or meat, bound to a stiff paste with sauce and wrapped in bacon, then coated with batter and fried. *Kromeski* may be served as an hors d'oeuvre or light main course.

KRUPEK (Krupuk) Similar to the Chinese prawn crisp and the Indian poppadom, the *krupek* is a large Indonesian crisp pancake made from dried prawns. These crisps are available ready-made in Indonesia and are deep fried before being drained and served as an accompaniment.

KUCHAI (*see* CHINESE CHIVE)

KUDZU (*see* KUZU)

KUGELHOPF (Gougelhopf, Guglhupf) A sweetened yeast cake of Austrian origin which contains dried fruit and is baked in a special deep, fluted tube tin.

KÜMMEL The German word for caraway, and the name of a caraway-flavoured, colourless liqueur of Dutch origin.

KÜMMELKASE A German cheese, flavoured with caraway. It is good served with cocktails.

KUMQUAT A close relative of the citrus fruit family, this is a tiny fruit with a smooth, orange, edible skin and an unusual sour-sweet flavour. Kumquats originated in China but are now cultivated in many countries, including Spain, Israel, Morocco, Brazil and California. They may be eaten raw, including the skin (which contains most of the sweetness), but may also be candied or made into preserves. Kumquat slices make attractive decorations for desserts or cakes.

In recent years, the kumquat has been used to produce a number of hybrid citrus fruits, including the limequat and citrangequat.

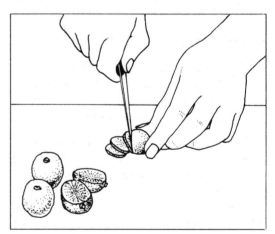

Slicing kumquats thinly for use as a decoration or garnish.

KUZU (Kudzu) A thickening agent used in Chinese and Japanese cooking, *kuzu* is derived from the edible roots of a type of vine. The roots are soaked in water until only the *kuzu* remains. This is dried and ground into a powder and can be used in the same way as arrowroot or cornflour to thicken sauces or to make a glaze.

KVASS A Russian home-brewed drink made from rye, malt and yeast and often flavoured with mint or juniper.

L

LABIATES The generic name for a group of plants with the same botanical structure, namely a corolla or calyx which is divided in two parts, suggesting lips. Labiates often have aromatic leaves and many of the most common herbs belong to the group, such as mint, basil, sage, thyme and rosemary. Some vegetables are also labiates, such as the Chinese artichoke.

LACHSSCHINKEN A German ham made from smoked fore loin of pork wrapped in white pork fat and tied with string. It is eaten raw, sometimes accompanied by horseradish.

LACTIC ACID An acid that is produced naturally by bacteria which develop in fermenting food, especially when sugar of some sort is present. It is produced in milk as it goes sour and acts as a preservative, turning conditions too acid for the development of other micro-organisms which would otherwise make the milk unfit for consumption. Lactic acid is also produced and acts as a preservative in the making of *sauerkraut* and other pickled foods, and is also present in yogurt.

LACTOSE (*see* SUGAR)

LADIES' FINGERS (*see* OKRA)

LAGER A type of beer which can be dark or pale. The original lager was produced in Bohemia for centuries and for a long time in Germany, but it is now produced in a lighter form in many other countries, including Australia, America and Canada. Although based on hops, the process is slightly different from beer-making. Lager is a carbonated drink which is at its best when served chilled. (*see also* BEER)

LAMB Sheep have been domesticated all over the world for thousands of years and are bred for their wool as well as their meat. In Victorian times, the meat of an older sheep was preferred and known as mutton. Nowadays, mutton is considered tough and only fit for boiling, and tender young lambs, killed before they are a year old, are preferred. Most of the lamb available in Britain is home-produced or imported frozen from New Zealand, where it is produced on a massive scale. It is an important meat in many countries, especially those where beef and pork are not eaten, such as in many Middle Eastern countries.

The meat of young sheep is particularly tender and all the joints can be roasted. This is because lambs are slaughtered before their connective tissues become tough, so the tissues dissolve easily in the meat's natural juices during cooking. Cuts, such as chops and cutlets from the neck, are also suitable for grilling or frying. Other neck cuts are ideal for casseroles, stews and pies.

The fat in lamb should be crisp and white with the lean fine-grained, firm and pinky-brown. There is usually very little gristle. Freshly cut surfaces should look slightly moist and the bones be pinkish-white. (*see also* MEAT)

Cuts and Methods of Cooking

Scrag and middle neck are usually sold as neck cuts on the bone and used for stewing or braising. They are the traditional cuts for Irish stew or Lancashire hot-pot. The main 'eye' of lean meat from the middle neck is now sold as 'fillet of lamb' and is ideal for grilling.

Shoulder is a succulent, tender roasting joint, whether on the bone, or boned, stuffed and rolled. Sold whole or halved into blade and knuckle, both of which are good for roasting or braising. The shoulder or forequarter can be cut into chop-size portions which are ideal for grilling or braising.

Best end of neck can be purchased as a roasting joint with a row of six or seven rib bones. The butcher will chine the backbone, to make carving easier. This is sometimes called 'rack of lamb'. It can be roasted on the bone, or boned, stuffed and rolled. It is also sold as cutlets with one rib bone to each, for grilling or frying. When boned and rolled, they are called noisettes. Two best end necks joined together and curved, bones outwards, make a 'crown roast'. Facing each other, fat-side outwards, they make a 'guard of honour'. Both these special occasion dishes can be stuffed before roasting (*see* CROWN OF LAMB OR PORK, GUARD OF HONOUR).

Loin consists of both chump and loin chops. It can be roasted in the piece, or boned, stuffed and rolled. Loin is usually divided into loin end and chump end, and cut into chops for grilling or frying. Chump chops are recognizable by the small round bone in the centre; loin chops are recognizable by the small 'T' bone.

Saddle of lamb is a large roasting joint for special occasions, which is the whole loin, from both sides of the animal, left in one piece. Double loin chops (Barnsley chops) are cut from a saddle of lamb. It is advisable to give the butcher notice if you require these cuts.

Leg is an excellent roasting joint on the bone, or boned, stuffed and rolled. The leg is often divided into fillet end and shank end. The round leg bone steaks are better for baking or braising than grilling or frying.

Breast is a long, thin cut, streaked with fat and lean. When boned, rolled and stuffed, it is the most economical cut for roasting or braising. Riblets of lamb breast make a suitable alternative to pork spare ribs for barbecuing, pan roasting, grilling, etc.

Minced or diced lamb is a quick and convenient way to purchase lamb for dishes such as shepherd's pie, moussaka, kebabs, casseroles, stews, etc.

To Roast Lamb

For succulent meat with less shrinkage, lamb should be roasted at 180°C (350°F) mark 4. Weigh the joint as it is to be cooked (on the bone or boned and rolled or stuffed) and cook for 25 minutes per 450 g (1 lb) plus 25 minutes.

Roast lamb is often flavoured with sprigs of rosemary; traditional accompaniments are mint sauce or jelly and redcurrant jelly. (*see also* CARVING)

Grilling and Frying Lamb

4 lamb chump or loin chops
15 ml (1 tbsp) vegetable oil

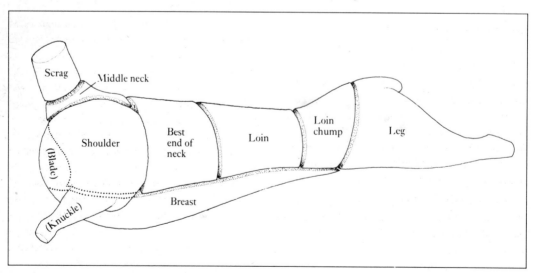

Major cuts of lamb to be found at your butcher.

Frying
Heat the oil in a frying pan and add the chops. Cook for about 15 minutes, turning frequently.

Grilling
Brush the chops with the oil. Place on the grill and grill under a moderate heat for 6–8 minutes each side.

LAMB'S FRY A collective name for lamb's liver, sweetbread, heart and some of the inside fat or 'leaf'.

LAMB'S LETTUCE (Corn Salad, Mâche, Marche) A small-leaved, green winter plant which is not a true lettuce, despite its name. It originated as a wild plant in Europe and is now cultivated in France and Italy. It is becoming increasingly available in Britain, usually separated in leaves and pre-packed. The leaves add a sweet flavour to winter salads, or it can be used as a garnish.

LAMB'S WOOL An old English drink, mentioned by Pepys, made by pouring hot ale over pulped roasted apples and adding sugar and spices.

LAMPERN A fish resembling a small lamprey which may be cooked like eel. (*see also* EEL, LAMPREY)

LAMPREY An eel-like fish, which can reach a considerable size, and was formerly considered a great delicacy. Like eels, lampreys are basically sea fish but they migrate upriver to spawn. The fish are still popular in Spain, Portugal and parts of France; they may be prepared like eels, but require longer cooking. (*see also* EEL)

LANCASHIRE CHEESE A fairly hard English cheese, crumbly in texture when cut. When new it has a mild, tangy flavour, which develops considerably as the cheese matures. Most Lancashire cheese is made in commercial dairies from pasteurized cows' milk. The farmhouse variety of Lancashire, made from the unpasteurized curds of two days' milking, has a much stronger flavour. Lancashire can be enjoyed cooked or uncooked. It has good melting properties and is ideal for making cheese on toast.

LANCASHIRE HOT-POT (*see* HOT-POT)

LAND CRESS (American Cress) This plant originated as a weed in Europe and America. It tastes somewhat like watercress but has the advantage of not needing the extremely wet conditions needed to cultivate watercress. Land cress is now cultivated in Europe and is a useful mustard-flavoured salad vegetable that is available in winter.

LAND JAGER (*see* SAUSAGE)

LANGOUSTE (*see* CRAWFISH)

LANGOUSTINE (*see* SCAMPI)

LANGUES DE CHATS Meaning, literally, 'cats' tongues', this French name is applied to small, flat, crisp, sweet biscuits that are a popular accompaniment to creamy desserts.

LAOS POWDER (*see* GALANGAL)

LAPWING (*see* PLOVER)

LARD The inside fat of a pig, which is melted down, freed from fibrous materials and stored in airtight containers for future use. The best-quality lard (sometimes called 'leaf' lard) comes from the abdomen and round the kidneys. Ordinary commercial lard comes from fat from all parts of the pig. It is a soft, white fat with a distinctive flavour.

Lard is suitable for pastry making, but is inclined to make cakes heavy, so is better mixed with butter or margarine for this purpose. It is suitable for both deep and shallow frying. As pure lard is 99 per cent fat, it does not splutter when heated and it has a high 'smoking' temperature (that is, it can be heated to a high temperature – not less than 182°C (360°F) – before it smokes and burns).

Being an animal fat, lard is high in saturated fatty acids and is best avoided by anyone wishing to reduce their blood cholesterol levels. Vegetable oils make good substitutes for frying purposes. Lard is also not suitable for vegetarian use and is usually replaced by solid hydrogenated vegetable oils. (*see also* FATS)

LARDING To insert small strips of fat bacon (called lardons) into the flesh of game birds, poultry and meat before roasting to prevent it drying out during cooking. A special larding needle is used. Today, because of the texture of British meat, larding is usually done more for decorative effect.

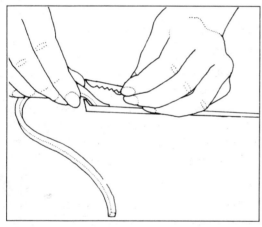

Attaching a thin strip of fat bacon *(lardon)* to a special larding needle before threading into meat.

LARDY CAKE A type of cake made in England with bread dough, lard, sugar and dried fruit. It is mostly found in Berkshire, Wiltshire and Oxfordshire.

LARK This small wild bird is seldom eaten in Britain today. Larks used to be served chiefly in pies, though they were also roasted, grilled and set in aspic. They are caught in nets and are still considered a great table delicacy on the Continent, though EC legislation may soon prohibit the capture of all species of lark. (*see also* BIRD)

LASAGNE (*see* PASTA)

LASSI A popular Indian yogurt drink, *lassi* is highly nourishing, refreshing and cooling and is a favourite all over India during the hot summer months. It consists of diluted natural yogurt and can be flavoured with all sorts of whole or ground and roasted spices. It can be sweet or savoury and flavoured according to taste.

LAVER (*see* SEA VEGETABLES)

LAX This is the Swedish, Norwegian and Icelandic name for salmon, but is generally applied to smoked salmon packed in oil. (*see also* GRAVAD LAX)

LAYER CAKE (Sandwich Cake) A sponge cake baked in two, three or more separate tins, the layers being put together when cold. Each layer can be spread with jam, cream, butter cream icing or other filling and the top or the complete cake may be coated with an icing. (*see also* CAKE)

LEAVEN Originally, this was the name of a piece of dough saved from one batch, refreshed and used to ferment and produce a rise in the next batch of bread. This method of leavening was used in the days before yeast was generally available. Nowadays, leaven is an alternative name for any raising agent (usually yeast or baking powder) used in dough. (*see also* RAISING AGENT)

LEBERWURST A German liver sausage made from pork, pigs' liver, onions and seasonings. (*see also* LIVER SAUSAGE)

LEEK A vegetable belonging to the same family as the onion and garlic, although it does not form a bulb. Its flavour is mild but distinctive. The lower part of the stem is 'earthed up' (that is the earth is built up around it) so that it remains white. Leeks are now available all year round, though they are at their best from November to March. They are excellent in soups (such as cock-a-leekie and *vichyssoise*), stews and casseroles or served as an accompanying vegetable. They make an excellent flavouring in a quiche and may also be used raw in salads.

To select: Choose small, young, firm leeks which have white stalks and fresh green leaves. Allow 1–2 leeks per person.

To prepare: Trim the root and top and slit down the length or slice crossways. Wash well under cold running water to remove all dirt and grit. It may require several washings to remove all the grit from between the layers. To use whole, trim and cut a slit of a few inches through the outer layers as these will harbour the most dirt. Put them, leaf downwards, tightly packed, into a deep container full of cold water and leave for at least 30 minutes.

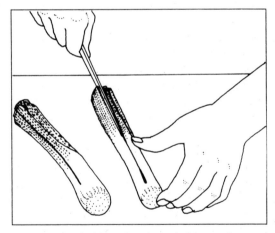

Cutting a slit of a few inches through the outer layers of whole leeks prior to thorough washing.

To cook: Cook in boiling salted water for 10–15 minutes, steam for 15–20 minutes or braise whole, in enough stock to cover, for about 1 hour.

To serve: Leeks are usually served hot with herbs or a sauce. Alternatively, allow to cool and serve with French Dressing.

LEGUME The generic name for a group of vegetables which consist of a bi-valved (two-sided) pod enclosing seeds attached along one join. Included in the group are peas, beans and lentils. Unlike most vegetables, legumes are a good source of protein and, when fresh, also supply some vitamins A and C. Dried legumes, called pulses, are important in various parts of the world where animal protein foods are scarce. They are also important in a vegetarian diet. (*see also* PULSES)

LEICESTER CHEESE Also known as Red Leicester, this is a hard English cheese with a mild, slightly sweet flavour and an orange-red colour. It is made from pasteurized cows' milk, the red colour being produced by the addition of annatto. It is a popular snack cheese.

LEIDEN (*see* LEYDEN)

LEMON One of the world's great fruits, the lemon is a member of the citrus family which, although too sour to eat raw, is used in countless ways in both sweet and savoury recipes. Lemons are available all year round, imported from such countries as Spain, Cyprus and South America.

The grated rind and juice of lemons can be used in puddings, cakes, pies, fruit drinks and in preserves such as lemon curd and marmalade, as well as in many savoury dishes, sauces and dressings. Lemon juice is an excellent source of pectin and is used in jams. It may also be brushed on the cut surfaces of fruits and vegetables to prevent discoloration. Lemon wedges are traditionally served with some foods, such as fish and pancakes, to be squeezed over just before eating. Lemon slices, twists, wedges and shreds make attractive garnishes for both sweet and savoury dishes.

To select: Look for lemons which are a strong 'lemon yellow' in colour, have a moist looking skin and feel heavy for their size. A shrivelled skin indicates that some of the juice has probably evaporated.

To prepare: If using the rind, lemons should be thoroughly scrubbed before use to remove any glazing or preservative substances. Lemons are quickly and easily sliced for adding to drinks or using as a garnish. To extract the juice, cut in half and use a lemon squeezer. When grating lemon rind, make sure that none of the bitter tasting white pith is grated. To thinly pare lemons, peel the rind with a vegetable peeler, avoiding any white pith.

LEMONADE Traditionally, this is the name of a refreshing home-made drink made from fresh lemons, water and sugar. Nowadays, however, it often refers to a commercially-produced sweet fizzy drink, the flavour of which bears little or no resemblance to lemon, but which is popular with children and as a 'mixer' with vermouth.

LEMON BALM (Balm) This herb is a member of the mint family with green, heart-shaped leaves and a tendency, like mint, to take over a whole garden unless controlled by being planted in a bottomless container sunk in the earth to contain the roots. It has a lemony smell and taste and is good with fish, poultry and ham dishes and in marinades. It also adds flavour to punches and fruit drinks and makes an excellent herbal tea.

LEMON CURD (*see* CURD)

LEMON GRASS Lemon grass is grown mostly in tropical and sub-tropical countries but is imported to the West in fresh and dried forms and as a powder (*sereh*). It has thick, grass-like leaves which smell and taste strongly of lemon. It is most often used in the cooking of Sri Lanka and South Asia to flavour curries and meat dishes. It can also be used with fish and to flavour sweet puddings.

LENTIL Classified as a pulse, a lentil is a small dried seed from a variety of leguminous plants which originated in the Middle East. Lentils may be red, brown or green. Unlike other pulses, lentils do not need soaking before cooking. The red lentils cook quickly to a purée and are good in soups and sauces. Brown lentils also cook quickly but keep their shape for use in casseroles or salads. (*see also* MASOOR, PULSES)

LETTUCE A common green leaf vegetable usually used raw in a salad, though it may also be braised or stir-fried and served as a vegetable or made into a chilled soup. The first lettuce was introduced into England in the sixteenth century and up until only a short time ago it was only possible to buy two or three varieties of lettuce. In recent years, however, our choice has widened greatly as more and more new varieties have appeared in the shops.

Types of Lettuce
Webb's Wonder, Iceberg and Great Lakes are large compact solid lettuces which stay very crisp.
Cos (Kos) or Romaine lettuces have long, crisp, green leaves, pale green hearts and a deliciously sweet taste.
Baby Cos lettuce (Little Gem, Sugar Cos) is excellent in salads.
Round (cabbage) lettuces are available all year round but have less flavour than other summer varieties and their soft leaves have a tendency to bruise. They are also known as butterhead lettuces.
Feuille de Chêne (Oak Leaf or Red Oak Leaf) is a lettuce with deep bronze, serrated leaves and a mild but distinctive flavour.
Lollo Rosso (Red Lollo) and Lollo Biondo (Green Lollo) are Italian lettuces with frilly leaves. They have a good flavour and are wonderfully decorative.
Quattro Stagioni (Four Seasons) is another Italian lettuce. It is round with dimpled, soft but glossy leaves tipped with red. Its leaves are less tightly curled than a normal round green lettuce.

Other vegetables which are similar to lettuce and may be used in the same way, but are not true lettuces, include lamb's lettuce (corn salad), dandelion leaves and Batavian endive.
To select: Choose lettuces with crisp green leaves and no brown or slimy patches. Allow one lettuce per person when cooked; $1/4$–$1/2$ of a medium lettuce served raw.

To prepare: Trim the base stalk and remove any damaged outer leaves. Separate the remaining leaves and wash in a bowl of cold water, *not* under running cold water which could wilt them. Dry thoroughly and tear the leaves into pieces. Try not to cut with a knife as this damages them, causing loss of vitamins and may cause discoloration.

To cook: The crisper leaves give the best results when cooked. To stir-fry, heat 15–30 ml (1–2 tbsp) vegetable oil in a large frying pan or wok, add whole or shredded leaves and stir-fry over a high heat for 2–3 minutes until the lettuce is just beginning to soften. Serve immediately with a good sprinkling of salt and pepper.

Whole lettuce hearts may also be braised for 25–30 minutes.

To serve: Lettuce is usually served raw in salads but may be cooked as above and served as a vegetable accompaniment.

LEUQKUAS (*see* GALANGAL)

LEVERET (*see* RABBIT)

LEYDEN (Leiden) A highly flavoured semi-hard Dutch cheese made from pasteurized whole or skimmed cows' milk. It has a red wax outer coating over a yellow rind and the cheese itself usually contains cumin and caraway seeds, though one version of the cheese is flavoured with cloves.

LIAISON Originating in classic French cookery, this term is used to describe any combination of ingredients which is used for thickening or binding sauces, soups, stews, etc. The ingredients of a liaison are usually flour, cornflour, arrowroot, rice or potato flour or egg yolk. Commonly used *liaisons* include *beurre manié* and roux.

LIGHTS The lungs of sheep, bullocks, calves or pigs, mostly used in Britain for pet food and only very occasionally for human consumption. Lights from cattle have now been banned for use in any meat product for human consumption, following concern over the disease BSE (*see* BOVINE SPONGIFORM ENCEPHALOPATHY). Lights may, however, be used in other countries in various meat preparations, such as pâtés and faggots, and are occasionally cooked in France.

LIMA BEAN (*see* BUTTER BEAN)

LIMBURGER (Limburg) A soft, whole cows' milk cheese made in Belgium (and also in Germany and Alsace), from December to May. It is full flavoured and strong smelling with a reddish-brown skin.

LIME This small green citrus fruit is far more widely available than it used to be and can usually be found all year round, imported from Florida, Brazil, the West Indies or Mexico. It is similar to the lemon, but with a thin green skin and a stronger, sharper flavour. The juice and rind are used in some ice creams and sorbets, curries and preserves (such as lime marmalade), and slices can be used in drinks and cocktails instead of lemon. Thin slices and twists of lime make popular garnishes. Limes should be selected and prepared in the same way as lemons (*see* LEMON).

LIME BLOSSOM The dried flowers of the lime (linden) tree can be infused to make a pleasant, delicately flavoured tea or tisane, which used to be regarded as a medicinal drink for debility, indigestion and sleeplessness.

LIME, DRIED Dried limes are frequently used in Middle Eastern and Oriental cooking. They can be bought in Asian or Chinese food shops in Britain either whole or in halves, or as shredded peel.

LIMEQUAT A hybrid citrus fruit produced by crossing a lime with a kumquat. Like the kumquat, it is a small fruit with thin edible skin, which is green in colour, but the flavour of limequats is very sour, too sour for most tastes when eaten raw. They make an attractive and unusual garnish, however.

LIMPET There are two varieties of this small single-shelled (univalve) sea creature – one is common on the Atlantic coast, while the other is found in the Mediterranean. Limpets can be prepared, cooked and served like cockles or periwinkles and may also be fried or used in soup and in scalloped dishes like mussels. They can sometimes be rather tough. (*see also* COCKLE, MUSSEL, SHELLFISH)

LINE To give a protective or decorative covering to the base and sides of a cooking container, for example with greaseproof or non-stick paper when baking cakes; with pastry when making suet puddings or flans; or with bacon for pâtés.

LING (Sea Burbot) This sea fish is a member of the cod family and, in fact, very much resembles cod, though it is longer and more slender. It was at one time prolific in the North Sea but is rarely available fresh these days, though it can be bought salted or smoked. If bought fresh, it should be prepared and cooked as for cod. (*see also* COD)

LINGONBERRY (*see* COWBERRY)

LINZERTORTE A classic Austrian torte named after the town of Linz. It is a type of flan with a base made from an almond-flavoured pastry, and filled with raspberry jam. The top of the torte is decorated with a lattice of pastry. *Linzertorte* may be served warm or cold as a dessert or with morning or afternoon coffee. It is traditionally served with *Schlagsahne*, an Austrian version of Chantilly cream lightened with whisked egg whites.

LIPTAUER A German cheese spread, traditionally made from fresh ewes' milk cheese mixed with cream, paprika, capers, anchovies, onions, caraway seeds and other flavourings according to taste. A simpler version can be made by combining cottage cheese and Cheddar cheese with butter and flavouring with chives, onion, caraway seeds and chopped anchovies. Liptauer can be served as a starter with wholemeal toast.

LIQUEUR An alcoholic drink that is served as a *digestif*, that is at the end of a meal, though various liqueurs are increasingly used in cooking sweet dishes too. Alcohol, an essential ingredient in all liqueurs, may be in the form of grape spirit, grain spirit or fruit spirit. Sweetening is added and the wide variety of flavourings come from herbs, spices or fruit. (*see also* ABRICOTINE, ADVOCAAT, AMARETTO DI SARONNO, ANISETTE, etc.)

LIQUORICE (Licorice) A leguminous plant which grows wild in Europe, though it was at one time cultivated in Yorkshire near Pontefract, the home of the famous liquorice-flavoured Pontefract cakes. The plant is now cultivated in other countries, including France. Black liquorice juice is prepared from the roots of the liquorice plant and is used to make many popular sweets, including Pontefract cakes, and to flavour medicines.

LISTERIA (*see* FOOD POISONING)

Opposite: Herbs: 1. Sage; 2. Parsley; 3. Chives; 4. Garlic; 5. Bay leaves; 6. Rosemary; 7. Tarragon; 8. Basil; 9. Dill; 10. Marjoram; 11. Mint; 12. Chives; 13. Fennel; 14. Curly leafed parsley; 15. Italian parsley; 16. Coriander; 17. Thyme

Overleaf: Left (from top to bottom), Escarole, Curly endive (Frisée), Radicchio, Chicory (Witloof), Broad leafed endive; **Right**, Moussaka
Centre Pages: Salmagundi

LITCHI (*see* LYCHEE)

LIVER The most popular of the offal meats, liver is renowned as a rich source of iron and is most often cooked with bacon and onions. The best liver is calf's (veal liver), followed by lamb's, pig's and ox, which is coarse and strong flavoured. Calf's, lamb's and pig's liver can be grilled, fried or used in braised dishes. Pig's and ox livers are mainly used in stews and casseroles or minced for pâtés and stuffings. The strong flavour of ox and pig's liver can be mellowed by soaking for an hour in milk. Chicken livers are also available, often frozen, and can be fried and served on toast or used to make pâté. (*see also* FOIE GRAS)

Calf's and lamb's liver are usually sold sliced. The outer membrane should be carefully peeled off and any internal ducts removed before cooking. Liver needs only a short cooking time – usually 5–10 minutes; overcooking will make it tough. It is particularly good stir-fried with garlic and spring onions.

LIVER SAUSAGE (Liverwurst) There are many varieties of liver sausage, made in many countries of the world. They are usually made from finely minced pigs' liver, pork and flavourings and have a soft, spreadable texture. All liver sausages have been cooked and are bought ready-to-eat, often sliced. They may be served with cold meats and salads, used in sandwiches or spread on toast like pâté. (*see also* LEBERWURST)

LOACH A small British river fish of the carp family; it is prepared like the smelt (*see* CARP, SMELT).

Previous Pages: Left, Kedgeree; **Right, Mushrooms**: (top row from left) Oyster mushrooms, brown closed cup cultivated mushrooms; (middle row from left) Horn of plenty, *Pied de mouton* (wood hedgehog), cultivated flat mushroom; (bottom row from left) Fairy ring mushroom, cultivated button mushroom, Chanterelles
Opposite: Stuffed papaya

LOAF A quantity of bread baked in a particular shape, usually of a standard weight. The name is also given to meat mixtures cooked in the same shape of tin, and to teabreads.

LOBSCOUSE A sailors' stew of meat and vegetables, dating back to the eighteenth century, now considered a Liverpudlian speciality.

LOBSTER A sea crustacean of which there are several types; the most common are the European lobster, which has the finest flavour, the spiny lobster (*see* CRAWFISH) and the flat lobster. Lobster is dark blue when alive and bright pink when cooked. It is often sold ready-boiled but many recipes call for a live lobster and, for absolute freshness, a lobster is best bought alive and killed and cooked at home. Female lobsters may contain eggs in the form of an orange coral. Lobster is in season all year but at its best in the summer months, and may be difficult to obtain from December to April. Lobster meat is often available frozen.

Lobster has long been considered a luxury and is generally reserved for special occasions or for when eating out. Classic lobster dishes include Lobster Newburg and Lobster Thermidor. (*see also* AMÉRICAINE, À L')

To select: Live lobsters should be active and feel heavy for their size. Their shells should feel hard and they should have good-sized claws. Cooked lobsters should smell fresh and their tails should spring back when opened out. A floppy lobster has probably been cooked for some time. Look for signs of discoloring at the front end of the tail – this is a sign that the lobster has not been cooked properly or had been dead for some time before cooking. One average-sized lobster (450 g-1.4 kg/1–3 lb) is enough to serve two people.

To prepare and boil: If a lobster has been bought alive, ask the fishmonger to weigh it, then kill and cook by one of the following methods:

Boil a large saucepan of water vigorously, then let it become completely cold. Immerse the lobster in the water and leave for 30 minutes. The lack of oxygen renders the lobster unconscious before it is put over the heat. Bring to the boil slowly, then simmer gently for 8 minutes per 450 g (1 lb). Lift the lobster out of the pan, set it aside and leave to cool completely.

Alternatively, bring a large saucepan of water to the boil, grasp the lobster by the back and drop it into the water, covering the pan with a lid and weighing it down for the first 2 minutes. Simmer gently for 12 minutes for the first 450 g (1 lb), 10 minutes for the next 450 g (1 lb) and 5 minutes more for each additional 450 g (1 lb). Lift out of the pan, set aside and leave to cool completely.

Alternatively, you can kill a lobster before cooking it or before grilling it, so it is not over-cooked. Keeping your hands clear of the claws, put the lobster, shell-side up, on a work surface. Place a cleaver in the centre of the cross-shaped mark behind the head and hammer it down with one sharp blow. The lobster may still twitch a little, but that is only reflex action. Cook the lobster in the same way as the second method above or prepare and grill as below.

To grill: Split the lobster lengthways and remove the intestine, stomach and gills. Brush the shell and flesh with melted butter and grill the flesh side for 8–10 minutes, then turn the lobster and grill the shell side for 5 minutes.

Dot the flesh with small pieces of butter, sprinkle with a little salt and cayenne pepper and serve with melted butter.

To serve: Lobster may be served in the half shell, or the meat may be removed from the shell before serving. The claw meat is considered by some to have the best flavour and it is necessary to break open the claws with a hammer or crackers in order to extract the meat. Cold cooked lobster meat may be sliced or shredded and served in a mayonnaise, with Green Goddess dressing or with hollandaise sauce.

LOCUST (*see* INSECTS)

LOCUST BEAN (*see* CAROB)

LOGANBERRY A hybrid fruit produced by crossing a blackberry with a raspberry. Loganberries look like large, dark red raspberries, with a flavour similar to raspberries but stronger. They may be used in the same ways as raspberries (*see* RASPBERRY).

LOIN A joint of lamb, pork or veal that consists of part of the backbone and some of the lower ribs from one side of the animal. The loin is considered one of the best parts of all these animals and the whole joint is suitable for roasting or braising, either on the bone or boned, stuffed and rolled. It is also often sold cut into chops for grilling or frying. The chump end of a loin of lamb is the end nearest the tail, the rib end being known as the loin end. A saddle of lamb consists of both loins and the backbone in one joint.

A loin of pork is divided into the fore loin and the hind loin. The hind loin is considered the best half of the loin and is an excellent roasting joint. It contains the kidney and fillet or tenderloin, which is often sold separately and is a very lean cut. The fore loin may also be roasted and is especially good boned, stuffed and rolled.

Loin of veal is usually sold in one piece and may be roasted on the bone or boned, stuffed and rolled. The fillet can be bought separately for frying or grilling.

(*see also* LAMB, PORK, VEAL)

LOLLIPOP A boiled sweet or toffee stuck on a small wooden stick. (*see also* SWEETS)

LOLLO BIONDO (*see* LETTUCE)

LOLLO ROSSO (*see* LETTUCE)

LONGAN A small round tropical fruit grown in South-East Asia and China and belonging to the same family as the lychee and rambutan. It has a brittle brown skin and sweet, aromatic, white flesh surrounding a central brown stone. Longans should be peeled and eaten raw, discarding the stone.

LOQUAT (Japanese Medlar) Originally an Oriental fruit, loquats are now grown in Mediterranean countries and the United States. They look similar to a small yellow plum with sweet, scented, slightly tart orange flesh. The seeds are within the large central stone. Loquats may be eaten raw, poached or made into ice cream or preserves.

To select: Look for firm fruit with smooth golden yellow skins.

To prepare: To eat raw, cut crossways and remove the stone. The outer skin can be eaten. To prepare for cooking, remove the stone and quarter the fruit.

To cook: Poach in a light syrup, then leave to cool.

To serve: Poached loquats may be skinned after cooking, then served chilled.

LOTE (*see* EEL POUT)

LOTUS The lotus plant is a member of the water-lily family and various varieties are cultivated in Asian countries for their underwater roots, seeds and leaves, as well as for their beautiful flowers. The lotus root is swollen and bulbous, looking rather like a series of turnips strung together, and may be used as a vegetable. There are numerous holes in the flesh of the root so that, when sliced, it has a lacy appearance which can be used to good decorative effect in stir-fries, salads and garnishes. Lotus root discolours quickly when cut so should be dropped straight into acidulated water (*see* ACIDULATE). Fresh, canned and dried lotus root are available from Chinese food stores. Lotus roots may also be dried and ground to a gluten-free flour that is used as a thickening agent in Chinese and Japanese cooking.

The seeds (or nuts) of the lotus plant are large and black and have a slightly almond-like flavour. They are a characteristic of Thai cooking. Smaller seeds may be eaten raw but they are usually boiled or grilled and used in sweet and savoury dishes. In Chinese cooking, they are most often used in a soup. The large leaves of the lotus plant may also be used as a wrapping for savoury mixtures.

LOVAGE A herb with a sharp peppery flavour, not unlike the flavour of celery, which is good in all strong-tasting savoury dishes and soups. Lovage leaves add an unusual tang to salads and are good in cold roast beef sandwiches. Lovage seeds can also be used, and the stems are sometimes cut and candied, rather like angelica.

Lovage is also used to make an alcoholic cordial of low strength, drunk as a *digestif* in the West Country.

LOW FAT CHEESES (*see* CHEESE)

LUGANEGA (*see* SALSICCIA)

LUKEWARM (Tepid) In cookery, this term is used to describe the temperature of a substance, usually a liquid, when it is about blood temperature, that is approximately 37°C (98.4°F).

LUMACHE (*see* PASTA)

LUMPFISH (*see* CAVIAR)

LUNGS (*see* LIGHTS)

LUTE In cookery, this name is given to a flour and water paste used to seal the lids of casseroles or terrines before cooking. The technique is known as luting and, as the paste bakes hard during cooking, it ensures lids are tightly sealed so that no steam or flavours can escape. The term luting is also used to describe the technique of placing a strip of pastry around the rim of a pie dish to seal on a pastry cover.

LYCHEE (Litchi) Originally a Chinese fruit, lychees are now grown in many other countries. They are stone fruit the size of plums, which grow in bunches. They have hard bumpy skins, ranging from pink to brown in colour, and sweet, aromatic, juicy, white flesh surrounding a shiny brown inedible stone. Lychees are available fresh in the winter months, and can be bought canned all year round. Lychees are also used dried in Chinese cooking and are known as Chinese nuts.

To select: Avoid fruit with shrivelled dry skins and choose those with the pinkest skins.

To prepare: To eat raw, simply peel and discard the central stone. To prepare for cooking or including in a fruit salad, peel and halve the lychees and remove the stones.

To cook: Lychees may be added raw to a fresh fruit salad, or may be poached in syrup and served chilled.

LYMESWOLD The first soft blue British cheese, made in Somerset since 1982. As it matures, Lymeswold develops from a firmer, more curd-textured and fresh-flavoured cheese to a softer, more mellow richness. The white rind can be eaten.

LYONNAISE, À LA A French name given to dishes which contain fried chopped or shredded onion as a principal ingredient.

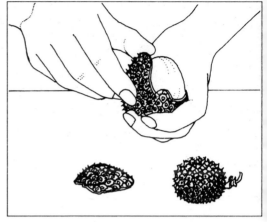

Breaking and removing the hard, bumpy skin from lychees.

M

MABOLO (*see* PERSIMMON)

MACADAMIA NUT (Queensland Nut) Looking rather like a large shelled and skinned hazelnut, the macadamia nut is native to Australia but now also grows in Hawaii, America, the Caribbean and the Mediterranean regions. Macadamia nuts are contained in shiny brown shells that are hard to crack. They are sold raw or roasted in oil and may be used as a dessert nut or chopped or grated and used in cakes, biscuits and desserts.

MACARONI (*see* PASTA)

MACAROON A small cake made from ground almonds, sugar and egg whites and baked on rice paper; small macaroons can be served as petits fours and the mixture may also be used as a filling for tartlets. A similar mixture is made with coconut. (*see also* RATAFIA)

MACE The outer covering (or aril) of the nutmeg which is bright red when harvested and dries to a deep orange. Both spices come from the same tree which is native to South-East Asia. Mace is sold in 'blades', which are useful for infusing, or ground. It has a stronger flavour than nutmeg and can be used in mulled wine and punches, potted meat, fish dishes, béchamel sauce, meat loaf, stews, pies and some puddings and cooked fruit dishes. (*see also* NUTMEG)

MACÉDOINE The French name for a mixture of fruit or vegetables cut into even-sized dice and usually used as a garnish.

MACERATE To soften and flavour raw or dried foods by soaking in a liquid. Fresh and dried fruits are frequently macerated before being cooked or added to a fruit salad. The liquid used may be water, fruit juice, sugar syrup, liqueur, wine or brandy.

MÂCHE (*see* LAMB'S LETTUCE)

MACKEREL A fairly small, round, oily sea fish with blue-black markings on the back, cream-coloured flesh and a very distinctive flavour. It is sold whole and can be cooked whole or filleted and cooked by any method suitable for herring (*see* HERRING). Mackerel must be eaten very fresh and is traditionally served with gooseberry preserve. It is available all year but at its best from August to May.

Horse mackerel (scad) are sometimes available. They are a darker colour than ordinary mackerel and their flavour is not as good. They do not belong to the same family of fish as mackerel.

Smoked Mackerel

Smoked mackerel is available whole or filleted and some are coated with peppercorns, and hot- or cold-smoked. Cold-smoked mackerel may also be known as 'kippered' mackerel. They can be poached or grilled. Fillets of smoked mackerel are popular served uncooked as a starter, accompanied by horseradish cream.

MACROBIOTIC The name given to a style of eating adopted by followers of the Zen sect of Japanese Buddhism. Each individual's diet takes into account spiritual as well as physical needs and is based on balancing the opposing principles of Yin (feminine) and Yang (masculine). The major foods included in a macrobiotic diet are whole grain cereals and vegetables, and many foods, including fruit and meat, are excluded.

MADAGASCAR BEAN (*see* BUTTER BEAN)

MADEIRA Named for the Portuguese island where it is made, Madeira is wine fortified by the addition of cane spirit and matured by cooking in heated lofts known as *estufagem*. The traditional varieties of Madeira are:

Sercial, the driest and lightest wine, a suitable aperitif, slightly chilled.

Verdelho, medium dry, darker in colour.

Bual, velvety, medium-sweet, deep golden-brown, suitable with dessert fruit and nuts.

Malmsey, the sweetest Madeira, rich and honeyed.

MADEIRA CAKE A type of rich sponge cake which, in Victorian times, was served with a glass of Madeira. It is often erroneously referred to as a 'plain' cake because it contains no fruit and is flavoured only with lemon. The characteristic decoration consists of candied citron peel which is placed on top during baking.

MADELEINE A small fancy cake baked in a dariole mould, coated with jam and coconut and often decorated with glacé cherries and angelica. Madeleines were originally made from a rich Victoria sponge mixture, but sometimes a Genoese sponge is used. In France, the name is applied to a sponge cake baked in a scallop-shaped mould.

MADRILÈNE, À LA A French name often given to dishes flavoured with tomato, and in particular to a tomato-flavoured chicken consommé usually served chilled.

MAGNESIUM A naturally-occuring mineral required by the body for efficient metabolism and a healthy nervous and skeletal system. Sources of magnesium include whole grain cereals, nuts and soya beans.

MAGNUM A large wine or champagne bottle the equivalent of two normal-sized wine bottles, containing 1.6 litres (1/3 gallon).

MAIDENHAIR FERN This popular houseplant also grows wild in parts of Europe and America and is sometimes used to make a flavoured syrup called *capillaire* (see CAPILLAIRE).

MAIDENHAIR TREE (*see* GINKGO)

MAID OF HONOUR This is a small tartlet with a filling made from flavoured milk curds. Maids of honour originated in Henry VIII's palace at Hampton Court, where they were popular with the Queen's Maids of Honour, and the recipe was a closely guarded secret. However, in George I's reign, a lady of the court gave the recipe to a gentleman who set up a shop in Richmond, where the tarts are still made. The recipe was made public in 1951 for a television programme about historic dishes of Britain.

MAIGRE, AU A French term meaning 'without meat'. It may be applied to a dish, a meal or to a fast day.

MAISON Meaning 'house', this French word is applied to dishes on a menu that are cooked in the style of the particular restaurant.

MAÎTRE D'HÔTEL In France, the *maître d'hôtel* is the man in charge of the dining room in a hotel or restaurant. The name is also given to simply prepared dishes garnished with *maître d'hôtel* butter, such as *filet de sole à la maître d'hôtel*. It is also the name of a sauce.

Maître d'Hotel Butter

25 g (1 oz) butter
10 ml (2 tsp) finely chopped parsley
5 ml (1 tsp) lemon juice
salt
cayenne pepper

Warm and cream the butter, then work in the parsley, lemon juice and seasonings. Roll the butter into a sausage shape in a piece of greaseproof paper, wrap and refrigerate until hard. Just before serving, unwrap the butter roll and cut into thin slices. When serving with hot food, add the butter only just before the dish is put on the table, or the butter will melt and lose its decorative effect.

MAIZE (*see* CORN)

MALAGA A sweet fortified Spanish wine. It is made from local wine to which Pedro Ximenez sherry and grape brandy are added.

MALDIVE FISH A type of dried fish which is frequently used in the cooking of Sri Lanka. Maldive may be prepared from a number of local fish species and is used in crumbled or powdered form.

MALIBU An alcoholic drink made from a mixture of coconut and rum.

MALLARD (*see* DUCK)

MALMSEY (*see* MADEIRA)

MALT A substance produced by soaking barley grains, then allowing them to germinate to a certain stage under controlled conditions, the starch being converted into dextrin (a type of gum) and malt sugar (maltose); when the correct stage of germination is reached, the grains are dried by gradual heating and become malt. The temperature to which the barley is heated at this stage determines the type of malt produced, ranging from pale to black. Malt is mostly used in the brewing industry; pale malts are used in pale beers, dark malts in stout and other dark beers.

Before malt can be used to make beer, it must be ground to grist, then soaked in warm water to develop the right proportion of maltose and dextrin for the type of beer to be produced. After soaking, the grist is strained and the soaking water, known as wort, can be used to make malt extract, a dark, sticky syrup made by evaporating malted barley wort at a low temperature or in a vacuum. When malt extract is used in cakes, breads and puddings, it imparts a distinctive flavour and a rather moist texture. Used in medicines, its flavour helps to mask other unpleasant-tasting ingredients such as cod and halibut liver oils. Malt extract is also known as barley syrup.

MALTOSE (*see* SUGAR)

MALT WHISKY (*see* WHISKY)

MANCHEGO A famous Spanish cheese made from ewes' milk. It has a strong taste and a firm texture and is sold fresh as well as matured, becoming harder and drier as it ages. It is a pale-coloured cheese, usually with a yellow wax rind, and is best eaten uncooked.

MANCHETTE The French name for a type of small paper frill used to decorate the exposed bones on a crown of lamb or pork or on lamb cutlets.

MANDARIN (*see* TANGERINE)

MANDARIN NAPOLEON The brand name of a liqueur made in Belgium from tangerines macerated in aged Cognac.

MANDOLINE (Mandolin) A vegetable slicer consisting of one or more metal blades fixed in a frame that can be supported in a tilted position. Some mandolines have as many as four blades, for cutting slices, chips and julienne strips of different thicknesses. Mandolines are most suitable for firm vegetables, such as carrots and potatoes, but can also be used for shredding cabbage or slicing apples.

MANGE-TOUT (Chinese Pea, Snow Pea, Sugar Pea, Sugar-snap Pea) This lovely vegetable has only become popular in Britain comparatively recently, though it has long been used in French and Chinese cooking. It is a leguminous vegetable, consisting of small, flat, green pods containing immature peas. Its French name means, literally, 'eat all' and, indeed, the whole pods of mange-tout are eaten when very young before the peas have developed. There are two main varieties of mange-tout; those known as

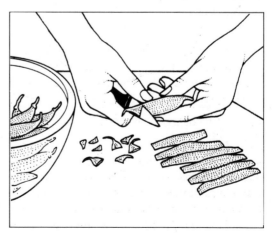

Preparing mange-tout by trimming off the ends with a sharp knife.

sugar-snap peas are rounder and fuller in shape and have a sweeter flavour.

To select: Choose bright green, fresh-looking pods that contain very small, underdeveloped peas. Allow about 100 g (4 oz) per person.

To prepare: Trim the ends and wash.

To cook: Cook mange-tout in boiling salted water for 2–4 minutes, or steam for about 5 minutes, or until just tender but still slightly crisp. Mange-tout can also be stir-fried with a little chopped shallot or onion for 5–10 minutes.

To serve: Mange-tout are usually served as an accompanying vegetable, sprinkled with herbs or tossed in butter, if liked. They can also be eaten cold in mixed vegetable salads.

MANGO This large stone fruit grows all over the tropical and sub-tropical regions of the world and has become readily available in Britain in recent years. There are many varieties of mango; some

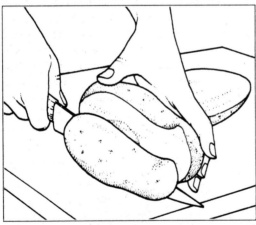

Cutting a large slice from either side of a mango, cutting close to the stone.

are round, others long and narrow or pear-shaped. Their juicy but fibrous, orange flesh has a distinctive, delicate flavour.

To select: Ripe mangoes are very juicy with a yellow or orange skin and 'give' if gently squeezed. Avoid soft or shrivelled fruit. Ripe mangoes are best used within three days.

To prepare: Mango skin is inedible and is best removed in the following way: Cut a large slice from one side of the fruit, cutting close to the stone. Cut another slice from the opposite side. Cut the flesh in the segments lengthways and crossways without breaking the skin, then push the skin inside out to expose the cubes of flesh which can then be cut (or bitten) off. Peel the remaining centre section and cut the flesh away from the stone in chunks or slices.

To serve: Mangoes can be served with ice cream, added to fruit salads, or puréed for mousses or ice cream. Green, unripe mangoes, can be made into chutney, popularly served with curry.

MANGO, DRIED Slices of mango are available dried and can be used as a flavouring in curries. They can also be chopped and used in fruit salads, cakes, desserts and puddings, or eaten as a snack. Like dried apricots, dried mangoes have usually been treated with sulphur; unsulphured varieties can be bought from health food shops.

MANGO POWDER (Amchur) Made from dried raw, green mangoes, this sour-tasting powder is much used in Indian cooking to give a piquant flavour to many dishes.

MANGOSTEEN A tropical fruit that originated in Malaysia but is now grown throughout South-East Asia and in the West Indies, Central America, Florida and Brazil, and is becoming increasingly available in Britain. It has a deep purple, fibrous outer shell enclosing juicy segments of creamy white flesh. When it reaches the shops, the fruit is usually still bearing its thick stalk and the curled leaves of its calyx.

Mangosteens are best enjoyed as a dessert fruit, eaten on their own, though they can be served with natural yogurt, cream or ice cream, if liked. (*see also* KOKUM)

To select: Choose mangosteens that 'give' slightly when gently squeezed. Avoid any that are hard or dry-looking.

To prepare: Cut the shell through the centre and remove the top part to reveal the fruit. The skin itself contains a deep pink juice that will stain.

MANIOC (*see* CASSAVA)

MANTIS SHRIMP This sea crustacean is usually somewhat large to be called a shrimp and has more the general appearance of a praying mantis, though it does share the shrimp's habitat. Mantis shrimps are mostly found in the Mediterranean and are popular in Italy and Spain, where they are prepared and cooked in the same way as prawns or shrimps, and are particularly good in fish soup.

MANZANILLA (*see* SHERRY)

MAPLE SUGAR As its name implies, this sugar is derived from the sap of various species of the maple tree. It has a characteristic flavour and may be used to replace part or all of the ordinary sugar in cakes, puddings, etc. It is also used in confectionery (often mixed with brown sugar) and in sauces for ice cream, waffles and blancmanges. It is particularly popular in Canada and the United States.

MAPLE SYRUP A very sweet syrup, made from maple sugar (see above). It has a distinctive but delicate flavour and is used in sweet dishes and as an accompaniment to ice cream, waffles, pancakes, etc. It is also used in the manufacture of confectionery.

MARASCHINO A bitter-sweet, water white liqueur made from maraschino cherries and their crushed kernels. It originated in Yugoslavia. (*see also* CHERRY)

MARC A rather coarse spirit produced from the debris that remains after grapes have been pressed to make wine. It can be used in cooking instead of brandy. The Portuguese equivalent is known as *bagaceira*. (*see also* GRAPPA)

MARCASSIN (*see* BOAR)

MARC DE RAISIN A French semi-hard cheese with a 'crust' of grape skins and pips replacing the usual rind.

MARCHE (*see* LAMB'S LETTUCE)

MARENGO A chicken dish named after the Italian village of Marengo. The dish is said to have been invented by Napoleon's chef and cooked after the battle of Marengo in 1800. Traditionally, the chicken is sautéed in oil and flavoured with tomato, garlic and brandy and garnished with eggs and crayfish, but there are many variations to this original recipe.

MARGARINE A yellow fat that first became popular as an economical substitute for butter. Nowadays, however, margarine is used instead of butter in most cases because it is made from vegetable oils which contain polyunsaturated fat rather than saturated animal fats.

Margarine first came into use in France in the late nineteenth century. The original margarines were made from beef fat and skimmed milk; today they are mostly based on vegetable oils which have undergone a process known as hydrogenation which hardens them. Unfortunately, the hydrogenation process transforms polyunsaturated fats into saturated fats, so even vegetable-based margarines contain a proportion of saturated fats; in general, the harder the margarine at room temperature, the more saturated fat it contains. Most vegetable margarines are still soft enough, however, to be spreadable and many are sold in plastic tubs rather than wrapped in foil.

By law, a margarine must contain 80 per cent fat and no more than 16 per cent water, the same proportions as in butter. Other ingredients may include salt and various preservatives, flavourings and colourings. Margarine must also contain vitamins A and D. The most frequently used vegetable oils are sunflower, soya and corn oil; some margarines are made from a blend of oils.

Margarine can be used in most of the ways in which butter is used, but the taste is never the same. Soft margarines are excellent for making one-stage sponge cakes and can be used in other types of baking as well. They are also suitable for frying and, of course, for spreading on bread, toast, etc. Margarines should be distinguished from low-fat spreads, which are excellent for reducing calories and cholesterol, but which contain high proportions of water and are not suitable for cooking. (*see also* FATS)

MARIE BRIZARD (*see* ANISETTE)

MARIGOLD (Calendula, Pot Marigold) The bright orange flowers of this garden plant were formerly used to make a cordial and to colour butter. Nowadays, marigold petals or leaves are occasionally used in salads, though the leaves tend to be tough unless very young.

MARINADE (*see* MARINATE)

MARINATE To steep raw meat, game or fish in a blend of oil, wine or vinegar and seasonings for periods of an hour up to several days before cooking, to make it more tender and flavoursome, and to give moisture to dry meats. The mixture, which is known as a marinade, may also be used to baste the food during cooking, to deglaze the pan after cooking, or to make a sauce.

MARINIÈRE A French word most familiar as the name of a mussel dish, *moules marinière* (*see* MOULES MARINIÈRE). The term is also applied, however, to other fish dishes cooked in white wine and garnished with mussels.

MARJORAM This small-leaved herb has a spicy, slightly bitter, nutmeg-like flavour and can be used to replace basil if not available. There are many varieties, the most common being the savoury pot (French) marjoram and the sweet marjoram. Wild marjoram is better known as oregano. Marjoram is a good herb to use in stuffings, rubbed over roasts (especially pork), in meat soups, on pizza and in home-made sausages. It is also used in egg dishes, on buttered vegetables and in cream soups. Marjoram is readily available fresh and dried. (*see also* OREGANO)

MARJORAM, WILD (*see* OREGANO)

MARLIN (*see* SWORDFISH)

MARMALADE A preserve traditionally served at breakfast in this country. The name is derived from the Portuguese word *marmalada*, from the Latin word for quince, since the preserve was originally made from that fruit. In English, the word now applies exclusively to a preserve made from Seville oranges (and sometimes other citrus fruits such as lemons, limes and grapefruit). In France, however, the term *marmelade* means thick purée, made by stewing fruit until considerably reduced; many different fruits can be cooked in this way.

In addition to its use as a spread on toast or bread, marmalade is sometimes used in making puddings, tarts and sauces.

Marmalade-Making

The equipment and method used for making marmalade are very similar to those used for jam (*see* JAM), but with a few special points to remember.

The Fruit

Seville or bitter oranges make the best marmalades with a pleasing flavour and appearance. Sweet oranges give marmalade a rather cloudy appearance and the pith does not turn as translucent as that of Seville oranges. Sweet oranges are usually only used in combination with other citrus fruits.

The best time to make marmalade is in January and February when Seville oranges are available. Fortunately, it is possible to freeze whole Seville oranges.

Preparing the Fruit

The peel of citrus fruits is tougher than that of most fruits used for jam-making and must therefore be evenly shredded, either by hand or in a food processor. The peel should not be minced as it produces a paste-like marmalade.

There are several methods of preparing and softening the fruit, each resulting in a different type of marmalade, such as coarse-cut, thin-cut and fine-shred jelly marmalade. It is sometimes suggested that the peel should be cut up and soaked in water overnight to help soften it. However, soaking is not essential and the long, first cooking stage is usually sufficient. Sometimes it may be more convenient to prepare the fruit one day and make the marmalade the next day, in which case the peel should be left in water overnight to prevent it drying out.

Cooking Marmalade

First cooking Cooking times required for marmalades are usually much longer than for jams – at least 1 hour and very often 2–3 hours. Consequently, larger quantities of water are needed to allow for evaporation. For the first cooking stage, the juice is squeezed from the oranges and put in the preserving pan with the water and shredded peel. The purpose of the first cooking stage is to extract the pectin (*see* JAM), reduce the contents of the pan by about half and to soften the peel thoroughly. Failure to do this is one of the most common reasons why a marmalade will not set.
Extracting the pectin Much of the pectin in oranges is contained in the pips and membranes, and it is important that it is all extracted. To do this, all the pips, and any membrane that has come away from the peel during squeezing, are placed in a clean piece of muslin. This is tied in a bundle with a long piece of string, then tied to the handle of the pan so that the bundle hangs down into the marmalade and can easily be removed after cooking. This is cooked with the fruit for the first cooking, then taken out and squeezed as much as possible, letting the pulpy juice run back into the pan.
Second cooking The sugar is added at the beginning of the second cooking stage and stirred in until it dissolves. The marmalade is then boiled rapidly for 15–20 minutes or until setting point is reached (*see* JAM). Prolonged boiling after the addition of sugar gives marmalade a dark colour. Test for a set in the same way as for jam (*see* JAM) .

As soon as setting point is reached, remove the pan from the heat and skim the marmalade with a slotted spoon to remove any scum.

Potting and Covering

Before potting, leave the marmalade to cool slightly for 10–15 minutes, then stir to distribute the peel. This will prevent the peel rising in the jars. Pot and cover as for jam (*see* JAM).

MARMITE A French metal or earthenware pot used for long, slow cooking of casseroles on the hob or in the oven.

MARRONS GLACÉS A popular delicacy, made from chestnuts treated with syrup, which is served as a dessert or used as decoration on desserts or cakes. *Marrons glacés* may also be sieved and beaten into a meringue mixture or blended with cream as a dessert.

MARROW A popular summer squash that is often allowed to grow quite large but is in fact best eaten when under 30 cm (12 inches) long and weighing about 900 g (2 lb). At that stage, the skin is tender and the seeds hardly formed. Older marrows, weighing up to 2.5 kg (5 lb), need peeling and the seeds and centre fibres removed. If left to ripen, marrows can be made into delicious jam.

Delicately-flavoured marrows are best either simply braised lightly in a little butter and black pepper or cooked with other vegetables such as tomatoes with herbs and spices. To turn marrow into a substantial main meal, they can be stuffed – whole or cut into thick slices. (*see also* SQUASH)
To select: Look for firm marrows with no blemishes or soft parts. Choose small marrows, as above. Allow 175–225 g (6–8 oz) per person.
To prepare: Wash the skin and, if thick, peel it off. Cut into small pieces or into halves, lengthways if it is to be stuffed. Discard the seeds and centre fibres. Place in a colander and sprinkle with salt. Leave for 30 minutes to extract the bitter juices, then rinse and pat dry thoroughly with absorbent kitchen paper.

To cook: Cook in boiling salted water for 10–20 minutes, steam for 20–25 minutes or sauté for 5-10 minutes. Stuffed marrow should be covered with foil and baked in the oven at 190°C (375°F) mark 5 for about 45 minutes or until tender.

To serve: Serve marrow as a vegetable accompaniment with cheese or béchamel sauce, or stuff and use as a main dish.

MARROW BONE (*see* BONES)

MARROW, SPAGHETTI (Vegetable Spaghetti) This winter squash is shaped like a short yellow marrow and is baked in its skin. The white flesh inside, which resembles spaghetti, is eaten seasoned with butter or a tomato sauce. (*see also* SQUASH)

MARSALA A Sicilian fortified wine made from a blend of local wines, brandy and unfermented grape juice. There are dry as well as sweet Marsalas. Its most famous use is in the Italian dessert, *zabaglione*.

MARSHMALLOW A sweetmeat of an elastic, spongy texture, which derives its name from the marsh-mallow plant, since a gum formerly used to make marshmallows was obtained from the plant's roots. Nowadays, gum arabic (*see* GUM) is used instead. Marshmallow may be tinted pink or other pale colours and is given various flavours; it is usually cut into cubes and these are rolled in icing sugar or occasionally coated with chocolate.

Marshmallows – either plain or toasted – are sometimes used as a decoration for a cold dessert. They may also be chopped up and added to ice creams and jellies or dissolved in frostings and sauces.

MARTINI (*see* VERMOUTH)

MARYLAND A name given to dishes served with a butter and cream sauce, often containing wine. Chicken Maryland is a traditional American dish and is served with a garnish of sweetcorn fritters and fried bananas.

MARZIPAN (*see* ALMOND PASTE)

MASA HARINA (*see* CORN)

MASCARPONE (Maschepone, Mascherpone) A rich unsalted cream cheese made from cows' milk in the Lombardy region of Italy. It is eaten fresh and is ready to eat within a day of making. It may be eaten plain, or flavoured with chocolate, coffee, brandy or liqueur and served as a dessert.

MASH (*see* BLACK GRAM BEAN)

MASKING To cover or coat a cooked meat or similar dish with a savoury jelly, glaze or sauce, or to coat the inside of a mould with jelly (*see* JELLY).

MASOOR (Egyptian Lentils) A type of lentil used in Indian cooking. They are available in two varieties: whole lentils (*saabat masoor*) are delicately flavoured lentils with a pale, pinky-orange centre. They are dark brown or pale green skinned flat beans which take a fair amount of time to cook. Split Egyptian lentils (*masoor dal*) are pinkish in colour and are easy and quick to cook. They are often used in lentil soup. (*see also* LENTILS, PULSES)

MASTIC A sticky resinous substance collected from a Mediterranean plant that belongs to the same family as the pistachio nut. Mastic is used as a flavouring in some Greek dishes, and is an ingredient in Turkish delight and the Greek liqueur *mastika*.

MATÉ (*see* YERBA MATÉ)

MATELOTE A rich, well seasoned French fish stew made with red or white wine.

MATJES HERRING (*see* HERRING)

MATZO A large, brittle, very thin biscuit of unleavened Jewish bread, eaten during the Passover. These biscuits resemble water biscuits and have become popular substitutes for them outside the Jewish community. Matzo biscuits can be crushed to make matzo meal for use in Jewish cooking.

MAY BOWL (May Drink, May Wine) A type of white wine cup, of German origin.

MAYONNAISE A thick rich sauce traditionally served with salads. Mayonnaise is made from an emulsion of oil and vinegar, combined with egg yolk and flavouring ingredients, and forms the basis of many other sauces such as tartare sauce and rémoulade sauce.

In addition to its use with salads, mayonnaise is served with such dishes as lobster mayonnaise, with certain vegetables (such as asparagus and globe artichokes) and to blend savoury fillings for canapés or sandwiches.

Commercially-produced mayonnaise can be bought in jars, but a more genuine mayonnaise can be made at home. Home-made mayonnaise does not keep as long as bought varieties because it lacks their added emulsifiers, stabilizers and preservatives. However, mayonnaise should keep for three to four days at room temperature and for at least a month in a screw-topped glass jar in the refrigerator. It should be allowed to come to room temperature before stirring or the mayonnaise may curdle.

Making Mayonnaise
The ingredients for mayonnaise should be at room temperature. Never use eggs straight from the refrigerator or cold larder as this may result in curdling. If a recipe requires thin mayonnaise, it can be thinned down with a little warm water, single cream, vinegar or lemon juice. The extra liquid should be added with care – too much will spoil the consistency.

1 egg yolk
2.5 ml (¹/₂ level tsp) mustard powder or 5 ml (1 tsp) Dijon mustard
2.5 ml (¹/₂ level tsp) salt
1.25 ml (¹/₄ level tsp) pepper
2.5 ml (¹/₂ level tsp) sugar
15 ml (1 tbsp) white wine vinegar or lemon juice
about 150 ml (¹/₄ pint) oil

Put the egg yolk in a bowl with the mustard, seasoning, sugar and 5 ml (1 tsp) of the vinegar or lemon juice. Mix thoroughly, then add the oil drop by drop, whisking constantly until the sauce is thick and smooth. If it becomes too thick, add a little more of the vinegar or lemon juice. When all the oil has been added, add the remaining vinegar or lemon juice gradually and mix thoroughly. *Makes about 150 ml (¹/₄ pint)*

Using an Electric Blender or Food Processor
Most blenders and food processors need at least a two-egg quantity of mayonnaise in order to ensure that the blades are covered. Put the yolks, seasoning and half the vinegar or lemon juice into the blender goblet or food processor bowl and blend well. If your machine has a variable speed control, run it at a low speed. Add the oil gradually while the machine is running. Add the remaining vinegar and season.

Rescue Remedies
If the mayonnaise separates, save it by beating the curdled mixture into a fresh base. This base can be any of the following: 5 ml (1 tsp) hot water; 5 ml (1 tsp) vinegar or lemon juice; 5 ml (1 tsp) Dijon mustard or 2.5 ml (¹/₂ tsp) mustard powder; an egg yolk. Add the curdled mixture to the base, beating hard. When the mixture is smooth, continue adding the oil as above. (If you use an extra egg yolk, you may find that you need to add a little extra oil.)

Variations
These variations are made by adding the extra ingredients to 150 ml (¹/₄ pint) mayonnaise.
Caper Mayonnaise Add 10 ml (2 tsp) chopped capers, 5 ml (1 tsp) chopped pimiento and 2.5 ml (¹/₂ tsp) tarragon vinegar. Serve with fish.
Cucumber Mayonnaise Add 30 ml (2 tbsp) finely chopped cucumber and 2.5 ml (¹/₂ level tsp) salt. This mayonnaise goes well with fish salads, especially crab, lobster or salmon.
Blue Cheese Dressing Add 142 ml (5 fl oz) soured cream, 75 g (3 oz) crumbled blue cheese, 5 ml (1 tsp) vinegar and 1 garlic clove, skinned and crushed, and pepper to taste.

Rémoulade Sauce Add 5 ml (1 tsp) chopped gherkins, 5 ml (1 tsp) chopped capers, 5 ml (1 tsp) chopped fresh parsley and 1 anchovy, finely chopped.

Tartare Sauce Add 5 ml (1 tsp) chopped fresh tarragon or snipped chives, 10 ml (2 tsp) chopped capers, 10 ml (2 tsp) chopped gherkins, 10 ml (2 tsp) chopped fresh parsley and 15 ml (1 tbsp) lemon juice or tarragon vinegar. Allow to stand for at least 1 hour before serving, to allow the flavours to blend. Serve with fish.

Thousand Island Mayonnaise Add 15 ml (1 tbsp) chopped stuffed olives, 5 ml (1 tsp) finely chopped onion, 1 shelled and chopped hard-boiled egg, 15 ml (1 tbsp) finely chopped green pepper, 5 ml (1 tsp) chopped fresh parsley and 5 ml (1 level tsp) tomato purée.

MEAD An old-fashioned drink made by fermenting honey with hops or yeast; spices or wild flowers were added for flavouring. Mead was drunk by Ancient Britons and also known as metheglin. It is fabled to have aphrodisiac qualities.

MEAL A name used to describe the edible parts of any grain that have been milled or ground to a powder, and used with particular reference to corn (maize), wheat and oats. In general, meals are thought to be coarser than flours, but finely ground meals can also be bought. (*see also* CORN, FLOUR, GRAINS, OATS, WHEAT)

MEALIE The South African name for maize or corn (*see* CORN).

MEALY PUDDING An oatmeal and suet pudding which is served with grilled sausages, bacon, herrings, etc. The mixture is flavoured with onions and may be stuffed into skins, like black pudding. It is boiled before serving.

MEAT The flesh of various animals and birds has been included in the diet of humans since ancient times. Although the flesh of fish and poultry is often called meat, in common use the term refers particularly to the flesh (mostly the muscles) of the ox (and calf), pig and sheep, known as beef (veal), pork and lamb or mutton. Beef, lamb and mutton are generally thought of as red meats, while pork, veal and poultry are white meats. (For detailed information about individual meats, see separate entries.)

Although not essential in the human diet, meat can form the basis of a good satisfying meal, and is a major supplier of nutrients including protein, some of the B vitamins and iron. It need not be the most expensive ingredient in a dish since price varies according to the type of cut or joint. Animals are cut into convenient-sized joints for selling, though the way in which an animal is cut up varies from region to region within Britain and from country to country. You pay most for those parts of an animal which are least exercised and thus tender enough to roast, fry or grill. Tougher cuts, which have more muscle, are cheaper and need long, gentle, moist cooking to soften them. Nutritionally, there is nothing to choose between tender and tough meat, and the flavour of both is good if correctly cooked.

Modern methods of transport and development in cold storage have done away with seasons for meat and you can buy good-quality beef, lamb and pork at any time of the year. Most butchers sell both fresh and frozen meat and it is worth searching out a good local butcher who is prepared to offer a wide choice of cuts. Bear in mind that the butcher is an expert on meat and take advantage of this. A friendly butcher can help with a lot of preparation problems by being prepared to bone, chop or mince to a particular degree of fineness for you.

Choosing Meat
A butcher will sometimes sell meat that has been frozen and that he has thawed, so do not re-freeze unless cooked first. If it still contains ice crystals, allow it to thaw thoroughly at room temperature before cooking. Pouring hot water over it or

putting it straight into a hot oven will lead to flavour loss.

Do not worry about the colour of meat. Bright red does not necessarily indicate good eating quality. The colour of cut lean beef displayed in butchers' shops will, for example, vary from bright red to dark brown. Long exposure to the atmosphere makes meat develop a brownish-red shade so some butchers may use tinted lighting to enhance the colour of the meat.

It is important to cut down the amount of fat we eat (*see* FATS), but when cooking meat a little fat is essential to prevent the meat drying out. It also enhances the flavour. Fat on meat should be firm and free from dark marks or discoloration. Meat for roasting, frying and grilling should be finely grained, firm and slightly elastic, with a fine marbling of fat throughout. Meat that is to be stewed or braised will have coarser-grained, lean areas and more fat. Trim off all but a little of the fat before cooking.

Calculating Quantities for All Meats

Although servings vary according to age, taste and appetite, as a guide, allow 100–175 g (4–6 oz) raw meat without bone and 175–350 g (6–12 oz) with bone per person.

Storing Meat

Meat should always be removed from the paper in which it is wrapped when bought. Either put it on a plate or wrap it in cling film, leaving the ends open for ventilation. Before using it, wipe with absorbent paper to remove any blood.

Meat should be stored in a cool place; the most suitable place is just below the frozen food storage compartment in the refrigerator, but you must be sure the raw meat is not going to drip on anything else in the refrigerator. Although the low, controlled temperature means that uncooked meat can be stored thus for three to five days, a refrigerator should not be regarded as a place for the long-term storage of meat. The low temperature merely slows down the process of deterioration; it

does not completely prevent it. When no refrigerator is available, store meat in a cool, well ventilated place, loose-wrapped. It must be used within two days.

Minced raw meat, sausages and offal are especially perishable and should be used within a day of being purchased.

If meat is cooked in advance, it should be cooled as quickly as possible, then stored in the refrigerator. Leftover casseroles should first be allowed to cool and then put into the refrigerator in a covered dish. They should be used within the next couple of days and reheated thoroughly before they are eaten. Bring the dish to boiling point and boil gently for at least 10 minutes.

Roasting Meat

The process known as oven roasting is in fact baking. The oven should be preheated to 180°C (350°F) mark 4. This low temperature will produce succulent meat with less shrinkage. The traditional, high temperature cooking is only suitable for top-quality meat.

Weigh the joint as it is to be cooked (on the bone, or boned and rolled, or stuffed as appropriate). Put in a shallow roasting tin, preferably on a grid. Cook for time shown below:

Roasting at 180°C (350°F) mark 4
Beef 15 minutes per 450 g (1 lb) + 15 minutes (rare); 20 minutes per 450 g (1 lb) + 20 minutes (medium); 25 minutes per 450 g (1 lb) + 25 minutes (well done)
Lamb 25 minutes per 450 g (1 lb) + 25 minutes
Pork 30 minutes per 450 g (1 lb) + 30 minutes
Veal 25 minutes per 450 g (1 lb) + 25 minutes

Use a meat thermometer to determine accurately whether the meat is cooked. Insert it into the thickest part of the joint before cooking, making sure the tip of the thermometer is well clear of the bone. Cook to 60°C (140°F), 70°C (160°F), 80°C (180°F) for rare, medium and well done. To allow for thermometer inaccuracy, the cook should discover which final internal temperature produces the desired result.

Covering the cooking container, covering in foil or cooking in a roasting bag is strictly pot roasting and the recommended roasting times will not be relevant.

Roasting on a Spit – Rotisserie Cooking

The meat is placed on a revolving spit, or skewers, and cooked under a direct source of heat, either in the oven or on a grill attachment. Allow 15 minutes per 450 g (1 lb) meat, plus 15 minutes extra.

Boiling Meat

The term boiling is a misnomer since meat cooked by this method should not be boiled but gently simmered. Boiling produces tough and tasteless meat. For this type of cooking the meat should be covered with liquid in a pan with a well-fitting lid so that evaporation is kept to a minimum. Vegetables and herbs added to the cooking liquid will produce excellent stock for soup.

Meat for boiling is usually salted and should first be soaked in cold water for several hours or overnight to remove excess salt. Change the water before bringing it slowly to the boil, then reduce to a gentle simmer. Large salted joints should be cooked for 25 minutes per 450 g (1 lb) plus an extra 30 minutes. Small joints should be cooked for a minimum of 1 1/2 hours. Calculate the cooking time from the moment the water reaches the boil. With vacuum packs, follow the instructions given.

Pressure cooking will cut the time needed to 'boil' meat by about two thirds, and less liquid is needed. Follow the pressure cooker manufacturer's instructions for exact times and quantities.

Grilling Meat

Grilling is a quick method of cooking by radiant heat which is only suitable for best-quality meat, such as tender chops, steaks, liver, kidneys, gammon, back and streaky bacon. Grilling toughens inferior cuts of meat as the fibres cannot be broken down.

An electric grill should be preheated but this is not necessary with gas. As the heat is fierce the meat must be basted with oil or melted butter before cooking. Meat for grilling is often greatly improved by first being marinated for at least 2 hours.

Frying Meat

It is the heat of the fat that cooks the meat when frying, and as it cooks, the meat absorbs some of the fat. Frying is not a suitable cooking method for anyone who is trying to cut down on fat.

Frying may be done in shallow fat that comes about halfway up the sides of the meat, or deep fat in which it is completely immersed.

Braising Meat

Braising is a combination of stewing, steaming and roasting. The meat is cooked in a saucepan or casserole, over a bed of vegetables, with just sufficient liquid for the steam to keep it moist. This gives a good flavour and texture to meat that otherwise would be tough and flavourless.

Stewing and Casseroling Meat

Strictly speaking, both stewing and casseroling describe a long, slow method of cooking in a simmering liquid at 96°C (205°F). The only difference between the two is that casseroling refers to the actual dish in which the food is cooked. This method of cooking is particularly suitable for tougher cuts of meat and since all the liquid is served, none of the flavour or food value is lost. A good, strong saucepan or casserole is needed to avoid burning it; it should have a tightly fitting lid to prevent evaporation. Keep the temperature below boiling, as boiling can often cause meat to become tough to chew.

MEAT EXTRACT Meat extracts are made by cutting up meat, removing the tendons, etc., mincing and boiling it; the mixture is then skimmed, filtered and reduced to a very concentrated liquid. Meat extracts contain small amounts of protein, minerals and some of the vitamins, and also have a strong flavour. A teaspoon of meat extract contains approximately as much riboflavin and nicotinic acid as 50 g (2 oz) roast beef (*see* VITAMINS). Meat extracts can be used to make a drink or can be added to soups, stews and gravies. They are commercially produced and readily available in small black jars. (*see also* EXTRACT)

MEDALLION A name derived from the French *médaillon* given to a small round or oval of meat, usually beef or veal. Medallions of beef are also sometimes known as *tournedos*. (*see* STEAK)

MEDLAR This is a small brown fruit, about the size of an apple, with sharp-flavoured flesh. It comes from a tree which can be found growing wild in warmer parts of Britain and Europe. The fruit is only edible raw in its over-ripe state, when it has become 'bletted', that is very soft and almost disintegrating. Medlars can be eaten raw or used to make preserves.
To prepare: Cut in half and spoon out the soft flesh.

MÉDOC A region of France famous for its red Bordeaux wines. The specific areas within the Médoc district produce slightly different wines, including St. Estèphe, Pauillac, St. Julien, Central Médoc, Margaux and Southern Médoc. The wine of the Southern Médoc region is considered the finest.

The river Gironde flows through the Médoc district, its gravel banks giving the area and its wines a characteristic quality. Although some of the Médoc wines are of excellent quality, others are not so good and are suitable for serving at family meals. (*see also* BORDEAUX)

MEGRIM (*see* SOLE)

MEKABU (*see* SEA VEGETABLES)

MELBA SAUCE A sweet sauce made from fresh raspberries and served with fruit sundaes and similar desserts, including peach Melba, a dessert created in 1892 by the great French chef Escoffier in honour of the famous nineteenth-century Australian opera singer, Dame Nellie Melba.

MELBA TOAST (*see* TOAST)

MELBURY CHEESE A mild, white mould-ripened soft British cheese. It has a mellow taste and is made in a distinctive loaf shape.

MELILOT (Sweet Clove) A rare and delicate herb plant that is a member of the clove family. It grows in many parts of Europe and can be used in stuffings and to flavour home-made wine. The most common variety of melilot has yellow flowers; a blue-flowering variety that originated in Turkey is an essential ingredient of an unusual Swiss green cheese called Schabzeiger or Sapsago.

MELON This popular fruit, of which there are many varieties, is now available all year round. Depending on the variety, melons can be smooth-skinned or have a light or heavy 'netting' over their yellow or green skins. All melons have perfumed, sweet, juicy flesh; usually the more fragrant the melon, the sweeter and juicier its flesh.

Melons are round or oval in shape and come in a variety of sizes. They have a hard skin enclosing juicy pale green, orange or red flesh, usually with a mass of inedible seeds in the centre. Melons were first cultivated in ancient Egypt, but are now grown all over the world. They are usually eaten raw and can be served as a starter, sometimes with smoked ham or other cold meat, or as a dessert. Melons can also be puréed for ice creams and sorbets.

The following are the best known types of melon:
Cantaloupe Has a green to yellow rough, segmented skin. The flesh is orange-yellow in colour and extremely fragrant.
Charentais A French variety of Cantaloupe, this is a small round melon with green skin and fragrant orange flesh.

Galia Round with green flesh and a lightly netted skin which ranges from green to yellow.

Honeydew Known as a 'winter' melon, this variety is oval in shape, usually with bright yellow skin. The flesh is pale green, sweet and delicate tasting.

Ogen Another variety of Cantaloupe, this melon is round with yellow to orange skin marked with faint green stripes, and very sweet, juicy, pale green flesh.

Tiger Melon A type of Cantaloupe melon that has only recently appeared in shops in Britain. It comes from Turkey and has orange, yellow and black stripes and fragrant, orange flesh.

Water Melon Originally from Africa, the water melon is not from the same family as other melons. It is a large round or oval fruit with dark green or striped green and yellow skin, and pink to deep red watery flesh with black inedible seeds set individually in rows within the flesh. Smaller varieties of water melon are becoming popular, such as Sweet Baby and Yellow Baby (or Golden Watermelon), which has yellow flesh.

To select: Melons should feel heavy for their size and slightly soft at the stalk end when ripe. Soft patches on the rind indicate bruising rather than ripeness. Some varieties smell fragrant when ripe. Melons should be stored tightly wrapped in the refrigerator as they can easily pick up the flavours of other foods, or the heady fragrance of melon can permeate other foods in the refrigerator. Buy ready-cut slices or wedges only if the cut surfaces are covered with cling film.

To prepare: Cut in segments and remove the seeds. To use in fruit salads, cut into cubes or balls (using a melon baller).

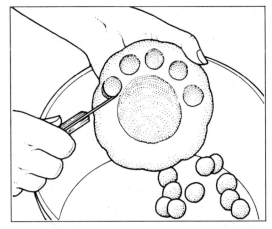

Using a melon baller to scoop out small balls of melon to use in fruit salads or cocktails.

To serve: Chilled melon wedges are often served as starters, sometimes garnished with a slice of orange. Ground ginger is a popular accompaniment.

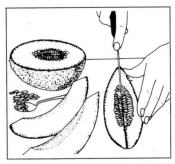

Cutting melon halves into wedges with a sharp knife and removing the seeds with a spoon.

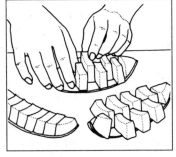

Arranging cubes of melon flesh in a zig-zag design on top of the skin before serving.

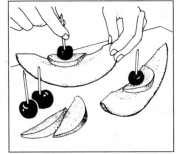

Decorating melon wedges with slices of orange and Maraschino cherries.

MELT (Milt) The spleen of certain animals, classified as offal. Melts are not commonly eaten in this country but can be used in stuffings.

MELTING Converting a solid (for example fat, sugar, chocolate) into a liquid by gently heating. Some food, such as chocolate, needs very careful handling and is best melted over hot water (*see* CHOCOLATE).

MERGUEZ (*see* SAUSAGE)

MERINGUE A sweet, light mixture made from whisked egg whites and sugar that is very lightly baked in the oven so it dries out and becomes crisp and firm. Meringue is used to make the basis of a dessert, such as Pavlova, or as a topping, such as on lemon meringue pie. The light texture is the perfect foil to creamy fillings and soft fruit.

There are three basic types of meringue, although for home cooking *meringue Suisse*, or simple meringue, is the most commonly used. It is made by incorporating sugar into stiffly whisked egg whites, usually in the proportions of 50 g (2 oz) caster sugar to each egg white used. Half the sugar is very gradually added, about 15 ml (1 tbsp) at a time, whisking after each addition, until the sugar is thoroughly mixed in and partially dissolved. Sugar added in large amounts at this stage may result in a sticky meringue. The remaining sugar is added by sprinkling it over the whisked egg whites and folding it in with a metal spoon. The egg whites should be firm and have a glossy appearance. Meringue mixtures can be flavoured with chocolate, vanilla, coffee or chopped nuts. The meringue used to make a Pavlova is based on *meringue Suisse* but vinegar and cornflour are added. This type of meringue is sometimes known as American meringue and is cooked at a higher temperature for a shorter time, producing a meringue with a crisp outside and a soft, sticky centre.

Meringue cuite is made by cooking the egg whites over boiling water while whisking them. This means that the meringue can be stored if necessary before shaping. These meringues are harder, whiter and more powdery than *meringue Suisse* and are used mostly by professional bakers as they require great care and long whisking.

Italian meringue is made by adding a hot sugar syrup to egg whites. It requires a sugar thermometer and is rarely used at home as other methods are simpler.

Before baking, meringue can be shaped in a variety of ways. Small 'shell' meringues are made by shaping spoonfuls of meringue between two spoons, then sliding them on to a lined baking sheet. To make meringue 'nests', the meringue is spooned on to a lined baking sheet in mounds which are then hollowed out with a spoon. Meringue can also be piped into small swirls or large rounds made from a continuous spiral of meringue. Swirling piped meringue makes an attractive topping for lemon meringue pie and other desserts.

Meringues are cooked slowly at a very low oven temperature so the mixture, in effect, dries out rather than bakes. It is sometimes necessary to leave the oven door open to achieve a low enough temperature. Once baked, meringues are very fragile and need careful handling. Leaving meringues to cool in the oven sometimes helps prevent cracking. Unfilled meringues can be stored for two to three weeks in an airtight container.

Small meringues can be sandwiched together with whipped cream; nests can be filled with fresh fruit topped with whipped cream; large rounds can be built up into a gâteau with a flavoured cream and fruit filling. Classic dishes made with meringue include Pavlova, baked Alaska, *oeufs à la neige* (floating islands) and *vacherin*. (*see also* BAKED ALASKA, VACHERIN)

MESCAL An alcoholic drink, similar to tequila, made in Mexico and South America from the Maguey or American sloe.

MESQUITE A North American leguminous tree that is mostly grown for its pods which are used as animal fodder. However, it is also used, particularly on the west coast of America, as a flavouring fuel that can be added to a barbecue fire when cooking fish. Like hickory, the smoke imparts a potent flavour that can be overpowering and is best suited to strong-flavoured oily fish.

METABOLISM In human nutritional terms, metabolism is the process by which the body converts the nutritive value of food in order to supply its needs. Food is metabolized to provide heat and energy as well as protein, vitamins and minerals needed by the body; excess is either stored (mostly as fat) or excreted. The efficiency of metabolism is often discussed in terms of metabolic rate, that is the speed at which food is metabolized and burnt up by the body.

Metabolic rate varies from one individual to another and is affected by various factors, such as lifestyle, and levels of exercise in particular. Basal metabolic rate is an individual's metabolic rate when at rest; as soon as the body is called upon to do anything, the rate increases. Ironically, eating is one activity that effectively increases metabolic rate, as does any form of exercise. Moreover, recent research has shown that metabolic rate is not only increased during activity, but also continues at a high level for some time afterwards. This is a point worth remembering by anyone on a weight-reducing diet. A high metabolic rate means food and energy are burned up more quickly and the body has a greater requirement for calories (energy). If the amount of calories consumed is less than this requirement, the body will turn to its fat stores to provide the shortfall.

(*see also* CALORIE, DIET, NUTRITION)

METRICATION The metric (or decimal) system of measurement has been in general use in Europe for many years, while in Britain the Imperial system has been used. Following decimalization of the currency, the British measuring system is gradually undergoing metrication in order that we may have the same system as other countries in the EC. At present, both systems are in use at the same time: weights on cans and packets of food are, in most cases, now given in metric units (grams, kilograms, millilitres and litres), but we still buy fresh food by the ounce or pound; petrol is sold by the litre, but beer is still sold by the pint; milk is still sold in pint-size bottles and cartons, but the metric equivalent (568 ml) is given on the container; we buy fabric and other materials by the metre and centimetre, but we discuss distance in terms of feet, inches and miles. Children now learn the metric system of measuring at school and gradually the Imperial system will be phased out, but it may take many more years.

In the meantime, for cooking purposes, all recipes give quantities of ingredients and cake tin sizes, etc., in both metric and Imperial units. It is usual to base a system of conversion on a unit that is rounded up or down from the exact equivalent. For example, 1 oz is equal to 28.35 g, but for simplicity, a conversion of 25 g may be used. For liquid measurements, 1 pint is equal to 568 ml, but a 600 ml conversion is usually recommended, except when using milk which is conveniently packaged in 568-ml quantities anyway. For most recipes (baking being the exception), these slight differences in quantities do not affect the finished result, as long as either the metric or Imperial quantities only are used; it is important not to mix the two within one recipe as they are not directly interchangeable. For quantities smaller than 25 g (1 oz), tablespoons and teaspoons are usually used. One tablespoon is equal to 15 ml of either a liquid or a dry ingredient; one teaspoon is equal to 5 ml. Sets of measuring spoons are available in both metric and Imperial sizes to give accurate measurement of these small quantities. Kitchen scales giving both metric and Imperial weights are readily available. (See also the conversion charts on page 7)

MEUNIÈRE, À LA A French term which refers to food cooked in butter, seasoned with salt, pepper and lemon juice and finished with parsley. It is usually applied to fish dishes.

MEXICAN BEAN (*see* BLACK BEAN)

MEXICAN TEA (*see* EPAZOTE)

MEZZALUNA An Italian two-handled, crescent-shaped chopping blade which can be used with a chopping board to chop herbs, vegetables and meat to the required degree of fineness Double- and triple-bladed *mezzalunas* are also available.

MEZZE (Mezes) The Greek or Turkish name for a selection of dishes served together as an hors d'oeuvre or light meal. *Mezze* usually consists of cold dishes such as *taramasalata*, stuffed vine leaves, cold meats, marinated vegetables and fish dishes, served with pitta bread, olives and ouzo or raki.

MICROWAVE COOKING Although microwave cookers have been used in the catering trade for many years, it is only comparatively recently that they have become commonplace in the home. They provide a quick, convenient and economical method of heating, thawing and cooking foods and can be used in conjunction with a conventional oven or to replace it completely. Microwave cookers run off ordinary household 13-amp socket outlets, can be placed on any flat surface, and save energy. However, there are certain foods that cannot be cooked in a microwave cooker, such as Yorkshire pudding and deep-fat fried foods, and some foods where the resulting texture or appearance is not very good, such as meat, pastry, cakes and breads which do not brown. For these items, it is sometimes preferable to use a conventional oven or a combination oven (*see* COMBINATION OVEN).

Choosing a Microwave Cooker
There are three different types of microwave cooker to choose from: the counter-top portable type, a built-in microwave in a conventional cooker, or a combination type of oven that can be switched either to microwave, to convection cooking or both simultaneously (*see* COMBINATION OVEN).

The main points to consider when choosing a cooker are the power settings, controls, timer settings and internal fittings.

The most useful type of cooker is one with variable power, ranging from full (usually 600-700 watts) down through various levels to defrost and warm (usually 200–300 watts). A wide choice of settings enables you to cook items with accuracy. Unfortunately, the terms used on different brands of microwave cooker have not yet been standardized. Thus, the setting 'reheat' on one model may be the equivalent of 'roast' on another. It is therefore important to familiarize yourself thoroughly with the instruction book supplied with your model and to experiment with the recipes contained in it. As you become more accustomed to cooking with microwaves it will become simple to use recipes from general microwave cookery books and also to adapt recipes you have formerly prepared with a conventional cooker.

Controls should be clear and easy to use; there is a choice of touch pads, buttons or dials. Some microwave cookers have memory programmes which can be set automatically to cook foods you eat often.

Timer settings should allow you to set the cooker for small accurate timings, such as 3 seconds (for softening ice cream served straight from the freezer) as well as longer times for cooking joints of meat.

Most microwave cookers incorporate a turntable or stirrers which distribute the microwaves (*see* MICROWAVES), so the food cooks evenly. If you buy a model without either of these, you can buy a rechargeable turntable. All models have an internal light which goes on when the oven is switched on, so you can see the food while it is cooking. This is essential as the food cooks so quickly.

All ovens have vents, either at the back, side or top, which allow moisture to escape during cooking. It is important that these are not obstructed by putting the oven under a low shelf or in too small a space.

Safety

Provided you buy a cooker which meets the British Standard specifications, a microwave cooker is one of the safest kitchen appliances. It has no moving parts or sharp edges and the dishes in which the food is cooked remain relatively cool.

For peace of mind, have your cooker checked once a year, or as often as the manufacturer recommends, for leakage as this could affect cooking results. Call in the manufacturer's service agent, who will have a special precision meter for doing this. Do-it-yourself meters are available, but they tend to be inaccurate.

If the cooker is dropped or has something dropped on it, have it checked before using it again. Although microwave cookers are portable appliances, it is best not to move them around too much.

Microwave cookers can affect older types of cardiac pacemaker. If necessary, consult your doctor about this and warn any visitors who have one to stay out of the kitchen when the oven is switched on.

To avoid any risk of food poisoning, it is important to follow instructions about stirring, turning and standing time when reheating precooked meals, to ensure they are sufficiently hot, especially in the centre. They should be piping hot right through before serving (*see* CHILLED FOOD).

(*see also* FOOD POISONING)

Caring for a Microwave Cooker

The most important thing to remember is never to switch on the microwave cooker when it is empty. If there is nothing to absorb the microwaves, they bounce back to the magnetron (*see* MICRO-WAVES) and will shorten its life. Leave a cup of water in the cooker when not in use, then no damage will occur if the oven is accidentally turned on.

Wipe the cooker with a damp cloth after each use and mop up spillages immediately or they will continue to absorb microwaves. Foods do not burn on to the interior of the cooker but if any spilled food does stick, do not scrape it off with a sharp instrument as this could damage the interior and distort the pattern of microwaves.

To clean the cooker, place a large bowl of water inside it and turn the cooker on to full power until the water gives off steam. Remove the bowl and wipe the oven with a damp cloth wrung out in washing up liquid, then rinse with clear water and dry with a clean cloth.

Suitable Containers for Microwave Cooking

A wide variety of containers can be used in a microwave cooker. Round containers are best, followed by square ones; rectangular ones are the least efficient. Choose containers with straight sides which allow you to spread the food in an even layer.

The containers must not be made of metal, or contain any metal; microwaves are reflected off metal dishes, causing arcing (*see* ARCING) which will damage the magnetron. Metal also acts as a barrier to the microwaves, preventing the food getting hot.

China, glass and some pottery dishes are suitable as long as they do not have metal trims and the pottery is not porous. To test if a dish is suitable, fill a heatproof cup with water and stand it in the dish to be tested. Put the dish in the cooker and switch on to full power for 1–2 minutes. If the dish is cool and the water hot, the dish is safe to use. If the dish is hot and the water cool, it means the dish has been absorbing the waves and is not suitable. If both dish and water are warm, the dish is safe to use but food will take longer to cook and it is preferable to use another, more suitable, container.

Plastics can be used in a microwave, though some plastics become distorted. Test for 15 seconds on full power with a little water in the dish to see if it is suitable. Also, avoid cooking food with a high proportion of fat and sugar in plastic as these ingredients become extremely hot in the cooker and may distort the plastic.

Other materials which are suitable include wicker and wood, which can be used for short periods, as for warming up bread rolls. Absorbent kitchen paper is useful for covering fatty foods, such as bacon, as it absorbs the fat and makes it crisper.

It is a good idea to have a plentiful supply of containers which can go into the freezer as well as the microwave cooker. Special microwave ware is available, in both permanent and disposable forms, and most of the containers can be used in the freezer as well. These containers are made of special materials which allow microwaves to pass through quickly so the food cooks faster than in ordinary glass or china. The range includes useful shapes like ring moulds, muffin pans, loaf dishes and pudding basins. Disposable plastic dishes, ovenproof boards, roasting bags and boil-in bags are also available.

Cooking in a Microwave Cooker

Cooking in a microwave cooker is very different from cooking by other methods and does require practice and special techniques. Your cooker will probably come with its own recipe book, with timings gauged exactly for that model. Be sure to keep your oven manufacturer's handbook for future reference.

In general, foods cook in a microwave cooker in between a quarter and a third of their conventional cooking time, but this varies according to the density, quantity and temperature of the food when it goes into the cooker.

Microwaves are attracted to water-bearing molecules. Fats and sugars will reach a higher temperature than in conventional cooking, so should be watched carefully. Bones in meat conduct heat and are best removed if possible.

Foods covered by a skin or membrane, such as sausages, egg yolks, potatoes and liver, should be pricked with a wooden cocktail stick to prevent a build-up of steam bursting them.

Make sure the container is the right size for the amount of food to be cooked. If it is too small, the food will bubble over the edges on to the base of the oven; if too large, the food will spread out too thinly and overcook in seconds.

The way food is arranged on a dish also affects the way it cooks. Place items like chicken pieces and chops in a circle with the thinner ends towards the centre, so that the thicker ends receive the most microwave energy. Other foods are best arranged around the edge of the dish. Most food will need turning, stirring or rearranging during cooking.

Foods are usually best covered, either with a lid or an inverted plate, or with absorbent kitchen paper if you want a crisp finish, as with bacon rashers. Take care when removing a lid after cooking, as the steam will be hot. Ordinary cling film should not be used for microwave cooking because of the risk of plasticizers migrating into the food. Special non-PVC films are available for use in microwave cooking.

Standing Time

Standing time is an important factor in both cooking and thawing in a microwave cooker. Once the heat action has started inside the food, it continues even after the power has been turned off. Most recipes specify the length of standing time and it is important to follow this, even if the food still looks uncooked when the power is turned off.

What Does and Does Not Cook Well

Fish and vegetables cook particularly well in a microwave oven and there is no loss of flavour or texture. Meat and poultry also cook well – care must be taken with unevenly-shaped joints to ensure even cooking.

Casseroles and soups can be made in a microwave cooker, but those requiring long, slow cooking to tenderize cheap cuts of meat and give depth of flavour are best cooked in a conventional oven or in a slow cooker and reheated in a microwave when required.

Many puddings can be made in a microwave cooker; it is particularly good for steamed or fruit puddings, using either fresh or dried fruit. Cakes can be cooked in a microwave cooker, but will look very pale because of the fast cooking and lack of applied surface heat. Ingredients (or flavourings) such as chocolate or ginger, can be added or the finished cake can be iced. Bread and pastry are best cooked in a conventional oven, but can be warmed through in a microwave cooker.

Egg and cheese dishes need to be cooked on a low setting and watched carefully, as they will become rubbery if overcooked. Sauces are excellent cooked in a microwave cooker. It can also be used for small batches of preserves; sweets, such as fudges; and for blanching vegetables for the freezer.

Dishes like soufflés and Yorkshire puddings, which need to rise, are not satisfactory cooked in a microwave cooker. Rice and pasta take just as long to cook in a microwave cooker as they do on a conventional hob.

(*see also* BROWNING DISH, BROWNING ELEMENT, MICROWAVE THERMOMETER)

Thawing in a Microwave Cooker

Frozen food can be thawed in a microwave cooker in minutes. Some cookers have a special control for automatic thawing. If your oven does not have this control, food can be thawed by turning on low power for a set period, then switching off and leaving the food to stand, before repeating this process as necessary.

MICROWAVES Microwaves are a form of electrical energy, similar to those used for transmitting radio and television, which is used in microwave cookers to cook food. The waves are of a high frequency and short length – hence the name. Microwaves cannot pass through metal – they are reflected off it – so they are safely contained within the cavity of the cooker.

Inside a microwave cooker is a magnetron, which converts electricity into microwaves. The microwaves pass through substances such as china and glass, but they are absorbed by the moisture molecules in food. They make the molecules vibrate at such a rapid rate that they produce intense heat, which cooks the food. Microwaves penetrate all the surfaces of the food simultaneously, to a depth of about 5 cm (2 inches), and the heat then spreads to the rest of the food.

MICROWAVE THERMOMETER A special thermometer that is useful when cooking meat in a microwave cooker that is not equipped with a temperature probe. It replaces a conventional meat thermometer which, because of its mercury content, cannot be used in a microwave cooker. A conventional meat thermometer should only be used *after* food has been cooked. (*see also* MEAT, TEMPERATURE PROBE)

MIGNARDISE A French name given to various small and dainty made-up dishes.

MIGNON A French word meaning small and dainty. In cookery, it is applied to small, tender portions of fillet of beef or chicken breast.

MILANAISE, À LA A French expression used to describe dishes garnished with spaghetti or macaroni, tomato sauce and ham or tongue. It also refers to food dipped in egg and a mixture of breadcrumbs and cheese (often Parmesan), then deep- or shallow-fried.

MILK In general, this refers to cows' milk, though in some countries goats' and ewes' milk are equally important for using fresh and for making into cheese and other milk products. Other types of milk used in various parts of the world include mares', buffaloes' and camels'. Soya milk, produced from the soya bean, is becoming increasingly available and is a useful substitute for cows' milk for anyone allergic to cows' milk (particularly babies) or following a vegan diet.

Milk is a highly nutritious food and a major source of protein and calcium. A cool refreshing drink in summer, or a warming one in winter, milk is one of the most versatile ingredients in the kitchen. It is vital for making a wide range of dishes – sauces, soups, batters, pancakes and many delicious desserts. Milk contains bacteria which, if allowed to develop, produce lactic acid which gradually turns the milk sour. Eventually, lactic acid acts on the protein in milk (casein), resulting in the separation of the milk into curds and whey. It is this property of milk that is put to good use in the production of all types of cheese and yogurt.

In Britain, the milk that is delivered to our doorsteps each morning, or that we buy in the supermarket, is cows' milk that has been pasteurized and, in some cases, homogenized. Pasteurization is a method of sterilizing the milk and destroying pathogenic (disease-carrying) organisms, while, at the same time, reducing the number of souring organisms present. Homogenization breaks down the globules of fat so the cream does not separate out so easily (*see* HOMOGENIZE, PASTEURIZE). Raw, untreated, unpasteurized milk is sometimes available (though not usually from supermarkets) and many people consider its creamy richness far superior to pasteurized milk. However, it can carry a health risk, despite thorough testing and the certifying of cows as brucellosis and tuberculosis free, and is not recommended for young children, elderly people or pregnant women. Unpasteurized milk is usually sold in green-topped bottles or clearly labelled cartons.

(*see also* BUTTER, BUTTERMILK, CHEESE, CREAM, YOGURT)

Types of Milk
Five different types of pasteurized milk are available, each classified according to fat content. The coloured foil caps on milk bottles act as a guide to the different types.

Channel Island (gold top) This is the richest, creamiest milk, with 4.8 per cent fat content.

Whole milk (silver top) Most of the cream rises to the surface to give a visible cream line. It contains 3.8 per cent fat.

Homogenized (red top) Whole milk (3.8 per cent fat) in which the cream has been evenly distributed throughout.

Semi-skimmed (silver and red striped top) A little over half the cream has been removed to give between 1.5 and 1.8 per cent fat.

Skimmed (silver and blue checked top) Almost all the cream has been removed to give 0.1 per cent fat. This milk is ideal for anyone trying to reduce fat consumption, but should not be given to babies or young children who need the additional energy and fat-soluble vitamins A and D provided by the fat contained in whole milk.

Other types of whole, semi-skimmed and skimmed milk widely available are:

Sterilized This is homogenized milk that has been heated to boiling point or above to ensure a sterile product. It will keep for several weeks without refrigeration, provided it is not opened, but must be refrigerated after opening. It is usually sold in tall bottles capped like beer bottles. The milk has a slightly 'cooked' flavour.

Ultra-heat treated Known as UHT or long-life milk, this has been homogenized, then ultra-heated (to 132°C/270°F) and aseptically packaged in foil-lined containers. It keeps unopened without refrigeration until the expiry date stamped on the container (usually several months ahead). Refrigerate after opening.

Condensed This is pasteurized, homogenized milk that is boiled under special conditions until it is reduced to about a third of its original volume. Condensed milk is often sweetened and its texture is thick and viscous. It is sold in cans, its high sugar content acting as a preservative. It is used to make desserts and sweets.

Evaporated Unlike condensed milk, evaporated milk is not pasteurized or sweetened but is sterilized by heat after canning. It is evaporated to half its original volume, then homogenized, canned and sterilized. Its consistency is thinner than condensed milk and it can be poured over desserts instead of cream, or used in coffee.

Dried milk powder This may be either whole or skimmed milk that is spray-dried or condensed and roller-dried. The most commonly available, however, is made from spray-dried skimmed milk. It is available in cans or jars and should be dissolved in a little cold water before being made up to the required amount. It can be used in cooking or for making hot drinks.

BST in Milk Bovine somatotropin (BST) is a natural growth hormone that is produced in the pituitary gland of the cow and regulates milk production. It is secreted by all cows and is present in minute quantities in all milk. Experiments have shown that by increasing the amount of this hormone in a cow, its milk production can be artificially increased. At first, BST was extracted from its natural source, the pituitary gland, but BST has now been genetically engineered in the laboratory and is available in large quantities for injection into cows.

Amid increasing controversy, at the time of going to press, the hormone is currently being tested on dairy herds in Britain, the locations of which are being kept a secret. BST is thought to be safe because residues of the hormone in milk from BST-treated cows do not exceed those found in other milk. While, at present, there is no reason to question the Ministry of Agriculture, Fisheries and Food's assurances that BST is safe for human consumption, many people are angry that they are not being given the choice of whether or not to use milk from BST-treated cows, especially since it is impossible to be certain that synthetic BST is as safe for human consumption as naturally-occurring BST. There is also some concern from animal welfare groups that intense milk production may reduce a cow's productive life. At the same time, anxiety has been expressed by dairy farmers who fear they will be put out of business by BST which could result in such an increase in milk production that proportionately fewer cows will be needed. It is not yet possible to say whether the use of BST will be permitted on a permanent basis.

MILK PUDDING Milk forms the basis of many puddings and desserts, including yogurt, junket and many custards and creams. However, a milk pudding is generally an old-fashioned hot dish made by cooking some kind of grain in milk. The grain used may be rice, sago, tapioca, semolina or oatmeal and puddings may be enriched by the addition of eggs or cream, flavoured with dried fruit or spices (especially nutmeg), or given a caramel topping.

MILK SHAKE Served chilled, this is a refreshing drink made by whisking milk with a flavouring, such as strong coffee, chocolate powder, fruit juice or fruit syrup. Milk shakes are best made in an electric blender, but can be made with a rotary whisk. Commercially produced milk shake flavourings are available. For an ice-cold milk shake, add a scoop of ice cream before serving.

MILK SUBSTITUTES A number of commercially produced milk substitutes are available, usually in powder form. They are known as 'filled' milks or 'non-dairy creamers' and are usually used as a substitute for milk in tea or coffee. They may be made from skimmed milk solids, animal fats or vegetable oils, emulsifiers and antioxidants.

MILL To reduce foods to a powder or paste. On a large scale, cereal grains are 'milled' to produce flour and, in the kitchen, some small, hand-operated implements which carry out this process are also known as mills, such as salt mills, pepper mills, spice mills and vegetable mills, though the coffee mill has mostly been replaced by the electric coffee grinder. (*see also* GRIND, MOULI-LEGUMES)

MILLE-FEUILLE This is the French name (meaning, literally, a thousand leaves) of a sweet pastry made from thin layers of puff pastry sandwiched together with jam and whipped cream; the top is iced with glacé icing. A savoury version can be made with cheese. *Mille-feuilles* are usually made in long strips which are then cut into small rectangular pastries, but can also be made in the form of a large round gâteau.

MILLET A general name given to a variety of grasses which produce small edible grains. Varieties of millet include common millet, sorghum, finger millet, kaffir corn, bulrush millet and the West African 'hungry rice'. They are hardy crops which, in the West, are grown mostly for bird seed or animal fodder, though in many parts of Africa and Asia millet is considered an important part of the diet, since it will survive in arid conditions when other cereals will not.

Millet is rich in iron and B vitamins and is gluten-free. The pale yellow husked grains are available from health food shops and can be cooked and served with hot savoury dishes, or cooled and used in a salad. Millet has a delicate, somewhat bland, flavour which combines well with other ingredients. If liked, the grains can be roasted or lightly fried before cooking. Millet grains can also be cooked in the same way as rice to make a sweet milk pudding. Millet flakes and millet flour are also sometimes available. Millet flakes can be added to a home-made muesli, while the gluten-free flour can be mixed with other flours to make bread or used to make scones, pancakes or crumble toppings.

MILT An alternative name for the soft roe found in female fish. It is also sometimes used for the spleen of animals (*see* MELT).

MINCE (Ground Meat) The name given to meat which is finely divided by chopping or passing through a mincing machine. The term usually refers to uncooked meat, but cooked meat is often minced before reheating.

As the meat is finely divided it is easy to assimilate and is suitable for those with weak digestions and for young children. Mince is often mixed with cereals, vegetables and pulses, to make the meat go further while still retaining its appetizing flavour; these added ingredients also serve to give body and interest to the dish. Mince needs careful serving if it is to appear appetizing; it may be served with potato rings and garnished with snippets of fried bread, tomatoes and mushrooms; or it can be made into hamburgers, rissoles, pies, bolognaise sauce or shepherd's pie. (*see also* BEEFBURGER, LAMB, SAUSAGEMEAT)

MINCEMEAT The preserve used as a filling for mince pies, which are part of the traditional Christmas fare in Britain. As the name suggests, the original mincemeat included cooked lean beef, though today this is invariably omitted. There are numerous treasured family recipes, all differing slightly; for example, some use Seville oranges and some use sweet oranges or tangerines, while others omit the orange flavour altogether. The remaining basic ingredients are currants, sultanas, raisins, chopped mixed peel, apples, almonds, sugar, shredded suet, nutmeg, cinnamon and lemon rind and juice.

A rich mincemeat is best allowed to mature for a month after it is made, but if a larger proportion of apple and no brandy are included it should not be kept for more than a week or it may ferment.

Mincemeat is usually made into mince pies or mince tarts, but may also be used in steamed suet or sponge puddings. It is also tasty in less traditional desserts; it blends well with apples and pears.

MINCE PIE A small, round individual pastry made from shortcrust or puff pastry and filled with mincemeat (*see* MINCEMEAT). In Britain, mince pies are traditionally served at Christmas time and may be eaten hot or cold, with or without cream. They are often served sprinkled with caster or icing sugar. Some people like to eat them with Stilton cheese.

MINCING The process of chopping or cutting food into very small pieces. Mincing may be done with a knife, a manual mincing machine or in a food processor. (*see also* MINCE)

MINEOLA (Minneola) A hybrid citrus fruit that is a cross between a grapefruit and a tangerine and bright orange in colour. It is about the size of an orange but its shape is less round than an orange, with the stem end tapering into a knob, rather like a lemon. The thick skin peels off easily to reveal a soft, juicy fruit with an aromatic flavour and very few pips. Mineolas are usually available from January to August and are imported from countries such as Israel, California and South Africa. They can be used in the same ways as oranges and tangerines. (*see also* ORANGE, TANGERINE)

MINERALS In nutritional terms, this refers to a number of chemical substances that occur naturally in food and are needed for the sustenance of a healthy body. They cannot be manufactured by the body and must therefore be obtained from food. At present, 15 minerals have been identified as being essential to health, and others are still under investigation. The majority of people obtain enough minerals provided a good variety of food is eaten.

The most important minerals are calcium, iron, magnesium, phosphorus, potassium, sodium chloride and sulphur. Others, required in minute amounts, are known as trace elements. (For details about individual minerals, see separate entries and TRACE ELEMENTS.)

MINERAL WATER A general name which can refer to any water collected from a natural spring and which contains various minerals. Many mineral waters are attributed with therapeutic properties and are usually much purer and better for drinking than the average tap water, though some of them do contain very high levels of some minerals.

Mineral waters are collected from springs in France, Germany, Italy and Britain. They have long been popular for drinking with a meal in France, Germany, Spain and Italy, but only recently has their popularity increased in Britain, partly because of concerns about drinking polluted tap water. Mineral waters may be drunk on their own or mixed with fruit juice, wine or other drinks.

Some mineral waters are naturally carbonated, while others are artificially aerated. All types are now readily available in large plastic or glass bottles. Popular French varieties include Perrier, Vichy and Evian, while British brands include waters from Malvern and the Highlands of Scotland. Most supermarkets sell their own brand of mineral water. By law, all mineral waters must be bottled at source, making them somewhat expensive – in fact 600 times more expensive than tap water.

MINESTRA An Italian word used as a general name for any type of thick soup, though usually applied to a thick vegetable soup, such as *minestrone*.

MINESTRONE The most celebrated Italian soup, made from a variety of vegetables and pasta and served with grated Parmesan cheese. A number of different recipes exist.

MINT There are many culinary varieties of this common herb, with different flavours and scents, such as peppermint, eau de cologne mint, spearmint and applemint. The herb known as spearmint or garden mint is the variety most often used in cooking. Mint is readily available dried but is very easy to grow; in fact it is almost impossible to get rid of once it has taken hold in the garden. Use fresh mint to make mint sauce or jelly to serve with roast lamb; add a sprig to the cooking water for new potatoes, peas and other vegetables; use to garnish wine and fruit cups. Mint is also good with fish or can be used to make a refreshing tisane. (*see also* PENNYROYAL)

MINT JULEP (*see* JULEP)

MINUTE, À LA A French term used to describe food that has been cooked quickly, such as grills and omelettes.

MIRABELLE (*see* PLUM)

MIREPOIX The French name for a mixture of cut vegetables, usually carrot, celery and onion, often combined with a little ham or bacon and used as a bed on which to braise meat. A *mirepoix* is also used in the preparation of some classic French sauces, specifically *sauce espagnole*.

MIRIN (*see* SAKE)

MISO (*see* BEAN PASTE)

MIXED GRILL A popular informal dish that may include a number of grilled meats, such as chops, sausages, bacon or ham, served with grilled tomatoes, mushrooms and chips. When cooking a mixed grill, the items which take the longest to cook should be placed on the grill first, so that all the food is ready at the same time.

MIXED HERBS A ready-made mixture of dried herbs, usually consisting of parsley, sage, thyme, marjoram and tarragon. Mixed herbs may be used to season savoury dishes which do not require individual herbs, e.g. soups and casseroles.

MIXED SPICE A mixture of sweet-flavoured ground spices, usually consisting of cloves, allspice, cinnamon, nutmeg and ginger. Mixed spice is most often used in sweet dishes, cakes, biscuits and confectionery, but can also be added sparingly to curries and spiced Middle Eastern dishes. Mixed spice is available ready-mixed, but, for the best flavours, can also be made up as required from whole spices.

MOCHA A strongly flavoured coffee produced in various countries (*see* COFFEE).

The word mocha is often also used to describe cakes and puddings flavoured with coffee and is sometimes applied to a mixture of coffee and chocolate flavourings.

MOCK TURTLE SOUP A brown gelatinous soup made from calf's head which is supposed to resemble real turtle soup. After cooking, the pieces of meat from the head are preserved and left until cold, then cut into tiny cubes which are added to the soup at the last minute.

MODE, À LA A French expression most often used to describe a dish of braised beef cooked in a classic style with veal, carrots and onions. However, it may also be applied to other dishes cooked in a certain regional style. In America, a pie *à la mode* is a fruit or other sweet pie served with ice cream.

MOLASSES A general term used for the thick, brown syrupy drainings from raw sugar or the syrup obtained from the sugar during the process of refinement. Molasses varies in texture, that drained from beet sugar being very bitter and disagreeable to taste. Cane sugar molasses is combined with refinery syrup to produce a variety of treacles, including black (West Indian) treacle, that are available for use in cakes, biscuits and confectionery. The darkest molasses of all is known as blackstrap molasses. Molasses has no nutritional value apart from its sugar content. (*see also* GOLDEN SYRUP, SUGAR, TREACLE)

MOLLUSC The general name for a group of creatures that have soft bodies and mostly live inside hard, solid shells. The molluscs can be divided into three smaller groups: gastropods (univalves), bivalves and cephalopods. The univalve or single-shelled molluscs are those with just one solid shell, such as snails, abalone, whelks and winkles. The bivalve molluscs all have a hinged shell that is in two parts, for example mussels, clams, oysters and scallops. The final group, the cephalopods, are not easily recognizable as molluscs since they have no external shell; the group includes squid, octopus and cuttlefish.

MONASTINE A yellow liqueur made in France. It resembles yellow Chartreuse in flavour.

MONGUETE (*see* BEAN, FRENCH)

MONKEY NUT (*see* PEANUT)

MONKFISH (Anglerfish) A round sea fish with a very large, ugly head, the monkfish is native to the Mediterranean and both sides of the Atlantic. Only the tail of the monkfish is eaten and it is sold as fillets which can be grilled, fried, poached or baked. The firm white flesh has a flavour not unlike lobster. It is available all year but at its best from October to January. Smoked monkfish fillets can also sometimes be found. The name is also sometimes given to a member of the shark family known as angel fish (*see* ANGEL FISH).

MONOSODIUM GLUTAMATE (MSG, Vetsin) A powder with little taste of its own but which enhances the flavour of meat and vegetables and is widely used in processed foods for home use. It is made from glutamic acid which occurs naturally in the gluten of some cereals. It is also called 'taste' powder and 'gourmet' powder, particularly when used in Chinese cooking. Monosodium glutamate can be bought from Chinese food shops and some supermarkets, where it is marketed under a variety of brand names.

MONTEREY JACK An American cows' milk cheese that originated in Monterey, California, but is now made in other parts of America. Its texture is similar to that of an English Cheddar but its flavour is rather bland. It can be used in much the same way as Cheddar.

MONTMORENCY, À LA The French name usually given to various sweet and savoury dishes and cakes which include Montmorency cherries. It is also given, however, to other dishes which do not include cherries, but which are dedicated to the family of the same name.

MOOLI (*see* RADISH)

MOONG DAL (*see* MUNG BEAN)

MOORFOWL (Moorcock, Moorgame) Names used in Scotland for grouse; in England, these names sometimes denote black grouse (*see* GROUSE).

MOREL (*see* MUSHROOM)

MORELLO (*see* CHERRY)

MORNAY A classic French sauce made by flavouring a béchamel sauce with grated Gruyère, Parmesan or Cheddar cheese. A Mornay sauce may be enriched with egg yolks and is usually used as a coating for a dish of cooked eggs, fish, chicken or vegetables which is then browned under the grill or in the oven. Dishes which include Mornay sauce are often called '*à la Mornay*'. (*see also* BÉCHAMEL)

MORTADELLA (Bologna Sausage) A large sausage traditionally made in Bologna, Italy; it consists of finely minced pork, ham and pork fat, flavoured with freshly ground white peppercorns, garlic and sometimes pistachio nuts. *Mortadella* is sold ready to eat and is usually thinly sliced and served as a cold hors d'oeuvre.

MORTAR (*see* PESTLE AND MORTAR)

MOSELLE (Mosel) The name given to wines made in vineyards in the regions of France, Luxembourg and Germany surrounding the river Moselle and its tributaries, the Saar and Ruwer. The best wines come from Germany; they resemble Rhine wines and hock, but have a very fine flavour, dry and clear. Wines from the central region (*Mittel-Mosel*) are more acid and zesty than the Rhine wines, the best coming from Bernkastel, though Piesport is also justifiably famous. Saar wines, including those of Wiltingen, Ayl and Ockfen, are brilliant and austere. Ruwer wines (Eitelsbach, Mertesdorf and Kasel) are fine and delicate. Moselle wines can be served as a drink without food or with light meals.

MOULD A hollow container which can be of varying shapes, used for making certain sweet and savoury dishes, which are then turned out of the mould to serve. Moulds can be made of plastic, metal, glass or china and usually have indentations which are printed on the food when it is turned out. The food is placed in the mould whilst in a liquid or very soft state, then chilled or cooked to transform it to a solid mass. Dishes made in a mould usually contain some form of setting or gelling agent, such as eggs, gelatine or butter.

The term also applies to a woolly, furry growth which consists of minute fungi. It will grow on meat, cheese, bread and sweet food if the correct conditions of warmth and moisture are present. The growth usually indicates that the food is not fresh. Although not harmful, the mould gives food an unpleasant taste and appearance.

Certain mould growths are responsible for the flavour and colour of cheeses such as Roquefort and Stilton, and on some cheeses, such as Camembert, a mould forms the outer skin. However, in these cases, the moulds are deliberately introduced and controlled. (*see also* CHEESE)

MOULE À MANQUÉ A classic French cake tin that resembles a deep sandwich tin but has slightly sloping sides. It is principally for cakes which are to be iced as the sloping sides allow the icing to run down easily.

MOULES MARINIÈRE Probably the best known mussel dish, often served as an hors d'oeuvre accompanied by brown bread and butter or hot garlic bread. It consists of mussels that have been cooked in a wine sauce flavoured with shallots and herbs. The mussels are served on the half-shell, that is with one shell removed, with the hot reduced sauce poured over. (*see also* MUSSEL)

MOULI-JULIENNE (*see* MOULI-LÉGUMES)

MOULI-LÉGUME An inexpensive hand-operated food mill found in most French kitchens, used for reducing cooked foods, including vege-

Using a mouli-légume to purée cooked vegetables to make a thick soup.

tables, to a purée. A similar gadget, known as a *mouli-julienne*, has five cutting discs and will shred and slice raw vegetables. Both these food mills are also available in Britain.

MOUNTAIN ASH (*see* ROWAN BERRY)

MOUSSAKA A savoury dish based on sliced aubergines and minced lamb. Moussaka originated in Greece, Turkey and the Balkans, but is now popular in many other countries, including Britain. It consists of alternating layers of minced lamb (browned and flavoured with onion, garlic and tomato) and fried aubergine slices in an ovenproof dish. The final layer is coated with a sauce made from yogurt and eggs and flavoured with cheese and nutmeg, or with béchamel sauce, before the dish is baked in the oven. Moussaka makes the perfect informal supper dish and is best served simply with a salad.

MOUSSE A mousse is a light, frothy dish which is usually served as a cold dessert, but may be sweet or savoury. It is similar to a soufflé, but does not rise above the dish in which it is served, as does a soufflé (*see* SOUFFLÉ). A mousse usually has as its base a flavoured egg mixture, or a fruit purée into which whisked egg whites and sometimes whipped cream are folded. Gelatine is sometimes used as a setting agent. Mousses are often made in a mould and turned out when set. A cold mousse can be frozen but when a gelatine mixture is used it is merely chilled. Savoury mousses, made from fish, shellfish or vegetables, are popular hors d'oeuvre, served with toast.

MOUSSELINE A savoury sauce based on hollandaise sauce to which beaten egg white or whipped cream has been added just before serving, giving a frothy effect. A *mousseline* sauce should be served as soon as possible; it is a good accompaniment to fish (especially sole) or green vegetables, such as asparagus. (*see also* HOLLANDAISE)

A sweet *mousseline* sauce can be made from eggs, sugar and sherry beaten together over hot water; it is served with sponge puddings and fruit.

MOZZARELLA An Italian curd cheese, pale-coloured and egg-shaped. When fresh, it is very soft and dripping with whey. Traditionally made from water buffaloes' milk, Mozzarella is now made from cows' milk. It should be eaten fresh, as the cheese ripens quickly and is past its best in a few days.

Mozzarella is now readily available from delicatessens and supermarkets, usually packed in brine, and can be used in salads (especially with tomatoes, onions and olives), pizzas, lasagnes and other Italian dishes. It becomes stringy and

chewy when cooked. If Mozzarella is not available, Bel Paese can be used as a substitute. A smoked version of Mozzarella is also available.

MSG (*see* MONOSODIUM GLUTAMATE)

MUESLI A cereal mixture which was first made in Switzerland for health reasons by a nutritionist called Bircher-Benner towards the end of the nineteenth century. It consists of a mixture of raw cereals which can include some or all of the following: oats, wheat, rye, millet and barley flakes; to these may be added dried fruit, nuts, sugar, bran, wheatgerm and grated apple. Muesli has now become a popular breakfast cereal served with milk or fruit juice and sometimes yogurt or cream.

There are many commercial varieties of muesli on the market, most of which have a high sugar content. A home-made muesli can be made from a bought muesli base which merely requires the addition of flavouring and sweetening; alternatively it can be made by buying each cereal separately and combining them with flavouring ingredients. The cheapest and easiest method is to use rolled oats as a base, but these tend to be floury and soft compared with other cereal bases.

Whichever variety of muesli is served, additional ingredients, such as fresh citrus fruits, extra nuts and sugar can always be added to suit individual tastes. (*see also* BREAKFAST CEREALS)

MUFFIN The traditional English muffin is a thick, flat yeast cake made from a soft dough and baked in rings on a griddle or hot plate, similar to a crumpet. This type of muffin is usually served warm with butter.

The American muffin is more like a small sweet sponge cake, baked in deep patty tins and sometimes flavoured with glacé cherries, dried fruit, fresh fruit, maple syrup or honey. The mixture uses baking powder as a raising agent and the baked muffins have a very soft and doughy texture. They can be eaten plain or split and buttered.

MULBERRY Similar in shape to a blackberry, but larger, the mulberry is a soft, juicy, fragile fruit which should be picked from the tree when very ripe. The two most common varieties are the black and white. Black mulberries are a wine-red colour with a sharp flavour; white mulberries are sweeter. In Asia, the leaves of the white mulberry provide food for silkworms.

Mulberries require careful washing. Place in a colander and dip into a bowl of water once or twice, then leave to dry in the colander. Mulberries are generally eaten raw or used to make jams and wines, and in other ways suitable for blackberries. The deep purple juice of the black mulberry is very staining.

MULLED WINE (*see* MULLING)

MULLET, GREY Grey mullet is a round sea fish which looks and tastes similar to sea bass. It is sold whole or as fillets. The white flesh is firm with a mild, nutty flavour and is suitable for baking, grilling, steaming or poaching. (For basic preparation and cooking, see FISH.)

Grey mullet roe is also available and is traditionally used to make the Greek *taramasalata*, although cod's roe is more frequently used these days. Dried grey mullet roe is known as *botargo* in Italy (*see* BOTARGO).

MULLET, RED (Goatfish) No relation to the grey mullet, red mullet is a smaller, crimson round sea fish with a unique and delicate flavour. One of the common varieties is known as golden mullet. The liver of red mullet is a delicacy and should not be discarded; the fish is often known as the woodcock of the sea because it is cooked with the liver still inside. Red mullet is sold whole and may be grilled, fried or baked. It is available all year, but at its best during the summer months. (For basic preparation and cooking, *see* FISH.)

MULLIGATAWNY A curry-flavoured soup of Anglo-Indian origin. The soup is based on beef or chicken stock to which may be added a variety of vegetables and rice. Flavouring ingredients may include bacon, tomatoes, curry paste, apple, mango chutney, herbs and spices and the finished soup may be enriched with cream.

MULLING To warm, spice and sweeten ale, cider or wine. Mulled wine is usually made with red wine spiced with cinnamon and nutmeg and sweetened with sugar. It should be served hot and makes a popular winter party punch. Mulled ale may be spiced with cloves, nutmeg and ginger, sweetened with sugar, and 'spiked' with rum or brandy.

MUM A strong, sweet ale made of wheat and malt, which was originally brewed in Brunswick.

MUNG BEAN (Green Gram, Moong Dal) This small, round, green dried bean is often used in Indian cookery or for sprouting (*see* BEAN SPROUTS). When cooked, the beans tend to be sticky but are good in stuffings and salads. In Indian cooking, the dried beans are sometimes soaked and ground to make a flour that is used to make various types of savoury pancakes, snacks and dumplings. (*see also* PULSES)

MÜNSTER There are both French and German versions of this semi-hard cheese which has been made in the Alsace region since the seventh century. French Münster is available as a farmhouse cheese, made from unpasteurized cows' milk, or as a commercially-produced cheese, made all year round from pasteurized cows' milk. Münster is also available flavoured with caraway or aniseed. The German cheese (called Münster) is made from pasteurized cows' milk and has a milder flavour. All types of Münster are yellow in colour and have a red rind. They may be eaten as they are or used in cooking. In Alsace, Münster is traditionally served with Gewürztraminer wine.

MUSCADET A fresh, dry white wine made from the Muscadet grape in the Loire region of France. It is a popular wine for drinking on its own or for serving with a light meal.

MUSCATEL A type of fine, large, juicy, sun-dried raisin from Spain. Muscatels are often served as a dessert, especially at Christmas time, and usually accompanied by blanched almonds. They may also be used in cooking. (*see also* VINE FRUITS)

The name Muscatel is also given to sweet white wines made in France, Spain and Italy from the Muscat grape.

MUSCOVADO SUGAR (*see* SUGAR)

MUSH A kind of maize (corn) porridge, resembling polenta, made in America. (*see also* CORN, POLENTA)

MUSHROOM An edible fungus of which there are many varieties. Some types of mushroom are cultivated on a very large scale, though it is still possible to gather mushrooms in the wild, provided they can be positively identified as an edible variety.

Mushrooms are an important ingredient in many dishes. They have an indispensable aromatic flavour that is essential to many soups, stews and casseroles, and they make a delicious filling for omelettes, quiches or vols-au-vent. On their own, they are popular fried and served for breakfast with bacon and egg or they can be served *à la grecque* as a dinner party starter. They are also an essential ingredient in many classic dishes, such as *coq au vin* and *boeuf bourguignon*. Mushrooms are also the main ingredient of a classic French preparation known as *duxelles*, for which chopped mushrooms are sautéed with onions and shallots and used as a stuffing or the basis of a sauce.

Large, flat mushrooms may be stuffed and served as a starter, while button mushrooms are popular coated in batter and deep fried.

Fresh Mushrooms

Cultivated Mushrooms
Most of the fresh mushrooms on sale in supermarkets and other shops are cultivated varieties of the field mushroom. They are picked and sold at varying stages of maturity.

Button mushrooms are picked when they are very young, before the caps have opened.

Cup mushrooms are picked when the cap has partially opened, and are available as closed cup (with the skin still closed beneath the cap) or open cup mushrooms, which have been allowed to grow a little longer until the skin has pulled away from the stalk, revealing pink gills.

Flat mushrooms are left to grow until the cap has opened out and become flat, with dark brown gills. The flavour of cultivated mushrooms improves with age, so that flat mushrooms have the most flavour.

Oyster mushrooms, which have a stronger flavour, are now cultivated and are available in some supermarkets. They are shaped like a fan and have a smooth, slippery texture reminiscent of an oyster.

Chestnut mushrooms are similar to closed cup mushrooms, but are larger, firmer and brown in colour with a stronger flavour.

Other types of cultivated mushroom include the Oriental *shiitake* which has recently appeared fresh in supermarkets and is also available dried. It is a hardy, dark brown mushroom with a pleasant, distinctive flavour.

Wild Mushrooms
Field mushrooms are the most commonly found wild mushrooms and are usually seen, as their name suggests, in fields, meadows and other open spaces. Other wild mushrooms to be found in Britain include the blewitt, chanterelle (girolle), honey fungus, horse mushroom, morel, orange peel fungus, oyster mushroom and parasol mushroom. Most mushrooms are found growing wild towards the end of the summer and in the early

autumn, and the best time to pick them is first thing in the morning. It is easy to confuse edible mushrooms with poisonous varieties, so it is essential that mushroom picking is done with the help of an expert or a detailed book that clearly identifies the many varieties. It is sometimes possible to buy some of the less common types of wild mushroom.

To select: Choose fresh cultivated or wild mushrooms that are firm-textured, with fresh-looking stalks that are not brown or withered. Use fresh mushrooms as soon as possible since they deteriorate quickly. Allow 100 g (4 oz) fresh mushrooms per person.

To prepare: Trim the stalk ends only and wipe with a damp cloth. If very dirty, wash them quickly but do not let them soak. Large mushrooms can be peeled, but only if really necessary, as much of the flavour is in the skin.

To cook: Sauté in butter or oil, steam or cook in a little salted water for 3–5 minutes.

To serve: Serve sautéed mushrooms hot as an accompaniment to grilled or fried foods. Young mushrooms can be eaten raw in salads.

Dried Mushrooms

Many wild mushrooms that are rare in this country, grow in greater abundance or are cultivated in other countries and are available here in dried form. Dried mushrooms should be soaked in warm water before use, then can be used as fresh. They are an important ingredient in Italian and Oriental cooking.

Chanterelles (girolles) grow throughout Europe but cannot be cultivated and are usually available dried or canned in Britain. They have a delicious delicately perfumed flavour.

Ceps and morels also have a very delicate flavour and are used in many European dishes. They are usually only available dried. Ceps are members of the boletus family of fungi and, in Italy, are known as *funghi porcini*.

Horn of plenty is a funnel-shaped mushroom with dark brown gills. It is also known as black trumpet.

Matsutake (pine mushroom) is a Japanese mushroom that is available dried in this country. It is considered one of the best and tends to be very expensive.

Wood ear is also known as Chinese black fungus and is used in many Chinese recipes.

Jew's ear may be used in the same way as wood ear, to which it is related. It has an unusual cupped shape. (*see also* AGARIC, BOLETUS, FUNGUS, TRUFFLE)

MUSSEL A common bivalve mollusc with very dark blue, almost black, shells, though some have brown shells and a variety imported from New Zealand has blue and green shells. Mussels are found in seas all over the world and are usually sold still alive or cooked and shelled. As mussels often come from polluted waters, they are usually kept in clean water before selling to enable them to flush themselves through. (*see also* SHELLFISH)

Probably the best known mussel dish is *moules marinière*, but they may be cooked in other ways and are a traditional ingredient of a Spanish *paella*. (*see also* MOULES MARINIÈRE)

Smoked mussels are also available. They are removed from their shells, then lightly smoked and usually bottled in brine or canned in oil.

To select: Mussels are usually sold by the quart (2 pints/1.1 litres) which is approximately equivalent to 900 g (2 lb). They are available from September to March. Never buy mussels with cracked or open shells.

To prepare: Put the mussels in a large bowl and, under running cold water, scrub off any mud, barnacles or seaweed. Trim off the 'beards' (byssus) with sharp scissors. Discard any mussels that are open and do not close when sharply tapped with the back of a knife. Rinse again until there is no trace of sand in the bowl.

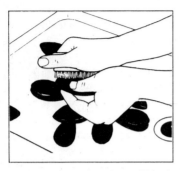
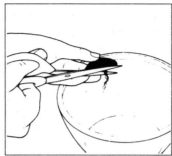

Scrubbing mussels with a stiff brush to remove mud, barnacles and seaweed.

Snipping off a mussel 'beard' (byssus) with a sharp pair of kitchen scissors.

Tapping mussels with the back of a knife to check that they will close. Discard any that will not.

To cook: Put the mussels in a frying pan and cover. Cook on a high heat for about 5 minutes, until the shells open. Discard any that do not open. Alternatively, put the mussels in a saucepan of water or wine, flavoured with onion and herbs. Cover and cook for 3–5 minutes or until the mussels open, shaking the pan frequently. Discard any that do not open and do not attempt to prise them open.

To serve: Mussels are often served on the half shell, that is the top shell is removed and the mussel is removed from the bottom shell. Any juices from inside the shell can be reserved and added to a sauce. Before replacing the mussel in the bottom shell to serve, remove the tough chewy ring surrounding the meat.

MUSTARD Classified as a spice, the seeds of the mustard plant are usually ground and used to make a condiment or flavouring paste known as mustard. There are three types of mustard seed – black, brown and white (or yellow); the dark seeds give aroma and white ones pungency and most made-up mustards are a combination of the two in varying proportions.

The seeds are either left whole, as when making whole grain mustards, or are ground to make mustard flour. Liquid such as wine, vinegar and cider are added to moisten it and add the characteristic flavours. Some English mustard is sold as

a dry yellow powder which is mixed with water; other mustards are sold ready-mixed in tubes, glass jars or stone pots. Mustard is used as a condiment, like salt and pepper, with a wide variety of savoury dishes and also to flavour dressings and sauces, with cheese dishes, especially Welsh rarebit and in beef, ham and bacon dishes. Mustard seeds are sometimes used whole in pickles and relishes, marinades and chutneys.

There are many different types of mustard now available, with many varying textures and flavours. Amongst those most recently developed are horseradish mustard, tarragon mustard, chilli mustard, honey mustard and fruit mustard. There are even green mustards, usually made from a variety of herbs.

English mustard is made from ground husked brown and white mustard seeds combined with wheat flour and coloured with turmeric. Its flavour is particularly pungent and it is usually served with meat dishes, such as roast beef, sausages and ham. It is available in powder form and ready-mixed in tubes and jars. The powder should be mixed with a little cold water and left to stand for at least 15 minutes before serving, to allow the flavour to develop. A whole grain English mustard is also available, made from coarsely ground whole mustard seeds, white wine, allspice and black pepper. It is a hot, pungent mustard.

French mustard is generally milder in flavour than English mustard. The best known of all French mustards is Dijon mustard, which is paler in colour than English mustard because it does not contain the husks of the brown and black seeds from which it is made and contains no colouring. It is a popular mustard for cooking or for adding to dressings and sauces. Traditionally, Dijon mustard is made with verjuice (*see* VERJUICE); mustards labelled 'Dijon style' are not made according to the traditional recipe. Meaux mustard (*moutarde de meaux*) is a whole grain mustard made from a mixture of grains. It has a grainy texture since it also contains the husks of the mustard seeds. Bordeaux mustard is the original brown French mustard. It is made from a mixture of black and brown seeds flavoured with vinegar and herbs. It is dark brown in colour and has a mild flavour.

German mustard is specially made to accompany the many types of sausage popular in Germany. There are many varieties, some more pungent than others. Düsseldorf mustard is a popular, mild variety.

American mustard is sweeter and milder than other mustards. It contains turmeric, giving it a bright yellow colour.

Cremona mustard (mostarda di Cremona) is more like a chutney than a mustard. It is made in Italy from a mixture of fruits preserved in a mustard-flavoured syrup, and is usually served with boiled meats.

MUSTARD AND CRESS (*see* CRESS)

MUSTARD GREENS (*see* CHINESE MUSTARD CABBAGE)

MUTTON In general, this name may be given to the meat of a sheep slaughtered when more than one year old. The meat of a younger sheep is known as lamb. However, since mutton does not have the good reputation it once had, it is quite common for meat from an older sheep to be given the label 'lamb'.

In Victorian times and later, mutton was considered far superior to lamb, since it had more flavour. Today, however, the more tender and succulent meat is preferred and lamb is more popular. Cuts of mutton are the same as for lamb, though larger, and the meat is darker in colour with a stronger flavour. Mutton is best braised or boiled, or cooked in a traditional dish, such as Lancashire hot-pot or Irish stew, though even these classic dishes are usually cooked with lamb these days. Recipes for mutton can be found in older cookery books. Roast or boiled mutton is traditionally served with onion or caper sauce. (*see also* LAMB)

MYCELLA A Danish semi-soft, full-fat cows' milk cheese similar to Danish Blue but with a milder flavour. It gets its name from the mould *mycelium* which produces its blue-green veins.

MYRTILLE (*see* EAU-DE-VIE)

MYRTLE Although not much used in cooking, myrtle is a very fragrant herb that goes particularly well with lamb. It produces white flowers and black berries which, along with the leaves, can be used to flavour marinades and stuffings. The myrtle is an evergreen shrub that is native to Mediterranean countries and is much used in Corsican and Sardinian cookery.

MYRTLE PEPPER (*see* ALLSPICE)

MYSÖST A whey cheese, principally made from cows' milk but sometimes with goats' milk added, which is produced in Norway. It is hard and dark brown, with a sweetish flavour. A similar, more traditional cheese, *gjetöst*, is made only from goats' milk. Both cheeses are popular served for breakfast.

N

NAARTJE A small South African tangerine.

NAM PLA A salty fish sauce from Thailand. It is used both in cooking and as a condiment.

NAN A soft, flat, pear-shaped bread from India. It is baked in a tandoor and, as there are no racks in a tandoor, the dough is slapped straight on to the inner walls of the hot oven. It sticks to the sides and bakes in a few minutes. The bread is removed from the oven with long, metal tongs. (*see also* TANDOOR)

NANTUA, À LA A French term used to describe dishes garnished or, in some cases, made with crayfish.

NAPOLITAINE, À LA The French name for a method of serving macaroni or spaghetti in a tomato sauce sprinkled with grated cheese. Pasta prepared in this way may be served as a main dish or as an accompaniment or garnish.

NARA NUT (Butternut, Butter Pit) The seed of a gourd produced by a spiny shrub that is found growing wild in the deserts of south-west Africa. It looks rather like a large melon seed.

NASEBERRY (*see* SAPODILLA)

NASHI (Asian Pear) This large, yellow-skinned fruit is more rounded than other pear varieties, looking something like a large, round, yellow apple. The crisp, white, scented flesh also tastes more like apple than pear. Asian pears are becoming increasingly available in shops and supermarkets and make an excellent snack fruit or can be used in fresh fruit salads.

NASI GORENG An Indonesian dish made by combining cooked rice, pork or chicken and seafood with fried onions, garlic and chilli. Just before serving, a shredded cooked omelette is arranged in a lattice pattern on top of the rice mixture. *Nasi goreng* is traditionally served with cucumber, peanuts and chutney.

NASTOIKA A Russian liqueur flavoured with galangal (*see* GALANGAL).

NASTURTIUM (Indian Cress) The round, hot-flavoured leaves of this familiar garden plant are occasionally eaten in salads. Young leaves are best and may be used whole or shredded. The yellow, orange or red flowers may be used to garnish salads. The green, berry-like seeds are also edible and, when pickled, make a reasonable substitute for capers.

NATUREL, AU A French term meaning plain, uncooked or very simply cooked. Raw oysters and fresh fruit, for example, are served *au naturel*.

NAVARIN The French name for a stew of lamb or mutton cooked with onions and potatoes. *Navarin printanier* is the name given to a lamb or mutton stew made with a selection of spring vegetables. (*see also* RAGOÛT)

NAVEL ORANGE (*see* ORANGE)

NAVET (French Turnip, Navette) *Navet* is the French name for any type of turnip but, in Britain, the name is most often applied to a small, tender variety that has recently become available in spring and summer. *Navets* are round and pink-tinged or elongated and white, often with their leafy tops still attached. They can be cooked in the same way as the winter turnip, but are much more tender and can be cooked without peeling. The green tops can be cooked like spinach or spring greens. (*see also* TURNIP)

NAVY BEAN (Boston Bean, Pea Bean, Yankee Bean) A small, white dried bean from the same family as the kidney bean and haricot bean. Navy beans look very similar to haricot beans and they can be used in many of the same ways. In America, they are used to make a stew known as Boston baked beans, and they were the original canned baked beans. (*see also* HARICOT BEAN, PULSES)

NEAPOLITAN A name frequently given to sweets, cakes and ice creams made in layers of two or more colours, such as white (or cream), pink, pale green and coffee or chocolate, each layer being appropriately flavoured. The layers are assembled before baking, setting or freezing or they can be sandwiched together afterwards, as is most convenient. Neapolitan dishes should be cut so that the different coloured layers show to the best advantage.

NECTARINE Nectarines are a variety of peach, but with a smooth skin that is usually a brighter red-orange colour. Many varieties of nectarine now find their way into shops and supermarkets in the summer months; some are paler-skinned and others have white rather than golden-coloured flesh. Nectarines can be eaten as they are when ripe and juicy, included in a fruit salad or used, like peaches, to make sorbets and other cold desserts, to decorate gâteaux and trifles, or to make jam. (*see also* PEACH)

To select: Look for plump, rich-coloured fruit softening along the indent. Avoid hard, extremely soft or shrivelled fruit. Nectarines will ripen at room temperature but, once ripe, should be refrigerated and used within five days.

To prepare: Simply wash, then stone and slice. If not eating immediately, brush exposed flesh with lemon juice to prevent browning. Nectarines can be eaten without peeling but, if preferred, they may be blanched and peeled like peaches.

NECTARINE, DRIED Dried nectarines are not very attractive but have a delicious flavour when reconstituted. They are available whole or halved and can be used in many of the ways dried apricots are used. Like dried apricots, dried nectarines have often been treated with sulphur in order to preserve their colour, and some Chinese varieties are preserved in sugar.

NEGUS A type of mulled wine, generally a mixture of port, claret or sherry, spice (such as nutmeg), lemon, sugar and hot water. (*see also* MULLING)

NESSELRODE PUDDING A rich and elaborate, originally French, dessert made from chestnut purée, egg yolks, cream and sometimes candied fruits, which is moulded and frozen. In French cooking, the name may also be given to other sweet or savoury dishes which contain chestnut purée.

NETTLE Young stinging nettles, which have a pleasant, slightly bitter taste, may be cooked as a vegetable, like spinach, or made into soup. Cooking completely removes the sting from the leaves, so this need not be a reason for avoiding them. Nettles are richer in iron than spinach and contain the same amount of vitamins A and C.

To select: Wearing gloves, gather the new, young tips of nettles in the spring from a patch that is not polluted by passing traffic or animals. Like spinach, nettles shrink during cooking so allow at least 225 g (8 oz) per person.

To prepare: Before cooking, it is necessary to don a pair of gloves and to sort through the gathered nettles to remove any weeds and the roots. Wash the nettles thoroughly, drain and immerse in boiling water for 2 minutes, then drain again.

To cook: Pack the nettles into a saucepan, cover and cook very gently without water until tender, as for spinach.

To serve: Drain and chop well, then add seasoning, a knob of butter and 15 ml (1 tbsp) cream for every 900 g (2 lb) nettles.

NEUFCHÂTEL A soft, creamy, cows' milk cheese prepared in Normandy and other parts of France. Neufchâtel may be eaten fresh and mild, or ripened (*affiné*), when it has a stronger flavour and red mottling on its white rind. It is usually made in small rectangular shapes, but is sometimes found in round or heart shapes.

NGAPI A dark grey paste made from decomposed fish. It is used in Burmese cooking as a flavouring or a relish; without it, Burmese food would be incomplete.

NIACIN (*see* VITAMINS)

NIÇOISE, À LA A French term used to describe a variety of dishes made or garnished with tomatoes and other ingredients typical of the southern area of France, around Nice. When used for a garnish for meat or poultry, the name implies the addition of tomatoes, olives and French beans. *Salade niçoise* is typical of southern France and contains tomatoes, cucumber, French beans, hard-boiled eggs, anchovy fillets and/or tuna, black olives, parsley and basil. It is usually dressed with a garlic-flavoured vinaigrette made with olive oil.

NICOTINIC ACID (*see* VITAMINS)

NIER BEURRE (*see* BUTTER, FRUIT)

NIGELLA Small, hard, triangular black seeds. They are used as a spice in India, Egypt and the Middle East and have a peppery flavour. They are sometimes confused with and referred to as black cumin, but the two have nothing in common and one should not be substituted for the other.

NITRATES (*see* WATER)

NOGGIN A liquid measure, usually 150 ml (¼ pint); however, the measure is variable and the term is often taken to mean simply a portion or ration of liquid, usually liquor.

NOILLY PRAT (*see* VERMOUTH)

NOISETTE A French name given to a neatly trimmed and tied boneless piece of lamb, not less than 1 cm (½ inch) thick. *Noisettes* of lamb are cut from the loin or best end of neck and are very tender cuts of meat suitable for frying or grilling. Lamb *noisettes* are usually prepared by the butcher, but they can be made at home by boning loin chops and rolling and tying them in a round shape. It is usual to wrap *noisettes* in a layer of fat before tying.

In French cooking, *noisettes* may also be cut from a boned saddle of lamb, and the name is also given to a neat, round, slice of beef fillet, or to a small grenadin of veal.

NON-DAIRY CREAMER (*see* MILK SUBSTITUTES)

NOODLES Noodles feature strongly in Chinese, Japanese and Asian cooking. They are very similar to pasta and may be used in the same way as ribbon pasta (*see* PASTA). Many types of noodle are available and are made from a variety of starchy substances. The following are the most widely available from supermarkets and specialist shops. Fresh noodles are available from Chinese supermarkets around the world.

Egg noodles are probably the best known noodles and are used a great deal in Chinese cooking. They are made from wheat flour, egg and water and are usually sold in compressed bundles of varying sizes.

Rice or *rice stick noodles* come in various thicknesses. They are made in long strands which are folded over for packaging. Very thin rice noodles are sold in compressed bundles and are known as *vermicelli*. Rice noodles can be fried until they puff up, or soaked and then stir-fried.

Transparent or *cellophane noodles* are made from mung beans, pea starch or wheat. They are made in long strands which are folded over for packaging. They need soaking before they are cooked and are usually mixed with other ingredients. In Japan, they are known as *harusame*.

Soba are Japan's most popular noodles. They are thin noodles made from buckwheat.

Chasoba (tea soba) are made from buckwheat and green tea.

Udon are very narrow, ribbon-like white noodles.

Somen are thin, very fine, white wheat noodles.

Shirataki are made from a glutinous tuber known as devil's tongue or snake palm plant.

NORFOLK DUMPLING (*see* DUMPLING)

NORI (*see* SEAWEED)

NORMANDE, À LA A French term applied to dishes containing cream, seafood, apples, cider or Calvados, for which the Normandy area of France is famous. Fish served *à la Normande* is served with Normande (Normandy) sauce and garnished with shrimps, truffles, crayfish or mussels.

NORMANDY SAUCE A white sauce served with fish. It is based on a rich velouté sauce made from fish liquor and cream and is further enriched with egg yolk and butter. It may be served with poached, grilled or steamed white fish dishes, or hot crab and lobster dishes.

NORWAY HADDOCK (*see* RED FISH)

NORWAY LOBSTER (*see* SCAMPI)

NOUGAT A hard sweet, usually white or pink, made from sugar and honey and containing chopped glacé or dried fruits, nuts, etc. Montelimar nougat is a famous white nougat made with boiled sugar, egg white, chopped nuts and cherries. (*see also* SWEETS)

NOUGATINE Similar to praline, this sweet preparation is made from a light caramel syrup and crushed almonds or hazelnuts. The mixture is spread on a marble slab or baking sheet and cut into small pieces or moulded into decorative shapes or baskets for holding other foods, or into a flat, round shape to be used as the base of a gâteau or dessert. (*see also* PRALINE)

NOUVELLE CUISINE A style of cooking which first became popular in France in the nineteen seventies. It is based on the basic principle that rich and elaborate *haute cuisine* dishes are unhealthy and unnecessary and it aims to promote a simpler, more natural style of cooking. The advocates of *nouvelle cuisine* insist on the freshest ingredients, served in natural ways without disguise and only accompanied by entirely appropriate garnishes. They aim to reduce the amount of fat used in cooking, and to serve only light sauces and lightly cooked vegetables. Favoured cooking methods include steaming, grilling and cooking *en papillote*.

Nouvelle cuisine is characterized by beautifully arranged small portions, simply but elegantly garnished, and by brightly coloured crisp vegetables cut into decorative shapes. The principles of this style of cooking have been adopted by cooks in countries other than France, though its popularity has waned in more recent years.

NOYAU A type of liqueur, originally made in France but now produced in other countries. It is rather sweet and is flavoured with fruit kernels, particularly apricot or cherry. The most famous of these liqueurs is Noyau de Poissy, which is flavoured with cherry stone kernels. It tastes rather like bitter almonds and it may be white or pink in colour. It can be drunk on its own as a liqueur, or used as a flavouring in sorbets, ice creams or fruit compotes.

NUOC-MAM (Nuoc-nam) A fish sauce much used in Vietnamese cooking, both as a condiment and a flavouring. It has a very strong smell and salty flavour and is sometimes used as a dipping sauce. It is made from small fish that have been marinated in brine, then pounded to a paste. It can be bought from specialist shops. (*see also* NAM PLA)

NUTMEG The seed of the nutmeg fruit which grows on a tree cultivated in South-East Asia. The nutmeg is hard, brown and nut-like in appearance and grows in the centre of the large round fruit. The spice known as mace also grows inside the nutmeg fruit, forming an outer web-like coating (the aril) surrounding the nutmeg. (*see also* MACE)

Nutmeg is sold whole or ground. As the flavour evaporates quickly, it is best bought whole and grated when required. Use it in chicken and cream soups, sprinkled on buttered corn, spinach, carrots, beans and Brussels sprouts, in cheese dishes, fish cakes, with chicken and veal, in custards, milk puddings, Christmas pudding and cakes.

NUTRIENT Any substance in food which provides the body with energy and the raw materials for growth, repair and reproduction. The nutrients we need are protein, fat, carbohydrate, minerals and vitamins. Hardly any foods contain only one nutrient. Most are complex mixtures of a variety of carbohydrates, fats, proteins and water, with minerals and vitamins present in much smaller amounts. Lack of an essential nutrient results in a specific deficiency disease; too much of some nutrients may cause ill-health. No one naturally-occurring food contains sufficient amounts of all the nutrients needed, so a wide variety of foods must be eaten to maintain health. (*see also* CARBOHYDRATE, FATS, MINERALS, PROTEIN, VITAMINS)

NUTRITION The process by which the body takes in food and uses it to provide the nutrients needed to keep the body alive and well. In its widest sense, this includes food production and processing, factors determining food choice, nutrient values of foods, effects of excess or inadequate food or particular nutrient intakes, and the role of diet in causing, preventing and curing disease.

NUTS The term 'nut' is used to describe any seed or fruit with an edible kernel inside a hard shell. Nuts are a highly concentrated food, rich in proteins, vitamins, minerals, fats and fibre. As well as being popular snacks, they are widely used in baking, sauces and sweet-making. Mixed with vegetables, they make a good substitute for meat, fish and eggs.

Shelled, flaked, chopped and ground nuts are best bought loose in small quantities or vacuum packed. Store them in airtight containers, preferably in the refrigerator. Nuts bought in their shells should feel heavy; if they feel light they are likely to be stale. Store nuts in their shells in a cool, dark place for up to three months.

(For detailed information about particular types of nut, see individual entries – ALMOND, BRAZIL NUT, CASHEW NUT, CHESTNUT, HAZELNUT etc.)

NUTWOOD CHEDDAR An English Cheddar cheese flavoured with cider, nuts and raisins. (*see also* CHEDDAR)

O

OAK LEAF (*see* LETTUCE)

OATCAKES An unleavened form of bread found in the north of England and Scotland. The ingredients include oatmeal, water, salt and fat. In Wales and Scotland, the mixture is made with pinhead oatmeal, rolled thinly and cut into rounds or triangles, then cooked slowly on a griddle or in the oven. In Yorkshire, the oatmeal is finely ground and made into a thick batter, then a thin layer is poured on to a heated griddle or hot iron plate and cooked until it can be removed and hung over a line in a warm room to dry and become crisp. All oatcakes should be crisp when eaten; they are popular served with butter and cheese. (*see also* OATS)

OATMEAL (*see* OATS)

OATS A cereal grass which is widely cultivated throughout the world. Oats will grow in colder and wetter climates and poorer soils than any other cereal and also in hotter climates than wheat or rye. Oats used to be the staple food in Scotland, but have now been replaced by wheat.

Oats are available in numerous forms, all produced from the husked seed or grain.

Whole oat grains (groats), with just the husks removed, are available and can be boiled and used to make a coarse porridge, though porridge made from rolled oats is usually preferred.

Oatmeal is made from cut or ground groats and is available in various grades. Pinhead oatmeal (sometimes called steel-cut) is made by cutting up whole groats into three or four pieces each. It can be used to make a coarse porridge that takes longer to cook than that made with rolled oats but is thought by many to have a better flavour.

The other grades of oatmeal available are rough-cut, medium, fine and superfine, though rough-cut and superfine can be hard to find. Rough-cut oatmeal can be used for thickening stews and making oatcakes; medium oatmeal for making cakes (such as Parkin) and for mixing with flours for scones; fine and superfine oatmeal for pancakes and coating grilled herrings.

Rolled oats or oat flakes are produced by treating the grains with heat (usually steam) while passing them between rollers. Quick-cooking or 'instant' rolled oats (for making quick porridge) are produced by the application of greater heat, which partially cooks the grain.

Jumbo rolled oats are made by rolling whole oat groats. They can be used to make a coarse porridge, eaten raw in muesli (*see* MUESLI), or toasted and used to make granola (*see* GRANOLA). Regular-sized rolled oats are made by rolling pieces of pinhead oatmeal, and are therefore smaller than jumbo rolled oats. They cook more quickly and produce a smoother porridge. Rolled oats of all sorts are frequently used to make flapjacks and biscuits.

Oat bran and oat germ are produced separately as a fine brown powder. The bran is the fibrous outer layer of the whole grain; the germ is the innermost part of the grain, the part from which the new plant would grow. Oat bran and germ can be used to make a thin porridge, can be sprinkled over savoury foods, or can be added to other flours and used in bread-making.

All types of oats have much the same food value and contain carbohydrates, protein, fat, iron, calcium and vitamin B. Oats have received publicity recently because they contain soluble fibre, a special kind of fibre which, when included in a low-fat, low-cholesterol diet, is thought to help reduce blood cholesterol levels. Oats contain very little gluten and can therefore only be used in leavened bread when combined with other flours. Since oatmeal contains fat, it does not keep as well as some other cereals, so it should be bought in small quantities and stored in a tin in a dry place.

OCTOPUS The octopus is the largest member of the cephalopod group of molluscs and has a hard beak and eight tentacles, each with two rows of suckers. There are many species of octopus, found in warm waters all over the world. Octopuses vary in size and can grow up to 3 metres (12 feet). Small octopuses may be sold whole; larger octopuses are sold ready-prepared in pieces. Octopus can be poached in water or red wine, then skinned and served cold or reheated in a sauce. It can also be used in soups and casseroles.

To prepare: Rinse the octopus, then hold the body in one hand and, with the other hand, firmly pull off the head and tentacles. The soft contents of the body will come out and can be discarded. Cut the tentacles just in front of the eyes.

Rinse the body and the tentacles, then beat well with a wooden mallet. Cut the flesh into rings or pieces or keep whole for stuffing. The ink sac has a musky flavour and is not usually used in British cooking.

OFFAL The edible, internal parts of an animal, which are cut out during the preparation of a carcass. Ordinary meat is composed mainly of muscle, but the structure of offal varies considerably according to the particular type; thus the heart, tongue and tail, which are used for active work, are very different from the liver, which is used for storage. Offal is one of the most economical meats to buy; the strong flavour and lack of bones in most offal means that only small amounts are needed.

The following parts of animals are available as offal: brains, chitterlings, feet or trotters, head, heart, kidney, liver, lungs (lights), spleen (melts), sweetbreads, tail, tongue, tripe. (For detailed information about particular types of offal, see individual entries.)

The most popular offal meats are probably liver and kidney, but all offal can be used to make interesting and nutritious meals. Offal must be very fresh and should be cooked as soon as possible as it goes off more quickly than other meat. It must not be overcooked or it will be tough.

OILS Oil is a fat which is liquid at normal room temperature. It can be produced from a wide range of seeds, nuts and fruit. Oils and fats are made up of fatty acids which are either saturated or unsaturated. The main constituents of oils are unsaturated fatty acids which make them liquid instead of solid (*see* FATS).

Types of Oil

The following is a guide to many of the oils available:

Almond oil is made by pressing bitter almonds to produce a colourless oil with a delicate flavour. It may be used in mayonnaise, particularly when it is to be served with seafood. It is also used in the manufacture of confectionery and for oiling moulds for desserts.

Coconut oil has an unexpectedly high level of saturated fat – about 75 per cent. For health reasons, it is not generally recommended, but its particular flavour does lend itself to some Caribbean and Indian dishes.

Corn oil is one of the most popular oils as it is economical and highly versatile. It is made from pressed sweetcorn kernels and is deep yellow in colour. It has a high percentage of unsaturated fats and is suitable for deep-frying and quick shallow-frying. It can also be used as a substitute for margarine when making pastry.

Cottonseed oil is used as a pure oil in the United States both for cooking and for salads. In Britain, it is generally used as an ingredient in blended oils and margarines.

Grapeseed oil has a delicate flavour and is used in the manufacture of margarine and in salads.

Groundnut (peanut or arachide) oil is pale in colour with a very mild flavour and is monounsaturated. It is suitable for salads, stir-frying and deep-frying.

Mustard oil is used in Indian cooking. It has a strong flavour which diminishes as it is heated. For this reason, it is not used as part of a cold dressing.

Olive oil has a unique flavour. Two types are produced – virgin and pure. Virgin olive oil is made from the pulp of high-grade olives without the stones and is never deodorized or bleached. It is green in colour with a rich flavour and is the more expensive of the two types. Pure olive oil is produced by pressing fruit, stone and pith and is yellow in colour without as rich a flavour. It is used for salad dressings and also as a dressing for cooked vegetables and pasta. It can be used in mayonnaise and is excellent for shallow-frying but, because of its low smoking temperature, is not suitable for deep-frying. It is a monounsaturated oil.

Palm oil is produced from the seed of the palm fruit. It has a pleasant flavour and is mainly used in the manufacture of margarine and in African and Brazilian cooking.

Poppy seed oil is made from opium poppy seeds and can be used as a salad oil as well as for cooking.

Rapeseed oil is not often used as a pure oil but is commonly an ingredient in margarines and blended cooking oils. It is also found in some curry pastes. Rapeseed oil is high in monounsaturated fats. One of its constituents is a fatty acid called eracic acid which, when fed to animals in large quantities, causes adverse changes in the circulatory system. For this reason, EC and British regulations limit the amount of eracic acid in edible oils and foods to 50 per cent of the total fat content.

Safflower oil has a polyunsaturated fat content of 75 per cent and is a good source of vitamin E. With its mild flavour it is excellent for salad dressings and mayonnaise. However, it is not suitable for deep-frying.

Sesame oil has a deep amber colour and pronounced nutty flavour. It can be used for stir-frying, sautéing and in salad dressings. It is also often used in Chinese cooking as a final garnish and to add gloss to a dish. Sesame oil is one of the more expensive oils.

Soya oil has either a light amber or pale green colour and a heavy texture. It may also have a slightly fishy flavour. It can be used for stir-frying and in salad dressings. It is often used as a constituent of blended oils (*see* below), margarines and commercial salad dressings. It is 55 per cent polyunsaturated fat, 25 per cent monounsaturated fat and 10 per cent saturated fat.

Sunflower oil is one of the most popular oils. It has a mild flavour, light texture and pale yellow colour. It is suitable for all types of salad dressing, including mayonnaise. Commercially, it is used to make margarines and some salad dressings.

Walnut oil is an expensive oil with a fine, nutty flavour. It is used in salad dressings and for moistening cooked vegetables and pasta.

Blended oils usually include soya, rapeseed and cottonseed. Blended oils are high in saturated fats and their flavour is generally poor.

Refined and unrefined oils Most oils have been refined as part of their manufacturing process. When oils are first pressed, they contain minerals and vitamins which include lecithin and a natural preservative, usually vitamin E. Most of these nutrients are chemically removed in the refining process, which lengthens the oil's shelf life. If an oil is unrefined, this will be marked on the label. A further process that the oil may go through is that of 'winterizing', a chilling process that prevents the oil becoming cloudy in cold conditions.

Cold pressed oils The best oils are 'cold pressed' which means that the nut, seed or fruit is not subjected to heat to extract the oil. In cold pressing, the nut or seed is pressed by a screw or press, to produce a highly-coloured, richly-flavoured oil that is excellent for salad dressings. Most other oils are solvent extracted. In this process a chemical solvent is added either to the complete nut or seed, or to the residue left from cold pressing. The oil dissolves into the solvent which then evaporates. Most solvent-extracted oils are then refined.

OKRA (Bhindi, Gumbo, Ladies' Fingers) This small dark green vegetable looks rather like a ribbed chilli. Okra are about 7.5 cm (3 inches) in length and both pods and seeds are eaten. Inside the pods is a sticky substance which melts away during cooking. Okra came originally from the West Indies but are also grown in India, South America, the United States and the Middle East. They are an important ingredient in Creole cooking, and are most readily available in this country from December to July, although they can now be found in specialist shops at other times of the year.

To select: Okra are best eaten when slightly under-ripe. Choose those which have no brown marks as they indicate staleness. Allow 100 g (4 oz) per person.

To prepare: Top and tail carefully, without cutting open the pod if the okra are to be used whole. If the ridges are tough or damaged, scrape them. Wash the okra thoroughly and slice or leave whole.

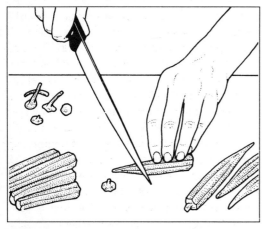

Carefully topping and tailing okra pods that are to be used whole.

To cook: Cook in boiling salted water for 5 minutes or sauté for about 10 minutes or until tender. Serve hot.

To serve: Okra can be added to soups, casseroles or mixed vegetable dishes, or served as a vegetable with or without a sauce.

OLIVE The small, oval fruit of the olive tree which is cultivated on a large scale in Mediterranean countries. There are many different varieties. Each fruit contains a large, single stone to which the flesh clings. The size of the olive varies considerably, according to the variety. Olives may be picked when green or when fully ripe and black. Violet-coloured olives are sometimes found; these have been picked before they are fully ripe. Fresh olives are very bitter and rarely eaten.

The most important use of olives is in the production of olive oil which is obtained by pressing the stoned fruit (*see* OILS). Olives and olive oil are widely used in the cooking of the Mediterranean area and are traditional ingredients in *salade niçoise*, pizza and Greek *mezze*. The olive itself has a sharp flavour and is therefore popular as an appetizer or cocktail snack. Some cocktails are served with an olive in them.

In this country, olives are usually bought pickled in brine in bottles or cans, though they can sometimes be bought loose from delicatessens, when they are marinated in flavoured olive oil. Green olives are often sold stoned and stuffed with red pimiento, red pepper, blanched almonds, hazelnuts, capers or anchovy; they make attractive garnishes or appetizers. Serve olives on cocktail sticks or piled in a dish. Any surplus may be returned to the brine.

OLIVE OIL (*see* OILS)

OLLA PODRIDA A traditional Spanish dish which is a type of soup or stew, usually containing meat or poultry, beans and sausages. It is named after the pot (*olla*) in which it used to be cooked. Nowadays, the stew is more likely to be called *cocido* or *puchero*.

OLOROSA (*see* SHERRY)

OMELETTE The French name, adopted elsewhere, for a method of cooking eggs, either to serve as a light meal or to use as part (usually the garnish) of another dish. A basic omelette is made by beating together whole eggs with a little seasoning and cooking the mixture in a hot greased frying pan or special omelette pan. A more elaborate type of omelette, known as a soufflé omelette, is made by whisking the egg whites separately and folding them into the beaten egg yolks, producing a fluffier texture when cooked.

Both types of omelette can be filled with a wide range of sweet and savoury ingredients. Flavouring ingredients can also be added to the beaten egg mixture. Plain omelettes are usually savoury and soufflé omelettes are most commonly served as a dessert, but there is no fixed rule and the fillings can be interchanged.

Omelette Pans

Special omelette pans are obtainable and should be kept for omelettes only. Alternatively, a heavy-based frying pan can be used. Non-stick pans are ideal for omelettes and do not require seasoning (*see* below) before use. Whether of cast iron, copper, enamelled iron or aluminium, the pan should be thick, so that it will hold sufficient heat to cook the egg mixture as soon as it is poured into the pan. This means the omelette can be cooked in about 2 minutes; both slow cooking and over-cooking make an omelette tough. A 15–18 cm (6–7 inch) pan takes a 2–3 egg omelette.

To season an omelette pan (to treat it before using for the first time), put 15 ml (1 level tbsp) salt in the pan, heat it slowly, then rub it well with a piece of absorbent kitchen paper. Tip out the salt and wipe the pan. To clean an omelette pan after use, do not wash it, but rub it over with absorbent kitchen paper, then rub the surface with a clean cloth.

Unless using a non-stick pan, gently heat the pan before use to ensure that it is heated evenly right to the edges – a fierce heat would cause the pan to heat unevenly. When the pan is ready for the mixture it will feel comfortably hot if you hold the back of your hand about 2.5 cm (1 inch) away from the surface. Manufacturers of non-stick pans advise that heating the empty pan will damage the surface, so read the instructions carefully and add fat before heating the pan.

A variety of fats or oils may be used for greasing an omelette pan. Undoubtedly, butter gives the best flavour, but margarine or oil can be used as a substitute. Bacon fat can also be used.

Plain Omelette

It is a good idea to have everything ready before beginning to make an omelette, including a warmed plate on which to serve it – an omelette must never wait, but, if possible should be waited for!

2 eggs
salt and pepper
15 ml (1 tbsp) milk or water
knob of butter or margarine

Whisk the eggs just enough to break them up; do not make them frothy as overbeating spoils the texture of the finished omelette. Season with salt and pepper and add the milk or water. Place an omelette or frying pan over a gentle heat and, when it is hot, add the butter or margarine, swirling it round as it melts to grease the surface of the pan. Add the beaten eggs. Stir gently with a fork or wooden spatula, drawing the mixture from the sides to the centre as it sets and letting the liquid egg from the centre run to the sides. When the eggs have set, stop stirring and cook for another minute or until the omelette is golden underneath and cooked but still creamy on top. Tilt the pan away from you slightly and use a palette knife to fold over one third of the omelette to the centre, then fold over the opposite third. Turn the omelette out on to a warmed serving plate, with the folded sides underneath, and serve at once.

Serves 1

Fillings

Fines herbes Add 15 ml (1 tbsp) finely chopped fresh herbs or 5 ml (1 level tsp) mixed dried herbs to the beaten egg mixture before cooking. Parsley, chives, chervil and tarragon are all suitable.

Cheese Grate 40 g (1½ oz) cheese and mix 45 ml (3 tbsp) of it with the eggs before cooking; sprinkle the remainder over the omelette after it is folded.

Tomato Skin and chop 1–2 tomatoes and fry in a little butter or margarine in a saucepan for 5 minutes or until soft and pulpy. Put in the centre of the omelette before folding.

Mushroom Wipe and slice 50 g (2 oz) mushrooms and cook in butter in a saucepan until soft. Put in the centre of the omelette before folding.

Bacon Rind and snip two rashers of bacon and fry in butter in a saucepan until soft. Put in the centre of the omelette before folding.

Ham or tongue Add 50 g (2 oz) chopped meat and 5 ml (1 tsp) chopped fresh parsley to the beaten egg before cooking.

Fish Flake some cooked fish and heat gently in a little cheese sauce. Put in the centre of the omelette before folding.

Shrimp or prawn Thaw 50 g (2 oz) frozen shrimps or prawns (or use the equivalent from a can) and fry gently in melted butter or margarine in a saucepan, with a squeeze of lemon juice. Put into the centre of the omelette before folding.

Soufflé Omelette

2 eggs, separated
salt and pepper (or 5 ml/1 tsp caster sugar
  for a sweet omelette)
30 ml (2 tbsp) water
knob of butter or margarine

Whisk the egg yolks until creamy. Add the seasoning or sugar and the water and beat again. Stiffly whisk the egg whites.

Melt the butter or margarine in an omelette pan over a low heat without browning. Swirl to coat the pan.

Turn the egg whites into the egg yolks and carefully fold in, using a metal spoon, but do not overmix.

Grease the sides of the pan with the fat by tilting it in all directions, then pour in the egg mixture. Cook over a moderate heat until the omelette is golden brown on the underside. Put under a heated grill until the omelette is brown on top.

Remove at once, as overcooking will make the omelette tough. Run a spatula gently around the edge and underneath the omelette to loosen it. Make an indentation across the middle of the omelette, at right angles to the pan handle, and add any required filling, then double the omelette over. Turn it gently on to a warmed serving plate and serve at once.

Serves 1

Fillings

Any of the savoury fillings given for a plain omelette can be used for a soufflé omelette. Alternatively, try one of the following sweet fillings:

Jam Spread the cooked omelette with warm jam, fold it over and sprinkle with caster or icing sugar.

Rum Substitute 15 ml (1 tbsp) rum for half the water added to the egg yolks before cooking. Put the cooked omelette on a hot dish, pour 45–60 ml (3–4 tbsp) warmed rum around it, ignite and serve immediately.

Apricot Add the grated rind of an orange or tangerine to the egg yolks. Spread some thick apricot purée over the omelette before folding it, and serve sprinkled with caster sugar.

ONION A common bulb vegetable that is a member of the *Allium* family, which also includes chives, shallots, leeks and garlic. Onion bulbs grow at the base of a few long, green tubular leaves, though these have usually dried out and been removed by the time the onions reach the shops. Under its brown, papery skin, the bulb of an onion consists of layers of very pale green, yellow or white, crisp flesh containing a white juice which escapes when the onion is cut. It is the vapour from this pungent juice that makes your eyes sting when preparing onions.

Onions are one of the most important vegetables in cooking and are used in countless savoury dishes as a basic ingredient. Few cooks would think of making a stew, casserole or soup that did not contain onions, and they are also used in savoury flans, hamburgers, pies, sauces, stocks, marinades, etc. Onions may also be served as a vegetable accompaniment in their own right, and fried onions are a classic accompaniment to steak. Onions are the main ingredient in dishes such as French onion soup, *pissaladière* and Soubise sauce.

Onions are usually used fresh but are also available pickled and as dried flakes. Pickled onions are traditionally served with cheese. Fresh onions are available all year round and keep well. *To select:* Choose clean, firm onions with dry, papery skin. Avoid any that are soft, damaged or beginning to sprout. Allow one onion per person if serving whole as a vegetable.

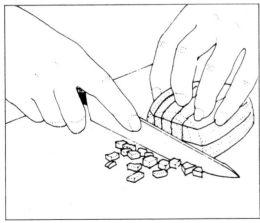

Cutting across a sliced onion half so that it falls into even-sized dice.

To prepare: Cut a slice from the top and peel off the skin. For onion rings, cut the onion crossways into slices and separate into rings. To chop, cut the onion in half lengthways and chop each half separately. Place one half cut-side down on the chopping board and make four or five cuts, towards the root but not through it, horizontally and vertically. Finally, slice the onion across so that it falls into even-sized dice. Repeat with the second half. Watering eyes can be prevented by preparing onions under running water, or by putting them in the freezer for 10 minutes, or the refrigerator for 1 hour, before preparing.
To cook: Boil whole onions for 30–40 minutes, bake for 1–1½ hours, steam for 40 minutes, braise for 30–40 minutes. Alternatively, slice and gently fry in butter for 5 minutes until soft or 10 minutes until golden brown.

Types of Onion

There are many different types of onion: some large, some small; some with red or brown skins, some with white; some strongly flavoured, some mild.

Globe onions These are the common onions that are widely available, either of British origin or imported from such countries as Spain, Italy and Holland.

Spanish onions These are larger and more delicately flavoured. They are most suitable for frying or serving raw. They do not necessarily come from Spain and may be brown- or red-skinned.

Italian red onions These are slightly oval-shaped and smaller than globe onions. They have a mild, sometimes sweet flavour and are attractive cut into thin rings. When cooked, they become white.

White onions The silvery-white papery skin of these onions makes them quite distinctive. They have a mild, sweet flavour and are ideal for serving raw.

Pickling (button) onions These small onions are about 2.5 cm (1 inch) in diameter. As their name suggests, they are ideal for pickling, but may also be added to stews and casseroles and are a traditional ingredient of *boeuf bourguignon*. They may also be called pearl onions. Such small onions can be fiddly to skin; it is best done after blanching.

Shallots These small, mild-flavoured onions grow like garlic, producing clusters of cloves rather than one bulb. They can be used for flavouring or pickling; blanch before skinning.

Silverskin onions As their name suggests, these onions have silver skin and white flesh. They are very small and are popular for pickling; they are often sold as 'cocktail' onions, for drinks.

Spring onions (scallions) These onions are nearly always used raw, though they are popular in Chinese stir-fried dishes. They are long, slim onions which are sold complete with leaves and root. When they are young they are mild in flavour, but as they mature and their bulbs develop, they become stronger. To prepare, cut off the roots and trim the green leaves to about 2.5 cm (1 inch) above the white. Use whole or sliced in salads or chop and add to stir-fried dishes. They are also sometimes known as green onions. Spring onions can be used to make an attractive garnish for use on savoury dishes.

Welsh onions These look very similar to spring onions but they are formed more in the fashion of leeks than spring onions, and a leaf can be broken off for use, leaving the remainder of the plant growing. For this reason, they are also sometimes known as everlasting onions. Their mild flavour is something between that of spring onions and leeks. Both green and white parts can be eaten. Welsh onions closely resemble another onion known as the Japanese bunching onion which is frequently used in Asian cooking.

ORANGE Probably the best known of all the citrus fruits, oranges are sweet and juicy and are popular for eating as a dessert fruit or snack, as well as for using in cooking. Oranges were originally grown in China, but are now cultivated in many of the warm areas of the world, including the Mediterranean, South America and Florida. There are two main types; bitter and sweet.

Bitter Oranges
Seville oranges are small, round Spanish oranges with a very sour taste. They are never eaten raw but are cultivated for culinary purposes, especially for making marmalade. They have a particularly high acid and pectin content and produce marmalade with a deliciously piquant flavour and a good set. They also have very thin peel which is ideal for shredding and adding to marmalade; any pith left on the shreds turns translucent and does not cloud the marmalade. Seville oranges are also sometimes used in meat and fish dishes and are the traditional ingredient of Bigarade sauce, although sweet oranges are often used instead. Seville oranges are in the shops during January and February.

Bergamot oranges are rarely seen in the shops and are used for extracting oil and for use in perfumes (*see* BERGAMOT).

Sweet Oranges
Like other citrus fruits, oranges are a rich source of vitamin C, and a sweet and juicy orange makes an ideal refreshing and healthy snack or dessert. Most types are easy to peel and can be separated into segments for easy eating. The flavour of freshly squeezed orange juice is far superior to any of the varieties available in bottles or cartons and is traditionally served for breakfast, although it can be enjoyed at any time of day. Fresh orange juice and segments can also be added to a fresh fruit salad.

Sweet oranges are also used in cooking, as a flavouring or main ingredient, in both sweet and savoury dishes. Duck is traditionally served *à l'orange* and oranges are often combined with carrots or raw cabbage in savoury dishes and salads. Orange-flavoured desserts include *Crêpes Suzette*, caramelized oranges and sorbets, soufflés and mousses. A little grated orange rind can be added to cakes and teabreads for a subtle orange flavour, and glacé icing can be made with orange juice instead of water.

Navel oranges are sweet and very juicy. They get their name from their unusual structure; when sliced lengthways, navel oranges appear to have a second, small orange growing inside them. The tip of this little orange is often visible at the base of the fruit, looking somewhat like a navel. Navel oranges are cultivated in Spain, Israel and South Africa and are available for most of the winter and spring months.

Shamouti oranges come from Israel and are usually available from January to April. They are large, oval oranges with thick pale orange skin that is thicker at the stalk end. The fruit of the shamouti is also pale in colour (yellow rather than orange) but sweet and juicy.

Valencia lates are cultivated in many countries, including Israel, Spain, South Africa, Cyprus, Australia and South America, and are available throughout the spring, summer and autumn months. They are fairly small and round with sweet, juicy flesh that is ideal for eating as a snack, or for squeezing to make juice.

Blood oranges were first cultivated in the Mediterranean in the middle of the nineteenth century, but not everybody finds their red juice and flesh appealing. In fact, they are extremely sweet and juicy and ideal for eating fresh or for squeezing to make juice. They can usually be recognized by a red flush on their skin. Blood oranges are imported from Spain and Sicily and are available from January to March.

To select: Choose firm fruit that feel heavy and have a glossy skin. Avoid oranges with hard or dry-looking skins. Oranges will keep for four days at room temperature; if wrapped and stored in the refrigerator they will keep for at least two weeks.

To prepare: When serving sliced oranges, remove the white pith and peel. To use orange peel in cooking, peel the rind with a vegetable peeler, avoiding any white pith, then blanch the peel for 3 minutes, rinse under cold water and then shred before using. Shreds of orange peel can also be used as an attractive garnish or decoration.

Other types of Orange

Other orange-like citrus fruits are dealt with under separate headings. Some, such as the tangerine, are true descendants of the original sweet orange, but many are hybrid fruits, produced by crossing one type of citrus fruit with another. See CITRANGE, CITRON, CITRUS FRUIT, CLEMENTINE, KUMQUAT, LIMEQUAT, MINNEOLA, POMELO, ORTANIQUE, SATSUMA, TANGELO, TANGERINE, UGLI FRUIT.

ORANGEADE A drink made from fresh oranges and sugar. It is usually served cold and may be flavoured with lemon juice. There are various proprietary brands on the market, but it can also be made at home.

ORANGE FLOWER WATER This potent flavouring is distilled from the flowers of the Seville orange. It is colourless and can be used sparingly in cakes, pastries and other sweet dishes.

OREGANO (Wild Marjoram) This herb is a member of the marjoram family and can be used instead of marjoram, though oregano is much more aromatic and strongly flavoured. It can be used with meat, sausages, soups, pizza and other Italian dishes, tomatoes, in salads, with cooked vegetables and in egg and cheese dishes. Oregano is available fresh or dried.

ORGEAT A beverage, originally made from barley, later from a syrup of almonds and sugar diluted with water.

ORIENTALE, À L' Rather confusingly, this French name is not given to dishes reminiscent of the Orient, but rather to dishes which use ingredients from the Mediterranean region, particularly Turkey and the Balkans. It is usually applied to fish, eggs and vegetables cooked with tomatoes and flavoured with garlic and often with saffron.

ORKNEY CHEESE This Scottish cheese was originally made in various farms on the Orkney

Islands, but is now made in a modern creamery. Each cheese weighs 454 g (1 lb), is similar to Dunlop cheese and is available as white cheese, red cheese (coloured with annatto) and as a more subtle smoked cheese.

ORMER (*see* ABALONE)

ORTANIQUE A hybrid citrus fruit produced in Jamaica, probably by crossing a sweet orange with a tangerine. Ortaniques have thin, orange-yellow skin, which is easy to peel, and sweet flesh which can be used in the same way as sweet oranges. They contain few, if any, pips. (*see also* ORANGE)

ORTOLAN A delicately flavoured wild bird, like the bunting in appearance and about 15 cm (6 inches) long. At one time it was found in this country, but is now extinct. The ortolan is now a protected species in France as it is also becoming rare in that country, mostly due to the traditional practice of catching the birds in nets and fattening them up for the table.

OSBORNE PUDDING (*see* BREAD AND BUTTER PUDDING)

OSSO BUCO (Osso Bucco) A popular Italian dish made from knuckle of veal which is cut into pieces, sautéed and then stewed with garlic, onion and tomato. The meat is served on the bone with spaghetti or rice. It is sometimes served *alla gremolata*, that is sprinkled with a mixture of chopped garlic, grated lemon rind and grated nutmeg. (*see also* KNUCKLE)

OUZO A Greek clear alcoholic drink, flavoured with aniseed. It is usually drunk diluted with water, which turns it a milky white. (*see also* PASTIS, PERNOD, RICARD)

OVEN TEMPERATURES Accurate temperatures are essential to ensure good results in cooking. Electric and gas cookers are thermostatically controlled; once the thermostat has been set, the oven heat will not rise above the selected temperature. New electric ovens use the Celsius scale of temperature, whereas older ovens use degrees Fahrenheit. The chart below gives the various equivalents for electric and gas ovens. Electric fan-assisted or convection ovens may need to be set at slightly lower temperatures than others – check in the manufacturer's handbook.

°C	°F	Gas Mark
110	225	1/4
130	250	1/2
140	275	1
150	300	2
170	325	3
180	350	4
190	375	5
200	400	6
220	425	7
230	450	8
240	475	9

OXTAIL (*see* TAIL)

OX TONGUE (*see* TONGUE)

OXYMEL A drink made from a syrup consisting of four parts honey to one part vinegar.

OYSTER Oysters are bivalve molluscs which are farmed intensively in oyster beds and sea lochs. There are many species: in Britain, the smaller ones from the Essex and Kent beds are the best for eating raw, while Portuguese oysters or the American blue points (now cultivated in Britain) are best cooked. At one time there was such an abundance of oysters that they could be enjoyed by everybody; nowadays a shortage means that they are very expensive and reserved for special occasions.

Oysters have hard craggy shells that vary in shape and can be quite sharp. They are hinged at one end and, like clams, can be hard to open. The top shell is shallower than the bottom one. All of the meat inside the shell is edible, as is the delicious juice which should be carefully reserved when opening.

Oysters can be served raw 'on the half shell' with a squeeze of lemon juice, or they can be cooked in various ways – as patties, as oysters *au gratin*, or added to steak and kidney pudding (*see also* ANGELS ON HORSEBACK). Local oysters are available fresh from August to April, but American varieties are usually available all year round. Shelled (shucked) oysters are available frozen or canned, or dried from oriental food shops. Oysters stuffed with various fillings are also available frozen, as are canned smoked oysters.

To select: When buying live oysters, the shells should be firmly closed. To keep fresh oysters, pack in a bowl, deep shell downwards, and cover with a damp cloth. Place in the refrigerator and eat within two days. Under no circumstances should the oysters be covered with water, and do not make any attempt to feed them while they are in the refrigerator.

To prepare: Oysters can be cleaned, opened and served in exactly the same way as clams (*see* CLAMS).

OYSTER, POULTRY A tiny succulent portion of meat found on the back of poultry birds, where the backbone joins the thigh. When a bird is jointed, the oyster meat is always cut away from the backbone and left attached to the thigh joint.

OYSTER PLANT (*see* SALSIFY)

OYSTER MUSHROOM (*see* MUSHROOM)

P

PADR SHKA An Eastern European root vegetable, similar to celeriac (*see* CELERIAC).

PAELLA A Spanish national dish, made from rice and a variety of ingredients according to taste and depending on what is available, although chicken and shellfish (especially crayfish and mussels) are regarded as traditional. Paella is usually cooked in and served from a special large, two-handled shallow pan which shares the same name.

PAIN PERDU (*see* FRENCH TOAST)

PAK CHOI (Bok Choi, Pak-choi, Pak Soi) A variety of Chinese cabbage, now cultivated in Holland. Like Chinese leaves, *pak choi* has a similar structure to celery, with broad white stalks topped with large, dark green leaves, but it does not form a heart. A smaller variety, known as Shanghai *pak choi*, is sometimes available, as is a 'baby' variety which can be cooked whole. Both leaves and stalks of all types of *pak choi* can be used, either steamed, braised or stir-fried. (*see also* CHINESE CABBAGE)

PALM HEARTS (Hearts of Palm) These are the edible inner parts of palm tree shoots, grown mostly in the West Indies. The firm, creamy-coloured flesh has a delicate flavour rather like artichoke or asparagus. They are rarely available fresh in Britain but are sold pre-cooked and canned in specialist food shops. They can be added to salads or sauces, eaten hot as a vegetable or sliced and fried.

PALMIER The French name for a cake consisting of puff or flaky pastry, sandwiched together with whipped cream or jam. *Palmiers* are so called because their distinctive heart shape and layered appearance is thought to resemble palm leaves, *palmier* being the French word for palm tree.

PALM OIL (*see* OILS)

PALM WINE In many tropical countries, a wine is made by fermenting the sap of various palms, particularly date and coconut palms.

PAN (Chewing Betel) This Indian speciality is served at the end of a meal as an aid to digestion, though in India it may be chewed at any time. It usually consists of a betel leaf (from one of a variety of palm-like trees) folded into a small parcel containing a betel nut and various spices which refresh the mouth and stimulate the digestive processes. *Pan* is intended for chewing, not for swallowing.

PANADA Derived from the French *panade*, a panada is a thick roux-based sauce or paste used for binding croquettes, stuffings and similar mixtures, and as the basis of choux pastry and some types of soufflé. A panada may be made from flour, breadcrumbs, potatoes or rice.

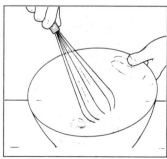

Beating pancake batter with a whisk, gradually incorporating the flour.

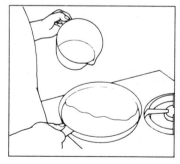

Pouring pancake batter into a frying pan and tilting it so that the base is covered.

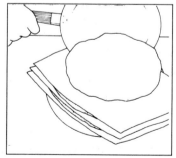

Stacking cooked pancakes between sheets of greaseproof paper ready for filling.

PANCAKE Traditionally eaten on Shrove Tuesday, pancakes are made from a thin pouring batter cooked on both sides in a frying pan, giving a round, wafer-thin cake which is served with lemon and sugar or filled with jam or some sweet or savoury filling. Pancakes are often called by their French name, *crêpes*.

A substantial main dish can be made by filling pancakes with a savoury mixture. The pancakes can then be rolled or folded into parcel shapes and served with a complementary sauce. (*see also* BATTER, CRÊPE)

PANCETTA Italian salted raw belly of pork. *Pancetta* looks rather like streaky bacon and can be bought in long rasher form or rolled up. It is usually chopped and used for frying in cooked dishes. It has a distinctive smoky flavour and aroma and, because it has a strong flavour, should be used sparingly.

PANCH FORAN Just as the Chinese have a favourite five-spice mixture, similarly the Bengalis in eastern India have their own five-spice blend. The *panch foran* mixture usually consists of cumin seeds, nigella seeds, aniseed, fenugreek seeds and brown mustard seeds. The spices can be mixed whole, then ground, or mixed after grinding to a fine powder.

PANEER (Panir) A fresh, soft cheese frequently used in Indian savoury dishes and puddings. It is often mixed with peas to make a dish known as *mattar panir*. In India, *paneer* can be bought in slabs but is often home-made. It is made by adding lemon juice or vinegar to warmed milk which curdles and separates. The mixture is then strained. The whey can be used in place of water in sauces, and the drained *paneer* is then usually pressed and cut into shapes.

PANETTONE A tall, yeasted cake with candied peel which comes from Milan in northern Italy. It is traditionally served with sparkling white wine after lunch on Christmas day and at midnight on New Year's Eve. The cakes are exported in attractive tall boxes which can be seen hanging in Italian delicatessens all over the world.

PANTOTHENIC ACID (*see* VITAMINS)

PANZANELLA An Italian bread salad from Tuscany. Coarse bread is soaked in water, squeezed dry and then mixed with tomatoes and other vegetables and basil. An oil and vinegar dressing is then poured over and it is left before serving, to allow the dressing to be absorbed.

PAPAW A variety of custard apple (*annona* fruit) which is said to resemble the papaya, hence the name. Papaw is grown in tropical regions and in the southern United States. It is green, with greenish-white flesh, and is generally not pleasant to eat, though one variety is edible, turning brown when ripe, with yellow flesh. (*see also* CUSTARD APPLE)

PAPAYA (Pawpaw) This is a large pear-shaped tropical fruit, cultivated in many tropical and sub-tropical areas of the world, including the Caribbean, Africa and Indonesia. The papaya has a

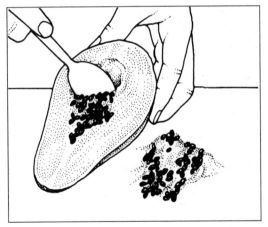

Using a spoon to scoop the seeds out of a halved papaya.

smooth skin which ripens from green to yellow or orange, and fragrant, juicy, orange-pink flesh the texture of avocado, with lots of black seeds in the centre. Although the seeds are edible, they have a somewhat peppery flavour. The papaya fruit is rich in vitamin C and is also thought to aid digestion.

To select: Papayas are ripe when the skin is yellow and the fruit feels slightly soft.

To prepare: Cut in half lengthways and scoop out the seeds, then cut in wedges or remove the flesh from the skin and cut into cubes.

To serve: Like melon, papaya can be cut in wedges and served for breakfast or as a starter, with a squeeze of lime juice. Alternatively, cut in cubes and serve in a fresh fruit salad.

PAPILLOTE, EN A French term applied to dishes that are baked and/or served in a greaseproof paper or foil case. A variety of foods, including fish, pork and veal chops and vegetables, can be cooked *en papillote*.

PAPRIKA Derived from a variety of sweet red pepper, paprika is a mild spice which is always sold ground to a red powder. It is good for adding colour to pale egg and cheese dishes. Some varieties (particularly Hungarian) are hotter than others. Paprika keeps poorly so buy little and often. Use it in salads, fish, meat and chicken dishes, with vegetables, on canapés and, classically, in goulash, where it adds the characteristic rich red colour.

PARADISE NUT (Sapucaya Nut) Similar to the Brazil nut, the Paradise nut is cultivated in tropical South America. It is a slightly larger nut, with one rounded end and a brittle shell that is more easily broken. The Paradise nut has a sweeter, more delicate flavour than the Brazil. (*see also* BRAZIL NUT)

PARAGUAY TEA (*see* YERBA MATÉ)

PARATHA An Indian unleavened bread. Plain *parathas* are made from a simple dough made from wholemeal flour and water, which is brushed with ghee, folded and shaped, then shallow-fried until crisp on the outside and soft inside. Alternatively, they may be dry-fried in a frying pan or on a griddle. *Parathas* are usually round, square or triangular in shape and may be flavoured with spices or filled with various vegetables. Plain *parathas* are excellent served with vegetarian and non-vegetarian Indian dishes, pickles and onion rings.

PAR-BOILING A term used to describe boiling food for part of its cooking time before finishing it by another method. For example, potatoes are often par-boiled before being roasted in the oven.

PARCHING A term used to describe browning food in dry heat, either in the oven or under the grill.

PARFAIT The French name for a type of frozen dessert, similar to a mousse, but somewhat richer. Like a bombe, a *parfait* is based on a flavoured custard mixture; beaten eggs are usually included to give a light consistency. The original *parfait* was flavoured with coffee, but the dessert may now be flavoured with chocolate, fruit, praline, liqueur or vanilla, as well as coffee. (*see also* BOMBE)

PARFAIT AMOUR An exotic, sweet citrus-oil-based liqueur made in several colours, mainly violet. It is scented and slightly spiced. It originated in Holland in the eighteenth century.

PARING An alternative name for thinly peeling vegetables or fruit, including trimming away any irregular parts.

PARIS-BREST A classic French gâteau made from a ring of choux pastry which is split horizontally and filled with praline-flavoured whipped cream. The top of the gâteau is decorated with icing sugar and flaked almonds. The gâteau was created in the late nineteenth century to commemorate the famous bicycle race that took place between Paris and Brest.

PARISIENNE, À LA A French name given to dishes served with a garnish that varies considerably, but usually includes *pommes de terre à la parisienne* (small potato balls, cut out with a melon baller, and fried in herb butter) and a variety of vegetables, often including artichoke hearts.

PARKIN A moist ginger-flavoured cake, usually served cut in squares. Parkin originated in Yorkshire, where oatmeal is always included in the mixture, which is sweetened with golden syrup and black treacle.

PARMA HAM (*see* PROSCIUTTO)

PARMENTIER The name of a Frenchman who was active in publicizing the nutritional merits of the potato in France in the eighteenth century. His name is now applied to a number of potato dishes.

PARMESAN (Parmigiano Reggiano) A very hard Italian *'grana'* cheese made from unpasteurized skimmed cows' milk. Only the genuine Parmesan cheese, made by a unique method in only one region of northern Italy, and only between 15th April and 11th November, is allowed to be stamped with the name *Parmigiano Reggiano*. After being specially processed, the curd is broken up, heated, packed into a large mould the shape of a millstone, and matured for at least two, usually three, years. When it is ripe, the crust of Parmesan is almost black, but the cheese itself should be of a pale straw colour and full of tiny holes, like pin-pricks.

Parmesan has a strong and distinctive flavour and is used finely grated for cooking or as a traditional accompaniment for soups, such as *minestrone*, and for all savoury rice and pasta dishes. Parmesan is available ready-grated in cellophane packets or cardboard drums, but is best bought in a wedge (from delicatessens) and freshly grated.

PARSLEY A mild, pleasantly-flavoured herb with flat or curly leaves which make an attractive garnish sprinkled on food. Most of the flavour of parsley is in the stalks which are used as a classic ingredient of bouquet garni and *fines herbes*. Use parsley in sauces for ham and fish, with vegetables, in stuffings and herb butters, salads and as a garnish, either as sprigs or chopped. Parsley is available fresh or dried from supermarkets, but can easily be grown in pots, window-boxes or gardens.

PARSNIP A common root vegetable with a nutty, sweet flavour which improves after several frosts. Parsnips resemble large, cream-coloured carrots and are at their best when young and well frosted.

The most mouthwatering way to cook parsnips is to par-boil them for a few minutes, then arrange them around a roasting joint of meat. They will absorb the meat juices, turn a rich golden brown and taste really sweet. Very young parsnips, blanched, make an interesting addition to winter salads. They are also good fried.

To select: Choose small, young parsnips with firm clean skins and no side shoots or brown marks. Allow 175–225 g (6–8 oz) per person.

To prepare: Scrub well, trim the top and root ends and peel thinly. Either leave young parsnips whole, or slice large old parsnips into quarters and remove the central core.

To cook: Boil or steam for 15–20 minutes, or blanch and sauté in butter or oil, or roast around a joint of meat after par-boiling for about 2 minutes.

To serve: Serve hot as a vegetable accompaniment with roast or grilled meats.

PARSON'S NOSE The nickname given in Britain to the fatty portion of meat remaining at the tail end of poultry, especially chicken and turkey, after the feathers have been removed. Traditionally, the same portion of a cooked duck or goose is known as 'the pope's nose'.

PARTRIDGE A greyish-brown game bird which, in Britain, is shot from 1st September to 1st

February, but is at its best in October and November. The two main species of partridge found in Britain are the red-legged and the common or grey partridge.

When young, the legs and feet of a partridge are yellowish, the beak supple and the wing feathers pointed. Old birds have slatey-blue legs and feet, hard beaks and rounded wing feathers. The feathers are the best guide to age as the feet change colour more quickly.

At the optimum age for eating, which is between two and four months, the partridge weighs about 450 g (1 lb). One bird per serving is usual. Young partridges are best barded and roasted at 200°C (400°F) mark 6 for about 40 minutes. Older birds should be braised for 1–2 hours. Partridges may also be grilled, poached and stewed in a variety of dishes.

For basic preparation, cooking and carving instructions, see CARVING, GAME, HANGING.

PASKHA (Pashka) A sweet dish originally made in Russia from curd cheese, cream, almonds and dried fruit set in a wooden mould. It may also be set in an earthenware pot (or a clean flower pot) or made in a muslin-lined sieve. The pot or mould, which should have a hole in the base, is lined with muslin before being filled with the *paskha* mixture. Weights are placed on top and the dessert is then left to drain and set in the refrigerator for at least 24 hours. The dessert is turned out and the muslin peeled off before decorating with glacé fruits and nuts. *Paskha* is a rich dessert, traditionally served at Easter.

PASSION FRUIT (Granadilla, Grenadilla) The fruit known as passion fruit in Britain is a tropical vine fruit that, when it reaches the shops, usually looks like a large wrinkled purple plum. Passion fruit originated in South America but are also grown in the West Indies, Africa, Australia and Malaysia. The fruit is also known as purple granadilla and, in Colombia, where it is cultivated on a large scale, as *maracuya*.

The inedible skin of the passion fruit is deeply wrinkled when ripe; smooth and green when unripe. The fragrant, yellow flesh is sweet and juicy and pitted with small edible black seeds. To eat raw, cut in half and scoop out the pulp with a spoon. Sieve the pulp to obtain the juice, which can be used to make drinks or to flavour ice cream.

A larger, smooth-skinned variety of passion fruit is sometimes available, usually labelled sweet granadilla, or simply granadilla (or grenadilla). It has a thick yellow skin mottled with red, and sweet yellow pulp full of edible black seeds. It can be used in the same way as passion fruit, but its flavour is less fragrant. (*see also* CURUBA)

PASTA The word *pasta* simply means dough in Italian, but it is also used to describe spaghetti, macaroni, lasagne and many other pasta shapes made from the basic dough mixture. There are said to be over 500 different varieties of pasta throughout Italy, although only about 50 of these are widely known. It falls into two main types – commercially dried pasta sold in packets (*pasta secca*) and fresh pasta (*pasta all'uovo* or *pasta fatta in casa*). The best commercially dried pasta is made from 100 per cent hard durum wheat (*semola di grano duro*).

Ingredients for commercially-produced dried pasta vary from one brand to another but, in general, the tubular types are not made with eggs, whereas the flat pastas are usually made with the addition of eggs. Although made with good-quality ingredients, commercially produced pasta cannot compare with the flavour and freshness of home-made pasta.

There is an increasingly wide choice of both fresh and dried pasta now available. Coloured pasta adds interest to meals – green pasta (*pasta verde*) is flavoured with spinach, pink or red pasta (*pasta rosso*) with tomatoes. Pasta is also available flavoured with basil or garlic. Wholewheat pasta is also available.

Pasta Shapes

The variety of pasta shapes is endless and new shapes are constantly being introduced. The following is a guide to the most common shapes, although you may see slightly different shapes or the same shape under different names – especially in Italy. This is because the different regions of Italy have their own individual pasta shapes and names – and so do the manufacturers.

Spaghetti comes in long straight strands of varying thickness. When cooking long dried spaghetti, coil it gently into the pan as it softens on contact with the boiling water.

Macaroni is a thicker hollow tube, sometimes cut into short lengths. *Bucatini, Tubetti lunghi, Zite* and *Penne* are all short macaroni.

Lasagne is the widest of the ribbon pastas. It comes in flat strips, rectangles or squares with either a smooth or a ridged edge. Some varieties do not need pre-cooking before incorporating into a dish which is to be baked.

Noodles are narrow, flat pasta strips which are either straight ribbons or are folded into a nest-shaped mass, which is easier to drop into boiling water. *Tagliatelle* and *fettucine* are the most familiar of the noodle pastas.

Vermicelli is the finest ribbon pasta, which comes in a nest-shaped mass and is mostly used in soups.

Cannelloni are large hollow tubes which can be stuffed with meat or vegetable mixtures and served with a sauce.

Lumache (snails), *conchiglie* (shells), *fusilli* (spirals), *ruotini* (wheels), *anelli* (rings) and *fiochetti* (bows) are all small shapes.

Ravioli, cappelletti, tortellini, tortelloni and *tortelli* are all stuffed pasta shapes.

Home-made Pasta

Making pasta at home is very easy – the actual dough is a simple mixture of flour, salt, eggs and olive oil. The best flour to use is semolina flour: a hard, very fine wheat flour. As this is difficult to obtain, a strong flour of the type used for making bread is a satisfactory alternative. General household plain flour can be used, but it produces a dough which cannot be rolled out as thinly by hand – it is best to use this only if you have a pasta-making machine. These can cut larger quantities more evenly and quickly than you can by hand. They can also cut various shapes such as spaghetti, macaroni and long strips for lasagne.

about 200 g (7 oz) semolina or strong
plain flour
2 eggs
pinch of salt
15 ml (1 tbsp) olive oil

Sift the flour into a mound on a clean working surface. With your fist, make a well in the centre and add the eggs, salt and oil. Start beating the eggs with a fork, gradually drawing in the flour from around the well. When the egg is no longer liquid, use your fingertips to mix in the remaining flour. Continue until the dough comes together. Then, using both hands, knead the dough for about 10 minutes or until smooth and not sticky. Wrap in cling film and leave to rest for 30 minutes before shaping as required.

Roll out the pasta on a floured work surface to a large rectangle which is nearly paper thin. If you are making cut pasta, such as tagliatelle, fettucine or lasagne, the dough must be allowed to dry. Place the dough on a clean tea towel, allowing one third to hang over the edge of a table or work surface and turn every 10 minutes. The pasta is ready to cut after about 30 minutes, when it is dry to the touch and beginning to look slightly leathery.

For tagliatelle, fold the dough over into a roll about 8 cm (3 inches) in depth. With a sharp knife, cut it into 1 cm ($\frac{1}{2}$ inch) wide strips. Try to cut them all the same width. When it has been cut, unfold and leave to dry for a minimum of 10 minutes.

For fettucine, proceed as for tagliatelle, but cut into 0.5 cm ($\frac{1}{4}$ inch) wide strips.

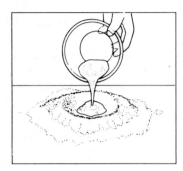

Pouring the beaten eggs, salt and oil into the well in the centre of the dry ingredients.

Beating the egg mixture with a fork, gradually incorporating the flour from around the well.

Using the fingertips to mix the remaining flour into the egg mixture.

For lasagne, cut into 10 x 15 cm (4 x 6 inch) rectangles.

Cooking Pasta

When calculating quantities of pasta per person, allow about 1¹/₂ times as much fresh as dried. Allow 50–75 g (2–3 oz) uncooked dried pasta per person if serving pasta as a starter before a substantial main course dish. If serving pasta as a main course dish for an informal meal, increase the quantity to 100–175 g (4–6 oz) dried pasta per person.

Pasta should be cooked in fast-boiling salted water in a large saucepan. Allow about 2–3 litres (3¹/₂–5¹/₄ pints) per 450 g (1 lb) pasta. Adding 15 ml (1 tbsp) oil to the water will prevent it boiling over and stop the pasta sticking together. Cooking times for dried pasta depends on the size of the pasta: long pasta takes about 8–10 minutes, short cut pasta 6–12 minutes and tiny pasta shapes 2–6 minutes. Lasagne takes about 12 minutes. Fresh pasta takes about 3 minutes.

Check just before the end of the cooking time by biting a piece of pasta. It should be what the Italians call *al dente*, firm but not too hard or soft. Once it has reached this stage it should be drained thoroughly. If it is for a cold dish, rinse it under cold running water. If for a hot dish, it is best eaten or mixed with other ingredients immediately, although it can be kept hot in a colander over a pan of boiling water for a short time before serving.

PASTE This name can be applied to any thick mixture of ingredients, usually made by combining ground (powdered) or very finely minced food with a little liquid, often water. For example, cornflour is mixed to a paste with a little water before being added to a hot dish to thicken it.

Fish and meat, when pounded and mixed with other ingredients and flavourings, give a smooth paste which is good for sandwich fillings, canapé spreads and so on. Many commercially made pastes are sold and these may be stored unopened for some time, as they contain preservatives. Once opened, however, these pastes should be stored in the refrigerator and eaten within two or three days. Delicious fish and meat pastes may also be made at home (usually with the help of a blender or food processor), but these should be prepared as required and used up within a day or two as they do not store well. (*see also* PÂTÉ)

PASTEURIZE To heat a substance, usually milk, to 60–92°C (140–180°F) and to keep it at that temperature for 15 seconds in order to destroy bacteria. This treatment is applied to almost all fresh milk destined to be delivered to doorsteps or sold in supermarkets in Britain, as well as to milk intended for other uses, such as for making cheese. The temperature is sufficient to destroy

99 per cent of the potentially harmful micro-organisms that may be found in milk, including any that could transmit disease, without making the milk taste as though it has been cooked, or affecting the nutritional content in any way. After heating, the milk is cooled rapidly and refrigerated. It will keep for two to three days. (*see also* MILK)

The pasteurization process is also used in the manufacture of beer and cider as well as in other areas of the food industry. It was first invented by Louis Pasteur (1822–1895), a French chemist and biologist.

PASTILLAGE A French confectioners' paste made from icing sugar, water and gum tragacanth. It is kneaded to form a thick dough-like paste that can be rolled out and shaped or used to cover cakes. It can be coloured as required and moulded to make cake decorations. (*see also* GUM)

PASTILLE A small gum lozenge, usually flavoured with fruit juice and often coated in crystallized sugar. (*see also* GUM)

PASTIS One of a number of aniseed or liquorice flavoured liquors that turn milky when water is added. Pastis is popular in the south of France; Pernod is more often drunk in the north. The best known brand of pastis is Ricard. (*see also* OUZO, PERNOD)

PASTRAMI A type of preserved beef popular in the United States. It is cut from the underside or brisket of beef, dry-cured and smoked. It is usually very thinly sliced and used for sandwiches, particularly made from rye bread.

PASTRIES A name loosely applied to fancy cakes, usually iced or decorated, but not always made of pastry. The name covers a vast assortment of different cakes, including meringues, éclairs, *mille-feuilles*, rum babas, cream horns and various types of small iced cakes.

PASTRY A mixture of flour and fat and sometimes egg, bound together with water. It was used by the Romans to enclose baked meat and therefore seal in the flavour and juices. The coating was then thrown away, until it was discovered that the paste was actually quite good to eat. Today there are several different types of pastry – short pastries, flaked pastries, suetcrust, hot water crust, choux and fillo (phyllo) pastry. The main difference between them is the method of introducing the fat. Each kind of pastry produces a different texture and variation in flavour and is suited to a certain range of recipes. It may be savoury or sweet and is usually baked, although some pastries are steamed or deep-fried.

Short Pastries

These are some of the easiest to make and the most versatile. They can be plain or flavoured, savoury or sweet, and form the basis of a wide range of flans, pies and tartlets. They are made by rubbing fat into flour until it is broken down into flour-coated crumbs which then bake to a light crisp texture.

Cool ingredients and conditions are essential and the dough should be handled as little as possible. It is not necessary to grease the baking equipment when cooking this type of pastry.

Shortcrust Pastry

This plain, short pastry is probably the most widely used of all pastries. For shortcrust pastry, the proportion of flour to fat is 2:1, or twice the quantity. Therefore, for a recipe using quantities of shortcrust pastry other than 225 g (8 oz) simply use half the quantity of fat to the flour weight specified.

225 g (8 oz) plain flour
pinch of salt
50 g (2 oz) butter or block margarine, chilled and diced
50 g (2 oz) lard, chilled and diced
chilled water

Place the flour and salt in a bowl and add the fat to the flour. Using the fingertips of both hands, rub the fat lightly into the flour until the mixture resembles fine breadcrumbs.

Add 45–60 ml (3–4 tbsp) water, sprinkling it evenly over the surface. (Uneven addition may cause blistering when the pastry is cooked.) Stir in with a round-bladed knife until the mixture begins to stick together in large lumps.

With one hand, collect the dough mixture together to form a ball. Knead lightly for a few seconds to give a firm, smooth dough. Do not over-handle the dough.

To roll out, sprinkle a very little flour on a working surface and the rolling pin (not on the pastry) and roll out the dough evenly in one direction only, turning it occasionally. The usual thickness is 0.3 cm (⅛ inch). Do not pull or stretch the pastry.

The pastry can be baked straight away, but it is better if allowed to 'rest' for about 30 minutes in the tin or dish, covered with foil or cling film, in the refrigerator. Bake at 200–220°C (400–425°F) mark 6–7, except where otherwise stated in a recipe, until lightly browned.

Variations
Wholemeal Pastry Follow the recipe and method for shortcrust pastry but use plain wholemeal flour instead of white. You may need a little extra water due to the absorbency of wholemeal flour.
Nut Pastry Follow the recipe and method for shortcrust pastry, but stir in 25 g (1 oz) very finely chopped, shelled walnuts, peanuts, cashew nuts, hazelnuts or almonds before adding the water. When using salted nuts, do not add salt to the flour.
Cheese Pastry Follow the recipe and method for shortcrust pastry, but stir in 100 g (4 oz) finely grated Cheddar or other hard cheese and a pinch of mustard powder before adding the water.

Rich Shortcrust or Flan Pastry
This pastry is made by the same rubbing in method as shortcrust pastry, but the liquid used is beaten egg instead of water. It is usually sweetened with caster sugar which improves the flavour and is ideal for flan cases, small tarts and other sweet pastries. If the sugar is omitted, it can be used for savoury flans and tarts. Quick and easy to prepare, flan pastry benefits from being chilled in the refrigerator for at least 30 minutes before being used.
100 g (4 oz) flour
pinch of salt
75 g (3 oz) butter or block margarine and lard, diced
5 ml (1 level tsp) caster sugar
1 egg, beaten
Place the flour and salt in a bowl. Rub the fat into the flour as for shortcrust pastry, until the mixture resembles fine breadcrumbs, then stir in the caster sugar.

Add the egg, stirring with a round-bladed knife until the ingredients begin to stick together in large lumps.

With one hand, collect the mixture together and knead lightly for a few seconds to give a firm, smooth dough. Roll out as for shortcrust pastry. Bake at 200°C (400°F) mark 6, unless otherwise stated, until lightly browned.

Pâte Sucrée (Sweet Pastry) This French, rich, sweet, short pastry is the best choice for Continental pâtisserie. *Pâte sucrée* is thin, crisp yet melting in texture; it keeps its shape, shrinks very little and does not spread during baking. It is fairly quick and easy to make. Although it can be made in a mixing bowl, the classic way to make it is on a flat, cold surface such as marble.
100 g (4 oz) flour
pinch of salt
50 g (2 oz) caster sugar
50 g (2 oz) butter (at room temperature)
2 egg yolks
Sift the flour and salt on to a work surface. Make a well in the centre and add the sugar, butter and egg yolks. Using the fingertips of one hand, pinch and work the sugar, butter and egg yolks together

until well blended. Gradually work in all the flour to bind the mixture together.

Knead lightly until smooth. Wrap the pastry in foil or cling film and leave to 'rest' in the refrigerator or a cool place for about 1 hour, or overnight if possible.

Bake at 190°C (375°F) mark 5, unless otherwise stated, until lightly browned.

Cheese Pastry

There are two types and methods of making cheese pastry. The plainer version is made by the shortcrust pastry technique with grated cheese added (as above) and is easy to handle and less liable to crack when shaped. It is the best type to use for pies, tarts and flans.

This cheese pastry is a little more difficult to make and handle; the fat and cheese are creamed together, then the flour is worked in. This type is best used for small savouries, such as pastry and cocktail appetizers and savouries. Use a hard, dry, well-flavoured cheese with a 'bite', such as Cheddar, Cheshire or Leicester, and grate it finely. A pinch of dry mustard added to the flour with the salt helps to bring out the cheese taste. Another flavour which blends well with cheese pastry is a pinch of cayenne pepper.

40 g (1½ oz) butter or block margarine
40 g (1½ oz) lard
75 g (3 oz) Cheddar or other hard cheese, finely grated
100 g (4 oz) flour
pinch of salt

Cream the butter, lard and cheese together until soft. Gradually work in the flour and salt with a wooden spoon or a palette knife until the mixture sticks together.

With one hand, collect the mixture together and knead very lightly for a few seconds to give a smooth dough. Cover with greaseproof paper or cling film and leave the pastry in a cool place until required.

Bake at 200°C (400°F) mark 6, unless otherwise stated, until lightly browned.

One Stage Short Pastry

This quick method for making pastry is completely different from the rubbed-in method for shortcrust. Soft tub margarine, water and a little of the flour are creamed together, then the remaining flour is mixed in until a dough is formed. One stage short pastry can be used in any recipe using shortcrust pastry.

100 g (4 oz) soft tub margarine
175 g (6 oz) flour, sifted
15 ml (1 tbsp) chilled water
pinch of salt

Place the margarine, 30 ml (2 level tbsp) flour and the water in a bowl. Cream with a fork for about 30 seconds until well mixed. Mix in the remaining flour with the salt to form a fairly soft dough and knead lightly until smooth. Roll out as for shortcrust pastry.

Bake at 190°C (375°F) mark 5 until lightly browned, or for the length of time indicated in individual shortcrust pastry recipes.

Oil or Fork-mix Pastry

Oil pastry is very quick to make and can be used instead of shortcrust pastry. As it is naturally slightly more greasy, it is best used for savoury rather than sweet dishes. Short and flaky in texture, oil pastry should be mixed quickly and used straight away, as it dries out and is too difficult to roll if left for even a short while or chilled.

40 ml (8 tsp) vegetable oil
15 ml (1 tbsp) chilled water
100 g (4 oz) flour
pinch of salt

Put the oil and water into a bowl. Beat well with a fork to form an emulsion. Mix the flour and salt together and gradually add to the mixture to make a dough.

Roll out on a floured surface or between pieces of greaseproof paper.

Bake at 200°C (400°F) mark 6 for the same length of time as shortcrust pastry.

Flaked Pastries

The light layered texture of flaked pastries is achieved by rolling and folding the dough to trap pockets of air between the layers of dough.

The proportion of fat to flour is much higher in all flaked pastries than shortcrust, and the methods of mixing it into the dough vary with the different types of flaked pastries.

Remember to rest all flaked pastries in the refrigerator for about 30 minutes after making and again after shaping and before baking. During baking, the air expands and the fat melts and is absorbed by the flour which leaves more air spacing. This gives the pastry its characteristic flaky texture.

Flaky Pastry

This pastry can be used instead of puff pastry in many savoury and sweet dishes where a great rise is not needed. The fat should be of about the same consistency as the dough with which it is to be combined, which is why it is 'worked' on a plate beforehand.

225 g (8 oz) plain flour
pinch of salt
175 g (6 oz) butter or a mixture of butter and lard
120 ml (8 tbsp) chilled water and a squeeze of lemon juice
beaten egg, to glaze

Mix the flour and salt together in a bowl. Soften the fat by 'working' it with a knife on a plate, then divide it into four equal portions. Add one quarter of the fat to the flour and rub it into the flour between finger and thumb tips until the mixture resembles fine breadcrumbs.

Add enough water and lemon juice, stirring with a round-bladed knife, to make a soft, elastic dough. Turn the dough on to a lightly floured surface, knead until smooth, then roll out into an oblong three times as long as it is wide.

Using a round-bladed knife, dot a second quarter of the fat over the top two thirds of the pastry in flakes, so that it looks like buttons on a card. Fold the bottom third of the pastry up and the top third down, then turn it so that the folded edges are at the sides.

Seal the edges of the pastry by pressing with a rolling pin. Wrap the pastry in greaseproof paper and leave in the refrigerator to 'rest' for 15 minutes. Re-roll as before and repeat twice more until the remaining fat has been used up.

Wrap the pastry loosely in greaseproof paper and leave it to 'rest' in the refrigerator for at least 30 minutes before using.

Roll out the pastry on a lightly floured work surface to 0.3 cm (1/8 inch) thick and use as required. Leave to rest in the refrigerator for 30 minutes before baking. Brush with beaten egg before baking to give the characteristic glaze.

Bake at 200°C (400°F) mark 6, unless otherwise stated.

Opposite: Spices: 1. White peppercorns; 2. Fennel seeds; 3. Ground white pepper; 4. Black peppercorns; 5. Ground black pepper; 6. Vanilla pods; 7. Juniper berries; 8. Cinnamon sticks; 9. Coriander seeds; 10. Ground coriander; 11. Whole nutmeg; 12. Blade mace; 13. Cardamom pods; 14. Whole dried chillies; 15. Chilli powder; 16. Cumin seeds; 17. Ground cumin; 18. Ground mace; 19. Dill seeds; 20. Black and white mustard seeds; 21. Dried root ginger; 22. Ground ginger; 23. Ground turmeric; 24. Fenugreek seeds; 25. Poppy seeds; 26. Caraway seeds; 27. Saffron; 28. Cloves

Overleaf: Left, Veal and ham pie; **Right**, Tagine
Centre Pages: Preserves

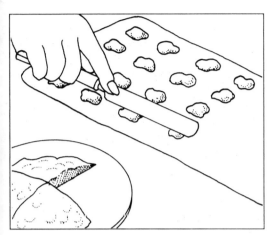

Using a round-bladed knife to dot an area of the dough with flakes of butter for flaky pastry.

Rough Puff Pastry

Similar in texture to flaky pastry, rough puff can be used instead of flaky, except when even rising and appearance are particularly important. Rough puff is quicker and easier to make than puff or flaky pastry.

225 g (8 oz) plain flour
pinch of salt
75 g (3 oz) butter or block margarine, well chilled
75 g (3 oz) lard
about 150 ml (¹/₄ pint) chilled water and a squeeze of lemon juice
beaten egg, to glaze

Mix the flour and salt together in a bowl. Cut the butter into 2 cm (³/₄ inch) cubes. Stir into the flour without breaking up the pieces. Add enough water and lemon juice to mix to a fairly stiff dough using a round-bladed knife. On a lightly floured

Previous pages: Left (from top to bottom), Star fruit, Nashi; **Right** (from top to bottom), Raspberry sorbet, Mango sorbet, Pineapple sorbet
Opposite: Old English syllabub

surface, roll out into an oblong three times as long as it is wide.

Fold the bottom third up and the top third down, then turn the pastry so that the folded edges are at the sides. Seal the ends of the pastry with a rolling pin. Wrap the pastry in greaseproof paper and chill for 15 minutes.

Repeat this rolling and folding process three more times, turning the dough so that the folded edge is on the left hand side each time. Wrap the pastry in paper and chill for 30 minutes.

Roll out the pastry to 0.3 cm (1/8 inch) thick and use as required. Leave to 'rest' in the refrigerator for 30 minutes before baking. Brush with beaten egg before baking to give the characteristic glaze. Bake at 220°C (425°F) mark 7.

Puff Pastry

The richest of all the pastries, puff requires patience, practice and very light handling. Whenever possible, it should be made the day before use. It is not practical to make in a quantity with less than 450 g (1 lb) flour weight. This is equivalent to two 368 g (13 oz) frozen packets.

450 g (1 lb) strong white flour
pinch of salt
450 g (1 lb) butter or block margarine
300 ml (¹/₂ pint) chilled water
15 ml (1 tbsp) lemon juice
beaten egg, to glaze

Mix the flour and salt together in a bowl. Cut off 50 g (2 oz) butter and flatten the remaining butter with a rolling pin to a slab 2 cm (³/₄ inch) thick. Cut the 50 g (2 oz) butter into small pieces, add to the flour and rub in. Using a round-bladed knife, stir in enough water and lemon juice to make a soft, elastic dough.

Quickly knead the dough until smooth and shape into a round. Cut through half the depth in the shape of a cross. Open out to form a star. Roll out, keeping the centre four times as thick as the flaps. Place the slab of butter in the centre of the dough and fold over the flaps envelope-style.

Press gently with the rolling pin and roll out into a rectangle measuring about 40 x 20 cm (16 x 8 inches).

Fold the bottom third up and the top third down, keeping the edges straight. Seal the edges by pressing with the rolling pin. Wrap the pastry in greaseproof paper and leave in the refrigerator to 'rest' for 30 minutes. Put the pastry on a lightly floured working surface with the folded edges to the sides and repeat the rolling, folding and resting sequence five times.

Shape the pastry as required, then leave to 'rest' in the refrigerator for 30 minutes before baking. Brush with beaten egg before baking. Bake at 220°C (425°F) mark 7 for about 15 minutes on its own, or longer if filled, except where otherwise stated.

Miscellaneous Pastries

This group includes the pastries like suetcrust, hot water crust, choux and fillo (phyllo) that are not made by either the traditional rubbing in or flaked pastry methods.

Hot Water Crust Pastry

This pastry is used to make savoury raised pies such as veal and ham pie and game pie. It is mixed with boiling water, which makes it pliable enough to mould into a raised pie that will hold its shape as it cools and during the baking. It is a 'strong' pastry, fit to withstand the extra handling that it must receive during the shaping and also the weight of the savoury filling it must hold. Care must be taken when moulding hot water crust pastry to ensure that there are no cracks through which the meat juices can escape during baking. Keep the part of the pastry that is not actually being used covered with a cloth or an upturned bowl, to prevent it hardening before use. (*see also* RAISED PIE)

450 g (1 lb) plain flour
10 ml (2 level tsp) salt
100 g (4 oz) lard
250 ml (9 fl oz) water

Mix the flour and salt together in a bowl. Make a well in the centre. In a small saucepan, melt the lard in the water, then bring to the boil and pour into the bowl. Working quickly, beat the mixture with a wooden spoon to form a fairly soft dough.

Use one hand to pinch the dough lightly together and knead until smooth and silky. Cover with cling film or a damp tea towel and leave in a warm place to rest for 20–30 minutes so the dough becomes elastic and easy to work. Use as required but do not allow the pastry to cool. Bake at 220°C (425°F) mark 7, usually reducing to 180°C (350°F) mark 4, depending on the individual recipe.

Suetcrust Pastry

This pastry may be used for both sweet and savoury basin puddings, roly-poly puddings and

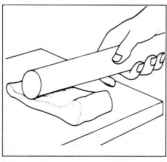 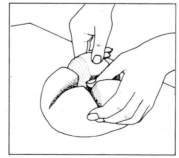 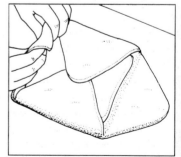

Using a rolling pin to flatten the butter for puff pastry to a slab 2 cm (¾ inch) thick.

Opening out the dough into a star shape, having cut through the depth in a cross shape.

Folding the flaps of dough over the butter like an envelope before re-rolling.

dumplings. It can be steamed, boiled or baked; the first two methods are the most satisfactory, as baked suetcrust pastry is inclined to be hard. Suetcrust pastry is quick and easy to make, and should be light and spongy in texture – the correct mixing, quick light handling and long, slow cooking will achieve this. For a lighter texture, or if using wholemeal flour, replace 50 g (2 oz) of the flour with 50 g (2 oz) fresh breadcrumbs.

225 g (8 oz) self raising flour
2.5 ml (¹/₂ level tsp) salt
100 g (4 oz) shredded suet
about 150 ml (¹/₄ pint) chilled water

Mix the flour, salt and suet together in a bowl. Using a round-bladed knife, stir in enough water to give a light, elastic dough. Knead very lightly until smooth. Roll out to 0.5 cm (¹/₄ inch) thick and use as required.

Steaming or boiling basin and roly-poly puddings takes about 2–4 hours, depending on filling and size. Roly-poly puddings can also be wrapped in foil and baked at 200°C (400°F) mark 6 for about 45 minutes, unless otherwise stated. Dumplings cooked in simmering liquid take about 25 minutes.

Lining a Pudding Basin with Suetcrust Pastry

Sweet and savoury filled and layered suet puddings in basins are a constant family favourite. The basin may be made of any heatproof material from glass or earthenware to certain kinds of plastic. It is important to use the size of basin specified in a recipe. The correct size basin should allow a space of about 1 cm (¹/₂ inch) at the top when the uncooked pudding is complete. Always grease the basin to prevent the pastry from sticking and if you do not have a steamer cook the pudding on a trivet in a saucepan at least 5 cm (2 inches) wider than the diameter of the basin, in boiling water that comes halfway up the basin.

For a 1.7 litre (3 pint) pudding basin, roll out the pastry to a round about 35.5 cm (14 inches) in diameter. Using a sharp knife, cut out one quarter of the dough and reserve. Lightly grease the pudding basin.

Dust the top surface of the large piece of pastry with flour and fold in half, then in half again. Lift the pastry into the basin, unfold, press into the base and up the sides, taking care to seal the join well. The pastry should overlap the basin top by about 2.5 cm (1 inch).

Spoon the filling into the lined pudding basin, taking care not to puncture the pastry lining. Gently spread out the filling so it is evenly distributed.

Roll out the remaining one quarter of pastry to a round 2.5 cm (1 inch) wider than the top of the basin. Dampen the exposed edge of pastry lining the basin.

Lift the round of pastry on top of the filling. Push the pastry edges together to seal.

Cut a piece of greaseproof paper and a piece of foil large enough to cover the basin. Place them together and pleat across the middle to allow for expansion. Lightly grease the greaseproof side and put them over the pudding with the greaseproof side down.

Tie securely on to the basin, running the string just under the rim. Make a strong handle of string across the basin top. Bring a large pan of water to the boil. Fit a steamer over the pan and put the pudding inside and cover. Steam for the specified time.

Choux Pastry

This light, crisp-textured pastry is used for making sweet and savoury éclairs, cream puffs, *aigrettes* and *gougères*. As long as the recipe instructions are strictly adhered to, choux pastry will always give good results. Always collect the ingredients together before starting to make choux pastry as all the flour needs to be added quickly as soon as the mixture has come to the boil.

Raw choux paste is too soft and sticky to be rolled out and is, therefore, piped or spooned on to a dampened baking sheet for baking. During baking, the moisture in the dough turns to steam and puffs up the mixture, leaving the centre hollow. Thorough cooking is important; if insufficiently cooked, the choux may collapse when taken from the oven and there will be uncooked pastry in the centre to scoop out.

When the cooked choux has cooled and dried out, it can be filled with whipped cream or a savoury filling. Choux pastry can also be deep-fried – pipe or spoon it directly into hot oil.

65 g (2½ oz) plain or strong white flour
50 g (2 oz) butter or block margarine
150 ml (¼ pint) water
2 eggs, lightly beaten (use size 2 when using an electric mixer)

Sift the flour on to a plate or piece of paper. Put the fat and water together in a saucepan, heat gently until the fat has melted, then bring to the boil. Remove the pan from the heat. Tip the flour at once into the hot liquid. Beat thoroughly with a wooden spoon.

Continue beating the mixture until it is smooth and forms a ball in the centre of the pan (take care not to overbeat or the mixture will become fatty). Leave the pastry mixture to cool for a minute or two.

Beat in the eggs, a little at a time, adding only just enough to give a piping consistency. It is important to beat the mixture vigorously at this stage to trap in as much air as possible. A hand-held electric mixer is ideal for this purpose. Continue beating until the mixture develops an obvious sheen and then use as required.

Bake in the oven at 200°C (400°F) mark 6. Immediately after the choux pastry is removed from the oven, it should be pierced to allow steam to escape.

Piping Choux Pastry

To fill a piping bag, usually fitted with a plain 0.5 cm (½ inch) nozzle, place it in a tall jug and turn back the open end over the jug rim. Spoon the pastry mixture into the bag and squeeze it down to eliminate air bubbles.

When making éclairs, it may help to mark evenly-spaced lines on the baking sheet with the end of a wooden spoon as a guide for piping.

Hold the piping bag in one hand and, with the thumb and one finger of your other hand on the nozzle to guide it, press out the pastry. When the required length is reached, cut off the paste with a wet knife. Choux puffs and profiteroles can be piped or spooned into mounds.

Fillo (Phyllo) or Strudel Pastry

Fillo is a pastry of wafer-like thinness from the Middle East which is used for both savoury and sweet pastries, such as the Greek *baklava*. It is identical to strudel pastry which originated in Europe and is used for the popular *apfel strudel*. Fillo or strudel pastry is fairly difficult and time-consuming to make. Unlike most pastries, it requires warm ingredients and, instead of light handling, it has to be kneaded and beaten. The dough is kneaded vigorously to enable the gluten in the flour to develop strength so the pastry can be stretched into a very thin, resilient sheet. For the same reason, strong plain flour is used as it yields more gluten to help produce an elastic dough. The thin sheet is either spread with a filling and rolled or folded, or it is cut into rectangles and stacked with a filling in between.

Ready-made fillo or strudel pastry (fresh or frozen) is available in sheets from continental shops, supermarkets and delicatessens.

225 g (8 oz) strong white flour
2.5 ml (½ level tsp) salt
1 egg, lightly beaten
30 ml (2 tbsp) vegetable oil
1.25 ml (¼ level tsp) lemon juice
75 ml (5 tbsp) lukewarm water
25 g (1 oz) butter, melted

Mix the flour and salt together in a large bowl. Make a well in the centre and pour in the egg, oil and lemon juice. Stirring with a fork, gradually add enough of the water to make a soft, sticky dough. Work the dough in the bowl until it leaves the sides. Turn out on to a lightly floured surface and knead for 15 minutes. The dough should feel smooth. Form it into a ball, place on a cloth and cover with a warmed bowl. Leave to 'rest' in a warm place for 30 minutes.

Warm a rolling pin and lightly flour a clean cotton cloth. Place the ball of dough on the cloth and roll out into a rectangle about 0.3 cm (1/8 inch) thick, lifting and turning to prevent it sticking to the cloth.

Brush the top of the dough with a little melted butter. Gently stretch the dough by carefully lifting it on the backs of the hands and fingertips, and pulling it from the centre to the outside, trying to keep it in a rectangle.

Continue lifting and stretching the dough until it becomes paper thin and the rectangle measures no less than 75 x 50 cm (30 x 20 inches). Trim off uneven thick edges with scissors or a sharp knife.

Leave the dough on the cloth to dry and 'rest' for about 15 minutes before lifting off carefully. Bake at 190°C (375°F) mark 5, except where otherwise specified, until lightly browned.

PASTY An individual savoury pastry pie made without a dish on a baking sheet. The best known pasty is the traditional Cornish pasty, containing a mixture of diced steak, potatoes, swede, onion and mixed herbs.

PÂTÉ A savoury mixture made from minced meat, flaked fish and/or vegetables cooked to form a solid mass. Pâtés are made in small individual ramekin dishes or large round or oblong terrines, in which case the pâté is often known as a terrine. Terrines are usually lined with bacon rashers, baked in a *bain marie*, then cooled and served cold. Their surfaces are often sealed with a layer of clarified butter or decorated aspic. Terrines may be turned out and served sliced, or the pâté may be scooped out with a spoon. Pâtés

may also be made *en croûte*, that is enclosed in a pastry case; this type of pâté is often served hot.

Pâtés vary a great deal in flavour and consistency. Some are made from coarsely minced meat, while others, such as chicken liver pate, are very smooth. They are usually highly flavoured with herbs, spices and sometimes garlic. Well known pâtés include *pâté de foie gras*, made from fattened goose livers, and *pâté de campagne*, which is a general name applied to various French regional pâtés. Pâté makes a good starter, served with toast, or it can be served for a light lunch, with crusty French bread.

PÂTE The French word for pastry. In English, the only pastry still called by its French name is *pâte sucrée* (see PASTRY).

PÂTE SUCRÉE (*see* PASTRY)

PÂTISSERIE When correctly used, this French term applies to highly decorated pastries, as produced by a French *pâtissier* or pastry cook. Examples include *mille-feuilles*, *palmiers*, cream horns and cream slices. In this country, the term is used more widely to denote any small fancy cakes and pastries. (*see also* PASTRIES)

PATTY An alternative name for a small pie, *bouchée* or *vol au vent*, often made of puff pastry and filled with a savoury mixture. A small, burger-like cake of minced meat may also be known as a patty. (*see also* BOUCHÉE, VOL AU VENT)

Patty tins are more often used for making small cakes and tartlets than for making patties.

PAUNCH To remove the stomach and intestines of a rabbit or hare (see RABBIT).

PAUPIETTE The French name for a thin slice of meat or fish rolled around a stuffing and secured with string or cocktail sticks. *Paupiettes* are usually braised or fried, though fish *paupiettes* may be rolled in greaseproof paper and gently poached.

PAWPAW (*see* PAPAYA)

PAYSANNE, À LA A French term used to describe dishes prepared in a simple country style. It is often applied to meat or poultry, usually braised and accompanied by a garnish of mixed chopped vegetables.

PEA BEAN (*see* NAVY BEAN)

PEA FLOUR (Pea Starch) A flour produced from ground dried, mature peas. It can be used for thickening sauces and as a basis for soup.

PEACH A delicious tree fruit that originated in China and is now grown in many of the warm parts of the world. Peaches are readily available in Britain in the summer months. They are round fruits, about the size of an apple, but with a marked groove running from top to bottom. They have a yellow and pink, sometimes red, downy skin enclosing soft and juicy orange flesh surrounding a central, crinkly stone. A new, excellent-flavoured small variety has white flesh.

There are many varieties of peach, but they can be roughly divided into two main types, the 'freestone' type with a stone that separates easily from the flesh, which are good for eating fresh, and the 'clingstone' type, which are good for cooking. Freestone peaches can be eaten on their own as a dessert or added to fruit salads; clingstones can be poached or made into jam or chutney. A well known peach dessert is peach Melba which consists of peach halves or slices topped with ice cream and Melba sauce (*see* MELBA SAUCE). Peaches can also be served with savoury dishes, especially duck or chicken.

To select: When ripe, peaches are slightly soft and have a yellow to red skin. Avoid green, bruised or 'sale' fruit. Eat within two days if kept at room temperature or, if wrapped and kept in the refrigerator, eat within five days.

To prepare: Peaches can be peeled by immersing them in boiling water for about 15 seconds, then cooling in cold water. Very ripe peaches are best skinned and stoned under running water, as scalding them will soften and slightly discolour the flesh. Brush cut fruit with lemon juice to prevent browning.

To cook: Slightly under-ripe peaches can be peeled, stoned, sliced and poached lightly in sugar syrup. Flavour with liqueur.

PEACH, DRIED Unlike dried apricots, dried peaches lack the flavour and fragrance of the fresh fruit. They are usually sold in packages of mixed dried fruits, either whole or halved. Dried peaches are often treated with sulphur to preserve their colour and some Chinese varieties may be preserved in sugar. They should be soaked before using in fruit salads, pies, teabreads, crumble toppings and stuffings for poultry.

PEACH BRANDY (*see* BRANDY)

PEANUT (Groundnut, Monkey Nut) Peanuts are a type of underground bean which grows in India, Africa and parts of America and the Far East. They consist of two kernels which grow in a dry, crinkly pod or shell, each one coated in a brown papery edible skin. They are available as whole nuts roasted in their shells, or as shelled nuts, which may be plain, dry roasted or roasted and salted. Ground peanuts are used to make peanut butter (*see* PEANUT BUTTER). Peanuts are also used to make oil, usually called groundnut oil (*see* OILS).

Peanuts are very nutritious, being rich in protein and oil. They are the most popular nuts for eating as a snack and can also be added to salads or used in vegetable dishes, or chopped and added to biscuits. Roasted peanuts are ground and used to make a sauce to serve with the Malaysian dish *satay* (*see* SATÉ).

PEANUT BUTTER Originating in America, this is a brownish-yellow, oily paste, with a somewhat coarse texture, made from peanuts. Commercially produced peanut butter is sold as 'smooth' or 'crunchy', the latter containing pieces of chopped peanut. True peanut butter is made simply by grinding whole peanuts, but commercial brands often contain salt and sugar. Peanut butter may replace butter for use with bread, water biscuits, etc., and is most palatable when spread thickly and sprinkled with salt. Mixed with celery, onion or pickles, it can be used in sandwiches. It is also used in making some cakes and biscuits.

PEAR This common tree fruit is popular as a dessert fruit and for cooking. It originated in the Middle East, but is now grown in many parts of the world, though the trees grow best in warm climates. Several varieties are now grown on a commercial scale in Britain, including Williams and Conference. There are many varieties of pear, each with a different shape, size and colour. Some are characteristically pear-shaped, while others are round or elongated; some are mottled yellow in colour, others green or red; some are soft and juicy, others firm and crisp. Most ripe pears are suitable for eating raw; Williams, Conference, Comice and Laxton's are good dessert pears. Different varieties of pear are available all year round.

Fresh pears are a delicious snack fruit, or they can be added to fresh fruit salads or eaten with cheese. They make an attractive tart topping and marry well with chocolate in the popular *poires belle-Hélène*, or in a chocolate upside down pudding. They can be used to make delicately flavoured soufflés or tangy chutneys. Commercially, they are used to make an *eau-de-vie* known as *poire William* (see EAU-DE-VIE).

To select: Choose well formed firm pears with no oozing or softness. Ripe pears 'give' a little at the stem end. They become overripe very quickly so are best refrigerated and eaten within three days.

To prepare: The skin of pears is edible, but tough in some varieties. They can be halved and cored in the same way as apples; if the fruit is very soft the core can be scooped out with a spoon, providing a useful container for sweet or savoury stuffings. Brush peeled pears with lemon juice to prevent browning.

To cook: Small firm pears can be stewed in sugar syrup; larger ones can be halved or sliced. Flavour with a liqueur, such as kirsch or port.

PEAR, ASIAN (*see* NASHI)

PEAR, DRIED Dried pears are usually sold in packets of dried mixed fruit but are also available separately, whole or halved. If whole, the skin, core and pips can be removed after soaking. Like other dried fruits, dried pears have usually been treated with sulphur to preserve their colour. Dried pears have a good flavour and can be eaten as a snack or cooked in compotes, dried fruit salads, puddings and some savoury dishes.

PEAR, TIENTSIN (*see* TIENTSIN PEAR)

PEARL BARLEY (*see* BARLEY)

PEARL MOSS (*see* CARRAGEEN)

PEAS Green peas are the seeds of a climbing plant, of which there are numerous varieties. The seeds are contained in a green pod which is not usually eaten, except in the case of mange-tout which are eaten whole before the peas begin to swell in the pods (*see* MANGE-TOUT). The peas themselves vary in size from the small petits pois, with a diameter of about 0.25 cm (1/8 inch) to large ones nearly 1 cm (^{1}/2 inch) across. Petits pois are sweet and tender and can be eaten raw or slightly cooked. Another good tasting pea is the variety known as the marrowfat pea.

The fresh pea season is short but they are available all year round frozen, canned, dried and dehydrated. Frozen peas are very popular as they taste similar to fresh peas and require no preparation.

To select: When buying fresh peas, choose crisp, well filled pods with some air space between the peas. Very full pods may have tough peas inside. Allow 100–175 g (4–6 oz) prepared weight per person. You will need to buy about 225–350 g (8-12 oz) per person in the pods.

To prepare: Remove the peas from the pods and discard any blemished or discoloured peas. Wash under cold running water.

To cook: Boil in lightly salted water, with a sprig of mint added, for 10–15 minutes, or steam for 3–5 minutes, or until just tender. Drain well and add a knob of butter, if liked.

To serve: Peas are usually served as an accompanying vegetable, especially with fish and roast or grilled meats.

PEAS, DRIED (*see* PULSES)

PEASE BROSE A kind of Scottish porridge, made with pea flour or meal. (*see also* BROSE)

PEASE PUDDING (*see* SPLIT PEAS)

PECAN NUT Pecan nuts belong to the walnut family and are grown in North America where they are also known as hickory nuts. They are available in their shells, which are smooth and brown, or shelled, looking rather like narrow, elongated walnuts.

The classic use of pecans is in pecan pie, but they can be used instead of walnuts in any recipe, though their flavour is somewhat sweeter and milder.

PECORINO A general name for several varieties of hard Italian cheese made from ewes' milk. When mature, it has a strong, sharp flavour and is mostly used, like Parmesan cheese, in cooking and for grating over pasta and other savoury dishes. There are many types of Pecorino, produced all over Italy. Some are eaten soft and fresh, while others, such as Pecorino Romano and Pecorino Sardo (from Sardinia), are left to mature and become hard. Pecorino Siciliano (from Sicily) is similar but it matures more quickly and has, if anything, a stronger flavour; it is best suited to cooking.

PECTIN A naturally-occurring substance found in most fruit (and some vegetables), the presence of which is necessary for setting jams and jellies.

Chemically, pectin is derived from carbohydrates, and develops as the fruit becomes ripe. It is concentrated in the pips, pith, core and skin of fruit. Once over-ripe, the pectin turns to pectic acid and methyl alcohol (*see* ALCOHOL), at which point most of its setting properties are lost. It is therefore best to use only just ripe fruit for making jams, jellies and marmalades. However, the set achieved is also dependent on the presence of sufficient acid (also found in fruit) and the correct amount of sugar.

The pectin content of fruits varies considerably; when making preserves, it is possible to carry out a test to check the pectin content of the food being used. If there is not enough pectin or acid present, more can be added in the form of home-made pectin extract (*see* below), lemon juice, or commercially-produced pectin liquid or powder.

Home-made pectin extract can be made from sour cooking apples, crab apples or apple peelings, cores and windfalls. Wash 900 g (2 lb) fruit and chop roughly without peeling or coring. Cover with 600–900 ml (1–1½ pints) water and stew gently for about 45 minutes, until well pulped. Strain through a jelly bag or muslin cloth, then carry out a pectin test on the juice (*see* JAM) to ensure that there is sufficient pectin present. Allow 150–300 ml (¼–½ pint) extract to 2 kg (4 lb) fruit which is low in pectin. Pectin extract can also be made, by the same method, using fresh gooseberries and redcurrants.

(*see also* JAM, JELLY, MARMALADE)

PEELING Removing the outer shell, rind or peel from a variety of foods, including prawns, fruit and vegetables.

PEKING DUCK A classic dish from Chinese Mandarin cuisine. Its main component is a stuffed, marinated, roast duck, the skin and meat of which is cut into strips and served with spring onions, cucumber, pancakes and a special plum-based sauce. Peking pancakes are made from a very plain dough made from flour and water.

Each item is served on a separate plate and each person takes a portion of duck skin and meat and puts it on a pancake with cucumber, spring onion and sauce. The pancake is then rolled and eaten with the fingers or chopsticks.

PELARGONIUM (*see* GERANIUM)

PEMMICAN Well-dried buffalo or deer meat which is ground and mixed with melted fat to form a cake which is then wrapped in animal skin. This concentrated food with good keeping qualities was used originally by North American Indians and then by trappers and other travellers. There is little demand for it today, though modern explorers take a similar preparation of dried beef on expeditions.

PENNE (*see* PASTA)

PENNYROYAL A small creeping plant, related to the mint family. It is strongly scented and for many centuries was used to repel insects. In the north of England, pennyroyal is popularly known as 'pudding grass' because it is a traditional flavouring in black pudding (*see* BLACK PUDDING).

PEPERONI (Pepperoni) A hot, dry Italian sausage made from coarsely chopped pork and beef, flavoured with hot pepper, fennel and spices. It is sold in long, thin sausages and needs no further cooking. It is often sliced and used as part of a pizza topping.

PEPINELLO (*see* CHAYOTE)

PEPINO (Melon Pear) An exotic fruit from the same family as the tomato, potato and aubergine. The pepino is a large, round or oval fruit with yellow or green smooth, shiny skin streaked with purple. The yellow flesh, which surrounds a central core of white seeds, is sweet tasting but slightly acid, the flavour being vaguely reminiscent of melon. The bitter-flavoured skin is best removed. The fruit can be eaten fresh, used in both sweet and savoury cooked dishes or cooked and served as an accompaniment to meat or fish.

PEPPER This spice is the berry of a tropical vine which produces hanging strings of berries. The berries, or peppercorns, are sold in several forms: green, black or white. Green or unripe berries are picked and either dried, canned or bottled. They have a milder flavour than black or white pepper and are used whole as a separate spice in pâtés, with rich meat like duck and in sauces and casseroles. Green peppercorns are sometimes used lightly crushed.

Black pepper consists of berries which are picked while green and dried in the sun which shrivels and darkens them. It has a strong, pungent, hot flavour and is best used freshly ground to season virtually all savoury dishes.

White pepper is made from the fully ripened berries with the red skin and pulp removed. It is more aromatic and less hot in flavour than black pepper. It can be interchanged with it, but its main use is in light-coloured dishes and sauces whose appearance would be marred by dark flecks.

Pink pepper berries are also sometimes available. These are not from the same family and are not in fact peppercorns, though they are the berries of a tropical bush known locally as a pepper tree. Pink peppercorns have little flavour, are flaky in texture and too many can have ill effects so are best used sparingly or reserved for use as a garnish.

PEPPER, SWEET (Bell Pepper) The pepper plant belongs to the capsicum family and produces fluted, pear-shaped fruits. Most peppers are green when first developed, and turn yellowy-orange and finally red when fully matured. Other colours available are white, yellow and black. Peppers can be eaten raw in salads or cooked in casseroles, savoury dishes and sauces. Stuffed peppers make a popular supper or lunch dish.

To select: Choose peppers with smooth, shiny skins. The flesh should be firm and free of blemishes. Allow 1 pepper per person when stuffed.

To prepare: Rinse the skins, then slice off the stem and remove the seeds and membrane. Leave whole, slice into rings or dice. When peppers are to be eaten raw, they are more digestible with the skins removed. Grill or turn the whole pepper over a gas flame until the skin is charred, then plunge straight into cold water. The skin will rub off between your fingers.

To cook: Blanch or stuff and bake in the oven at 190°C (375°F) mark 5 for about 45 minutes.

PEPPERMINT A European plant that is a member of the same family as garden spearmint, but with a more pronounced odour and taste. An oil and a flavouring essence are made from the plant, the oil being obtained by distilling the plant with water, and the essence consisting of the plant's essential oils mixed with spirit. The oil has the stronger flavour, while the strength of the essence varies according to the degree of dilution.

Peppermint forms a popular flavouring for confectionery, drinks and occasionally for desserts, and it is also used medicinally. Sweets, jellies, liqueurs, etc., that have been flavoured with peppermint are often coloured green.

PERCH A large, round freshwater fish with firm, sweet, white flesh. Perch is rarely available from the fishmonger but can be caught in rivers and lakes in Europe, Britain and parts of the United States. It should be cleaned and scaled as soon as possible after being caught. Treat the dorsal fins with respect as they can wound. Perch can be fried or poached. If poaching, cook first, then scale. (*see also* FISH)

PÉRIGORD (*see* TRUFFLE)

PÉRIGUEUX, À LA A French expression usually used to describe dishes made or served with truffles and sometimes *foie gras*. Other terms used to describe similar preparations include *à la Périgord* and *à la Périgourdine*. These expressions may also be used to describe other dishes from the Périgord region of France which do not, in fact, include truffles or *foie gras*.

PERIWINKLE (*see* WINKLE)

PERNOD An aperitif that takes its name from a French firm which used to distil absinthe. The modern Pernod is based on aniseed and contains no absinthe, a bitter liqueur made from wormwood, which is now prohibited in France due to its habit-forming properties. Pernod is usually served with water, which turns the clear liquid a milky white, and topped up with chunks of ice. (*see also* OUZO, PASTIS, RICARD)

PERPETUAL SPINACH (*see* SPINACH)

PERRY An alcoholic drink made from the fermented juice of a hard, astringent type of pear (unsuitable for eating raw). Perry is made in a similar way to cider, the pears being crushed between rollers. The resulting pulp (or pomace) is packed in cloths between frames and the juice is pressed out and collected in a cask, in which it is left to ferment. Perry is a speciality of south-west England and western France, especially Normandy and Brittany, where it has been made since ancient times.

PERSILLADE A flavouring from classic French cuisine. It consists of chopped parsley and garlic, mixed together and sprinkled over certain dishes towards the end of the cooking time.

PERSIMMON (Kaki, Mabolo, Sharon Fruit) This is a large, tomato-like tropical fruit with a leathery skin which turns from yellow to bright orangey red. It is usually sold with its large calyx still attached. The most common variety of persimmon found in Britain is the Sharon fruit, which is grown in Israel. Unlike other persimmons, it is seedless and both skin and flesh can be eaten. It is developed from an oriental type of persimmon, known as kaki, cultivated in Japan and China. The mabolo (velvet apple) is closely related to the persimmon.

To select: Kaki persimmons should be ripe when eaten; look for those that are so soft and swollen-looking that they appear, if anything, over-ripe. Under-ripe fruit are bitter and very acidic; they cause an unpleasant drying sensation in the mouth. Sharon fruit, however, can be eaten when still quite firm. Avoid fruit with broken or bruised skins.

To prepare: Wash the fruit and slice. The flesh can be spooned out and added to fruit salads, or puréed and used in ice creams and mousses.

PESTLE AND MORTAR Consisting of a bowl (the mortar) and a round-ended implement (the pestle), these are invaluable kitchen items, especially for grinding small amounts of spices, crushing garlic, softening butter or grinding or pounding a variety of other foods. The food is placed in the mortar and is pounded and worked round and round with the pestle until reduced to a paste or powder. Pestles and mortars may be made of wood, stone, glazed or unglazed porcelain, glass or marble and are usually very heavy. Those with a rough, unglazed surface are best for grinding small, hard, dry spice seeds. Pestles and mortars come in a variety of sizes but are most efficient when the mortar is only half-full, so it is wise to buy pestles and mortars of a reasonable size.

PESTO A classic Italian sauce, originally from Genoa, and made from fresh basil, garlic, pine nuts, Parmesan cheese and olive oil. It is usually served over various types of hot pasta, but can also be used as a flavouring in other cooked dishes.

PETIT FOUR The French name, adopted elsewhere, for a variety of small sweets, pastries and biscuits served as a dessert at the end of a meal, often with coffee. They may also be served with morning coffee or afternoon tea. Popular petits fours include macaroons, meringues, fondants, almond paste fruits, small iced cakes and crystallized, candied or glacé fruits.

In France, the term may also be used for savoury filled pastries served with aperitifs and cocktails, or plain sweet biscuits, such as sponge fingers and *langues de chat*, served with creamy desserts.

PETITS POIS (*see* PEAS)

PETIT-SUISSE (Petit-Gervais) An unsalted French cream cheese, often sold in foil-wrapped packs. It is cylindrical in shape with a very soft texture and mild flavour. It is so soft it is sometimes sold in small plastic cartons. It is made from cows' milk enriched with cream, giving it a very high fat content. It can be eaten and used in much the same way as *fromage frais*, and is also available flavoured with fruit, like *fromage frais*. (*see also* FROMAGE FRAIS)

PE-TSAI (*see* CHINESE CABBAGE)

PETTITOES (*see* PIGS' TROTTERS)

PHEASANT A game bird which is at its prime in October and remains in season until 1st February; the actually shooting season is 1st October to 1st February. At its best, pheasant is one of the choicest game birds available.

In the fields, it is the cock bird, with its colourful feathers, which delights the eye, but on the table, the duller brown hen bird is preferred. After shooting, the birds should be hung for about a week before being plucked and drawn. When buying pheasant, look for pointed flight feathers and downy under-wing feathers; in the case of a cock bird, the spurs should be short and blunt.

A pheasant will serve two to three people, depending on size. It is common to serve a 'brace', that is one male and one female. Oven-ready pheasants are available fresh and frozen.

Pheasants are best roasted in the oven at 230°C (450°F) mark 8 for 10 minutes, then the oven temperature should be reduced to 200°C (400°F) mark 6 for 30–50 minutes. The meat can be dry so pheasants are often barded with a few bacon rashers before roasting. The usual accompaniments are browned crumbs, bread sauce and thin gravy. Cranberry sauce, redcurrant jelly, green salad, orange salad or stuffed oranges can also be served with roast pheasant.

Pheasant may also be mixed with veal, ham and mushrooms in a pie, or cooked in a casserole with onion, tomato, bacon and sherry or other ingredients, such as apple, celery, grapes, cream and wine.

For basic preparation, cooking and carving instructions, see CARVING, GAME, HANGING.

PHOSPHOROUS (Phosphorus) A naturally-occurring mineral that is essential to health. It is mainly laid down in the skeleton with calcium. The rest interacts with some of the B complex vitamins to release energy from foods and is present in small quantities in many body cells. Phosphorous is present in a wide variety of foods and a deficiency is very rare. (*see also* MINERALS, VITAMINS)

PHULKA (*see* CHAPPATI)

PHYLO (*see* PASTRY)

PHYSALIS FRUIT (*see* CAPE GOOSEBERRY)

PICCALILLI A bright yellow English mustard pickle of Anglo-Indian origin. It is rather coarse in flavour and is made from mixed vegetables, such as cauliflower, marrow, cucumber, beans and onions, which are salted overnight, then pickled in a sauce made from sugar, mustard, spices, vinegar, flour and turmeric. It is usually served with cold meats.

PICKLE Pickles are made by preserving fresh raw or lightly cooked vegetables or fruits in clear, spiced vinegar. They add interest to a dish, especially to foods such as cold meat and cheese, and can be either sweet or sharp, or an interesting blend of both. Only crisp, fresh fruits and vegetables should be pickled.

PICKLED FISH (*see* CAVEACH)

PICKLING SPICE A pungent mixture of varying spices added to the vinegar when making pickles. Varying proportions of black peppercorns, mace, red chillies, allspice, cloves, ginger, mustard seeds or coriander may be included. Pickling spice can be stored in an airtight, screw-topped jar and kept for up to 1 month. The spices may be tied in a muslin bag before being added to the vinegar.

PIE The name given to various large and small combinations of pastry with sweet or savoury fillings. In single-crust pies, the filling is placed in a deep dish or plate and covered with pastry; in 'open-faced' pies (usually called tarts or flans), a pastry shell or case is filled with the mixture. Some pies, known as 'double-crust' pies, have both a top and a bottom layer of pastry; many of those having a pastry base are given a topping of meringue or something similar.

Shortcrust, rich shortcrust (flan) or puff are the most usual types of pastry used for pies, but other kinds are sometimes used and occasionally a sweet pie has a shell made of biscuit crumbs.

(*see also* FLAN, PASTRY, RAISED PIE, TART)

PIEDMONTESE (*see* TRUFFLE)

PIG (*see* PORK)

PIGEON Though not as popular as they used to be, both wild and tame pigeons may be eaten. Wild and wood pigeons may be classified as game, while domesticated birds are, strictly speaking, poultry. Young pigeons, known as squab, are reared commercially for the table. When selecting a bird, choose one with small eyes; soft, red feet; short rounded spurs; and bright neck feathers, of the same colour as the body feathers.

Wild birds (which can be recognized by their large feet) are excellent if hung for two or three days after shooting; domestic pigeons should be starved for 24 hours before they are killed, then plucked while still warm. Young pigeons may be roasted or grilled, while the older, tougher birds are excellent for making raised pies, rich stews and curries. Allow one pigeon per person as the largest weigh only 700 g (1½ lb). Pigeons can be bought frozen.

Pigeons are plucked, drawn, singed, washed and trussed like other poultry or game, except that the feet are not cut off but are scalded and scraped; the wings are not drawn across the back in trussing (*see* POULTRY).

To roast pigeon, prepare, stuff (if liked) and truss, then cover the breasts with rashers of streaky bacon and place a small shallot inside each bird. Roast at 200°C (400°F) mark 6 for 20-30 minutes. Serve each bird on a *croûte* of fried bread, garnish with watercress and serve with gravy.

PIGEON PEA (Gunga Pea, Red Gram, Toor Dal) Although most frequently available dried, this unusual pea can sometimes be found fresh. The green peas grow in coarse, curved green pods and have a nutty flavour and floury texture. They originated in Africa, but are also eaten in India and the West Indies.

In their dried form, pigeon peas are small, round, cream-coloured peas streaked with red. They are an important food in the Caribbean. (*see also* PULSES)

PIGNOLI (*see* PINENUT)

PIGNUT (*see* CHUFA NUT)

PIG'S CHEEK This portion of the pig is usually pickled and may be dried and cured, when it is known as a Bath chap. It is usually sold ready cooked and can be served cold, cut in slices.

PIG'S EAR Although still popular in France, this part of the pig is now rarely eaten in Britain as a separate dish, though it can be cooked together with the trotters, after being washed and cleansed. It is generally used in sausages and other commercial preparations.

PIG'S FRY (Haslet) A country-type dish in which the heart, liver, lights (lungs) and sweetbreads of a pig are cooked together. As the name suggests, the mixture is usually fried, but may also be stewed, casseroled or made into faggots (*see* FAGGOT). It should be eaten immediately after cooking.

PIG'S HEAD (*see* HEAD)

PIG'S TONGUE (*see* TONGUE)

PIG'S TROTTERS Pig's trotters (feet) are available fresh or salted. They may be boned, stuffed and roasted, or the meat from them used in brawn. When cooked, they produce a protein-rich gelatine. To prepare, singe off any hairs over an open flame. Scrub the trotters well and pat dry. Par-boil in salted water for 5 minutes before using in a recipe. (*see also* BRAWN)

PIGWEED (*see* PURSLANE)

PIKE (Freshwater Shark, Waterwolf) Pike is a sharp-nosed, duck-billed freshwater fish with large jaws and sharp teeth. It is found in European and North American lakes and streams, where it feeds on other fish, hence its alternative names. The flesh is quite dry, but has an excellent flavour. Smaller fish up to 900 g (2 lb) are best for cooking. Pike is often used for *quenelles* and stuffings, and can also be poached or stuffed and baked. Unfortunately, the flesh contains a number of fine bones which are difficult to remove.

If the fish has a muddy film on it, it can be soaked in cold water for a few hours before cooking. (*see also* FISH)

PIKELET The name of various types of British teacake. In Yorkshire, it is an alternative name for crumpet (*see* CRUMPET), but in other parts of the country, the name refers to a flatter type of cake made from a Scotch pancake (drop scone) mixture, yeasted or unyeasted, and cooked on a griddle. Pikelets are usually eaten warm, spread with butter. (*see also* SCONE)

PILAF (Pilau, Pilav, Pilaw) A national dish of Turkey, made of rice or bulgar wheat, oil and stock or water, to which are added meat, poultry, game, fish, vegetables or nuts, herbs and/or dried fruit. It is covered and cooked in an oven until all the liquid has been absorbed. In Europe it is known as *pilaf* and a Polish version, to which lamb and tomato purée are added, is known as *pilaw*. The dish is also eaten in Greece.

PILCHARD This small, round, oily seafish is, in fact, the mature sardine. Most pilchards are caught off the coasts of Devon and Cornwall and are sold canned in oil, brine or tomato sauce. Fresh pilchards can be grilled or fried whole. They are available from February to July. (*see also* FISH, SARDINE)

PIMENTO (*see* ALLSPICE)

PIMENTON A spice, made from ground pimiento, which is the Spanish equivalent of paprika. It is sold loose in Spanish markets and should be a bright red colour with a strong aroma. If it is brown, it is probably stale. It is used in many traditional Spanish dishes and sausages, such as *chorizo* and *sobresada*. When cooking with it, it is best to mix it into the hot fat of fried dishes as this gives it a good colour and helps to amalgamate it.

PIMIENTO (Pimento) The Spanish name for a variety of red or green sweet peppers with a sweet, pungent flavour, used in salads and as a vegetable. The name is often corrupted to pimento in Britain, where the peppers are mostly available canned.

PINA COLADA A Caribbean cocktail made from rum, pineapple juice and coconut cream. It is shaken together with crushed ice and traditionally served in a hollowed-out pineapple. It may be decorated with pineapple and cherries.

PINEAPPLE Probably the most familiar of the tropical fruits, the pineapple is a large oval fruit with hard knobbly skin, that grows in most tropical and sub-tropical countries. The skin varies from deep yellow to orange-brown. Most pineapples are quite large, anything up to 5 kg

(9 lb), but a miniature variety has recently become available.

The pale yellow flesh of the pineapple can be eaten raw on its own or mixed with other fruit. Pineapple can also be served with cheese, ham or bacon. Alternatively, cut off the leaf crown and carefully cut out the flesh in chunks, leaving the skin intact to use as a bowl for fruit salad. Fresh pineapple contains an enzyme that breaks down protein, so it cannot be used with gelatine to make a jelly, as it will not set. Pineapple is also available in cans, as rings, chunks, cubes or pieces, in syrup or natural juice.

To select: Ripe pineapples give off a sweet aroma and a leaf pulls easily from the crown. Avoid pineapples that are bruised, discoloured or have wilting leaves. Pineapples continue to ripen after picking and are often sold slightly unripe. However, an unripe fruit with no aroma will not ripen properly.

To prepare: Cut off the leaf crown and cut the fruit crossways into thick slices. Trim off the outer skin and remove the brown spots from the flesh. Remove the central core. Alternatively, the pineapple can be cut in wedges lengthways and the central core removed. The skin can also be removed from the whole fruit before slicing, by cutting down the length of the fruit, removing the skin. The 'eyes' can be removed separately by cutting deep spiral grooves around the pineapple.

PINEAPPLE GUAVA (*see* FEIJOA)

PINE NUT (Indian Nut, Pignolia, Pine Kernel) This is the small, pale cream-coloured seed of the Mediterranean stone pine tree. Pine nuts are always sold shelled and may be roasted and salted. They have a strong, resinous flavour and soft oily texture.

Pine nuts are popular in Middle Eastern rice dishes and stuffings and are also used to make the Italian pesto sauce (*see* PESTO). They can also be eaten raw, sprinkled over cooked vegetables or added to fruit salads. Pine nuts are also used to make a fine, and expensive, oil that is ideal for salad dressings.

PINHEAD OATMEAL (*see* OATS)

PINK FIR APPLE (*see* POTATO)

PINTO BEAN A variety of kidney bean that is popular in Spain and Mexico. It is pale in colour with bright red markings. (*see also* KIDNEY BEAN, PULSES)

PIPÉRADE A type of ragoût of eggs, peppers and tomatoes, which is a speciality of the Basque country. The tomatoes and peppers are cooked in olive oil or (more traditionally) goose fat with onions and garlic until they are soft and pulpy. Herb-flavoured beaten eggs are then added and the mixture is lightly scrambled. *Pipérade* is usually served with fried or grilled ham, and garnished with triangles of fried bread.

PIPING Forcing cream, icing, mashed potato, cake mixtures, choux pastry and meringue through a nozzle fitted into the end of a greaseproof paper, plastic or fabric piping bag to create fancy patterns and shapes. The mixture must be of a stiff enough consistency to hold its shape. Piping techniques are used to decorate cakes and desserts; to make duchess potatoes; to make éclairs, choux puffs and other choux pastry items; to make meringues and biscuits. Piping nozzles are available in different shapes and sizes; some are plain, while others are fluted.

PIPO CREM' A blue-veined French cows' milk cheese sold in a log shape. It is a semi-soft cheese with a flavour similar to Bleu de Bresse.

PIQUANT SAUCE A well flavoured sharp sauce served with fish and hot or cold meat dishes, especially pork. It is based on *sauce espagnole* and is flavoured with shallots, vinegar, gherkins and parsley.

PIRI-PIRI The name given to meat or fish dishes served with a hot pepper sauce. The sauce in piri-piri dishes originates from a combination of Portuguese and African cooking, particularly from Mozambique. The sauce is made from small fresh or dried chillies which are very hot.

PIROSHKI (Pirozhki) Small Russian or Polish savoury pastries served as an accompaniment to soups or as a meal in themselves. They may be made of choux or puff pastry and are usually filled with a meat, fish, vegetable, cheese or rice stuffing. They may be baked or deep-fried.

PISCO A South American brandy made from muscat wine, aged in clay jars and traditionally said to have the taste and aroma of beeswax.

PISSALADIÈRE A savoury flan or tart filled with tomatoes, onions, black olives and anchovy fillets, eaten hot or cold. The dish is said to have originated in Greece, but it is mainly found in the south of France.

PISTACHIO NUT (Green Almond) The fruit of a small tree native to the Middle East and Central Asia, but now grown in other parts of the world. The bright green kernels have purple skins and beige-coloured shells. The shells split when the kernels are ripe. Commercially, pistachios are used as a flavouring in sweets, particularly nougat and the Greek speciality known as *halva*, and they add colour to slices of *mortadella*.

Pistachios are available in their shells or shelled (plain or salted). The purple skins can be removed after blanching (*see* ALMOND). Pistachios can be eaten as a snack or used as a colourful garnish or ingredient in desserts, ice creams, pâtés, terrines and rice dishes.

PITAHAYA This unusual fruit comes from a cactus that grows in Central and South America. It is round in shape, with a scaly, red or purple skin. The flesh is a vivid pink in colour, speckled with tiny, black, edible seeds, and rather like passion fruit in texture. The flavour is sweet but quite bland and best combined with other fruits in a fruit salad. A yellow variety of the fruit can also sometimes be found.

PITH The white lining found under the rind of citrus fruits, which is thicker in some varieties than in others. Pith tends to be bitter in flavour and is always removed when eating fresh citrus fruits. In some varieties, the pith peels away easily, while in others it is quite difficult to remove. When grating the rind of citrus fruits, it is important not to grate into the pith as it will impart a bitter flavour. Pith contains a high concentration of pectin, so it is always used in making marmalade (*see* MARMALADE, ORANGE, PECTIN).

PITTA BREAD (Pita Bread) A Middle Eastern flat bread made from a yeast dough and shaped in an oval. It is baked in the oven until puffy and brown. Both large and small pitta breads are available, sometimes made from wholemeal flour. They can be opened up to make a pocket which is perfect for filling with meat from a kebab or other savoury fillings. Pitta bread is often warmed and served as an accompaniment to *taramasalata* and *hummus*.

PIZZA An Italian dish made from yeast dough, rolled into a flat round and covered with a variety of ingredients, such as tomatoes, cheese, anchovies, ham, mushrooms, olives and onion. Pizzas are best eaten straight from the oven, either as an individual serving or cut into wedges. In Italy, they are not often made in the home but eaten at a *pizzeria* as a snack. This is because the domestic oven is not as good for baking pizza as the old-fashioned brick varieties.

PLAICE A flat sea fish with brown skin and orange or red spots on the top side. The underside is white. Plaice are found on both sides of the Atlantic and in the North Sea. The flesh of plaice is soft and white with a very delicate flavour. It is sold whole or as fillets and can be cooked by most methods, including steaming, frying, grilling and baking. It is popular coated in egg and breadcrumbs and fried. Plaice is available fresh all year but at its best from April to December. It is also available frozen. (*see also* FISH)

PLANKING Popular in the United States, this is a method of cooking or, more usually, serving meat or fish on a special wooden board. The plank should be of well-seasoned hardwood, oblong or oval in shape, with a groove or well to catch cooking juices. It is heated in the oven, then oiled with olive oil or melted butter and the meat or fish is placed on it, dabbed with pieces of butter or bacon and cooked in a hot oven or under a grill (provided it can be placed at a safe distance from the heat). The food to be cooked on a plank is usually seared in advance, either under the grill or in a frying pan, and a border of duchess or mashed potatoes is often piped around the edge of the board before cooking. Other vegetables may also be added to the plank with the meat or fish. Traditionally, planks are wiped and thoroughly scraped after use, never washed.

PLANTAIN (Green Banana, Kayla) These large, green bananas have a high starch and low sugar content. As they ripen they become sweeter and change from green to yellow to black, but they must always be cooked. They are treated as a vegetable rather than a fruit and can be fried, baked or dried and ground into flour.

Plantains are much used in South American, African and West Indian cuisines. The original homeland of this fruit was South-East Asia, from where it travelled to the Middle East, Africa and the other tropical parts of the world.

PLAT DU JOUR The French name for the main dish of the day served at a restaurant.

PLOVER A small, wild wading bird, several varieties of which have been popular for eating since the Middle Ages. The green plover, also known as bustard plover or lapwing, is the most common, and is in season from August to March. The golden plover, grey plover, stone curlew and ring-dotted plover are also found in the British Isles, the golden plover being the most sought after. However, as with many edible species of wild bird, plovers are no longer common and are rarely eaten. (*see also* BIRD)

PLUCK The liver, heart and lights (lungs) of a sheep or other animal.

PLUCKING Removing feathers from poultry and game birds. Commercially-produced oven-ready birds are plucked by machine. Any remaining feathers are usually quite easy to pull out; remaining down can be removed by singeing. Hand plucking must be done carefully to avoid tearing the skin. Chilling the bird in the refrigerator beforehand may make feathers easier to remove.

PLUM There are many different varieties of this stone fruit, varying in size and colour of skin and flesh. The original cultivated plum is a hybrid fruit, produced from the cherry plum and the sloe. Plums grow in most temperate climates and are available all year round, though most abundant in late summer. Sweet or dessert plums can be eaten raw on their own or added to fruit salads, and all varieties can be cooked. They can be stewed, used in pies and puddings or made into preserves.
To select: Avoid plums that are bruised or damaged or very soft. Dessert plums should be firm and some varieties have a distinct 'bloom' on the skin. They can be bought slightly under-ripe and left to ripen before eating.
To prepare: Wash, halve and stone the plums. They can also be skinned after blanching in boiling water.
To cook: Stew gently in a little water, adding sugar as required.

Plum Varieties
Greengages are sweet, amber-coloured plums with a good flavour. They make delicious jam.
Damsons are small, dark blue to purple coloured plums with yellow flesh. They need to be cooked as they are often sour. They are usually stewed, or made into pies or preserves, particularly damson

cheese (*see* CHEESE, FRUIT). They are available from August to October.
Cherry plums are usually stewed or bottled.
Mirabelle is a small, golden, French variety of plum with a delicate flavour. It can be made into preserves and is also used to make an *eau-de-vie* (*see* EAU-DE-VIE).
Quetsch plums are small, dark cooking fruit from eastern Europe. They are also used to make an *eau-de-vie* (*see* EAU-DE-VIE).
Bullace is a small, wild plum that is blue-black in colour and has a tart flavour. It can be used to make preserves.
Japanese plums are small, round, yellow, orange or red, fruit that, in fact, come from China.
Victoria plums are probably the best known of the dessert plums. They are large and oval in shape with pink or red skins streaked with yellow. When ripe, the flesh is sweet and juicy and delicious eaten raw, though Victoria plums can also be used for compotes, pies and crumbles.

PLUM, DRIED (*see* PRUNE)

PLUM PUDDING (*see* CHRISTMAS PUDDING)

POACHING A method of cooking food gently in a liquid at simmering point so that the surface is just trembling. Poaching can be done in an open pan, in the oven or using an egg poacher with a lid. The term is used most commonly for eggs and fish.

PÔELÉ A French term, meaning braised or pot-roasted. In France, a small, lidded, long-handled saucepan, known as a *poêlon*, is used for such slow cooking methods.

POIRE WILLIAM (*see* EAU-DE-VIE)

POISONING (*see* FOOD POISONING)

POITRINE FUMÉE A French term, generally meaning bacon, but referring more specifically to smoked breast.

POLENTA A fine golden cornmeal produced in Italy and used to make a thick savoury porridge also called *polenta*. It may be served as it is with fish, meat and vegetable dishes, or it can be left to cool and harden, then cut up, fried and served with bacon as a breakfast or supper dish. *Polenta* can also be used to make *gnocchi* (*see* GNOCCHI) and some breads and cakes. (*see also* CORN)

POLLACK (Green Cod) A sea fish that is a member of the same family as cod, haddock, whiting and hake. It is found on both sides of the North Atlantic and may be prepared and cooked in any of the ways suitable for cod (*see* COD), though it lacks the flavour of cod. It has fairly firm white flesh and is usually sold in fillets or cutlets. (*see also* FISH)

POLLOCK (*see* COLEY)

POLONAISE, À LA A French expression most often used to describe a number of vegetable dishes, especially made with asparagus and cauliflower, in which the cooked vegetables are covered with a mixture of chopped hard-boiled egg and parsley and topped with fried breadcrumbs. However, the expression is also used to denote dishes derived from Polish cooking, often containing soured cream, beetroot and red cabbage.

POLONY (*see* BOLOGNA SAUSAGE)

POLYUNSATURATES (*see* FATS)

POMEGRANATE Pomegranates are the size of oranges with thin, tough, shiny yellow, pink or red rind and a characteristic crown-like calyx. Probably originating in Persia, pomegranates are now cultivated in many tropical and sub-tropical areas of the world. They are available in Britain in the autumn months and are a delicious, refreshing fruit that is generally neglected, perhaps because they are time-consuming to prepare.

The inside of a pomegranate is a mass of edible seeds, each one surrounded by beautiful, red, translucent, juicy flesh. The seeds can be removed one by one, but must be carefully separated from the inedible yellow internal membrane of the fruit which divides the inside into numerous sections. Pomegranates are used in Middle Eastern dishes, soups and stews. The fruit can be turned into a purple juice which is rather acidic. The seeds can also be used to decorate some dishes, and are also used to make a French flavouring syrup known as grenadine (*see* GRENADINE).

To select: Buy fruit with hard, undamaged skins. Keep refrigerated and use within seven days.

To prepare: Cut a slice off the stem end, then slice the skin into sections lengthways and draw the sections apart. The seeds can then be removed, individually or in small groups. To extract the juice, halve the fruit and press gently on to a lemon squeezer, or put the seeds in a sieve over a bowl and crush with the back of a wooden spoon.

POMELO (Pummelo, Shaddock) Looking rather like a very large, pale green grapefruit, this is a citrus fruit which has firm, sharp-flavoured flesh. The variety imported from Israel has white flesh and is available from November to April; a pink-fleshed variety is imported from South Africa during July and August. Both varieties have very thick, pithy skin which must be removed before segmenting and serving the fruit in a fruit salad or as a dessert with sugar to taste.

POMFRET (Ray's Bream) An attractive but unusual sea fish found in tropical waters and important in the cooking of India, China and South-East Asia. Its white flesh is similar in texture to that of turbot or sole, though its flavour is not as good. It can be prepared and cooked in many of the ways suitable for turbot or sole (*see* SOLE, TURBOT). (*see also* FISH)

POMMEL A double cream cheese, unsalted and not unlike Petit-Suisse. Pommel is made in France all the year round.

POMPANO A small, round, oily sea fish found in the Mediterranean, the Caribbean and around the coasts of Florida and Louisiana. It features particularly in the cooking of New Orleans. As the sweet, white meat tends to be dry, pompano fillets are often cooked *en papillote*.

PONT-L'EVÊQUE A soft paste cheese with a thickish orange rind, about 10 cm (4 inches) square and 4 cm (1½ inches) thick. It is made practically all year round in the Pont l'Evêque district of Normandy. Made from cows' milk, the cheese is golden or orange in colour with a tangy smell that is stronger than the taste. The cheese should be soft when bought, not runny, and the rind should not be dry or cracked. The cheese is best served at the end of a meal.

POPCORN (*see* CORN)

POPE (Ruffe) A freshwater fish resembling the perch (*see* PERCH).

POPE'S EYE The small circle of fat in the centre of a leg of lamb or pork. In Scotland, 'pope's eye' is a name given to prime rump steak.

POPE'S NOSE (*see* PARSON'S NOSE)

POPOVER An individual batter (Yorkshire) pudding, served with roast beef. Popovers can also be flavoured with grated cheese, a little chopped onion, bacon or herbs to serve for lunch or supper. A sweet variation can be made by adding a little finely chopped apple or some other fruit to the basic batter mixture. (*see also* BATTER, YORKSHIRE PUDDING)

POPPADOM A savoury Indian biscuit or bread which is thin, round, very light and crisp. There are several ready-made varieties available, made from rice flour or dried pulse flours, either plain, or flavoured with spices and seasonings such as chillies, garlic or black pepper. They can be shallow-fried or grilled and are served with savoury dishes, especially curries.

POPPY SEEDS Classified as spice seeds, these are the small blue-black seeds of the opium poppy, which have no narcotic effect, but are nutty-flavoured, very hard and usually sold

whole. They are used to add flavour and give an attractive appearance to baked goods, and they are also used in curry powder, dips, spreads, onion soup, salads and dressings and pasta dishes. Poppy seeds are widely used in Jewish and central European cookery. Cream-coloured poppy seeds are also available from Indian food shops. Both types of poppy seed can be used for sprouting (*see* BEAN SPROUTS), and they are used commercially to produce a pale-coloured oil.

PORGY (*see* BREAM)

PORK The meat of the pig eaten fresh, as distinct from bacon and ham, which are cured. Pork can be bought all the year round, thanks to modern refrigerating methods, and is particularly good value in the summer. All joints can be roasted and the individual cuts from them grilled or fried. In addition, the forequarter cuts can be used for casseroles, stews and pies.

The lean part of pork should be pale pink, moist and slightly marbled with fat. There should be a good outer layer of firm, white fat with a thin, elastic skin. Small pinkish bones denote a young animal. If the joint is to be roasted, either get the butcher to score the rind or do it yourself with a sharp knife just before cooking. Pork must be well cooked to prevent the risk of infection by trichinosis, caused by worms which may be present in the meat. When thoroughly cooked, pork should look white; pink-coloured pork should never be eaten. It requires long, slow cooking, but because of the large amount of fat it contains, roast pork seldom requires to have much extra fat added or to be basted during cooking. To counteract its richness, roast, grilled or fried pork is often accompanied by something sweet and tart, such as apple sauce. (*see also* MEAT)

Cuts and Methods of Cooking
Neck end (spare rib and blade bone) is a large, economical roasting joint, particularly good when boned, stuffed and rolled. It is often divided into blade and spare rib, these two smaller cuts being

suitable for roasting, braising or stewing. Spare rib pork makes the best filling for pies. Spare rib chops are suitable for braising, grilling or frying. *Hand and spring* is a large roasting joint, often divided into the smaller cuts, hand and shank. As well as being suitable for roasting, hand and shank can be used for casseroles and stews.

Belly is a long, thin cut with streaks of fat and lean meat. Stuffed thick end of belly makes an economical roast. Belly is sometimes rather fatty and is best sliced and grilled or fried, rather than braised or stewed.

Spare ribs (American) are from the belly and are removed in one piece, leaving the meat between the rib bones. Chinese spareribs are bones with a very small amount of meat on them. They are usually barbecued or used in Chinese dishes.

Leg can be cut into four or more succulent and popular roasting joints, often divided into fillet end and knuckle end. The fillet end (the top of the leg) is the prime roasting joint, which can be boned and stuffed. It is sometimes sliced into steaks for grilling and frying. The feet (trotters) are usually salted and boiled or used to make brawn.

Loin is a popular roast on the bone or boned, stuffed and rolled. It is often divided into loin chops (with or without kidney) and large, meaty chump chops, both of which are excellent for grilling, frying or roasting. The loin produces good crackling (*see* below). Two loins of pork are used to make a crown roast of pork (*see* CROWN OF LAMB OR PORK).

Tenderloin, as its name suggests, is a tender, lean cut, found underneath the backbone of the loin, in the same position as beef fillet. It is sometimes called pork fillet, not to be confused with the fillet end of the leg. Tenderloin is most often served sliced or cubed for frying, or coated with a sauce. It can be stuffed and rolled for roasting.

To Roast Pork

For good crackling, score the rind deeply and evenly. Brush the cut surfaces with oil and rub salt into the scoring. Place the joint, with the rind uppermost, in a roasting tin. Do not baste the pork during cooking. Alternatively, the rind can be removed before cooking, treated in the same way, and roasted separately until crisp and golden.

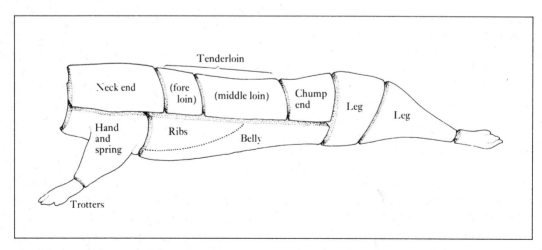

Major cuts of pork to be found at your butcher.

For succulent meat with less shrinkage, pork should be roasted in the oven at 180°C (350°F) mark 4. Weigh the joint as it is to be cooked, that is on the bone or boned and rolled or stuffed, and put in a shallow roasting tin, preferably on a grid. Cook for 30 minutes per 450 g (1 lb), plus 30 minutes.

Traditional accompaniments for roast pork include apple, gooseberry or cranberry sauce and sage and onion stuffing. Try baked or fried apples or redcurrant jelly as an alternative. (*see also* CARVING)

Grilling and Frying Pork

4 pork chops

30 ml (2 tbsp) vegetable oilTrim any excess fat from the chops. Large loin chops often have a thick strip of fat around the edge. To prevent this fat curling during cooking, snip it with scissors at 2.5 cm (1 inch) intervals.

Frying

Heat the oil in a large frying pan and add the chops. Cook for about 20 minutes, turning frequently.

Grilling

Brush the chops with oil. Place on the grill pan. Grill the chops for 8–10 minutes each side.

Serves 4

PORRIDGE An oatmeal breakfast dish which originated in Scotland but is now common throughout the British Isles. The name is also given to a type of thick soup made from maize, buckwheat, etc.

There are many different ways of making and eating porridge. Fine, medium or coarse oatmeal, pinhead oatmeal, rolled oats or 'instant' porridge oats can all be used, with water or a mixture of milk and water. In Scotland, porridge is often eaten with milk and salt, some people liking to accentuate the savoury touch by sprinkling over a few pieces of crisply fried bacon. Others prefer milk or cream and sugar, syrup or honey.

Partially cooked porridge is available as a breakfast cereal. This just requires the addition of hot milk.

(*see also* OATS)

PORT A fortified wine made from grapes grown in the upper valley of the Douro river (in Portugal) and shipped from Oporto.

Vintage port is the great wine, unique in style. It spends most of its life in a bottle and that can be for 10–20 or even more years for a fine vintage. Vintage port must be decanted or filtered to remove sediment, before it is served. When decanting port, it is important to keep the bottle level. This prevents the sediment passing into the decanter.

Wood ports are blends of wines of different years and ages which are matured in the cask; they may be ruby, tawny, 'crusted' or of vintage character. Ruby is generally a blend of young wines; tawny can be either a fine old matured port which started as a ruby, or a blend of ruby port and older or white wine. White port, made entirely from white grapes, is pale gold and slightly dry.

Port is most often served with the cheese course at the end of a meal. Tradition has it that the decanter should be passed around the table in a clockwise direction, each diner pouring his own port with his right hand, then passing it on to the next person with his left.

PORTER A dark brown beer, the colour and flavour being due to roasted malt and sometimes to added caramel. Stout can be made by adding molasses to porter (*see* STOUT).

PORTERHOUSE STEAK (*see* STEAK)

PORT-SALUT A semi-hard cheese, made originally by Trappist monks in the west of France. It is made from cows' milk in a flattened round shape, weighing 1.5–1.75 kg (3–4 lb), with an orange rind. Port-Salut has a fairly mild flavour that is best enjoyed as a dessert cheese; it is scarcely strong enough for use in cooking. Serve with black grapes, crusty French bread or crisp crackers. (*see also* SAINT-PAULIN)

PORTUGUAISE, À LA A French term used to describe dishes which usually include tomato, onion and garlic.

PORTULACA (*see* PURSLANE)

POSSET A drink made from sweetened milk curdled with treacle, ale or wine. At one time, posset was thought to be a good remedy for a cold.

POTAGE The French word, generally adopted elsewhere, for a thick soup.

POTASSIUM Potassium is a mineral involved in maintaining the correct amount of fluid inside and outside the body cells. It is also important for nerve and muscle function. Most foods, with the exception of fats, oils, sugar and alcohol, are good sources of potassium.

The main sources in the diet are fruit and vegetables. Boiling vegetables reduces their potassium content by half, but this can be recovered by using the cooking water. Potassium is not lost during baking or steaming. A deficiency of potassium is rare in healthy adults and children. People with kidney failure may need to restrict the amount of potassium in their diet.

POTATO The most familiar of all vegetables, the potato has long been a staple food in many countries. It originated in South America and was introduced into Europe in the sixteenth century. It is grown for its starchy underground tubers which grow to knobbly rounded shapes of varying size, with thin brown or red skin. The colour of the flesh beneath the skin varies from white to yellow, depending on the variety.

A great many varieties of potato are available for home planting, and a large number are grown commercially, though it is unusual to see more than three or four different varieties together in the shops. The range can be divided into two groups – early or new potatoes and maincrop potatoes. New British potatoes are available from May to August, though imported new potatoes are available at other times of the year. Maincrop British potatoes are lifted during September and October and stored for sale over the next eight months.

The potato is a nutritious vegetable, being a source of vitamin C, carbohydrate, dietary fibre and some protein. Amongst slimmers, it once had a reputation for being very fattening, but it is usually the cooking method or accompaniments that are responsible for the high calorie content of a potato dish. Plain boiled, steamed or baked potatoes are, in fact, low in calories.

To select: Choose potatoes with smooth, firm skins. New potatoes should feel slightly damp and their skins should rub off easily. Buy new potatoes in small quantities and use up quickly. Never buy potatoes that are turning green or beginning to sprout, or that are soft and wrinkled. See below for the most common varieties and the best methods of cooking them. Allow 175–225 g (6–8 oz) potatoes per person.

To prepare: Prepare potatoes just before you cook them; leaving them in water after peeling causes loss of vitamin C. Scrub or scrape new potatoes. They contain more vitamin C than maincrop potatoes, which is why they are only scrubbed or scraped and eaten with their skins on. The vitamin C in older potatoes is just under the skin so they are better cooked in the skin and peeled afterwards. If they must be peeled, peel as thinly as possible.

To cook: For *boiling*, peel maincrop potatoes and, if necessary, cut into smallish, even-sized pieces. Place in cold salted water and bring to the boil. Cook for 10–15 minutes (new potatoes), 15–20 minutes (maincrop) or until tender.

To make *chips*, peel larger potatoes and cut into slices, then into sticks. Put into a bowl of cold water for 30 minutes to remove excess starch. Drain and dry in a clean tea towel or on absorbent kitchen paper. In a deep frying pan or electric deep-fat fryer, heat the oil to 190°C (375°F). If you do not have a thermostat on the pan, nor a cooking thermometer, check the temperature by dropping in one chip, which should rise to the surface immediately, surrounded by bubbles. Put enough chips into the frying basket to quarter-fill it, lower into the oil and cook for 6–7 minutes or until starting to colour. Raise the basket and tip the chips on to absorbent kitchen paper to drain. When all the chips have been fried once, repeat the process and fry this time for 3 minutes, or until they are golden and crisp. Drain and serve at once.

For *game chips*, cut very thin slices, then deep fry until golden.

To *bake* potatoes in their jackets, choose quite large vegetables, wash and dry and prick with a fork or impale on a potato baking spike. For crisp skins, brush with oil or melted butter. Bake near the top of the oven at 200°C (400°F) mark 6 for 1–1 $1/2$ hours or until tender right through. Cut a cross in the top or cut in half and serve with a knob of butter.

For *mashed* and *creamed* potatoes, boil as above, then drain and mash until smooth with a fork or potato masher. Season, then put on a low heat and dry for 2–3 minutes, stirring continuously. For creamed potatoes, add a little butter or margarine, a little warm milk and beat until fluffy. To make *duchess* potatoes, beat an egg and a little grated nutmeg into creamed potatoes and pipe in pyramid shapes (using a large rosette nozzle) on to a greased baking sheet and cook in the oven at 200°C (400°F) mark 6 for about 25 minutes or until set and golden brown. Serve as a vegetable or use to garnish serving dishes for a dinner party.

To make *roast* potatoes, place peeled potatoes in cold salted water and bring to the boil. Cook for 2–3 minutes, then drain thoroughly. Either add to the fat around a roasting joint at 180°C (350°F) mark 4 for about 1$1/4$–1$1/2$ hours or heat vegetable oil or dripping in a roasting tin in the oven at 220°C (425°F) mark 7 and put the potatoes into it.

Cook for 45–60 minutes, basting regularly and turning once or twice, until golden brown all over.

To *steam*, scrub potatoes and remove a 1 cm ($1/2$ inch) strip of peel from around the centre of each. Steam for about 45 minutes or until tender.

For *sauté* potatoes, boil potatoes for 15 minutes or until just cooked. Drain, peel and cut into large chunks. Sauté gently in hot butter and oil until golden and crisp on all sides. Drain thoroughly on absorbent kitchen paper and sprinkle with salt.

Potato Varieties

New Potatoes
Arran Comet has creamy white flesh which does not break up when cooked. Good for boiling, sautéing, potato salad and chips.
Carlingford can be treated as a new or maincrop potato. It is a round potato that is available in late summer and winter. Good eaten cold.
Duke of York is yellow in colour with a good flavour and smooth texture. It was once commonplace but is now unfortunately quite rare and in limited supply.
Home Guard has creamy white flesh which does not break up or discolour when cooked. Good for boiling and potato salad.
Jersey Royal is usually the first new potato to appear in the new British season. It has creamy-yellow skin and flesh and is good for boiling or steaming.
Maris Bard is oval in shape with a white waxy flesh. It does not disintegrate during cooking or discolour when cold.
Maris Peer has pale yellow firm flesh. Good for boiling, sautéing, potato salad, chips or roasting.
Pentland Javelin has very white firm flesh. Good for boiling and potato salad.
Red Craigs Royal has creamy close-textured flesh. A good all-rounder.
Ulster Sceptre is a very early variety with white flesh which does not discolour. A good all-rounder.

Wilja is a variety of potato that can be lifted early and treated as a new potato, but is also available amongst other maincrop potatoes from July to April. It has yellow skin and flesh and is a good all-rounder.

Maincrop Potatoes

Cara is a large, round potato with creamy flesh. A good all-rounder, but best boiled or baked.

Desirée has pinkish-red skin and pale yellow flesh which is of consistently good quality and not as dry as many maincrop varieties. A good all-rounder.

Dunbar Standard originated in Scotland. A white potato good for making chips or mashed potato.

Golden Wonder is a dark-skinned potato with a soft floury texture. It is best roasted or baked.

King Edward has a pale skin with red patches and pale yellow floury flesh. A good all-rounder, especially good roasted or baked. A red variety of King Edward is also sometimes available.

La Ratte is a French variety with a nutty flavour. It is long and thin with glossy yellow skin which may be left on during cooking. Good eaten cold in salads.

Linzer Delikatess is an Austrian potato now cultivated in Britain for its high number of small tubers and fine flavour. Its availability is limited.

Majestic has a white skin and creamy white floury flesh. It does tend to discolour after cooking. Good for chips, sautéing and roasting.

Maris Piper has a pale skin and creamy white floury flesh which does not discolour after cooking. Good for chips, cooking in its jacket, boiling, sautéing, mashing and roasting.

Pentland Crown has pale skin and creamy white flesh but is of only moderate cooking quality as it tends to be wet. It is best used for jacket potatoes.

Pentland Dell has a pale skin and tends to disintegrate. It is best for jacket potatoes.

Pentland Hawk has pale skin and creamy flesh but only moderate cooking quality. It is best for boiling, mashing and cooking in its jacket.

Pink Fir Apple is an unusual potato with an irregular shape. It has pink skin with smooth, yellow, waxy flesh with a nutty flavour. Good served cold in a potato salad.

Romano is a red-skinned potato with a firm texture. A good all-rounder that is available all year round.

POTATO FLOUR (Potato Starch) The flour extracted from potatoes by means of pulverizing and washing. Potato flour is of special importance for people on a gluten-free diet. It can be used for thickening but tends to have a pronounced flavour. It can also be used in cakes and biscuits where a softer flour is required. (*see also* FECULA)

POTATO, SWEET (*see* SWEET POTATO)

POT-AU-FEU A traditional French dish of meat or poultry and vegetables. A *pot-au-feu* is often divided into separate dishes, the broth being served as a soup and the meat and vegetables as a main course.

POT BARLEY (*see* BARLEY)

POT ROASTING A method of cooking meat slowly in a covered pan or casserole with fat and a very little liquid. Pot roasting may be done on the hob or in the oven. It is good for small and less tender joints of meat. The meat is first browned over a high heat. Vegetables may be added, if liked.

PO TSAI (*see* CHINESE CABBAGE)

POTTAGE A thick, well-seasoned meat or vegetable soup, usually containing barley or a similar cereal, or a pulse such as lentils. When cooked, the soup should be of the consistency of thin porridge.

POTTING A method of preserving cooked meat or fish for a few days. Many commercially made brands are sold and these may be stored unopened for some time, as they contain preservatives. After cooking, the meat or fish is formed into a paste, or left whole (as in the case of prawns or shrimp), potted and stored under a seal of fat or clarified butter. The seal excludes air and moisture which encourage the growth of bacteria.

Meat can also be prepared in the form of *rillettes* and stored in the refrigerator for up to two months before serving. This method of preserving best suits meats that are naturally fatty, such as duck or pork. It is important to remove all moisture from the meat, so it is first salted and then cooked for a long time until it is very tender. After cooking, the fat is strained off the meat and reserved. The meat is then separated into strands, usually with two forks, and piled into small pots before being covered with the reserved fat.

POTTEEN (Potheen) An Irish whiskey illicitly made from barley. It is very crude and can be injurious to health.

POULETTE, À LA A French term used to describe a variety of dishes served with *sauce poulette*, which is made from egg yolks, white stock, lemon juice, butter and chopped parsley. The sauce was originally a traditional accompaniment for chicken but is now more often served with fish, offal, snails or mushrooms. Dishes given this name are sometimes garnished with onions or garlic.

POULTRY A general name given to all domesticated birds bred for the table, as distinct from the edible wild birds which are classed as game (*see* GAME). It includes chicken, turkey, duckling and goose. Guinea fowl, which used to be regarded as game, is now farmed and classified as poultry. Methods of breeding and rearing poultry have changed dramatically, so that now it is cheap and plentiful and no longer served only on special occasions. Oven-ready poultry birds are available fresh or frozen and need little preparation prior to cooking, unless the bird is to be jointed or boned (*see* below).

(For detailed information about buying and cooking poultry, see CHICKEN, DUCK, GOOSE, GUINEA FOWL, TURKEY)

Storing Poultry

Remove any wrappings from the bird as soon as possible, and the giblets if there are any. The bird can be stored on a plate, covered with greaseproof paper or foil, in the refrigerator for two to three days. The giblets are best cooked the same day.

Frozen birds should be transferred to the freezer while still solidly frozen. If possible, freeze the giblets separately as they only have a freezer life of 1 month.

Jointing and Boning Poultry

Jointing Poultry

With the bird breast-side up, cut through the skin between leg and breast. Bend the leg back until the joint cracks. Remove the leg from the body by cutting through the joint. Repeat with the other leg.

Separate the thighs from the drumsticks by bending each leg to crack the joint. Cut through the joint with a sharp knife to separate. Remove the wings by bending them back and cutting the joint at the breast.

Place the carcass on its side; with poultry shears, cut from the leg joint to the backbone and along the backbone to the neck. Turn and cut along the other side to detach the breast. (The backbone will remain intact.)

Hold the breast skin-side down and bend it back to crack the breastbone. With poultry shears, cut along each side of the breastbone and remove.

Halving a Bird

With the bird breast-side up, using poultry shears or a sharp knife, cut straight along one side of the breastbone from the body cavity to the neck cavity. Spread open and cut along the side of the backbone to halve.

Boning Poultry

Use a very sharp knife, strong scissors and a darning or trussing needle with a large eye.

If using a frozen bird, first remove the giblets. Snip off the wing pinions at the second joint and remove the parson's nose. Wipe and pat dry. Place the bird on its breast and cut straight down the back to the bone. Ease the flesh and skin away from the backbone and rib-cage. Work down towards the joints, turning the bird as you go.

Clasping one leg in each hand, press firmly outwards to release the ball and socket joints. Ease the knife point into the joints and separate the legs from the body. Repeat for the wings.

Return to the main body and fillet the flesh from the breastbone. There is little flesh below the skin. Work down both sides and continue along the tip until the whole carcass is free.

Taking hold of the thigh end of the leg joint in one hand, scrape the flesh down from the bone towards the hinge joint. Use the point of the knife – a cartilage has to be removed too. Continue filleting the flesh off the lower leg joint until the knobbly end is reached. Clasp the exposed bones in one hand and the skin and flesh in the other. Pull the leg completely inside out to remove the bone, snipping any sinews.

Remove the wings in a similar way, easing out any pieces of breast bone, and remove the wishbone.

Trussing

Trussing is done to keep the bird in a compact shape. You need a trussing needle or fine skewer and thin thread.

Fold the neck skin under the body and fold the wing tips back towards the backbone so they hold the neck skin in position. Put the bird on its back and press the legs well into the side. Slit the skin above the vent and push the parson's nose through.

Thread the needle with a length of thread and insert it close to the second joint of the right wing; push it right through the body, to catch the corresponding joint on the left side.

Insert the needle again in the first joint of the left wing, pass it through the flesh at the back of the body, catching the tips of the wings and the

neck skin, and pass it out through the first joint of the wing on the right side. Tie the ends in a bow.

To truss the legs, re-thread the needle and insert it through the gristle at the right side of the parson's nose. Pass the thread over the right leg, over the left leg, through the gristle at the left side of the parson's nose, carry it behind the parson's nose and tie the ends of the thread firmly.

If using a skewer, insert it right through the body of the bird just below the thigh bone and turn the bird over on to its breast. First, catching in the wing tips, pass the thread under the ends of the skewer and cross it over the back. Turn the bird over and tie the ends of the thread together around the tail, at the same time securing each of the drumsticks.

Cooking Poultry

Detailed instructions for cooking the various types of poultry are given under individual entries. To test when a whole bird is cooked, push a fine skewer into the thickest part of the thigh. If the juices run clear, the bird is cooked but if they are still pink, it needs longer cooking. (*see also* CARVING)

POUND CAKE A fruit cake, so called because all the ingredients used to be added in 450 g (1 lb) quantities. A more practical version is the 'half-pound' cake. Despite metrication, these cakes are still called by their traditional names.

POUNDING The process of crushing or bruising in order to reduce a hard ingredient to small pieces or a soft one to a smooth consistency. For example, kipper fillets are pounded to break them down to a suitable texture for a fish pâté. Pounding can be done in a pestle and mortar or in a strong bowl using the end of a rolling pin.

POUSSIN (*see* CHICKEN)

POUTARG (*see* BOTARGO)

PRAGERSCHINKEN (Prazskasunka)
Although called Prague ham, this is a delicately smoked ham from Czechoslovakia. It is salted and

then left in a mild brine for several months before being smoked over beechwood ashes and matured in airy cellars. It is either baked or boiled whole and served hot for a main course.

PRAIRIE OYSTER A drink, sometimes recommended as a cure for a hangover. It consists of a shelled but unbroken raw egg flavoured with Worcestershire sauce, lemon juice and salt.

PRALINE A confection consisting of almonds caramelized in sugar, then left to set, crushed and used to flavour or decorate sweet dishes or as a filling for sweets and chocolates. In France, sugar coated almonds (sugar almonds) are called *pralines*.

PRAWN Prawns are small crustaceans which are available in a variety of sizes, called by many different names. The common pink prawns from the cold waters of the North Atlantic have a better flavour than those from the warm waters of the Indian and Pacific Oceans, such as Malaysian prawns and Pacific (jumbo) prawns. The Mediterranean has several different species, known generally as Mediterranean or King prawns.

Fresh prawns are usually cooked as soon as they are caught and are sold in the shell by weight or volume. Frozen prawns come from different areas of the world and are usually peeled. Prawns are also available canned, or dried from oriental food stores.

Prawns have a sweet, delicate flavour and may be used in cooked dishes as well as salads. Combined with thousand island dressing, they are a popular filling for avocados or for making a common starter known as prawn cocktail. Prawns can also be used to make attractive garnishes.
(*see also* SCAMPI, SHRIMP)
To prepare: To peel, hold the head of the prawn between thumb and forefinger, then using the fingers of the other hand, hold the tail and gently pinch and pull off the tail shell. Holding the body, gently pull off the head, the body shell and the claws. Using a skewer or the point of a knife,

carefully remove and discard the black vein running down the prawn's back. Frozen prawns should be thoroughly thawed before use. They usually contain a lot of water and need thorough draining.

PRE-FORM (*see* FREEZING)

PRÉ-SALÉ A French name given to mutton and lamb raised on salt marshes. The meat is considered especially well flavoured.

PRESERVATION To take fresh foods in prime condition and to store or preserve them in such a way that they will remain in the same condition for long periods of time. Deterioration of food is caused by micro-organisms and by enzymes present in the food itself; preservation either kills the micro-organisms or makes them dormant. Methods of preservation include freezing, canning, drying, salting, bottling, irradiation and preserving with sugar (jams, jellies and marmalades), vinegar (chutneys, relishes and pickles) or alcohol.

PRESERVATIVES This term legally denotes any substance added to food which is capable of inhibiting, retarding or arresting the process of fermentation, acidification or other decomposition of food. Preservatives are nearly all manufactured, although a few do occur in nature. Traditional preservatives include salt, sugar, vinegar, saltpetre, acetic or lactic acid, alcohol or spirits, spices, herbs, hop extract, essential oils used for flavouring, glycerine, or any substance added to the process of curing. The food industry also makes use of gases, such as sulphur dioxide, for preservative purposes and a number of synthetically produced chemicals, including phosphates and nitrates. Preservatives permitted for use in foods within the EC can be identified on food labels by the numbers E200-E283. (*see also* ADDITIVE)

PRESS To shape meat by pressing it under a weight. The cold pressed meat – often spiced meat or tongue, boned stuffed chicken or meat roll – is turned out and sometimes glazed. Some fruit desserts are also pressed.

PRESSURE COOKING To cook food quickly in steam under pressure; a 'pressure cooker' is used. Foods suitable for pressure cooking include vegetables, pulses, meat, poultry, steamed puddings and preserves.

PRETZEL A hard, brittle biscuit, originally made in Germany and Alsace, and formed in the shape of a loose knot, somewhat resembling a letter B, sometimes said to be the initial of the alternative name, Bretzel. The biscuits are firstly poached in boiling water, then baked hard in the oven. Pretzels are sprinkled with salt and sometimes cumin seeds, and are traditionally served with beer.

PRICKLY PEAR (Cactus Pear, Indian Fig) This small pear-shaped fruit comes from a type of cactus which originated in America and now also grows in India, Africa and the Mediterranean. It has a greenish-orange skin and is covered with fine, needle-sharp prickles which can become embedded in your hands. The sweet, juicy, pink flesh contains edible seeds.

Prickly pears have to be prepared carefully because of their prickles. Wearing rubber gloves, wash and scrub off the prickles, cut off each end, slit the skin lengthways and peel back the skin. Slice the flesh and serve with a squeeze of lemon juice. The flesh can also be included in a mixed fruit compote or fruit salad, or it can be cooked, puréed and used to flavour sauces, ice creams and sorbets.

PRIMEURS A general French name given to early forced vegetables and fruit.

PRINCESSE A French name given to dishes served with a garnish of asparagus tips and truffles or noisette potatoes.

PRINTANIÈRE, À LA A French term used to describe various dishes garnished with a mixture of (usually spring) vegetables tossed in melted butter. (*see also* NAVARIN)

PROCESSED CHEESE (*see* CHEESE)

PROFITEROLE This term originally meant a kind of light cake, baked on hot ashes and filled with cream or custard. Nowadays, it refers to a small choux pastry bun the size of a walnut filled with whipped cream, Chantilly cream, ice cream or confectioners' custard. Profiteroles are usually served as a rich dessert, with hot, dark chocolate sauce poured over them.

A savoury filling can also be used for small choux puffs. Very small ones can be used to garnish consommé.

(*see also* PASTRY)

PROOF (*see* SPIRIT)

PROSCIUTTO The Italian word for fresh ham, and more particularly for various types of raw smoked ham (*prosciutto crudo*), including *prosciutto di Parma* (Parma ham) and *prosciutto di San Daniele*. Parma ham comes from the area around the town of Parma in Emilia-Romagna and must have the authentic brand burned into its skin. All Parma hams have been dried for at least eight months, some for as long as two years, giving them a sweet, smoky flavour and tender flesh. Parma ham is considered the finest *prosciutto* and is most often very thinly sliced and served as a starter accompanied by slices of fresh melon or fig.

Most of the *prosciutto* on sale in Italian shops is air-dried, which gives it a wonderful smoky flavour – boiled hams sold in supermarkets make poor substitutes.

PROTEIN The main body-building nutrient. Proteins are made up of substances called amino acids. There are 20 amino acids which join together in different ways to make different proteins. Eight of these are not produced naturally in the body and these essential amino acids must be provided from proteins in the daily diet.

(For growing infants, there are nine essential amino acids.) Dietary protein is broken down in the digestive system into amino acids which are then used to build different proteins for body tissues such as muscle, hair, skin, blood, etc.

Meat, fish, cheese, eggs and milk provide most of the protein intake, with the remainder coming from cereals and vegetables. For vegetarians, nuts, beans and pulses are the main sources of protein in the diet. Cooking and processing do not normally affect the nutritional value of protein. Light cooking may indeed improve digestibility. (*see also* AMINO ACID)

PROVENÇALE, À LA A French term used to describe various dishes typical of the Provence region of southern France, and usually containing olive oil, garlic and often tomatoes.

PROVING In bread-making, this term refers to the process of leaving dough to rise (often for a second time) after shaping. Proving ensures an even textured loaf.

PROVOLONE An Italian cheese made from unpasteurized cows' milk. It is moulded by hand into a variety of shapes and is popular for cooking, as well as for eating as a dessert cheese. It has a soft, smooth texture and is pale yellow in colour. The flavour varies from mild to strong, depending on how long it has been matured. One type of provolone, coagulated with kid's rennet and known as *provolone piccante*, is left to mature for up to two years and is dark, hard and strong, making it a good grating cheese.

PRUNE Prunes are whole dried plums, with or without the stones. Some varieties are tenderized and do not need soaking before using; otherwise, soak in cold tea or red wine rather than water for a better flavour.

Prunes can be eaten on their own or they can be used in biscuits, puddings, cakes and savoury stuffings. They go particularly well with pork (*see* DEVILS ON HORSEBACK). Prunes are also available canned.

PRUNELLE (*see* EAU-DE-VIE)

PTARMIGAN A small wild bird of the grouse family, which is found in Northern Europe, including Scotland, and is in season from 12th August to 10th December; it turns white during the winter months. Other names for the ptarmigan are willow or rock partridge and mountain grouse. It is now rarely seen in shops.

The flavour of ptarmigan is not so good as that of grouse, but the bird may be treated in the same way; serve it with fried breadcrumbs, bread sauce and thin brown gravy, and garnish with watercress. One bird will serve one to two people. (*see also* CARVING, GAME, GROUSE)

PUDDING A general name given to a very wide range of sweet and savoury dishes, usually served hot and often made in a pudding basin or other mould. Sweet puddings include suet puddings, steamed puddings, baked puddings, boiled puddings, batter puddings, milk puddings, bread and butter pudding, summer pudding and a large number of other dishes served as a sweet or dessert course at the end of a meal. Savoury puddings include Yorkshire pudding, black pudding, steak and kidney pudding and cheese pudding.

The term can also be used in a more general way to refer to any sweet dish served after the main course at the end of a meal, including pies, tarts, fruit salads, ice creams, custards, etc. A distinction is usually made, however, between a pudding and a dessert, the latter referring more especially to cold dishes. (*see also* DESSERT)

PUDDING RICE (*see* RICE)

PUFFBALL (Giant Puffball) The largest member of a family of fungi that are all rounded in shape. The giant puff ball may grow to 30 cm (12 inches) or more in diameter and while young and small, the flesh is white and cheesy, and can be eaten. To cook, first skin, then cut into 1 cm ($^{1}/_{2}$ inch) slices, coat with egg and breadcrumbs and fry. (*see also* FUNGUS)

PUFF PASTRY (*see* PASTRY)

PULASAN A tropical fruit belonging to the lychee family. Its skin is covered with short red or yellow projections and, like the lychee, although the skin comes away from the flesh easily, the flesh is firmly attached to the central stone. The fruit is strongly scented and is sweet and juicy. Use pulasans in the same way as lychees. (*see also* LYCHEE)

PULLET A young hen or female fowl.

PULSES The generic name given to all dried beans, peas and lentils, of which there are many varieties. Pulses are versatile ingredients and can be used in savoury dishes of all kinds. Nutritionally, they are an excellent food; they contain plenty of dietary fibre, protein, B group vitamins, iron and potassium. They have virtually no fat and are best eaten with a cereal such as bread, rice or pasta. Pulses are sold in packets or loose and should be bought in fairly small quantities from a shop with a high turnover. Use them up within six to nine months, or they will start to shrivel and become tough. (For detailed information about particular pulses, see individual entries.)

Cooking Pulses

Before cooking, wash pulses thoroughly and pick out any pieces of dirt or damaged beans. All pulses, except lentils, need to be soaked, preferably overnight, before cooking in fresh boiling water. If you do not have enough time for this, put the pulses in water and bring to the boil simmer for 2 minutes, then leave them to soak in the water for 2–3 hours before cooking. When cooking, allow double the volume of water to beans and do not add salt until the end of the cooking time, or the beans will be tough.

Cooking times vary from one bean to another. Some beans, including red kidney and soya beans, must be boiled rapidly for at least 10 minutes at the start of the cooking time to kill the toxic haemoglutinens.

Cooking Times for 100–125 g (4 oz) Dried Beans

Aduki beans	30 minutes
Black beans	1 hour
Black-eyed beans	45 minutes
Butter beans	50 minutes
Cannellini beans	1½ hours
Chick peas and peas	1½ hours
Dal and lentils	1 hour
Flageolet beans	1¼ hours
Haricot beans	1¼ hours
Mung beans	30 minutes
Red kidney beans	50 minutes
Soya beans	1½ hours
Split peas	45 minutes

PUMMELO (*see* POMELO)

PUMPERNICKEL A German black bread made from coarse rye flour. It is a very heavy, dense-textured bread that is often sold ready-cut in very thin slices.

PUMPKIN One of the largest of the winter squashes (the same family as the marrow), pumpkin can be used as a vegetable or a fruit and is available from October to December. Pumpkins usually appear in the shops just in time for Hallowe'en (31st October) when they are traditionally hollowed out and made into lanterns.

The colour of pumpkin varies from green to orange, depending on variety, but most pumpkins seen in the shops are yellow or orange in colour. They are round in shape, with flattened tops and bottoms, and their skin is often deeply grooved. They can grow to an enormous size, much bigger than usually required, so are often sold in slices. One variety, known as Jack-be-little, is much smaller.

Pumpkin can be served as a vegetable, or it can be made into a traditional American highly spiced pumpkin pie.

To select: Choose firm pumpkins weighing about 4.5–6.8 kg (10–15 lb). Allow 225 g (8 oz) per person.

To prepare: Cut in half and scoop out the seeds. Cut into sections and peel and chop the flesh into even-sized pieces. Alternatively, it is possible to buy ready-cut slices of pumpkin, sold by weight. *To cook:* Cook pumpkin in boiling salted water for about 15 minutes or until tender. Alternatively, pumpkin may be steamed or roasted. For roasting, treat like potatoes and add to the hot fat around a roasting joint. Pumpkins can also be stuffed and baked (like marrow), or used in stews – the flesh makes a good thickener for gravies.

PUMPKIN SEEDS These large, flat, green seeds can be eaten raw or cooked in sweet or savoury dishes, or added to a muesli or granola mixture. They are highly nutritious and can also be sprouted (*see* BEAN SPROUTS).

PUNCH A drink made from a mixture of ingredients, one of which should be a spirit. It is said to derive its name from the Hindu word *panch*, meaning five, because punch was originally made from five ingredients – the spirit arrack, sugar, spice, lemon juice and water. Punches became popular in this country in the seventeenth century. Nowadays a punch may have a base of red or white wine, cider, ale, lager, cold tea or champagne and small quantities of sherry, whisky, rum, brandy or a fruit liqueur may be added.

There are many types of punch, some served hot and some cold; they provide useful drinks for parties, as they are generally less expensive than spirits or fine wines. A glass of hot rum punch makes an excellent welcome to guests arriving on a cold winter's night, and milk punch is a warming 'night-cap', while a refreshing cold fruit punch is a popular addition to a summer buffet party. Fruit punches can be made without any alcoholic ingredient, the sparkle being provided by ginger ale or soda water. Fresh fruits, cut in a decorative fashion, are often served in a fruit-based punch.

PURÉE Fruit, vegetables, meat or fish which has been pounded, sieved or liquidized (usually after cooking) to give a smooth, finely divided pulp. A soup made by sieving or liquidizing vegetables together with the liquor in which they were cooked is also called a purée. Purées can be made by rubbing food through a sieve, pounding in a mortar, or processing in an electric blender or food processor. In some cases, food is puréed in a blender or food processor, then sieved to produce a very smooth purée.

The thickness of a purée depends on the amount of liquid present before puréeing; a purée of thoroughly drained cooked green peas or potatoes, for example, is very stiff and can be piped for decoration. Tomato purée, on the other hand, is soft and runny and usually requires thickening before it can be used. When making a fruit purée for gelatine desserts, it is advisable to use very little water for stewing the fruit, otherwise the purée will be too thin.

The food is usually sieved or liquidized while still warm; in the case of meat and fish, the bones and gristle must first be removed and the flesh can then be pounded in a mortar.

A wire sieve may be used for vegetables and meat, but a nylon one is better for fruit, to avoid discoloration and a metallic taste.

PURI A type of Indian chapatti, made on special occasions. It is fried in deep fat. (*see also* CHAPATTI)

PURL An old-fashioned English winter drink, based on warmed ale, either flavoured with bitters and spiked with whisky or brandy, or mixed with sweetened milk and a measure of gin, brandy or whisky.

PURPLE GRANADILLA (*see* PASSION FRUIT)

PURSLANE (Pigweed, Portulaca) An unusual annual herb grown and used as a salad leaf or for cooking as a vegetable. It has red stems and lobe-shaped, fleshy, green leaves and is sometimes available during the summer months, though it is less common than it used to be. It is a good source of iron but, like sorrel, contains oxalic acid which inhibits the absorption of calcium and magne-sium. Its acid content also gives it quite a sharp, vinegar-like flavour.

PYRIDOXINE (*see* VITAMINS)

Q

QAWWRAMA A type of Lebanese preserved meat, consisting of mutton preserved in its own fat. The mutton comes from sheep that have been fattened specially for the purpose. After slaughter, the fat is removed from the sheep and rendered down separately, while the lean meat is cut in pieces and pressed to remove moisture. The meat is then fried in the fat, then both fat and meat are packed into earthenware pots which are sealed with clay. *Qawwrama* prepared in this way will keep for several months and can be used in stews and stuffings. The fat is used for frying.

QUAIL The quail, which used to nest in large quantities in Britain, was formerly treated as a game bird, but it has now become so scarce that it has been given complete protection under the Protection of Birds Act 1954, and can no longer be classed as game. However, quails are now being cultivated as a domesticated bird on quail farms and are available all year, fresh or frozen. The domestic quail is a species known as the Japanese quail, which is slightly different from the common quail.

The quail is a very small bird, weighing only 100–125 g (4–5 oz) and it is usual to serve two birds per person. Quail are usually sold oven-ready and are cooked and eaten without being drawn. Quail can be casseroled, pot-roasted or braised, but are most often roasted.

(*see also* GAME)

Roast Quail

8 quail
8 rounds of bread, toasted or fried
thin rashers of streaky bacon
watercress, to garnish

Pluck and singe the birds, if necessary, but do not draw. Cut off the head and neck and take out the crop.

Place each bird on a round of toast or fried bread and cover the breast with thin rashers of bacon. Roast in the oven at 220°C (425°F) mark 7 for about 25 minutes, basting with butter.

Serve on the toast or fried bread with the bacon and thin gravy. Garnish with watercress.
Serves 4

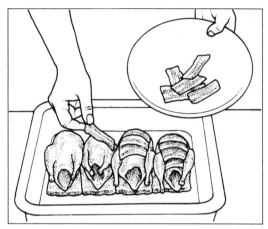

Covering quail with bacon rashers prior to roasting on slices of fried bread or toast.

QUAILS' EGGS (*see* EGGS)

QUARK A soft curd cheese that is often eaten on its own with a spoon. It is sometimes flavoured with fruit or herbs. It may be made from skimmed or whole milk or buttermilk and may also include added cream. The name, which is German, means simply curds and the cheese is also sold as Buttermilchquark, Labquark and Speisequark. It has a mild, slightly sour flavour and may be used to make desserts.

QUASSIA A tree found in South America and the West Indies, from which is extracted a bitter oil, used for medicinal purposes and also to make a flavouring for tonic wines, aperitifs and bitters.

QUATRE-ÉPICES (Four Spices) A classic spice mix, used in French cookery, and usually consisting of ground pepper, grated nutmeg, ground cloves and ground cinnamon, though ginger is often also included. The spice mixture is used in a wide variety of savoury dishes.

The same name is also sometimes given to allspice or nigella (*see* ALLSPICE, NIGELLA).

QUEEN CAKE A small, light, rich cake, containing dried fruit and baked in patty tins or paper cases.

QUEEN OF PUDDINGS A pudding made of custard and breadcrumbs, with a meringue topping. Usually it is flavoured with lemon rind and vanilla but, for variety, apricots or peaches may be placed on top of the custard mixture instead of jam when it is set and before it is covered with the meringue.

QUEENSLAND NUT (*see* MACADAMIA NUT)

QUENELLE Fish, meat or poultry which has been blended to a fine forcemeat and bound with eggs or fat, then shaped into round or oval dumplings and cooked in liquid. *Quenelles* may be served either as a garnish for soup or as a main course with a sauce.

QUETSCH (*see* EAU-DE-VIE)

QUICHE A savoury custard tart, originally a speciality of Lorraine and Alsace. For the famous Quiche Lorraine, a shortcrust pastry base is filled with chopped bacon and slices of Gruyère cheese, then a mixture of egg, cream and seasoning is poured over. The quiche is baked for about 30 minutes or until set and golden. There are many variations for the filling, such as mushrooms, fish, sweetcorn, peppers, ham, onion, etc. A quiche may be served hot or cold and makes a popular buffet party or picnic dish.

QUICK FREEZING The commercial process of freezing food. It is a very much quicker process than freezing done at home, even when using the fast freeze facility on a domestic freezer. The difference is that the temperature drops at great speed through the water-freezing zone (known as 'the zone of maximum crystal formation'). Between 0°C (32°F) and -4°C (25°F), water freezes into ice crystals. If this happens slowly the crystals are large and tend to damage the cells of the food; if it takes place rapidly, the crystals are small, the cells remain undamaged and less deterioration takes place in the appearance and texture of the food. It is therefore best to freeze food as fast as possible.

After quick freezing, food is transferred to a cold store at -29°C (-20°F), until required for distribution. It leaves the factory in insulated lorries at -28°C (-18°F) and is stored in the shop cabinet at less than -18°C (0°F). Freezing preserves the colour and flavour of foods better than other methods of preserving, and also retains the nutritional value. (*see also* FREEZING)

QUINCE An apple- or pear-shaped fruit with yellow skin and scented yellow flesh. The quince probably originated in Iran, but is now grown in the Mediterranean region and South America. Quinces cannot be eaten raw but are excellent cooked and used in a number of ways. Quinces are rich in pectin and make good jams and jellies. They can also be stewed with apples and pears, or used to make a sauce to serve with pork and other meats. (*see also* JAPONICA)
To select: Avoid scabby, split or very small fruit.
To prepare: Simply peel, core and slice.

QUININE A bitter drug obtained from the bark of the South American *cinchona* bush. It is used as a medicine to treat malaria and other fevers, and as a flavouring in Indian tonic water. Like caffeine, quinine is an alkaloid substance with stimulant properties.

QUINOA The seeds of a small plant recently introduced from South America. Quinoa is a tiny, golden seed with a delicate flavour. It has been cultivated since 3000 BC in the South American Andes, the home of the Incas.

Like buckwheat, quinoa is not a true cereal grain, but is treated like one. It can be used in the same ways as rice and is quick and easy to prepare. It is light, tasty and easy to digest, and has a higher protein content than most other grains. Cook in boiling, salted water for 10–15 minutes, then drain and serve as an accompaniment to hot dishes, such as casseroles and curries, or use cold in salads or stuffed vegetables.

QUORN A vegetarian meat substitute developed from a fungus by Rank Hovis McDougall (RHM) Limited. The fungus, which was originally found in a field near High Wycombe, has proved to be remarkably efficient at producing high quality protein that can be made into a surprising range of foods, from biscuits to meat substitutes. Quorn contains 45 per cent protein and 13 per cent fat, is high in dietary fibre and contains no animal fats. Quorn is widely used in a number of vegetarian ready-prepared meals, such as savoury pies, flans and casseroles and is also available for use as an ingredient in a variety of dishes.

R

RABBIT AND HARE Rabbits and hares look similar but are two different species. Hares are available from late summer to early spring. Rabbits are available all the year around and may be tame (farmed) or wild. Hares have a darker, more gamey-flavoured flesh than rabbits.

Hares are hung by the hind feet without being paunched (entrails removed) for five to seven days to improve the flavour. During this time, the blood collects in the chest cavity. When paunching (*see* below), collect the blood if required for jugged hare and add 5 ml (1 tsp) vinegar to stop it coagulating. It can be stored, covered, in the refrigerator for two to three days.

If you want the butcher to collect the blood, you will probably have to order the hare and specify that you want the blood. Add vinegar to it as above. The butcher will skin and paunch the hare after hanging.

Very young hares (leverets) may be roasted whole but for larger hares, the body alone is used. This is known as saddle or baron of hare.

Rabbits are available both fresh and frozen. Unlike hares, they are paunched within a few hours of killing and are not hung. Tame rabbits, which have a delicate flavour, are always tender. Wild rabbits have darker, stronger-flavoured flesh and they should be eaten young. Fresh rabbit can be cooked in the same way as hare. Frozen rabbit is best used for pies, stews and casseroles.

Preparing a Rabbit or Hare
Skinning
Cut off the feet at the first joint. Loosen the skin round the back legs. Hold the end of one leg and bend up at the joint, then pull the skin over the end of the hind leg. Do the same with the other legs.

If keeping the head on for roasting, cut the skin around the eyes and mouth and remove the eyes. If not, cut the head off. Pull the skin towards the head, stripping it off inside out.

Paunching
Using kitchen scissors, snip the skin at the fork and cut it up the breastbone, then open the paunch by cutting the inside skin in the same direction. Draw out the entrails. Cut away the gall-bladder and the flesh it rested on and discard. Reserve the kidneys and liver. Cut the diaphragm and draw out the heart and lungs. Discard the lungs but keep the heart. If paunching hare, reserve the blood.

Trussing
Cut the sinews in the hind legs at the thigh, bring the legs forward and press closely against the body. Bend the forelegs back in the same way. Secure with two skewers or a trussing needle and thread.

Jointing
Cut off the hind legs at the thighs and the forelegs round the shoulder bone. Cut off the head. Cut the back into pieces, giving the back of the knife a sharp tap with a hammer to cut through the bone, then cut the ribs in two lengthways.

Roast Hare
The hare's heart, liver and kidneys may be added to the stuffing, if wished. Wash well, put into a saucepan, cover with cold water, bring to the boil, then strain and chop finely.

1.6 kg (3¹/₂ lb) hare or saddle of larger hare
streaky bacon rashers
dripping or margarine
gravy and redcurrant or guava jelly, to serve
FOR THE STUFFING
100 g (4 oz) lean veal
75 g (3 oz) lean bacon, rinded
25 g (1 oz) butter or margarine
1 small onion, skinned and finely chopped
75 g (3 oz) fresh breadcrumbs
25 g (1 oz) mushrooms, wiped and finely chopped
5 ml (1 tsp) chopped fresh parsley
salt and pepper
a pinch of cayenne pepper
a pinch of ground mace

1 egg, beaten

First, make the stuffing. Put the veal and bacon through a mincer or food processor twice, then beat them well in a bowl. Melt the butter in a saucepan, add the onion and fry for 2–3 minutes or until soft but not coloured, then add to the meat. Add the breadcrumbs, mushrooms, parsley and seasonings. Mix together well, then bind with the egg.

Stuff the hare, fold the skin over and sew in position (*see* above). Lay bacon rashers over the back and cover with greased greaseproof paper. Put in a roasting tin, dot with dripping and roast in the oven at 180°C (350°F) mark 4 for 1¹/₂–2 hours. Baste frequently as the flesh is apt to be dry.

Remove the paper and bacon 15 minutes before the end of the cooking time to allow the joint to brown. Remove the skewers and trussing thread and serve the hare with gravy and redcurrant or guava jelly.

Serves 4

Jugged Hare

1.6 kg (3¹/₂ lb) hare, paunched and jointed, with its blood
75 ml (5 level tbsp) seasoned flour
125 g (4 oz) streaky bacon, rinded and diced
50 g (2 oz) butter or margarine
900 ml (1¹/₂ pints) beef stock
150 ml (¹/₄ pint) port
5 ml (1 level tsp) dried marjoram
45 ml (3 level tbsp) redcurrant jelly
2 medium onions, skinned and stuck with 12 cloves
salt and pepper
chopped fresh parsley, to garnish

Wipe the hare and toss in the seasoned flour. Brown the bacon in its own fat in a large flameproof casserole, then remove and drain.

Add the butter to the casserole and lightly brown the hare portions. Add the stock, port, marjoram and redcurrant jelly with the onions. Replace the bacon and season. Bring to the boil, cover and cook in the oven at 170°C (325°F) mark 3 for 3 hours or until tender.

Transfer the hare to a deep serving dish, cover and keep warm. Discard the onions. Mix the blood with the cooking juices until smooth. Pour into the casserole and heat gently, adjust the seasoning and pour over the hare. Garnish with chopped parsley.

Serves 6

RACLETTE In popular use, this is the name of a Swiss method of toasting cheese over an open fire or in a special appliance. As the cheese melts, it is scraped off and eaten with potatoes, pickled onions and gherkins. In fact, *raclette* is the generic name of a semi-hard cheese (the name means scraper), which is golden with a few small holes and a rough, grey-brown rind. It tastes full and fruity and somewhat like Gruyère. There are many local Swiss varieties.

RADICCHIO (*see* CHICORY)

RADISH There are several varieties and sizes of this root vegetable, which may be red, white or black. The radish originated in China but is now grown all over the world. The most familiar red radishes are sold in bunches, with their green leafy tops intact, or ready-prepared and pre-packed. They are a popular salad ingredient.

Radish Varieties

Red radish is the most readily available; cultivated varieties are sold all year round. They have a peppery flavour which is milder in the spring. They are usually eaten raw in salads or with bread and butter as an hors d'oeuvre, or they can be made into attractive garnishes, such as radish roses. The leaves add pungent flavour to salads. *Daikon radish (Japanese radish or mooli)* is a long, white tube-like vegetable which can be grated and eaten raw or cooked. It may be sliced and added to soups and stews, in the same way as turnip.

Spanish black radish is a round radish the size of a small turnip which can be eaten raw or cooked.

To select: Choose radishes with fresh green tops or, if these have been cut off, look for radishes with firm bright white flesh. Allow 3–4 red radishes per person; 175–225 g (6–8 oz) raw weight, 100–175 g (4–6 oz) cooked weight white or black radish per person.

To prepare: If necessary, trim off the tops and root ends. Wash, then slice or grate for use in salads, or cut into decorative shapes for garnishes.

RAFRAÎCHI A French word, meaning chilled or refreshed.

RAGOÛT The French name, adopted elsewhere, for a type of stew of meat or poultry and vegetables. For a brown *ragoût*, the meat is first browned in a little fat before being gently simmered. For a white *ragoût*, the meat is first sealed, but not browned. A *ragoût* can be flavoured with mushrooms, port wine, tomatoes, etc. A mutton *ragoût* is often known by the French name *navarin* (see NAVARIN).

RAINBOW TROUT (*see* TROUT)

RAISED PIE A meat pie made with hot water crust pastry (*see* PASTRY) which becomes firm during baking and retains its shape. A raised pie can be made and baked in a special (sometimes hinged) mould or a greased cake tin, or can be moulded by hand, sometimes with a jam jar or small tin as a basis. After baking, raised pies are usually filled up with stock which sets into a jelly. Raised pies are often highly decorated and glazed and are usually served cold. Popular examples include pork pies and veal and ham pies. They can be bought whole or in slices from delicatessens and supermarkets.

RAISIN (*see* VINE FRUITS)

RAISING AGENT Any substance or method used to introduce air or gas (carbon dioxide) into bread, cake, pastry or pudding mixtures to make them rise during the cooking process. For example, in the making of sponge cakes, air is introduced by the whisking of egg and sugar over hot

water, and this air produces the rise. Batters, such as Yorkshire pudding, depend principally on the conversion of water into steam to make them rise, for the steam has 1,600 times the volume of the original water. The most usual raising agent, however, is carbon dioxide, produced either by the action of yeast or by chemicals (*see* BAKING POWDER, BICARBONATE OF SODA, CREAM OF TARTAR, YEAST). (*see also* BREAD, CAKE)

RAITA Indian raitas are yogurt-based vegetable or fruit side dishes. Their cool, refreshing flavours make an excellent, yet simple, accompaniment to all spiced foods. The most popular raita combines natural yogurt with cucumber, sometimes with fresh mint and spices added. Other combinations are yogurt with aubergine, tomatoes, mixed vegetables, potatoes or bananas.

RAKI (*see* ARRACK)

RAKIA (*see* ARRACK)

RAMBUTAN These are the dark red-brown fruit of a tree that originated in Malaysia but is now cultivated in the United States and parts of South-East Asia. The shell, which is covered with soft spines, is peeled off to reveal white, translucent, juicy flesh similar in taste and appearance to a lychee. At the centre of a rambutan is a long inedible stone. Rambutans can be eaten on their own, or chopped and added to fruit salads.

RAMEKIN A small, round, straight-sided ovenproof dish, often used to make and serve individual portions of pâté or *crème brûlée*. Ramekin dishes may be made from porcelain, earthenware or glass and are usually sold in matching sets of four or six. (*see also* COCOTTE)

RAM'S-HEAD PEA (*see* CHICK PEA)

RAPE There are a number of varieties of rape, all probably descending from a hybrid vegetable produced from varieties of turnip and cabbage. The most familiar rape is now cultivated on a large scale, partly as an animal fodder but also for its seeds which are crushed to produce rapeseed oil (*see* OILS). It is a tall plant that produces bright golden flowers in April and May, turning vast expanses of arable land a glorious yellow. The sprouted seeds are also sold in punnets mixed with cress, sometimes masquerading as mustard (*see* CRESS).

RAREBIT (*see* WELSH RAREBIT)

RĀS AL-HĀNOUT A north African spice mixture used to flavour meat and game dishes, rice and couscous. The mixture varies enormously, with any number of spice combinations being used, according to personal taste. It may even be perfumed with dried rosebuds.

RASPBERRY A soft, juicy fruit with a central hull, the raspberry has a delicious sweet yet slightly acidic flavour. Most raspberries are red, but yellow, white and black varieties are also available.

Homegrown raspberries are available in June and July and are sold hulled which makes them liable to crushing. When buying, avoid stained containers and wet fruit. After damp weather they are likely to go mouldy quickly. Raspberries can be eaten fresh with cream, used in desserts with other fruit, lightly stewed or made into jam. Ripe fruit can easily be puréed by pressing through a nylon sieve, making an instant dessert sauce for serving with ice cream. Raspberries are traditionally used to make Melba sauce (*see* MELBA SAUCE) and included in a summer pudding. They are also used to flavour a fruit vinegar (*see* VINEGAR).

RASPINGS (*see* BREADCRUMBS)

RATAFIA The name of a liqueur or cordial flavoured with the kernels of cherries, almonds, peaches or other fruits; also a flavouring essence used in cookery.

The name is also given to a type of sweet biscuit formerly eaten with the liqueur and now usually flavoured with ratafia essence. These biscuits somewhat resemble macaroons, but are smaller and browner; they may be served as a wine biscuit, used whole to decorate trifles and other cold desserts, or crushed and mixed with cold desserts. Similar Italian biscuits are known as *amaretti*.

RATATOUILLE A casserole or stew of vegetables, originating in Provence. It can be served hot as a vegetable or cold as a starter. Traditional ingredients include tomatoes, aubergines, sweet peppers, onions, courgettes and garlic.

RAVIGOTE BUTTER A green-coloured savoury butter, made by adding fresh aromatic herbs to creamed butter, which is served with grilled meat, etc. The herbs used can include tarragon, parsley, chives, chervil and burnet (if available). Shallot or garlic may also be added and the mixture is pounded together and mixed with creamed softened butter. The butter is chilled, then sliced and served on top of hot meat.

RAVIGOTE SAUCE A French salad dressing containing pounded hard-boiled egg yolks and highly flavoured with chopped herbs and garlic.

A hot sauce of the same name is made by adding a generous amount of ravigote butter (see above) and some wine and vinegar (reduced by boiling) to a *velouté* sauce base. It is served with boiled poultry, etc.

RAVIOLI (*see* PASTA)

RAY'S BREAM (*see* POMFRET)

RAZOR SHELLS A variety of clam found on all British coasts, burrowing in the sand on the lower shores and in shallow water. Razor shells are oblong in shape, about 12.5 cm (5 inches) long and 2.5 cm (1 inch) wide; when open they resemble an old-fashioned cut-throat razor. They are not easy to catch and are not often seen for sale, but they can be eaten raw, like oysters, or steamed, like mussels, or they can be used in soup. (*see also* CLAM, SHELLFISH)

RÉCHAUFFÉ The French name for a made-up dish of reheated food. A variety of *réchauffés* can be made from leftovers of cooked food, so that they become appetizing dishes in their own right. In general, the aim should be to reheat rather than to re-cook the food and it is usually necessary to combine it with a well-flavoured sauce or other accompaniment. As cooked food does not absorb flavour, this must come from other ingredients. It is often a good idea to heat and serve *réchauffés* in individual dishes or small pastry cases, etc., to make them look more attractive. Examples of *réchauffés* include cottage pie, croquettes, rissoles, fish pie and hash.

It is important to take great care when storing and reheating leftover cooked food. Meat, fish, milk products and vegetables, in particular, are easily contaminated with the germs that cause food poisoning, especially if left in a warm state for any length of time. Leftover cooked food intended for reheating should therefore be cooled as quickly as possible, then stored in the refrigerator. When reheating, ensure that food is piping hot right through before serving so that any micro-organisms that might have developed in the food will have been destroyed. (*see also* FOOD POISONING)

RECIPE The list of ingredients and instructions for making a dish. With some types of dish it is possible to vary the nature and amount of the ingredients and the method of mixing and cooking, so that there are often many different recipes for one dish. With certain classic or specialized recipes, however, particularly those devised by the great chefs of the last century or so, there is only one really 'correct' and authentic version.

Beginners should follow recipes carefully and learn the basic methods for cakes, pastry, sauces, etc., before attempting too much variation.

The quantities given in a recipe can usually be doubled or halved without further alteration, but when quantities are varied beyond this, the proportions of the ingredients often require modification: this applies particularly to such ingredients as raising agents, flavouring and mixing liquids, which may need to be used in slightly smaller proportions when the quantities are increased. When you want to cook a large quantity of some particular mixture it is often better to make two moderate-sized batches rather than one very big one.

RED BREAM (*see* BREAM)

RED CABBAGE (*see* CABBAGE, RED AND WHITE)

REDCURRANT (*see* CURRANTS)

RED FISH (Norway Haddock) This sea fish has a flattened body and bright orange-red skin with dark blotches. It is found in the deep waters of the North Atlantic and is sold whole or as fillets. The white flesh is lean and firm and has a good flavour. It is excellent for soup, but can also be cooked like bream (*see* BREAM). (*see also* FISH)

RED GRAM (*see* PIGEON PEA)

RED HERRING (*see* HERRING)

RED KIDNEY BEAN (*see* KIDNEY BEAN)

RED MULLET (*see* MULLET, RED)

RED SNAPPER This round sea fish has a distinctive red skin and delicious white flesh. It is usually sold whole, but steaks and fillets are also available. Whole fish may be baked with scales left on, or stuffed and baked. Alternatively, grill, braise or steam with scales removed. Red snapper is available all year. Other varieties of snapper are also sometimes available, including one with grey skin that is not considered as good as the red snapper.

REDUCE To fast boil a liquid (especially when making a soup, sauce or syrup) in an uncovered pan, in order to evaporate off surplus liquid and give a more concentrated result.

REFORM SAUCE A brown sauce of the espagnole type, enriched by the addition of port wine and redcurrant jelly. It is traditionally served with a dish of breaded and fried lamb cutlets devised by the chef of the Reform Club in London. The traditional Reform garnish consists of a julienne of cooked carrot, truffle or mushroom, lean ham or tongue, hard-boiled egg white and gherkin, heated together and placed in the centre of the dish of cutlets. (*see also* ESPAGNOLE SAUCE)

REFRESH To pour cold water over blanched and drained vegetables in order to set the colour and to stop the cooking process. Also, to revive or keep salad ingredients, especially lettuce, crisp by putting them back in the refrigerator after washing. (*see also* RAFRAÎCHI)

REFRIGERATION A method of storing foods at a temperature low enough to arrest deterioration, at least for a short period. Few homes are without a domestic refrigerator and they are indispensable for storing perishable foods such as dairy produce, meat, fish and vegetables.

Refrigerators work by transferring the heat from inside the cabinet to the outside by means of a refrigerant substance such as ammonia or freon. Most domestic refrigerators also incorporate a small freezing compartment or ice-box, in which frozen food can be stored or ice can be made, but food cannot be frozen. The coldest part of the refrigerator is usually the area immediately below the ice-making compartment.

The cabinet of a refrigerator should be kept at a temperature between 1°C and 5°C to ensure foods remain in good condition. Any higher and foods will deteriorate more rapidly and harmful micro-organisms may begin to develop. It is a good idea to keep a refrigerator thermometer in the refrigerator in order to check regularly on the temperature. It is worth remembering that the temperature rises each time the door is opened and it can take the refrigerator up to an hour to return to a sufficiently low temperature, even after opening the door for only 10 seconds. New designs of refrigerator incorporate many more separate sections with individual doors within the main cabinet, preventing warm air entering every area of the refrigerator when the door is opened. Some new models also include a special compartment with a thermostatically-controlled temperature of 0°C to 1°C, specifically intended for storing ready-made cook-chill foods which are best stored at a lower temperature.

REHEATING (*see* RÉCHAUFFÉ)

REINDEER A large deer found in Arctic regions, the meat of which can be classified as venison. The meat of young reindeer, both cows and steers, is mild-flavoured; the tongues are excellent when smoked. The milk of reindeer can be used to make cheese. (*see also* VENISON)

REINE, À LA A French term used to describe a variety of elaborate dishes made from chicken.

RELISH Similar to a chutney, a relish is a mixture of fruits and/or vegetables cooked with vinegar and spices which act as preservatives. The ingredients for a relish should be cut into chunks and cooked for a fairly short time so that the fruit and/or vegetables retain their shape. Some relishes do not need cooking at all. Like chutneys, relishes are served as a condiment with cold meats, cheese and hamburgers. A number of commercially prepared relishes are readily available. (*see also* CHUTNEY)

RÉMOULADE SAUCE A cold, mayonnaise-based sauce usually served with cold meat, fish and shellfish. (*see also* MAYONNAISE)

RENDERING Extracting fat from meat trimmings by cutting them into small pieces and heating in the oven at 150°C (300°F) mark 2 until the fat runs out and can be strained.

RENNET A substance extracted from the lining of calves' stomachs. Rennet contains an enzyme called rennin which, when added to milk, causes the milk protein to curdle or coagulate. This process is used to make junket and cheese. A vegetarian version of rennet, extracted from certain plants (such as cardoon) is also available and is used to make vegetarian cheeses. (*see also* CHEESE, JUNKET)

RESIN A substance that exudes from certain plants and trees. Pine resin is used in the making of the Greek wine, *retsina*. The resin from the asafoetida plant is used in Indian cookery as a seasoning and a digestive, in minute quantities.

RETINOL (*see* VITAMINS)

RETSINA This famous white or red Greek wine is flavoured with pine resin while still in the cask.

RÉVEILLON The name of a feast held in France on Christmas Eve after Midnight Mass. It consists of a very elaborate supper and is often provided by the wealthy members of the town or village. The chief dish is usually *boudin noir* (black pudding). The name *réveillon* is also given to a feast held on New Year's Eve.

RENVERSÉ A French word meaning turned out, as of a cream or jelly.

RHUBARB Strictly speaking, rhubarb is a vegetable, not a fruit, as it is the stem of the plant that is used in cooking, but it is always eaten in sweet dishes. Early forced rhubarb (available in early spring) is pink and tender looking and sweet tasting; maincrop rhubarb has a stronger colour, a thicker stem and is more acid tasting. Many varieties of rhubarb are cultivated, one of the best being champagne rhubarb which is a forced variety, available at the beginning of the season.

Rhubarb is always cooked for eating and can be used in pies, crumbles, fools, puddings and jams. The leaves must not be eaten as they are poisonous.

To select: Look for young pink rhubarb; once the stems are thick and green they are coarse and sour. Avoid limp or damaged stalks.

To prepare: For young rhubarb, simply cut off the leaves and roots, then wash and chop the stems. Older stems can be stringy and may need peeling.

To cook: Stew gently in water or orange juice, adding sugar as required.

RIBOFLAVIN (*see* VITAMINS)

RICARD (*see* PASTIS)

RICE Rice is the most important cereal grain in the world. It is an aquatic plant, grown in rice or paddy fields in hot, moist climates, such as India, Java, China, Japan and parts of the United States. There are countless varieties, with long, medium or short grains. It may be sold as brown, natural, unpolished or wholegrain rice, still retaining its outer bran layers, or as white or polished rice, having been milled to remove the bran. All rice contains protein, carbohydrate, vitamins and minerals, but no fat. The brown types also contain dietary fibre, which makes them a better choice nutritionally, but they do need longer cooking than white rice.

Some rice is sold as 'easy-cook', pre-cooked or pre-fluffed. This has usually been steam treated before the husk is removed. This helps retain some of the vitamins and minerals which would normally be removed with the husk and also helps to keep the grains separate during cooking. (*see also* GRAINS)

Types of Rice
Long grain rice consists of slender grains about four times as long as they are wide. When cooked they become fluffy and dry and remain separate. Long grain rice is particularly suitable for savoury dishes. The two main types are *patna* and *basmati*. Basmati is the best rice to eat with Indian food, with its slimmer, dense grains giving a delicate nutty flavour when cooked. It should be rinsed before cooking to remove excess starch.
Medium grain rice is about three times as long as it is wide. It absorbs more liquid than long grain and is moister and stickier when cooked. It can be used in both sweet and savoury dishes.
Short grain (pudding) rice has small, chalky round

or oval grains which absorb a large quantity of liquid and produce a moist sticky mass when cooked. It is used mainly for milk puddings and other sweet dishes.

Italians use a special short grain rice, called *arborio*, for making risottos. *Arborio* rice swells during cooking and the grains cling together – unlike most other savoury rice dishes in which long grain rice needs to be fluffy and the individual grains separate. *Arborio* rice is available in specialist delicatessens and Italian shops. Two other varieties which can also be used for risottos are *superfino* and *avorio*, which are pre-fluffed and a golden yellow colour.

Glutinous rice (also sold as sticky or sweet rice) has oval cream-coloured grains which cook into a sticky mass. It is popular in Chinese and other eastern cuisines.

Wild (Indian) rice is not rice at all but the seed of an aquatic grass. It has long dark brown grains which are cooked in the same way as long grain rice and served with savoury dishes. It is considerably more expensive than other types of rice, but has a very distinctive flavour.

Rice flakes consist of grains that have been processed into flakes, making them very quick to cook. They can be used in milk puddings or to thicken soups and stews.

Ground rice is available in coarse, medium and fine grains. It can be used in milk puddings, added to shortbread to provide a fine, crisp texture, or used as a thickener.

Cooking Rice
During cooking, the starch in rice swells, the grain softens and the rice increases to two or three times its original weight and bulk. Allow about 50 g (2 oz) uncooked rice per person as an accompaniment and about 40–50 g (1½–2 oz) when it is to be mixed with other ingredients.

Rice can be cooked either on the hob or in the oven. Check when it is done by biting a grain between your teeth; like pasta, it should be *al dente*. For easy-cook, pre-cooked or pre-fluffed rice, follow the manufacturer's instructions on the can or packet.

Cooked rice can be stored, covered, in the refrigerator for up to 1 week or frozen for up to 6 months. To reheat, either put it in a saucepan with a little water, steam in a colander over boiling water, or place in a tightly covered greased dish in the oven.

Boiled Rice
3.4 litres (6 pints) water
salt
225 g (8 oz) long grain white rice
Bring a large saucepan of water to a fast boil, then add salt and the rice. Stir once to loosen the grains at the base of the pan, then leave uncovered to cook for 12 minutes or until tender.

Drain well, rinse with hot water and drain again. Pour into a warmed serving dish and separate the grains with a fork.
Serves 4

Variations
An alternative method is to use an exact amount of water which is completely absorbed by the rice. For this method, allow 600 ml (1 pint) water, 5 ml (1 level tsp) salt to 225 g (8 oz) long grain white rice.

Place the rice, salt and water in a large saucepan and bring quickly to the boil, stir well and cover with a tightly fitting lid. Reduce the heat and simmer gently for about 15 minutes or until tender and the water has been absorbed. Remove from the heat and separate the grains with a fork before serving.

Brown rice should be cooked in plenty of fast-boiling salted water for about 35 minutes or until just tender.

Oven-cooked Rice
225 g (8 oz) long grain white rice
600 ml (1 pint) water
5 ml (1 level tsp) salt

Place the rice in an ovenproof dish. Bring the water and salt to a fast boil, pour over the rice and stir well with a fork.

Cover tightly with a lid or foil and bake in the oven at 180°C (350°F) mark 4 for 35–40 minutes, or until the grains are just soft and all the cooking liquid has been absorbed by the rice.
Serves 4

RICE BEAN A small dried bean that is native to south-east Asia and grown in China, India and the Philippines. Its shape is similar to that of the aduki bean, but it is less rounded and has a much larger hilum, running almost the whole length of the bean. Rice beans vary in colour from yellow to deep red or black and are so called because they are said to taste like rice when cooked. They are a rich source of calcium. (*see also* PULSES)

RICE NOODLES (*see* NOODLES)

RICE PAPER A very fragile, sweet-tasting type of edible paper made from the pith of a Chinese tree. It is used as an edible base for sticky baked goods such as macaroons.

RICE STICK NOODLES (*see* NOODLES)

RICE WINE A potent wine made in China. It resembles sherry in appearance and flavour.

RICHELIEU, À LA A French name given to meat dishes served with Richelieu sauce (a rich brown Madeira sauce) or garnished with mushrooms, potatoes, or stuffed tomatoes. The name is also given to other dishes, such as a sweet pastry, dedicated to the Duc de Richelieu (the Cardinal's great-nephew).

RICING A method of puréeing foods, especially cooked potatoes. They are pressed through a ricer or sieve, emerging like little grains of soft rice, hence the name. Ricers are conical in shape with a pestle to push the food through. Other foods which produce light, fluffy results by ricing are cooked parsnips, carrots and turnips.

RICKEY An unsweetened long drink made from a liqueur or spirit and ginger ale; it is flavoured with fresh fruit.

RICOTTA A fragrant Italian cheese made from ewes' milk whey left over when producing other cheeses. It is usually used in its soft, fresh, unripened state, though a hard, matured, grating version of Ricotta is also made. Fresh Ricotta is unsalted and has a delicate, smooth flavour which makes it very suitable for cooking in such things as ravioli or cannelloni. It can also be eaten with sugar or used layered in fruit tarts and puddings.

RIESLING A type of white grape used to make wines which are usually given the same name. It is the classical German grape, producing the best German wines.

Most of the grapes are grown in the Mosel and Rheingau areas. The wines are comparatively expensive as the Riesling only gives about half as much wine per plant as other varieties of grape. Good Riesling wines are also produced in Austria and Alsace, and the grapes are also grown in Australia, South Africa, Chile and California, but the climates of these countries are too hot for producing the excellent wine made in Germany.

A Riesling wine must be labelled with the country of origin.

RIGATONI (*see* PASTA)

RILLETTE (*see* POTTING)

RISE To allow a yeast dough to double in size before baking. When it has risen, the dough is sometimes knocked back (*see* KNOCK BACK), shaped and then allowed to rise for a second time. The second rising is sometimes known as proving (*see* PROVING).

RISOTTO A famous Italian dish made by boiling rice in stock until the stock has been absorbed, flavouring it with onion, cheese, mushrooms, chicken, seafood, kidneys, white wine, etc., according to the type of risotto. Italian, risotto or Arborio rice give the best results. The rich and creamy *risotto alla milanese*, from Milan, contains onion, bacon, mushrooms, saffron and prawns. (*see also* RICE)

RISSOLE In Britain nowadays, this word is usually taken to mean a small roll or patty, made of cooked minced meat bound with mashed potatoes, which is coated in egg and breadcrumbs and fried in hot fat. Rissoles may also be made of vegetarian ingredients such as cooked vegetables and nuts. In France, however, a *rissole* is a small sweet or savoury pastry, rather like a turnover, which may be filled with a wide range of fillings made from fish, meat, poultry, shellfish, fruit or jam. French *rissoles* are usually made from puff pastry and deep-fried.

Rissoles may be served as a supper or light lunch dish, with a brown or tomato sauce.

RIVER TROUT (*see* TROUT)

ROACH This small, freshwater fish of the carp family is in season from September to March. It has white flesh, which turns red when cooked. To counteract the muddy flavour, rub it well with salt (or hang it up with salt in its mouth) and leave it for a while. Clean and wash the fish thoroughly, then soak it in salted water for 2–3 hours before cooking.

Frying and grilling are the usual methods of cooking. Garnish with parsley and serve accompanied by anchovy sauce.

ROASTING A method of cooking foods (usually meat) by dry heat in the oven. Originally, the term meant cooking by a fierce dry heat over an open fire. Nowadays, it refers to oven-roasting or baking. The heat is still fierce, but confined to the oven space, so the meat retains its juices. (*see also* MEAT)

ROBALO (*see* SNOOK)

ROBERT SAUCE A piquant sauce based on espagnole or demi-glace sauce and flavoured with onion, dry white wine, vinegar and mustard. It is served with hot or cold meats, especially chops, steaks, pork and goose, when the tangy sauce will liven up the bland flavour of the meat. (*see also* DEMI-GLACE SAUCE, ESPAGNOLE SAUCE)

ROBUSTA (*see* COFFEE)

ROCAMBOLE (Spanish Garlic) A kind of onion grown in southern France which bears 'fruits' at the top of the stem; these resemble garlic, but are not so pungent.

ROCK CAKES Plain buns containing fruit and spice, which are baked in small heaps on a baking sheet. The mixture must not be too wet or the buns will spread and lose their 'rocky' shape.

ROCK CANDY (*see* SUGAR)

ROCK SALMON (*see* HUSS)

ROCKET (Arugula) A green salad vegetable that has long been popular in Mediterranean countries. A member of the cabbage family, rocket has long, spear-shaped leaves (similar to dandelion leaves) which have a slightly bitter, peppery flavour. It is delicious served with a hot bacon dressing.

ROE The spawn or milt of a fish. In many cases it is only suitable for cooking as part of the fish, but the roes of grey mullet and cod, amongst other fish, are often used to make separate savouries or made-up dishes. Sturgeon's roe, commonly called caviar, is an expensive delicacy used as an appetizer or for cocktail savouries. (*see also* CAVIAR, COD, MULLET, TARAMA)

ROE DEER (*see* VENISON)

ROGAN JOSH A rich, red-coloured lamb or beef curry from India. The meat is cooked in a yogurt sauce with chilli powder or cayenne and paprika pepper providing the colour. Although there are several recipes for the dish, peppers and tomatoes usually feature. It is served with Indian bread or rice.

ROLLS, BREAD Bread rolls may be made in

numerous shapes and from many kinds of dough: certain textures are traditionally associated with certain shapes. Thus, finger-shaped sandwich or bridge rolls are soft; Vienna rolls are crisp and very light; milk rolls (which may be made in various shapes) are soft; croissants are made from a dough with extra fat added.

Rolls become rather tough when stale, but this can be remedied by sprinkling with water and reheating in a moderate oven, to crisp them up. This process cannot be repeated or the rolls become hard.

(*see also* BREAD, CROISSANT)

ROLLMOP (*see* HERRING)

ROLY-POLY A family steamed pudding made with suetcrust pastry. The pastry is rolled out into an oblong and spread with jam or mincemeat. It is then rolled up like a Swiss roll, wrapped in foil and steamed for $1\frac{1}{2}$–2 hours. A pressure cooker cooks the roly-poly more quickly, or it can be baked in the oven. Serve with custard. (*see also* PASTRY)

ROMAINE (*see* LETTUCE)

ROOT VEGETABLES A general name for a group of vegetables all grown for their swollen roots. The group includes carrots, beetroot, turnips, swedes, parsnips, radishes and salsify.

Most root vegetables are cooked and eaten hot, though some, such as carrots, may be used raw in salads. Cold cooked beetroots, carrots, turnips and parsnips may be included in salads. Radishes are seldom cooked, but are usually used raw as an appetizer or in salads.

(For detailed information about particular root vegetables, see individual entries.)

ROPE A bacterial contamination of bread dough, which can make bread turn 'ropy' in hot, moist conditions. In the tropics, it is sometimes necessary to add a little vinegar to bread dough to prevent the infection.

ROQUEFORT A delicious blue, ewes' milk cheese which has obtained a world-wide reputation. It is made during the lambing season in the village of Roquefort in the Cévennes mountains of France. It can be made only in this district, partly because the sheep-grazing land here is particularly suitable, but also because of the limestone caverns of Roquefort itself, which play a very important part in the maturing of the Roquefort cheese.

The same mould as that used in the making of Stilton is introduced into the curd as a maturing agent when making Roquefort. The cheese has a sharp, pungent flavour and a soft, creamy, crumbly texture. It is very good for salads, mixed with the dressing.

ROSE HIPS Hips, the fully ripe, dark red fruits of the wild rose, are valuable on account of their high vitamin C content, but they are not suitable for eating raw, as they are somewhat sour and have many hard seeds and irritating silky hairs. When cooked, however, they may be made into an agreeable preserve or a pleasant-flavoured syrup, which may be taken by itself or used to add extra sweetness and food value to sauces and cold sweets.

ROSELLA (*see* JAMAICA FLOWER)

ROSEMARY A strong, pungent herb with spikey leaves. The flavour of rosemary overpowers other herbs so use it on its own and sparingly in meat, fish, poultry and some sweet dishes. It marries well with all lamb dishes and is excellent used with barbecued meats.

ROSE PETALS Pretty, scented rose petals have all kinds of uses in the culinary world as well as making wonderfully fragrant pot pourri and cosmetics. They can be transformed into delicious jams, jellies, conserves and drinks, or they can be used as a flavouring in many desserts. Rose petals make attractive, delicate decorations for all sweet dishes, desserts, cakes and drinks. They can also be frosted or crystallized.

To use rose petals at their best, gather scented roses after the dew has disappeared and before the sun gets hot. This is when the petals will have the most fragrance and flavour. If the petals are to be eaten, use fragrant roses only. Choose undamaged petals, free of blemishes and disease. Avoid roses that have been sprayed with insecticide, etc. Detach the petals gently and, if required, remove the white or cream parts at the bases. Rose petals should be used as soon as possible.

ROSE WATER Highly fragrant rose flavoured water, which is either distilled from rose petals or prepared from rose oil. It is used to make Turkish Delight, baking and sweet dishes and in other Middle Eastern dishes.

ROSOLIO A bright red liqueur made in Italy and France; it is flavoured with either oil of roses or tangerine rind, orange juice and orange blossom.

ROTI (*see* CHAPATTI)

ROTISSERIE COOKING A method of cooking meat and poultry which has developed from the old fashioned spit over an open fire. The joint or bird is impaled on a shaft and held securely by holding forks at each end. The shaft is positioned close to a heat source (either under the grill or in the oven) and is continuously rotated by a motor as the meat cooks. A tray is positioned beneath the joint to catch the drippings from the meat as it cooks. The main advantages are that the meat bastes itself, there is little splashing, and the excellent flavour, which some consider to be better than oven-baked meat. Rotisserie units are fitted on many gas or electric cookers, and separate electrically operated units are also available.

ROUGH PUFF PASTRY (*see* PASTRY)

ROULADE The French name for a stuffed meat roll or galantine (*see* GALANTINE).

ROULÉ This French processed cheese resembles a Swiss roll in shape and comes in several varieties. All are full fat soft cheeses; one is spread with and rolled in *fines herbes* and garlic, and another (Roulé Acapulco) with spices, including cumin, pepper and chilli. They look very attractive when sliced and served as part of a cheese board.

ROUT CAKES AND BISCUITS Confections somewhat similar to petits fours which were formerly served at 'routs' or evening parties. Many different types were made.

ROUX A mixture of equal amounts of fat and flour cooked together to form the basis of a sauce or panada. The cooking time for a roux varies depending on whether the sauce is to be brown or white. For a brown sauce, the roux is cooked until browned; for a white sauce, the roux is cooked until just beginning to colour (blond). (*see also* PANADA, SAUCES)

ROWANBERRY (Sorb) The bright orange-red fruit of the mountain ash tree. Rowanberries are occasionally used to make a jelly which may be served with game and may also be sieved and added to apple sauce to vary the flavour.

ROYAL ICING The hard, white icing, made from egg whites and icing sugar, which is used for coating Christmas and other cakes that are to be decorated and kept for some time. It is usually applied over a coating of almond paste. Royal icing may also be made using dried albumen powder instead of fresh egg whites, if preferred (*see* ALBUMEN POWDER). Follow the instructions on the packet.

Royal Icing
Royal icing may be made in an electric mixer but take care not to overbeat or the icing will become fluffy, resulting in a rough surface, and will break easily if piped.
4 egg whites
900 g (2 lb) icing sugar
15 ml (1 tbsp) lemon juice
10 ml (2 tsp) glycerine

Whisk the egg whites in a bowl until slightly frothy, then sift and stir in about a quarter of the icing sugar with a wooden spoon. Continue adding more sugar gradually, beating well after each addition, until about three-quarters of the sugar has been added.

Beat in the lemon juice and continue beating for about 10 minutes or until the icing is smooth.

Beat in the remaining sugar until the required consistency is achieved, depending on how the icing will be used.

Finally, stir in the glycerine to prevent the icing hardening. Cover and keep for 24 hours to allow any air bubbles to rise to the surface.

Makes about 900 g (2 lb) or enough to coat one 20.5 cm (8 inch) square or one 23 cm (9 inch) round cake

Using Royal Icing

Just before using a made-up quantity of royal icing, beat lightly and adjust the consistency if necessary. Royal icing dries out quickly, so keep the bowl covered with a clean, damp cloth or cling film while in use.

To Flat Ice a Cake

Place a small spoonful of icing on the cake board and place the cake on top, making sure it is in the centre of the board. Stand the cake and board on a non-slip surface. Spoon almost half the icing on top of the cake and spread it evenly over the surface with a palette knife, using a paddling action to remove any air bubbles that may remain. Using an icing ruler or palette knife longer than the diameter of the cake, without applying any pressure, draw it steadily across the top of the cake at an angle of 30°, to smooth the surface. Neaten the edges with a palette knife, removing any surplus icing. For best results, leave to dry for about 24 hours before applying the icing to the side of the cake.

To make icing the side of a cake easier, place it on an icing turntable or up-turned plate. Spread the remaining icing on the side of the cake and smooth it roughly with a small palette knife, using

a paddling action. Hold the palette knife or icing comb upright and at an angle of 45° to the cake. Draw the knife or comb towards you to smooth the surface. For a square cake, apply icing to each side separately. Neaten the edges with a palette knife, removing any surplus icing.

For a really smooth finish, apply a second thinner coat of icing, allowing the first coat to dry for one or two days first. Use fine sandpaper to sand down any imperfections or slight marks in the first coat. Brush the surface of the cake with a grease-free pastry brush to remove the icing dust. Leave the final coat to harden for two or three days.

To Rough Ice a Cake

Coat the cake with royal icing as above and, while the icing is still soft, use a palette knife or the back of a spoon to draw the icing up into peaks over the top and round the sides. Simple decorations can be added before the icing sets.

ROYAL JELLY The food given to certain bee larvae, which causes them to become queen bees. It is claimed, without any scientific proof, to have certain magical effects on human health.

ROYAL MINT CHOCOLATE A popular modern liqueur with a subtle flavour blend.

ROYALE, À LA A French term used to describe dishes cooked and served by a variety of methods. *Consommé à la royale* is garnished with tiny savoury custard shapes.

ROYAN A delicately flavoured fish similar to a sardine. It is caught off the coast of France, near the town of the same name.

RUBANÉ A French term used to describe dishes built up of ribbon-like layers.

RUBBING IN A method of incorporating fat into flour when a 'short' texture is required. It is used for pastry, plain cakes, scones and biscuits. 'Rubbing in' is a literal description of the method: the fat is lightly 'worked' into the flour between the fingers and thumbs until the mixture resembles fine breadcrumbs. The fat is usually cut into small cubes before being rubbed in. While rubbing in, the hands should be held high above the bowl to keep the mixture cool and light.

Lightly rubbing fat into flour between fingers and thumbs until the mixture resembles breadcrumbs.

RUE A hardy evergreen shrub with blue-grey foliage and a pungent aromatic smell. It has long been cultivated for its medicinal and culinary properties. For use in cooking, gather the sprigs fresh, or dry, then store in airtight containers. The leaves may be finely chopped and added sparingly to salads to impart a bitter flavour.

RUM A spirit distilled from molasses and made chiefly in the West Indian and Caribbean region, especially in such sugar cane districts as Jamaica, Barbados, Trinidad, Demerara (Guyana), Martinique, Cuba and Puerto Rico. Rum can be sold as 'white' rum, but is usually coloured with caramel and often flavoured with fruits.

Many hot and cold drinks and punches may be made with rum; it is popular made into a long drink with cola. It is also used for making rum butter (*see* BRANDY BUTTER) and a syrup for babas, as well as for flavouring cakes, omelettes, sauces, chocolates, truffles, etc.

RUM BABA (*see* BABA)

RUM BUTTER (*see* BRANDY BUTTER)

RUMP STEAK (*see* STEAK)

RUNNER BEAN (*see* BEAN, RUNNER)

RUSH NUT (*see* CHUFA NUT)

RUSK This may mean a type of sweetened tea biscuit, a piece of bread or cake crisped in the oven, or a commercially made product intended especially for young children and invalids. Both the last two types of rusk are frequently given to babies when they are teething, and to older children to keep their teeth in good condition. Plain rusks are sometimes served with cheese as an alternative to biscuits or bread.

RUTABAGA (*see* SWEDE)

RUTLAND CHEDDAR A Cheddar cheese flavoured with beer, garlic and parsley. (*see also* CHEDDAR)

RUOTINI (*see* PASTA)

RYE A hardy cereal which will grow in cold climates and in poor soil. The grain, which is brown and hard, with a slightly sour taste, is ground to a flour which is often mixed with other flours in bread-making, and is used on the Continent for making 'black' bread. It is also used for making special thin, dry, crisp biscuits.

Whole rye grains are available for including in soups and stews, or for sprouting (*see* BEAN SPROUTS). Cracked rye is similar to cracked wheat and is used mainly in the making of coarse rye breads in northern and eastern Europe. Toasted rye flakes and rye bran are also available and may be added to a muesli mixture.

The composition of rye flour varies with its source and the milling, the protein content being double and the calcium treble in the wholemeal version, as compared with a low-extraction rye flour. The calorific values of high-extraction flour are about the same as those of white flour, but the calcium content is slightly higher in rye flour. The gluten content of rye flour is very poor and unless some other flour is mixed with it it makes a damp, heavy bread.

A whisky distilled from rye is popular in the United States, and the Russian drink *kvass* is also made from rye.

(*see also* FLOUR, GRAIN)

S

SABAYON This French version of the Italian word *zabaglione* denotes a sweet sauce served with a rich sponge or fruit pudding (often steamed). It is a light frothy mixture made from eggs, sugar and rum or sherry; it is not as thick as *zabaglione*. (*see also* ZABAGLIONE)

Sabayon Sauce

50 g (2 oz) caster sugar
2 egg yolks, beaten
grated rind of ¹/₂ a lemon
juice of 1 lemon
30 ml (2 tbsp) rum or sherry
30 ml (2 tbsp) single cream

Put the sugar in a saucepan with 60 ml (4 tbsp) water and heat gently until the sugar has dissolved. Bring to the boil and boil for 2–3 minutes or until syrupy. Pour slowly on to the yolks, whisking constantly until pale and thick.

Add the lemon rind, lemon juice and rum and whisk for a further few minutes. Fold in the cream and chill well.
Serves 4

SACCHARIN A white crystalline powder, manufactured from coal tar, which has remarkable sweetening properties, being around 400 times sweeter than sugar. However, it has no food value and passes through the body unchanged. In the past, therefore, it has been much used in foods specially prepared for people with diabetes or on slimming diets. It fell into disrepute, however, when it was suspected, along with cyclamates (*see* CYCLAMATE) of being linked with bladder cancer, and its use is banned in some countries. In Britain, saccharin and its derivatives are currently approved for use in soft drinks, cider, sweetening tablets, sugar-free jams and similar products, but they do not have 'E' numbers and are therefore not approved for use throughout the EEC (*see* ADDITIVES). To some extent, saccharin has been replaced by newer sweeteners, such as aspartame (*see* ASPARTAME).

SACK An old name for various white wines, particularly those from Spain and the Canaries; sherry is the only modern representative of the family.

SADDLE OF LAMB This comprises the whole of the back of the sheep, from the end of the loin to the best end of neck. It is usually divided into smaller joints.

Saddle of lamb is a prime roasting joint, an ideal choice for special occasions or when cooking for large numbers. (*see also* LAMB)

SAFFLOWER (Saffron Thistle) A thistle-like plant with large orange-red flower heads. A pale, delicately-flavoured oil is extracted from the seeds (*see* OILS). The dried and powdered flowers are used medicinally and as a colouring in foods and cosmetics.

SAFFLOWER OIL (*see* OILS)

SAFFRON The most expensive of the spices, saffron is the dried stigmas of the purple flowering saffron crocus. Once cultivated around the town of Saffron Walden in Essex, it is now imported, mostly from Spain. It has an aromatic, slightly bitter taste and only a few threads are needed to flavour and colour dishes such as *bouillabaisse*, chicken soup, rice and *paella*, and saffron cake. The threads are usually infused in a little hot liquid, then stirred into the dish. Powdered saffron is also available. Where just a touch of colour is needed, a pinch of turmeric can be used instead, but the flavour is not the same.

SAFFRON CAKE An old English cake or sweet bread made from a saffron-coloured and flavoured yeast dough containing currants. It is thought to have originated in Cornwall. Small cakes made from the same mixture are known as saffron buns.

SAFFRON THISTLE (*see* SAFFLOWER)

SAGE A large-leaved herb with a strong, slightly bitter taste. Common sage has pale green leaves but other varieties have purple or variegated leaves. Use on its own, sparingly, in stuffings, casseroles, salads, meat dishes (especially pork), egg and cheese dishes. It is most commonly combined with onions in sage and onion stuffing (*see* STUFFING), and is also familiar as a flavouring for cheese (*see* DERBY CHEESE).

SAGO Although often treated as a cereal grain, sago in fact consists of dried starch granules derived from the pith of the sago tree, a type of palm tree native to Asia. Sago is mainly used in milk puddings but is also ground into a flour.

SAINTE-MAURE A soft and creamy French goats' milk cheese made in a long, cylindrical shape, often with a long straw inserted through the centre.

SAINT-GERMAIN A French name usually given to dishes which include green peas.

SAINT PAULIN A French semi-hard cheese, round in shape and originally made by the monks of Port du Salut. Saint Paulin is sometimes sold as Port Salut, but is now made in various other parts of France. It is creamy yellow in colour and has a very mild and delicate flavour; it should be eaten while still slightly soft.

SAITHE (*see* COLEY)

SAKE (Mirin, Saki) A Japanese alcoholic drink made by fermenting rice. It is colourless and still and is usually served warm, in tiny porcelain bowls. It is also used in Japanese cooking.

SALAD The term 'salad', which is used in some form in most European languages, is derived from the Latin word *sal*, for salt, since a salad originally meant any food dipped in salt. The most widely used kind of salad is probably that made from raw vegetables (such as lettuce, cucumber, tomato, radish, sweet pepper, spring onion), but an infinite variety of vegetables and fruits can be used, either cooked or uncooked, to make delicious dishes, many of which form a

meal in themselves when combined with a portion of a food such as fish, cheese, egg, cold meat, etc. Salads can also include cooked rice or pasta, nuts, dried fruit and herbs. Savoury salads may be served as starters, main course dishes or accompanying side salads.

No savoury salad is complete without a dressing, even if only a simple vinaigrette. A wide variety can be used (*see* SALAD DRESSING).

Fruit salads are served for dessert. They may be made from a mixture of fresh and canned or dried fruits combined in a sugar syrup or fruit juice. A mixture of three or more fruits is usual, often including exotic fruits such as papaya, mango or lychees.

SALAD BURNET (*see* BURNET)

SALAD DRESSING A term used to describe any of a number of sauce-like mixtures poured over salad. Every salad benefits from being dressed and there are a huge number of dressings to choose from, though basically only two main types – mayonnaise and vinaigrette (French dressing). (*see also* MAYONNAISE)

The dressing can make or mar a salad. The most usual mistake is to use too much dressing, swamping the salad instead of making it appetizing. No surplus dressing should be seen at the bottom of the bowl – there should be just sufficient clinging to the salad ingredients to flavour them. Before dressing a salad, make sure all the ingredients are dry so that the dressing will cling to the salad and will not be diluted and make a watery salad.

Dressing Ingredients

Most salad dressings are made from combinations of oil and vinegar or lemon juice, though other ingredients like yogurt, soured cream and various fruit juices can be used.

Different oils and vinegars have their own distinct flavours. *Olive oil* is traditional for salads and very popular with its distinctive flavour. Virgin oil is best, with its dark green colour and strong rich flavour and aroma. *Corn* or *maize oil* has a bland flavour which is useful with strongly flavoured salad ingredients. *Groundnut (peanut, arachide) oil* is also bland and light, while *soya bean oil* has a strong flavour which some people dislike. *Sunflower and safflower seed oil* are also fairly bland and have a high polyunsaturated content. *Sesame seed oil* is expensive but has a delicate nutty flavour that goes well in dressings, while *walnut oil* – the most expensive of all – has a strong nutty flavour and is thought by many people to be the best of all for salad dressings. *Hazelnut oil* also has a delicate nutty flavour.

Blended vegetable oil and *salad oil* are usually a mixture of different oils and are acceptable in dressings, provided the flavour is not too pronounced.

Wine and cider vinegars are in general more suitable than malt vinegars which tend to mask other flavours in salad dressings. Vinegars flavoured with garlic, herbs such as tarragon, or fruit such as raspberries, add unusual flavours to dressings. You can buy them or make your own more cheaply (*see* VINEGAR).

Dressing a Salad
Some salads need to be dressed in advance so that the flavours have time to blend. This applies particularly to cooked ingredients, which are best dressed when warm so they absorb the flavours while cooling. Others, like a plain green salad, should be tossed in dressing just before serving. If you are serving the salad in individual dishes, you will find it easier to dress the salad in a large bowl and then divide it. Thicker dressings, like mayonnaise and aïoli, may be served separately at the table.

French Dressing (Vinaigrette)
When making French dressing, the proportion of oil to vinegar can be varied according to taste. Here it is in the ratio of three to one. Use less oil if a sharper dressing is preferred.

90 ml (6 tbsp) oil (see above)
30 ml (2 tbsp) vinegar (see above) or
  lemon juice
2.5 ml (1/2 level tsp) sugar
2.5 ml (1/2 level tsp) mustard (whole grain, Dijon,
  French, or English mustard powder)
salt and pepper

Place all the ingredients in a bowl or screw-topped jar and whisk or shake until well blended. The oil separates out on standing, so whisk or shake the dressing again, if necessary, immediately before use. The bottle can be stored in a bottle or screw-topped jar for a few months in the refrigerator, but shake it vigorously just before serving.
Makes 120 ml (8 tbsp)

SALAMANDER A heavy metal instrument that is heated over a gas flame or in a fire until red-hot, then held over the sugar-coated top of a *crème brûlée*, or other dessert, to brown or caramelize the surface.

SALAME (Salami) A type of dry sausage produced in Italy, Hungary and various other European countries. It is made from finely chopped lean pork and pork fat, and is highly seasoned, flavoured with garlic and moistened with red wine. The sausages are air-dried or smoked and, if properly stored, will keep for a very long time. Salame is often eaten as an appetizer or as a lunch dish with other cold meats and salad. It can be filled with a savoury mixture and rolled up, used in open sandwiches, as a pizza topping or as a garnish.

SALLY LUNN A plain type of teacake baked in cake tins of various sizes. Sally Lunns are served hot, split and buttered. Alternatively, they may be served cold, topped with glacé icing.

The name is said to have come from a pastry cook in Bath.

SALMAGUNDI (Salmagundy) An old English supper dish of the eighteenth century, consisting of meat, salad, eggs, anchovy, pickles and beetroot, diced and carefully arranged to form a pattern on a bed of salad.

SALMIS A stew made from game birds; the bird is partly roasted, then cooked with wine or port. A *salmis* may be made with pheasant, partridge or wild duck.

SALMON An important round fish with bright, silvery scales and flesh which is deep pink when raw and pale pink when cooked. Although generally classified as freshwater fish, salmon spend much of their life in the sea, only returning to their freshwater birthplace to spawn. Small salmon returning after just one year are known as grilse.

Salmon are sold whole, weighing from 3–13 kg (7–30 lb), or as steaks or cutlets. When buying a whole salmon, look for a small head and broad shoulders, as the head can represent up to one fifth of the weight.

Home-caught salmon has such a delicious flavour and excellent firm texture that the simplest cooking is best. Whole fish can be baked or poached and steaks and cutlets can be baked, poached or grilled. Canadian, Norwegian, Alaskan and Japanese salmon tend to be less tender and delicate, but can be made more interesting with sauces.

Salmon is in season in England and Scotland from February to August and in Ireland from January to September, but it is imported and sold frozen all year round. Farmed Scottish salmon, reared in large numbers in the remote lochs of the Western Highlands and Islands, are always available. Although salmon farming is helpful in meeting the huge demand for the fish, it is an unnatural and intensive method of rearing salmon which can be unhealthy. The salmon are therefore routinely treated with anti-biotic chemicals to control pests such as sea lice. The farmed salmon are also deprived of their natural diet, normally responsible for their pink colour. To counteract this, a colouring material called canthaxanthin is added to their feed. (*see also* FISH)

Smoked Salmon
Smoked salmon is cold smoked for a long period and is sold ready to eat. Scottish smoked salmon, which is quite pale in colour, is the best quality. Canadian and Pacific smoked salmon are a deeper colour. Thin slices of smoked salmon are considered a delicacy, accompanied by lemon, freshly ground black pepper and brown bread and butter. Smoked salmon offcuts can sometimes be bought at a reduced price and used for pâtés and pastes.

SALMONELLA (*see* FOOD POISONING)

SALMON TROUT (*see* TROUT)

SALPICON The French name given to many different mixtures of chopped fish, meat and vegetables in a sauce, used as stuffings or fillings. It usually means minced or diced poultry or game, mixed with ham or tongue and mushrooms (or truffles) bound with sauce and used for croquettes, appetizers, *bouchée* fillings and canapés. A *salpicon* may also be sweet, made from fresh or poached fruits flavoured with liqueurs, and used for filling various desserts and pastries.

SALSA This word is both the Italian and Spanish for sauce and is applied to a number of international sauces.

SALSICCIA (Luganega) The Italian word for sausage, usually used with reference to a small pork cooking sausage, of which there are many varieties.

SALSIFY (Oyster Plant, Vegetable Oyster) Originating in central and southern Europe, salsify is an unusual vegetable grown for its long, tapering roots. It looks rather like an under-developed parsnip with a white skin and a flavour similar to oysters, hence its various names.

Salsify is a winter vegetable, available from October to March or April. The roots may be blanched and served in a salad, cooked and served *au gratin* or simply tossed in butter and lemon juice and served sprinkled with chopped fresh herbs. (*see also* SCORZONERA)

To select: Choose firm undamaged roots; they bleed badly when broken. Allow 100–175 g (4–6 oz) per person.

To prepare: Scrub and peel the roots. Trim the ends and cut into about 5 cm (2 inch) lengths. Place immediately in a bowl of water with a little lemon juice added, to prevent discoloration.

To cook: Cook in boiling salted water with a little added lemon juice for 25–30 minutes or until tender but still crisp. Drain well. Boiled salsify can be coated in batter and fried to make delicious fritters.

To serve: Toss boiled salsify in melted butter and lemon juice. Serve sprinkled with chopped herbs.

SALT A mineral (sodium chloride) used for seasoning savoury dishes. Sea or bay salt is fairly coarse and is produced by evaporating sea water naturally or over a fire. As it is produced from sea water, it contains iodine. Rock salt is mined or pumped up with water, which is then evaporated off. Table salt (free-flow) is mixed with magnesium carbonate and ground small so that it flows easily. Iodized salt is land salt to which iodine has been added.

Salt (as a compound of sodium and chloride) is necessary for the healthy functioning of the human body, but too much salt can cause high blood pressure. Approximately 70 per cent of the salt we eat is present in food, much of it added during manufacture. The other 30 per cent is added at the table or in cooking. It would seem advisable at least to reduce the amount of salt we eat, by using smaller amounts in cooking and eating fewer products with a high salt content, such as preserved meats and meat products, smoked foods and savoury snacks like salted peanuts. Salt substitutes are available for those who want to reduce their salt intake. These may be low-sodium or sodium-reduced and are bulked out with potassium chloride.

SALT BEEF A type of cured beef, preserved by soaking the whole joint (usually brisket) in a spiced brine. It is cooked and served hot (like silverside) or cold.

SALT COD (*see* COD)

SALT HERRING (*see* HERRING)

SALTING A method of preserving food in dry salt or brine, dating back to Roman times. It was widely used domestically until the advent of refrigeration, sometimes combined with smoking or drying. Home salting is not recommended for fish or meat, but some vegetables, such as French or runner beans, can successfully be preserved in this way. The German speciality *sauerkraut* is made by salting cabbage. Salting is, however, carried out on a commercial basis, producing salted fish, such as cod and herring; salted meat, such as bacon and salt beef; salted nuts, such as peanuts, cashews, etc.

SALTPETRE Saltpetre, or potassium nitrate, is a white, crystalline substance. It is odourless with a piquant, fresh taste. Saltpetre is used extensively in conjunction with common salt for the preservation of meat, such as in pickling and preparing salt and corned beef. It gives a pleasant, reddish colour to the meat. The use of saltpetre is strictly regulated as excessive amounts can be harmful.

SAMBAL One of several foods served in small individual dishes as accompaniments to Indian and Pakistan dishes, particularly curries. Typical *sambals* include chopped tomato, chopped sweet peppers, chutneys, chopped cucumbers, sliced bananas, grated fresh coconut and sliced mangoes.

SAMBUCA An Italian liqueur tasting of elderberry and liquorice. It is traditional to float coffee beans on each glass and to set fire to the liqueur for a few minutes to roast them, and to release their flavour, before drinking the liqueur.

SAMOSA A triangular, deep-fried, savoury pastry, served mainly as a snack in India, but also as a starter. *Samosas* are filled with all kinds of spicy meat or vegetable mixtures; traditional stuffings are made from spiced potato or minced meat. Once deep-fried, they are served warm with an Indian chutney or *raita*.

SAMPHIRE (Glasswort, Rock Samphire) There are two types of this green seashore plant. The first is also known as marsh samphire or glasswort. It is a small plant that grows in European salt marshes. It has green fleshy tips that are harvested in summer and may be used in salads or as a vegetable accompaniment to fish. It may also be served with melted butter, like asparagus, or pickled.

The other type of samphire, known as rock samphire, is a piquant-flavoured succulent plant found along various rocky European coasts. The leaves can be pickled in vinegar or served fresh in salads or cooked in soup or as a vegetable.

SAMSOE (Samsø) Named after the Danish island of Samsoe, this is a firm cheese, made from whole cows' milk. It has a few irregular-sized small holes and a delicate, nutty flavour. The flavour acquires greater pungency as the cheese matures. Samsoe is best used uncooked, and is a popular addition to open sandwiches.

SAND-EEL This small, long fish is found on sandy beaches. It buries itself in the sand at low tide. Sand-eels, gutted and heads removed, can be substituted for elvers (young eels) in recipes. They are often used by anglers as bait.

SAND CAKE A Madeira-type cake made from cornflour, ground rice or potato flour. It is a traditional British tea-time cake.

SANDWICH Two slices of bread enclosing some kind of filling. Sandwiches are said to have been invented in the eighteenth century by John Montagu, Fourth Earl of Sandwich, from whom they take their name, but in fact sandwich-type dishes were popular long before that time. Sandwiches are quick and easy to make and are acceptable at any time. They are also very portable and ideal for packed lunches and picnics. They are also capable of endless variation, and can be highly nutritious if made with wholemeal bread and low-fat spreads and fillings.

Sandwich fillings can be anything from a plain slice of cheese, perhaps with pickle or salad, to an elaborate filling of cold roast beef with horseradish sauce, onion or gherkins and French mustard. Any type of bread can be used, though sliced loaves obviously make sandwich making easier and quicker. French loaves (*baguettes*) are popular cut into chunks, sliced horizontally and filled with cold meats and salad. Wholemeal, granary and rye breads, as well as white bread, are all suitable for making sandwiches. The bread is usually spread with softened butter or a polyunsaturated margarine or low-fat spread. Some sandwiches, such as cucumber sandwiches, are traditionally cut into small shapes, without crusts, and are served at formal teas, while others are thick and chunky, perhaps made with two different fillings and three slices of bread (double decker sandwiches). Hot toasted sandwiches can be made under the grill or in an electric sandwich maker (*see* CONTACT GRILL). Open sandwiches consist of a filling arranged on a bread base. They are popular as buffet party food (*see* SMÖRREBRÖD).

SANDWICH CAKE (*see* LAYER CAKE)

SAPODILLA (Naseberry, Tree Potato, Zapote) This delicious-tasting fruit, also known as Naseberry plum, is grown in the East Indies and Java. The size of a plum with greyish-brown skin, the sweet granular flesh is reddish yellow, with a flavour similar to that of banana and pear. They should only be eaten when ripe, and should feel slightly soft to the touch; hard fruit will ripen at room temperature. Sapodillas are usually eaten as a dessert fruit; the seeds have little hooks and should not be eaten.

SAPSAGO (*see* SCHABZIEGER)

SAPUCAYA NUT (*see* PARADISE NUT)

SARACEN CORN (*see* BUCKWHEAT)

SARDINE The small, round, oily sea fish known as sardines are, strictly speaking, young pilchards, but the name is also applied to the young of other fish (sprats and herrings). The majority of sardines are canned in olive oil, soya oil, brine or tomato sauce, but fresh sardines are becoming more readily available. Sardines can be grilled or baked or fried like smelts, sprats and whitebait. They are available from February to July. (*see also* FISH, PILCHARD, WHITEBAIT)

SARSAPARILLA A flavouring made from the dried roots of a tropical American plant; it was formerly used to make a refreshing still cold drink and is now used to flavour carbonated ones.

SASHIMI A Japanese delicacy of raw seafood, usually served as an hors d'oeuvre. Paper thin slices of raw, colour-contrasting fish fillets, such as flounder, monkfish, sea bass, cod, salmon, tuna and swordfish, are arranged exquisitely on a bed of salad or grated daikon (giant white radish). The presentation is all-important. *Sashimi* is served rather like a fondue with a soy sauce dip, flavoured with mustard, lemon juice, grated root ginger or horseradish. In Japan, the fish are kept alive until the last minute to ensure absolute freshness.

SASSAFRAS This distinctive lauraceous tree originates in the United States. The leaves vary from oval to fig-leaf-shaped and produce attractive autumn colour. The roots, bark and leaves are used to produce a lemon-scented oil with a spicy flavour, which is used in soft drinks, confectionery and ice cream. The dried leaves are used to make filé powder (*see* FILÉ POWDER).

SATÉ (Satay) An Indonesian dish of small grilled or barbecued pieces of marinated meat on fine wooden skewers or saté sticks, served with a peanut sauce. The sauce can be either sweet or fiery with chilli. Fried rice or noodles make the perfect accompaniment.

SATSUMA A small orange citrus fruit related to the tangerine and Japanese in origin. Its shape is distinctly flattened, not round like the tangerine, and it has thick loose skin. In general, satsumas are sweet and juicy, but some can be rather dry and pithy; most are seedless. They are available in the early winter months and are traditionally served at Christmas time. (*see also* TANGERINE)

SAUCE A sauce is used to flavour, coat or accompany a dish and may also be used in the actual cooking to bind the ingredients together. Sauces of all kinds are intended to enhance the foods with which they are served. A good, well-flavoured sauce, simple or elaborate, will add a gourmet touch to any meal. For this reason, it is well worth making your own; commercial packet sauces are often highly seasoned and coloured, as well as more expensive. Once the basic techniques of sauce-making have been mastered, the variations are endless, and original and distinctive sauces can easily be created.

A great deal of mystique is attached to successful sauce-making, but in fact all that is required is a little time and your undivided attention. Roux-based sauces are probably the most common type, but there are also egg-based types and the classic British favourites like bread, mint and apple sauce.

Roux-based Sauces
These are made by melting butter (or another fat), adding flour and cooking, then adding liquid. For a white sauce, the butter and flour, or roux, are cooked but not coloured; for a blond sauce they are allowed to cook to a light biscuit colour; while for a brown sauce the roux is cooked until brown, thus giving the sauce its colour. Brown sauces range from simple gravies made with meat juices to the classic espagnole sauce and sauces based on it. For the best flavour, use home-made beef stock when making brown sauces. (*see also* BÉCHAMEL

SAUCE, CHAUDFROID, DEMI-GLACE SAUCE, ESPAGNOLE SAUCE, GRAVY, REFORM SAUCE, ROBERT SAUCE, SOUBISE SAUCE, SUPRÊME SAUCE, VELOUTÉ SAUCE)

Liquid Choice

For white and blond sauces, such as *velouté*, the liquid used is usually milk or milk and white stock. Brown sauces need meat stock and/or vegetable water. Fish should be served with a sauce made from a liquid produced by boiling up the fish bones in water and adding milk if necessary.

There is no doubt that real stock does add an excellent flavour to sauces. If you are short of time, or do not have any stock, you can use a cube flavoured with beef, chicken, ham, fish or vegetables, but bear in mind that many contain monosodium glutamate and other sodium compounds and give a salty flavour. Check the seasoning. (*see also* STOCK)

White Sauce (Roux method)

15 g (¹/₂ oz) butter or margarine
15 g (¹/₂ oz) flour
300 ml (¹/₂ pint) milk
salt and pepper

Pouring Sauce

Melt the butter in a saucepan, stir in the flour and cook gently for 1 minute, stirring. Remove the pan from the heat and gradually stir in the milk. Bring to the boil slowly and continue cooking, stirring all the time, until the sauce comes to the boil and thickens. Simmer very gently for a further 2–3 minutes. Season with salt and pepper. *Makes 300 ml (¹/₂ pint)*

Coating Sauce

Follow the recipe for pouring sauce above, increasing the butter and flour to 25 g (1 oz) each.

Binding Sauce

Follow the recipe for pouring sauce above, increasing the butter and flour to 50 g (2 oz) each.

One-stage Method

Use ingredients in the same quantities as for pouring or coating sauce above. Place the butter, flour, milk and seasonings in a saucepan. Heat, whisking continuously, until the sauce thickens and is cooked.

Blender or Food Processor Method

Use ingredients in the same quantities as for pouring or coating sauce above. Place the butter, flour, milk and seasonings in the machine and blend until smooth. Pour into a saucepan and bring to the boil, stirring, until the sauce thickens.

Variations

Anchovy sauce Follow the recipe for pouring sauce or coating sauce above, using half milk and half fish stock. Before seasoning with salt and pepper, stir in 5–10 ml (1–2 tsp) anchovy essence to taste, a squeeze of lemon juice and a few drops of red colouring to tint a pale pink (if liked). Serve with fish.

Caper sauce Follow the recipe for pouring sauce or coating sauce above, using all milk or – to give a better flavour – half milk and half stock. Before seasoning with salt and pepper, stir in 15 ml (1 level tbsp) capers and 5–10 ml (1–2 tsp) vinegar from the capers, or lemon juice. Reheat gently before serving with lamb dishes.

Cheese sauce Follow the recipe for pouring sauce or coating sauce above. Before seasoning with salt and pepper, stir in 50 g (2 oz) finely grated Cheddar cheese or 50 g (2 oz) crumbled Lancashire cheese, 2.5–5 ml (¹/₂–1 level tsp) prepared mustard and a pinch of cayenne pepper. Serve with fish, poultry, ham, bacon, egg and vegetable dishes.

Egg sauce Follow the recipe for pouring sauce or coating sauce above, using all milk or (if possible) half milk and half fish stock. Before seasoning with salt and pepper, add a hard-boiled egg, shelled and chopped, and 5–10 ml (1–2 tsp) snipped chives. Reheat gently before serving with poached or steamed fish or kedgeree.

Mushroom sauce Follow the recipe for pouring sauce or coating sauce above. Fry 50–75 g (2–3 oz) sliced button mushrooms in the butter before adding the flour. Serve with fish, meat or eggs dishes.

Onion sauce Follow the recipe for pouring sauce or coating sauce above. Soften 1 large onion, skinned and finely chopped, in the butter before adding the flour. Serve with grilled and roast lamb, tripe and freshly hard-boiled eggs.

Parsley sauce Follow the recipe for pouring sauce or coating sauce above. After seasoning with salt and pepper, stir in 15–30 ml (1–2 tbsp) finely chopped fresh parsley. Serve with bacon, ham and fish.

Egg-based Sauces

Egg yolks rather than flour are the thickening agent for these sauces. They must be cooked very slowly and gently. The water in the double saucepan should be barely simmering; a fierce heat will produce a granular texture and, if overcooked, the eggs will scramble. If not serving immediately, remove the sauce from the heat and keep warm over warm (not hot) water. Traditional egg-based sauces include hollandaise and bearnaise. (*see also* BÉARNAISE SAUCE, HOLLANDAISE SAUCE, MOUSSELINE SAUCE)

Cornflour Sauces

Cornflour is used in a different way to wheat flour. Blend the required amount with a little cold liquid, bring the rest of the liquid to the boil and gradually stir in the cornflour mixture and cook for a few minutes. Cornflour tends to give a more glutinous texture to a sauce than the roux-based method.

White Sauce (Blending method)

For a savoury sauce, use half milk and half stock.

25 ml (5 level tsp) cornflour
300 ml (¹/₂ pint) milk
knob of butter or margarine
salt and pepper

Pouring Sauce
Put the cornflour in a bowl and blend with 75 ml (5 tbsp) milk to a smooth paste. Heat the remaining milk with the butter until boiling, then pour on to the blended mixture, stirring all the time to prevent lumps forming. Return the mixture to the saucepan. Bring to the boil slowly and continue to cook, stirring all the time, until the sauce comes to the boil and thickens. Simmer gently for a further 2–3 minutes, to make a white, glossy sauce. Add salt and pepper to taste.
Makes 300 ml (¹/₂ pint)

Coating Sauce
Increase the quantity of cornflour to 30 ml (2 level tbsp) and blend with 90 ml (6 tbsp) milk.

Arrowroot Sauces

Arrowroot can be used in the same way as cornflour to thicken a clear liquid. It gives the sauce a gloss, unlike cornflour which makes a cloudy sauce. Once added to the sauce, bring to the boil, then remove from the heat.

Vegetable Purée Sauces

Leaf vegetables can be briefly cooked and puréed to make sauces. Root vegetables and pulses need to be cooked until they are really soft. Purées such as onion, need to be thickened with equal quantities of white sauce to give the desired consistency, while others, like pulses, need thinning with stock or their cooking liquid.

Miscellaneous Sauces

There are many other groups of sauces:

Barbecue sauces are usually fairly strongly flavoured with spices, herbs, tomato, onion and Worcestershire sauce. These sauces add piquancy to chops, steaks, chicken and kebabs.

Butter sauces are made solely from melted butter with one or two additions. They are served mainly with fish and vegetables.

Classic Italian sauces include a number of sauces to serve over pasta, such as bolognese sauce (with minced beef), Neapolitan tomato sauce and *pesto* (*see* PESTO).

Traditional British sauces include apple sauce for pork, duck and goose; bread sauce for roast chicken and turkey; cranberry sauce for turkey; Cumberland sauce with red wine or port and redcurrant jelly for gammon, ham and pork; curry sauce for meat, chicken and vegetables; gooseberry sauce for goose, duck and mackerel; mint sauce with vinegar for lamb; raisin sauce for ham, tongue, lamb and duck; tomato sauce for meat, poultry, fish and eggs.

Sweet sauces There are no classic sweet sauces. Sweet white sauces are made by the roux or blending method described earlier, and are probably our most traditional sauces. Others include custard sauce with eggs or custard powder for fruit pies, tarts and flans, steamed or baked puddings (*see* CUSTARD); chocolate sauce with cocoa powder or plain chocolate for puddings and ice creams; hard butter sauces (*see* BRANDY BUTTER); jam sauce for baked or steamed puddings; Melba sauce (*see* MELBA SAUCE); syrup sauce with golden syrup for steamed puddings; sabayon sauce for cold fruit desserts (*see* SABAYON).

SAUCISSE A general French name given to smaller types of fresh sausage that are cooked and, usually, eaten hot. (*see also* SAUSAGE)

SAUCISSON A French name given to larger sausages which are either lightly preserved but still need further cooking, or are ready to eat. The ready-to-eat sausages are often called *saucissons sec* (dried). (*see also* SAUSAGE)

SAUERKRAUT This is cabbage which has been allowed to ferment in salt; it is a favourite dish on the Continent, especially when it is served with sausages. *Sauerkraut* may often be bought ready prepared in delicatessen shops and it is also obtainable in canned form.

SAUSAGE The name sausage is derived from the word salt, referring to the practice of preserving meat with salt. Sausage-making is one of the oldest methods of preserving. Sausages are made in a wide variety of sizes and flavours. Most countries have a sausage-making tradition, but Europe produces the majority. All sausages are preserved in some way, and fall roughly into three categories. (*see also* GERMAN SAUSAGE)

Fresh Sausages
These require cooking soon after buying or making, and storing in the refrigerator. They are usually grilled, fried or baked. Fresh sausages are made from pork, beef, bacon, lamb, venison, turkey, some with herb and spice flavourings. The majority are enclosed in natural casings, made from the cleaned guts of pigs, sheep or cattle. High meat, more than 65 per cent meat, and low fat sausages are becoming increasingly available as a healthy alternative. Fresh sausages are usually smaller sausages with skins, the long, coarse-textured Cumberland sausage being one of the exceptions. Other types of fresh sausage include: links, chipolatas, skinless, breakfast, German *bratwurst*, French Toulouse, English Cumberland, Italian Luganeghe, spiced French, Chinese *lap cheong*, French *andouilles* and *andouillettes*, Algerian *merguez*, Spanish *salchicha* and Greek *Soudzoukakia*.

Medium Keeping Sausages
These have been lightly smoked or brined, and cooked or scalded. Some require further cooking by boiling or steaming, others can be sliced or spread and eaten cold. Types of medium keeping sausage include liver sausage, black and white pudding, French *boudin*, saveloy, frankfurter, Italian *zampone*, German *knackwurst*, German *bratwurst*, German *extrawurst*, Mortadella, *mettwurst*, *bierwurst* and polony.

Long Lasting Sausages
These are made of raw meat, usually pork or beef, which is cured, air-dried and/or smoked. Those with natural casings can last literally for years in a cool, dry place. Salame is the best example of this type of sausage. Others include Italian *peperoni*, German *cervelat*, Polish *kabanos*, Polish *kielbasa*,

French *saucisson fumé aux herbes*, German Land Jager (*Landjager*).

SAUSAGEMEAT A mixture similar to that used for sausages, but not put into skins. It is cheaper and more convenient to buy the meat in this form for sausage rolls, pies or stuffings.

SAUTÉ To cook food in fat to brown it lightly. The word is derived from the French verb *sauter*, to jump, and suggests the action of tossing the food in the hot fat.

The vegetables used in making soups, stews and sauces are often sautéed to improve the flavour of the finished dish. Sauté potatoes are boiled, cut into slices and cooked in a little fat until lightly browned.

SAUTERNES The sweet white wine from the vineyards in the Gironde, near the village of Sauternes. Château Yquem is the best of the Sauternes, which also include Bommes, Barsac, Preignacs and Fargues. Sauternes is not a highly alcoholic wine, the average alcoholic content being 10 per cent. It may accompany fish, poultry and white meat, but is is particularly suitable to serve with the dessert course of a meal.

SAVARIN A rich yeast mixture (similar to a *baba* dough but without the currants or raisins) baked in a ring mould; it is served soaked with a rum syrup and accompanied by cream or fruit salad. The dessert was named after Brillat-Savarin, a famous gastronomic writer of the eighteenth century.

SAVELOY A short, thick sausage made from salted pork, lightly seasoned and coloured red with saltpetre. Saveloys are dried, smoked and sold ready cooked. They are served skinned and sliced as an appetizer or savoury.

SAVORY A herb which comes in summer and winter varieties and is best when fresh. Savory has a distinctive peppery flavour which has a particular affinity with beans and brings out their taste. Use also with egg dishes, tomatoes and other vegetables, soups and cheese.

SAVOURY This term is applied to three different kinds of food. Firstly, the titbits eaten with the fingers, which are often known as cocktail savouries; secondly, the highly seasoned type of dish, frequently hot, which is served after the sweet course and before the dessert at a formal dinner; finally, a more substantial dish which can form the main course of a simple lunch, high tea, supper or a snack meal.

SAVOY CABBAGE (*see* CABBAGE, SAVOY)

SAVOY BISCUITS Small sponge fingers, used particularly for making such desserts as *charlotte russe* (*see* CHARLOTTE RUSSE).

SBRINZ A hard Swiss cheese made from unpasteurized cows' milk. It is dark yellow in colour with a dark rind, and is most suitable for grating and using in cooking.

SCALD (*see* SOLE)

SCALDING Pouring boiling water over fruit (such as tomatoes and peaches) to make it easy to remove skins, and over pork to loosen hairs from the skin or to treat trotters. Food should be removed from the boiling water before it starts to cook. Scalding is also used to treat milk or to cleanse jelly bags.

SCALING Removing the scales from fish. This can be done using an old knife or scallop shell, or with a scaler. (*see also* FISH)

SCALLION (*see* ONION)

SCALLOP (Coquilles St. Jacques, Scollop) Scallops are bivalve molluscs with ribbed shells that are almost circular. There are several types which vary in size; the *great scallop* and the *queen scallop* are the varieties most commonly available in Britain. The colour of their shells varies from whitish, brown, yellow or orange to pinkish or purple.

To select: Look for shells that are tightly closed. If slightly open, tap the shell sharply and, if fresh, they will close up instantly. Do not buy any that do not close. Scallops are in season from October to March. Frozen scallops are available all year from supermarkets.

To prepare: Scrub the scallop shells under cold running water to remove as much sand as possible. Discard any that are open and do not close when sharply tapped. Place on a baking sheet with their rounded sides uppermost. Cook in the oven at 150°C (300°F) mark 2 for about 10 minutes or until the shells open. Set aside and leave until cold.

Using your fingers, gently push the shells slightly apart until there is a gap into which a knife blade can be slipped. Slide the blade through the opening against the rounded upper shell, then gradually ease the scallop flesh away from the top shell.

Detach the scallop from the top shell and prize apart the top and bottom shells by pushing the shell backwards until the small black hinge at its back snaps. Rinse the scallops, still attached to the lower shells, under cold running water to remove as much sand as possible.

Using a small knife, cut and ease away all the grey-coloured beard-like fringe surrounding the scallop. Make sure that you do not detach the orange roe (or coral) and try not to tear the delicate flesh.

Slide the point of a small knife under the black thread on the side of the scallop. Ease this up and gently pull it off, with the attached black intestinal bag. Ease the scallop away from the bottom shell, and wash in a bowl of cold water until all traces of sand have gone. Scallops may be eaten as they are or cooked in a variety of recipes.

Scrub the rounded shells thoroughly to remove all traces of sand and grit; drain carefully under cold running water and gently pat dry with absorbent kitchen paper. They can be used for serving the scallops.

SCALLOPED DISHES Food (often previously cooked) baked in a scallop shell or similar small container; it is usually combined with a creamy sauce, topped with breadcrumbs and surrounded by a border of piped potato.

SCALLOPING (Fluting) Decorating the double edge of a pastry pie with small horizontal cuts which are pulled up with the back of a knife to produce a scalloped effect. Traditionally, sweet dishes should have about 0.5 cm (¼ inch) scallops and savoury dishes 2.5 cm (1 inch) scallops.

SCAMPI (Dublin Bay Prawn, Norway Lobster) This crustacean, which is related to the lobster, has a variety of names. It is known as Norway lobster, *langoustine* in France, *cigale* in Spain and *scampi* in Italy. In Britain, it is usually called Dublin Bay prawn when whole, and the peeled, uncooked tail meat is known as *scampi*.

Scampi can be cooked whole as for lobster (*see* LOBSTER) and served cold with mayonnaise, or the tail meat can be fried or used in hot dishes. It is available all year.

SCARLET RUNNER (*see* BEAN, RUNNER)

SCHABZIEGER (Green Cheese, Sapsago) This unusual green cheese comes from Switzerland. It is made from soured skimmed milk and whole milk and is flavoured and coloured with a type of clover (*see* MELILOT). It is a strong-flavoured, hard cheese that is best grated and used in cooking.

SCHROD (*see* SCROD)

SCHNAPPS (Schiedam, Schnaps) A strong, clear German spirit, reminiscent of gin. It is also made in Scandinavia and the Netherlands; there are many varieties, including aquavit (*see* AQUAVIT). Schnapps should always be served ice-cold. (*see also* HOLLANDS)

SCHNITZEL The Austrian name for a thin slice of meat, usually veal, which is coated in egg and breadcrumbs and fried. (*see also* WIENER SCHNITZEL)

SCONE A light, plain cake, quickly made and containing very little fat, which is baked in a very hot oven or cooked on a griddle, and is usually eaten split open and spread with butter or a filling. Scones can be eaten hot or cold, as a tea-time dish, with morning coffee, or as a base for open savouries for cocktail or supper parties. A scone mixture is sometimes used as a base for pizzas or as a topping for dishes called cobblers (*see* COBBLER). Scones are best eaten fresh, but can be kept in a cake tin for a day, then reheated in the oven or toasted. Scones also freeze very well for up to 3 months.

Oven Scones

These can be made with a variety of flours and other ingredients, such as mashed potato, etc. When a plain flour is used, raising agent is added in the form of cream or tartar plus bicarbonate of soda, or baking powder. The liquid may be fresh or soured milk or buttermilk and may be diluted with water or mixed with golden syrup; eggs may be used with any of these liquids. Salt and sugar are added as required and the scones may, if liked, be flavoured with dried fruit, ginger, cheese or mixed herbs (fresh or dried).

Griddle and Drop Scones

Griddle scones have similar ingredients to the oven type, but are cooked on a hot griddle, electric hotplate or heavy-based frying pan. Griddle scones are best when served warm and spread thickly with butter.

Drop scones, which are thin, light and spongy, are also known as Scotch pancakes; they are made from a type of batter mixture and are also cooked on a griddle, hotplate or heavy-based frying pan. Drop scones are served hot or cold, with butter and syrup or jam. Though northern in origin, they are now equally popular in the south of England.

SCOLLOP (*see* SCALLOP)

SCORING To make shallow cuts in the surface of food in order to improve its flavour and appearance or to help it cook more quickly. Thus, fish has a better flavour if scored before being marinated or soused; the crackling of pork is scored before roasting to prevent it pulling the joint out of shape and to facilitate carving.

SCORZONERA (Black Salsify) Closely related to salsify, this root vegetable looks very similar but has a brownish black skin. It has a stronger flavour than salsify and is at its best in the late autumn. It should be selected, prepared, cooked and served like salsify (*see* SALSIFY).

SCOTCH (*see* WHISKY)

SCOTCH BEAN (*see* BEAN, BROAD)

SCOTCH BUN (*see* BLACK BUN)

SCOTCH EGG Scotch eggs make excellent picnic food or packed lunch fare. Cold, shelled, hard-boiled eggs are coated in seasoned flour, then sausagemeat. Next, they are dipped in beaten egg and breadcrumbs, and finally deep-fried until golden. Serve either hot with a tomato sauce, or cold with salad.

SCOTCH KALE A thick broth or soup, resembling *pot-au-feu*, containing shredded cabbage.

SCOTCH PANCAKE (*see* SCONE)

SCOTCH WOODCOCK The popular name for a light lunch or supper dish consisting of toast spread with anchovy paste and topped with scrambled egg.

SCREWPINE (*see* KEWRA)

SCROD (Schrod) Alternative names for baby cod or halibut. These small fish have a delicate flavour and are very popular along the coast of New England.

SEA BREAM (*see* BREAM)

SEA CUCUMBER A primitive sea creature, looking more like a plant, and belonging to a group of creatures called holothurians. Dried sea cucumber is used in Chinese cooking and is known as trepang.

SEA DATE (Date Mussel) A tiny bivalve mollusc the size, shape and colour of a date. Sea dates are found in the Mediterranean and enjoyed in surrounding countries. They are usually eaten raw.

SEA-EAR (see ABALONE)

SEAKALE This looks like a cross between blanched forced rhubarb and celery. It has crisp, white stalks topped with tiny green leaves. The variety of seakale most commonly available in shops is forced in a greenhouse. Seakale grown outdoors like celery is available in specialist shops in the spring. Seakale stalks have a nutty flavour and should be quite crisp.
To select: Choose stalks which are not discoloured or wilting. Allow 100–175 g (4–6 oz) per person.
To prepare: Trim the stalks and wash well.
To cook: Tie in bunches of five or six stalks as for asparagus (see ASPARAGUS). Steam for 20–25 minutes, or boil in lightly salted water with a little lemon juice for 15–20 minutes. Drain well.
To serve: Serve hot with melted butter, hollandaise or cheese sauce.

SEAKALE BEET (see SPINACH)

SEA LETTUCE (see SEA VEGETABLES)

SEA-MOSS (see CARRAGEEN)

SEA PIE This is not, as the name might suggest, a pie made of fish, but a beef stew with a suetcrust 'lid' cooked on top. The pie is first cooked as a stew in a casserole, then a layer of suetcrust pastry is placed on top of the stew (resting on the food itself, not sealed to the edge of the casserole), the lid of the casserole is replaced and cooking is continued until the meat is tender. The dish is served straight from the casserole.

SEARING Browning meat quickly in a little hot fat before grilling, roasting or stewing.

SEASONED FLOUR Flour mixed with a little salt and pepper, usually used for coating meat or fish before frying.

SEASONING Adding salt, pepper, herbs and spices to a dish for added flavour. The seasoning is usually checked and possibly adjusted towards the end of the cooking time.

SEA TROUT (see TROUT)

SEA VEGETABLES Mostly, this refers to a variety of seaweeds (algae) which have long been used in Japanese cookery, and have recently increased in popularity in other countries too. Other seashore plants can also be classified as sea vegetables, however (see SAMPHIRE).

There are many varieties of seaweed, with differing tastes and textures. Some taste very strongly of the sea, while others are quite mild in flavour. Some, such as agar-agar and carrageen, have gelling properties and are used to produce gum-like substances (alginates) for use in the food industry, and for home-use as a vegetarian alternative to gelatine (see AGAR-AGAR, CARRAGEEN).

Seaweeds are high in protein and rich in minerals and trace elements, particularly iodine, calcium, potassium and iron. They can therefore form an important part of the diet, particularly for vegetarians. They are also high in sodium (salt), however.

Seaweeds are mostly available washed and dried from health food shops. They need a good soaking in clean boiling water before use, partly to remove some of the salt.

Types of Seaweed
Arame comes from Japan and, after gathering, is par-boiled, then dried in the sun before being shredded and packed. After soaking, it can be

Opposite: Squashes (clockwise from top):Golden nugget, Butternut, Custard, Courgette, Pumpkin, Little gem, Acorn
Overleaf: Left, Simnel cake, **Right** (from top to bottom), Pomelo, Ugli fruit
Centre Pages: Fruit and herb vinegars

added to soups and stews or cooked separately in boiling water for 20–30 minutes. It has a mild, sweet flavour, is rich in calcium and can be eaten hot or cold.

Dulse is harvested on the shores of Canada and North America, Iceland and Ireland. It is one of the tougher seaweeds, with large, dark red leaves. After soaking, it should be cooked in boiling water for about 45 minutes, then served as a vegetable. Its strong flavour combines particularly well with potatoes.

Hiziki (hijiki) is another Japanese seaweed. It is sun-dried and coarsely shredded. It has a sweet, delicate flavour and is high in iron and calcium. After soaking, it can be added to soups and stews or cooked separately in boiling water for 30 minutes.

Kelp is a collective name, generally used for a variety of brown seaweeds. Varieties are commonly found on British coasts. It has a good flavour and can be eaten cooked or raw. When cooked with pulses and other foods, it helps to soften them.

Kombu also comes from Japan and comes in thick dark green strips. It is a type of kelp, has a strong flavour and is high in sodium. It can be used to make a stock for soups, or infused to make a tea, as is done in Japan. To cook as a vegetable, cook in boiling water for 30 minutes.

Laver is found around the coasts of South Wales and Ireland. It is red in colour and is shaped rather like spinach. In Wales, it is rolled in oatmeal, fried and served with bacon and eggs as a traditional breakfast dish. It has a very strong, salty flavour. It is also used to make laverbread.

Mekabu is a black-green seaweed from Japan. It is similar to kombu and is used in the same ways.

Nori is the Japanese version of laver. It is used extensively in Japanese cooking and is specially cultivated around the coast of Japan. After drying, it is pressed into thin sheets which can be crumbled over savoury dishes and soups. Its shape also makes it useful for wrapping round stuffings. For crumbling, the sheets of nori first need to be toasted quickly to make them crisp. Nori can also be soaked and cooked as a vegetable in the same way as arame.

Sea lettuce is a green British seaweed which resembles lettuce leaves, as its name suggests. It is also called sea laver or green laver and can be used in similar ways to laver.

Wakame also comes from Japan and looks and tastes very like kombu, though it is somewhat softer. It has a mild taste, reminiscent of ordinary green vegetables. After soaking, it can be shredded for use in salads, or cooked in boiling water for 10–15 minutes.

SEED CAKE A type of Madeira cake, flavoured with caraway seeds and lemon. (*see also* MADEIRA CAKE)

SEITAN A processed form of wheat gluten extracted from a dough by washing under running water. The seitan is then marinated in a flavouring, such as tamari, seaweed and ginger, which turns it a pale brown colour, before being packaged for selling in wholefood shops. It is very rich in protein and can be chopped and added to soups, stews and pâtés. (*see also* GLUTEN)

SELF RAISING FLOUR (*see* FLOUR)

SELSHCAREE A type of bacon popular in northern Europe. It consists of trimmed back bacon cured in spiced brine, then lightly smoked. It is usually boiled and eaten with *sauerkraut*.

SEMOLINA A granular, creamy coloured flour ground from hard wheat, especially the variety known as durum wheat. It has a high protein and gluten content and is the main ingredient in all types of dried pasta. Semolina is also used to make *gnocchi* and is combined with wheat flour to make couscous. Its most familiar use, however, is

Previous Page: Left, Summer pudding; **Right**, Yule log
Opposite: Zabaglione

in a milk pudding. (*see also* COUSCOUS, GNOC-CHI, PASTA)

SERCIAL (*see* MADEIRA)

SEREH (*see* LEMON GRASS)

SESAME OIL (*see* OILS)

SESAME PASTE (*see* TAHINA)

SESAME SALT (*see* GOMASHIO)

SESAME SEEDS These small spice seeds have a rich, sweet, slightly burnt flavour which is enhanced by toasting or frying in butter. They come from a plant that originated in Africa but is now cultivated in most tropical and sub-tropical parts of the world. Most of the sesame seeds found in shops are cream or white in colour, but black sesame seeds are also available from specialist shops. Sesame seeds can be used in salads and dressings, with mashed potato, sprinkled on to fish and chicken dishes, in fruit salads, added to pastry for meat pies and sprinkled on to bread and other baked goods. They are also suitable for sprouting (*see* BEAN SPROUTS). Sesame seeds are also used to produce an oil, a flavouring salt and a paste (*see* GOMASHIO, OILS, TAHINA).

SEVICHE (*see* CEVICHE)

SEVILLE ORANGE (*see* ORANGE)

SHAD (Allis) A European white sea fish of reasonably good flavour, belonging to the herring family. Like salmon, shad migrates from the sea to the rivers for spawning, and is caught during the winter months only. There are several types, varying in length from about 30 cm (12 inches) to 1 metre (3¼ feet).

Shad may be boiled, but is better grilled or baked, either plain or stuffed. When baked, it is served with anchovy, hollandaise or other piquant sauces. Shad may also be pickled, like herrings. (*see also* FISH, HERRING)

SHADDOCK (*see* POMELO)

SHALLOT (*see* ONION)

SHALLOW FRYING (*see* FRYING)

SHARK One of a family of sea fish which includes the dogfish (*see* HUSS) and skate. Although sharks caught for eating are large, they are not of the giant species famed for their ferocious behaviour. Edible varieties of shark include tope, guitar fish and angel fish (*see* ANGEL FISH). It has a good flavour and few bones and is usually sold in steaks. It can be fried or casseroled. Shark's fin, from a species of shark found in the Indian Ocean, is available dried and is used in Chinese cooking, particularly in soups.

SHARK-RAY (*see* ANGEL FISH)

SHARK'S FIN (*see* SHARK)

SHARON FRUIT (*see* PERSIMMON)

SHELL BEAN (*see* BEAN, BROAD)

SHELLFISH The collective name for a wide range of sea creatures caught or farmed for their meat. They can be divided into two different types – molluscs and crustaceans. Molluscs, such as cockles and winkles, have soft bodies and live inside a solid, hard shell. The exceptions are the cephalopods, which belong to the mollusc family, but have no shells. Crustaceans have hard external skeletons, which are segmented to allow for movement. All shellfish, except crayfish, are sea fish. (*see also* BIVALVE, CEPHALOPOD, CRUSTACEAN, MOLLUSC and individual shellfish entries).

Occasionally shellfish and crustaceans become contaminated with toxic algae which can cause illness if consumed. Paralytic Shellfish Poisoning (PSP) is a naturally occurring and naturally variable algal problem, believed to be dependent mainly on weather and sea conditions. In Britain, the period of greatest risk is during the months of May and June, when large increases in populations of the algae concerned occur. Toxin levels are monitored weekly during the period from March to August, results are passed to local Environmental Health authorities and the

Department of Health. Occasionally a warning will be issued by the Department of Health when toxin levels remain high; during this period the consumption of all shellfish, including crustaceans such as crabs, lobsters, shrimps and prawns could cause illness and should be avoided until further notice.

SHEPHERD'S PIE A dish consisting of well-flavoured cooked meat, usually minced but sometimes sliced, with a 'crust' of mashed potato, which is baked long enough to reheat the meat thoroughly and brown the potatoes. If leftover potatoes are used, they should be mashed while still hot. Some people say that only lamb or mutton should be used in a shepherd's pie. (*see also* COTTAGE PIE)

SHERRY Sherry comes from Spanish vineyards around the towns of Jerez de la Frontera, Puerto de Santa Maria and Sanlucar de Barrameda, which is on the coast and where, specifically, Manzanilla is produced.

Sherry is a blend of wines, matured by what is called the *solera* system, to ensure a continuing supply of wines of the same style and quality. There are five main types of sherry.
Fino, driest to the taste, pale gold in colour, this is a wine best drunk chilled.
Manzanilla is a special type of Fino, bone-dry and with a slightly salty flavour.
Amontillado at its finest is a matured Fino, with deep fragrance and a slightly 'nutty' flavour.
Oloroso is tawny-gold sherry with a rich bouquet and not by nature sweet at all, although many are sweetened for export as cream sherries.
Brown sherries are dark and sweet.

SHERWOOD CHEESE A Double Gloucester cheese flavoured with chives and onions (*see* GLOUCESTER CHEESES).

SHIITAKE (*see* MUSHROOM)

SHIN The name given to the lower part of the fore leg of beef (*see* BEEF).

SHIRATAKI (*see* NOODLES)

SHIRRING To bake food (usually eggs) in small shallow containers or ramekin dishes in the oven. Shirred eggs, sometimes called *oeufs sur le plat*, are popular in the United States.

SHOULDER In veal and lamb butchery, this is an alternative name for the joint known as the forequarter (*see* LAMB, VEAL)

SHORTBREAD A thick, crisp cake of 'short', biscuit-like texture, which is particularly associated with Scotland but is widely popular. Recipes vary but all have a high proportion of butter to flour, therefore no liquid is required to bind the mixture. The dough is traditionally pressed into a wooden or earthenware mould to shape it, then turned out on to a baking sheet, but it can simply be shaped into a round on the baking sheet or in a cake tin. It is cut into wedge-shaped pieces to serve, usually sprinkled with caster sugar. Shortbread keeps well if stored in an airtight tin. It can also be frozen.

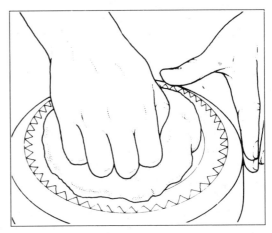

Pressing shortbread dough into a floured, round shortbread mould.

SHORTCAKE This is a dessert of American origin, consisting of two rounds of a rich type of scone, with a filling of fruit and cream. Small individual shortcakes can also be served.

SHORTCRUST PASTRY (*see* PASTRY)

SHORTENING The fat used in a dough, cake mixture, etc., is so named because it makes the mixture 'short', or tender. Such fats and oils as butter, dripping, lard, margarine, suet and nut oils all come under this heading.

Fats differ in their shortening powers; generally speaking, the more 'workable' the fat, the greater its shortening power; thus lard is good for the purpose, but oils lack 'workability' and must therefore be used somewhat differently to obtain good results.

SHOYU (*see* SOY SAUCE)

SHREDDING Grating cheese or slicing raw vegetables into very fine pieces or strips.

SHREWSBURY BISCUIT A traditional English biscuit made by the rolling method (*see* BISCUIT) and cut out into round shapes. The basic dough is flavoured with lemon or orange rind, but variations are flavoured with mixed spice, dried fruit and cocoa powder.

SHRIMP In Britain, only very small crustaceans are called shrimps, as distinct from prawns. They are greyish-brown and translucent when alive and pink when cooked. In America, larger crustaceans – which are known as prawns in Britain – are called shrimps. Shrimps are available fresh nearly all the year. They are also available throughout the year frozen, canned and potted in butter from supermarkets. Fresh shrimps are nearly always ready-cooked when bought as they should be cooked very soon after catching. They may be used in many of the ways prawn are used (*see* PRAWN). Shrimps are also available salted and dried and are much used in Chinese cooking. They can be bought from Chinese food stores.

SHROPSHIRE BLUE CHEESE (*see* BLUE SHROPSHIRE)

SHRUB A bottled cordial, made of different fruits, spirits and sugar, which used to be popular.

SIEVING Pushing food through a perforated sieve to achieve a soft, even texture.

SIFTING Shaking flour and similar dry ingredients through a sieve. If more than one ingredient is being used, they should be mixed before sifting. When making cakes, sifting helps to ensure any raising agent or dry flavouring is evenly distributed throughout the mixture, and also helps to add air to the mixture for a better rise.

SILD A small type of herring, caught in large quantities off the coast of Norway and exported in canned form. They are used like sardines (*see* SARDINE).

SILVER BEET (*see* SPINACH)

SILVER LEAF (*see* VARAK)

SILVERSIDE (*see* BEEF)

SIMMERING Keeping a liquid just below boiling point. The liquid is first brought to the boil, then the heat is adjusted so that the surface of the liquid is kept just moving or 'shivering' – bubbling indicates that the temperature is too high.

Simmering is the method of cooking used for many dishes which require long, slow cooking.

SIMNEL CAKE A spiced fruit cake with a layer of almond paste on top and sometimes another baked in the centre of the cake. Originally, this cake was baked for Mothering Sunday, in the days when many young girls went into domestic service and Mothering Sunday was one of the few days in the year they were allowed home. It is now more usual to have Simnel cake at Easter, and the top of the cake is very often decorated with 11 almond paste 'eggs', representing the 11 faithful Apostles.

SINGEING Using a flame, such as on a lighted taper, to burn off any residual traces of feather on plucked game or poultry.

SINGIN' HINNY A type of griddle cake traditionally associated with Northumberland. It is made from a currant scone mixture shaped into a large round and cooked on a griddle. It is usually cut in half, buttered and eaten while hot. During cooking, the cake is turned on the griddle, at which point it releases a hissing sound – hence the name.

SIRLOIN (*see* BEEF)

SKATE A flat-bodied, kite-shaped sea fish. Its upper side is bluish-grey and its belly is greyish-white. Only the wings (side parts) and nuggets of flesh known as 'nobs' are eaten and they are usually sold already cut from the body. They can be fried, grilled or poached.

The wings of small skate are often sold whole, but those of larger fish are usually sold cut into slices. Pieces of small skate can be cooked without any preparation, but large skate tend to be rather tough and flavourless and are better if first simmered in salted water or *court bouillon* until just tender. They can then be skinned, cut into 5–7.5 cm (2–3 inch) pieces and cooked in any way you wish. (*see also* COURT BOUILLON)

Skate 'nobs' are nuggets of flesh cut from under the boney part of the fish and sold separately. Skate is available from September to February.

SKIMMING Removing froth, scum or fat from the surface of stock, gravy, stews and jam. Use either a skimmer, a spoon or absorbent kitchen paper.

SKINNING Removing the skin from meat, fish, poultry, fruit or vegetables. (*see also* PARING, PEELING)

SKIPJACK (*see* TUNA)

SLING A toddy made with gin and fruit, sometimes known as a gin sling.

SLIPCOTE A soft English cheese produced at Wissenden, Kent. It is made up into little cheeses which are placed between cabbage leaves for a week or two to ripen. When ripe, its skin or coat becomes loose and slips off – hence the name.

SLIVOVITZ A colourless, dry plum brandy, notably from the Balkans.

SLOE Sloes are the small, round, bluish-black fruit of the blackthorn tree which grows wild. They are used to make sloe gin and other country wines. Sloe gin is made by macerating washed and pricked sloes in gin, with sugar and almond flavouring added, if liked, for three months, after which time the liquor should be strained through muslin until clear.

SLOE GIN (*see* SLOE)

SLOW COOKER (*see* ELECTRIC CASSEROLE)

SMELT A small, round silvery sea fish, which can be very oily. Its flavour is similar to trout. Smelt are usually served as a starter. They are prepared by making a small cut with scissors just below the gills and gently pressing out the entrails. They can be threaded on to skewers through the eye sockets and deep-fried, or larger ones may be baked. Smelt are available fresh from November to February.

SMETANA (Smatana, Smitane) A soured cream that is much used in Russia and Eastern Europe, and is also made commercially in Britain from skimmed milk and single cream. It is lower in fat than ordinary soured cream and is a good alternative for using in cooking.

SMOKED CHEESE Most of the smoked cheese on sale in Britain is of Austrian and German origin. It is sold in small rounds or 'sausages' wrapped in brown plastic. The cheese is a pale creamy colour and has a mild, smoky flavour with a very smooth, soft texture. It is excellent served with wine.

SMOKED FISH There are two methods of smoking fish – hot and cold. Cold smoking is done at relatively low temperatures and most cold-smoked fish needs to be cooked before eating. The exception is salmon, which is smoked for a longer period and can be eaten raw. Hot smoking is done at higher temperatures and the fish is ready to eat. Smoking is done more for flavour than as a means of preserving these days, and smoked fish should only be kept in the refrigerator for three to five days. (*see also* COD, EEL, HADDOCK, HALIBUT, etc.)

SMOKED SALMON (*see* SALMON)

SMOKED TURKEY (*see* TURKEY)

SMOKIES These are whole haddock or whiting, gutted and with the heads removed. They are hot-smoked and only need reheating in the oven or under the grill. Originally, smokies came from Arbroath in Scotland and were very dark in colour. Nowadays, they are smoked mechanically and are much paler.

SMOKING The process of preserving meat and fish by drying them in the smoke of a wood fire. It is essential to use a wood fire and sawdust is usually thrown over it to create dense smoke. The flavour given to the food depends on the variety of wood employed: juniper, oak, beech, etc., all give their own special flavour. Some old houses had chimneys specially constructed for smoking; in others a special outhouse was used.

A new form of home-smoker is now available for use domestically. It is particularly suitable for fish, poultry, meat and cheese. Food smoked in this way is for immediate consumption and not for preservation.

SMÖRGASBORD In Sweden and, to a lesser extent, in the rest of Scandinavia, this is the traditional way of serving food. It resembles a buffet meal or cold table and can be either an appetizer course or a full meal.

No matter how elaborate it may be, a *smörgasbord* starts with bread and butter and herring dishes, accompanied by boiled potatoes and followed by one or two small piquant dishes. The plates are then changed and egg dishes are served, with salads, cold meats, perhaps some dishes in aspic, and finally (for a fairly elaborate meal) some hot dishes such as kidneys or meat balls; then come rye bread, cheese and coffee.

SMÖRREBRÖD Danish open sandwiches, consisting of an oblong slice of bread, generously buttered, topped with meat, fish or cheese (often combined with egg or salad ingredients) and attractively garnished. They may be served for lunch, high tea or supper and are very suitable for informal entertaining. In Denmark, rye bread is traditionally used, but other firm-textured types can be substituted. The Danes serve schnapps or lager with *smörrebröd*, with perhaps a liqueur to accompany a cheese *smörrebröd*.

SNAIL (Escargot) A cultivated variety of snail, most esteemed in France; the best are said to be those fed upon vine leaves. Snails have a good flavour (thought by some people to resemble that of oysters), but little food value. After being cleaned and boiled for 5 minutes, the snails are taken from their shells, the intestine is removed and the flesh is stewed with herbs, garlic, etc., before being returned to the shells for serving. They may also be fried or prepared in various other ways. Snails may be bought in cans, ready-prepared and often accompanied by cleaned shells ready for serving.

SNAP BEAN (*see* BEAN, FRENCH)

SNIPE A small bird with a long bill and striped plumage, in season from 15th August to 15th March. Snipe should be eaten really fresh, so make sure when buying that the bill is dry and the feet supple. (*see also* GAME)

SNOEK A fish related to the mackerel, the tuna and the swordfish, which is found in South African waters, in Australian waters (where it is known as Australian barracuda), and off the coast of Chile, where it is called sierra. The fish grows to about 1.2 metres (4 feet) in length and may weigh up to some 8 kg (18 lb).

SNOOK (Robalo) The general name for several varieties of fish resembling pike. It comes from tropical Atlantic and Pacific waters and its well-flavoured, firm flesh is very popular locally.

SNOW The name given to a mixture of sweetened fruit pulp and whisked egg whites; it may be coloured and is usually accompanied by biscuits or sponge fingers. Alternatively, it may be served on a bed of sponge cake previously soaked in a little fruit juice. Apples, apricots and prunes are excellent for use in this way. A similar sweet may be made with gelatine.

SNOW PEA (*see* MANGE-TOUT)

SOAKING Many foods are soaked prior to cooking, especially dried pulses, dried fruits, seaweeds, dried meats and salty gammon joints. Dried pulses should be soaked overnight in cold water, in order to soften them before cooking. Dried fruits may be soaked in cold tea, fruit juice, liqueur or water before stewing. Seaweeds and gammon joints are soaked in boiling water to remove some of the saltiness. (*see also* MACERATE)

SOBA (*see* NOODLES)

SODA BREAD A traditional Irish bread in which the raising agent is bicarbonate of soda combined with buttermilk. The bread is shaped in a round and baked on a baking sheet. It should be eaten while still fresh.

SODA WATER (Carbonated Water) Water aerated with carbon dioxide and sold in bottles or syphons. Soda water also contains a little bicarbonate of soda, the proportion varying in different makes. It is alkaline and may help to neutralize the acidity of the gastric juices. The chief value of soda water, however, is to add sparkle and therefore to accentuate the flavour of certain drinks such as claret cup and lemon squash. It is also used with spirits, such as in whisky and soda.

SODIUM BICARBONATE (*see* BICARBONATE OF SODA)

SODIUM GLUTAMATE (*see* MONOSODIUM GLUTAMATE)

SOFT CHEESE (*see* CHEESE)

SOFT DRINKS Non-alcoholic bottled or canned drinks, ready to drink or requiring dilution. They include carbonated beverages, such as various tonic waters, fizzy lemonades and herbal infusions, as well as still beverages which are ready to drink, and the fruit squashes and drinks which may or may not need dilution. Many soft drinks these days are also sold in cartons. (*see also* FRUIT JUICE)

SOJA (*see* SOYA BEAN)

SOLE The name sole is given to several species of flat fish which resemble the sole of a sandal. Dover sole is the only true sole. Sole is sold whole or as fillets and is excellent grilled, fried, baked or steamed.

Dover sole is considered one of the finest flat fish. It has dark brown-grey skin and pale, firm flesh with a delicious flavour. It is available all year, but at its best from November to April.

Lemon sole is lighter in colour, slightly longer and its head is more pointed than Dover sole. The flesh is more stringy and has less flavour. It is at its best from December to March. Similar fish include the megrim and the scald.

Witch or Torbay sole is shaped like Dover sole and has slightly greyish-pinkish skin. Its flesh is similar to that of lemon sole. It is at its best from August to April.

SOMEN (*see* NOODLES)

SORB (*see* ROWANBERRY)

SORBET Originally an iced Turkish drink the modern sorbet is a soft water ice, flavoured with either fruit or liqueur and sometimes containing whisked egg white. A sorbet was previously served at a formal dinner before the main meat course, to clear the palate, but nowadays it is more often served at informal meals as a refreshing dessert, sometimes combined with diced fruit or fruit salad. Sorbets are too soft to mould and are served in goblets or glasses. (*see also* GRANITA)

SORBITOL A sugar substance that occurs naturally in some types of fruit, including the rowanberry (sorb). It is also produced synthetically and is used as an artificial sweetener (E420) in sugar-free confectionery, ice cream, diabetic jam and pre-packaged cakes. It is often used in combination with saccharin as it masks the bitter flavour of saccharin in drinks. However, its use is strictly limited as some people have a low gastric tolerance to sorbitol. (*see also* ADDITIVE, SWEETENERS)

SORGHUM (*see* MILLET)

SORREL There are several varieties of this green leafy vegetable, but the main ones are wild sorrel and French sorrel. It can be used raw in salads, though it has a distinctive acidic flavour which prevents it being used alone. It also has a high oxalic acid content so should not be eaten in any quantity (oxalic acid inhibits the absorption of certain important minerals). (*see also* JAMAICA FLOWER)

To select: Choose leaves which are small, fresh looking and bright green. Sorrel is not widely available commercially, but is easily grown in the garden. It should be picked when young, before it flowers. Allow 50 g (2 oz) per person.

To prepare: Wash well and tear up any large leaves into smaller pieces.

To cook: Soften the leaves in butter or margarine and use in soups, sauces or as a filling for omelettes.

SOUBISE SAUCE A velvety, onion sauce made by adding puréed cooked onions to a béchamel sauce and enriching it with cream. It can be served with any egg or vegetable dish and is a traditional accompaniment for cutlets.

Soubise Sauce
25 g (1 oz) butter or margarine
2 medium onions, skinned and chopped
300 ml (¹/₂ pint) béchamel sauce (see BÉCHAMEL SAUCE)
15–30 ml (1–2 tbsp) chicken stock or water
salt and pepper

Melt the butter in a saucepan, add the onions and cook gently for 10–15 minutes or until soft. Sieve or purée with the béchamel sauce and the stock in a blender or food processor until smooth. Season and reheat gently for 1–2 minutes before serving.
Makes about 300 ml (¹/₂ pint)

SOUFFLÉ A fluffy dish, either sweet or savoury, which is lightened by the addition of stiffly beaten egg whites. The success of a soufflé depends largely on the adequate whisking of the egg whites and their very light but thorough incorporation into the flour or other mixture. As the soufflé cooks, the air expands making the soufflé rise. Hot soufflés are usually based either on a thick white sauce called a panada (or *panade*), to which egg yolks and flavourings are added, or on a *crème pâtissière*, a sauce in which the egg yolks are already incorporated. Hot soufflés are usually baked and should be eaten at once, as they rapidly sink. Special ovenproof, straight-sided soufflé dishes are available.

Cold soufflés are not true soufflés but mousses which are set in a dish with a collar to give a 'soufflé-like' appearance. When the collar is removed, the soufflé looks as if it has risen like a baked soufflé. Cold soufflés are set with gelatine. The egg whites must be beaten very stiffly and are folded in at the last moment.

To Prepare a Cold Soufflé Dish
Cut a strip of greaseproof paper long enough to wrap right around the soufflé dish with the ends overlapping slightly, and deep enough to reach from the bottom of the dish to about 7 cm (2³/₄ inches) above the top. Tie the paper around the outside of the dish with string, or stick it with

adhesive tape, so that it fits closely to the rim of the dish and prevents any mixture escaping.

Place the prepared soufflé dish on a baking tray. This makes it easier to move the filled dish from the work surface to the refrigerator for chilling.

To take off the paper when the soufflé has set, remove the string and ease the paper away from the mixture with a knife dipped in hot water.

SOUP The term soup covers an astonishingly wide range of liquid dishes, ranging from thin, light consommés to thick hearty stews containing chunks of meat and vegetables which serve as a meal in themselves. Soups are ideal for using up small quantities of leftovers – just put them in a blender or food processor with some stock or other flavoursome liquid – but may also require time and skill to create perfect flavour and texture.

Most soups fall into one of six groups:

Consommés are light soups, consisting of completely clear, well flavoured broths, made from good brown stock. The soup is boiled with an egg white, then carefully strained through muslin or a jelly bag to remove all impurities. Consommé may be served hot or cold, plain or with one of a number of garnishes, in which case the soup takes on the name of the garnish, for example *consommé julienne* (garnished with small strips of even-sized vegetables).

Cream soups are smooth and rich and are usually based on a purée of cooked vegetables enriched with cream or egg yolks. They may also be thickened with flour or cornflour. They include a variety of vegetable soups, such as cream of mushroom, cream of celery and cream of asparagus soup.

Meat soups may contain meat, poultry or offal, such as in Scotch broth, oxtail soup and cock-a-leekie.

Vegetable soups can be thick and chunky, like *minestrone* and winter hotchpotch. Ingredients can include pasta and grains such as barley.

Fish soups include bisques and chowders as well as *bouillabaisse*.

Chilled soups are perfect for summer entertaining. Some of the classic soups are usually served chilled, such as *vichyssoise*, *borshch* and *gazpacho*. They may be served with cubes of ice floating on top.

All types of soup are made with a meat, fish, or vegetable stock of some sort. Stock cubes and stock powders tend to be strong and salty. If you find them too salty, use less of the cube than recommended and do not add extra salt to the soup. If you make your own stock, you can reduce it to quite small quantities which can be diluted with water when required. Concentrated stock also freezes well. (*see also* STOCK)

There is nothing to beat the flavour of a really good home-made soup: you know exactly what has gone into it; there are no additives in the form of preservatives or colourants and you can adjust the flavour and texture to suit your taste. With the use of electrical equipment, soups can easily be processed to exactly the right texture.

Serving Soup

When serving soup as a starter, allow about 150-200 ml (5–7 fl oz) per person, depending on how substantial it is; for soup that is a meal in itself, allow about 250–300 ml (8–10 fl oz), depending on appetites and the ratio of solids to liquid.

Hot soup should be served piping hot, unless it is served with cream added which would curdle. Warm the soup bowls well and, if possible, do not pour it out until the last minute.

Chilled soup should not be so cold that its flavour is masked.

Accompaniments for Soup

Some soups have a traditional accompaniment like the croûtons and grated cheese that are served with French onion soup; others, such as *vichyssoise*, can look pale and bland unless garnished with chopped chives or parsley. Most soups, especially those served in wide soup plates, look better garnished, while others can be bulked out or given a contrasting texture by adding an accompaniment.

Croûtons are fried or toasted cubes of bread. For fried croûtons, cut the bread into small dice and fry in vegetable oil until golden brown. Drain on absorbent kitchen paper and serve in a separate bowl so they remain crisp. For toasted croûtons, toast the bread and then cut it into dice. Croûtons can be made in advance and stored in an airtight container. Add to individual bowls of soup just before eating.

Cream or yogurt swirled on top of a soup just before serving looks attractive.

Rice and pasta make a soup more substantial. Either add cooked leftovers and heat through just before the soup is served, or cook the rice or pasta in the soup itself. Use small pasta shapes in soups or break up large varieties so that it is easy to eat with a soup spoon.

Fried vegetables, such as onion rings, chopped leeks and sliced mushrooms add colour, texture and flavour to bland soups such as potato or bean soups. Cook, then drain well before using.

Bacon rashers, rinded and cut into small strips or dice, can be fried or grilled until crisp and then crumbled. Sprinkle over a soup to add flavour and texture but take care that the soup itself is not salty to start with.

Fresh vegetables, such as thin slices of cucumber, snipped celery tops, or julienne strips of carrot, will decorate the soup and add a crunchy texture. They are best used on chilled soups.

Lemon, thinly sliced, or curls of lemon rind are good with clear soups. Orange slices and rind go well with tomato.

Grated hard cheese, such as Cheddar and Parmesan, melts deliciously into hot soups. Serve separately in a bowl and sprinkle on the soup just before it is served.

Fresh herbs, whether of one or several types, will liven up almost any hot or cold soup. Dried herbs will always look dried if sprinkled on top and are best cooked in the soup itself.

Melba toast is a popular accompaniment which makes a change from bread rolls (*see* TOAST).

SOURDOUGH A type of bread, usually made with a sourdough 'starter', which is made from 15 g ($\frac{1}{2}$ oz) dried yeast, 5 ml (1 level tsp) caster sugar, 450 ml ($\frac{3}{4}$ pint) tepid water and 225 g (8 oz) strong white flour. The starter should be prepared at least three days in advance and stored in the refrigerator until required. The advantage of using a starter is that it can be replenished and used over and over again so that you need never buy more yeast.

To make the starter, sprinkle the yeast and sugar on to 150 ml ($\frac{1}{4}$ pint) of the water and leave until frothy. Mix in the remaining water and flour. Cover and leave in a warm place for 48 hours, stirring occasionally, until it has risen and bubbled, then separated. Stir well before using 225 ml (8 fl oz) starter to make two 900 g (2 lb) loaves. Replenish the remaining starter by beating 100 g (4 oz) strong white flour with 225 ml (8 fl oz) tepid water until smooth. Stir this into the remaining 225 ml (8 fl oz) starter. Leave until the mixture begins to bubble, then cover loosely and refrigerate until required for the next batch of bread.

This method of making sourdough bread is rather old-fashioned now, but was frequently used when yeast was not so readily available. Some is still made this way simply because people like the taste. (*see also* BREAD)

SOURED CREAM (*see* CREAM)

SOURING Adding acid, often in the form of lemon juice, to cream to give it a sour taste. Soured cream made this way can be used in recipes when commercially prepared soured cream is not available. The lemon juice should be added to fresh single cream in the proportions of 15 ml (1 tbsp) lemon juice to 300 ml ($\frac{1}{2}$ pint) cream, then left in a warm place for about 30 minutes before use.

SOUR SOP (*see* CUSTARD APPLE)

SOUSING The name given to a method of pickling in brine or vinegar, and especially used with reference to fish.

SOUTHERN COMFORT The most popular of America's indigenous liqueurs – a Bourbon whiskey flavoured with peaches, oranges and herbs. (*see also* BOURBON)

SOUTHERN LOBSTER (*see* LANGOUSTE)

SOYA BEAN These round, brown beans are the most useful of the pulses nutritionally. They contain first class protein and so do not need to be eaten with a cereal to release it. Soya beans came originally from China and are widely used in vegetarian cookery as a basis for soups and casseroles. Soya beans with a yellow tinge have a mild flavour; the blacker ones taste sweet. Soya beans are also suitable for sprouting (*see* BEAN SPROUTS). (*see also* PULSES)

Soya Bean Products

Soya flour is made from partially cooked, ground soya beans. It is rich in protein and can be mixed with other flours to make bread. Soya flour contains no gluten. It can also be used in cakes, biscuits and puddings.

Soya milk is useful as a substitute for cows' milk (*see* MILK).

Soya oil is a light vegetable oil available for cooking and also used in canned sardines (*see* OILS).

Bean paste is also known as miso and is made from fermented soya beans (*see* BEAN PASTE).

Shoyu and tamari are naturally fermented soy sauces (*see* SOY SAUCE).

Tofu is also known as bean curd and is used in a wide range of sweet and savoury dishes (*see* BEAN CURD).

Soya flakes are similar to flakes produced from grains such as oats and wheat. They are made by toasting and rolling whole soya beans and can be used to make a porridge or biscuits.

Soya grits are crushed and cooked soya beans. They can be used instead of whole soya beans and take less time to cook.

Soya bran is made by removing and grinding the coarse outer layer of soya beans. It can be used in the same way as wheat bran, sprinkled on breakfast cereals or added to savoury dishes to increase dietary fibre.

SOY SAUCE (Soya Sauce) A light or dark brown sauce with a salty, sweetish taste, made from soya beans which have been boiled and then fermented. Light soy sauce has a more delicate flavour and is not as salty as the dark soy sauce. It is widely used in oriental cookery and for flavouring a variety of savoury dishes.

Many proprietary brands of soy sauce are available from supermarkets and shops, but most of these contain sugar and other additives. Shoyu and tamari, on the other hand, are naturally fermented soya sauces, made from soya beans. Shoyu may have barley or wheat added, but true tamari is a by-product of the manufacture of miso (*see* BEAN PASTE), contains no wheat and is therefore suitable for gluten-free diets, but it is quite hard to find. Tamari has a slightly stronger flavour than shoyu.

SPAGHETTI (*see* PASTA)

SPAGHETTI MARROW (*see* MARROW, SPAGHETTI)

SPARE RIBS (*see* PORK)

SPATCHCOCKING A method of preparing a small whole bird for grilling. The bones are left in but the body is opened flat. It is suitable for poussins, spring chickens and guinea fowl. Once cut open and flattened, the bird is held in position with two long skewers threaded across the body.

SPEARMINT (*see* MINT)

SPECK (Spek) This is the German word for bacon but is used more specifically to refer to an extremely fatty type of fat bacon which may be smoked or green. It can be rendered down and used for cooking.

SPECULAAS (Flemish Spiced Biscuits)
Popular in the Netherlands, these biscuits are flavoured with ginger, allspice and cinnamon. They are made from a soft dough that is chilled, then sliced before cooking. They may be decorated with flaked almonds.

SPICES
The dried parts of aromatic plants that are used for flavouring sweet and savoury dishes. Spices may be derived from the fruit, bark, seed, root or flower bud of various plants. Most come from hot countries. Once rare and expensive commodities, spices are some of the most useful ingredients available to every cook.

Most spices are sold dried, either whole or ground. Whole spices which you grind yourself will give a more pungent flavour than those which are ready ground. For the strongest flavour, grind the spice immediately before use. Use either a pestle and mortar or an electric coffee bean grinder. If the latter, first clean it by grinding a slice of stale bread which will absorb the flavour of the coffee. If you grind spices regularly it is worth keeping a separate grinder for this purpose. Spices should be bought in small quantities since their flavour deteriorates quite quickly. Keep them in small, airtight jars stored away from the light as this affects their flavour. Discard spices not used within a year.

(For detailed information about particular spices, see individual entries.)

SPINACH
Delicately flavoured summer spinach is light green in colour with tender leaves and stalks, while winter spinach is much darker green in colour, has coarser-textured leaves and stalks and a much stronger flavour. Spinach is a tasty vegetable to flavour a savoury quiche, and the tender summer variety makes an excellent salad ingredient. It is rich in iron. Spinach is also available frozen, in chopped and puréed forms.

To select: Choose bright green leaves and avoid spinach that is yellow or wilted. Summer spinach should be light green and fine textured, while winter spinach is darker and coarser. Allow at least 225 g (8 oz) per person.

To prepare: Wash spinach well as it collects dirt. Use several changes of water and handle the leaves gently as they bruise easily.

To cook: Summer spinach is best steamed for 5–10 minutes in just the water that clings to it after rinsing. Winter spinach needs to have the stalks and central ribs removed before boiling in salted water for 5–10 minutes or until tender. Drain well and press the water out of the leaves with the back of a wooden spoon.

To serve: Cooked spinach is usually chopped or puréed and served with butter or cream stirred into it. It is often served topped with a poached egg. Some people like to sprinkle vinegar over spinach.

Types of 'Spinach'
As spinach can be quite a difficult vegetable to grow, hardier varieties have been developed. The 'spinach substitutes' available are listed below – plants that produce leaves similar in colour, texture and flavour:

Spinach beet (perpetual spinach) looks very much like winter spinach but the leaves have a coarser centre rib and stalk and a stronger flavour.

Seakale beet (silver beet) is two vegetables in one. Although unrelated, its leaves are used as spinach and the centre ribs cooked as for seakale (*see* SEAKALE).

Good King Henry, with its charming name, is a native of Britain. It has been grown for centuries in cottage gardens and has recently become popular again. The plant produces leaves on a centre stalk rather than many leaves grown from the root.

SPINACH BEET (*see* SPINACH)

SPINY LOBSTER (*see* CRAWFISH)

SPIRIT Beverages made from an alcohol-bearing liquid, the result being of a high alcoholic content. The five main spirits of the world are brandy, whisky, gin, vodka and rum. (*see also* ALCOHOL)

Food can be both preserved and flavoured with spirits; thus fruit is often preserved in brandy or gin, while rum, whisky or brandy may be added to such things as rich cakes and mincemeat. Spirits can also be used in savoury dishes. (*see also* FLAMBÉING)

SPIT-ROASTING Originally, meat was always roasted by turning it on a spit in front of an open fire. Meat cooked in a modern oven, although referred to as a roast, is really baked. However, a rotary spit, worked by an electric motor or a clockwork mechanism, can now be fitted to many cookers. The spit can be situated inside the oven or made into an eye-level fitment, usually combined with the ordinary grill.

This method of cooking is very successful for good cuts of meat, rabbit, poultry and game. It ensures very even cooking and an excellent flavour, as the meat is basted by its own juice. (*see also* ROTISSERIE COOKING)

SPLEEN (*see* MELTS)

SPLIT A type of yeast bun made in the south-west of England which is split open and served with cream or butter and jam. The buns are also known as Devonshire splits. The term can also refer to a liquid measurement of 250 ml (8 fl oz). It is also the popular name for a half-sized bottle of aerated water.

SPLIT PEA Split peas are varieties of dried pea that split naturally during the drying process. There are two main varieties – yellow and green – both of which are sweeter than the whole, dried marrowfat pea. They do not need soaking before cooking and, compared with other pulses, cook very quickly. They can be used to make delicious purées and can be used in soups and pâtés. In particular, they are traditionally used to make pease pudding, a famous north-of-England speciality. (*see also* PULSES)

SPONGE CAKE A light cake, made of eggs, sugar, flour and flavouring and mixed by the whisking method. (*see also* CAKE, GENOESE, VICTORIA SPONGE SANDWICH)

SPOTTED DICK (Spotted Dog) A favourite type of steamed or boiled suet pudding containing currants, sultanas or other dried fruit and shaped in a roll.

SPRAT (Brisling) A fairly small, round sea fish of the same family as the herring. To prepare sprats, wash and draw them through the gills, as for smelt. Coat in seasoned flour and deep-fry for 4–5 minutes. They may also be grilled. They are available from September to March. (*see also* FISH, SMELT)

Smoked Sprats
These are smoked whole and may be grilled or fried.

SPRING GREENS (*see* CABBAGE)

SPRING ONION (*see* ONION)

SPROUTED SEEDS (*see* BEAN SPROUTS)

SPROUTS (*see* BRUSSELS SPROUTS)

SPRUCE A coniferous tree, the essence of which is used to flavour spruce beer. Various types of spruce are used in different parts of the world to make spruce beer. In western Canada, the black spruce is used, while in northern Europe, the Norway spruce is used to make 'black beer'. Spruce oil, derived from yet another species of spruce (also known as hemlock, though not the poisonous variety) is used as a flavouring in root beer, ice cream and chewing gum in North America.

SPRUE (*see* ASPARAGUS)

SQUAB A young pigeon. Confusingly, squab pie is a West Country dish made of meat, apples and onions, having nothing to do with pigeon. (*see also* PIGEON)

SQUASH, FRUIT A drink made from sweetened fruit pulp and intended to be diluted with water. Various types of squash are sold ready-prepared in concentrated form. There are legal requirements for their composition, but unfortunately most of them still contain artificial colourings and flavourings and large amounts of sugar. Some contain very little real fruit or fruit juice, though new high-juice varieties can contain as much as 40 per cent real fruit juice. Popular squash flavours include orange, lemon, 'tropical' and 'exotic'. (*see also* FRUIT JUICE)

SQUASH, VEGETABLE The term used in the United States, and to some extent adopted in Britain, for gourd-like fruits, such as the vegetable marrow. There are many types, some edible and some inedible but used for decorative purposes. Most varieties can be categorized as either winter squashes or summer squashes.

Summer squashes are tender vegetables with thin green skins, soft seeds and pale, watery flesh. Good examples of summer squashes are cucumbers, courgettes and marrows.

Winter squashes have tough, thick skins which are often bright yellow or orange in colour, the best example being the pumpkin. Others are quite unusual in shape, such as the turban squash and the golden nugget.

(For detailed information about particular squashes, see individual entries.)

SQUID (Calamare) Squid is the most commonly available member of the cephalopod group (*see* CEPHALOPOD) of molluscs. There are several species, varying in size. Only the tentacles and body pouch are eaten, the other parts being discarded. The tentacles are usually chopped and the body is either sliced into rings, cut into sections or kept whole and the body stuffed.

A popular practice in Mediterranean cookery is to cook squid in their own ink. For this, the ink sac must, therefore, be removed intact. Small squid can be sautéed, poached, grilled or deep-fried; larger ones are often stewed.

To clean: Rinse the squid, then hold the body in one hand and, with the other hand, firmly pull off the head and tentacles. As you do this, the soft contents of the body will come out and can be discarded. Cut off the tentacles just in front of the eyes. Remove the ink sac from the head, if wished.

Remove the plastic-like quill and rinse the body under cold running water.

Rub the fine dark skin off the outer body and rinse again under cold running water. Cut the flesh into rings or pieces, or keep whole for filling with stuffing.

STANDING TIME In microwave cooking, standing time is an essential part of the cooking process in which the food is usually left to stand after it has been removed from the cooker. Although the food is no longer being cooked by microwave energy, the cooking is being completed by the conduction of the heat existing in the food to the centre. (If standing time were incorporated into the microwave cooking time, the outside of the food would be overcooked, while the centre remained uncooked. This is because microwave energy cooks from the outside in towards the centre.)

The length of standing time necessary will depend on the density and size of the food. Very often (as in the case of potatoes), it will take no longer than the time taken to serve the dish. However, for large joints of meat, poultry and cakes, standing time could be up to 10 minutes; this time should always be followed when specified in a recipe. Meat should be wrapped in foil during standing time to keep in the heat. (*see also* MICROWAVE COOKING)

STAPHYLOCOCCUS (*see* FOOD POISONING)

STAR ANISE The most decorative of spices, this is the star-shaped fruit of an evergreen tree native to China. When dried, the dark husk contains shiny red-brown seeds and the flavour and aroma is one of pungent aniseed. It can be used to flavour stewed and simmered duck, beef, chicken and lamb. It can also be placed under whole fish for steaming. It is used whole and one star is quite sufficient to flavour a large dish. Star anise is one of the ingredients of five-spice powder (*see* FIVE-SPICE POWDER).

STAR FRUIT (Carambola) One of the most recent tropical fruits to arrive on supermarket shelves, the star fruit comes originally from Indonesia and Malaysia but is now grown in many tropical parts of the world, in the United States and in Brazil. It is a fluted, yellow, waxy-looking fruit with a sweet and sour taste. The fruit is shaped in such a way that individual slices are star-shaped – hence the name. To prepare, peel off the skin and slice. Eat on its own or add to fruit salads.

STARCH A form of complex carbohydrate, made up of lots of units of glucose joined together in a long chain. It is the major store of energy in most plants, occurring in roots, tubers and seeds. Starch is present in plants as granules which, when heated in water or steam, swell and burst. The starch then dissolves and thickens the food. Stirring sauces helps to rupture the granules and thus makes the sauce smoother and thicker. Dry heat, as used when toasting bread, breaks down starch into dextrins, producing the characteristic brown colour and slightly sweet taste. Starchy foods such as bread, potatoes, rice, pasta, flour and pulses tend to be low in fat and play an important role in a healthy, balanced diet. During digestion, starch is broken down into glucose which is absorbed into the blood stream and used either at once for energy or stored as fat or glycogen (complex carbohydrate in animals) for use another time. (*see also* CARBOHYDRATE)

STEAK Steaks are lean slices taken from the tenderest cuts of beef. They take very little time to cook and need careful watching to ensure they do not overcook.

Steaks need very little preparation; trim them to a good shape if necessary and wipe well. Cut off excess fat but do not remove it all, then slash the remaining fat at regular intervals before cooking to prevent the edges of the meat curling while it is cooking.

Cuts of Steak

Rump is the joint next to the sirloin and one of the commonest cuts used for grilling or frying. The 'point' is considered the best part for tenderness and flavour.

Fillet, the undercut of the sirloin, is probably one of the best known and the most expensive of the cuts used for grilling or frying. It is very tender, although it usually has less flavour than rump. The 'centre' or 'eye' of the fillet is considered the best part. The fillet is often cut and shaped into small rounds, known as *tournedos*, weighing 100 g (4 oz) each.

A *filet mignon tournedos* is a small round steak, weighing 75 g (3 oz), cut from the end of the fillet. *Châteaubriand*, a thick slice taken from the middle of the fillet, is generally regarded as the most superb cut of all. It can weigh about 350 g (12 oz) and is best grilled.

Sirloin (or *contre-filet*) is cut into two parts. Porterhouse steak is cut from the thick end of the sirloin, giving a large juicy piece that can weigh 800 g (1¼ lb); when it is cooked on the bone it is called T-bone steak. Minute steak is a very thin steak from the upper part of the sirloin, weighing 125–150 g (4–5 oz), without any trimmings of fat.

Entrecôte, by definition, is the part of the meat between the ribs of beef, but a slice cut from the sirloin or rump is often also served under this name.

Steak Tartare is not a cut of steak, but a dish of finely chopped or minced steak served raw. It is garnished with raw egg yolks and served with capers, onions, anchovies and seasoning.

Cooking Steaks

To grill: Brush with melted butter or oil and put under a preheated grill. Cook under a medium heat, turning regularly with a blunt tool so as not to pierce the meat and allow the sealed-in juices to escape.

To fry: If the steak is large, brown it quickly on both sides in shallow hot oil and/or butter, then reduce the heat and cook gently for the remaining time. With small steaks, fry over a medium heat for half the cooking time on one side, then turn and cook for the remaining time. Use a heavy-based frying pan, heating it well before adding the fat.

To serve: To make quick sauces for fried steaks, remove the steaks from the pan and keep warm. Add whisky or brandy to the pan juices and ignite. Pour the sauce over the steaks. Another variation is to add mustard and single or double cream to the pan juices and heat without boiling, then pour over the steaks.

A piece of *maître d'hôtel* butter placed on each steak before it is served is one traditional accompaniment. Other accompaniments are matchstick or chipped potatoes, grilled tomatoes and fried mushrooms, or a green or mixed salad, or green vegetables.

Cooking Time for Steaks

(total in minutes)

Thickness	Rare	Medium-rare	Well-done
2 cm (³/₄ inch)	5	9–10	12–15
2.5 cm (1 inch)	6–7	10	15
4 cm (1¹/₂ inches)	10	12–14	18–20

STEAMING Cooking food in the steam of rapidly boiling water. This is a method of cooking gently, particularly good for fish and vegetables. Special perforated steamers are available; they either fit inside saucepans or stand on top.

STEEPING Covering food with hot or cold water and leaving it to stand, either to soften it or extract its flavour and/or colour.

STERILIZATION The destruction of bacteria in foods by heating to very high temperatures. Such processes cannot be carried out efficiently at home, even when using a pressure cooker.

STERLET A small sturgeon; the swimming bladder is used to make isinglass, the flesh is highly prized and the roe yields the finest-quality caviar (*see* CAVIAR).

STEWING A long, slow cooking method where food is placed in liquid which is kept at simmering point. It is a good method for tenderizing coarse meat and vegetables. Stewing may be done in a saucepan on the hob or in an ovenproof dish or casserole in the oven. (*see also* CASSEROLING)

STICK BEAN (*see* BEAN, RUNNER)

STILTON Stilton, one of the best known of English cheeses, is made in Leicestershire, Nottinghamshire and Derbyshire. It is a white full-cream milk cheese now produced all the year round although it used to be a seasonal cheese. Stilton is semi-hard and has a blue veining, caused by a mould which in most cases is a natural growth throughout the curd, accelerated by the use of stainless steel skewers piercing the cheese to allow the mould to enter. The veins of blue mould should be evenly distributed throughout. The rind, of a dull, drab colour, should be well crinkled and regular and free from cracks. Stilton is at its best when fully ripe, that is four to five months after it has been made. If bought in small quantities, eat it as soon as possible. A whole or half Stilton will keep well if the cut surface is covered and the cheese is kept in a dry, airy larder. It needs no port or anything else added to it. It should be cut in slices from the top and not scooped out.

White Stilton bears little resemblance to blue Stilton in flavour but it is the same cheese before the blue mould has grown into it. It has a slightly crumbly texture and is white in colour without the characteristic blue veining. This cheese has a pleasant, mild flavour.

STIRABOUT The Irish equivalent of porridge.

STIR-FRYING (*see* FRYING)

STIRRER Most microwave cookers have a built-in 'stirrer' positioned behind a splatter guard or cover in the roof of the cooker. This has the same effect as a turntable and it circulates the microwaves evenly throughout the cooker.

STOCK (Fumet) The liquid produced when meat, bones or vegetables are simmered with herbs and flavourings in water for several hours. Stock forms the basis of soups, sauces, stews and many savoury dishes, giving a far better flavour than when plain water is used. It has no food value apart from some minerals. Making stock takes about 3 hours in an ordinary saucepan on the hob; 1–1$\frac{1}{4}$ hours in a pressure cooker. When it is done, allow the stock to cool and remove the layer of fat from the top before storing. Stock can be kept in the refrigerator for up to a week but boil up every 1–2 days.

STOCK CUBES These small cubes are made of a mixture of flavouring ingredients and can conveniently be used to make stock quickly for use in sauces, soups, stews and casseroles. Stock cubes can be crumbled dry into a dish, or they can be dissolved in boiling water. Beef, chicken and vegetable are the most common stock cube flavours. Most of them are very high in salt, a fact which is worth remembering when seasoning.

STOCKFISH (*see* COD)

STOLLEN A type of German Christmas cake, made from a sweetened yeast dough flavoured with dried fruits.

STOUT A beer made with a dark malt. It is thus darker (and sweeter) than most other beers. (*see also* BEER)

STRAWBERRY Widely grown in Britain, strawberries are one of the most popular summer fruits. The juicy red fruit grows round a central hull and has tiny seeds embedded in the outer surface.

When buying, check the base of the punnet for staining as this indicates squashed fruit. Buy plump, glossy berries with the green hulls still attached. Only wash the strawberries just before hulling. Strawberries can be eaten raw or stewed and used in flans, pies and/or made into a variety of preserves.

STRAWBERRY TOMATO (*see* GROUND CHERRY)

STRAWBERRY, WILD (Alpine Strawberry, Fraise des Bois) This variety of strawberry is smaller and more aromatic than its cultivated relative. It is found in woods and on sheltered banks in June and July.

STREGA An aromatic herb liqueur made from a centuries-old Italian recipe combining the flavours of some 70 herbs and barks. It is sometimes used to make a liqueur coffee known as Witch's coffee (*see* COFFEE).

STRING BEAN (*see* BEAN, RUNNER)

STRUDEL PASTRY (*see* PASTRY)

STUFFING Stuffings, also known as forcemeats, fillings and, sometimes, *farces*, may be used in various ways. They can help keep a dry food moist during cooking or absorb some of the fat and juices from meat, or they can be used to extend small amounts of ingredients into meal-sized portions. They can also be used to provide contrasting colour, flavour or texture to a dish. Stuffings are most commonly used with meat and poultry, but they are equally good with fish or vegetables such as peppers and tomatoes.

Stuffing Ingredients

Most stuffings are based on one of the following:
Breadcrumbs Home-made ones are best, as bought ones are dry and powdery and often artificially coloured. Use brown or white bread that is 2–3 days old and make the breadcrumbs in a blender or food processor. A grater can also be used to make them.

Rice This should be cooked first, then mixed with a little fat, egg or liquid to bind it with the other ingredients.

Suet This adds flavour and moisture to a stuffing. Suet is available shredded, ready for use.

Sausagemeat This can be bought fresh from the butcher or supermarket, or frozen.

Small amounts of other foods such as meat, fish, nuts, vegetables and cheese can be added to the basic ingredient. Depending on the mixture, it may need moistening with a little water, stock or fruit juice or binding with a raw egg.

Making Stuffings

When making a stuffing, assemble all the ingredients but do not mix with any egg or liquid until ready to use. Do not put the stuffing into poultry, meat or fish until ready to cook it; bacteria could penetrate the stuffing which might not reach a sufficiently high temperature during cooking to kill them. When cooking food that is stuffed, calculate the cooking time on the total weight of the food to make sure it is cooked thoroughly.

Watchpoints

* Do not make the stuffing too wet or too dry; if too wet it will be stodgy and if it is too dry it will be crumbly and difficult to handle.

* Season stuffings well as the flavours may well need to penetrate a fairly solid mass.

* If stuffing poultry, put the stuffing in to the neck end only as it might not cook sufficiently in the body cavity.

* Do not pack the stuffing too tightly into meat and poultry as the meat juices will make the stuffing swell during cooking and it may burst the skin and spill out. If you have too much stuffing, cook the surplus in a separate casserole or form into small balls and cook with the meat.

* It is not advisable to stuff meat or poultry prior to freezing.

Sage and Onion Stuffing

50 g (2 oz) butter or margarine
450 g (1 lb) onions, skinned and chopped
10 ml (2 level tsp) dried sage
225 g (8 oz) fresh breadcrumbs
100 g (4 oz) medium oatmeal
salt and pepper

Melt the butter in a saucepan, add the onions and sage and fry for 4–5 minutes. Stir in the breadcrumbs. Toast the oatmeal under the grill for a few minutes, then stir into the breadcrumb mixture and season well. Cool before use.

STURGEON Sturgeon is not usually available in Britain; it is found mainly in the Black and Caspian Seas. It is a large sea fish – it can grow up to 4 metres (13 feet) – and has a head covered with hard, boney plates and a snout with four barbels (thin feelers) hanging from it. Its flesh is white to pink with a flavour similar to veal. Caviar is the roe of the female sturgeon (*see* CAVIAR).

Smoked Sturgeon

This is not widely available, but is sometimes sold sliced very thinly. It does not.need cooking.

SUCCOTASH An American dish made from sweetcorn kernels and green or lima beans. The dish is said to be borrowed from the Narrangansett Indians.

SUCROSE (*see* SUGAR)

SUET Suet is most often bought in packets from the supermarket, though at one time it could be bought in a lump from the butcher. Suet consists of the fat from around beef kidneys which is shredded and floured for domestic use. It is used to make many traditional baked goods, such as suetcrust pastry, steamed suet puddings and dumplings. A vegetarian version is also available, made from hydrogenated vegetable oils.

SUETCRUST PASTRY (*see* PASTRY)

SUET PUDDING A number of popular sweet and savoury puddings are made either with suetcrust pastry (*see* PASTRY) or with a somewhat wetter, slacker mixture, which is steamed or boiled in a pudding basin or cloth.

SUGAR A crystalline, sweet-tasting substance obtained from various plants. The type normally used in the home is sucrose, derived both from sugar cane, grown in tropical and sub-tropical countries, and from sugar beet, a root crop grown commercially in Britain. Contrary to some people's belief, beet and cane sugar are of equal value. Other sources of sugar of various kinds are maple trees, sorghum, millet, maize, certain varieties of palm trees and malted substances.

Types of Sugar

Sucrose is contained in sweet fruits and in roots such as carrots, as well as in sugar cane and beet, which give a product that is chemically the same.
Glucose is contained in honey, grapes and sweetcorn.
Fructose is contained in fruit, fruit juices and honey.
Lactose is contained in milk.
Maltose is formed during the germination of any grain.

Food Value of Sugar

Sugar is a good source of energy and is easily and speedily digested. Most of the sugar we eat, or is added to processed foods, is white, highly refined sugar. Sugar cane and beet are reduced to a juice which goes through a long process of evaporation and crystallization to produce, in the end, a product which is 99 per cent sucrose, all the other original nutrients of the cane or beet, including the molasses, having been taken away. On average, a quarter of our calorie intake is supplied by sugar, but these are so-called 'empty calories', bringing with them no vitamins, minerals or fibre. It is easy to consume too many, bringing with it the risk of obesity. Sugar, particularly in the form of sucrose, is also linked with dental caries (tooth decay).

Unrefined or 'raw' sugars do not undergo such a stringent purification process, and still contain some of the molasses from the original cane. As beet molasses is inedible, all unrefined sugars are made from sugar cane. Many people believe that brown sugar is 'healthier' than white sugar – this is not the case.

Commercially Prepared Sugars

Caster sugar is a fine, crystalline white sugar that is mostly used for baking and for sprinkling over fruit, cakes and biscuits.
Granulated sugar is the most commonly used sugar, for adding to coffee and tea as well as for sprinkling on desserts. It is a refined white sugar with coarse granules.
Lump or loaf sugar is refined white sugar which is compressed into cubes for convenient table use.
Preserving sugar is specially made for use in jams, jellies and marmalades. It has large crystals which dissolve slowly and produce less scum than granulated sugar. Some types of preserving sugar have pectin added to them to help produce a good set when making preserves.
Icing sugar is refined white sugar ground to a fine powder. As its name suggests, it is used to make cake icings, as well as sprinkling over cakes and desserts.
Rock candy is a crystal sugar that is often coloured a pale brown for use in coffee. It is also available as rainbow rock candy, the crystals coloured in a variety of colours, for use in coffee and as a cake decoration.
Demerara sugar is named after its place of origin. It is a moist, golden brown crystal sugar which is traditionally an unrefined (raw) cane sugar. However, it is often made from refined sugars with some molasses put back in. It can be used in coffee, baking or desserts.
Barbados or Muscovado sugars are 'raw' cane sugars that are available in light and dark varieties. They are both very soft and sticky and finely grained. Both contain B vitamins (including thiamin) which help to digest them, and small amounts of minerals including calcium and potassium.
Soft brown sugar generally refers to any fine, moist, brown sugar which may be made from a

genuine unrefined sugar but is usually refined sugar combined with some molasses. It is commonly used in baking to produce a rich sweet flavour of molasses.

Molasses sugar is the raw sugar which contains the most goodness. It is the least refined of all the sugars and is very dark and sticky. It is also called Black Barbados or Demerara Molasses. It has a very strong molasses flavour and is best used in baking. (*see also* SWEETENERS)

SUGAR APPLE (*see* CUSTARD APPLE)

SUGAR BOILING Sugar boiling is the basis of nearly all sweet making, and the process is also used to produce caramel for flavouring desserts such as caramel custard. The sugar is first dissolved in the liquid, then brought to the boil. The temperature continues to rise as the water evaporates and the syrup thickens and becomes darker. The following are the most important stages; they are best checked with a sugar thermometer but simple tests are described for those who do not own one.

Smooth 102–104°C (215–220°F) Used for crystallizing purposes. The mixture looks syrupy. To test, dip your fingers in water and then very quickly in the syrup. The thumb will slide smoothly over the fingers but sugar will cling to them.

Soft ball 116–118°C (240–245°F) Used for fondants and fudges. Test by dropping a little of the syrup into very cold water. It should form a soft ball. At 116°C (240°F) the soft ball will flatten when you take it out of the water; the higher the temperature the firmer the ball.

Firm or hard ball 120–130°C (250–265°F) Used for caramels. When dropped into cold water the syrup forms a ball which is hard enough to hold its shape, although still pliable.

Soft crack 132–143°C (270–290°F) Used for toffees. When dropped into cold water the syrup separates into hard but not brittle threads.

Hard crack 149–154°C (300–310°F) Used for hard toffees. When dropped into cold water, a ball of syrup separates into hard and brittle threads that break easily.

Caramel 174°C (345°F) Used for pralines. The syrup turns golden brown when it reaches this temperature.

Avoiding Crystallization

Sugar must be dissolved and boiled with great care, as syrup has a tendency to re-crystallize if incorrectly handled. The main causes of crystallization are agitation of the mixture by stirring or beating whilst the sugar is dissolving, and the presence of undissolved sugar particles during boiling.

Watchpoints
* Make sure the pan is clean.
* Make sure the sugar has dissolved completely before boiling.
* If crystals do form, brush the sides of the pan with a brush dipped in cold water.
* Do not stir the mixture unless the recipe specifically instructs you to. If necessary, use a wooden spatula to tap the grains of sugar on to the bottom of the pan to hasten the dissolving process.
* Once the sugar has dissolved, boil rapidly to the required temperature. When it is reached, remove the pan from the heat immediately.

SUGAR PEAS (*see* MANGE-TOUT)

SUKIYAKI A traditional Japanese dish that is cooked at the table, like a fondue. It usually consists of small strips of meat, vegetables and noodles which are fried in a shallow pan over a table burner. The cooking is usually done by one person, while guests help themselves from the pan as food is cooked.

SULPHUR (*see* PRESERVATIVES)

SULTANA (*see* VINE FRUITS)

SUMAC (Shoomak, Sumach) A purple powder produced from the petals and berries from a variety of sumac shrub that originated in Turkey and is now grown in southern Italy and Sicily. The powder is much used as a tart flavouring in Middle Eastern cookery.

A variety of sumac is also grown in Britain, but its leaves cannot be used in cooking.

SUMMER PUDDING A delicious, striking, cold dessert made by lining a pudding basin with slices of bread and filling with a variety of lightly cooked summer fruits, especially raspberries, redcurrants and loganberries. The fruit mixture is covered with more slices of bread and a weight is placed on top. The pudding is left for several hours; when turned out, the fruit juice has soaked through the bread, producing a deep red-coloured pudding. It is usually served with cream.

SUN-DRIED TOMATOES (*see* TOMATO)

SUNFLOWER A tall annual plant, grown in Britain since the sixteenth century and now cultivated for its seeds which can be eaten as a snack or added to salads and savoury dishes. They are also suitable for sprouting (*see* BEAN SPROUTS). The seeds are also used to produce an oil which can be used in cooking and is also the basis for a variety of polyunsaturated margarines (*see* FATS, OILS).

SUNFLOWER OIL (*see* OILS)

SUPRÊME A French word meaning the best or most delicate part, for example boned breast of chicken is known as a *suprême*.

SUPRÊME SAUCE A white sauce made like a velouté sauce, with a base of well-reduced chicken stock; cream, butter or egg yolks may be added just before the sauce is served. (*see also* VELOUTÉ SAUCE)

SUSHI A traditional Japanese method of serving raw fish. It usually consists of delicacies made from raw fish or shellfish moulded on top of rice 'fingers', seasoned with vinegar and accompanied by a dab of *wasabi* (*see* WASABI). *Sushi* is prepared with great skill and care, always using the freshest of fish. (*see also* SASHIMI)

SUZE (*see* BITTERS)

SWEATING Gently cooking food (usually vegetables) in melted fat in a covered pan until the juices run.

SWEDE (Rutabaga, Swedish Turnip) A heavy, coarse-skinned root vegetable with orange flesh. It is available from late autumn to spring and can be served as a separate vegetable or used in soups or savoury dishes, often combined with bacon or cheese.

To select: Choose small swedes as large ones can be tough. Avoid those with damaged skins. Allow 175–225 g (6–8 oz) per person.

To prepare: Peel thickly to remove all the skin and roots, then cut into chunks.

To cook: Place in cold salted water and boil for 20 minutes or steam for the same amount of time, then mash or purée with a knob of butter and seasoning. Alternatively, roast chunks of swede in hot fat or around a joint of meat for 1–1½ hours at 200°C (400°F) mark 6.

SWEDISH TURNIP (*see* SWEDE)

SWEET BASIL (*see* BASIL)

SWEETBREADS These consist of two portions of a calf's or lamb's thymus gland, are sold in pairs and are considered a delicacy. Calf's sweetbreads are considered the finest, while lamb's are smaller and have a less pronounced flavour. Ox sweetbreads are large, reddish, tough and coarse in flavour. (*see also* BOVINE SPONGIFORM ENCEPHALOPATHY)

Sweetbreads may have a strong smell, which will disappear during preparation. Buy 450 g (1 lb) sweetbreads to serve 3–4 people. Soak in cold water or milk for 2 hours. Rinse. Cover with cold water, flavoured with the juice of half a lemon and 5 ml (1 level tsp) salt and bring to simmering point. Simmer for 15 minutes and plunge into cold water to firm the meat. Remove the tubes and outer membrane. Use as required.

SWEET CICELY An aromatic herb with a sweet flavour resembling aniseed. The herb looks a little like parsley and grows wild in the north of England. It can be used in salad dressings, herb butter, soups, cream desserts, fruit salad and trifles. It also adds sweetness to sharp fruits such as rhubarb and apple.

SWEETCORN Sweetcorn (maize) originated in America but is now grown all over the world. The cob's sweet, nutty flavour is at its best just after picking. Once the cob is cut from the plant the natural sugar in the kernels begins to change to starch and the cob loses the sweetness and flavour quite quickly.

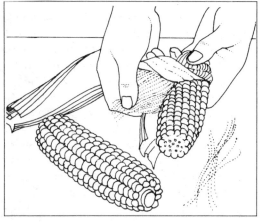

Removing the leaves and silky fibres from cobs of sweetcorn.

Baby sweetcorn, which looks like miniature corn on the cob, is sometimes sold fresh and also in cans. When cooked, the whole cob is eaten.
To select: Choose cobs with a pale green, tightly fitting husk with kernels inside that are not dry. Once they turn gold some of the sweetness goes and the corn becomes tougher. Allow 1 whole cob per person and 75–100 g (3–4 oz) loose corn.
To prepare: Remove the stem, leaves and silky fibres. Trim the pointed end if the corn is not fully formed there. If the corn is to be served off the cob, remove it by holding the cob upright on a work surface and cutting off the corn with a sharp knife, working downwards.

To cook: Cook in boiling unsalted water (salt makes corn tough) for 5–15 minutes, until a kernel comes away from the cob easily. Cook loose corn in a little unsalted boiling water for 5–10 minutes, then drain.
To serve: Serve with melted butter or margarine. The easiest way to eat corn on the cob is from special cob-shaped dishes, holding it between two forks or special tiny skewers. Serve corn kernels hot with melted butter, or cool and add to salads.

SWEETENERS This name may be given to any substance that adds a sweet flavour to foods, including sugar, syrups and a range of other natural and synthetic substances that are added to processed foods and drinks. (*see also* SUGAR, SYRUP)

Of the artificial sweeteners used in processed foods, there are currently 12 permitted for use in Britain, but only three have 'E' numbers and are therefore permitted for use throughout the EC. Among the others are aspartame and saccharin and its derivatives. (*see also* ASPARTAME, SAC-CHARIN, SORBITOL)

SWEET GALE (*see* BOG MYRTLE)

SWEETIE (*see* GRAPEFRUIT)

SWEET LAUREL (*see* BAY)

SWEET PEPPER (*see* PEPPER, SWEET)

SWEET POTATO Despite its name, this vegetable is not related to the potato. It is a tuber vegetable, usually of an elongated shape, though there are some rounder varieties. The flesh is orange orwhite and is sweet and slightly perfumed. The outer skin may be white or purplish red.
To select: Choose sweet potatoes which are small and firm; large ones tend to be fibrous. Allow 225 g (8 oz) per person.
To prepare: Scrub them well and, if boiling, peel after they are cooked as the flesh is soft and rather floury.

To cook: Boil, bake, fry or roast as for ordinary potatoes.

To serve: Serve as a vegetable accompaniment to roast or grilled meats.

SWEETS A general term used with reference to a wide range of sweet confections and chocolates, either home-made or widely available from shops and supermarkets. They include boiled sweets, toffees, caramels, fudges, jellies, etc. Home-made sweets can be roughly divided into fondants; marzipan sweets; fudges; toffees, butterscotch and barley sugar; caramel and nougat; and a miscellaneous group including marshmallows, jellies, Turkish delight and truffles. (*see also* SUGAR BOILING)

Fondants may be made from cooked or uncooked fondant and form the basis of many sweets and chocolate centres. Fondants may be dipped in melted chocolate or decorated with crystallized flower petals, nuts or glacé fruits. (*see also* FONDANT)

Marzipan (almond paste) can be coloured with a wide range of edible colourings and moulded into different shapes. It can be combined with other ingredients such as dried or glacé fruits and nuts and made into a wide variety of sweets. Marzipan sweets can be made with bought or home-made marzipan. (*see also* ALMOND PASTE)

Toffee can be made successfully at home, but it will not be exactly like the commercially-made variety. It does, however, need care and accuracy. Toffees include treacle toffee, peanut brittle, butterscotch, caramels and humbugs. (*see also* TOFFEE)

Fudge is very popular and is also quite simple to make. It can be flavoured with such things as chocolate, coffee, nuts or glacé fruits. Cooked fudge is made from sugar, butter and milk or cream that is gently heated and then boiled to the required temperature. (*see also* FUDGE)

SWEET SOP (*see* CUSTARD APPLE)

SWEET WOODRUFF A white-flowering woodland herb that grows wild over much of Europe. It is not usually used in cooking but is an essential flavouring in the young German wine served on 1st May and known as *Maibowle*. The herb may also be used in punches and fruit cups.

SWISS CHARD This vegetable is related to seakale beet (*see* SPINACH) and is grown mainly for its leaves which look very similar to spinach.

To select: Choose fresh looking bulbs with unblemished ribs and crisp leaves. Allow 225 g (8 oz) leaves per person and 100–175 g (4–6 oz) ribs per person.

To prepare: Prepare in the same way as for winter spinach: wash thoroughly in several changes of water and handle the leaves gently as they bruise easily. Remove the central ribs and prepare in the same way as seakale: trim and wash well.

To cook: Boil the leaves in salted water for 5-10 minutes or until tender. Drain well and press the water out of the leaves with the back of a spoon. Tie the central ribs in bunches of five or six stalks as for asparagus. Steam for 20–25 minutes or boil in lightly salted water with a little lemon juice added for 15–20 minutes. Drain well.

SWISS ROLL A sponge cake (usually Genoese) which is made in a large shallow rectangular Swiss roll tin, then spread with jam, cream or some other filling and rolled up. It is usually served cold as a cake, but it also makes an excellent pudding if served hot, covered with hot coffee, chocolate or fruit sauce. Swiss rolls may be made of plain or chocolate-flavoured sponge cake. (*See also* GENOESE)

SWORDFISH (Marlin) This sea fish is not commonly sold, but when available it is usually sold cut into steaks. It has pale pink flesh which, when cooked, has a firm texture and a good flavour, though it can be dry. Swordfish is best grilled or baked. Marlin are similar fish that can be treated in the same way, though their flavour is not so good. Smoked swordfish is also available and can be cut in very fine slices and served as an hors d'oeuvre.

SYLLABUB An old English dessert, traditionally made by gently pouring fresh milk, in a thin stream, over wine, cider or ale, resulting in a frothy mixture which was sweetened to taste and flavoured with spices and spirit. Alternatively, cream was whisked with wine, sugar and grated lemon rind until frothy; as the froth formed, it was skimmed off, to be served piled on ratafia biscuits. Modern syllabubs are made from whisked egg whites mixed with whipped cream and flavoured with sugar, lemon juice, wine or spirit.

SYRUP A concentrated solution of sugar in water, used in making water ices, drinks and fruit juices. (*see also* GOLDEN SYRUP, MOLASSES, SWEETENERS, TREACLE)

SZECHUAN A large region of western China which has its own style of cooking. Szechuan cooking is hot and spicy, though the people of Szechuan have a preference for multi-flavoured dishes: they like them sour, salty, hot and sweet all at the same time, creating a sophisticated range of flavours. Typical of the type of spice used is the Szechuan pepper (*see* ANISE PEPPER). There is a strong tradition of peasant cooking in Szechuan, with an emphasis on preserving. Szechuan dishes are very often served in Chinese restaurants in Britain.

SZECHUAN PEPPER (*see* ANISE PEPPER)

T

TABASCO (*see* CHILLI SAUCE)

TABBOULEH A Middle Eastern salad made from bulgar wheat flavoured with tomatoes, parsley, lemon and mint. It may be served as a main dish or as an accompanying salad. (*see also* BULGAR)

TABLE D'HÔTE The French name for a meal consisting of a certain number of courses at a fixed price; there is usually some choice of dishes within each course.

TACOS A Mexican dish consisting of corn tortillas which are folded and fried until crisp, then stuffed with a variety of savoury fillings, such as minced meat mixtures, avocado purée or black beans. Tacos may be served as a snack or supper dish.

TAGINE A North African dish which is a type of highly spiced meat or vegetable stew, traditionally cooked in a special earthenware lidded cooking pot of the same name. The stew is usually served with *couscous* which is steamed above the stew as it cooks (*see* COUSCOUS).

TAGLIATELLE (*see* PASTA)

TAHINA (Tahini) A thick creamy paste made from ground sesame seeds and sesame oil, which has long been popular in the Middle East. Light and dark varieties of *tahina* are available, the dark being made from unhusked sesame seeds and having a stronger, slightly bitter flavour. The paste can be used in a variety of savoury dishes or eaten with vegetables, beans or grains.

TAIL The tails of various animals can be eaten and are classed as offal. Oxtail is usually the main type sold, ready-skinned and jointed, though pigs' tails are sometimes available. On an oxtail, there should be a good proportion of lean meat with a layer of firm, white fat. One oxtail weighs about 1.4 kg (3 lb). The joints are usually cooked to make oxtail soup or braised with a selection of vegetables.

Oxtail is sold skinned and jointed. One large oxtail will serve about four people.

TALEGGIO An Italian unpressed, uncooked cows' milk cheese with a pinkish-grey rind and white soft flesh. The flavour becomes stronger and more aromatic as the cheese ripens. Taleggio made with unpasteurized milk is considered a special Italian delicacy.

TAMALE FLOUR (*see* CORN)

TAMARI (*see* SOY SAUCE)

TAMARILLO (Tree Tomato) This large yellow or red hard fruit is related to the tomato and the kiwi fruit. It came originally from South America but is now grown in a number of tropical and sub-tropical countries. It is an acid fruit, rich in vitamin C, and somewhat sour when eaten raw. It should be peeled but the seeds are edible. It can also be added to fruit salads.

TAMARIND (Indian Date) A spice derived from the large pod of the Indian tamarind tree. It is seeded, peeled and pressed into a dark-brown pulp which is sold dried. It is then soaked in warm water and made into a juice that is used to add a sour flavour to chutneys, sauces and curries.

TAMMY To squeeze a sauce through a fine woollen cloth to strain it and make it glossy.

TANDOOR An unglazed clay oven used in ndia. It is heated by charcoal and it is the unique aroma of the clay and the coals that gives the food cooked in it its delicious taste. There are no racks in the oven and food, such as *nan*, is either cooked on the sides of the oven walls or on skewers, on the top. (*see also* NAN)

TANDOORI The Indian name given to dishes cooked in a *tandoor* oven (*see* TANDOOR). Tandoori chicken is the best known of these dishes and is a popular choice in Indian restaurants.

TANGERINE (Mandarin) A small type of orange with loose, easy-to-peel skin, traditionally served at Christmas time. There are many varieties, including the satsuma and clementine, and many hybrids produced by crossing the tangerine with other fruits.

Tangerines have sweet, juicy flesh, making them a popular snack and dessert fruit. Canned segments are available labelled 'mandarin oranges'. (*see also* CLEMENTINE, SATSUMA)

TANGELO (*see* UGLI FRUIT)

TANGLEBERRY A type of huckleberry or blueberry grown in the United States. They are dark blue and very sweet, with a pleasant, sharp flavour. Like all these berries, they are good in pies and puddings, as well as for dessert.

TANNIN The name given to a group of strong acids which occur naturally in certain plants. They have the ability to coagulate and toughen protein and were first used in the leather tanning business. Tannin is present in tea and wine, though it is rarely consumed in any harmful quantity. However, many people prefer to avoid tannin by drinking herbal 'teas' (*see* TEA SUBSTITUTES).

TAPAS The Spanish name for a collection of hors d'oeuvre or cocktail snacks usually served with drinks. They may consist of cubes of meat, vegetable sticks, pieces of filled omelette, olives, seafood and various vegetables in a vinaigrette dressing. The different foods are served in individual dishes from which the food is eaten with the fingers or cocktail sticks.

TAPENADE This is a purée made from capers, black olives and anchovies pounded together with olive oil. It takes its name from the Provençal dialect word *tapeno*, meaning capers. *Tapenade* is sometimes known as 'poor man's caviar'. It can be used as a dip or a spread, or used to fill hardboiled eggs or hollowed-out cucumber. Marinated tuna, lemon juice and mustard are included in some versions.

TAPIOCA This 'cereal' is obtained from the roots of the cassava plant (*see* CASSAVA) which grows in hot countries like Central and South America, Malaysia and the East and West Indies. Tapioca is sold in different forms, the most common being flakes (large, irregularly shaped pieces) and 'pearls', which cook more quickly.

Tapioca contains very little protein and consists almost entirely of starch. Its chief uses are for making milk puddings and moulds.

TARAMA The orange-coloured, salted and dried roe of the grey mullet fish. In Greece it is considered a great delicacy and, as the name suggests, it is traditionally used to make the popular dip *taramasalata*.

TARO Taro tubers (also known as coco yams) are a staple food in the diet of the Pacific islands; they can be boiled or baked or made into a kind of bread. Taro must be well-cooked or fermented before eating, to break down the poisons it contains.

TARRAGON A herb with a distinctive, unusual flavour. There are two main species, the French variety being better than the Russian. It is one of the herbs used in the *fines herbes* mixture and is also used in hollandaise, béarnaise and tartare sauces. It is also used to flavour vinegar, in marinades, with fish and chicken, in aspic glaze, tarragon butter and sauce for ham.

TART A large or small (tartlet) open pastry case with a filling such as fruit, jam, lemon curd, golden syrup, custard, etc. The term is often used interchangeably with 'pie' or 'flan'.

Tarts are usually made of shortcrust or rich shortcrust (flan) pastry. The filling is usually cooked in the pastry case, as for treacle (syrup) or Bakewell tarts, but in the case of a custard tart, the pastry may be baked blind for a short time before the filling is added. (*see also* BAKE BLIND)

Metal, enamel or heatproof glass or china plates, sandwich tins and flan rings may all be used for tarts, and patty tins of various sizes for tartlets.

TARTARE SAUCE A mayonnaise-based sauce flavoured with herbs, chopped capers and gherkins, which is served with fish, salads and such vegetables as globe artichokes.

TARTARIC ACID (*see* CREAM OF TARTAR)

TASSE, EN A French expression meaning served in a cup, and is especially used with reference to soups, etc.

TEA Tea is the leaf of a tropical evergreen shrub, *Camellia sinensis*, whose dried leaves are used to make an infusion with boiling water. The plant has sweet-smelling white flowers and leaves similar to bay leaves. It is grown all around the world in regions with a warm tropical climate and good rainfall, particularly China, India, Indonesia, Sri Lanka and Japan.

While tea has been drunk by the Chinese for centuries, it was only brought to Europe in the seventeenth century by Dutch traders. It was known as 'cha' from the Cantonese word for tea *ch'a*. Even today it is still referred to as a 'cup of cha'. By the end of the seventeenth century the drink was known as 'tay' or 'tee' from the Cantonese Amoy word *tay* for tea.

The flavour of tea depends on the variety and on the soil and climate. For black tea, the most popular type in England, the leaves are wilted, then bruised by rolling to mix the chemical components of the leaf together. During rolling, the colour, flavour and astringency of the tea begin to develop. The leaves are then left in contact with air to ferment so that they are oxidized, developing a red-brown colour. They are then dried, turning black in the process. For green tea, the leaf is steamed and dried without being allowed to ferment. This preserves the green colour and yields a tea with an astringent taste. For brown (oolong) tea, the leaves are partially fermented before drying.

There are three main grades of tea, but these are not classified according to quality but to the size of the leaf: leaf tea takes the longest to release its flavour; tea made from broken leaves makes a strong, quick-brewing infusion; smaller leaf tea, also known as 'dust', is usually blended with other leaves.

A good infusion of tea, properly made, contains little tannin, but tea that has been standing a long time will contain an excessive amount of tannin which can be harmful if drunk in large quantities. (*see also* TANNIN)

To enjoy tea at its best, use freshly drawn cold water (hot or reheated water has a flat, stale taste). Warm the pot and add the tea. The quantity varies according to the type and blend – more is required with China tea than with Indian, for example; an average amount is 10 ml (2 tsp) tea to 450 ml (³/₄ pint) water. Make the tea as soon as the kettle boils or the water will go flat and spoil the taste of the brew. Take the hot teapot to the kettle and pour the boiling water on the leaves, then cover the pot to keep it warm. Allow the infusion to stand for 3 minutes in the case of ordinary Indian teas, 5–6 minutes for China or high-grade Indian tea.

Tea should be served really hot. Milk is usually served with black tea, but lemon can be offered as an alternative.

Types of Tea

Green tea is the original tea. The leaves are picked, withered on racks and steamed to stop oxidization/fermentation. They produce a weak brew which is best drunk on its own or with lemon.

Oolong tea is semi-fermented; after withering, the leaves are slightly crushed and half-fermented before being dried. This process produces a brown tea with delicate flavour.

Black tea is the most popular type sold in Britain. The leaves are fermented until they are a dark brown and then dried.

Smoked tea is produced in much smaller quantities. A few teas are given a distinctive, slightly, tarry flavour by being dried over smoke.

Indian, Ceylon and African teas are sold black and usually blended in the UK and sold under brand names whose flavour and quality are consistent. Most popular brand teas are a blend of different types. The best teas are those sold under their own names. The following is a list of some of the most readily available.

Assam Strong tea with a rich malty flavour. It is often blended with other teas.

Ceylon Although Ceylon is now called Sri Lanka, the tea has not been re-named. A light flavoursome tea with a slightly lemony or astringent taste.

Darjeeling Indian high-grown tea with a brisk flavour. Often known as the Champagne of tea.

Earl Grey A tea flavoured with oil of bergamot. It is best drunk without milk.

English Breakfast Two different types: originally a fragrant blend of China teas, now usually a stronger blend of Ceylon and Assam tea.

Formosa Oolong A delicate semi-fermented tea with a peachy flavour. The only oolong tea to be found in the west.

Gunpowder Top quality green tea which gets its name from its metallic grey sheen.

Jasmine Green or black tea, or a mixture, with jasmine flowers. Goes well with Chinese food and is best without milk or sugar.

Keemun Considered the best China tea available in the UK. Has an aromatic flavour strong enough to be drunk with milk.

Lapsang Souchong A pungent China tea with a smoked flavour.

Lemon tea Usually a black tea mixed with lemon peel and scented with lemon oils. Can be served hot or cold without milk.

Nilgris A bright black tea from India.

TEA SUBSTITUTES 'Teas' or tisanes can be made from a variety of herbs and other plants to drink as a substitute for tea. Herbal teas have become very popular in recent years, although the practice of drinking such infusions is very old, particularly as they have long been thought to have therapeutic effects.

Herbal teas can be made from dried or fresh herbs. It is possible to buy 'tea' bags containing dried herbs which can conveniently be put in a cup, filled with boiling water and left to infuse. Herbs that can be used to make herbal teas include camomile, comfrey, fennel, lemon verbena and mint. Mu tea is a macrobiotic tea made from a combination of natural herbs. Other leaves that can be used are nettle, raspberry leaf, vervain or coltsfoot. A variety of fruits can also be used, including rosehips.

Other 'teas' that are also available, mostly from health food shops, are bancha tea (a macrobiotic green tea that is low in tannin), luaka tea (a black tea from Sri Lanka, also low in tannin) and twig (or kukicha) tea, which is made from the same plant as bancha tea, but uses the twigs instead of the leaves.

TEACAKE A flat, round cake made with yeast dough flavoured with currants and mixed peel. Teacakes are usually split, often toasted, and served with butter.

TEAL One of the smaller wild ducks, averaging about 36 cm (14 inches) in length. Teal, which is highly prized, is in season from September to February and is at its best at Christmas time. One bird per person is served and it is usually roasted in the oven at 180°C (350°F) mark 4 for 25–30 minutes, then served garnished with watercress and slices of lemon. (*see also* DUCK)

TEFF A plant with very small grains about the size of a pin head, which grows in Abyssinia, where a bread made of meal ground from these grains is the staple food.

TEMPEH This is an Indonesian soya bean cake. Soaked and boiled soya beans are treated with a fungus and then left to ferment. *Tempeh* has a rich, cheese-like flavour. It can be cut into thin slices or cubes, then shallow-fried in oil and eaten dipped in tamari (*see* SOY SAUCE). It is also sometimes smoked, giving it a flavour similar to the flavour of bacon.

TEMPERATURES (*see* OVEN TEMPERATURES)

TEMPERATURE PROBE (Food Sensor) In microwave cooking, a temperature probe is used to cook joints of meat and poultry. It enables you to control cooking by the internal temperature of the food, rather than by time. The probe is inserted into the thickest part of the food being cooked and the other end is plugged into a special socket in the cooker cavity. The desired temperature is then selected, according to manufacturer's instructions. When the internal temperature reaches the pre-set level, the cooker switches itself off. It is, however, important that the probe is inserted in the thickest part of the flesh and not near a bone as it will give a misleading temperature reading. For this reason, conventional thermometers inserted after cooking, or conventional techniques for testing to see if food is cooked, are usually more reliable than temperature probes or food sensors.

TENCH This small freshwater fish is a member of the widespread carp family, inhabiting English and Continental rivers. To counteract its muddy flavour, rub it well with salt and leave for a while, then clean and wash it and soak in salted water for 2–3 hours before cooking. Frying and grilling are the most suitable methods.

TENDERIZING Beating raw meat with a spiked mallet or rolling pin to break down the fibres and make it more tender for grilling or frying.

TEPID (*see* LUKEWARM)

TEQUILA A Mexican spirit distilled from *pulque*, a kind of beer.

TERRAPIN A small turtle of North America, the flesh of which is considered a great delicacy.

TERRINE A china or earthenware dish used for pâtés and potted meats. Foods cooked in a terrine are often called by the same name. (*see also* PÂTÉ)

TEXTURIZED VEGETABLE PROTEIN (TVP) A meat substitute made from vegetables, usually soya beans. It generally takes on the flavour of anything it is cooked with.

THIAMIN (*see* VITAMINS)

THICKENING Any substance added to sauces, soups, etc., to give them a thicker consistency and to bind them. In the case of sauces, the thickening or *liaison* is an integral part of the mixture, for example the flour used in many sauces and the butter used in hollandaise and béarnaise sauces. A thickening also ensures a smooth texture and holds heavy ingredients (whether sieved or not) in suspension – without a *liaison*, ingredients such as lentils would separate out from a soup and settle at the bottom. (*see also* LIAISON)

The most commonly used thickeners are types of flour, such as cornflour and potato flour. A paste of butter and flour (known as *beurre manié*) is often added to hot stews towards the end of cooking to thicken and enrich. Arrowroot is used to thicken fruit juices to make a sauce or glaze for fruit flans and other desserts.

(*see also* ARROWROOT, BEURRE MANIÉ, CORNFLOUR, FARINA, FECULA)

THRUSH (*see* BIRD)

THYME This small-leaved herb comes in many varieties, of which garden and lemon are the most common. It has a strong, aromatic flavour and is a constituent of a bouquet garni. Rub over beef, lamb and veal before roasting and use in soups, stuffings, bread sauce, with carrots, onions and mushrooms and in dishes cooked with wine. Lemon thyme is especially good in stuffings for veal and in egg and fish dishes.

TIA MARIA A Jamaican rum liqueur, based on coffee extracts and local spices.

TIENTSIN PEAR A smooth, yellow-coloured fruit which is more rounded than pear-shaped. It is usually still bearing its long stalk when it appears in the shops. Its flesh is crisp and sweet with a typical pear-like grainy texture. It should be peeled, cored and eaten raw.

TIFFIN An Anglo-Indian name for a light midday meal, which is not used very much these days.

TIGER NUT (*see* CHUFA)

TILSIT A European semi-hard cows' milk cheese, originally from East Prussia. It has a firm texture and is made either in wheel shapes or blocks. It has a slightly sharp flavour and is a good cheese for serving with fruit.

TIMBALE A round mould with straight or sloping sides, made from heatproof china or tinned copper and used for moulding meat or fish mixtures. Moulds for hot timbales are lined with macaroni, potato, pastry or breadcrumbs, and cold moulds are lined with aspic and decorated. Dishes cooked in the mould are usually also called timbales. They are a good way of using up leftover meat, fish, vegetables, etc.

TIPSY CAKE A tall sponge cake made into a trifle, but reassembled into its original shape and decorated with split blanched almonds. Its name comes from the fact that it is soaked in wine and fruit juice and it has a tendency to topple sideways in the serving dish in a drunken fashion.

TISANE (*see* TEA SUBSTITUTES)

TOAD-IN-THE-HOLE A dish made by cooking sausages or chopped cooked meat in a Yorkshire pudding batter.

TOADSTOOL (*see* FUNGUS)

TOAST Bread browned on each side under a grill, in an electric toaster or in front of an open fire. Toast is popular breakfast fare, spread with butter or margarine and marmalade. Toast may be buttered immediately on removal from the heat and placed in a covered dish to keep warm, but this uses more butter and it is less digestible than dry toast served with separately butter.

Fingers of hot buttered toast can be spread with savoury pastes such as anchovy, *foie gras*, etc. The popular cinnamon toast is made by sprinkling buttered toast with a mixture of equal quantities of cinnamon and sugar, then returning it to the grill to melt the sugar. (*see also* FRENCH TOAST)

Fingers, rounds, triangles and other shapes of toast are often used as bases for canapés.

TOAST, MELBA This light, crisp toast can be served instead of rolls with soup and other appetizers. It is made by cutting bread into slices 3 mm (1/8 inch) thick and toasting them slowly on both sides, so that they become very crisp; or they can be dried slowly in the oven until crisp and golden in colour. Alternatively, it can be made from thicker slices, toasted on both sides, then split through the middle.

TOCINO The Spanish name for salted fat belly or other fat pork similar to the German *speck*. It is not smoked and is often covered with a layer of crystalline salt. It can be rendered down to produce fat for frying. (*see also* SPECK)

TODDY A drink made with rum or whisky, hot water, sugar and lemon. In tropical countries, the word is also used for the sap of various palm trees and for the fermented drinks made from them.

TOFFEE A sweet confection made from a simple sugar mixture boiled to a temperature of 138–

154°C (280–310°F). The majority of toffees contain butter, but some are made merely from sugar and water, with flavouring and sometimes colouring. (*see also* SWEETS)

TOFU (*see* BEAN CURD)

TOHEROA A shellfish found in the sand of certain beaches in New Zealand. It is very scarce and the greenish-coloured soup made from it is a highly-prized delicacy.

TOKAY The best known Hungarian wine. The highest grades, known as Essencia and Aszu, are sweet and rich; they keep longer than any other wine and may be served with dessert or as a liqueur. They should be stored for some years before using.

Other grades of Tokay are drier and not in the same class, being more like ordinary table wines. The word *puttonys* applied to Tokay indicates the amount of over-ripe grapes used in the making; the higher the number of *puttonys*, the richer the wine.

TOMATE VERDE (*see* TOMATILLO)

TOMATILLO (Ground Tomato Jamberry) This tropical fruit belongs to the same family as the cape gooseberry and Chinese lantern – the physalis fruits. It is about the size of a tomato, with a large version of the papery calyx that is characteristic of this family of fruits. The berry within is green in colour, with rather sticky, bland flesh.

TOMATO Although, strictly speaking, the tomato is a fruit, it is nearly always used as a vegetable. The varieties range in colour from red to orange, yellow to green, and in size from tiny cherry tomatoes to large beef varieties. Tomatoes feature in a wide range of cooked dishes and can also be eaten raw in salads and sandwiches. They can be turned to a purée very easily to make a quick tomato sauce, or they can be used to make attractive garnishes. Peeled tomatoes are also available canned, either whole or chopped. Some brands are flavoured with 'Italian' herbs (oregano and marjoram) and are ideal for using in sauces for pasta, or spreading on a pizza. Sun-dried tomatoes are also available; they have a rich tomato flavour and can be added to casseroles and stews. Unripe green tomatoes can be used to make chutney.

To select: Look for firm tomatoes with not too dark a colour. Unripe tomatoes will ripen quickly in a brown paper bag with one ripe tomato amongst them. Allow 1–2 tomatoes per person if serving raw, 1 large tomato when stuffed. The following are the most common varieties of tomato available:

Red and 'pink' tomatoes are the most common varieties, available all year round but at their best in the late summer.

Spanish tomatoes are large and misshapen with skin varying from deep pink to green. They are good raw or stuffed.

Italian plum tomatoes are bright red with a strong flavour. They are excellent for soups, sauces and casseroles. This is the variety of tomato that is most often canned.

Cherry tomatoes are tiny tomatoes about the size of large marbles, which are very sweet and delicious eaten raw. There are red and yellow varieties.

Beef and marmande varieties are very large, weighing up to 450 g (1 lb) each. They can be stuffed or used raw.

Tigerella tomatoes are streaked with green.

Yellow pear tomatoes are tiny pear-shaped fruits. They are rarely seen but make an excellent garnish when available.

To prepare: For using in cooked dishes, tomatoes often need skinning. Cover with boiling water for about 30 seconds, then plunge into cold water and the skins will peel off. Slice or quarter tomatoes if using raw, or remove the top and the seeds, and cut a small sliver from the base, if they are to be stuffed. Over-ripe tomatoes can be used to make juice or sauces for pasta, meat, fish and vegetables.

To serve: Serve raw tomatoes in salads or with herbs and a dressing as a starter. When stuffed, they may be served hot or cold.

TOMATO PURÉE (Tomato Paste) A deep red, thick tomato paste sold in tubes or tins that is widely used as a flavouring in savoury dishes. It is much thicker and stronger-flavoured than tomato ketchup, which is used as a condiment. (*see* KETCHUP)

TOM COLLINS A famous cocktail made of gin, lemon or lime juice, sugar and crushed ice, shaken together and served with soda water.

TOMME The name of various small cheeses produced during the summer months in Savoie, France. They are mostly made from skimmed cows' milk. *Tomme du Raisin* is ripened in a mixture of grape skins, pips and stalks to give the cheese its distinctive flavour. *Tomme de Savoie* is cylindrical in shape and has a pleasant, light flavour resembling Saint Paulin.

TONGUE Ox and lambs' tongues are the most common, calves' and pigs' usually being sold with the head. Lambs' and ox tongues can be bought fresh or salted. Lambs' tongues weigh about 225 g (8 oz) but an ox tongue can weigh from 1.8–3 kg (4–6½ lb). To prepare lamb's tongue: soak for 1–2 hours if fresh or 3–4 hours if salted. For ox tongue, soak for 2–3 hours if fresh or overnight if salted. Drain, place in cold water (salt only if fresh) and bring slowly to the boil. Skim, then add peppercorns, bay leaves and root vegetables. Simmer gently for 2–3 hours, until tender. Remove the skin carefully and use as required.

TORBAY SOLE (*see* SOLE)

TORTA SAN GAUDENZIO A mixture of the semi-hard blue-veined Gorgonzola and the rich creamy Mascarpone cheeses, which are layered together to form a gâteau effect. A variety flavoured with anchovy and caraway seeds is sometimes available. This cheese is also known as *torta gorgonzola*.

TORTE An international name given to an open tart or rich cake-type mixture baked in a pastry case. An Austrian 'torte' called *Linzertorte* is a flan case of rich spiced pastry filled with raspberry jam, then topped with latticed strips of pastry. A 'torte' can include other ingredients, such as nuts, fruit, chocolate and cream. In France, savoury mixtures are often used as the filling for a rich savoury base. The richness is offset by serving with a green salad.

TORTELLI (*see* PASTA)

TORTELLINI (*see* PASTA)

TORTELLONI (*see* PASTA)

TORTILLA A kind of thin pancake eaten throughout Mexico, which is made from a dough of *masa harina* (*see* CORN). The pancakes are shaped and flattened by hand and cooked on both sides on a hot griddle until dry. Tortillas are served sprinkled with salt and rolled into a cylinder; if they are filled with beans, meat and a spicy sauce before rolling they are called *tacos* (*see* TACOS) (*see also* ENCHILADA).

TOURNEDOS (*see* STEAK)

TOURTE A French name for a round, shallow tart (rather like a flan case), made of puff pastry, which can be filled with a savoury or sweet mixture.

TRACE ELEMENTS These are minerals needed in tiny amounts in the diet for good health. They include iron, zinc, copper, cobalt, iodine, fluorine, chromium, manganese, molybdenum, selenium and vanadium. Other minerals occur in traces in the body, food and water, but as yet are not thought to be essential for life and health. The risk of having too much or too little in the diet is minimized by eating a wide variety of foods in moderation. (*see also* MINERALS)

TRAGACANTH GUM (*see* GUM)

TRAIL A general name given to the entrails of such game birds as woodcock, snipe and plover, and to the red mullet fish, all of which are cooked without removing the entrails, which are considered a delicacy.

TRANSPARENT ICING A very thin icing which is used to give a professional finish to royal-iced cakes. The surface of the royal icing should be very smooth, and if necessary should be shaved with a sharp knife or sanded down and brushed well with a clean, soft brush before the transparent icing is applied. It is rarely used in home cake decorating. (*see also* ROYAL ICING)

TREACLE The sticky fluid remaining after sugar cane has been processed. Black treacle, which contains more of the harmless impurities than light treacle (golden syrup), has a somewhat bitter taste, but it gives a good flavour and colour to treacle tart, gingerbread and some type of rich fruit cake.

Treacle is a good source of energy and it contains useful amounts of calcium and iron. It has considerable sweetening power, though less than sugar, weight for weight, owing to the higher proportion of water which it contains. (*see also* GOLDEN SYRUP)

TREE POTATO (*see* SAPODILLA)

TREE TOMATO (*see* TAMARILLO)

TREPANG (*see* SEA CUCUMBER)

TRESTERBRANTWEIN (*see* MARC)

TRICHINOSIS Infestation with the slender, unsegmented parasitic worm *Tricinella spiralis*, which also lives in pigs, rats and other animals. Humans can get trichinosis from eating infected pork. When measly, worm-infected meat is eaten and digested, the worms bore into the gut and deposit their offspring in the lymph system.

Although meat sold today is subject to vigorous inspection, it is sensible not to eat raw pork. Cooked or smoke-cooked sausages are safe because the worms are killed at temperatures as low as 70°C (140°F) maintained for a period of time. Raw pork products, such as raw ham and salame, are safe as they have been hung long enough for any worms to have been killed by the salt, saltpetre and spices.

TRIFLE A cold English dessert made with a basis of sponge cake soaked in a liquid such as sherry or fruit juice, then covered with layers of fruit, jelly, custard and whipped cream. Trifles for entertaining can be quite elaborately decorated with such things as glacé fruits, angelica, almonds, sweets, small silver balls, ratafias, grated chocolate and whipped cream. They may be made either in a large glass dish or in individual glasses or dishes.

Variations on the traditional trifle can be made with the use of convenience foods, such as instant desserts and canned fruit.

TRIPE Tripe is the stomach linings from the ox. The smooth first stomach is known as 'blanket', the second 'honeycomb' and the third 'thick seam'. All should be thick, firm and white and there is no difference in taste. Tripe is sold bleached (dressed) and partly boiled.

TRIPLE SEC A strong white curaçao (*see* CURAÇAO).

TRITICALE This is a cross between wheat and rye. It was originally developed to create a grain with the generous yield of wheat and the hardiness of rye. It has a higher protein content than wheat and a higher amount of the amino acid lysine. However, crop yields proved disappointing and it failed to become a 'super food'. It comes in the form of flour or flakes, but is seldom available in Britain.

TROUT There are several different varieties of this popular freshwater fish.

Sea trout (salmon trout) is the name given to a trout which has spent a season or more in the sea, living on a diet of crustaceans so that its flesh takes on a pink colour and flavour similar to that of salmon. However, because its flesh is coarser and less succulent than salmon, it is slightly cheaper. Sea trout can be prepared and cooked like salmon (*see* SALMON).

Rainbow trout spends all its life in fresh water. It is readily available all year round, as it is reared on trout farms. The delicate-flavoured flesh may be white or pink. Farmed fish which are fed on shrimps have pinkish-red flesh and may be called 'red trout'. Rainbow trout is sold, and usually cooked, whole. It can be either grilled, poached or baked in foil.

River or brown trout is a golden brown fish with whitish flesh. It spends all its life in rivers or streams and is considered to have a better flavour than rainbow trout. It is rarely available in the shops. It can be cooked like rainbow trout and is at its best from March to September.

Smoked Trout

Smoked trout is usually rainbow trout, cleaned but with the head left on. They are hot smoked and do not need cooking.

TRUFFLE Truffles, which are renowned for their flavour and scent, are actually tubers which grow near the roots of oak and beech trees, particularly in France and Italy. The two main, highly prized, varieties are the black Périgord, which is used as a garnish (for *pâté de foie gras* in particular), and the white Piedmontese, which is usually used grated raw on pasta or egg dishes.

TRUFFLE, CHOCOLATE These mouthwatering sweets are believed to have originated in France, where larger truffles were served as part of a selection of cakes and biscuits. Although traditionally associated with Christmas, smaller truffles make ideal after-dinner sweets. They are usually chocolate based with added flavourings such as rum, brandy, coffee, fruit and nuts. They are usually shaped into small balls and, when completely set, are rolled in chocolate or cocoa powder, coconut or chopped nuts, or dipped in chocolate.

TRUSSING Tying or skewering into shape before cooking. The term is usually applied to poultry and game.

TUBETTI LUNGHI (*see* PASTA)

TUNA (Tunny) Fresh tuna fish is not widely available in Britain – it is usually sold canned. Tuna is a very large, round sea fish with a dark blue back and silvery grey sides and belly. The deep reddish-pink flesh is oily and much heavier than the flesh of other fish, almost like meat. It may be sold in slices or pieces; the belly is the best part. Fresh tuna can be braised, poached in foil, grilled or fried. Canned tuna (often called skipjack tuna) can be used in both hot and cold dishes.

Smoked Tuna

This is not widely available, but may be found in slices of fillet. It does not need cooking.

TUNA FIG (*see* PRICKLY PEAR)

TUNNY (*see* TUNA)

TURBOT Turbot is a flat, diamond-shaped sea fish with very small scales. The upper sides can be various shades of dappled brown. It has creamy white flesh with a delicious flavour and is considered to be the finest of the flat fish. It is usually cut into steaks and grilled, baked or poached – often with wine. It is in season all year, but is best from March to August.

TURKEY A large poultry bird that is readily available, especially at Christmas time. Its meat has an excellent flavour and its size makes it useful for large gatherings.

Buying Turkey

Oven-ready turkeys are available in sizes ranging from 2.3 kg (5 lb) up to 13.5 kg (30 lb).

Frozen turkeys are also available in a range of sizes from 2.3 kg (5 lb) upwards. Some are self-basting oven-ready frozen birds with fat incorporated. Follow the cooking instructions on the wrapping. *Chilled oven-ready* birds are prepared as for frozen but sold chilled and loosely wrapped.

Turkey roast is rolled dark or light meat of a convenient size for about four people. Roast as other joints, allowing about 20 minutes per 450 g (1 lb) at 170°C (325°F) mark 3.

Turkey steaks look similar to gammon steaks. They can be fried or grilled.

Turkey escalopes are thin slices carved from the breast of the bird for frying or grilling.

Turkey drumsticks, wings and thighs can be either roasted or casseroled.

Turkey chops are cut from the top of the drumstick or the thigh and can be grilled, fried or casseroled. They are sold fresh or frozen.

Turkey casserole meat is sold in packs of dark or light meat. It needs less cooking time than stewing beef, veal or lamb and there is no fat to trim.

Turkey sausages are made from turkey meat with a little pork fat and flavoured with herbs and spices. They can be bought fresh and frozen.

Turkey burgers are also flavoured with herbs and spices and come plain or coated with crumbs. When cooked they shrink less than beefburgers because of their low fat content.

(For information on jointing, boning, storing and trussing turkey, *see* POULTRY. *see also* CARVING)

Roasting Turkey

When roasting a turkey, remember you are cooking two different types of meat, the delicate light breast meat, which must not be allowed to dry out, and the darker leg meat which takes longer to cook. The turkey must be roasted long enough for the legs to cook so frequent basting is necessary. To calculate the required size of turkey, use the following guidelines: 3.6–5 kg (8–11 lb) serves 10–15; 5–6.8 kg (11–15 lb) serves 15–20; 6.8–9 kg (15–20 lb) serves 20–30.

1 oven-ready turkey
stuffing
a little melted butter or vegetable oil
salt and pepper
streaky bacon rashers, rinded (optional)

Wash the inside of the bird and stuff at the neck end before folding the neck skin over. Make the turkey plump and as even in shape as possible, then truss it with the wings folded under the body and the legs tied together. Weigh the turkey and calculate the cooking time, allowing 20 minutes per 450 g (1 lb) plus 20 minutes. Place the turkey in a roasting tin, brush with melted butter and sprinkle with salt and pepper. Place streaky bacon rashers over the breast to prevent it from becoming dry, if wished. Roast in the oven at 180°C (350°F) mark 4, basting from time to time. Put a piece of foil over the bird if it shows signs of becoming too brown. Serve with gravy and bread sauce. Small sausages, bacon rolls and watercress may be used to garnish the turkey. Cranberry sauce is a traditional sharp accompaniment.

TURKEY EGGS (*see* EGGS)

TURKISH COFFEE (*see* COFFEE)

TURKISH DELIGHT A popular jelly-like sweet. The genuine Turkish delight sold in the East is made with dextrin or dextrinized flour and is flavoured and perfumed with flower essences, but a fair substitute can be made by using either gelatine or cornflour. (*see also* SWEETS)

TURMERIC A spice derived from the dried root of a plant of the ginger family. Whole pieces of turmeric are available – they look like fresh ginger but are bright orange inside the peel – but it is most commonly sold ground. It has an aromatic, slightly bitter flavour and should be used sparingly in curry powder, pickles and relishes and to colour cakes and rice dishes.

TURNIP A root vegetable with a thick skin and white or yellow flesh. Sweet, tender, early turnips are slightly mustard flavoured. They have green and white skins and are sold from April to July. Maincrop turnips, which are available for the rest of the year, have thicker skins and coarser flesh. Young turnips can be served raw, sliced thinly or grated into salads.

To select: Choose turnips that are smooth and unblemished. Allow 175–225 g (6–8 oz) per person.

To prepare: Peel young turnips thinly, older ones thickly, then slice, dice or cut into chunks.

To cook: Place in cold salted water and boil for 20–30 minutes or until tender

To serve: Young turnips may be cooked whole, but older ones should be cut up and served either in chunks or mashed. Their strong flavour benefits from being mashed with an equal part of mashed potato or carrots. Use older turnips sparingly, diced or thinly sliced, in soups and casseroles.

TURNIP, SWEDISH (*see* SWEDE)

TURNOVER A large or small piece of pastry, folded over on itself and containing a filling of fruit, mincemeat, jam or some savoury mixture. Apple turnovers are particularly popular.

TURNTABLE To ensure even cooking in a microwave cooker, food should be turned; a turntable built into the floor of the cooker does this automatically. However, it is still sometimes necessary to reposition food by hand. Some cookers are also equipped with automatic stirrers which are situated in the roof of the microwave.

TURTLE Various types of saltwater turtles are found in the warmer seas of the world and other types inhabit the rivers and lakes of the New World.

Turtles vary in size and the so-called green turtle from the South Atlantic, which is used to make the famous turtle soup, may weigh several hundred pounds. The soup must be made from freshly killed turtles, so for this reason, and because the method of making the soup is very complex, it is out of the question except for commercial firms or for skilled staff catering for special functions.

Ready-made turtle soup may be bought in bottles or cans and a version may be made from canned or diced turtle. The soup should be served accompanied by forcemeat balls.

TUSCARORA RICE (*see* RICE)

TVP (*see* TEXTURIZED VEGETABLE PROTEIN)

TZATZIKI A Greek salad of yogurt and cucumber flavoured with mint. It is usually served with warm pitta bread. Different versions of this salad are found in the countries stretching from the Near East to India. The Turkish version is known as *cacik*, and the Middle Eastern version is called *raita*.

U

UDDER Rarely available these days, the fatty white meat of cow's udder was once quite popular. It was also, at one time, used in Italy as an ingredient in pasta stuffings.

UDON (*see* NOODLES)

UGLI FRUIT (Tangelo) A very large hybrid citrus fruit produced by crossing a tangerine with a grapefruit. It is round and knobbly in shape with thick, coarse yellowish-brown or yellowish-green skin. The thick skin is easily peeled off to reveal large segments. The fruit has a rich, fragrant flavour and very few pips.

UMBELLIFER The *umbelliferae* family of plants have umbrella-shaped flower clusters on stalks of equal lengths arising from a common point. Carrots, parsnips, celery and celeriac all belong to the umbellifer group, as do the herbs chervil, angelica and parsley, and the spices ajowan, anise, caraway and cumin.

UMBLES The edible entrails of a deer or other animal, which used to be made into a pie – hence the expression 'to eat (h)umble pie'.

UMEBOSHI PLUMS A variety of pickled plums from Japan. They have a tart, salty flavour and are popular served at the end of a meal to aid digestion. They can also be cooked with grains or added to savoury dishes.

UNDERBERG (*see* BITTERS)

UNLEAVENED BREAD (*see* FLATBREAD)

UPSIDE-DOWN PUDDING This is made by lining a baking tin or dish with fruit and placing a sponge mixture over it, so that when the pudding is cooked and turned out, the fruit decoration will be on top. Fruits such as apricots, prunes, peaches and pineapple are especially suitable for this purpose, as they keep their shape well. Fresh or canned fruit may be used. To give variety, the sponge mixture may be flavoured with ginger, chocolate or lemon. When it is served as a pudding it should be accompanied by a sauce made from the fruit juice, thickened with arrowroot, or by cream.

URD BEAN (*see* BLACK GRAM BEAN)

USQUEBAUGH The Celtic form of the word whisky, meaning literally 'water of life'. It is also the name of an Irish liqueur made of whisky or brandy flavoured with spices and infused overnight. (*see also* EAU-DE-VIE)

V

VACHERIN A fairly elaborate dessert, consisting of a 'basket' made of meringue, or macaroon mixture, built up in rings on a pastry base, which is filled with cream or ice cream and fruit. It is also the name of a Jura cheese; a soft runny cheese with a firm rind, usually served with cream.

VALENCAY A soft French goats' milk cheese. It is usually made in a small pyramid shape.

VAN DER HUM A South African liqueur, flavoured with the South African tangerine or *naartje* (*see* NAARTJE).

VANILLA A spice derived from the dried pods of a climbing orchid. The long, thin, black pods are sold whole or are made into a synthetic bottled flavouring. Infuse a pod in the milk or cream when making custard or sweet sauces.

VANILLA ESSENCE True vanilla essence is extracted from vanilla pods. It is not widely available but is sold at some high-class food shops and herbalists. It may be sold as an essence or natural vanilla. Vanilla flavouring, which is made from an ingredient in clove oil, is sold in supermarkets. Both can be used to flavour sweet dishes, particularly to bring out the flavour of coffee and chocolate.

VANILLA SUGAR This is made by leaving a vanilla pod in a jar of caster sugar so that the flavour of vanilla is absorbed by the sugar. Vanilla sugar can be used in ice creams, chocolate and coffee dishes and custards.

VARAK (Silver Leaf) This unusual decorative ingredient is unique to Indian cooking. To make *varak*, tiny pellets of silver are placed between sheets of tissue paper, which are then enclosed in a leather pouch which is beaten with a heavy, metal hammer. This effectively flattens the pellets into paper-thin sheets. These sheets are spread on finished desserts and on festive meat and rice dishes. *Varak* is not only used for its decorative effect but, as it is edible, can provide essential minerals in the diet. A gold version of *varak* is also sometimes used.

VEAL The meat of a young calf. As it comes from a young animal the flesh is comparatively light in colour and should be fine-textured, pale pink, soft and moist. The pale colour of the meat is considered a sign of good quality and calves are often given a diet of nothing but milk so that their meat will be pale. Avoid really flabby, wet meat. The fat – of which there is very little – should be firm and pinkish or creamy white. Veal bones make excellent jellied stock or gravy when simmered – they give the special flavour to veal stews and fricassees. The best known veal dishes are the Italian *osso buco* and the Austrian *wiener schnitzel*.

Cuts and Methods of Cooking

Leg is a prime cut, used mainly for escalopes (also known as *schnitzels*) for frying. Occasionally, leg is sold as a small joint for roasting. (**3**)

Fillet, which is usually the most expensive cut, is sold in a piece for roasting. It can also be cut in thin slices, which are beaten and fried. It is also sold as medallions. (**2**)

Knuckle, usually sold as *osso buco*, already sawn into 5 cm (2 inch) pieces, for stewing. (**5**)

Loin is usually sold as cutlets (with rib in) and chops. It can be boned and sold as entrecôte steak. Otherwise it is rolled for roasting. (**6**)

Shoulder is usually boned and rolled into oyster and shoulder roasting joints. The oyster cut is slightly leaner than the shoulder. (**1**)

Breast is usually the least expensive. It is divided into breast and flank joints, boned and rolled and sometimes ready-stuffed for roasting. (**4**)

Pie or diced veal consists of trimmings and small pieces of shoulder, breast, neck or knuckle, bought ready cut up. This needs long slow cooking.

Best neck is a good-value cut. It can be chined and roasted on the bone, or boned, stuffed and rolled for roasting, or used for braising and stewing.

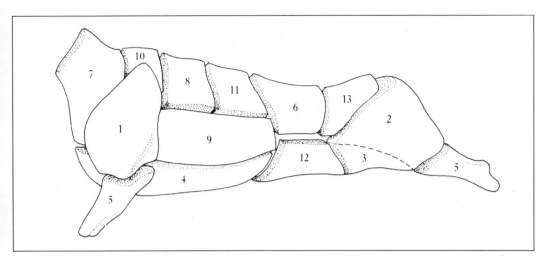

Major cuts of veal to be found at your butcher.

Cutlets can be cut if the 'eye' muscle is sufficiently large. (**8**)

Neck is a stewing cut which needs slow, moist cooking. It can be cut into small peices for pies. (**7**)

Ribs, when boned, are sliced and braised or casseroled. (**9**)

Middle neck is usually sliced into cutlets for braising. (**10**)

Cutlets are trimmed neatly of most fat and used for grilling or frying. (**11**)

Flank is a tough cut that can be stewed or minced and cooked slowly for a long time. (**12**)

Rump is a tender cut usually sliced into excalopes or medallions to be fried or grilled. (**13**)

Roasting Veal

For succulent meat with less shrinkage, roast veal at 180°C (350°F) mark 4. Weigh the joint as it is to be cooked, that is on the bone or boned and rolled or stuffed, and put it in a shallow roasting tin, preferably on a grid. Cook for 25 minutes per 450 g (1 lb), plus 25 minutes. (*see also* CARVING, MEAT)

VEGAN A person who practises a strict form of vegetarianism, eating a wide range of plant foods but no products of animal origin. With the excep-

tion of vitamin B12, which may be low in intake, all the nutrient requirements can be met by such a diet only with careful planning and the use of as wide a selection of foods as possible. Good quality protein can be obtained from cereals, legumes, peas, beans and nuts. Vitamin B12 is found only in foods of animal origin with the exception of miso, tempeh, baker's yeast, brewer's yeast and fortified soya milks. If such foods are not eaten regularly in sufficient amounts, a supplement may be needed. Calcium can be obtained from nuts (especially almonds), soya (beans and milk), dried fruit and dark green vegetables. (*see also* VEGETARIANISM)

VEGETABLE GELATINE (*see* AGAR-AGAR)

VEGETABLE MARROW (*see* MARROW)

VEGETABLE OYSTER (*see* SALSIFY)

VEGETABLE PEAR (*see* CHAYOTE)

VEGETABLE SPAGHETTI (*see* MARROW, SPAGHETTI)

VEGETARIANISM This term covers a wide range of eating habits, based around the avoidance of meat. Lacto-vegetarians include milk and milk products in their diet but avoid meat, poultry, fish and eggs. Lacto-ovo-vegetarians include milk, dairy products and eggs but no flesh foods. Vegans consume no animal foods or food products at all. Partial vegetarians include anyone who excludes some groups of animal foods but eat others, for example non-meat eaters who eat fish and/or poultry; non-red-meat eaters. As nuts, pulses and dairy products supply the same range of essential nutrients as meat and fish, most vegetarians are able to eat a balanced diet without too much difficulty.

VEGETARIAN CHEESE Types of cheese made with non-animal rennet are now available in supermarkets as well as health food shops. As well as vegetarian Cheddar, there are now vegetarian versions of other English hard cheeses. (*see also* RENNET)

VELOUTÉ SAUCE A rich white sauce made with a foundation of white stock, which is used as the basis of many more elaborate sauces, such as *allemande*, *mousseline*, etc. The liquid used may be veal, chicken or fish stock, according to the dish in question.

Velouté Sauce
knob of butter
30 ml (2 level tbsp) flour
450 ml (³/₄ pint) chicken or other white stock
30–45 ml (2–3 tbsp) single cream
few drops of lemon juice
salt and pepper
Melt the butter in a saucepan, stir in the flour and cook gently for 1 minute, stirring well, until the mixture is a light golden colour. Remove the pan from the heat and gradually stir in the stock. Bring to the boil and continue to cook, stirring, until the sauce thickens. Simmer until slightly reduced and velvety. Remove from the heat and add the cream, a few drops of lemon juice and seasoning.
Makes 450 ml (³/₄ pint)

VELVET APPLE (*see* PERSIMMON)

VENISON Venison is the meat of the red, fallow or roe deer. The meat is inclined to be tough so it is hung for 1–2 weeks before cooking. Unless your butcher specializes in game, you will probably have to order venison, though venison roasting joints such as legs, saddles and shoulders, are becoming more widely available at butchers and supermarkets, and some stewing venison is now sold cut up ready for cooking.

The meat should be dark and firm with clear white fat. As there is only a little fat on venison, the meat tends to be dry, so additional fat or liquid is added for cooking. This is done either by marinating the meat overnight or adding melted fat or oil and basting frequently during cooking.

Roast Venison
saddle, leg or shoulder of venison
melted butter or margarine or vegetable oil
thick gravy and redcurrant jelly, to serve
Pat the joint dry with absorbent kitchen paper and place on a large piece of foil. Brush generously with butter. Fold the foil to make a parcel. Weigh.

Place the parcel in a roasting tin and roast in the oven at 170°C (325°F) mark 3, allowing 25 minutes per 450 g (1 lb). Fold back the foil 20 minutes before the end of the cooking time to allow the meat to brown. Serve with gravy and redcurrant jelly.

VERBENA (Lemon Verbena) A herb with a faint lemon flavour, which used to be used for making a herb tea.

VERDELHO (*see* MADEIRA)

VERJUICE The juice of unripe grapes, apples or crab apples. It was at one time used in sauces, etc., instead of lemon juice or vinegar.

VERMICELLI (*see* PASTA)

VERMOUTH Dry, medium or sweet, vermouth may be served chilled and straight or with ice cubes and/or soda water and a slice of lemon; or to make mixed drinks (dry white with gin for a dry

Martini; sweet red with whisky for a Manhattan, for instance). Chambéry is the most subtle, delightful vermouth of France and has its own *appellation d'origine*. Made from light, dry wine of the southern Alps, its pink version, Chambéryzette, is flavoured with wild strawberries. Noilly Prat is another well known French bone-dry and pale. Vermouth. It is Cinzano, Martini and Gancia are famous Italian vermouth names. They can be red (sweet), white (dry) or *bianco* (meaning white, but on the sweet side of medium).

VERT-PRE, AU A French expression applied to dishes garnished with watercress and straw potatoes and often served with maître d'hôtel butter; also, coated with green mayonnaise.

VESOP A concentrated vegetable extract used in Chinese and other Eastern cookery.

VETIVER (*see* KHAS-KHAS)

VE-TSIN (*see* MONOSODIUM GLUTAMATE)

VIBRO PARAHAEMOLYTICUS (*see* FOOD POISONING)

VICHY CARROTS Young carrots, lightly scraped and cooked in water and butter until all the liquid has evaporated and the carrots are glazed with the butter. Originally, Vichy water was used as the cooking liquid – hence the name. The French term, *à la Vichy* indicates that carrots have been used in a dish or its garnish.

VICHYSSOISE A cold leek and potato cream soup created by Diat, Chef des Cuisines of the Ritz-Carlton Hotel, New York.

VICHY WATER (*see* MINERAL WATER)

VICTORIA SPONGE SANDWICH This popular type of cake is made with a creamed mixture based on equal amounts of flour, sugar and fat; the fat enables it to keep moist longer than the fatless or 'true' sponge. Victoria sandwich cakes are made in two sandwich tins and sandwiched together with a filling, such as butter cream icing, jam or cream. Both sponge and filling can be flavoured with chocolate, orange or lemon or coffee.

VIEILLE CURE, LA A sweet French liqueur, of high alcoholic strength, brown in colour and with a distinctive aromatic flavour.

VINAIGRETTE (*see* SALAD DRESSING)

VINDALOO Vindaloo is an exceptionally hot curry which comes from Goa in western India. It is always fiery hot. The locally grown red chillies, which are mixed with vinegar, give the vindaloo curry its characteristic hot-sour taste. Traditional vindaloos are made from pork, which the Christians in western India are able to eat, but if you see vindaloo on an Indian restaurant menu, it will usually be made with lamb or beef – depending on whether the proprietors of the restaurant are Muslim or Hindu.

VINE FRUITS Currants, raisins and sultanas are all types of dried grapes. They do not need soaking and are often sold pre-washed. Currants are dried small black seedless grapes. Seedless raisins are dried seedless grapes and are the most popular type for cooking. The largest and sweetest raisins come from the Spanish Muscatel grapes. Sultanas are dried small white seedless grapes.

The main use for all vine fruits is in baking, such as in cakes and steamed puddings, and desserts.

VINE LEAVES These are the young leaves of the grape vine which originated in the Mediterranean region and are now found all over the world.
To select: Vine leaves are sold fresh, canned or packed in brine. Choose fresh leaves that are undamaged. Allow 4–5 leaves per person if stuffing.
To prepare: If using fresh vine leaves, plunge a few at a time into boiling water for a few minutes

until softened. When using vine leaves packed in brine, drain them, then pour over boiling water and leave to soak for about 20 minutes. Drain, then soak in fresh cold water for a further 20 minutes, drain again, then soak once more to remove any remaining excess salt.

To serve: Serve in salads or stuffed. They can also be wrapped around game or used as an attractive base for fresh fruit dishes and salads.

VINEGAR The word vinegar comes from the French *vin aigre*, or 'sour wine' and vinegars should, strictly speaking, be made from wine, but the term vinegar is also used for other sour liquids produced in the same way.

Vinegars are produced when a vinegar plant (a floating raft of yeast cells called the vinegar mother) is added to alcoholic liquids such as wine, beer or cider, and causes fermentation, oxidizing the liquid into acetic acid.

The most common vinegars are made from beers (malt vinegar), red and white wines and cider, although fruit and sherry vinegars are becoming increasingly popular and widely available. In the Orient, vinegars are commonly made from fermented sake (rice wine). Balsamic vinegar is a particularly fine vinegar produced in Italy from fermented grape juice. A huge variety of ingredients can be steeped in wine vinegar to produce flavoured vinegar: herbs, fruit and garlic are particularly popular.

Apart from their use in preserving, vinegars are indispensable for flavouring all kinds of different foods. Malt vinegar is used in pickles and relishes and strong-flavoured sauces, such as mint and horseradish, flavoured wine vinegars are used to give a subtle tang to salad dressings, sauces and marinades. Cider vinegars can be used in pickles and relishes and sherry vinegars can be used to give an unusual flavour to salad dressings. Rice wine vinegars are mostly used in Chinese and Japanese cooking.

The ancient Egyptians are known to have used vinegar not only as a seasoning for food but also as a refreshing medicine for fevers and as an aid to digestion. The Greeks and Romans used vinegar to preserve herbs, flowers and vegetables and combined it with oil and brine to tenderize and flavour meat before cooking.

VINTAGE The word is derived from the French *vendage*, which means 'grape harvest'. Although there is a vintage each year, the term is usually used as 'vintage year', meaning that the wines made in that year are of excellent quality.

Vintage wines are made from one grape harvest which is particularly good. Individual wine growers may decide when a year can be termed a 'vintage year' or it may be a trade association decision. The greatest vintages are usually small harvests as the fewer grapes on a vine the more flavour there is in each grape.

VIOLET The old-fashioned sweet violet which grows wild in southern England and Europe is a tiny perennial plant with heart-shaped leaves and sweet-scented mauve and white flowers. In medieval England, violets were widely used in soups, sauces, salads and desserts. Nowadays, they are mostly used in crystallized form for decorating cakes and desserts. They can also be used to make an unusual vinegar to flavour all kinds of sauces and stews. The petals are placed in a glass bottle about one-third full, and then topped up with red or white wine vinegar. The bottle is sealed and left in a warm place for 2–3 weeks before straining.

VIPER'S BUGLOSS A hairy biennial plant found in chalky soil in southern England and Europe. It has edible blue flowers and is very similar to borage. It can be used for decoration in the same way as borage flowers, particularly in summer wine and fruit cups. (*see also* BORAGE)

VITAMINS A diverse group of natural substances essential for growth and health. Diets lacking in a particular vitamin may produce a specific deficiency disease. Vitamins can not be made in the body and must be supplied by food. The amounts needed are small, varying from a few micrograms to several milligrams a day. Vitamins are sometimes divided into fat soluble vitamins (A, D, E and K) and water soluble vitamins (B complex and C). The fat soluble vitamins are less vulnerable to cooking and processing than the others. Water soluble vitamins leach out of foods into cooking water and most are readily destroyed by heat. Some foods are rich sources of a particular vitamin, for example liver for vitamin A, oranges for vitamin C. A good mixed diet usually provides enough of all the necessary vitamins each day.

Folic acid (folacin) is needed to produce healthy red blood cells. Deficiency is being increasingly recognized in pregnant women, old people and Asian immigrants, who may need supplements. Good food sources include liver, green leafy vegetables, pulses, bread, oranges and bananas. Other fruit, meat and dairy products contain little.

Pantothenic acid is needed for all tissue growth as it plays a large part in releasing energy from fats and carbohydrates. It is found in a wide variety of foods, particularly animal produce, cereals and legumes.

Vitamin A (retinol) is needed for growth, good vision in dim light, healthy skin and surface tissues, especially those that secrete mucus. Vitamin A is the vitamin in its active form and is known as retinol. Provitamin A, vitamin A precursors or caratenoids are substances which the body can turn into vitamin A. These are found in animal foods, dairy products and vegetables. Good sources include offal, green leafy vegetables, yellow and orange-coloured fruit and vegetables e.g., carrots, tomatoes, apricots, peaches and Cantaloupe melons, butter and margarine.

Vitamin B was originally thought to be one vitamin, but has turned out to be a complex of substances. There are at present thought to be about eight vitamins in the B group and they often appear in the same foods. The three best known are thiamin (vitamin B1), riboflavin (vitamin B2) and niacin or nicotinic acid (which used to be referred to as vitamin B3). These three are always known by their chemical names, while most of the others are known by their numbers.

Thiamin (B1) helps the body release energy from carbohydrates. Good sources include milk, offal, eggs, vegetables, fruit, wholegrain and fortified cereals–including bread and breakfast cereals–pulses and nuts.

Rivoflavin (B2) is also vital for the release of energy from food. About one third of our daily intake comes from milk. Other good sources include offal, eggs, cheese and yeast extract.

Niacin helps in the conversion of food to energy. The main sources are meat, fish, fortified breakfast cereals, vegetables and yeast extract.

Vitamin B6 (pyridoxine) helps the body utilize protein and contributes to the formation of haemoglobin for red blood cells. It is found in a wide range of foods including meat, fish, eggs, wholegrain cereals, some vegetables, pulses and yeast extract.

Vitamin B12 (cyanocobalamin) is essential for the production of healthy red blood cells. Deficiency leads to a type of anaemia. The only people at risk of not getting enough of this vitamin are vegans, as it is found only in animal foods. Useful sources include liver, meat, eggs, fish, milk and cheese.

Vitamin B13 (orotic acid) is little known; its function and its deficiency effects are not known.

Biotin also belongs to the B complex. It is made by bacteria in the intestine and is also found in offal, egg yolk, vegetables, cereals, fruit and nuts.

Vitamin C (ascorbic acid) is needed to keep the connective tissue between cells healthy. Vitamin C is found almost exclusively in fresh fruit and vegetables, including potatoes. A glass of orange juice will supply a day's requirements. Despite the popular belief that vitamin C will prevent or cure colds, the evidence is not conclusive.

Vitamin D (cholecalciferol) is needed for the growth and formation of bones and teeth as it helps in the absorption of calcium and controls the amount that is retained. Children, pregnant women and lactating women have particularly high requirements, while elderly people and Asian women and children may be at risk of deficiency.

Vitamin D is obtained by the action of sunlight on a substance in the skin. It is also found in a few sources such as some dairy products, some fish and margarine. Most of the body's supply comes from sunlight.

Vitamin E can be found in different forms under the names tocopherols and tototrienols – tocopherols is the most common name. It is thought to be essential for muscular health and blood circulation. Rich sources include wheat-germ, vegetable oils, some vegetables and nuts.

Vitamin K is needed for the normal clotting of the blood. It is found in green and some other vegetables, cereals and pulses. It is also made by bacteria in the intestines.

VODKA This strong, fiery, colourless spirit distilled mainly from wheat (though rye or potatoes can be used) has been the national drink of Russia ever since it was first produced there in the twelfth century. It can be drunk chilled and neat, as a long drink, or as the base for cocktails such as Harvey Wallbanger, White Russian and Screwdriver.

VOL AU VENT A round or oval puff pastry case which is filled with diced meat, poultry, fish or vegetables in sauce. Individual vol au vents are also popular for inclusion in a buffet. To make the lidded pastry cases, the pastry is stamped out into fluted rounds, then smaller rounds are cut out from the centre of the larger ones, though the pastry should not be cut right through. After baking, the small 'lids' can be lifted out, then replaced after the vol au vents have been filled.

W

WAFER A very thin, crisp, sweetened biscuit, served with ice cream, etc. In addition to the conventional oblong, various fancy shapes are made. Smaller wafer biscuits are also produced sandwiched together with a sweet or savoury cream filling.

WAFFLE A crisp, golden-brown type of pancake, with deep indentations, made by baking a batter mixture in a special waffle iron, which cooks on both sides at once. The irons may be made for use over a gas flame or electric ring or they may be electrically heated. Waffles, which are quickly prepared, are usually served hot with butter or golden or maple syrup. Alteratively, they may be layered with whipped cream or ice cream and fresh fruit.

WAKAME (*see* SEA VEGETABLES)

WALEWSKA, À LA A French name given to fish dishes served with a lobster sauce and garnish.

WALNUT These are one of the most popular nuts and are grown in many parts of the world. They have a round, crinkly shell with a wrinkled looking kernel. They are available in their shells, shelled, in halves, chopped or ground. Fresh unripe green walnuts are sometimes available pickled in jars. Walnuts have a moist, oily flavour and are used in cakes, stuffings and salads. They are also used to produce an oil (*see* OILS).

WALTON CHEDDAR An English cheese made from Cheddar and Stilton, and flavoured with walnuts.

WASABI The name translates from the Japanese as 'mountain hollyhock'. It is also known as Japanese horseradish as the flavour is similar, though more fragrant, than horseradish. The edible part of the plant is the root. Outside Japan, fresh *wasabi* is almost impossible to find, but it is available powdered or as a paste. The powder can be reconstituted by blending it with enough water to form a firm paste. It should then be left to stand for 10 minutes to allow the flavour to develop before using. It is used as a condiment to serve with *sushi* (*see* SUSHI).

WASSAIL BOWL A kind of spiced ale formerly served on Christmas Eve.

WATER Water is essential to life. It makes up two-thirds by weight of the human body. Water is continually being lost from the body – normally about 1.2 litres (2 pints) per day are lost in urine, sweat and through breathing, and this has to be replaced by drinking liquid and eating foods containing water. This is easily provided by, for example, 300 ml (½ pint) milk, one glass of water and four cups of tea. Also, many foods consist largely of water. This applies not only to such obvious things as gravy and custard; vegetables and fruit, for example, are up to 90 per cent water, and even cheese, meat, bread and other apparently solid foods supply an appreciable amount of water.

While it is possible to go without food for weeks, someone without water will die in a matter of days, depending on the climate.

Pure water is a colourless, tasteless and odourless liquid. At normal atmospheric pressure, water boils at 100°C (212°F) and freezes at 0°C (32°F). Most water contains dissolved gases, minerals and minute particles of dust. Hard water is particularly found in chalk, limestone or dolomite areas, and the chemicals responsible for hardness are mainly bicarbonates, sulphates and chlorides of calcium, magnesium, sodium and potassium. When water containing bicarbonates of calcium and magnesium is boiled, the bicarbonates are changed to insoluble carbonates – producing furring in kettles. Hard water is not good for making tea and cooking. Soft water, which does not contain these chemicals, is best for washing and making tea.

Water is used in large quantities for drinking, cooking, other domestic uses and for industrial purposes. Part of its value to life lies in the fact that it will dissolve many substances; it is not chemically changed but it acts as a vehicle in the body for oxygen and food and for removing waste products. It is also involved in many other processes.

Clean water is taken very much for granted in this country. The basic supplies are treated by filtering and other methods to make them safe. However, the purifying ingredients can sometimes be detected in the taste and bottled water is becoming increasingly popular. Bottled mineral water has been drunk in European countries for years, but it has only become popular in Britain in the last few years. Bottled waters may be still, naturally full of gas or artificially carbonated. (*see also* MINERAL WATER)

WATER BISCUIT A thin, crisp, plain biscuit, usually served with butter and cheese.

WATER CHESTNUT Small tubers, related to the myrtle, eaten in China and other parts of the East. They are similar in appearance and flavour to ordinary chestnuts. They are available canned in this country.

WATERCRESS A plant with small green leaves, sometimes tinged with brown, which grows in water. Commercially grown watercress is now available all the year round. The leaves have a pleasant, slightly hot, peppery flavour and are excellent as an accompaniment to fish, game or grilled food, in a salad or sandwiches, or made into a soup.
To select: Choose watercress that looks fresh with dark green leaves and no sign of yellowing. Allow one bunch for four people when raw.
To prepare: Wash well and trim off the tough stalks before use.
To serve: Watercress is usually eaten raw in salads or used as a garnish on hot or cold dishes.

WATER ICE A refreshing frozen dessert, made from a sugar syrup flavoured with fruit juice or purée. Water ices are best made in an ice cream machine, but they can be made in a refrigerator if the mixture is stirred frequently during the freezing, although there will be a certain amount of crystallization. Two especially delicious types of water ice are made by adding stiffy beaten egg white or by flavouring with a liqueur. (*see also* GRANITA, SORBET)

WATER MELON (*see* MELON)

WATER WOLF (*see* PIKE)

WATERZOIE (Waterzoetje) In Brussels this is a dish of boiled chicken and white wine served in a creamy white sauce containing julienne strips of mixed vegetables. Elsewhere in Belgium and Holland, it consists of a mixed fish stew containing julienne strips of vegetables. It us usually eaten like soup.

WEDDING CAKE In Britain, the traditional wedding cake consists of a rich fruit cake with one, two, three or more tiers, covered with almond paste and decorated with royal icing. The cake is always served at the wedding reception. The bride and groom make the first cut and the rest of the cutting up is then usually done in the background. The top tier of a wedding cake is often saved for the first christening, for the cake is rich enough to keep if wrapped well. The almond paste and icing may well have to be renewed, however.

WELSH ONION (*see* ONION)

WELSH RAREBIT Melted cheese on toast. Welsh rarebits are often served as a savoury and, when eaten with tomatoes or similar vegetables, they can make a nourishing main course for a light meal. When topped with a poached egg, Welsh rarebit becomes buck rarebit.

WENSLEYDALE CHEESE An English cheese made in the vale of Wensleydale in Yorkshire. Originally, it was a double cream cheese, cylindrical in shape, which matured until it became blue – in this form it was considered one of the best English blue cheeses, second only to Stilton. Since

1954, much of the Wensleydale production has been sold when white and in this form it is a mild, creamy-coloured cheese with a rather flaky texture. Blue Wensleydale is also available.

WESTPHALIAN HAM (*see* HAM)

WHALE Whales have long been hunted for their oil more than their meat. At one time the oil was used a great deal in the manufacture of margarine and oils, but is it now rarely used. (*see also* OILS)

WHALE OIL (*see* OILS)

WHEAT Wheat has been grown for 10,000 years, since it was first cultivated in Mesopotamia. Now, it is grown in most parts of the world to provide flour for human consumption and is the most important food for a third of the world's population.

There are two main types of wheat, hard wheat which is rich in gluten and soft wheat which is richer in starch. The two varieties are blended according to availability and requirement. Hard wheat flour is used to make bread as the gluten stretches like elastic when it is heated. As it expands it traps the carbon dioxide released by the yeast, giving bread its open texture. Soft wheats are used for cakes and pastries. Durum wheat, which produces a large grain with a lower gluten content than common wheat, is used to make pasta. (*see also* BREAD, FLOUR, GLUTEN)

The nutritional value of wheat is similar to that of barley, oats and rye, though it varies somewhat with different varieties and in different climates. As well as containing protein, wheat products also provide varying amounts of the B group vitamins, calcium and iron.

Wheat is available in many different forms, other than flour. Whole wheat grains (or berries) are the grains with just the outer husk removed. They look like brown grains of rice with a split down the middle. The whole grains can be cooked or sprinkled over loaves of bread before cooking. Wheat flakes are produced by flattening whole grains between rollers. They can be added to

muesli. Malted wheat grains are larger and darker than plain whole wheat grains and have a sweet, nutty flavour. Wheat bran may be sprinkled over breakfast cereals or desserts. (*see also* CRACKED WHEAT, GRAINS, WHEATGERM)

WHEATGERM This is the heart of the wheat grain – the part of the plant that gives rise to the new plant – and is the part that is removed when milling white flour. However, it is sold as a commercial preparation, either plain or toasted, and is a rich source of the B group vitamins. It can be added to cooked dishes or sprinkled over the top of breakfast cereals.

WHEATMEAL (*see* FLOUR)

WHELK These are molluscs with greyish or brownish shells. They are usually sold ready-cooked and shelled and can be eaten plain with vinegar. They are available all year but at their best from September to February.

To prepare raw whelks: Wash the whelks in several changes of water, then leave to soak for 2–3 hours. Cook in a saucepan of boiling salted water for 15–20 minutes, until tender.

WHEY The watery liquid which separates from the curd when milk is clotted, as during the making of cheese. It contains lactose, a trace of easily digested protein (lactalbumin) and calcium.

WHIFF (*see* SOLE, LEMON)

WHIPPING (Whisking) Beating air rapidly into a mixture either with a manual or electric whisk. The most frequently whisked or whipped foods are egg whites and cream. It is usual to describe cream as having been whipped, while egg whites are nearly always said to have been whisked.

WHISKY (Whiskey) The alcoholic spirit distilled from the fermented grain of cereals, chiefly barley, rye and maize. The best known type is distilled in Scotland, but whisky is also made in Ireland (where the spelling 'whiskey' is preferred). The Canadian and American types are made from rye or maize. Liqueur whiskies are good quality spirits well matured, while Drambuie is a liqueur made from Scotch whisky and heather honey.

The quality of whisky depends on the grain used, the process followed in its manufacture, the time allowed for maturing and the blending. Distillers usually aim at achieving by blending a more or less standard spirit, so that people will know what to expect when they ask for a certain brand. Whisky is drunk neat or with water or soda water; rye whisky is often drunk with ginger ale.

Scotch whisky is the most popular spirit distilled from grain. It is made from malted barley and blended with an unmalted grain spirit. The different brands depend on the part of Scotland from which the malt whisky comes. Both the malt whisky and the plain grain spirit must, by law, be matured for 3 years before being blended. The blending is very important and has to be carefully carried out to produce a whisky of the same flavour and colour each year. (*see also* BOURBON)

WHITEBAIT These are the tiny, silvery fry (young) of sprats or herring which are eaten whole and require no gutting. Rinse thoroughly and drain well. Whitebait are usually coated in flour, either seasoned with salt and pepper and/or cayenne pepper, and deep-fried. They are best from February to June.

WHITE PUDDING In different parts of the country and at different times, this name has been applied to a variety of farmhouse sausages. Probably the commonest type was made at pig-killing time from the cooked brain, tongue, lights, heart, kidneys, etc., mixed with cooked pearl barley or oatmeal (or breadcrumbs), seasoned and flavoured to taste. The puddings are fried and eaten hot.

WHITING Whiting is a smallish sea fish with a pale brown to olive-green back and a cream-coloured belly. The flesh is soft, white and flaky with a delicate flavour. It is sold whole or as fillets.

It can be poached, steamed or shallow-fried. It is available all year round. (*see also* SMOKIES)

WHOLEMEAL (*see* FLOUR)

WHORTLEBERRY (*see* BILBERRY)

WIDGEON A small bird of the wild duck family, in season from 1st September to 28th February. It is plucked, drawn and trussed like a duck, but is cooked for only 20–25 minutes in the oven at 220°C (425°F) mark 7. Widgeon should be served with a rich gravy flavoured with redcurrant jelly or port wine. Carve as for game (*see* CARVING). Orange salad, watercress and lemon should be served as accompaniments.

WIENER SCHNITZEL An Austrian dish consisting of veal escalope that is beaten, dipped in flour, in beaten egg and finally in white breadcrumbs, then fried in deep fat. Schnitzels are traditionally served quite simply with a wedge of lemon, although a more elaborate garnish of sliced hard-boiled egg, olives and anchovies may be used.

WILD BOAR (*see* BOAR)

WILD DUCK (*see* DUCK)

WILD MARJORAM (*see* OREGANO)

WILD RICE (*see* RICE)

WINE The product of the alcoholic fermentation of fresh or dried grapes or grape juice. Wines vary according to the varieties of grape used; where and how they are grown; how the wines are made and treated; and according to the weather in each year. Not only can wines from the same grape varieties grown in different countries be completely different from each other, but the same wine from the same vineyards will vary from vintage to vintage, too.

Wine is fermented grape juice. The fermentation turns grape sugar into alcohol. The amount of alcohol in wine may vary from as little as 5 or 6 per cent by volume (the amount is usually shown on labels) to 16 per cent. In wines such as port and sherry, additional alcohol is added to arrest fermentation and preserve more of the wine's natural sweetness. These are fortified wines, with alcoholic strengths from 17–22 per cent.

Most wine is sold when it is ready to drink. Blended wines from chain stores are intended, and best used, for prompt consumption. But fine wines need bottle age, which may vary from five to as many as 20 or more years for great Bordeaux, Hermitage, or or vintage port. Your wine merchant, or his list, should advise about the quality and maturity of vintage wines. All but the finest white wines, and all cheap reds, should be drunk as young as possible.

There are no hard and fast rules about which wine should be served with which food. However, helpful guidelines are that light wines should be served before fuller ones; dry before sweet; red before sweet white; lesser wines before fine ones. When one wine only is served throughout a meal, it should be the wine most appropriate to the main course.

Dry white wines which stimulate the palate are good as an apéritif or with hors d'oeuvre or shellfish (Chablis, Muscadet, Portuguese Vinho Verde, Champagne or other sparkling wine if dry).

Dry or medium dry white wines suit plainly cooked veal, chicken and fish dishes and drink well throughout the meal (white Burgundy, Sancerre, Alsace Riesling, Moselle, Soave, Verdicchio).

Rosé wines, of a medium dryness are pleasant summer wines for cold plates and picnic dishes (Tavel, Rosé de Cabernet).

Lighter bodied red wine is pleasant with lamb chops, veal escalopes and milder casserole dishes (light clarets, Beaujolais, Valpolicello, Bardolino).

Fuller red wine suits red meats, rich stews, casseroles, game dishes (St. Emilion and Pomérol among the clarets; red Burgundy, Côtes du Rhône, Chianti, Rioja).

Sweet white wines are drunk chilled, on their own or to go with certain sweet puddings and dessert fruits (Sauternes, sweeter hocks, Muscat de Beaumes de Venise).

WINE VINEGAR (*see* VINEGAR)

WINKLE (Periwinkle) A small mollusc usually sold ready-cooked, with or without shells. A long pin is needed to remove the flesh from the shells. Prepare and cook raw winkles as whelks and eat with vinegar and bread. They are available from September to April. (*see also* SHELLFISH)

WITCH (*see* SOLE)

WINDSOR BEAN (*see* BEAN, BROAD)

WINDSOR RED CHEESE A mature Cheddar cheese flavoured and coloured with English fruit wine. This produces a cheese with a red veining and gives a very mature flavour. Serve as part of a cheese board.

WITLOOF (*see* CHICORY)

WOK A Chinese cooking pan used for stir-frying. The food cooks on the sloping sides of the pan as well as in the rounded base.

WOLF-FISH (*see* CATFISH)

WOODCOCK A small wild bird with mottled plumage, long bill and large eyes. The young birds are best and can be recognized by the fact that the feathers beneath the wing are like down, the spurs are short and round, the flight feathers are rounded and the feet supple. Woodcock are in season from 1st October (1st September in Scotland) to 31st January, and at their best from October to November.

Woodcock are cooked without drawing and with their heads still on. They are usually roasted and should be barded with bacon beforehand. Place the birds on a square of toast in the bottom of the pan and cook in the oven at 190°C (375°F) mark 5 for 15–25 minutes. Serve on the toast, garnished with watercress and lemon. A rich brown gravy should be made in the roasting tin to serve with the birds.

WOOD GROUSE (*see* CAPERCAILZIE)

WOOD PIGEON (*see* PIGEON)

WOOD EAR (*see* MUSHROOM)

WOODRUFF (*see* SWEET WOODRUFF)

WORCESTERSHIRE SAUCE A pungent anchovy-flavoured sauce made from a secret recipe. It can be used to flavour sauces, meat casseroles and cheese dishes, as well as a drink of tomato juice.

WORMSEED (*see* EPAZOTE)

WORMWOOD This is a bitter aromatic herb with grey foliage covered with fine hairs and yellow flowers. It has been used for thousands of years as a medicine (to cure worms) and in the preparation of various aperitifs and herb wines. Nowadays, its use is forbidden as it has been proved to cause blindness.

WORT Beer is made from a mixture of malted grain, water, sugar, yeast and hops. The malted, dried grain is boiled with water in a large container and the liquid that is strained off this mash is called the wort. Sugar and yeast are added to it, fermentation starts and the sugar is converted to alcohol.

Y

YAM A member of the tuber family, yams originated in Africa but have become widely available in British markets and supermarkets. Yams have a brownish-pink skin and white flesh.
To select: Choose undamaged yams when buying.
To prepare: Wash and peel, then dice.
To cook: Cook in boiling salted water, with a little lemon juice added to avoid discoloration, for 20 minutes, or until tender, or steam. Yams can also be roasted, baked or fried like ordinary potatoes.
To serve: Serve hot as an accompanying vegetable with meat.

YARD-LONG BEAN (*see* ASPARAGUS BEAN)

YARROW This is a common perennial herb which grows in hedges and meadows in Britain and other parts of Europe. It has furrowed, downy stems and clusters of small white flowers. The plant's healing properties were known to the ancient Greeks who named yarrow *archillea* after the Greek hero Achilles. The young leaves can be used in salads and can replace chervil as a garnish.

YEAST Yeast is a microscopic single-celled plant, and there are many different varieties all around us in the air and on the leaves and fruit of plants. In the right conditions yeast will reproduce rapidly and produce ferments which are capable of breaking down starch and sugars, converting them into carbon dioxide and alcohol. It is the production of carbon dioxide gas in bread making which makes the dough rise, while the by-products that are formed during the working of the yeast ferments give the bread its special flavour. A different type of yeast is used in beer and wine making. This has a higher alcohol tolerance than other yeasts.

Carbohydrates, air, water and warmth, in suitable proportions, are all necessary for the rapid growth of yeast. A certain amount of sugar enables it to grow quickly, though too much shrinks the cells and prevents budding. Too much salt and fat also slow down the budding process. All liquids used for yeast mixtures should be lukewarm, as cold retards the growth, and excess heat kills the yeast plant. (This happens when bread is put in the oven, but by that time it has done its work.)

Yeast is a source of the B group vitamins, and is sometimes prescribed medically, either in its natural form or as one of the manufactured yeast extracts.

Types of Yeast
Baker's yeast is the type used for bread making. It is available fresh or as dried granules. Fresh yeast will only keep for two or three days, after which it crumbles easily, becomes darker in colour and has a stale smell. It is best to buy just enough for immediate use. It can, however, be stored in the freezer for up to a year.

There are different varieties of dried yeast granules and the manufacturers' instructions should be followed. When using dried yeast in a recipe specifying fresh yeast, allow half the quantity of the dried type. To add it to other ingredients in bread making, dissolve the dried yeast with 5 ml (1 tsp) sugar in some of the liquid taken from the amount stated in the recipe (the liquid should be lukewarm). Leave in a warm place for about 10 minutes, or until frothy, then mix with the dry ingredients and the remaining liquid to make a dough. Easy-blend dried yeast can be mixed with the dry ingredients without adding to liquid first.
Brewer's yeast (*barm*) is used for brewing. There are two types in general use. Top fermenting yeast works on the surface of the vat and is used for making beer; bottom fermenting yeast is used for brewing lager.

Wine yeasts come in powdered, granular or tablet form as well as in liquid yeast cultures.

YEAST EXTRACT This product, which is made by treating yeast with acid, is rich in the B vitamins.

Yeast extracts resemble meat extracts, with which they are often confused, the main difference being that they contain the nitrogenous substance called adenine, while the meat extracts contain the nitrogenous substances creatine and creatinine. They can be used to flavour soups, stews, etc., and as a sandwich spread.

YERBA MATÉ A South American shrub, the leaves of which are dried and used to make a drink called Paraguay tea. The natives prepare it by putting the leaves in a hollowed-out gourd and pouring on boiling water. A small tube, like a metal straw, is used to suck up the tea.

YOGURT Yogurt is a fermented milk product. Its nutritional and medicinal properties have been known in the Middle East, Far East and eastern Europe for hundreds of years, but it has only been appreciated in the West in the last few decades.

It is made by introducing two harmless bacteria, *Lactobacillus bulgaricus* and *Streptococcus thermophilus* into either whole or skimmed milk. These bacteria feed on the milk sugars and produce an acid which coagulates the protein, resulting in a semi-solid consistency and tart flavour. Vitamins and minerals remain similar in proportion to those in whole or semi-skimmed milk. Yogurt is higher in protein than milk, but contains less vitamin A, unless this vitamin is added artificially. It is richer in B vitamins and minerals and, since the milk sugars have been partially fermented, contains fewer carbohydrates. It is easier to digest than milk and has a beneficial effect on the digestive system.

Most natural or unflavoured yogurts on the market are 'live' to the extent that they all contain the two types of introduced bacteria and no pasteurization or sterilization has taken place. Some fruit yogurts have been pasteurized or sterilized after they are made. This prevents the fruit from fermenting but unfortunately it also removes 95 per cent or more of the beneficial bacteria. Some smaller manufacturers sell live fruit yogurts. These obviously have a shorter shelf life.

There are a number of different varieties of yogurt which can vary from brand to brand so always check the label:

Very low fat yogurt is based on skimmed milk and contains less than 0.5 per cent fat and is often sweetened artificially for slimmers.

Low fat yogurt contains 0.5–2 per cent fat.

Creamy yogurt is made with whole milk and may be enriched with cream.

Greek-style yogurt is made from whole milk (cows' or ewes') and has a very thick, creamy consistency.

Set yogurt is inoculated, packaged and incubated in the container in which it is sold.

Natural yogurt contains no colour, preservatives, stabilizers or thickeners.

Fruit yogurt contains at least 5 per cent of the whole fruit as pieces or purée.

Flavoured yogurt is flavoured with a variety of fruits and other flavourings. Honey and chocolate are the most common flavourings used, apart from fruits and nuts.

Using Yogurt

Yogurt can be eaten at any time of the day and can be used in either sweet or savoury dishes. It is particularly delicious served with breakfast cereal or muesli, and can make a refreshing summer drink. It can be mixed with fruit purées, nuts, honey or jam and served as a dessert, or used instead of cream to top fruit salads and other desserts, or used to make light mousses, ice creams and fruit fools.

It makes a perfect, low-fat salad dressing and is an excellent meat tenderizer when used in a marinade. Swirl it into soups, make into a sauce for grilled meats, use to top casseroles and stews or pour over white fish before baking.

When cooking with yogurt, take care not to heat it too vigorously or it will curdle. Let the yogurt come to room temperature before adding to a hot dish and, if adding to a soup or sauce, whisk it into the hot liquid just before serving.

Making Yogurt

It is not necessary to invest in a commercial yogurt machine to make your own yogurt; a wide-necked vacuum flask and a thermometer are the only essential equipment. Use either skimmed or semi-skimmed milk, skimmed milk powder, raw, pasteurized milk, or UHT (UHT is already sterilized so it is the most convenient to use and results in a richer texture. It does not have to be boiled; just heated to the correct temperature. Sterilized. condensed and evaporated milks do not always give such good results. You can buy special yogurt starter cultures, but it is simpler to use bought unpasteurized natural yogurt. For your next batch, keep back a little from the first yogurt you make. You can do this about three times, then buy a new starter tub of natural yogurt. To obtain a thick, creamy yogurt, add skimmed milk powder (see recipe below). Flavour the finished yogurt with fruit or honey if liked.

568 ml (1 pint) milk

15 ml (1 tbsp) natural yogurt (not pasteurized)

15 ml (1 tbsp) skimmed milk powder (optional)

Sterilize a vacuum flask and a small saucepan with boiling water or sterilizing solution. Warm the vacuum flask. Pour the milk into a saucepan and bring to the boil. If you want a thick yogurt, keep the pan on very low heat after this for 15 minutes. Remove from the heat and allow to cool to 45°C (113°F). (If you are using UHT milk, heat gently to 45°C/113°F.)

Spoon the natural yogurt into a bowl and stir in a little of the cooled milk. Add the skimmed milk powder, if using, to make a smooth paste. Stir in the remaining milk. Pour into the warmed insulated jar. Cover and leave for 8–9 hours, undisturbed.

Transfer the yogurt to small pots or cartons and place in the refrigerator immediately. It will keep for up to 10 days.

Makes about 600 ml (1 pint)

YORK HAM (*see* HAM)

YORKSHIRE PUDDING A batter pudding traditionally eaten with roast beef. In Yorkshire it is usually served separately, before the meat, accompanied by some of the hot beef gravy, but in much of the rest of the country, the pudding is served with the meat. It can be cooked either in a separate tin, or round or under the joint. If preferred the mixture can be made up as small individual puddings or popovers. (*see also* BATTER)

YUCCA (*see* CASSAVA)

YULE LOG (Bûche de Noël) A traditional Christmas cake, consisting of a Swiss roll filled and coated with chocolate and vanilla butter cream and decorated to represent a log of wood, using a fork to give the effect of bark. Other seasonal decorations may be added.

Z

ZABAGLIONE An Italian dessert, a frothy mixture of wine (usually Marsala), egg yolks and sugar, beaten over a gentle heat until thick; it is served in hot glasses. The sauce called *sabayon* is a variation of *zabaglione* (*see* SABAYON SAUCE).

ZAKUSKA The Russian form of appetizer. It consists of many types of caviar, *blinis* (savoury pancakes), smoked sausages, cold meats, pickled fish and *tvoroinki* (cheese dumplings).

ZAMPONE A northern Italian sausage whose casing is a boned pig's trotter. Made from a mixture of pork and spices, it goes particularly well with the bland flavour of potatoes and lentils and is traditionally served with these in Italy. Although a fairly fatty sausage, it is considered a great delicacy in Italy. Some *zampone* needs boiling for 3 hours, but the pre-cooked variety, *zampone lampo* does not need boiling.

ZAPOTE (*see* SAPODILLA)

ZEDOARY (Kentjoer) A spice derived from the dried rhizome of a South-East Asian plant related to the ginger and turmeric. It is used in Malaysian and Indonesian cooking and can sometimes be found in the form of dried pieces in specialist food shops.

ZEST The coloured outer layer of citrus fruit which contains essential oil. (*see also* RIND)

ZEERA (*see* CUMIN)

ZITE (*see* PASTA)

ZUCCHINI (*see* COURGETTE)

ZUPPA INGLESE This is the famous Italian dessert of custard and sponge cake flavoured with rum or Marsala. Literally translated, the name means 'English soup' and theories vary about how it came by its unusual name – some say it is derived from English trifle, others that it acquired the name because of the association of English sailors and their issue of rum. (*see also* TRIFLE)

ZWIEBACK The German name for small type of rusk, usually bought ready-made, to serve with cocktails, sherry, etc.

RECIPES ILLUSTRATED ON COLOUR PAGES

Bagna Cauda (Hot Anchovy Dip)

Illustrated between pages 64 and 65

225 g (8 oz) asparagus, washed, trimmed and freshly cooked
3 globe artichokes, trimmed and freshly cooked
1 small cauliflower
1 large red pepper
1 large green pepper
4 carrots, peeled
6 celery sticks, trimmed
3 courgettes, trimmed
1 bunch radishes
150 ml (¼ pint) olive oil
75 g (3 oz) butter
2 garlic cloves, skinned and finely chopped
two 50 g (2 oz) cans anchovy fillets, drained and finely
    chopped

While the asparagus and artichokes are cooling, prepare the remaining vegetables. Cut the cauliflower into florets, discarding any tough stalks. Cut the peppers in half lengthways and remove the cores and seeds. Wash the peppers inside and out, dry and cut into strips. Cut the carrots, celery and courgettes into finger-sized sticks. Trim the radishes.

Heat the oil and butter in a saucepan until just melted, but not foaming. Add the garlic and cook gently for 2 minutes. Do not allow it to colour. Add the anchovies and cook very gently, stirring all the time, for 10 minutes or until the anchovies dissolve into a paste.

To serve, transfer the dip to an earthenware dish and keep warm over a fondue burner or spirit lamp at the table. Each guest dips the vegetables in the hot anchovy sauce. Serves 6

Marmalade Teabread

Illustrated between pages 64 and 65

200 g (7 oz) plain flour
5 ml (1 tsp) ground ginger
5 ml (1 tsp) baking powder
50 g (2 oz) butter, diced
50 g (2 oz) light soft brown sugar
60 ml (4 tbsp) orange marmalade
1 egg, beaten
45 ml (3 tbsp) fresh milk
25 g (1 oz) candied orange peel, chopped

Grease a 750 ml (1½ pint) loaf tin, then line the base with greaseproof paper and grease the paper.

Put the flour, ginger and baking powder in a bowl and rub in the butter until the mixture resembles fine breadcrumbs. Stir in the brown sugar thoroughly.

Mix together the marmalade, egg and most of the milk. Stir into the dry ingredients and mix to a soft dough. Add the rest of the milk, if necessary.

Turn the mixture into the prepared tin, level the surface and press the candied orange peel on top. Bake at 170°C (325°F) mark 3 for about 1¼ hours or until golden brown. Turn out on to a wire rack to cool.
Makes 8–10 slices

Cheese and Chive Scones

Illustrated between pages 64 and 65

225 g (8 oz) self raising flour
pinch of salt
50 g (2 oz) butter, diced
100 g (4 oz) Lancashire cheese, grated
15 ml (1 tbsp) snipped fresh chives
150 ml (¼ pint) fresh milk, plus extra for brushing

Put the flour and salt into a bowl and rub in the butter until the mixture resembles fine breadcrumbs. Stir in 50 g (2 oz) of the cheese and the chives.

Add the milk and mix to form a soft dough, then knead quickly until smooth. Roll out on a floured work surface until 1 cm (½ inch) thick. Cut into 10 rounds with a 5 cm (2 inch) plain cutter and brush the tops with milk. Transfer to baking sheets.

Bake at 230°C (450°F) mark 8 for 7–10 minutes, until well risen and golden brown.

Immediately put the remaining cheese on top of the scones and allow to melt before serving hot or cold.
Makes 10

Chelsea Buns

Illustrated between pages 64 and 65

15 g (½ oz) fresh yeast or 7.5 ml (1½ tsp) dried
100 ml (4 fl oz) warm milk
225 g (8 oz) strong plain white flour
2.5 ml (½ tsp) salt
40 g (1½ oz) butter, diced
1 egg, beaten
100 g (4 oz) mixed dried fruit
50 g (2 oz) light soft brown sugar
clear honey, to glaze

Grease a 17.5 cm (7 inch) square tin. Blend the fresh yeast with the milk. If using dried yeast, sprinkle it into the milk and leave in a warm place for 15 minutes, until frothy.

Put the flour and salt in a bowl, then rub in 25 g (1 oz) of the butter until the mixture resembles fine bread-crumbs. Make a well in the centre, pour in the yeast liquid and the egg, then beat together until the mixture forms a dough that leaves the sides of the bowl clean.

Turn the dough on to a lightly floured surface and knead well for 10 minutes, until smooth and elastic. Cover with a clean tea-towel and leave in a warm place for about 1 hour, until doubled in size.

Knead the dough lightly on a floured surface, then roll it out to a large rectangle, measuring about 30× 23 cm (12×9 inches). Mix the dried fruit and sugar together. Melt the remaining butter, then brush over the dough. Scatter with the fruit mixture, leaving a 2.5 cm (1 inch) border around the edges.

Roll the dough up tightly like a Swiss roll, starting at a long edge. Press the edges together to seal them, then cut the roll into 12 slices. Place the rolls, cut side uppermost, in the prepared tin. Cover and leave in a warm place for 30 minutes, until the rolls have doubled in size.

Bake the rolls at 190°C (375°F) mark 5 for 30 minutes, until they are well risen and golden brown. Brush them with the honey while still hot. Leave them to cool slightly in the tin before turning out. Serve the Chelsea Buns warm. *Makes 12*

Marbled Chocolate Teabread

Illustrated between pages 64 and 65

225 g (8 oz) butter
225 g (8 oz) caster sugar
4 eggs, beaten
225 g (8 oz) self raising flour
finely grated rind of 1 large orange
15 ml (1 tbsp) orange juice
few drops orange flower water (optional)
75 g (3 oz) plain chocolate
15 ml (1 tbsp) cocoa powder

Grease a 900 ml (2 pint) loaf tin and line the base and sides with greaseproof paper.

Cream the butter and sugar together until pale and fluffy, then gradually beat in the eggs, beating well after each addition. Fold in the flour.

Transfer half of the mixture to another bowl and beat in the orange rind, juice and orange flower water, if using.

Break the chocolate into pieces, put into a small bowl and place over a pan of simmering water. Stir until the chocolate melts. Stir into the remaining cake mixture with the cocoa powder.

Put alternate spoonfuls of the two mixtures into the prepared tin. Use a knife to swirl through the mixture to make a marbled effect, then level the surface.

Bake at 180°C (350°F) mark 4 for 1¼–1½ hours, until well risen and firm to the touch. Turn out on to a wire rack to cool. Serve cut in slices. *Makes about 10 slices*

Herbed Granary Bread Stick

Illustrated between pages 64 and 65

15 g (½ oz) fresh yeast or 7.5 ml (1½ tsp) dried and a pinch of sugar
450 g (1 lb) Granary flour
5 ml (1 tsp) salt
30 ml (2 tbsp) chopped fresh parsley
30 ml (2 tbsp) chopped fresh mixed herbs, such as mint, thyme, marjoram, rosemary, chives
1 garlic clove, skinned and crushed (optional)
10 ml (2 tsp) clear honey
fine oatmeal, for sprinkling

Blend the fresh yeast with 300 ml (½ pint) warm water. If using dried yeast, sprinkle it into 300 ml (½ pint) warm water with the sugar and leave in a warm place for 15 minutes, until frothy.

Put the flour, salt and herbs in a bowl and mix together. Make a well in the centre. Stir the garlic, if using, and the honey into the yeast liquid, then pour into the centre of the dry ingredients. Beat together until the dough leaves the sides of the bowl clean.

Turn on to a lightly floured surface and knead well for about 10 minutes, until smooth and elastic. Place in a clean bowl. Cover with a clean tea-towel and leave in a warm place for about 1 hour, until doubled in size.

Turn the dough on to a floured surface and knead lightly. Shape into a sausage shape about 40 cm (16 inches) long. Place on a greased baking sheet. Cut several slashes on the top of the loaf. Cover and leave in a warm place for about 30 minutes, until doubled in size.

Brush with a little milk and sprinkle with oatmeal. Bake at 230°C (450°F) mark 8 for 10 minutes, then reduce the oven temperature to 200°C (400°F) mark 6 and bake for a further 15–20 minutes. Leave to cool on a wire rack. *Makes 1 bread stick*

Cottage Loaf

Illustrated between pages 64 and 65

15 g (½ oz) fresh yeast or 7.5 ml (1½ tsp) dried
300 ml (½ pint) warm milk
450 g (1 lb) malted brown flour, strong wholemeal flour or strong white flour
5 ml (1 tsp) salt
beaten egg, to glaze
poppy or sesame seeds, for sprinkling (optional)

Dissolve the fresh yeast in the milk. If using dried yeast, sprinkle it into the milk and leave in a warm place for 15 minutes, until frothy.

Put the flour and salt in a bowl. Make a well in the centre, then pour in the yeast liquid. Beat well together until the dough leaves the sides of the bowl clean.

Turn on to a lightly floured surface and knead for about 10 minutes, until smooth and elastic. Place in a clean bowl. Cover with a clean tea-towel and leave in a warm place for about 1 hour, until doubled in size.

Turn the dough on to a floured surface and knead lightly. Cut off one-third of the dough and shape into a round. Shape the remaining dough into a round. Place the larger round on a greased baking sheet and brush with a little water. Place the smaller round on top.

Push the lightly floured handle of a wooden spoon down through the centre of the loaf right to the bottom. Using a sharp knife, slash the dough at 5 cm (2 inch) intervals around the top and bottom edges to make a decorative pattern. Cover and leave in a warm place for about 30 minutes, until doubled in size.

Brush with a little beaten egg to glaze and sprinkle with poppy or sesame seeds, if liked. Bake at 230°C (450°F) mark 8 for 10 minutes, then reduce the oven temperature to 200°C (400°F) mark 6 and bake for a further 20–25 minutes, until the loaf sounds hollow when tapped on the bottom. Transfer to a wire rack to cool. *Makes 1 large loaf*

Peking Duck

Illustrated between pages 128 and 129

1.8 kg (4 lb) oven-ready duck
15 ml (1 tbsp) brandy
12 spring onions
FOR THE PANCAKES
450 g (1 lb) plain flour
450 ml (¾ pint) boiling water
30 ml (2 tbsp) sesame oil
FOR THE BASTING SAUCE
30 ml (2 tbsp) clear honey
30 ml (2 tbsp) dark soy sauce
150 ml (¼ pint) cold water
FOR THE PLUM SAUCE
60 ml (4 tbsp) hoisin sauce
1.25 ml (¼ tsp) sesame oil
5 ml (1 tsp) clear honey

Wash and dry the duck thoroughly. Rub the brandy all over the skin. Tie a piece of string under each wing and hang the duck in a cool, dry, airy place overnight.

To make spring onion tassels for the garnish, trim the root ends and all but 5 cm (2 inches) of the leaves from two spring onions. Skin the onions and cut the green leaves two or three times lengthways. Drop them into iced water and leave for 2 hours, or until the ends open and curl up. Slice the white part only of the remaining spring onions lengthways into thin strips. Wrap until needed.

To make the pancakes, sift the flour into a bowl and stir in the boiling water. Mix to a dough. Knead in the bowl or on a lightly floured surface for 3 minutes. Cover with cling film or a clean tea-towel and rest for 30 minutes.

Meanwhile, mix all the basting sauce ingredients together. Place the duck on a rack in a roasting tin half filled with cold water. Pour some of the basting sauce over the breast. Roast, breast side up at 200°C (400°F) mark 6 for 35 minutes, basting every 10 minutes or so

with the sauce. Using two wooden spoons, turn the duck over on to its breast and baste with more sauce. The wooden spoons prevent the skin from being pierced and the juices escaping. Roast for a further 30 minutes, basting frequently. Turn the duck over on to its back and cook for a further 10 minutes, basting with the sauce.

While the duck is roasting, make the pancakes. Knead the dough briefly. Divide in half and keep one half covered. Roll the first half into a sausage shape about 40 cm (16 inches) long and cut it into 16 equal pieces. Flatten each piece into a 6.5 cm (2½ inch) round. Brush half the circles with sesame oil, then press the remaining circles on top of them, making eight pairs. Make more pancakes with the remaining dough in the same way, to give 16 pairs. Roll out the circles until they measure 15 cm (6 inches) in diameter. Heat a heavy-based frying pan and cook the pancakes in the dry pan for 2 minutes on each side. When ready, the pancake will look dry on the underside and have brown flecks. The pancake will puff when turned over. Remove from the pan, and while still hot, peel the two pieces apart. Keep hot, wrapped in a cloth.

Mix all the plum sauce ingredients together. Remove the skin from the duck in one piece and cut into 5 cm (2 inch) squares. Using two forks, pull the meat into shreds. Arrange the meat on a serving platter and garnish with the onion tassels.

To serve, spread a little plum sauce over a pancake. Top with duck skin and meat, sprinkle with spring onion strips, and roll up. *Serves 4–6*

Christmas Pudding

Illustrated between pages 128 and 129

50 g (2 oz) plain flour
2.5 ml (½ tsp) ground mixed spice
2.5 ml (½ tsp) grated nutmeg
2.5 ml (½ tsp) ground cinnamon
2 eggs
50 g (2 oz) shredded beef suet
50 g (2 oz) fresh breadcrumbs
50 g (2 oz) soft light brown sugar
175 g (6 oz) raisins
175 g (6 oz) sultanas
25 g (1 oz) mixed peel, chopped
1 eating apple, grated
1 carrot, peeled and grated
25 g (1 oz) blanched almonds, chopped
grated rind and juice of ½ lemon
grated rind of ½ orange
10 ml (2 tsp) treacle
65 ml (2½ fl oz) barley wine
15 ml (1 tbsp) brandy

Grease a 1.1 litre (2 pint) ovenproof pudding basin. Mix all the ingredients together, cover and leave overnight in the refrigerator.

Spoon the mixture into the prepared basin, cover with

pleated greaseproof paper and foil and secure with string. Steam for 6 hours. Cool, then remove the covers.

Turn the pudding out of the basin and cover tightly with greaseproof paper. Store for at least 1 month in a cool place.

To serve, uncover, place in a basin, re-cover and steam for 2 hours. *Serves 6–8*

Croquembouche

Illustrated between pages 128 and 129

treble quantity choux pastry (see page 324)
1 quantity pâté sucrée (see page 318)
quadruple quantity confectioners' custard (see page 122) or
* 900 ml (30 fl oz) double cream, 300 ml (10 fl oz) single*
* cream and 90 ml (6 tbsp) caster sugar*
1.1 kg (2¼ lb) granulated sugar
900 ml (1½ pints) water
crystallized rose petals and violets, to decorate

Dampen three baking sheets with water. Put the choux pastry into a piping bag fitted with a medium plain nozzle and pipe about sixty 2 cm (¾ inch) buns on to the baking sheets.

Bake in the oven at 200°C (400°F) mark 6 for 20–25 minutes until well risen and golden brown. Make a small slit in the side of each bun to release the steam, then transfer to a wire rack and cool for 30 minutes.

Roll out the pâté sucrée on a lightly floured working surface to a 22 cm (8½ inch) round. Place on a baking sheet, crimp the edge and prick all over with a fork.

Bake in the oven at 180°C (350°F) mark 4 for 20 minutes until light golden brown. Cool for 30 minutes on a wire rack, then transfer to a cake stand; use a highly ornamental one for a very special occasion.

Fill each choux bun with a little crème pâtissière. Or whip the double and single cream together until stiff, fold in the caster sugar and use to fill the buns.

Make the caramel. Put one-third of the granulated sugar with one-third of the water into a heavy-based saucepan. Heat gently to dissolve the sugar, then bring to the boil and boil to 143°C–154°C (290°F–310°F) on a sugar thermometer or until the mixture reaches the hard crack stage (see page 404). Remove from the heat and place the pan on a mat so it is tilted.

Dip one side of the filled choux buns into the caramel. Arrange around the edge of the pâte sucrée base, sticking the edges together. Fill the centre with more caramel choux buns. When the first layer is completed, make another on top.

Continue in this way, building up into a cone shape and making more caramel as necessary.

When the cone is completed, make up more caramel using the remaining sugar and water and drizzle over the Croquembouche. Decorate with crystallized rose petals and violets. *Serves 25–30*

Coeurs à la Crème

Illustrated between pages 128 and 129

225 g (8 oz) cottage cheese
25 g (1 oz) caster sugar
300 ml (10 fl oz) double cream
5 ml (1 tsp) lemon juice
2 egg whites, stiffly whisked
150 ml (5 fl oz) single cream, and fresh raspberries or
* strawberries, to serve*

Press the cottage cheese through a nylon sieve into a bowl. Add the sugar and mix well.

Whip the double cream until stiff, then add the lemon juice. Mix into the cheese and sugar mixture.

Line four or six small heart-shaped moulds with muslin (this is unnecessary if serving in the moulds). Fold the stiffly whisked egg whites into the cheese mixture. Spoon the mixture into the moulds. Drain overnight in the refrigerator. Serve with cream and fruit. *Serves 4–6*

Gravad Lax with Dill Sauce

Illustrated between pages 192 and 193

15 g (½ oz) white peppercorns, coarsely crushed
100 g (4 oz) coarse salt
150 g (5 oz) granulated sugar
1.8 kg (4 lb) fresh salmon, filleted
25 g (1 oz) chopped fresh dill
FOR THE SAUCE
30 ml (2 tbsp) mild Swedish or German mustard
10 ml (2 level tsp) caster sugar
1 egg yolk
150 ml (¼ pint) vegetable oil
30–45 ml (2–3 tbsp) white wine vinegar
30 ml (2 tbsp) chopped fresh dill or 10 ml (2 tsp) dried dillweed

Mix the coarsely crushed peppercorns with the salt and sugar.

Lay one salmon fillet, skin side down, in a dish and spoon over the peppercorn mixture. Sprinkle over the dill and then place the remaining fillet on top, skin side up.

Place a board on top of the fish and put weights on top to compress. Refrigerate. Turn the fish and baste with the juices daily, for 3 days.

To make the sauce, mix the mustard with the sugar and egg yolk. Gradually whisk in the oil as if making mayonnaise, until the sauce is thick. Add the vinegar and dill and mix well. Keep in a cool place for at least 24 hours to allow the flavours to blend.

To serve, remove the weights from the salmon, lift off the top fillet and scrape off the dill and peppercorns. Slice the salmon thinly, cutting down towards the skin across the width of the fillet. Arrange on serving plates with the dill sauce. *Serves 4, or 6–8 as a starter*

Roast Grouse with Bread Sauce, Game Chips and Chestnuts

Illustrated between pages 192 and 193

4 young grouse
juice of 1 lemon, strained
salt and pepper
16 slices of unsmoked streaky bacon
50 g (2 oz) butter
5 ml (1 level tsp) flour
FOR THE BREAD SAUCE
450 ml (¾ pint) milk
2 cloves
1 small onion, skinned and sliced
salt and pepper
pinch of grated nutmeg
75 g (3 oz) fresh white breadcrumbs
30 ml (2 tbsp) single cream
FOR THE GAME CHIP BASKETS
350 g (12 oz) potatoes
oil for deep-frying
50 g (2 oz) butter
550 g (1¼ lb) canned whole unsweetened chestnuts, drained
25 g (1 oz) pine kernels
small bunch white grapes, to garnish (optional)

Remove the giblets from the grouse and use for the gravy. Cover the giblets with water, bring to the boil and simmer for 30 minutes. Set aside.

Wipe the birds inside and out and truss. Sprinkle with lemon juice and season. Bard with the bacon and place the birds in a roasting tin with the butter. Roast at 230°C (450°F) mark 8 for 15 minutes. Remove the bacon and return the grouse to the oven for a further 5 minutes to brown the breasts. Remove from the pan and keep hot. Skim off the excess fat from the pan juices. Stir in the flour then strain in the giblet stock. Bring to the boil and boil until well reduced. Season and strain. Remove the trussing string from the grouse.

To make the bread sauce, bring the milk, cloves, onion, seasoning and nutmeg to the boil. Reduce the heat and barely simmer for 10 minutes. Cool and strain. Return the infused liquid to the pan and stir in the breadcrumbs and cream. Simmer for 10 minutes, stirring often to prevent it from sticking. Adjust seasoning.

To make the game chip baskets, slice the potatoes finely on a mandoline, or slice very thinly with a sharp knife. Dip a double wire mesh basket into the hot oil, remove, then line the bottom of the basket with overlapping potato slices. Push the top basket into place and plunge into the hot oil. Deep-fry until crisp and golden. Make three more baskets in the same way. Drain on absorbent kitchen paper, sprinkle with salt and keep hot. Melt the butter in a saucepan and add the chestnuts and pine kernels. Stir until they are heated through, then use to fill the baskets. Serve garnished with white grapes, if liked. *Serves 4*

Gâteau Saint-Honoré

Illustrated between pages 192 and 193

1 quantity pâte sucrée (see page 318)
beaten egg, to glaze
1 quantity choux pastry (see page 324)
300 ml (10 fl oz) double cream
45 ml (3 tbsp) sugar
45 ml (3 tbsp) water
1 quantity confectioners' custard (see page 122)
angelica and glacé cherries

Roll out the pâte sucrée on a lightly floured working surface to an 18 cm (7 inch) round. Place on a baking sheet and prick all over with a fork. Brush a 1 cm (½ inch) band round the edge with beaten egg.

Put the choux pastry into a piping bag fitted with a medium plain nozzle and pipe a circle round the edge. Brush with beaten egg.

Dampen a baking sheet and pipe about 20 walnut-sized choux balls on to it. Brush with beaten egg.

Bake both the flan and the choux balls in the oven at 190°C (375°F) mark 5 for about 15 minutes or until well risen and golden brown.

Make a slit in the side of each bun to release the steam, then transfer with the flan on to a wire rack and leave for 15–20 minutes to cool.

Whip the cream until stiff. Reserving a little cream for the top of the gâteau, put the rest into a piping bag fitted with a medium plain nozzle and pipe some into each of the cold choux buns.

Put the sugar with the water into a heavy-based saucepan and boil until the edge just begins to turn straw-coloured. Dip the tops of the choux buns in this syrup, using a skewer or tongs to hold them.

Use the remainder of the syrup to stick the buns on to the choux pastry border to form a wall. Fill the centre of the gâteau with the confectioners' custard mixture.

Pipe the reserved cream around the edge, in between the choux balls. Decorate with angelica and cherries. *Serves 6*

Moussaka

Illustrated between pages 256 and 257

2 medium aubergines
salt and pepper
about 150 ml (¼ pint) olive or vegetable oil, or a mixture of both
1 large onion, skinned and roughly chopped
1–2 garlic cloves, skinned and crushed
450 g (1 lb) minced lamb
227 g (8 oz) can tomatoes
30 ml (2 tbsp) tomato purée
10 ml (2 tsp) dried oregano
5 ml (1 tsp) ground allspice
2 bay leaves
410 g (14½ oz) can evaporated milk

40 g (1½ oz) cornflour
25 g (1 oz) butter or margarine
25 g (1 oz) plain flour
pinch of grated nutmeg
1 egg, beaten

Slice the aubergines thinly and place in a colander, sprinkling each layer with salt. Cover with a plate, place heavy weights on top and leave the aubergines to dégorge for 30 minutes.

Meanwhile, heat 30 ml (2 tbsp) of the oil in a heavy-based saucepan, add the onion and garlic and fry gently for 5 minutes until soft and lightly coloured. Add the minced lamb and fry until well browned, stirring and pressing with a wooden spoon to break up any lumps.

Add the tomatoes with their juice, the tomato purée, oregano, allspice and salt and pepper to taste, then add the bay leaves. Cover and simmer for about 20 minutes, stirring occasionally to break up the tomatoes.

Meanwhile, rinse the aubergines under cold running water, then pat dry with absorbent kitchen paper. Pour enough oil into a heavy-based frying pan just to cover the base. Heat until very hot, then add a layer of aubergine slices. Fry until golden on both sides, turning once, then remove with a spatula and drain on absorbent kitchen paper. Continue frying and draining all the aubergine slices, adding more oil as necessary.

Make the sauce for the topping. Dilute the evaporated milk with water to make up to 1 litre (1¾ pints) as directed on the can. In a jug, mix the cornflour to a smooth paste with a few spoonfuls of the milk.

Melt the butter in a saucepan, add the flour and cook gently, stirring, for 1–2 minutes. Remove from the heat and gradually blend in the milk. Bring to the boil, stirring constantly, then simmer for 3 minutes.

Stir in the cornflour paste and continue simmering and stirring until the sauce is thick. Remove the pan from the heat, add the nutmeg and salt and pepper to taste, then stir in the beaten egg.

Arrange the meat and aubergines in layers in a baking dish, then pour over the sauce. Bake, uncovered, in the oven at 180°C (350°F) mark 4 for 40 minutes. Leave to stand at room temperature for at least 15 minutes before serving. *Serves 4–6*

Salmagundi

Illustrated between pages 256 and 257

1 oven-ready duckling, weighing about 2.3 kg (5 lb), thawed
*   if frozen*
salt and pepper
1 oven-ready chicken, weighing about 2 kg (4½ lb), thawed
*   if frozen*
450 g (1 lb) carrots, cut into 0.5 cm (¼ inch) wide strips
450 g (1 lb) potatoes, peeled
150 ml (¼ pint) vegetable oil
75 ml (5 tbsp) lemon juice
pinch of mustard powder

pinch of sugar
450 g (1 lb) shelled peas, cooked
1 cucumber, sliced
225 g (8 oz) tomatoes, thinly sliced
4 celery sticks, thinly sliced
4 eggs, hard-boiled (optional)
mayonnaise (optional)
slices of stuffed olives and radishes, to garnish

Weigh the duckling, prick the skin all over with a skewer or sharp fork and sprinkle with salt. Place breast-side down on a rack or trivet in a roasting tin. Roast in the top of the oven at 200°C (400°F) mark 6, basting occasionally, for 20 minutes per 450 g (1 lb).

Weigh the chicken and sprinkle with salt and pepper. Place in a shallow roasting tin and roast below the duck on the lowest shelf of the oven for 20 minutes per 450 g (1 lb) plus 20 minutes. Cool both birds for 1–2 hours or until cool enough to handle.

Using a sharp knife, make a slit along each side of the breastbone of both the chicken and duck. Remove and discard the skin.

Carefully remove all the flesh from the carcasses of both birds. Discard the carcasses and cut the flesh of the birds into thin strips, about 5 cm (2 inches) long.

Cook the carrots in boiling salted water for 8 minutes or until just tender. Drain and rinse in cold water. Cook the potatoes in boiling salted water for 15 minutes until tender. Drain and leave to cool, then dice finely.

Make the dressing by whisking the oil, lemon juice, mustard and sugar together with salt and pepper.

Choose a large oval platter for making up the salmagundi. Place the potato and peas in the bottom of the dish to give a flat base. Arrange the carrot strips or a layer of cucumber on top, following the oval shape of the platter.

Pour over a little dressing. Next, arrange a layer of cucumber or carrot, slightly inside the first layer so that it may be easily seen.

Top with more layers of chicken meat, peas, tomato slices, celery and duck meat. Make each layer smaller than the previous one so that the lower layers can all be seen. Sprinkle each one with dressing. Continue layering until all the ingredients are used.

If using the eggs, shell and halve them, then top each half with a little mayonnaise, if used. Garnish with a few radish slices and stuffed olives, arranged round the edge of the dish. *Serves 8*

Kedgeree

Illustrated between pages 256 and 257

175 g (6 oz) long grain rice
salt and pepper
450 g (1 lb) smoked haddock fillets
2 eggs, hard-boiled and shelled
50 g (2 oz) butter
chopped fresh parsley, to garnish

Cook the rice in a saucepan of fast-boiling salted water until tender. Drain well and rinse under cold water. Drain again and spread out to dry – this prevents the kedgeree from becoming stodgy.

Meanwhile, put the haddock in a large frying pan with just enough water to cover. Bring to simmering point, then simmer for 10–15 minutes, until tender. Drain, skin and flake the fish, discarding bones.

Chop one egg and slice the other into rings. Melt the butter in a saucepan, add the cooked rice, fish and chopped egg. Season to taste and stir over a moderate heat for about 5 minutes, until hot. Pile on to a warmed serving dish and garnish with chopped parsley and the sliced egg. *Serves 4*

Stuffed Papayas

Illustrated between pages 256 and 257

2 papayas
30 ml (2 tbsp) vegetable oil
1 onion, skinned and finely chopped
1 large garlic clove, crushed
1 slice of unsmoked streaky bacon, rinded and finely chopped
450 g (1 lb) minced pork
1 small green hot chilli, seeded and finely chopped
15 ml (1 tbsp) tomato purée
75 ml (3 fl oz) dry white wine
175 g (6 oz) ripe tomatoes, peeled and chopped
salt and pepper
45 ml (3 level tbsp) freshly grated Parmesan cheese
15 g (½ oz) butter
parsley, to garnish
FOR THE TOMATO SAUCE
45 ml (3 tbsp) olive oil
2 garlic cloves, crushed
1 kg (2 lb) ripe tomatoes, quartered
5 ml (1 level tsp) sugar
1.25 ml (¼ level tsp) salt

Peel the papayas, cut them in half lengthways and remove the black seeds with a teaspoon. Par-boil the fruit in gently boiling, salted water for 10 minutes, then drain them upside down on absorbent kitchen paper.

Heat the oil in a large frying pan and fry the onion, garlic and bacon together until the onion is soft. Add the pork and chilli and fry until browned, stirring to break up the meat. Add the tomato purée, and cook, stirring, for 2 minutes. Pour over the white wine and stir in the tomatoes. Bring to the boil, reduce the heat and simmer for 5 minutes. Season to taste, remove from the heat and allow the mixture to cool slightly.

Grease a baking dish just large enough to hold the papaya shells and place them, cavity side up, in the dish. Pile the meat mixture into the centre of each papaya. Sprinkle with Parmesan cheese and dot with butter. Bake at 180°C (350°F) mark 4 for 30–40 minutes, or until the papaya is tender.

Meanwhile, to make the tomato sauce, heat the oil and fry the garlic, stirring, for 1 minute. Add the tomatoes and sugar and bring to the boil. Reduce the heat, cover the pan, and simmer for 15 minutes. Sieve the tomatoes, using a soup ladle to push every scrap of pulp through, so that only the skin and seeds remain. Return the pulp to the pan, season with salt and simmer for 10 minutes, or until the sauce has reduced to the required consistency.

Serve the papaya hot, with tomato sauce poured around each papaya half. Garnish with parsley. *Serves 4*

Veal and Ham Pie

Illustrated between pages 320 and 321

450 g (1 lb) minced veal
100 g (4 oz) boiled ham, minced
30 ml (2 tbsp) chopped fresh parsley
2.5 ml (½ tsp) ground mace
1.25 ml (¼ tsp) ground bay leaves
finely grated rind of 1 lemon
2 medium onions, skinned and finely chopped
salt and pepper
100 g (4 oz) lard, plus extra for greasing tin
350 g (12 oz) plain wholemeal flour
1 egg yolk
3 eggs, hard-boiled and shelled
10 ml (2 tsp) powdered aspic jelly

Grease a 1.4 litre (2½ pint) loaf tin and line the base with greased greaseproof paper.

Put the first seven ingredients in a bowl, 5 ml (1 tsp) salt and 1.25 ml (¼ tsp) pepper. Mix well to combine.

Put the lard and 200 ml (7 fl oz) water in a saucepan and heat gently until the lard has melted. Bring to the boil, remove from the heat and tip in the flour with 2.5 ml (½ tsp) salt. Beat well to form a soft dough.

Beat the egg yolk into the dough. Cover with a damp tea-towel and rest in a warm place for 20 minutes, until the dough is elastic and easy to work. Do not allow the dough to cool.

Pat two-thirds of the pastry into the base and sides of the prepared tin, making sure it is evenly distributed. Press in half of the meat mixture and place the eggs down the centre. Fill with the remaining meat mixture.

Roll out the remaining pastry for the lid. Cover the pie with the pastry and seal the edges. Use the pastry trimmings to decorate the top, then make one large hole in the centre of the pie.

Bake at 180°C (350°F) mark 4 for 1½ hours. If necessary, cover the pastry with foil towards the end of cooking to prevent over-browning. Leave to cool for 3–4 hours.

Make up the aspic jelly to 300 ml (½ pint) with water. Cool for about 10 minutes. Pour the liquid aspic through the hole in the top of the pie. Chill the pie for about 1 hour. Leave to stand at room temperature for about 1 hour before removing from the tin. *Serves 8–10*

Tagine

Illustrated between pages 320 and 321

4 chicken portions
50 g (2 oz) butter
15 ml (1 tbsp) olive oil
1 onion, skinned and sliced
10 ml (2 tsp) ground ginger
10 ml (2 tsp) paprika
10 ml (2 tsp) turmeric
2.5 ml (½ tsp) ground cinnamon
300 ml (½ pint) chicken stock
225 g (8 oz) dried prunes and apricots
salt and pepper

Cut each chicken portion into two pieces and strip off the skin. Melt the butter with the oil in a flameproof casserole, add the chicken in batches and fry over moderate heat until golden on all sides. Remove with a slotted spoon and place in the bottom of a tagine.

Add the onion to the casserole and fry gently for about 5 minutes until softened. Add the spices and fry for a further 2 minutes, stirring. Pour in the stock and bring to the boil. Add the fruit and salt and pepper to taste, then pour over the chicken. Cover tightly with the tagine lid. Cook at 150°C (300°F) mark 2 for 2 hours without lifting the lid.

To serve, carry the covered tagine to the table and very carefully lift the lid, taking care that the casserole juices do not spill out. *Serves 4*

Stock Syrup for Sorbets

100 g (4 oz) granulated sugar
300 ml (½ pint) water

Put the sugar in a heavy-based saucepan. Add the water and heat gently until the sugar dissolves. Do not stir the mixture but occasionally loosen the sugar from the base of the pan to help it dissolve. Bring to the boil and boil for 2 minutes. Cool and use as required. *Makes about 350 ml (12 fl oz)*

Raspberry Sorbet

Illustrated between pages 320 and 321

450 g (1 lb) raspberries
30 ml (2 tbsp) lemon juice
30 ml (2 tbsp) kirsch
350 ml (12 fl oz) Stock syrup
2 egg whites

Purée the raspberries with the lemon juice and kirsch in a blender or food processor. Press through a nylon sieve.

Add to the stock syrup and pour into a shallow freezer container. Cover and freeze for about 3 hours or until mushy.

Whisk the egg whites until stiff. Turn the sorbet into a bowl and beat gently to break down the ice crystals.

Fold in the egg whites.

Return the sorbet to the freezer container, cover and freeze for 4 hours or until firm.

Leave in the refrigerator for about 40 minutes to soften slightly before serving. *Serves about 6*

Mango Sorbet

Illustrated between pages 320 and 321

2 large ripe mangoes
350 ml (12 fl oz) Stock syrup
juice of 1 large lime
1 egg white

Peel the mangoes and remove the flesh from the stones. Purée the flesh in a blender or food processor. Press through a sieve. Mix with the stock syrup and lime juice.

Freeze as for raspberry sorbet, adding the egg white as directed. Serve straight from the freezer. *Serves 8*

Pineapple Sorbet

Illustrated between pages 320 and 321

Stock syrup made with 100 g (4 oz) sugar and 150 ml
(¼ pint) water
450 ml (¾ pint) pineapple juice
juice of 1 orange
1 egg white

Mix the stock syrup, pineapple juice and orange juice together.

Freeze as for raspberry sorbet, adding the egg white as directed. *Serves 4*

Old English Syllabub

Illustrated between pages 320 and 321

1 clove
1 allspice
2.5 cm (1 inch) cinnamon stick
little grated nutmeg
50 g (2 oz) caster sugar
finely grated rind and juice of 1 lemon
90 ml (6 tbsp) pale cream sherry
300 ml (½ pint) double cream
24 ratafia biscuits

Very finely grind the clove, allspice and cinnamon stick with a pestle and mortar, then sift through a fine sieve. Put the ground spices, nutmeg, sugar, lemon rind, lemon juice and sherry into a bowl. Stir well until the sugar dissolves, then cover and leave to stand for 1 hour.

Strain the sherry mixture through a fine nylon sieve into a clean bowl. Pour in the cream in a continuous stream, whisking all the time, then whip until it is just thick enough to hold a trail when the whisk is lifted.

Place four ratafias in each of four serving glasses, then fill each glass with the spicy syllabub. Chill for about 1 hour. Decorate with the remaining ratafias and a few fresh flower petals. *Serves 4*

Simnel Cake

Illustrated between pages 384 and 385

225 g (8 oz) plain flour
50 g (2 oz) potato flour
5 ml (1 level tsp) baking powder
2.5 ml (½ level tsp) ground mixed spice
225 g (8 oz) currants
175 g (6 oz) sultanas
50 g (2 oz) raisins
75 g (3 oz) mixed candied peel
50 g (2 oz) glacé cherries, quartered
225 g (8 oz) butter, softened
225 g (8 oz) soft light brown sugar
4 eggs
finely grated rind of 1 lemon
15–30 ml (1–2 tbsp) brandy
45 ml (3 tbsp) apricot jam, warmed and sieved
1 egg, beaten, to glaze
FOR THE ALMOND PASTE
225 g (8 oz) ground almonds
100 g (4 oz) icing sugar, sifted
100 g (4 oz) caster sugar
1 egg yolk
15 ml (1 tbsp) lemon juice
15 ml (1 tbsp) orange flower water
2–3 drops vanilla essence
FOR THE GLACÉ ICING
100 g (4 oz) icing sugar
15 ml (1 tbsp) warm water
5 ml (1 tsp) orange flower water

First make the almond paste. Mix the ground almonds, icing and caster sugar together. Add the remaining ingredients and mix to a smooth paste. Knead the almond paste lightly but do not over-work, or the almonds will become oily. Divide in half and shape into rounds. Wrap in a double layer of cling film and set aside.

Sift the plain and potato flour, baking powder and mixed spice together. In a separate bowl, mix together the dried fruits, peel, glacé cherries and 45 ml (3 level tbsp) of the sifted flour.

Cream the butter and sugar together until pale, light and fluffy.

Roll out half the almond paste into a circle, just under 20.5 cm (8 inches) wide.

Add the eggs to the creamed butter, beating well after each addition. Add a little flour if the mixture starts to separate. Add the lemon rind and fold in the flour. Fold in the fruit mixture and stir in the brandy. Spoon half the mixture into a 20.5 cm (8 inch) round cake tin, double-lined with greaseproof paper. Place the layer of almond paste over the cake mixture, then spoon the remaining cake mixture on top, making a slight hollow in the centre.

Wrap the outside of the cake tin with a double layer of brown paper and secure with string. Bake at 170°C (325°F) mark 3 for 3 hours. Do not test the cake in the normal way with a skewer, as the almond paste layer tends to stick to it and gives the appearance of under-done cake mixture. Simply press the top of the cake with your fingers – it should feel firm. Cover the top of the cake with greaseproof paper if it becomes too brown. Leave to cool in the tin for 30 minutes, then turn out on to a wire rack to cool. Wrap in aluminium foil and leave the cake for 24 hours before decorating.

Divide the remaining almond paste in half. Roll out one half into a 20.5 cm (8 inch) circle to fit the top of the cake. Turn the cake over, trimming the base if necessary. Glaze the top with apricot jam and place the almond paste circle on top. Divide the remaining almond paste in half. Divide one half into 11 small balls and place on a baking tray. Divide the second half in half again and roll each half into strips, long enough to go around the top of the cake. Twist these strips together and press around the outer edge of the cake. Place a circle of greaseproof paper over the circle of almond paste. Brush the ring and almond paste balls with beaten egg. Place the cake under a hot grill, for 1–2 minutes, to brown the almond paste. Remove the paper carefully, then grill the almond paste balls until brown.

Make the glacé icing by sifting the icing sugar into a bowl and adding the water and orange flower water. Mix until smooth then pour immediately into the centre of the cake. Leave to set for 2–3 hours before placing the almond paste balls around the edge and adding any decorations. Tie a ribbon around the outside of the cake, if wished. *Makes one 20.5 cm (8 inch) cake*

Summer Pudding

Illustrated between pages 384 and 385

175 g (6 oz) redcurrants, stalks removed
350 g (12 oz) blackcurrants, stalks removed
225–275 g (8–10 oz) granulated sugar
thinly pared rind of 1 large orange, in one continuous spiral
   if possible
225 g (8 oz) raspberries
225 g (8 oz) loganberries
12 thick slices of white bread, about 2 days old, crusts removed

Place the currants, sugar and orange rind in a large saucepan. Cover and cook gently until the juices flow and the sugar has dissolved. Add the raspberries and loganberries, and continue cooking for about 5 minutes until they are softened. Remove from the heat and leave to cool.

Cut a round from one of the slices of bread, large enough to fit in the base of a 1.7 litre (3 pint) pudding basin. Place the round in the basin, then line the sides of the basin with slightly overlapping slices of bread. Reserve the rest for the centre and top.

Remove the orange rind from the fruit. Spoon half of the fruit and juice into the lined basin, then place a layer of bread on top. Add the remaining fruit and juice, then cover completely with the remaining bread.

Cover the top of the pudding with cling film, then

place a small, flat plate on the top. Stand the basin on a plate to catch any juices that overflow. Place some heavy weights on top of the plate. Chill overnight.

To serve, gently loosen the pudding from the sides of the basin with a palette knife, then turn out on to a flat plate. Serve with cream. *Serves 8*

Yule Log (Bûche de Noël)

Illustrated between pages 384 and 385

1 egg white
175 g (6 oz) caster sugar, plus a little extra for dredging
3 eggs, size 2
75 g (3 oz) plain flour, plus a little extra for dredging
30 ml (2 tbsp) cocoa powder
225 g (8 oz) unsalted butter
50 g (2 oz) plain chocolate
450 g (1 lb) icing sugar, plus a little extra for decorating
440 g (15½ oz) can sweetened chestnut purée
holly sprigs, to decorate

Line a baking sheet with non-stick paper. To make the meringue mushrooms, whisk the egg white until stiff, add 25 g (1 oz) of the sugar and whisk again until stiff. Fold in another 25 g (1 oz) sugar.

Spoon the meringue into a piping bag fitted with a plain nozzle. Pipe the meringue on to the prepared baking sheet to resemble small mushroom caps and stalks. Bake in the oven at 110°C (225°F) mark ¼ for about 1½ hours until dry. Leave to cool for at least 15 minutes.

Grease a 33×23 cm (13×9 inch) Swiss roll tin. Line with greaseproof paper and grease the paper. Dredge with the extra caster sugar then flour, knocking out any excess.

Put the eggs and measured caster sugar in a deep bowl which fits snugly inside the rim of a saucepan of simmering water. Whisk the eggs and sugar until thick enough to leave a trail on the surface when the beaters are lifted. Do not overheat the bowl by letting it come into contact with the simmering water or by having the heat under the saucepan too high.

Take the bowl off the saucepan and whisk the mixture for 5 minutes until cool. Sift in the measured flour and cocoa and gently fold through the mixture. Fold in 15 ml (1 tbsp) water.

Pour the mixture gently into the prepared tin and lightly level off the surface. Bake in the oven at 200°C (400°F) mark 6 for about 12 minutes until slightly shrunk away from the tin.

Meanwhile, place a sheet of greaseproof paper over a tea-towel. Dredge the paper with caster sugar and turn the cake out on to it. Trim off the crusty edges with a sharp knife. Roll up with the paper inside. Transfer to a wire rack, seam side down. Leave to cool for 20 minutes.

Put the butter in a bowl and beat until soft. Put the chocolate and 15 ml (1 tbsp) water in a bowl over a pan of hot water. Melt, then leave to cool slightly. Grad-

ually sift and beat the icing sugar into the softened butter, then add the cool chocolate.

Unroll the cold Swiss roll and spread the chestnut purée over the surface. Roll up again without the paper inside. Place on a cake board or plate.

Cut a thick diagonal slice off one end of the Swiss roll and attach with butter cream to the side of the roll.

Using a piping bag and a large star nozzle, pipe thin lines of butter cream over the log. Pipe one or two swirls of butter cream to represent knots in the wood. Sandwich the meringues together with a little butter cream to form mushrooms. Decorate the log with the mushrooms and sprigs of holly. Dust lightly with sifted icing sugar. Store in an airtight container for up to 2–3 days. *Serves 6–8*

Zabaglione

Illustrated between pages 384 and 385

4 egg yolks
65 g (2½ oz) caster sugar
100 ml (4 fl oz) Marsala

Beat the egg yolks and sugar together in a large bowl. Add the Marsala and beat until mixed.

Place the bowl over a saucepan of simmering water and heat gently, whisking the mixture until it is very thick and creamy.

To serve, pour the zabaglione into six glasses and serve immediately, with sponge fingers. *Serves 6*

Sponge Fingers

Illustrated between pages 384 and 385

75 g (3 oz) caster sugar
3 eggs, separated
5 ml (1 tsp) vanilla essence or almond flavouring
75 g (3 oz) plain flour
25 g (1 oz) cornflour
pinch of salt
icing sugar, for dredging

Grease two large baking sheets.

Using an electric whisk, beat half of the caster sugar and the egg yolks in a bowl until very pale and creamy.

Whisk the egg whites until stiff, then gradually add the remaining sugar, whisking between each addition. Fold into the egg yolk mixture, using a large metal spoon. Fold in the vanilla essence.

Sift the flours and salt together, then sift into the mixture. Fold in lightly, using the spoon.

Spoon the mixture into a piping bag fitted with a 1 cm (½ inch) plain nozzle. Pipe 10 cm (4 inch) fingers on to the prepared baking sheets. Dredge with sugar.

Bake in the oven at 150°C (300°F) mark 2 for about 20 minutes or until crusty on the surface. Transfer to wire racks and cool. Store in an airtight container. *Makes about 32*